"This comprehensive study of mal
Second Temple literature and New Testament texts makes clear the continuity between early Judaism and nascent Christianity. The reader is treated to detailed examination of both well-known and less familiar traditions by one of the foremost experts of this literature."

— KELLEY COBLENTZ BAUTCH
St. Edward's University

"As one would expect from Stuckenbruck, the studies in this volume are carefully considered, thoroughly researched, and salutary for comprehending early Jewish and Christian literature."

— *Review of Biblical Literature*

"For a number of years, Loren Stuckenbruck has been at the forefront of all that is good about the study of Judaism in antiquity. This has not simply been due to his brilliance—although that has been repeatedly demonstrated—but is also due in no small part to the humility with which he treats both the primary sources and his fellow scholars, the sensitivity with which he approaches often difficult topics . . . and the respect and grace he displays to a variety of religious traditions. These qualities are clearly and amply demonstrated throughout this volume."

— *Journal of Jewish Studies*

David
Skelton

The Myth of Rebellious Angels

*Studies in Second Temple Judaism and
New Testament Texts*

Loren T. Stuckenbruck

WILLIAM B. EERDMANS PUBLISHING COMPANY
GRAND RAPIDS, MICHIGAN

Wm. B. Eerdmans Publishing Co.
2140 Oak Industrial Drive N.E., Grand Rapids, Michigan 49505
www.eerdmans.com

First published 2014 in Germany by
Mohr Siebeck, Tübingen
© 2014 Mohr Siebeck
All rights reserved
Eerdmans edition published 2017
Printed in the United States of America

23 22 21 20 19 18 17   1 2 3 4 5 6 7

ISBN 978-0-8028-7315-6

Library of Congress Cataloging-in-Publication Data

Names: Stuckenbruck, Loren T., author.
Title: The myth of rebellious angels : studies in Second Temple Judaism and New Testament
    texts / Loren T. Stuckenbruck.
Description: Grand Rapids : Eerdmans Publishing Co., 2017. | Originally published:
    Tübingen : Mohr Siebeck, 2014. | Includes bibliographical references and index.
Identifiers: LCCN 2016046688 | ISBN 9780802873156 (pbk. : alk. paper)
Subjects: LCSH: Demonology. | Angels. | Apocryphal books—Criticism, interpretation, etc.
Classification: LCC BL480 .S783 2017 | DDC 202/.16—dc23
    LC record available at https://lccn.loc.gov/2016046688

in honor of Hermann Lichtenberger

Contents

Preface

The present volume brings together some unpublished and mostly published (yet updated and augmented) material. The common thread that links the chapters of this book is a concern to explore the myth of rebellious angels in some of its Second Temple Jewish setting and to inquire into possible aspects of its reception, including among writings belonging to what we now call the New Testament. While the ancient storyline about the "fallen" angels and its consequences has garnered my formal attention for nearly two decades, it continues to hold my interest, not only because of the important place it occupies in the early Enoch writings, the Dead Sea Scrolls and related Jewish literature, but also because of potential ways reflection on this tradition may contribute to the interpretation of texts more familiar to scholars, students, and interested readers in biblical studies.

The influence of the collection of traditions known as *1 Enoch* or *Ethiopic Enoch* on Second Temple Judaism and Early Christianity has, of course, been documented and worked out in various ways, and the "fallen angels" mythology has played a role in some of these studies. The more obvious among New Testament texts that receive and sustain scholarly attention in this respect include 1 Peter 3:18–22, 2 Peter 2:4–5, and Jude 6 and 14–15, the last text of which contains the explicit and much discussed quotation of 1 Enoch 1:9. Given the recent published interest in each of these texts (text-critical, tradition-historical, and exegetical), the discussions offered in this book, especially chapters 8 through 14, attempt to draw other New Testament passages into the conversation, here the Synoptic Gospels (chs. 8 and 9), the Johannine tradition (ch. 10), the Book of Acts (ch. 11), Pauline thought (chs. 12 and 13), and the Apocalypse of John (ch. 14). Without making any claim to be comprehensive in relation to either the Second Temple traditions (chs. 1 through 7) or the New Testament, I hope that these studies will open up and stimulate pathways for further tradition-historical research and, indeed, theological reflection.

This book appears at a time when research, some of it groundbreaking, is being carried out in relation to the myth of disobedient angels in several areas. First, much needed attention is being directed at the ancient Near Eastern context within and in relation to which the earliest account of the fallen angels in the *Book of Watchers* (esp. *1 Enoch* chs. 6–11) took shape. Here, the continuing and recent studies of Helge Kvanvig, Brian Doak, and especially Henryk Drawnel merit attention.

Second, there is currently a resurgent interest in the giants, who in the early Enoch tradition are presented as violent offspring of the malevolent angels and the daughters of humankind just prior to the time of the Great Flood (cf. Gen. 6:1–4). The presentation in the *Book of Watchers* of the giants, as that of the angels who sired them, picks up symbols, motifs, and characters otherwise known through literature of the ancient Near East, in addition to drawing on the same in Greek mythology. Along with throwing light on such backgrounds for "giants" in Second Temple Jewish tradition, recent study is also turning in the direction of reception history, that is, within Graeco-Roman culture, patristic sources, Rabbinic literature, Byzantium, and even Jewish, Christian, and Manichean sources from the medieval period. Here I am thinking of the research being carried out by Matthew Goff, Ken Penner, Joseph Angel, Andrew Perrin, Kelley Coblentz Bautch, Jan Bremmer, Annette Yoshiko Reed, Andrei Orlov, Gábor Kósa, Jens Wilkens, Enrico Morano, John Reeves, and Philip Alexander.

Third and more profoundly, whether or not "influence" of the angels and giants mythology preserved in *1 Enoch* on this or that tradition can be firmly established *per se*, the tradition in question allows us to explore what it means to place Second Temple Jewish and emerging Christian traditions in the late 1st and 2nd centuries in a conversation that furthers both historical and theological interpretation and that takes account of socio-political and religious contexts while being sensitive to the permutation and transformation of ideas.

Fourth, an area of study not addressed in the present volume but which is on the verge of receiving sustained formal attention is the further critical study of the *1 Enoch* text tradition. Although much discussion has been and is being devoted to the relevant texts and traditions, their precise form bears further investigation at each stage. While considerable advances have been made since the initial publication of fragments from the Dead Sea Scrolls regarding the shape of the early Enochic tradition that refers to rebellious angels, a number of text-critical and early reception-historical questions remain. Further research is not only needed in relation to the Aramaic fragments of the early Enoch tradition (including the *Book of Giants*) and the more extensive yet still fragmentary Greek texts, emerging manuscript evidence in Ge'ez, some of it textually significant, is making a new textual edition of the materials a desideratum. The latter project is one centered at Ludwig-Maximilians-Universität in Munich and on which Ted Erho and I are currently engaged, in collaboration, as appropriate, with colleagues in Ethiopia, Israel, Europe and North America.

Fifth and finally, the study of *Ethiopic Enoch* in the Ethiopian Tewahedo Orthodox Church is currently being augmented by growing work on its rich commentary tradition (Andemta). An increasing number of scholars has become involved in this and related areas of the reception of *1 Enoch* in Ethiopia. In addition to some of the names mentioned above, these scholars include Jonathan Ben-Dov, Daniel Assefa, Eshbal Ratson, Randall Chesnutt, Ted Erho,

Ralph Lee, Archie Wright, and Amsalu Tefera. It is in forthcoming publications that I shall address some of the issues raised above in the third, fourth, and fifth points.

The content of this book has benefited from a large number of conversation partners, especially during the last several years. The names already mentioned can be augmented by the following: Stephen Barton, Leslie Baynes, Eve-Marie Becker, Michael Becker, Shane Berg, Gabriele Boccaccini, Markus Bockmuehl, James Charlesworth, Esther Chazon, John Collins, Christopher Cook, Devorah Dimant, Esther Eshel, Jörg Frey, Sean Freyne, Beverly Gaventa, Maxine Grossman, Robert Hayward, Desta Heliso, Matthias Henze, Matthias Hoffmann, Chris Keith, Menahem Kister, Anders Klostergaard-Petersen, Matthias Konradt, Robert MacLennan, Hindy Najman, Judith Newman, George Nickelsburg, Alexandra Parvân, Claire Pfann, Stephen Pfann, Émile Puech, Paul Rorem, Christopher Rowland, Daniel Seife-Mikael, Michael Stone, Eibert Tigchelaar, Michael Tuval, William Telford, James VanderKam, Ross Wagner, Rodney Werline, Benjamin Wold, and Benjamin Wright.

At an important stage of manuscript preparation, Seth Bledsoe and Blake Jurgens, both beneficiaries of grants to conduct their research at Ludwig-Maximilians-Universität, have contributed significantly, not only in attending to some of its formalities, but also in reflecting with me about the arguments set forth in individual chapters. Amanda Davis Bledsoe has also contributed by casting a meticulous eye on the manuscript during perparation of the indices. In addition, Ursula Danninger, my secretary in the faculty, Lina Aschenbrenner, and Elisabeth Fischer, research assistants, have no less been involved in attending to several matters as the manuscript has gone to press. Of course, any errors in the manuscript remain my sole responsibility.

The final chapter of this book (ch. 14) was initially authored with Mark D. Mathews, whose own published doctoral dissertation had touched upon several important aspects of the argument. I am very grateful for the opportunity to have worked with him collaboratively on the Apocalypse of John and its reception of Enochic tradition.

As always, one's institutional context contributes significantly to the intellectual and collegial climate within which research comes to publication. I am now especially grateful to members of the Protestant, Catholic, and Orthodox Faculties of Theology at Ludwig-Maximilians-Universität München for their warm reception of me as a colleague, for inter- and cross-disciplinary opportunities to exchange ideas and perspectives, and for interest in research questions taken up in this project. In addition, I am grateful to Dr. Henning Ziebritzki at the Mohr Siebeck publishing house in Tübingen for the support given in bringing the present book to publication.

It is surely an understatement for me to thank my wife Lois for being as significant a conversation partner as anyone else mentioned above. Endlessly, and often with great profit, we have discussed matters such as "giants", "angels", "demons", "evil" and "Enoch". I am grateful to her for many insights and ideas that have come about through our daily discussions.

Lastly, I wish to mention Hermann Lichtenberger, Prof. Emeritus at the Institut für antikes Judentum und hellenistische Religionsgeschichte at Eberhard Karls Universität Tübingen. I am but one among many who are grateful for his consistent example, through numerous publications, support, and collegial conversations, in advocating for a serious reading of Second Temple literature as it is placed in conversation with New Testament and Early Christian texts and traditions. So many of his accomplishments have set the tone for work being carried out by a next generation of scholars. It is to him that this book is dedicated.

LOREN STUCKENBRUCK
Munich
Ethiopian Calendar 27th of Terr 7506
(4th February 2014)

Acknowledgments

The chapters in this book draw on material from the following articles, which their respective publishers have kindly given permission to reuse:

"The Origins of Evil in Jewish Apocalyptic Tradition: The Interpretation of Genesis 6:1–4 in the Second and Third Centuries B. C. E.". In *The Fall of the Angels*, eds. Christoph Auffarth and Loren T. Stuckenbruck (Themes in Biblical Narrative 6; Leiden: Brill, 2004), pp. 87–118 (Chapter 1)

"Giant Mythology and Demonology: From the Ancient Near East to the Dead Sea Scrolls". In eds. Armin Lange, Hermann Lichtenberger, and K. F. Diethard Römheld, *Die Dämonen – Demons. Die Dämonologie der israelitisch-jüdischen und frühchristlichen Literatur im Kontext ihrer Umwelt* (Tübingen: J. C. B. Mohr [Paul Siebeck], 2003), pp. 318–338 (Chapter 2)

"The Lamech Narrative in the *Genesis Apocryphon* (1QApGen) and *Birth of Noah* (4QEnoch^c ar): A Tradition-Historical Study", in eds. Katell Berthelot and Daniel Stoekl Ben Ezra, *Aramaica Qumranica* (STDJ 94; Leiden / Boston: Brill, 2010), pp. 253–274 (Chapter 3)

"The Demonic World of the Dead Sea Scrolls". In eds. Ida Fröhlich and Erkki Koskenniemi, *Evil and the Devil* (ISCO and LNTS 481; London: Bloomsbury T & T Clark, 2013), pp. 51–70 (Chapter 4)

"Daniel and Early Enoch Traditions in the Dead Sea Scrolls". In *The Book of Daniel: Composition and Reception*, eds. John J. Collins and Peter W. Flint (Supplements to Vetus Testamentum 83.2; Leiden/Boston/Köln: Brill, 2001), pp. 368–386 (Chapter 5)

"The Book of Tobit and the Problem of 'Magic'". In *Jüdische Schriften in ihrem antik-jüdischen und urchristlichen Kontext*, eds. Hermann Lichtenberger and Gerbern S. Oegema (JSHRZ Studien 1; Gütersloh: Gütersloher Verlagshaus, 2002), pp. 258–269 (Chapter 6)

"To What Extent Did Philo's Treatment of Enoch and the Giants Presuppose a Knowledge of the Enochic and Other Sources Preserved in the Dead Sea Scrolls?" *Studia Philonica Annual* vol. 19 (2007), pp. 131–142 (Chapter 7)

"The Human Being and Demonic Invasion: Therapeutic Models in Ancient Jewish and Christian Texts". In ed. Christopher C. H. Cook, *Theology, Spirituality, and Mental Health* (London: SCM, 2013), pp. 94–123 (Chapter 9)

"'Protect Them from the Evil One' (John 17:15): Light from the Dead Sea Scrolls". In eds. Mary L. Coloe and Tom Thatcher, *John, Qumran and the*

Dead Sea Scrolls: Sixty Years of Discovery and Debate (Early Judaism and Its Literature 32; Atlanta: Society of Biblical Literature, 2011), pp. 139–160 and "Evil in Johannine and Apocalyptic Perspective: Petition for Protection in John 17." In eds. Catrin H. Williams and Christopher Rowland, *John's Gospel and Intimations of Apocalyptic* (London: Bloomsbury, 2013), pp. 200–232 (Chapter 10)

"The 'Cleansing' of the Gentiles: Background for the Rationale behind the Apostles' Decree in Acts 15". In ed. Markus Oehler, *Aposteldekret und antikes Vereinswesen: Gemeinschaft und ihre Ordnung* (WUNT I/208; Tübingen: Mohr Siebeck, 2011), pp. 65–90 (Chapter 11)

"Overlapping Ages at Qumran and 'Apocalyptic' in Pauline Theology." In ed. Jean-Sébastien Rey, *The Dead Sea Scrolls and Pauline Literature* (STDJ 102; Leiden/Boston: Brill, 2014), pp. 309–326 (Chapter 12)

"Why Should Women Cover Their Heads Because of the Angels?" *Stone-Campbell Journal* vol. 4 (2001), pp. 205–234 (Chapter 13)

"The Apocalypse of John, *1 Enoch*, and the Question of Influence", in eds. J. Frey, J. Kelhoffer, and F. Toth, *Die Apokalypse: Kontexte – Konzepte – Wirkungen* (WUNT I/287; Tübingen: Mohr Siebeck, 2012), pp. 191–235, coauthored with Mark D. Mathews (Chapter 14).

Abbreviation List

AB	Anchor Bible
ABRL	Anchor Bible Reference Library
AGSU	Arbeiten zur Geschichte des Spätjudentums und Urchristentums
AJEC	Ancient Judaism and Early Christianity
AOAT	Alter Orient und Altes Testament
AoF	Altorientalische Forschungen
BAC	Biblioteca de autores cristianos
BBB	*Bulletin de bibliographie biblique*
BBR	*Bulletin for Biblical Research*
BECNT	Baker Exegetical Commentary on the New Testament
BETL	Bibliotheca ephemeridum theologicarum lovaniensium
BFCT	Beiträge zur Förderung christlicher Theologie
BibAn	*Biblical Annuals*
BibOr	Biblica et orientalia
BSOAS	*Bulletin of the School of Oriental and African Studies*
BTS	*Bible et terre sainte*
BZ	*Biblische Zeitschrift*
BZAW	Beihefte zur Zeitschrift für die alttestamentliche Wissenschaft
BZNW	Beihefte zur Zeitschrift für die neutestamentliche Wissenschaft
CBQ	*Catholic Biblical Quarterly*
CBQMS	Catholic Biblical Quarterly Monograph Series
CEJL	Commentaries on Early Jewish Literature
CJA	Christianity and Judaism in Antiquity
CNT	Commentaire du Nouveau Testament
CRINT	Compendia rerum iudaicarum ad Novum Testamentum
CSCO	Corpus scriptorum christianorum orientalium. Edited by I. B. Chabot et al. Paris, 1903–
DSD	*Dead Sea Discoveries*
FB	Forschung zur Bibel
FRLANT	Forschungen zur Religion und Literatur des Alten und Neuen Testaments
HBS	Herders Biblische Studien
HNT	Handbuch zum Neuen Testament
HSM	Harvard Semitic Monographs
HTKNT	Herders theologischer Kommentar zum Neuen Testament

HUCA	*Hebrew Union College Annual*
HUCM	Monographs of the Hebrew Union College
HUT	Hermeneutische Untersuchungen zur Theologie
ICC	International Critical Commentary
IEJ	*Israel Exploration Journal*
IOS	*Israel Oriental Studies*
JAJ	*Journal of Ancient Judaism*
JAJSup	Journal of Ancient Judaism Supplements
JCTCRS	Jewish and Christian Texts in Contexts and Related Studies
JECS	*Journal of Early Christian Studies*
JJS	*Journal for Jewish Studies*
JNES	*Journal of Near Eastern Studies*
JSJ	*Journal for the Study of Judaism in the Persian, Hellenistic, and Roman Periods*
JSJSup	Journal for the Study of Judaism Supplements
JSNT	*Journal for the Study of the New Testament*
JSNTSup	Journal for the Study of the New Testament Supplement Series
JSOT	*Journal for the Study of the Old Testament*
JSOTSup	Journal for the Study of the Old Testament Supplement Series
JSP	*Journal for the Study of the Pseudepigrapha*
JSPSup	Journal for the Study of the Pseudepigrapha Supplement Series
JSSSup	Journal for Semitic Studies Supplement
JTS	*Journal of Theological Studies*
KEK	Kritisch-exegetischer Kommentar über das Neue Testament
LCL	Loeb Classical Library
LNTS	Library of New Testament Studies
LSTS	Library of Second Temple Studies
MNTC	Moffatt NT Commentaries
NEBAT	Die Neue Echter Bibel. Altes Testament
NHC	Nag Hammadi Codices
NICNT	New International Commentary on the New Testament
NICOT	New International Commentary on the Old Testament
NovT	*Novum Testamentum*
NRSV	New Revised Standard Version
NTD	Das Neue Testament Deutsch
NTL	New Testament Library
OBO	Orbis biblicus et orientalis
ÖTK	Ökumenischer Taschenbuch-Kommentar
OtSt	*Oudtestamentische Studiën*
PVTG	Pseudepigrapha Veteris Testamenti Graece
RB	*Revue biblique*
RevQ	*Revue de Qumran*
RHR	*Revue de l'histoire des religions*

RSR	Recherches de science religieuse
RTRSup	Reformed Theological Review Supplement
SB	Sources bibliques
SBL	Society of Biblical Literature
SBLECL	Society of Biblical Literature Early Christianity and Its Literature
SBLEJL	Society of Biblical Literature Early Judaism and Its Literature
SBLSBS	Society of Biblical Literature Sources for Biblical Study
SBLSP	*Society of Biblical Literature Seminar Papers*
SBM	Stuttgart Bible Monographs
SBT	Studies in Biblical Theology
Sem	*Semeia*
SJS	Studia Judaeoslavica
SNTSMS	Society for New Testament Studies Monograph Series
SP	Sacra Pagina
SUNT	Studien zur Umwelt des Neuen Testaments
SVTP	Studia in Veteris Testamenti pseudepigraphica
TA	*Tel Aviv*
TANZ	Texte und Arbeiten zum neutestamentlichen Zeitalter
TBN	Themes in Biblical Narrative
THNT	Theologischer Handkommentar zum Neuen Testament
TKNT	Theologischer Kommentar zum Neuen Testament
TSAJ	Texte und Studien zum antiken Judentum
VT	*Vetus Testamentum*
VTSup	Supplements to Vetus Testamentum
WBC	Word Bible Commentary
WMANT	Wissenschaftliche Monographien zum Alten und Neuen Testament
WUNT	Wissenschaftliche Untersuchungen zum Neuen Testament
ZA	*Zeitschrift für Assyriologie*
ZAW	*Zeitschrift für die alttestamentliche Wissenschaft*
ZBK	Zürcher Bibelkommentare
ZNW	*Zeitschrift für die neutestamentliche Wissenschaft und die Kunde der älteren Kirche*

Chapter One

Origins of Evil in Jewish Apocalyptic Tradition: The Interpretation of Genesis 6:1–4 in the Second and Third Centuries B. C. E.

Introduction

During the last several decades, specialists in ancient Judaism have increasingly devoted attention to traditions about the "sons of God" (Gen. 6:2) in Jewish literature from the Second Temple period, in which they are also referred to as "watchers"[1] who, by convention, are often described under the heading "fallen angels". It is frequently observed that in a number of early Jewish writings such angels were regarded as evil beings whose activities, whether in the past or present, are inimical to God's purposes for creation.[2]

---

[1] The designation (Aram. עירין; Grk. ἐγρήγοροι) is applied to the rebellious angelic beings in a number of texts; cf. *1 Enoch* 1:5; 10:7, 15; 12:3a; 13:10; 14:1, 3; 15:2; 16:1, 2; 91:15; *Book of Giants* at 4Q203 7A 7; 7B i 4; 4Q532 2.7; *Genesis Apocryphon* (1QapGen ii 1–2, 15); *Damascus Document* (CD ii 18–19 par. 4Q266 2 ii 18). The Aram. עיר functions as a designation for good angelic beings in *1 En.* 12:2, 3 and Dan. 4:13, 17, and 23.

[2] The literature from the early 1970's until the turn of the 21st century is considerable. From this period, see especially Devorah Dimant, e. g. in "'The Fallen Angels' in the Dead Sea Scrolls and in the Apocryphal and Pseudepigraphic Books Related to Them" (Ph.D. thesis, Hebrew University, 1974) (mod. Heb.) and "The 'Pesher on the Periods' (4Q180 and 4Q181)", *IOS* 9 (1979), pp. 77–102; Lionel R. Wickham, "The Sons of God and the Daughters of Men: Gen 6:2 in Early Christian Exegesis", *OtSt* 19 (1974), pp. 135–147; Martin Delcor, "Le myth de la chute des anges et de l'origine des géants comme explication du mal dans le monde dans l'apocalyptique juive histoire des traditions", *RHR* 190 (1976), pp. 3–53; Józef T. Milik, in "Turfan et Qumran: Livre des géants juif et manichéen", in eds. Gerd Jeremias, Heinz-Wolfgang Kuhn, and Hartmut Stegemann, *Das frühe Christentum in seiner Umwelt. Festgabe für Karl Georg Kuhn zum 65. Geburtstag* (Göttingen: Vandenhoeck & Ruprecht, 1971), pp. 117–127 and *The Books of Enoch: Aramaic Fragments from Qumrân Cave 4* (Oxford: Clarendon Press, 1976); Paul D. Hanson, "Rebellion in Heaven, Azazel and Euhemeristic Heroes in 1 Enoch 6–11", *JBL* 96 (1977), pp. 195–233; George W. E. Nickelsburg, "Apocalyptic and Myth in 1 Enoch 6–11", *JBL* 96 (1977), pp. 383–405; David W. Suter, "Fallen Angel, Fallen Priest. The Problem of Family Purity in 1 Enoch 6–16", *HUCA* 50 (1979), pp. 115–135; Ida Fröhlich, "Les enseignements des veilleurs dans la tradition de Qumran", *RevQ* 13 (1988), pp. 177–187; Paolo Sacchi, *Jewish Apocalyptic and its History*, trans. William J. Short (JSPSup 20; Sheffield: JSOT Press, 1990); Maxwell J. Davidson, *Angels at Qumran: A Comparative Study of 1 Enoch 1–36, 72–108 and Sectarian Writings from Qumran* (JSPSup 11; Sheffield: JSOT Press, 1992); John C. Reeves, *Jewish Lore in Manichaean Cosmogony: Studies in the Book of Giants Traditions* (HUCM 20; Cincinnati: Hebrew Union College Press, 1992); William R. Adler and James C. VanderKam, *The Jewish Apocalyptic Heritage in Early Christianity*

Such a view, however correct it may be, is often taken as axiomatic. To be sure, there is ample reason for such a view. Traditions that refer to both evil angels and their gigantic offspring are variously preserved in a number of apocalyptic and sapiential writings dated mostly to the first three centuries before the Common Era. The literature includes the following: *1 Enoch* (*Book of Watchers* chs. 1–36; *Animal Apocalypse* chs. 85–90, *Apocalypse of Weeks* (93:1–10 + 91:11–17); *Book of Giants*; *Jubilees*; *Damascus Document*; Ben Sira; Wisdom of Solomon; *3 Maccabees*; *3 Baruch*; plus a number of fragmentary texts only preserved among the Dead Sea Scrolls: *Genesis Apocryphon* (1Q20), *Ages of Creation* (4Q180–181), *Exhortation Based on the Flood* (4Q370), *Incantation* (4Q444), *Songs of the Sage* (4Q510–511), and *Apocryphal Psalms* (11Q11). For all the apparently one-sided emphasis of these writings in regarding "the sons of God" and their progeny as evil, nothing in Genesis 6 itself unambiguously prepares for such an understanding (see below). It is misleading, therefore, to suppose that the writings just cited were simply adapting a tradition inherent to Genesis 6.

In order to give shape to the particular concerns that allowed early Jewish apocalyptic authors to regard the angelic "sons of God" in Genesis 6:2 as malevolent beings, it is necessary to consider the biblical tradition itself and to give some attention to the wider Hellenistic world within which the apocalyptic ideas took shape; in particular, we shall consider those documents in which the gigantic offspring of the "sons of God" are not categorically branded as evil.[3] In view of the biblical background and contemporary context, it is thus remarkable how uniformly the ambiguous Genesis 6:1–4 (or at least tradition relating to this passage) was being read, that is, as a story about irreversibly rebellious angels and giants. In addition to the special and respective circumstances of communities that inspired a trajectory of biblical interpretation in this direction, it seems that the myth about "fallen angels" took on a life of its own as it became subject to a relatively widespread surge of interest during the third and second centuries B. C. E. More than merely coming

---

(CRINT III.4; Assen: Van Gorcum and Minneapolis: Fortress Press, 1996); Loren T. Stuckenbruck, *The Book of Giants from Qumran: Texts, Translation, and Commentary* (TSAJ 63; Tübingen: Mohr Siebeck, 1997); Philip S. Alexander, "Wrestling Against Wickedness in High Places: Magic in the Worldview of the Qumran Community", in eds. Stanley E. Porter and Craig A. Evans, *The Scrolls and the Scriptures: Qumran Fifty Years After* (JSPSup 26; Sheffield: Sheffield Academic Press, 1997), pp. 319–330 and "The Demonology of the Dead Sea Scrolls", in eds. Peter W. Flint and James C. VanderKam, *The Dead Sea Scrolls after Fifty Years. A Comprehensive Assessment* (2 vols.; Leiden / Boston / Köln: Brill, 1999), 2:331–353; and Andy M. Reimer, "Rescuing the Fallen Angels: The Case of the Disappearing Angels at Qumran", *DSD* 7 (2000), pp. 334–353.

[3] For an early, though brief attempt in this direction, see Thomas Francis Glasson, *Greek Influence in Jewish Eschatology with Special Reference to the Apocalypses and Pseudepigrapha* (London: SPCK, 1961). In addition and esp. see Benjamin Zion Wacholder, "'Pseudo-Eupolemus' Two Greek Fragments on Abraham", *HUCA* 34 (1963), pp. 83–113 and, of course, the more general approach reflected in Martin Hengel's *Judaism and Hellenism*, trans. by John Bowden (2 vols.; London: SCM Press, 1974), esp. 1:231–234, in addition to which the articles by Hanson and Nickelsburg mentioned in n. 2 above continue to be useful. For two more recent, though contrasting studies, see John C. Reeves, "Utnapishtim in the Book of Giants?", *JBL* 112 (1993), pp. 110–

to terms with social oppression or political persecution, there was something genuinely theological at stake as writers, whether "apocalyptic" or not in orientation, attempted to understand their location and the location of those for and to whom they spoke in the experienced world. New circumstances generated fresh ways of coming to terms with received tradition (whether from Genesis directly or from early or proto-Enochic sources). Hence the following question arises: What theological interests account for the reason(s) why a tradition known through Genesis 6 could be read as a story about the introduction of evil into the world?

In what follows, I would like to describe the various approaches to this question among the earliest Jewish apocalyptic writings while, at the same time, suggesting how their respective treatments of the "fallen angels" and "giants" might be broadly thought to cohere. To achieve this aim, we may begin with a brief, but necessary look at the interpretive horizon of Genesis 6 which, in turn, is followed by a description of the role of "angels" and "giants" in two Hellenizing euhemeristic sources. I shall argue that it is against this (Hellenizing) background that, finally, the early apocalyptic traditions themselves can best be understood.

A. Interpretive Possibilities in the Biblical Tradition

For Second Temple Jewish authors, the pericope that perhaps most inspired speculation about the "fallen angels" myth is the enigmatic passage of Genesis 6:1–4.[4] Beyond the reference to "the daughters of men" (v. 1) and "humankind" (v. 3), the Masoretic tradition distinguishes at least three, perhaps even four, categories of beings. The first is "the sons of God" – that is, בני אלהים (*bny 'lhym*) in verses 1 and 4b (rendered literally as οἱ υἱοὶ τοῦ θεοῦ in LXX, while Cod. Alexandrinus reads "the angels [οἱ ἄγγελοι] of God"). The second is the beautiful "daughters of men" with whom the sons of God have consorted. Later tradition would debate the degree to which the women might be held responsible for the sons' descent to earth.[5] Third, the text refers to the offspring of sons of God and the human women; they are called "the mighty men ... men of renown" (v. 4b – הגברים ... אנשי השם; LXX οἱ γίγαντες ... οἱ ἄνθρωποι οἱ ὀνομαστοί). Fourth and finally, there is a somewhat indefinite mention of "the Neph[i]lim"[6] (הנפלים) who are described as having been

---

113 and Ronald V. Huggins, "Noah and the Giants: A Response to John C. Reeves", *JBL* 114 (1995), pp. 103–110.

[4] It is not necessary to claim that it is precisely the text of the Hebrew Bible that, in all aspects of its wording lies behind all adaptations of the storyline. Nevertheless, it is more difficult, for example, to explain Genesis chs. 6–9 on the basis of *1 En.* chs. 6–11 than the other way around. If the Enochic tradition underlies Gen. 6 at all, it did not bear much of the embellished form it now has.

[5] See a review of this tradition in Kelley Coblentz Bautch, "Decoration, Destruction and Debauchery: Reflections on 1 Enoch 8 in Light of 4QEn^b", *DSD* 15 (2008), pp. 79–95, though it is not a view that can already be detected in the Aram. Dead Sea Scroll fragments.

[6] The transliteration "Neph[i]lim" is given on account of the ambiguous form in the Heb.

"on the earth in those days" (v. 4a). By translating both "the mighty men" and "the Neph[i]lim" in verse 4 with the same expression, "the giants" (οἱ γίγαντες), the Old Greek tradition has identified these groups with one another.[7] As is frequently noted, the thematic coherence of the text is not easy to trace. How, for example, is God's decision to cut short human life in verse 3 related to the account of the Nephilim and mighty men in verse 4?[8] Moreover, it is anything but clear how "the sons of God," "the mighty men", and "the Neph[i]lim" contribute to the story of Noah and the Flood that follows (6:5–9:29). Given these difficulties within the text, one may wonder whether several questions could have emerged for later interpreters: How, if at all, do any of these groups play a role in God's decision to punish evil on the earth through a deluge (see 6:3, 5–7, 13)? Do, for example, "the sons of God" and their offspring have anything to do with the "great evil", "corruption", and "violence" that had consumed the earth (6:5, 11–13)? In relation to *whose* wickedness does the Flood constitute a divine response? Does the destruction of "all flesh" through the Flood include "the mighty men" and "the Neph[i]lim"? While answers to these questions may, on first reading of the Flood narrative, be readily forthcoming, the juxtaposition of the story about "mighty men" with the silence about them and their parentage in what follows creates a problem if one wishes to read the passages *together*. Hence some interpreters during the Second Temple period would find points of departure for a more coherent picture on the basis of the larger literary (i.e. Genesis and Pentateuchal) context.

Although the tradition in Genesis 6 seems, on the surface, to underscore that a complete destruction took place through the Flood (Gen. 6:13, 17) and to restrict its survivors to Noah, his family and selected animals (6:18–21; 7:1–3), there are enough clues in the narrative of Genesis, indeed in the Pentateuch as a whole, that may have provided Jewish readers sufficient reason to suppose that "the mighty men" (assuming their identification with "the Neph[i]lim") actually outlived the Flood. Such a conclusion could have been reached either by supposing that Noah and his family somehow belonged to their number or by inferring that they survived through a means not narrated in the text. The former possibility might have been raised by coordinating Genesis 6:4 with the brief story of Nimrod in Genesis

---

text: נפלים. While the Masoretic pointing, as well as some early renderings (Heb. נפילים / Aram. נפילין/א) identify the vowel of the second syllable as an -*i*-, the form is likewise consistent with an *a*-class vowel.

[7] The same assimilation of the different Hebrew expressions of v. 4 into one group is also carried through by the Aramaic targumic traditions of *Onqelos* and *Neophyti*, which render both with גיבריא and גיבריה, respectively; cf. further n. 12 below. Both LXX and these targumim presuppose a more coherent tradition about giants than does the Hebrew.

[8] For a description of the problems encountered in the text of Gen. 6:1–4 as it stands, see esp. Claus Westermann, *Genesis 1–11. A Continental Commentary*, trans. J.J. Scullion (Minneapolis: Fortress Press, 1994), p. 366 and, more recently, Jacques T. A. G. M. van Ruiten, "The Flood Story in the Book of Jubilees", in eds. Florentino García Martínez and Gerard P. Luttikhuizen, *Interpretations of the Flood* (TBN 1; Leiden / Boston: Brill, 1998), pp. 66–85 (here p. 83).

10:8–12,[9] while a double-reference to "the Nephilim" in Numbers 13:33 (LXX has γίγαντες) would have made it possible to consider the latter.[10] Each of these alternatives for reading the biblical tradition bears further comment.

Nimrod. As a post-Flood descendent of Noah through the line of Ham, Nimrod is in Genesis 10:8–11 described as "a mighty man (גבר) in the land" (v. 8) and as "a mighty hunter (גבר ציד) before the Lord" (v. 9). To Nimrod is also attributed the building of several cities in Assur (v. 11), after he had already established his rule in the cities of Babel, Erech, and Accad in the land of Shinar (v. 10). Shinar, of course, is identified in the subsequent narrative (11:1–9) as the very location in which the tower of Babel was built. It may be significant that the Greek translator of Genesis 10:8–9 used the term γίγας each of the three times Nimrod is described as a גבר. This correspondence between the Hebrew and Greek versions is the same as found in Genesis 6:4 (where, however, the Masoretes have pointed גבר as *gibbôr*), and it is not impossible that the Greek translation reflects some coordination between the passages. Nimrod's identification as a "mighty man" or "giant" may have given readers cause to infer that the offspring of the sons of God in 6:4 may, at least in part, have survived the Flood,[11] whether this survival took place directly through the lineage of Noah (who in this case would have been a "giant" too; see more on this below) or through some other means not recounted in the narrative.

Nephilim in Canaan. The passage from Numbers 13 picks up on another aspect of Genesis 6 through an enigmatic double-reference to "the Nephilim" (v. 33). The Israelites spying out the land of Canaan, except for Caleb, advise against taking possession of the land because of the menacingly great size of its inhabitants (vv. 28, 32–33). In verses 32–33, the spies are made to say:

[32]The land that we have gone through to spy it out is a land devouring its inhabitants. And all the people whom we saw in it were men of great stature. [33]And there we saw the Nephilim (הנפילים) – *the sons of Anak are from the Nephilim* (חנפלים) – and we were in our eyes as grasshoppers, and so we were in their eyes.

---

[9] In this passage Nimrod, described as a גבר ("a mighty man"; LXX renders γίγας), is identified as the son of Cush, the son of Ham, the son of Noah (Gen. 10:6–8).

[10] Although an allusion to Gen. 6:4 in Num. 13 is not impossible, the reference to the גבורים נפלים in Ezek. 32:27 (translated in LXX as "the giants of those who fell" οἱ γίγαντες τῶν πεπτωκότων) neither refers specifically to the Flood nor specifies just when this group "descended to Sheol with their weapons of war".

[11] This seems to be the shape of the tradition behind Philo's discussion of Nimrod in *De gigantibus* 63–66. A vestige of Nimrod's connection with the gigantic offspring of the sons of God survives in Josephus (*Ant.* 1.114) who explains that by overseeing the erection of the tower of Babel to reach "higher than the [flood] waters", Nimrod wished "to avenge the destruction of their forefathers" (μετελεύσεσθαι δὲ καὶ τῆς τῶν προγόνων ἀπωλείας). Although Josephus describes Nimrod as the great-grandson of Noah and not, with the LXX tradition, as a "giant", does he or the tradition upon which he drew from presuppose a genetic connection between Nimrod and his contemporaries, on the one hand, or between him and those who were destroyed by the deluge, including the "giants", on the other?

The gloss (in italics), which explains the unexpected nomenclature of "Nephilim" in relation to Anakim already mentioned in verses 22 and 28, is perhaps a later addition that seems to coordinate this passage with Genesis 6:4 (as suggested by the same spelling without the first *yod*). Similarly, the Greek translation tradition may be cognizant of the pre-diluvian Nephilim, since here, as in Genesis 6:4, they are likewise rendered as οἱ γίγαντες.[12] Although in Numbers 13 the inhabitants of Canaan are considered enemies of the Israelites, both the use and coordination (LXX) or derivation from the designation (MT) in an allusion to Genesis 6 betrays an assumption that one or more of the Nephilim must have escaped the Great Flood. An account that relates how any of the Nephilim might have survived is, of course, not given. However, it is not impossible that some ancient readers, in considering the literary context of the Pentateuch as a whole, might have come to the conclusion that Noah, as sole survivor with his family, was one of their number.

Nephilim and Further Groups. The specific correlation between the Nephilim in Numbers 13:33 and "the sons of Anak" (vv. 22, 28) would have widened the horizon for ancient readers to have inferred links between groups of various names within the biblical tradition, whether in the Masoretic text or the LXX tradition.[13] For example, in Deuteronomy 2:10–11 an apparent gloss refers to inhabitants of Ar called "the Emim ... a great and numerous and tall people" who "like the Anakim are thought to be the Rephaim" (see also vv. 20–21).

The correspondence chain of Giborim = Nephilim = Anakim = Rephaim, which could be inferred from reading synthetically the Hebrew of Genesis 6, Numbers 13, and Deuteronomy 2, is consistent with a translation strategy in the Greek tradition that often applied, as we have seen above, the term γίγας, for these words.[14] By implication, Og king of Bashan could have been related to this circle, as may be suggested by the gloss at Deuteronomy 3:11 (see also 3:13) about the unusually large size of his bed and the claim that he "alone was left remaining from the remnant of the Rephaim (מיתר רפאים)". In the Greek translation at Joshua 12:4 the same phrase מיתר רפאים is rendered ἐκ τῶν γιγάντων ("from the

---

[12] However, only the first instance of "Nephilim" is translated (as in Targums *Onqelos* and *Neophyti*) in LXX: καὶ ἐκεῖ ἑωράκαμεν τοὺς γίγαντας καὶ ἤμεν ἐνώπιον αὐτῶν ὡσεὶ ἀκρίδες ("and there we saw the giants, and before them we were as grasshoppers ..."). It is possible that the gloss in Masoretic tradition of Num. 13:33 was either inserted after the time the Greek translation was made or, and less likely, the Greek tradition reflects a copyist or reader's error through *homoioteleuton* (הנפילים ... הנפלים ...).

[13] Unfortunately, none of the biblical manuscript fragments from the Dead Sea preserves anything corresponding to the passages relevant to the present discussion.

[14] For instances of גבור, רפאים, and עֶנָקִים (only once: Deut. 1:28) rendered as γίγαντες throughout the Septuagint tradition, see the listing with discussion by Brook W. R. Pearson, "Resurrection and the Judgment of the Titans: ἡ γῆ τῶν ἀσεβῶν in LXX Isaiah 26.19", in ed. Stanley E. Porter, Michael A. Hayes and David Tombs, *Resurrection* (JSNTSup 186; Sheffield: Sheffield Academic Press, 1999), pp. 33–51 (here pp. 36–37 and ns. 6 and 7) and Brian R. Doak, *The Last of the Rephaim: Conquest and Cataclysm in the Heroic Ages of Ancient Israel* (Ilex Foundation Series; Cambridge, Massachusetts / London: Harvard University Press, 2012), pp. 51–118.

giants") in a way that could have identified Og's ancestry with the pre-diluvian giants. This possibility for interpretation was later given explicit shape in several traditions preserved in rabbinic and targumic literature.[15]

The foregoing consideration of biblical tradition has been necessarily brief. However, it is sufficient to allow for the following inferences to be made about the gigantic offspring of "the sons of God". Firstly, there is no coherent picture in the biblical narratives that clarifies their status in relation to the Great Flood. Though Numbers 13 and Deuteronomy 2–3 present giant men as enemies of the Israelites in the wilderness, the initial reference to them in Genesis 6 does not specify that the Flood was sent as a punishment for anything they had done. Secondly, despite the annihilation of "all flesh" in the Flood account (with the exception of Noah, his family, and the selected creatures on the ark), traditions persisted that assumed the "giants" had survived the Flood. Viable for later interpretation, therefore, was the possibility that the giants, whether it was one or more of them, escaped from the Flood and that they were not necessarily perpetrators of an evil introduced into the world by fallen "sons of God".

B. The Euhemeristic Citations Preserved through Alexander Polyhistor

Brief, but significant fragmentary accounts of early history that refer to "the giants" were preserved in the first century B.C.E. by Alexander Polyhistor (112–30). Alexander Polyhistor's work "On the Jews" was, in turn, quoted in the fourth century C.E. by Eusebius in his *Praeparatio Evangelica* 9.17.1–9 (fragment 1) and, quite possibly, 9.18.2 (fragment 2).[16] Despite the likelihood that both "fragments"

---

[15] See *b.Niddah* 61a and *Tg. Ps.-Jon.* to Deut. 2:2 and 3:11 in which both Sihon and Og are identified as giants insofar as they are the "sons of Ahijah the son of Shemihazai" (the latter, of course, being the chief of the fallen angels in the Enoch tradition). In *b.Niddah* 61a Og is, in addition, said to have reported the destruction of Sodom and Gomorrah to Abraham, and is singled out as one "who escaped from the generation of the flood" (זה עוג שפלט מדור מבול). – Another passage in *b.Zebahim* 113 refers only to "Og king of Bashan". Its brief account suggests that Og escaped the scalding waters of the Flood by (presumably) holding onto the ark that was miraculously protected by cooled water; on Og as a giant, see further *b.Erub.* 30a, 48a; and *b.Yoma* 80b. Indeed, Milik has speculated whether these texts presuppose a knowledge of giants traditions that ultimately derive from the *Book of Giants* ('Og being a derivational equivalent for the giant 'Ohyah); cf. Milik, *The Books of Enoch*, p. 320 and further Reeves, *Jewish Lore in Manichaean Cosmogony*, p. 22. It is possible that the dream vision of the giant Hahyah in 4Q530 2 ii + 6–7 i + 8–12, lines 7–12, which refers to fire and water, contains imagery of hot waters in describing divine judgment against the giants; see further the *Animal Apocalypse* at *1 En.* 89:3 (Eth.).

[16] The Greek text was published in 1970 by Albert-Marie Denis, *Fragmenta Pseudepigraphorum Quae Supersunt Graeca. Una Cum Historicum et Auctorum Judaeorum Hellenistarum Fragmentis* (PVTG 3; Leiden: Brill, 1970), pp. 197–198. For English translations, see Robert Doran, "Pseudo-Eupolemus: A New Translation and Introduction", in ed. James H. Charlesworth, *The Old Testament Pseudepigrapha* (2 vols.; Garden City: Doubleday, 1983–1985), 2:873–879 (with discussion); Carl H. Holladay, *Fragments from Hellenistic Jewish Authors. I. Historians* (Texts and

stem ultimately from difference sources,[17] there is little doubt that they share an anti-Egyptian perspective on the origin and dissemination of learning and culture,[18] instead favoring a view that assigns the provenience of such knowledge to Babylonia, Abraham's original homeland. If Alexander's citation of these texts in the first century B. C. E. may be allowed to provide a broad *terminus ad quem*, it is probable that the texts go back to works composed sometime during the second century; and, if they, in turn, draw on previous traditions, the dates in which the ideas were generated may possibly be even earlier. As shall presently become obvious, the references to giants in these citations are of particular importance for this study; they exemplify the fusion of biblical and other traditions in a way that is consistent with the possible interpretations of Jewish scripture noted in section A above. In this vein, the Alexander Polyhistor fragments provide a contrast to the way early Jewish apocalyptic traditions developed their interpretations of Genesis 6:1–4.

The citations vary in length. The second fragment, which is considerably shorter, contains both a brief citation and a foregoing introduction by Alexander based on his apparent summary of "anonymous sources". The longer, first fragment is more detailed and, at the same time, more ambiguous with respect to the relationship of the figures mentioned in the text. Despite these differences, the frag-

---

Translations 20; Chico: Scholars Press, 1983), pp. 157–187 (with Grk. text and commentary); and Ben Zion Wacholder, *Eupolemus. A Study of Judaeo-Greek Literature* (HUCM 3; Cincinnati: Hebrew Union College Press, 1974), pp. 105–106 (discussion) and 313–314. See further Harold W. Attridge, "Historiography", in ed. Michael E. Stone, *Jewish Writings of the Second Temple Period* (CRINT II.2; Assen: Van Gorcum, and Minneapolis: Fortress Press, 1984), pp. 165–166; Stuckenbruck, *The Book of Giants from Qumran*, pp. 32–40 (esp. pp. 33–34 and ns. 126 and 127); and Pearson, "Resurrection and the Judgment of the Titans", pp. 42–44.

[17] Those who trace both passages to the same author include Jacob Freundenthal, *Alexander Polyhistor und die von ihm erhaltenen Reste judäischer und samaritanischer Geschichtswerke, Hellenistische Studien* (Breslau: Grass, 1875), pp. 90–92; Benjamin Zion Wacholder, "Pseudo-Eupolemus' Two Greek Fragments on the Life of Abraham" (bibl. in n. 3); see also Hengel, *Judaism and Hellenism*, 1:88–89; Harold W. Attridge, "Historiography", pp. 165–166; Reeves, "Utnapishtim in the Book of Giants?", p. 112; and Holladay, *Fragments from Hellenistic Jewish Authors*, pp. 159 and 163 n. 18. Due to slightly different emphases, however, the fragments attributed respectively to "Eupolemus" (fragment 1) and to "anonymous sources" (fragment 2) stem from a circle of similar traditions. Doran, "Pseudo-Eupolemus", pp. 874–876, followed by Pearson ("Resurrection and the Judgment of the Titans", pp. 42–44), argues that the Samaritan traits of fragment 1 stem derive from Eupolemus himself (though see Stuckenbruck, *The Book of Giants from Qumran*, pp. 34–35, esp. n. 128), while fragment 2 derives from a different tradition, whether oral or written. See further Wacholder's change of mind in *Eupolemus*, p. 287 n. 112; Nikolaus Walter, "Pseudo-Eupolemos (Samaritanischer Anonymus)", in ed. Werner Georg Kümmel, *Jüdische Schriften aus hellenistisch-römischer Zeit* (I/2; Gütersloh: Gerd Mohn, 1976), pp. 137–143 and Huggins, "Noah and the Giants", pp. 104–107 (see bibl. in n. 3 above).

[18] This is especially clear in frg. 1 (9.17.8b – "Enoch first discovered astrology, not the Egyptians"; 9.17.8a – only after Abraham taught the Phoenicians is he said to have taught among the Egyptian priests), while it is implied in frg. 2; whereas Abraham passes his knowledge on to the Phoenicians, nothing is said about such activity when he went to Egypt.

ments, with regard to giants, do have a number of significant features in common that may be described as follows.

First, "the giants" in both fragments are linked with *Babylonia* (9.17.2; 9.18.2) from where, as noted above, higher forms of knowledge originated and spread to other parts of the world.

Second, and obviously, the giants in each fragment relate to the biblical events of *the Great Flood* (9.17.2; 9.18.2)[19] and the building of a tower (i. e. of Babel; 9.17.2; 9.18.2).

Third, *the astrological knowledge* that eventually passed on to the Phoenicians and the Egyptians had itself already been *inherited by Abraham*. Where did Abraham get his knowledge from? After identifying the founders of Babylon as giants "who were delivered from the Flood" (οἱ διασωθέντοι ἐκ τοῦ κατακλυσμοῦ, 9.17.2), fragment 1 goes on to derive the knowledge of astrology from Enoch (9.17.8),[20] the same knowledge that the text attributes to Abraham (9.17.3, 8) who taught it to the Phoenicians and to the Egyptian priests (9.17.4 and 8, respectively). The more cursory citation in fragment 2 (9.18.2) likewise focuses on Abraham's astrological learning that he conveyed to the Phoenicians and, by implication, to the Egyptians. Of special interest in Alexander's introduction to this citation is the claim, more explicit than in fragment 1, that Abraham's ancestry is to be traced back to the giants "who lived in the land of Babylonia".[21]

Fourth, and more generally, both fragments share a series of details about the giants that, nevertheless, are preserved in a somewhat different form. In particular, a certain "Belos" is in each fragment linked with Babylon.[22] In fragment 2, Alexander's introduction unambiguously identifies Belos as a giant who, unlike the other giants who had been "destroyed by the gods because of their impiety", had been able to escape destruction and who dwelt in Babylon where he built a tower. Although the kind of "destruction" is not specified, it may be an allusion to the Flood. Belos thus seems at this point to correspond to the figure of Noah in the biblical tradition,[23] while the activity of building the tower corresponds more to

---

[19] The mention in this fragment of "destruction" is probably an allusion to the Flood.

[20] Enoch is identified in 9.17.9 with Atlas; see n. 26 below.

[21] It is not clear that Alexander's genealogical correlation between Abraham and the giants in the introduction, as Walter argues, is due to the non-Jewish misinterpretation of fragment 1 at v. 3; cf. Walter, "Pseudo-Eupolemos", pp. 137–138 n. 4. This correlation is in fact a plausible inference from fragment 1 and, given both fragments' attempt to relate their histories to the Genesis story, would be consistent with the residual ambiguities in the biblical tradition.

[22] The association of Belos with Babylon stands much in contrast with the works of Herodotus (2.82) and Diodorus Siculus (1.81.6), in which ancestry is used to derive the origin of astrology from Egypt; cf. Doran, "Pseudo-Eupolemus", p. 877.

[23] See Reeves, "Utnapishtim in the Book of Giants?", p. 115, who discusses the possibility of Noah as a giant on the basis of his interpretation of the name "Atambish" in two fragmentary Manichaean texts preserved in Middle Persian and published by Werner Sundermann: "M5900 Recto? and Fragment 'L' page 1, Verso, line 5", in *idem, Mittelpersische und partische kosmogonische und Parabeltexte der Manichäer* (Berlin Turfan Texte 4; Berlin: Brepols, 1978), p. 78 and *idem,*

Nimrod. In fragment 1 Belos is "the son of Kronos" and regarded as "before the Egyptians". As the tradition about Belos is attributed to the Babylonians (9.17.9), Belos functions as part of the writer's emphasis on the pre-eminence of Babylon as the place of the origin and dissemination of culture. No relationship between this Belos and the "giants", however, is delineated. It remains unclear in fragment 1 whether Belos was the first among the giants[24] or merely the first human being (πρῶτον γενέσθαι Βῆλον).[25] Moreover, unlike in fragment 2, the motif of destruction is associated with the tower, and the "escape" (here, from the Flood) is not made by one figure alone, but by a group of "giants" (9.17.2–3). Furthermore, and significantly, the fragments each associate the giants, whether directly (frg. 2: through Abraham's lineage) or indirectly (frg. 1: as the only link between the pre-diluvian Enoch and post-diluvian Abraham), with what is considered to be an innocuous and inoffensive role, namely, that of introducing culture. In neither source are the giants *per se* consigned to punishment. Instead, a distinction is drawn between "good" and culpable giants: Fragment 1 assumes that the giants who built the tower were culpable, as it is "by the power of God" that the tower was destroyed and that, therefore, the giants were scattered from Babylon throughout the earth. At the same time, it was Abraham, born generations later in Babylon, who "pleased God because he eagerly strove to be pious". If the section 9.17.3–4 on Abraham is coordinated with 9.17.8–9 on Enoch, it is implied that Abraham's learning is being derived from or linked to Enoch whose knowledge, in turn, came through instructions revealed to him "by the angels of God". Although the text of fragment 1 does not explicitly identify either Enoch or Abraham as a giant, the reference to Babylon as the birthplace of Abraham, which occurs immediately after the brief account about the giants' building of a tower, certainly allows for such a connection to be inferred.[26] Just how the commendable learning might

---

"Ein weiteres Fragment aus Manis Gigantenbuch", in *Orientalia J. Duchesne-Guillemin emerito oblata* (Textes et Memoires 12; Leiden: Brill, 1984), pp. 491–505, esp. p. 495 n. 19 and p. 497. Reeves and Sundermann both argue that Atambish refers to one of the giants who functions as an anti-Noah figure in the story. The name is, unfortunately, not preserved among the Dead Sea *Book of Giants* fragments. Huggins' contention that, instead, the Manichaean Atambish is to be identified with Enoch is less convincing; cf. Stuckenbruck, *The Book of Giants*, p. 73 n. 43. Grounds for considering Noah as a "giant" (γίγας) might already have been seen as implicit in the biblical story itself, if the notion of the giants' or Nephilim's survival of the Flood is coupled with the view that only Noah and his family (along with the animals) escaped destruction.

[24] As argued by Wacholder, *Eupolemus*, p. 314.

[25] In my opinion, Doran is too quick to use the emendation of the Grk. text (i. e. in designating Belos as the son of Kronos [Κρόνου] rather than as Kronos himself [Κρόνον] to differentiate between the traditions in fragments 1 and 2; cf. Pearson, "Resurrection and the Judgment of the Titans", pp. 43–44 n. 23. In the end, the possibility that Belos is being correlated to one of the Titans of Greek mythology (as is the case with Kronos) or even to a giant cannot be discounted. On the merging of the Titan and giants mythologies into one story during the Hellenistic period, see e. g. Timothy Gantz, *Early Greek Myth. A Guide to Literary and Artistic Sources* (Baltimore/London: The Johns Hopkins University Press, 1993), pp. 44–56 and 445–454.

[26] Fragment 1 may thus assume that Enoch was a giant or perhaps even a progenitor therefore

have been passed down from the ante-diluvian Enoch through the generations to the postdiluvian Abraham is not explained. Nevertheless, the escape of the giants from the Flood leaves the impression that precisely these giants have acted as tradents of the knowledge initially revealed to Enoch. The portrait preserved by fragment 2, together with Alexander's introduction, distinguishes between the calumniable giants who were "destroyed by the gods on account of their impiety" (διὰ τὴν ἀσέβειαν ὑπὸ τῶν θεῶν ἀναιρεθῆναι) and one of their offspring, Abraham, from whom the Phoenicians learned astrology. Perhaps it is significant that no negative overtones are associated with Belos the "giant" who built and inhabited the tower and that this tower, therefore, is not destroyed (*contra* the narratives in frg. 1, 9.17.3 and Gen. 11:1–9).

The description in fragment 1 of the tower builders as "giants" can, of course, be explained on the basis of a possible reading or interpretation of Genesis 10:8–11 (which is concerned with Nimrod the גבר, γίγας) in conjunction with the tower of Babel episode in 11:1–9. Moreover, an allusion at least to Genesis 11:1–9 may even be at work in the introduction to fragment 2, in which the giants' continued existence after the Flood is taken for granted. Thus both fragments, as preserved through Eusebius, can be understood to assume a reading of the biblical tradition, namely, that, if the Great Flood did indeed destroy "all flesh" and if the giants did indeed survive this cataclysm, then the only survivors (i.e. Noah and his family) may have been "giants". In this way, the biblical giants would have been made to function as an important link in introducing and spreading culture, beginning in Babylonia. Significantly, the fragments draw no distinction between commendable and reprehensible knowledge; there is, in fact, no doubt that the authors of these traditions approved of the learning attributed to Enoch and Abraham. Hence, although the link between the "giants" and culture is nowhere made explicit, the fragments both suggest that this spread of knowledge took place through several links in an unbroken chain of transmission: from (a) angels to (b) Enoch to (c) a giant (Belos?) or giants, who then escaped the Flood, to (d) their descendants all the way down to the time of Abraham.

(see n. 25 on the convergence in the Hellenistic period of the myths about the Titans and giants). This notion is strengthened by Enoch's identification with the Titan Atlas who, the writer claims, is said by the Greeks "to have discovered astrology" (9.17.9). As the son of Iapetos, Atlas was consigned to bearing up the sky with a pillar because of his prominent role in the Titans' conflict against Zeus (cf. Hesiod, *Theogony* 517–520). The association of Atlas with the knowledge or discovery of celestial sciences, though unconventional, is nevertheless widely attested; see the cited fragmentary texts in Felix Jacoby, *Fragmente der griechischen Historiker. Erster Teil: Genealogie und Mythographie* (Leiden: Brill, repr. 1957 from 1923), sections 31 (Herodoros of Heracleia, F 13), 32 (Dionysius of Scytobrachion, F 7 c. 60,2), and Xenagoras of Heracleia (F 31, associated with lunar calculations). Cf. further Wacholder, "Pseudo Eupolemus' Two Greek Fragments on the Life of Abraham", p. 96 and n. 83. If fragment 1 identifies Belos (as a Noachic figure) with Kronos and Enoch with Atlas, it should be noted that the chronological sequence of Enoch to Belos, as opposed to that of Kronos to Atlas, shows no concern to retain the sequence of the Greek myth.

Fifth and finally, a feature that both Pseudo-Eupolemus fragments share has to do with the events of destruction: whether occurring through the Flood (frg. 2) or through God's punitive response to the tower episode (frg. 1), they are not associated with any enduring cosmic significance. In contrast to the emerging apocalyptic accounts relating to the diluvian period (on which see below), these euhemeristic traditions functioned to locate Jewish origins, as known through the biblical story, within the context of propaganda in Hellenistic antiquity when it was concerned with the provenience of culture. In order to assert the superiority of Jewish culture, Abraham as progenitor of the Jews is placed within a larger story, as the authors assigned to him a prominent role in the dissemination of learning that originated in Babylon, bringing it first to the Phoenicians and then to Egypt.

C. The Early Enoch Tradition

The early apocalyptic traditions associated with Enoch (*Book of Watchers* = *1 En.* 1–36, *Book of Giants*, *Apocalypse of Weeks* = *1 En.* 93:1–10 + 91:11–17, and *Animal Apocalypse* = *1 En.* 85–90) stand much in contrast to the euhemeristic passages (i. e. Pseudo-Eupolemus) conveyed to Eusebius by Alexander Polyhistor discussed in section B. On the whole, these works emphasize that the biblical Flood was a divine punishment against the evil carried out by the disobedient watchers and their giant offspring. In turn, the Flood, or at least imagery associated with that event, is adapted as the authors attempted to describe divine judgment anticipated in the eschatological future. As the views of these documents are distinguishable, we shall presently discuss them according to the chronological sequence in which they were composed.

C.1. Book of Watchers (1 Enoch 1–36)

The palaeographical date of the earliest manuscript of the *Book of Watchers*, 4Q201 (4QEnoch[a]), can plausibly be set within "the first half of the second century" B. C. E.[27] There are indications, however, that compositional elements of the text date to an earlier period. For example, different strands of tradition in *1 Enoch* chapters 6–11 and 12–16 can be identified, indicating that the text preserved by

---

[27] Cf. the paleographical evaluation by Milik, *The Books of Enoch*, pp. 140–141. For a discussion of this ms. and its contents (23 frgs. corresponding to identifiable parts of the first 12 chs. of *1 En.*), see Loren T. Stuckenbruck, "The Early Traditions Related to 1 Enoch from the Dead Sea Scrolls: An Overview and Assessment", in eds. Gabriele Boccaccini and John J. Collins, *The Early Enoch Literature* (JSJSup 121; Leiden / Boston: Brill, 2007), pp. 41–63 (here pp. 44–46; on the confusion of frg. numbers, p. 44 n. 15). For a detailed the study, see Michael Langlois, *Le premier manuscrit du Livre d'Hénoch. Étude épigraphique et philologique des fragments araméens de 4Q201 à Qumrân* (Paris: Éditions du Cerf, 2008).

4Q201 is itself a conflation of several originally independent traditions.[28] Moreover, given evidence in this manuscript of scribal confusions, it is clear that the manuscript is a copy of an earlier *Vorlage* (which Josef T. Milik plausibly dated back to the 3rd cent.[29]).

In its early received form, the story, especially the tradition associated with ʿAsaʾel, focused on the pre-diluvian dissemination of *reprehensible forms of knowledge* attributed to the "fallen angels" (*1 En.* 7:1; 8:3; 9:6–8a; 13:2b; cf. 16:3). The activities of their offspring, the giants, are held responsible for the increase of violence and oppression on the earth in the time before the Flood (7:3–6; 9:1, 9–10; cf. 10:15).[30] Whereas there is no trace of an attempt among the Pseudo-Eupolemus fragments to distinguish between the angels who instructed Enoch in the sciences and the giants who apparently learned this from Enoch and acted as its tradents, the *Book of Watchers* draw a clear line of demarcation between rebellious angels who fathered the giants and introduced humans to rejected forms of knowledge, on the one hand, and those angels that instructed Enoch concerning the nature and structure of the universe, on the other. The instructions brought to humankind by the fallen angels are listed in the *Book of Watchers* at *1 Enoch* 8:1–3 and are more briefly referred to in 7:1b, 9:8, and 10:7.[31] According to the passage in 8:1–3, which was originally associated with the ʿAsaʾel tradition,[32] these teachings during the pre-diluvian period included:

(a) the production of weapons leading to violence (8:1a);
(b) techniques of fashioning jewelry and cosmetics leading to acts of fornication (8:1b–2); and
(c) activities associated with "magic" and astrological forms of divination (8:3; cf. also 7:1b).

The specificity of these instructions suggests that the fallen angels are being made to represent aspects of culture that the author(s) knew, regarded as a threat, and rejected as contrary to the divine ordering of the world.[33] By association, anyone

---

[28] See e.g. Carol A. Newsom, "The Development of 1 Enoch 6–19. Cosmology and Judgment", *CBQ* 42 (1980), pp. 310–329. Fragments of 4Q201 correspond to chs. 1–5 (in 4Q201 1 i–ii), 6–11 (in 1 iii–vi, in which the ʿAsaʾel and Shemiḥazah traditions are combined), and ch. 12 (in 1 vi). Similarly the early Hasmonean ms. 4Q202 (= 4QEnoch[b]): from chs. 1–5 (1 ii, line 1), chs. 6–11 (1 ii–iv), and ch. 14 (1 vi). On 4Q201 and 4Q202, see also Milik, *The Books of Enoch*, pp. 139–163 and 164–178, respectively.

[29] Milik, *The Books of Enoch*, p. 141.

[30] *1 En.* 10:15 seems to refer, however, not strictly to the giants but to the post-diluvian "souls" that survive them, as in chs. 15–16; cf. Devorah Dimant, "1 Enoch 6–11: A Methodological Perspective", *SBLSP* 13 (1978), pp. 323–339, esp. pp. 333 n. 8.

[31] This list of objectionable teachings is adapted and expanded, respectively, in the later *Book of Parables* at *1 En.* 65:6–11 and 69:1, 6–15.

[32] As shown, e.g., by Newsom, "The Development of 1 Enoch 6–19", p. 313.

[33] It is possible that the attribution of these teachings to the disobedient angels marks a protest against trends associated with the growing influence of Hellenistic culture and/or a perceived corruption among the priesthood; see, respectively, Nickelsburg, "Apocalyptic and Myth in 1 Enoch

involved in or cooperating with such practices is, as the watchers, subject to divine judgment (cf. *1 En.* 1:9).

Of course, the watchers' instructions are intended to contrast with the sort of knowledge mediated through the visions given to Enoch by the good angels. According to the *Book of Watchers*, several angels, with Uriel playing a prominent role among them as an *angelus interpres* (*1 En.* 17:1–20:7), mediate to Enoch visions of two journeys through the cosmos. In these journeys Enoch is led to observe the positions of the stars and luminaries, the places of punishment and reward, and the contours of the earth that has Jerusalem at its center (*1 En.* 17:1–36:4).[34]

It is clear that in the *Book of Watchers* the spread of culture among humanity (albeit in reprehensible forms) is attributed to the disobedient angels, not to the giants. Similarly, as discussed above, there is no explicit reference to giants playing such a role among the Pseudo-Eupolemus fragments in which such a function on their part is nevertheless strongly implied.[35] In the *Book of Watchers* the extent of the giants' involvement in culture is that, in addition to humans (*1 En.* 7–8), they are recipients of the watchers' teaching (*1 En.* 10:7–8). This, however, does not explain why it is that the author(s) of the *Book of Watchers* placed such emphasis on the giants' culpability. According to the Shemiḥazah strand of the narrative, the giants are the product of an unsanctioned sexual union between the angels as heavenly beings and the women on earth (*1 En.* 6:1–4; 7:1a, 2; 9:7–8; 10:9a, 11; 15:3–7, 12). In 15:3–7 the reason for specifying this union as especially loathsome is expressed: the sexual intermingling between spiritual, heavenly beings and earthly human beings of flesh and blood violates, by definition, the natural order (15:4, 9–10).[36] The giants are misfits; as the progeny of an illegitimate union, they are neither fully angelic nor fully human. Thus they are called "bastards" (10:9 – τοὺς μαζήρεους in Codex Panopolitanus, a transliteration from Heb./Aram. ממזרים).[37]

6–11", pp. 383–405 and Suter, "Fallen Angel, Fallen Priest", pp. 115–135. Nevertheless, the myth, given its inherent polyvalent capacity to be reapplied to different situations and its incorporation of the gargantuan oppressors who violently oppress humanity, resists any wholesale reduction to this or that meaning.

[34] In the *Astronomical Book* (*1 En.* 72–82), which was likely known to the writer of *1 En.* 17–36, instructions to Enoch concerning the movements and positions of the sun and moon are likewise mediated by Uriel. See further, e. g., the *Book of Parables* at *1 En.* 71:3–4.

[35] See the discussion of the Pseudo-Eupolemus passages in section B above.

[36] This transgression is in analogy with explanation offered in the *Astronomical Book* for the existence of wrong calendars: disobedient stars have veered off the paths designed for them from the beginning; cf. *1 En.* 80:6–8. The *Book of Watchers* prefaces the story of the watchers with calls to heed the obedience of the created order (*1 En.* 2:1–5:3) and draws inferences from this in denouncing those who transgress the law.

[37] No doubt, therefore, the phrase רוחות ממזרים ("spirits of the bastards") in 4Q510 1.5 (among a list of demonic forces) and 4Q511 35.7 (singled out as needing to be subjugated by God) refers to the giants who have only existed beyond the Flood as spirits. See further 4Q444 1 i 8; 4Q511 2 ii 3; 48.3; 182.3; 48+49–51.2–3; and 1QHᵃ xxiv 3. Depending on the correctness of the restoration at the beginning, a further possible reference to a giant demonic being is the incantation in

As inherent to their mixed nature, the giants in the pre-diluvian period are the embodiment of the violation of the created order; correspondingly, they subject the natural order, both animals and humans, to oppression and death (7:3–5; 9:1, 9b; cf. 10:15).[38] It is ultimately their destructive deeds, not those of humans themselves (as in the Genesis 6 narrative), which result in God's response to human souls' pleas for divine retributive intervention (9:2–3, 10).

In addition to the role of the giants in relation to knowledge, the *Book of Watchers* differs markedly from the Pseudo-Eupolemus fragments with respect to the fate of the giants. Whereas according to the latter, a giant (or giants) escaped the Flood, the former draws on the story of the Flood (both in relation to the past and eschatological future) to describe the giants' punishment. To be sure, the *Book of Watchers* does refer to an escape from the Flood (10:3). However, this escape is restricted to the righteous Noah (called "the son of Lamech") and his offspring. There is, in contrast to the tradition about Belos in Pseudo-Eupolemus fragment 2, no possibility of identifying Noah with one of the giants. Similarly, Enoch, "the scribe of truth/righteousness" (*1 En.* 12:1–3), is dissociated from any connection to a tradition of learning that includes the giants, again in contrast to the impression left by Pseudo-Eupolemus fragment 1 (9.17.8–9).

Although Noah is the only one who escapes divine punishment in the *Book of Watchers* (10:1–3), this does not mean that the giants are left without any post-diluvian existence. Despite the emphasis of the work on the giants' culpability and their punishment, they are allowed to survive, albeit in a radically altered form, that is, as "evil spirits" (15:8–9). The extant textual witnesses to *1 Enoch* 15 do not specify how this change has come about. Nevertheless, the following etiology may be inferred from a reading of 15:3–16:3 as an elaboration on parts of 10:1–22: As a mixture of heavenly and earthly beings, the giants were composed of flesh and spirit. When, on account of their destructive activities they came under divine judgment, the fleshly part of their nature was destroyed, whether through violent conflict among themselves (7:5; 10:12) or through the Flood itself. At this point, spirits or souls emerged from their dead bodies, and it is in this disembodied form that the giants continue to exist until the final judgment (16:1). Since these spirits were the products of a reprehensible union (a *mala mixta*), they are inherently evil. And so, after the time of the Great Flood, they continue to engage in the sort of destructive activities that characterized their existence before. In particular, as before, they wished to bring affliction to human beings (15:12), that is, to the offspring of Noah, because they are jealous that humans – and not they – have escaped the time of destruction associated with the Flood with their bodies.[39]

11Q11 v, in which the demon who visits during the night is addressed in line 6 as ‏ילוד[אדם וזרע‏ ‏הקד]ושים‏ (i. e. "offspring of] Adam and the seed of the ho[ly ones").

[38] On 10:15, however, see n. 30 above.

[39] For a similar etiology (though with some different details), see Alexander, "Demonology of the Dead Sea Scrolls", pp. 337–341. I am, however, uncertain that this explanation from the *Book*

This reconstructed etiology explains how it is that the giants could become so openly identified as demons at a later stage.[40] Moreover, it would have provided one possible way of explaining why demons were thought to be especially intent on entering the bodies of human beings. Finally, the myth serves to place the problem of demonic evil into an apocalyptic perspective. Since the giants are permitted to survive into the post-diluvian period (as disembodied spirits), neither their punishment through internecine battles nor their possible destruction through the Great Flood represent God's final triumph over evil. While the Flood is a clear sign of divine punishment in the past, it is but a proleptic event. Thus in chapter 10 the Flood motif refers back to an event of the sacred past (10:2) and, at the same time, is adapted into imagery that alludes to the eschatological judgment when evil will once and for all be destroyed (10:22). The meantime – that is, between the time of the Flood and the end when evil is eradicated – is characterized as an age during which the evil spirits stemming from the giants can only operate as defeated powers that know that their time is limited.

For all its emphasis on the spirits of the giants, the *Book of Watchers* in the visions suggests that their progenitors, fallen angels, also continue to exert their influence following the Flood. Whereas according to the separate tradition of 10:12 the fettered watchers are consigned seventy generations to a place "below the hills of the ground", in the account of Enoch's journey through the cosmos they are said to lead people to sacrifice to demons until the time of their eschato-

---

of Watchers was as comprehensively influential on "the Qumran demonology" as Alexander seems to suggest.

[40] In particular, see the Christian *Testament of Solomon* 5:3 and 17:1. In 5:3 (within the section 5:1–11), the author reinterprets the demon Asmodaeus – this is a deliberate reference to the Book of Tobit that follows the longer recension (cf. Codex Sinaiticus at 3:7–8, 17; 6:14–15, 17; 8:2–3; 12:15) – one born from a human mother and an angel. In the latter text (in the passage 17:1–5) the demonic power thwarted by Jesus (in an allusion to Mk. 5:3) is identified as having been one of the giants who died in the internecine conflicts (cf. *1 En.* 7:5 and 10:12). Similarly, *Pseudo-Clementine Homilies* 8.12–18 refers to the giants, which are designed as both "bastards" (18; cf. 15) and "demons" (14; 17) in the ante-diluvian phase of their existence. Here they are said to have survived the Flood in the form of disembodied "large souls" whose post-diluvian activities are proscribed through "a certain righteous law" given them through an angel; on this see James C. VanderKam, "1 Enoch, Enochic Motifs, and Enoch in Early Christian Literature", in James C. VanderKam and William Adler, *The Jewish Apocalyptic Heritage in Early Christianity* (bibl. in n. 2 above), pp. 33–101, esp. pp. 76–79 and Yoshiko Reed, *Fallen Angels and the History of Early Christianity and Judaism* (Cambridge: Cambridge University Press, 2005), p. 128. Furthermore, one may consider Tertullian's *Apology* 22, a passage deserving more detailed analysis, in which the offspring of the fallen angels are called a "demon-brood" who "inflict ... upon our bodies diseases and other grievous calamities ...". According to Lactantius, in his *Institutes* 2.15, there are two kinds of demons, "one from heaven and one from earth", that is, demons who are the fallen angels and demons who are spirits derived from these angels' union with human women. Finally, and not mentioned by VanderKam, see the *Instructions* by the 3rd century North African bishop Commodianus (ch. 3), according to which the disembodied existence of the giants after their death is linked to the subversion of "many bodies". The implications of the giants traditions for concepts of demonology at the turn of the Common Era have until now been insufficiently recognized.

logical judgment (19:1).[41] The Greek recension in Codex Panopolitanus adds that the spirits of these angels "will harm people" (λυμαίνεται τοὺς ἀνθρώπους), a function that is generically reminiscent of what the spirits of the giants do (cf. 15:11).[42]

C.2. Book of Giants

This composition has been subject to increasing scholarly attention since John Reeves' study on *Jewish Lore in Manichaean Cosmogony* (1992).[43] The book is nowhere preserved in a complete version; it exists only in Manichaean manuscript fragments in several languages[44] and is distributed among a number of even more fragmentary manuscripts among the Dead Sea materials.[45] Since there is sufficient

[41] Cf. e.g. George W.E. Nickelsburg, *1 Enoch 1* (Hermeneia; Minneapolis: Fortress Press, 2001), pp. 287–288.

[42] I am much in agreement with Reimer, "Rescuing the Fallen Angels", pp. 337–340, who cautions against an assumption that the Dead Sea documents preserve a consistent demonology that is based on the giants' myth and may be attributed to the Qumran community. Significant here is his interpretation (in my opinion correct) of the phrase כול רוחי מלאכי חבל in 4Q510 1.5 as a reference to the watchers.

[43] See bibl. in n.2 above. Between 1992 and 2003 (after which a number of studies have appeared) the following studies have been published (not including dictionary entries and editions): Florentino García Martínez, "The Book of Giants", in *idem, Qumran and Apocalyptic. Studies on the Aramaic Texts from Qumran* (STDJ 9; Leiden / New York: Brill, 1992), pp. 97–115; Robert Eisenman and Michael O. Wise, *The Dead Sea Scrolls Uncovered* (Shaftsbury, UK and Rockport, Maine: Element, 1992), pp. 94–96; Klaus Beyer, *Die aramäischen Texte vom Toten Meer. Ergänzungsband* (Göttingen: Vandenhoeck & Ruprecht, 1994), pp. 119–124 and *Die aramäischen Texte vom Toten Meer. Band 2* (Göttingen: Vandenhoeck & Ruprecht, 2004), pp. 155–162; Huggins, "Noah and the Giants: a Response to John C. Reeves" (bibl. in n.3 above); Stuckenbruck, *The Book of Giants from Qumran* (bibl. in n.2 above); *idem,* "The Sequencing of Fragments in the Qumran Book of Giants: An Inquiry into the Structure and Significance of an Early Jewish Composition", *JSP* 16 (1997), pp. 3–24; *idem,* "The Throne-Theophany of the Book of Giants: Some New Light on the Background of Daniel 7", in *The Scrolls and the Scriptures* (bibl. in n.2 above), pp. 211–220; *idem,* "Giant Mythology and Demonology: From the Ancient Near East to the Dead Sea Scrolls" in eds. Armin Lange, Hermann Lichtenberger, and K.F. Diethard Römheld, *Die Dämonen – Demons. Die Dämonologie der israelitisch-jüdischen und frühchristlichen Literatur im Kontext ihrer Umwelt* (Tübingen: Mohr Siebeck, 2003), pp. 318–338; Émile Puech, "Les fragments 1 à 3 du Livre des Géants de la grotte 6 (pap 6Q8)", *RevQ* 19 (1999), pp. 227–238; *idem,* "Les songes des fils de Semihazah dans le *Livre des Géants* de Qumrân", *Comptes Rendus de l'Académie des Inscriptions et Belles Lettres* janvier-mars (2000), pp. 7–26; *idem,* "Quand on retrouve le Livre des Géants", *Le Monde de la Bible* 151 (2003), pp. 24–27; Andrei A. Orlov, "Overshadowed by Enoch's Greatness: 'Two Tablets' Traditions from the Book of Giants to Palaea Historica", *JSJ* 32 (2001), pp. 137–158; *idem,* "The Flooded Arboretums: The Garden Traditions in the Slavonic Version of 3 Baruch and the Book of Giants", *CBQ* 65 (2003), pp. 184–201.

[44] The three most significant treatments and publications of the Manichaean materials before 2000 are by (1) Walter B. Henning, "The Book of Giants", *BSOAS* 11 (1943–1946), pp. 52–74; (2) Werner Sundermann, "M5900 Recto? and Fragment 'L' page 1, Verso, line 5", in *Mittelpersische und partische kosmogonische und Parabeltexte der Manichäer*, pp. 76–78 (bibl. in n.23 above) and "Ein weiteres Fragment aus Manis Gigantenbuch" (bibl. in n.23 above); and (3) Reeves' *Jewish Lore in Manichaean Cosmogony*. Further work on the Turfan materials is a *desideratum.*

[45] Attention to the presence of the *Book of Giants* among the caves near Khirbet Qumran was given by Józef T. Milik, "Turfan et Qumran: Livre des géants juif et manichéen" (bibl. in n.2). It

evidence to support the likelihood that the *Book of Giants* was composed under the influence of chapters 6–16 of the *Book of Watchers*,[46] the latter may be said to provide its general *terminus a quo* (i. e. late 3rd cent. B. C. E.). More difficult is the question of a *terminus ad quem*. As I have argued elsewhere, a date sometime between the composition of the *Book of Watchers* and Daniel 7 is possible, though this must remain uncertain. At the very least, a date during the first half of the 2nd century B. C. E. is likely.[47]

More significant for the present discussion is that the *Book of Giants* may be said to have adapted and reinforced the view known through the *Book of Watchers* that the giants were destroyed through intramural conflict and perhaps through the Great Flood (see below). Unfortunately, the limited material evidence requires that any arguments about what the document may have originally contained must be accompanied by caution.[48] Nevertheless, the extant fragments from the Dead Sea do preserve enough clues to make it possible to offer some observations about the *Book of Giants'* distinctive view of the watchers and their offspring.

As in the *Book of Watchers* the writer(s) of the *Book of Giants* categorically regarded the giants – under the influence of Genesis 6:4 they are designated both גברין/א and נפילין/א[49] – and their angelic progenitors as evil and, thus, as deserving of an irrevocable punishment.[50] Furthermore, similar to the *Book of Watchers* the work draws on the motif of the giants' destruction through internecine fighting (1Q23 9 + 14 + 15?; 4Q531 7)[51] and through the Flood (2Q26; 4Q530 2 ii + 6–12(?), lines 4–7; 6Q8 2). Finally, the *Book of Giants* also recounts the story about the fall of the angels (so esp. 4Q531 1).

---

was not until 30 years later with the publications at Oxford Press of fragments from the work in the DJD series volume 36 (2000, by Loren T. Stuckenbruck) and 31 (2001, by É. Puech) that the materials have been the focus of closer readings based on direct study of the fragments.

[46] See Stuckenbruck, *The Book of Giants from Qumran*, pp. 24–25 for a listing of the relevant passages and a discussion of the influence of *Book of Watchers* on *Book of Giants*.

[47] Stuckenbruck, *The Book of Giants from Qumran*, pp. 31, 119–123; *idem*, "The Throne Theophany of the Book of Giants" (bibl. in n. 43 above). Though the vision of judgment contained in 4Q530 2 ii + 6–7 i + 8–12, lines 16b–20 is less well developed than the parallel phrases in its counterpart in Dan. 7:9–10, this does not necessarily mean that the *Book of Giants* as a composition was written before Daniel 7. What has been shown, however, is that one can no longer assume that the parallels between these passages suggest a dependence of the *Book of Giants* on the Daniel text.

[48] For an earlier attempt to reconstruct the contents and outline of the document, see Stuckenbruck, "The Sequencing of Fragments in the Qumran *Book of Giants*" (bibl. in n. 43 above).

[49] Thus the "mighty ones" and "Nephilim" of Gen. 6:4 are, as in the Septuagint tradition, identified with one another; so in 4Q531 1.2 and further 4Q530 2 ii + 6–7 i + 8–12, lines 6, 13, and 15.

[50] This view does not mitigate the fact that the disobedient watchers are originally thought to have been "gardeners" whose task it was before their rebellion to act as angelic protectors of the earth (4Q530 2 ii + 6–12(?), line 7 and perhaps 7 ii 11); see Stuckenbruck, *The Book of Giants from Qumran*, pp. 113–116.

[51] On the intramural violence, see also the *Book of Giants* fragments published by Henning, "Book of Giants", p. 60 (Middle Persian frg. *j*, lines 23–32) and pp. 65–66 (Sogdian frg. pp. 1–2,

The *Book of Giants*, however, bears some features that distinguish it from its predecessor in the Enoch tradition. Firstly, the direct communication between Enoch and the watchers that has so characterized *1 Enoch* 12–16, according to which Enoch acts as a mediator between the reprobate angels' vain petitions and God's declaration of judgment, gives way in the *Book of Giants* to a story that centers more narrowly around direct communication between the patriarch and the giants themselves.[52] Secondly, whereas the *Book of Watchers* places an emphasis on how it is that the fallen angels learn of their judgment, the *Book of Giants* casts the spotlight of judgment as it is anticipated by the giants. Given that more space is devoted to describing the exploits of the giants that led to pre-diluvian chaos (4Q531 1; 1Q23 9 + 14 + 15; 4Q532 2), the *Book of Giants* recounts what may be two series of dream visions given to the giants that portend the inevitability of their punishment (2Q26; 6Q8 2; 4Q530 2 ii + 6–12(?), lines 4–20).[53] Thirdly, the *Book of Giants* describes the nature of the giants' plight more fully and with far more detail than either the *Book of Watchers* or *Jubilees* (e.g. 4Q203 8; 4Q530 1 i 5–7; 4Q531 22.4–7, 11–12).[54] In line with this focus on the giants is the fact that, in contrast with other known contemporary Jewish apocalyptic literature, the *Book of Giants* actually provides names for some of the giants: for example, Mahaway, Gilgamesh, Ḥobabish, Ahiram, and the brothers ʿOhyah and Hahyah.[55]

For all the comparisons drawn above between the Pseudo-Eupolemus fragments and the *Book of Watchers*, the notion of fallen or rebellious *angels* does not, as such, occur in the former. This observation renders the comparison of the Pseudo-Eupolemus fragments with the *Book of Giants* especially interesting. Given the fragments' interest in "giants", the importance of the *Book of Giants* within the 2nd century B.C.E. Jewish milieu becomes more than merely an interpretive elabora-

---

lines 1–18). Significantly, as in *1 En.* 10:12, the internecine conflicts may involve the watchers as well, who in 4Q531 4 are included among the list of those killed "by the sword" (line 5). The motif of infighting among the giants is further attested in *Jub.* 5:9 and 7:22–24a (see below) and *Sib. Or.* 1.104–108.

[52] The mediator between Enoch and the giants is none other than one of the giants, Mahaway; see 4Q530 2 ii + 6–12(?), line 21–7 ii 11 and the Manichaean Uygur fragment, in which Mahaway's equivalent is spelled "Mahawai" (see the English translation by Henning, "The Book of Giants", p. 65). In *Genesis Apocryphon* in 1Q20 ii–v and the *Birth of Noah* at *1 En.* 106–107, the mediator between Lamech (who suspects that Noah is one of the giants) and Enoch is Methuselah.

[53] Despite Émile Puech's substantive arguments and reconstruction to the contrary (in "Les fragments 1 à 3 du *Livre de Géants*", pp. 227–238), I am not yet convinced, due to the variable spacing produced by the merging of text from the different fragments, that 6Q8 2 provides the missing portion of Hahyah's dream vision in 4Q530 2 ii + 6–7 i + 8–12, lines 7–12.

[54] The miserable state of the giants is not only represented by their dread of coming judgment, but also manifests itself in restless sleep (despite tiredness) and inability to eat (despite hunger); so in particular 4Q530 1 i 6–7; 4Q531 22.11–12 and the Manichaean fragment "L" Verso, lines 1–4 published by Sundermann, "Ein weiteres Fragment", p. 497. See Matthew J. Goff, "Monstrous Appetites: Giants, Cannibalism, and Insatiable Eating in Enochic Literature", *JAJ* 1 (2010), pp. 12–42.

[55] See Chapter Two below.

tion of Genesis 5–6 as found in the earlier Enochic tradition. We may reckon with the possibility that the author(s) of the *Book of Giants* attempted to refute just the sort of tradition that the euhemeristic fragments contain. Of course, similar to the materials cited by Alexander Polyhistor and preserved for us through Eusebius, the *Book of Giants* associates the story about the biblical "giants" with Babylonian tradition.[56] Furthermore, as in the euhemeristic fragments, the motif of an escape from punishment for at least some of the giants also occurs in the *Book of Giants*.[57] These parallels, however, throw the differences between the traditions into sharp relief. Unlike the Pseudo-Eupolemus fragments, the *Book of Giants* goes to great lengths to draw two unambiguous distinctions: (1) a distinction between the hopeless position of the rebellious angels and the giants, on the one hand, and the knowledge revealed to Enoch, on the other; and (2) a distinction between the culpable giants who did not escape punishment, on the one hand, and the righteous human beings (Noah and sons) who escaped the Flood, on the other. A reconstruction of the book – based on the physical evidence, on inferences from content, and on a comparison with the Manichaean sources – reveals that the work contained a relatively elaborate narrative that focuses on how it was that the giants became cognizant that the punishment for their heinous crimes is indeed inevitable.[58] Inspired by the earlier Enoch tradition, the *Book of Giants* insists that the biblical גברים = נפילים of Genesis 6:4 (who are considered evil) met with a decisive form of punishment in the Great Flood, a destruction from which Noah and his sons were rescued.

This is not, however, the end of the matter. The etiology for the origin of evil spirits given in *1 Enoch* 15:8–16:1[59] seems to be presupposed by some of the *Book*

---

[56] The link is *inter alia* suggested by the preservation of names for giants in the work that derive from Babylonian tradition (though there is no overlap in the names themselves), such as the *Gilgamesh Epic*, so esp. Ḥobabish (4Q203 3.3) from Ḥumbaba (in the Neo-Assyrian version of the *Epic*) or Ḥuwawa (Old Babylonian version) and Gilgamesh (4Q530 2 ii + 6–12 (?), line 2; 4Q531 22.12). See Reeves, *Jewish Lore in Manichaean Cosmogony*, pp. 119–120 and 158 (n. 365); and Matthew J. Goff, "Gilgamesh the Giant: The Qumran *Book of Giants'* Appropriation of *Gilgamesh* Motifs", *DSD* 16 (2009), pp. 221–253.

[57] Perhaps the illusionary hope of such an escape may in the narrative have been associated with the figure of Gilgamesh (4Q531 22.11–12; 4Q530 1.2–7 and 2 ii + 6–12 (?), line 1–3); cf. Stuckenbruck, *The Book of Giants from Qumran*, pp. 23, 103–109, and 161–167. For a different view, however, see Goff, "Gilgamesh the Giant", pp. 240–246.

[58] The plot is not straightforward in the sense that the giants are merely informed of their fate through a series of communications (a "letter" [4Q203 8] and dreams). Along the way, the giants somehow (cf. 4Q531 22.11–12; 4Q530 2 ii + 6–12 (?), line 2) find reason to think that at least some of them will escape destruction; see the text in 4Q530 2 ii + 6–12 (?), lines 1–3 (the giants "rejoiced" on account of what ʿOhyah had told them about what Gilgamesh has said). The story narrates how such optimism on the part of the giants is replaced by their realization that their punishment is imminent.

[59] For the most thorough study of the "origin" the early Enoch tradition, see Archie T. Wright, *The Origin of Evil Spirits* (WUNT 2.198; Tübingen: Mohr Siebeck, 2005), esp. pp. 138–165.

of Giants fragments. Though divine punishment of the giants through intramural fighting and the Great Flood is presented as decisive and irreversible, it remains incomplete; the giants seem to expect that they will survive the Flood in a different form of existence. Of particular interest in this regard may be the very fragmentary text in 4Q531 19.3–4:

3]we (are) [neither] bones nor flesh
4 fl]esh, and we will be blotted out from our form

This text, which is preceded and followed by one line of incomplete text of similar length, assumes a distinction between an existence (line 3) in the form of flesh (בשר) and bones (גרמין) and a subsequent existence (line 4) when a "form" has been "blotted out", that is, when they have assumed an incorporeal or disembodied state (נתמחה מן צורתנא).[60] If the first person plural subjects in both lines are identical, then the words are more likely to be those of the giants rather than of the disobedient angels. The text suggests that, instead of being completely wiped out, the giants will continue to exist, though in an altered state; after their bodies have been destroyed,[61] they can only persist in what remains: disembodied spirits (i. e. what they have inherited from the fallen angels in their being). As such, they have an awareness of being ultimately powerless before God, unable to reverse their punishment (like the watchers, *1 En.* 12–16), and faced by the inevitable certainty that their destruction will come to completion in the eschatological future.

C.3. Animal Apocalypse (1 Enoch 85–90)

This allegorical review of sacred history, which spans from Adam until the initial victories of Judas during the Maccabean crisis, was likely composed between 165 and 160 B. C. E..[62] Much as in the *Book of Watchers*, this work describes the rebellion of the angels (designated initially as "stars"; cf. *1 En.* 86:3–4; 88:3) as having begun in heaven. The angels' act of disobedience occurs in two stages: at first, a single star falls from heaven (86:1) and then "many stars" descend after him and

---

[60] I assume that in line 3 the phrase נתמחה מן צורתנא ("we will be blotted out from our form") is (a) spoken by giants in relation to themselves; and (b) refers to the destruction of the body only, not to the entire being. This body is the result of the watchers' deplorable union with the human daughters and, therefore, becomes the object of divine punishment (cf. *1 En.* 15:8–9; *Jub.* 10:5–6); cf. Émile Puech, "531. 4QLivre des Géants^c ar", in ed. *idem, Qumrân Grotte 4 XXI: Textes Araméens Première Partie 4Q529–549* (DJD 22; Oxford: Clarendon Press, 2001), pp. 49–94 (here p. 79–84).

[61] If 2Q26, 6Q8 2 and 4Q530 2 ii + 6–12(?), lines 4–7 represent dreams of the giants about their punishment, allusions to the Great Flood in these texts may imply that their destruction would be at that time.

[62] Soon after the initial composition (just following 166 B. C. E.), the document was edited through additional content in *1 En.* 90:13–14 (before Judas' death in 160); cf. Patrick A. Tiller, *A Commentary on the Animal Apocalypse of 1 Enoch* (SBLEJL 4; Atlanta: Scholars Press, 1993), pp. 61–79.

impregnate the women on earth (designated "cows").[63] Moreover, like both the *Book of Watchers* and *Book of Giants* (and *Jubilees*; see section D below), the *Animal Apocalypse* preserves the tradition of internecine fighting among at least some of the giants (designated "elephants, camels, and asses"; cf. 86:4; 87:4; 88:2, 6) who kill one another before the time of the Flood. Furthermore, the binding by hand and foot of the first star that fell into the abyss (88:1) is reminiscent of the binding of ʿAsaʾel by hand and foot in the *Book of Watchers* (*1 En.* 10:4–5).[64] The binding of the angels as a whole into the earthly depths (88:3) likewise reflects influence from the Shemiḥazah tradition in *1 Enoch* 10:11–12. However, the throwing down and binding of culpable angels (cf. *Jub.* 5:6 and *1 En.* 10:5) derives ultimately from widespread images associated with the binding and incarceration of the Titans in Tartarus known through Greek mythologies, as told, for example, in Hesiod's *Theogony* (713–721) and which was later adapted with a number of modifications in the *Sibylline Oracles* Book 3 (105–158; esp. 150–151).[65] It is presumably in the netherworldly place of imprisonment where the disobedient angels are thought to be kept until the end of time, when they are to be judged and thrown into the abyss for good (*1 En.* 90:24).

Like the *Book of Watchers* and *Book of Giants*, the *Animal Apocalypse* distinguishes between the angelic wayward progenitors and the giants. However, in the *Animal Apocalypse* this differentiation becomes more pronounced. The author(s)

---

[63] If the *Book of Watchers* (at *1 En.* 8:1) lies behind the text, then perhaps the *Animal Apocalypse* assumes that ʿAsaʾel descended first to teach the women the art of beautification through jewelry and cosmetics. Once the women have made themselves attractive, the other angels are seduced and descend as well; cf. Coblentz Bautch, "Decoration, Destruction and Debauchery: Reflections on 1 Enoch 8 in Light of 4QEn^b", pp. 79–95 (bibl. in n. 5 above); cf. esp. *1 En.* 19:1 and *Test. Reub.* 5:6. The two-stage descend (ʿAsaʾel – the other angels) to earth may be reflected in *4QPesher of the Periods* (4Q180) 1.7, which represents an early stage of designating the leader of the fallen angels as ʿAzazʾel; cf. Devorah Dimant, "The 'Pesher on the Periods' (4Q180) and 4Q181", *IOS* 9 (1979), pp. 77–102.

[64] See Tiller, *A Commentary on the Animal Apocalypse*, pp. 84–85.

[65] See the cursory discussion in Pearson, "Resurrection and the Judgment of the Titans", pp. 38–41 and esp. Jan N. Bremmer, "Remember the Titans", in eds. Christoph Auffarth and Loren T. Stuckenbruck, *The Fall of the Angels* (TBN 7; Leiden/Boston: Brill, 2004), pp. 35–61 (here pp. 55–60). In terms of how the *Animal Apocalypse* retains details from the myth (i.e. casting down, incarceration, binding in chains), the text comes much closer to the Hesiod account than, for instance, the adaptation thereof in *Sib. Or.* 3, which, though recounting the defeat of the Titans (105–158 and 199–201), makes reference to neither their being hurled down nor to their fettered imprisonment. It is possible that the verb *wagara* (the Ethiopic may mean either "to stone" or "to throw") is not so much an allusion to the casting down of the fallen angels alone (as argued by Tiller, *A Commentary on the Animal Apocalypse*, pp. 254–255), but has its origin in the Hesiodic version of the Titan myth, which more broadly narrates that the Titans are defeated when 300 stones are hurled upon them and they are cast in chains into Tartarus. For an abbreviated adaptation of the tradition, see 2 Pet. 2:4: "for when the angels sinned, God did not spare them but put them in Tartarus (ταρταρώσας) with ropes of gloom and handed them over to be kept in judgment" (translation my own; see the parallel passage in Jude 6, which does not contain the verbal form alluding to Tartarus).

of the *Animal Apocalypse* stressed that the Flood resulted in the complete annihilation of the giants. In *1 Enoch* 89:6, this fate of the giants is made explicit[66]:

And that vessel floated on the water, but all bulls, elephants, camels and asses sank along with all (remaining) animals to the bottom, so that I could no longer see. And it was not possible for them to emerge (from there), and they were destroyed and sank into the depths.

This passage reflects a shift of emphasis away from other early Jewish apocalyptic traditions (i. e. *Book of Watchers, Book of Giants, Jubilees*) that leave room for a post-diluvian existence for the giants in altered form. The author of this text in the *Animal Apocalypse* does not qualify the giants' destruction, however it may have occurred. The allegorical narrative, in contrast to the fallen angels, leaves no trace of a survival or continuing presence for them. In this respect, the *Animal Apocalypse* contrasts even more with the Pseudo-Eupolemus sources than either the *Book of Watchers* or *Book of Giants*.

C.4. Apocalypse of Weeks (1 Enoch 93:1–10 + 91:11–17)

Composed only a few years before the *Animal Apocalypse*,[67] the *Apocalypse of Weeks* refers explicitly to the disobedient angels only once. The writing recounts sacred history within a scheme of ten periods of time called "weeks", the first seven of which cover the beginning until the time of writing, while the end of weeks seven through ten plus "many weeks without end" (*1 En.* 91:17) are concerned with events in the eschatological future. It is within this future, in the final week ten, that an "eternal judgment ... will be executed against the watchers of the eternal heaven, a great judgment that will be decreed in the midst of the angels" (91:15).[68]

Given the indebtedness of the *Apocalypse of Weeks* to prior Enochic tradition, this final judgment of disobedient angels comes as no surprise (*1 En.* 10:4–8; 18:14–15; cf. *Animal Apocalypse* at *1 En.* 88:1 and *Jub.* 5:6, 10–11; 7:21; 10:5–9). This is, however, the first time in the composition that the "watchers" are mentioned. This emphasis on their future judgment may reflect the opening of the *Book of Watchers* (*1 En.* 1:5), according to which, at the time of divine judgment, an eschatological theophany, "the watchers will quake" and that "great fear and quaking will seize them until the ends of the earth".

Nevertheless, it is possible that the *Apocalypse of Weeks'* description of events in the second week (i. e. the time of the Flood) already allude to the disobedience of

---

[66] The translation below is adapted from that of Siegbert Uhlig, "Das äthiopische Henochbuch", *Jüdische Schriften aus hellenistisch-römischer Zeit* (V/6; Gütersloh: Gütersloher Verlagshaus, 1984), here p. 684. The extant fragment in 4QEnoch[c] = 4Q206 IV 1.20–21 does not preserve any divergent reading; cf. Milik, *The Books of Enoch*, p. 238.

[67] For discussions of the date, see Nickelsburg, *1 Enoch 1*, pp. 440–441 and Loren T. Stuckenbruck, *1 Enoch 91–108* (CEJL; Berlin: Walter de Gruyter, 2007), pp. 60–62.

[68] Translation of the Eth. is from Stuckenbruck, *1 Enoch 91–108*, p. 145, with the reading "great judgment" following the Aram. text in 4QEnoch[g] = 4Q212 1 iv 23.

the angels and its consequences. According to *1 Enoch* 93:4 in the second week, which follows upon the advent of Enoch, "great evil will arise and deceit will have sprouted up" (Aram. of 4Q212 1 iii 24–25 reads: "the second [week] in which there will sprout deceit and violence"). The language of sprouting, combined with violence and deceit, is strongly reminiscent of planting imagery associated with the evil angels and their offspring (*Book of Giants* at 4Q530 2 ii + 6–12 (?), lines 5–12; and *Genesis Apocryphon* at 1Q20 xvi–xvii).[69] The "sprouting" would allude to the insemination of women by the angels that led to the birth of the giants.[70] This planting imagery functioned as a contrasting counter-image to Noah, his offspring, the elect community of Israel, or, for example, the Enochic community who are presented as "plant of truth" and related designations.[71]

The *Apocalypse of Weeks* does not assign the defeat of the watchers to the eschatological future. If the image of sprouting recounting within the second week has its background in the disobedient angels story, it is significant that afterwards, yet within that same week, the text specifies that, "there will be the first end" (*1 En.* 93:4). The end is not simply an allusion to the Great Flood, but may, more specifically, refer back to a judgment or punishment that came into effect at that time against those involved with the evil just described. The "eternal judgment" in week ten (91:15) is then a defeat of evil that is permanent, whereas the initial one took place during the Deluge. The text thus implies the continued existence of a form of evil that had its beginnings during the second week, when it was held to account, but not annihilated. Somehow, the wrongdoing carried out in the weeks that follow may be understood as a continuation of what had gotten underway before the Flood.

D. The Book of Jubilees

The *Book of Jubilees* was composed sometime during the middle of the 2nd century B. C. E.[72] The narrative follows a sequence that broadly corresponds to what we find in the biblical story from the beginning of Genesis until Israel's exodus from

---

[69] As I have argued in *1 Enoch 91–108*, pp. 94–95; cf. further Orlov, "The Flooded Arboretums", pp. 184–201 and Daniel A. Machiela, *The Dead Sea Genesis Apocryphon: A New Text and Translation with Introduction and Special Treatment of Columns 13–17* (STDJ 79; Leiden / Boston: Brill, 2009), pp. 96–98.

[70] Cf. 1QapGen ii 15, in which Lamech is assured that "the planting of fruit" (נצבת פריא) in his wife did not come from the watchers.

[71] See Loren T. Stuckenbruck, "4QInstruction and the Possible Influence of Early Enochic Traditions: An Evaluation", in eds. Charlotte Hempel, Armin Lange, and Hermann Lichtenberger, *The Wisdom Texts from Qumran and the Development of Sapiential Thought* (BETL 159; Leuven: Leuven University Press and Peeters, 2002), pp. 245–261.

[72] See the thorough discussion of date by James C. VanderKam, *Textual and Historical Studies in the Book of Jubilees* (HSM 41; Missoula: Scholars Press for Harvard Museum, 1977), pp. 207–285 and George W. E. Nickelsburg, *Jewish Literature between the Bible and the Mishnah* (Minneapolis: Fortress Press, 2005, 2nd ed.), pp. 73–74 (early 160's B. C. E.).

Egypt. Accordingly, the work offers a complex network of storylines, five in all, that each explain the beginnings of evil, sin and wrongdoing; and it is among these five that *Jubilees'* adaptation of tradition relating to Genesis 6:1–4 takes its place. In addition to the story of disobedient angels, *Jubilees* draws on the following distinguishable, yet interconnected traditions found in Genesis: (1) the garden scene involving the first woman, Adam and the serpent (*Jub.* 3:8–31); (2) the murder of Abel by Cain (4:1–6, 9, 31–32); (3) Noah's nakedness and the cursing of Canaan (7:7–15 and 8:8–9:15); and (4) the tower of Babel incident (10:18–11:6).

Jubilees, however, does not simply interpret material familiar through Genesis; the work draws on a number of interpretations and elaborations of Pentateuchal traditions, some of which were in Aramaic.[73] Among the latter, *Jubilees* seems to have been aware of Enoch tradition in the *Book of Watchers* (5:1–11; 7:22–25; cf. 10:1–11), *Astronomical Book* (4:17) and, with less certainty, *Apocalypse of Weeks* (cf. 4:18) and the *Epistle* (cf. 4:19).[74] The account about disobedient angels in *Jubilees* cannot be easily explained on the basis of reading the Genesis account alone. As shown by the writer's interest in the figure of Enoch (4:17–26) and his view that the "sons of God", as rebellious beings, sired malevolent giants, it is likely that the Enochic tradition provided at least one source. In particular, this Enochic influence is reflected in the statement that Enoch "testified to the Watchers who had sinned with the daughters of men because these had begun to mix with earthly women so that they became defiled" (*Jub.* 4:22; cf. *1 En.* 9:8, 15:3; cf. *Book of Giants* at 4Q531 1.1–3).

Though admitting some dependence on the earliest Enochic tradition (the *Book of Watchers*), the writer of *Jubilees* departs from the Enochic predecessors in several points. We may distinguish the emphases of *Jubilees* from the *Book of Watchers* at *1 Enoch* chapters 6–16 in at least four ways: (1) the location of the rebellious angels' transgression; (2) the means of punishment carried out on these angels and their

---

[73] This matter is debated esp. in relation to *Aramaic Levi Document* and *Genesis Apocryphon*; contrast e. g. Esther Eshel, "The *Imago Mundi* of the *Genesis Apocryphon*", in eds. Lynn R. LiDonnici and Andrea Lieber, *Heavenly Tablets: Interpretation, Identity and Tradition in Ancient Judaism* (JSJSup 119; Leiden/Boston: Brill, 2007), pp. 111–131 and Loren T. Stuckenbruck, "Pseudepigraphy and First Person Discourse in the Dead Sea Documents: From the Aramaic Texts to Writings of the Yahad", in eds. Adolfo Roitman, Lawrence H. Schiffman and Shani Tsoref, *The Dead Sea Scrolls and Contemporary Culture. Papers in Celebration of the 60th Anniversary of the Discovery of the Dead Sea Scrolls* (STDJ 93; Leiden: Brill, 2011), pp. 295–326 with James Kugel, "Which is Older, *Jubilees* or *Genesis Apocryphon*? An Exegetical Approach", pp. 257–294 in the same volume; Daniel K. Falk, *The Parabiblical Texts: Strategies for Extending the Scriptures in the Dead Sea Scrolls* (LSTS 63; London: T. & T. Clark, 2007), pp. 26–106 (esp. pp. 29–30). See the nuanced arguments on the *Genesis Apocryphon* by Machiela, *The Dead Sea Genesis Apocryphon*, pp. 8–17 (*Genesis Apocryphon* and *Jubilees* rely on a common source). See further chapter 3 n. 3 below.

[74] For arguments in favor of *Jubilees'* use of the latter two, see James C. VanderKam, *Enoch and the Growth of an Apocalyptic Tradition* (CBQMS 16; Washington D.C.: The Catholic Biblical Association of America, 1984), pp. 142–44 and Stuckenbruck, *1 Enoch 91–108*, pp. 60–61 and 214–215.

malevolent offspring; (3) the explanation for the origin of demons; and (4) the motif of angelic instruction. Each of these aspects are discussed below.

D.1. The Location of the Angels' Transgression

According to *Jubilees* and unlike the Enochic tradition, the angels' disobedience takes place on earth. The Hebrew word-play that relates the descent (the vb. ירד) of the angels during the time of Jared (ירד) is picked up by the writer (cf. *1 En.* 6:6; 106:13; *1QGenesisApocryphon* iii 3) and coordinated with the time the angels begin to carry out their mission to instruct humanity "and to do what is just and upright upon the earth" (4:15; cf. 5:6). It is only once on earth that the angels are distracted from their mission by the beauty of the daughters of humanity (5:1). In addition to the forbidden sexual union that leads to the birth of gargantuan offspring, they are held responsible for teachings that lead to sin (see discussion of *Jub.* 8:3 in section D.4 below).

By contrast, according to the *Book of Watchers*, it is in heaven, where the "sons of God" take the decision to reproduce through the women on earth. By postponing the angels' transgression to the time after their descent, the text of *Jubilees* accomplishes two things that are of theological import. First, "heaven" is preserved as a place of complete sanctity where the God of Israel reigns. While the early Enochic tradition insists on God's transcendent rule (*1 En.* 14:8–25), it does not reflect on the question of how divine rule in heaven could be reconciled with the heavenly angels' decision to be disobedient (6:1–8).[75] The earthly location of the angels' decision to sire offspring in *Jubilees* relieves this theological tension; the transgression of breaching cosmic boundaries, so emphasized in the *Book of Watchers* (*1 En.* 15:8–11), plays no role here. The earthly setting of their sin served to keep the heavenly and earthly spheres distinct, so that the boundaries established at creation are not violated.[76] Second, the strong etiological component of the fallen angels and giants narrative in the *Book of Watchers* is less prominent in *Jubilees*, in which the paradigmatic function of the story is more clearly in focus[77]: the angels' reprehensible actions, both their union with women and their culpable teachings,

---

[75] Such a problem emerges only when reading *1 En.* chs. 6–11 and 12–16 in synthesis, as is to be understood because different hands were responsible for the traditions, for example, behind chs. 6–11 (which do not refer to Enoch at all), on the one hand, and chs. 12–16 (the earliest part of the *Book of Watchers* that relates to the figure of Enoch), on the other.

[76] This comparison may reflect a mild critique of the Enoch tradition on the part of *Jubilees* that, at the same time, affirms the former's concern to distance the generation of evil from heaven. Thus *Jubilees* does not speculate on the origin of Mastema, the chief of demons whose role is not harmonized with that of the angels and is not mentioned until ch. 10.

[77] By "paradigmatic function" I refer to the paraenetic use of the story of the angels, i.e. to warn the audience from behaving as they did (cf. e.g. Jude 5–9; 2 Pet. 2:4–10). The paradigmatic is also at work in the *Book of Watchers* since it is implied that those who participate in activities and follow the teachings attributed to the angels and giants are culpable. See, however, the nuance in n. 79 below.

serve as a warning to anyone who would behave in the same way. This is illustrated best in Noah's exhortations to his children that they "keep themselves from fornication, uncleanness, and from all injustice" (7:20), precisely those activities which the angels and their progeny have spread to humanity (7:22–24).[78]

So, at this stage of the storyline in *Jubilees*, the negative consequences of the angels' sin relates primarily to the violence their gigantic offspring bring upon the earth (7:22–25) and the reprehensible instructions they have introduced and disseminated among humans (8:3). Whereas in the *Book of Watchers* it is primarily the wayward angels and giants' activities that lead to divine punishment (cf. *1 En.* 10:1–15), in *Jubilees* the picture is more nuanced: it is because the sins of the angels and giants have caused humanity to do the same that the Flood was sent upon the earth (7:21a, 25).[79] This additional, more transparent, emphasis on human responsibility in *Jubilees* mirrors the culpability of the angels; just as the angels were steered away from the mission they were originally given by God, so also the people of Israel should be wary of doing likewise.

D.2. The Purpose of the Flood

In its account of the Great Flood, *Jubilees* negotiates conceptually between emphases found in the *Book of Watchers* (*1 En.* 10) and the story in Genesis chapters 6–9, and in the later take-up of both in the Enochic tradition (*1 En.* 1–5; the *Epistle* at 98:4–8). Unequivocally, in Genesis chapter 6 the flood comes as God's response to the violence and sin committed by human beings on earth (see Gen. 6:3, 13, 17). By contrast, the *Book of Watchers* and *Book of Giants* treat the Flood tradition as but one manifestation of divine judgment against the angels and giants (see *1 En.* 10:2–3; the motif is at least as prominent in the *Book of Giants*: 2Q26; 4Q530 2 ii + 6–12 (?), lines 4–7; 6Q8 2). Analogous to the *Book of Giants*' reception of the *Book of Watchers*, *Jubilees* places greater emphasis on the Flood and, in addition, picks up on the motif of the giants destroying one another (*1 En.* 7:5; 10:9, 12; *Book of Giants* 1Q23 9 + 14 + 15?; 4Q531 4), a motif noticeably absent from Genesis. The narrative of *Jubilees* thus weaves together elements from received traditions to create a new account: the Great Flood comes as a divine response to ante-diluvian sins committed by human beings (as in Gen. 6) whose wrongdoings were fuelled by the transgressing angels and giants who, in turn, have likewise been punished, though by other means (*Jub.* 10; as in *Book of Watchers* at *1 En.* 10:4–15). Since *Jubilees* contributes its own voice to the tradition, it is appropriate to elaborate this storyline a little further below.

---

[78] Citations of Jubilees are taken from the English translation by James C. VanderKam, *The Book of Jubilees: Translated* (CSCO 511 and Scriptores Aethiopici 88; Leuven: Peeters, 1989).

[79] Though the *Book of Watchers* implicates people who have been taught by the fallen angels, the story of punishment does not so much focus on them as upon the angels and the giants.

As just suggested, in contrast to the *Book of Watchers, Jubilees* does not clearly link the Flood itself to God's punishment of the angels and giants. On the one hand, in *1 Enoch* 10:1–3 a deluge is announced to "the son of Lamech" after the corrupt instructions and horrific misdeeds of the watchers and giants have been described (cf. 7:1–8:3) and after the complaints by the murdered of humanity have been mediated by angels to God (cf. 8:4–9:10). On the other hand, two passages in *Jubilees* (5:3–5 and 7:20–25) suggest that it is sinful humanity – whatever the role of the fallen angels and giants in the narrative – whose deeds, as in Genesis 6, need to be held accountable and provide the immediate reason for the Flood.[80]

While in *Jubilees* the Flood is primarily a response to sins among humans, the divine punishments against the angels and giants take different forms, respectively (as in *1 En.*). *Jubilees* recounts the punishment of the angels by having them bound and sent to the nether regions of the earth (5:6; 10:7–8), a scenario that according to the *Book of Watchers* is carried out against ʿAsaʾel (*1 En.* 10:4–6, 8). This motif, as is the case in the *Animal Apocalypse* (*1 En.* 88:3; cf. section C.3 above), may reflect the influence of the Tartarus tradition preserved, for example, in Hesiod's *Theogony*. As for the giants, their punishment in *Jubilees* is manifested through their intramural violence (5:7, 9; 7:22–24) that again may be compared with the *Book of Watchers* (*1 En.* 7:3; 10:12) where, however, in 10:12 this includes the fallen angels as well.

The form of punishment meted out to the giants in *Jubilees* may go back to a double interpretation of the ambiguous Hebrew verb ידין of Genesis 6:3: (1) In *Jubilees* 5:8 the verb is understood in the sense of "to dwell" (as in the LXX) – "My spirit will not *dwell* on people forever, for they are flesh. Their lifespan is to be 120 years". (2) Distinguishable from the Greek translation, however, *Jubilees* applies the term "flesh" (בשר) in Genesis 6:3 not to human beings, but to the giants who, though they have bodies like humans, are made to destroy one another in advance of the Flood (*Jub.* 5:9). In this way, the text makes clear that the giants are not expected in the unfolding narrative to survive the Flood, nor does the text leave one to imagine that they were allowed to live long enough to be punished through it; the Flood itself is not their only form of punishment.

If the angels and giants have introduced, or at least increased, evil in the world, their malevolent deeds do not in *Jubilees* lead to a wholesale corruption of human nature. Quite the contrary: after their punishments are recounted and their condemnation on the final day of judgment confirmed (*Jub.* 5:10–11), the text states that God "made a new and righteous nature for all his creatures so that they *would not sin with their whole nature* until eternity. Everyone will be righteous – each according to his kind – for all time" (5:12; italics my own). This re-creation or

---

[80] As mentioned above, the watchers' fornication with the women of the earth and the violence of several generations of their progeny (7:21b–24a) contribute to conditions which make divine judgment through the Flood necessary, though they themselves are not expressly punished through the Flood.

renewal of human nature may seem puzzling in the aftermath of the ante-diluvian upheavals. However, it is not unqualified: the writer allows for a propensity to sin within human beings while maintaining that the punishment of the watchers and their offspring addressed something within humanity that had gone irretrievably wrong on account of them. *Jubilees* thus hints at, but does not develop a theological anthropology that views the human race as a whole as having been affected by the angelic rebellion, a consequence that is partially dealt with through God's restorative activity.

D.3. The Residual Effect of Past Punishment of Evil

While the punishment through the Flood and intramural violence has led to a renewal of humanity (*Jub.* 5:12), *Jubilees* explains the continuing reality of human wrongdoing and suffering after the Flood as a manifestation of residual influences left by ante-diluvian evils. The explanation of human suffering is based on *Jubilees'* particular version of "the origin of demons". The etiology for evil spirits in *Jubilees* can be compared to that in both the *Book of Watchers* and *Book of Giants*, which identify such spirits with the spirits or souls of the dead giants (compare e.g. *Jub.* 10:5 with *1 En.* 15:8–11). Another similarity is that, ultimately, the demonic forces behind evil in the world are regarded, in effect, as powers whose judgement is assured; they are already defeated beings whose complete destruction is only a matter of time (until the day of judgement; cf. *Jub.* 10:7, 8, 11).

Although *Jubilees* seems to depart from the Enoch traditions in having the giants killed through intramural violence alone,[81] the writer adapts the Enochic etiology of demons, holding out for a continued existence of giants in some form after the Flood. Both traditions share the view that the giants become disembodied spirits as a consequence of their destruction of one another (*1 En.* 15:9, 11–16:1; cf. *Jub.* 10:5 and 5:8–9); both traditions perhaps even imply that the giants' disembodied spirits could already have been active before the Flood was sent.[82] There are, however, differences between these traditions on a smaller scale. The *Jubilees* account differs from the Enochic traditions in that the nature of demonic evil is not articulated in anthropological terms (cf. *1 En.* 15:4–10[83]), that is, in *Jubilees*

---

[81] The author perhaps did not find a warrant in the Genesis tradition known to him that the giants died through the Flood (see the allusion to Gen. 6:3 in *Jub.* 5:8). Similarly, see the text of 4Q252 i 2–3 which, drawing on Gen. 6:3, focuses only on the cutting short of humans living before the Flood. See Devorah Dimant, "The Flood as Preamble to the Lives of the Patriarchs: The Perspective of Qumran Hebrew Texts", in eds. Reinhard Kratz and Devorah Dimant, *Rewriting and Interpreting the Hebrew Bible* (BZAW 439; Berlin: Walter de Gruyter, 2013), pp. 101–134 (here, pp. 119–125).

[82] While the *Book of Watchers* is silent on this point, Noah's prayer in *Jub.* 10:5 implies that the giants' spirits, alongside the watchers, were active before the Flood.

[83] Like the *Book of Watchers*, Philo, *Quaest. Gen.* 1.92 is concerned with human nature, though to the point that the angels and giants function as a projection of what Philo wishes to emphasize

the impurity of the giants as mixtures between rebellious angels and earthly women is not expressed as an *inherent* characteristic. Though it is possible that the aetiology of demons in *1 Enoch* 15 is presupposed by *Jubilees* – after all, the union between the watchers and human daughters is considered a form of "pollution" (4:22; cf. 7:21) – it is not clear that they are described as evil *per se*. The effect of this is, in effect, to strengthen the analogy between the giants' responsibility for their deeds and the responsibility that humans bear when they disobey in similar fashion. Punishment in *Jubilees* comes not because of what one is or has become by nature, but is essentially the result of wilful disobedience.

In terms of how it is that demons contribute to the post-diluvian suffering of humans, *Jubilees* goes into the kind of detail for which there is no trace in the Enoch traditions. The demonic spirits, which bring affliction to humanity after the Flood, are but a tenth of their original number. Nine-tenths are completely destroyed[84] while one tenth are permitted to carry on with their destructive malevolence. This permission is granted as a divine concession to the petitions of Mastema, their chief, who, after God has commanded the angels to bind all the spirits for judgement, requests that some spirits be allowed to corrupt humans, lead them astray and to cause suffering through illness (*Jub.* 10:8, 12; cf. 7:27-Noah's words: "For I myself see that the demons have begun to lead you and your children astray ...").[85]

The writer of *Jubilees* thus attempts to steer a fine line between human responsibility, on the one hand, and demonic cause, on the other. While evil in its various forms is regarded as a manifestation of activities of the spirits of the giants, humanity is capable of rising above such influences and, to some degree, even able to manage afflictions by applying the herbal remedies given to Noah by one of the angels (*Jub.* 10:10–13). If in comparison with the *Book of Watchers*, the situation of disobedient humans and the giants in *Jubilees* is less distinct and more analogous, the rebellious angels tradition serves not only to explain why humans in the author's day fall prey to wrongdoing and suffering from external influences, but also and especially to serve as a warning that Jews should stay away from engaging in the giants' "fornication", "uncleanness" and "injustice" (7:20; cf. 7:21–25).

---

about humanity; they are a mixture of "spiritual" and "somatic" realms that should be kept separate and, therefore, function as examples for what people should likewise avoid. See Chapter Seven below.

[84] Cf. *Animal Apocalypse* at *1 En.* 89:5–6, according to which all the giants are destroyed by the Flood and have no afterlife.

[85] For a study of this tradition, also in its reception, see James C. VanderKam, "The Demons in the *Book of Jubilees*", in *Die Dämonen – Demons. Die Dämonologie der israelitisch-jüdischen und frühchristlichen Literatur im Kontext ihrer Umwelt* (bibl. in n. 43 above), pp. 339–364.

D.4. The Disobedient Angels' Teachings

One aspect of the fallen angels tradition has been mentioned above but not developed: the reprehensible instructions traced back to the rebellious angels (see section C.1). According to *Jubilees* their teaching was mainly concerned with "the omens of the sun, moon, and stars and every heavenly sign", that is, with astrological lore associated with wrong calendrical reckonings and objectionable forms of divination (*Jub.* 8:3; 11:8).[86] The calendrical calculations of the disobedient angels do not disappear when they are punished. After the Flood, Cainan, great grandson of Noah, discovers this teaching inscribed on a stone and "read what was in it, copied it, and sinned on the basis of what was in it" (8:3; cf. *1 En.* 80:1–8 and 82:5). This learning, which is kept secret for fear that knowledge of it would incur Noah's anger (8:4), eventually finds its way down to Noah's descendants, that is, down to the time of Nahor, Abraham's grandfather (11:8). In *Jubilees*, then, while the watchers are originally good when sent to instruct human beings on earth (cf. 5:6), their knowledge becomes skewed through their illicit sexual union with women. Once the watchers transgressed the purpose of their mission, the author distinguishes sharply between two tracks of learning that are subsequently kept distinct: (1) the wrong astrological knowledge introduced by the wayward angels and conveyed through Cainan down to Noah's descendants and, in stark contrast, (2) the correct knowledge about the movements of heavenly bodies from which agricultural cycles and calendrical reckonings are to be derived. This latter divinely revealed learning is traced back to instruction given to Enoch by the heavenly angels (cf. 4:18, 21); it is bound up with the 364-day solar calendar that the writer uncompromisingly supports throughout the work. From Enoch, it was transmitted through Noah and his family who escaped the flood and then finally re-emerges as a component of the piety attributed to Abraham (12:16) and his descendants through the line of Jacob.

The sharp differentiation in *Jubilees* between opposed traditions of learning is best perceived against the background of the euhemeristic traditions discussed above (see section B), especially fragment 1 of Pseudo-Eupolemus. In Pseudo-Eupolemus, the figure of Enoch is, as in *Jubilees*, also the recipient of angelic instruction centred on astrological knowledge (*Praep. Evang.* 9.17.8–9; cf. *4QPsJub*^c = 4Q227 2.1–4 and *Genesis Apocryphon* at 1Q20 ii 20–21). This knowledge is also attributed to Abraham (9.17.3) who, in turn, is said to have passed it on to the Phoenicians. As we have seen, *Jubilees* shares the view that the knowledge revealed to Enoch eventually comes down to Abraham. There is, however, a big difference. In Pseudo-Eupolemus fragment 2, the lineage of a Noahic figure (9.17.2) and Abraham

---

[86] On this, see Armin Lange, "The Essene Position on Magic and Divination", in eds. Moshe Bernstein, Florentino García Martínez and John Kampen, *Legal Texts and Legal Issues. Proceedings of the Second Meeting of the International Organization for Qumran Studies, Published in Honour of Joseph M. Baumgarten* (STDJ 23; Leiden: Brill, 1997), pp. 377–435 (pp. esp. 401–403).

(9.18.3, if this second fragment belongs to the same work) is associated with "the giants" who escaped the destruction of the Flood and built a tower (9.17.2; cf. 9.18.2, where only one "giant" called "Belos" is in view). Furthermore, the Pseudo-Eupolemus text makes no effort to specify whether the angels who revealed astrological knowledge to Enoch were good or bad. The resulting picture – which blends the traditions of giants, the learning given to Enoch, and the figures of Abraham and Noah – is one that in *Jubilees* is bifurcated into the two streams of tradition. In doing this, *Jubilees* is following the path already set in the *Book of Watchers* and especially the *Book of Giants*, in which the strict distinction between Enoch and Noah, on the one hand, and the angels-giants, on the other, is maintained.[87]

Another area in which *Jubilees* distinguishes between good and bad instruction reflects a departure from the early Enoch tradition: knowledge about the use of herbs as medicines. *Jubilees* not only has the angels instruct Enoch regarding the calendar (4:17; cf. *1 En.* 72–82), the work also has one of them instruct Noah on the medicinal properties of herbs (10:10, 13), a teaching that comes in response to Noah's petition that God deliver his offspring from the evil spirits who have been corrupting them after the Flood (10:1–6).[88] The use of herbs to combat the damage caused by those spirits permitted to afflict humans (thanks to Mastema's request), contrasts markedly from the Enoch tradition. In the *Book of Watchers* at *1 Enoch* 8:3, the "cutting of roots" (so Grk. Codex Panopolitanus) is unequivocally rejected as a practice associated with the disobedient angels. Thus, while *Jubilees* takes over from Enoch tradition the attribution of good and bad knowledge to good and bad angels, respectively, the content of what is good and bad is not entirely the same. Whereas the *Book of Watchers* has condemned the use of medicines by attributing them to the fallen angels who have eventually generated the giants that became oppressive evil spirits (*1 En* 8:3; 15:8–11), in *Jubilees* such knowledge is revealed by good angels in order to combat the attacks of the evil spirits which have originated from the giants.[89]

Thus, the rebellious angels tradition in *Jubilees* and its relationship to the beginnings of evil can be summarized as follows: in adapting the myth from various received traditions, the writer of *Jubilees* does not actually deliberate about the origin of evil *per se*. Instead the tradition about rebellious angels serves the book to underline two main points. First, it functions to explain "why things are the way they are experienced and perceived" in the world of the author and his readers

---

[87] For the similar insistence that denies Noah's identity as an offspring of the watchers, see *Genesis Apocryphon* (at 1QapGen ii–v) and *Birth of Noah* (at *1 En.* 106–107); for a discussion, see Stuckenbruck, *1 Enoch 91–108*, pp. 630–655.

[88] On Noah's prayer in the context of *Jubilees*, see Loren T. Stuckenbruck, "Deliverance Prayers and Hymns in Early Jewish Documents", in eds. Gerbern S. Oegema and Ian Henderson, *The Changing Face of Judaism and Christianity* (Gütersloh: Gerd Mohn, 2005), pp. 146–165. See further Chapter Ten below.

[89] On this contrast, see Bernd Kollmann, "Göttliche Offenbarung magisch-pharmakologischer Heilkunst im Buch Tobit", *ZAW* 106 (1994), pp. 289–299 (esp. pp. 298–299).

Second, as in the *Book of Watchers*, the storyline of *Jubilees* provides assurance that, to the extent they are caused by the tenth of Mastema's cohort of disembodied spirits, present afflictions and sins are temporary; the evil powers are, in effect, already defeated. Unlike the *Book of Watchers*, however, the writer of *Jubilees* goes to greater lengths to avoid any inference that demonic causality undermines human, especially Israel's, responsibility. This is achieved not only by analogies that are drawn between human misdeeds and those attributed to the watchers' offspring (7:20–21), as we have seen, but also by the degree to which the notion of the giants as primarily responsible for the ante-diluvian violence at the expense of humanity is diminished.[90]

Conclusion

The tradition of Genesis 6:1–4 is sufficiently ambiguous to have allowed for a wide range of interpretations with respect to the character of the "sons of God", the "Nephilim", and "the mighty men". As we have observed, however much Genesis and, in particular, subsequent apocalyptic writings thought the latter two groups were destroyed through the Flood, the versions preserved in the Pseudo-Eupolemus fragments allow for one or more of the giants to have escaped the destruction unleashed during the diluvian period. Thus the fragments imply that the giants came to play an important role in disseminating culture from the pre-diluvian period down to Abraham, whose lineage is traced to them.

The apocalyptic traditions retold the story of disobedient angels in a variety of ways, each of which denied the giants and their progenitors any role in the spread of divinely sanctioned learning. The internecine conflicts among the giants and destruction through the Great Flood were important, paradigmatic events of the past in which divine action against the increase of evil on the earth was manifested in a definitive way. In writings composed after the influential *Book of Watchers*, the Flood took on increasing significance as an event that signifies, contrary to the Pseudo-Eupolemus traditions, the eradication of the giants. The *Book of Giants* interpreted the Flood as a past, yet proleptic, sign of divine judgment, and in *Jubilees* the Flood functions as an interruption of the increase of evil among humankind; it put into effect a definitive, yet partial judgment that anticipates full implementation at the end of the present world order. For the *Animal Apocalypse* the

---

[90] In 7:22 there is an element of oppression by the giants (the Elyo killed humankind), though what follows are statements that people killed one another and, in 7:23, that "When everyone sold himself to commit injustice and to shed innocent blood, the earth was filled with injustice." Whereas the *Book of Watchers* holds the giants responsible for destroying humanity and spilling their innocent blood (*1 En.* 7:3; 9:1, 9), the writer of *Jubilees* comes close to calumniating humans for this activity (cf. 7:23–25) and has Noah warn his children against both the shedding and consumption of blood (7:27–33).

Flood simply spelled the end of the giants, who are not given any further role to play in the remainder of the work's recounting of Israel's sacred history. The disobedient angels continue to exist after the Flood; their punishment is reserved for the end time.

The diversity of traditions, from Genesis 6 through to the Enochic materials, bequeathed a legacy that lasted well into the first two centuries of the Common Era.[91] A number of traditions maintained, with the *Animal Apocalypse*, that the giants were simply destroyed by the Flood, sometimes (and unlike the *Animal Apocalypse*) without even addressing the status of the disobedient angels who fathered them. Thus the writer of *4QExhortation Based on the Flood* (= 4Q370) affirms the view that, along with evil humankind and other creatures, "the gi[ant]s did not escape (הג]בור[ים לוא נמלטו)" the Flood (4Q370 i 6).[92] A similar emphasis is preserved by the writer of *3 Maccabees* 2:4: the prayer attributed to the high priest Simon addresses God as the one who "destroyed (διέφθειρας) those who perpetrated wickedness in the past, among whom were the giants who were convinced by (their own) strength and confidence, bringing upon them immeasurable water". Moreover, according to the Wisdom of Solomon 14:6 the escape of Noah (called "the hope of the world") through divine help was taking place "while the arrogant giants were perishing (ἀπολλυμένων ὑπερηφάνων γιγάντων)". According to the Greek and Slavic recensions of the later *3 Baruch* 4:10, a large number of giants were destroyed by the Flood along with "all flesh" (Greek) or "every firstborn" (Slavic).[93] More veiled, though disputed allusions to punishment of the giants have been detected in the language of Ben Sira 16:7 ("he [God] did not forgive the giants of old", οὐκ ἐχιλάσατο περὶ τῶν ἀρχαίων γιγάντων)[94] and the *Damascus Document* in CD ii 19–20 ("... and their sons whose height was as the height of cedars and whose bodies were as mountains [were caught] because they fell. All flesh which was on dry land decayed and became as if they never were").[95]

---

[91] With apocalyptic tradition, Philo, writing in Greek in the 1st century CE, regarded the "giants" of Gen. 6:4 as evil; cf. Chapter Seven below. In addition, Philo denies the figure of Abraham from having any connection with the giants, associating Nimrod with them instead.

[92] Cf. Carol A. Newsom, "4Q370: An Admonition Based on the Flood", *RevQ* 13 (1988), pp. 23–43 and *idem*, in eds. Emanuel Tov *et al.*, *Qumran Cave 4 XIV: Parabiblical Texts, Part 2* (DJD 19; Oxford: Clarendon Press, 1995), pp. 85–97 (esp. pp. 90–91, 95).

[93] See Alexander Kulik, *3 Baruch* (CEJL; Berlin: Walter de Gruyter, 2010), pp. 187–222. While the Slavic version numbers the giants killed at 104,000, the Greek version has 409,000.

[94] For a nuanced interpretation of this text, see Matthew J. Goff, "Ben Sira and the Giants of the Land: A Note on Ben Sira 16:7", *JBL* 129 (2010), pp. 645–655, who argues that not the Flood, but rather the conquering of the archaic Canaanite ruler in the Land (cf. the Nephilim in Num. 13:31–33) is in view.

[95] Ambiguous in meaning is a passage in *Sib. Or.* 2.227–232, as it is unclear whether the Titans and giants mentioned in the text are to be included among "such ones that the Flood destroyed" (εἰς κρίσιν ἄξει εἰδώλων τὰ μάλιστα παλαιγενέων Τιτήνων ἠδέ τε Γιγάντων καὶ ὅσας εἷλεν κατακλυσμός); cf. the text in ed. Johannes Geffcken, *Die Oracula Sibyllina* (Leipzig: J. C. Hinrichs, 1902).

The other traditions allowed – similar to the *Book of Watchers, Book of Giants, Jubilees* – for the giants to persist beyond death, perhaps alongside the fallen angels, in a disembodied form of existence as spirits.[96] This emphasis is presupposed in the sapiential songs document, *Songs of the Maskil*, in 4Q510 1.5 and 4Q511 35.7, in which the "spirits of the bastards" are reckoned as powers with which the righteous and elect community still has to content. In the later Christian *Testament of Solomon* (5:3; 17:1), the link between the post-diluvian demons and the giant offspring of the rebellious angels is made explicit (see n. 40 above). This raises the possibility that would require more analysis than is possible here,[97] namely, that mythological traditions about the giants may have been adapted in passages of the New Testament gospels in which the desire of spirits to enter into human bodies is assumed (so e. g. Mk. 5:1–20; Mt. 12:43–45 par. Lk. 11:24–26).

The later Second Temple Jewish and early Christian traditions are clear-cut in associating the "sons of God" and their progeny in Genesis 6:1–4 with evil, whether or not some were thought to have been destroyed in the past or to have persisted as malevolent powers into the present. Indeed, they assume, without explanation, that their respective audiences would have been familiar with such a perspective. By contrast, the earlier authors of apocalyptic traditions could not take such a view for granted; they found it necessary to delineate a position that contrasted with and, indeed, was opposed to those interpretations that fused the early biblical narrative with accounts of the history and origins of culture. Along these lines, they dissociated divine knowledge revealed to Enoch, Noah and Abraham from other traditions that they thought illegitimately aligned these patriarchs with reprehensible realms of knowledge. Against the backdrop of a horizon informed by an apocalyptic expectation that evil powers and instructions will be eradicated once and for all at the end of the present age, a number of Second Temple period authors reviewed above sought to remove ambiguity from the tradition by pressing it in a particular direction. They contributed to a trajectory that moved towards a conception of reality that drew clear lines of distinction between good and evil in the sacred past in order to do the same in the present between the faithful, on the one hand, and the unfaithful in the community of Israel and beyond, on the other. This overriding concern shaped the apocalyptic reading of received sacred tradition; correspondingly, good and bad angels and, respectively, the areas of learning attributed to each, were kept distinct.

---

[96] See the work by Wright, *The Origin of Evil Spirits* (bibl. in n. 59 above).

[97] On which, however, see Chapter Nine below.

Chapter Two

Giant Mythology and Demonology:
From the Ancient Near East to the Dead Sea Scrolls

A. Introduction

Ever since the *Book of Giants* was identified among the fragments recovered from caves near Khirbet Qumran,[1] the distinguishing features of its account of the disobedient "watchers" and their offspring, the "giants" or "Nephilim", have been increasingly recognized. Although a number of early Jewish writings refer to traditions about the giants in some form,[2] the *Book of Giants* stands out in the way it

---

[1] For a partial edition, mostly of 4QEnGiants[a] (= 4Q203), see the early work of József T. Milik, *The Books of Enoch: Aramaic Fragments from Qumrân* (Oxford: Clarendon Press, 1976), pp. 4, 6–7, 57–58, 230, 236–38, and 298–339 (on 4Q203, pp. 311–317 and PLATES XXX–XXXII). Preliminary discussions of some or all of the material were published, respectively, by John C. Reeves, *Jewish Lore in Manichaean Cosmogony: Studies in the Book of Giants Tradition* (HUCM 14; Cincinnati: Hebrew Union College Press, 1992) and Loren T. Stuckenbruck, *The Book of Giants from Qumran* (TSAJ 63; Tübingen: Mohr Siebeck, 1997). Though some issues remain, these discussions have been updated and substantively corrected in Stuckenbruck, "1Q23–24; 2Q26; 4Q203; 6Q8", in eds. Stephen J. Pfann et al., *Qumran Cave 4, XXVI: Cryptic Texts and Miscellanea, Part 1* (DJD 36; Oxford: Clarendon Press, 2000), pp. 8–94 (hereafter DJD 36) and, especially Émile Puech, "4Q530–4Q533, 203 1. 4QLivre des Géants[b–e] ar", in *Qumran Cave 4, XXII: Textes araméens, Volume 1* (DJD 31; Oxford: Clarendon Press, 2001), pp. 9–115 (hereafter DJD 31). For the sake of clarity, it is important to note that the numerical designations for fragments in the case of 4Q530–4Q533 and 4Q206a 1–2, subject previously to some confusion, should now be taken from the *editio princeps* in DJD 31.

[2] See *1 En.* 7–8; 10; 15–16; 39:1; 86–89; *Jub.* 5; 7–10; Sir. 16:7; *3 Macc.* 2:4; Wisd. 14:6; Philo, *Gig.*; *3 Bar.* 4:10 (Grk., Slav.); *4QExhortation Based on the Flood* i 6 (= 4Q370); Pseudo-Eupolemus (in Eusebius, *Praep. evang.* 9.17.1–9; 9.18.2); 4Q180–4Q181; CD ii 19–20; 11Q11 v; 4Q510–4Q511; 4Q444. In addition, a number of texts in the Hebrew Bible and early Greek translation may reflect an awareness of the apocalyptic and Hellenistic giants traditions; see esp. Gen. 10:8, 9 (cf. 1 Chr. 1:10); Num. 13:31–33; Deut. 1:28; 2:10–11; 3:10, 13; Josh. 12:4; 17:15; Prov. 2:18; 9:18; Isa. 14:9; Ezek. 32:27; for a discussion of these texts, see Brook W. R. Pearson, "Resurrection and the Judgment of the Titans", in eds. Stanley E. Porter, Michael A. Hayes and David Tombs, *Resurrection* (JSNTSup 186; Sheffield: Sheffield Academic Press, 1999), pp. 33–51 and, in relation to Prov., see Matthew J. Goff, "Subterranean Giants and Septuagint Proverbs: The 'Earth-born' of LXX Proverbs", in eds. Károly Dániel Dobos and Miklós Kószeghy, *With Wisdom as a Robe: Qumran and Other Jewish Studies in Honour of Ida Fröhlich* (Sheffield: Phoenix Press, 2009), pp. 146–156. An important recent contribution that studies the theme of "giants" in relation to the diluvian period, the conquest of Canaan narratives, and the Davidic monarchy, see Brian R. Doak, *The Last of the Rephaim: Conquest and Cataclysm in the Heroic Ages of Ancient Israel* (Ilex Foundation Series; Cambridge, Massachusetts / London: Harvard University Press, 2012), esp. pp. 51–118.

develops the watchers tradition. The following discussion shall draw attention to the distinctiveness of this composition in several of its aspects and, in turn, explore – with primarily the question of demonology in view – the degree to which it picks up or reflects some traditions attested in sources from the Ancient Near East.[3]

The very fragmentary remains of the *Book of Giants*, preserved in versions transmitted in Manichaean circles and among the Dead Sea materials, provide evidence for a document which is to be taken seriously in its own right, that is, apart from traditions preserved in *1 Enoch*.[4] The features that distinguish the work from other Second Temple writings that refer to the giants may be identified in relation to three basic areas. The first has to do with the role assigned to the pre-diluvian patriarch Enoch. Whereas the other early Enoch compositions (i.e. *1 Enoch, Slavonic* or *2 Enoch*) largely claim to be written by Enoch himself,[5] the *Book of Giants*

---

[3] The study of Ancient Near Eastern backgrounds to the watchers and giants mythologies preserved in the Enochic and related traditions has been undertaken, with varying degrees of success, by Paul D. Hanson, "Rebellion in Heaven, Azazel, and Euhemeristic Heroes in 1 Enoch 6–11", *JBL* 96 (1977), pp. 195–233; Siam Bharyo, *The Shemihazah and Asael Narrative of 1 Enoch 6–11: Introduction, Text, Translation and Commentary with Reference to Ancient Near Eastern and Biblical Antecedents* (AOAT 322; Münster: UGARIT-Verlag, 2005); Matthew J. Goff, "Gilgamesh the Giant: The Qumran *Book of Giants'* Appropriation of *Gilgamesh* Motifs", *DSD* 16 (2009), pp. 221–253, whose discussion is esp. relevant for the literature covered here; Amar Annus, "On the Origin of Watchers: A Comparative Study of the Antediluvian Wisdom in Mesopotamian and Jewish Traditions", *JSP* 19 (2010), pp. 277–320; Ida Fröhlich, e.g. in "Theology and Demonology in Qumran Texts", *Henoch* 32 (2010), pp. 101–129 and "Evil in Second Temple Texts", in eds. Ida Fröhlich and Erkki Koskenniemi, *Evil and the Devil* (LNTS 481; London: Bloomsbury T & T Clark, 2013), pp. 23–50; Helge S. Kvanvig, *Primeval History: Babylonian, Biblical, and Enochic. An Intertextual Reading* (JSJSup 148; Leiden: Brill, 2011), esp. pp. 13–316 (focus on the Atrahasis Epic and the *Poem of Erra* and Mesopotamian origins – esp. the Akkadian *apkallu* – of the watcher myth); Doak, *The Last of the Rephaim* (bibl. in n. 2 above); and Henryk Drawnel, e.g. in "Knowledge Transmission in the Context of the Watchers' Sexual Sin with the Women in *1 Enoch* 6–11", *BibAn* 2 (2012), pp. 123–151. The work of Drawnel potentially throws new light on the background of both the disobedient angels and giants tradition and firmly anchors the composition of the storyline in the *Book of Watchers* within a Babylonian environment. Ancient Near Eastern backgrounds explored in two important monographs by James C. VanderKam, *Enoch and the Growth of an Apocalyptic Tradition* (CBQMS 16; Washington D.C.: Catholic University of America Press, 1984) and Helge S. Kvanvig, *The Roots of Apocalyptic: The Mesopotamian Background of the Enoch Figure and of the Son of Man* (WMANT 61; Neukirchen/Vluyn: Neukirchener Verlag, 1988) were more immediately concerned with the figure of Enoch himself.

[4] For a synoptic comparison of the *Book of Giants*, the Manichaean materials, and the later *Midrash of Shemḥazai and ʿAzaʾel* (cf. n. 24 below), see Ken M. Penner, "Did the Midrash of Shemḥazai and Azael Use the Book of Giants?", in eds. James H. Charlesworth, Lee Martin McDonald, and Blake Jurgens, *Sacra Scriptura: How "Non-Canonical" Texts Functioned in Early Judaism and Early Christianity* (JCTSRS; London: Bloomsbury T & T Clark, 2014), pp. 15–45 (here pp. 27–42). Penner cautions that the later materials cannot be relied upon to reconstruct the shape of the *Book of Giants* among the Dead Sea Scrolls, they provide evidence for the way the work was being received in later contexts.

[5] I hesitate to describe these writings as "pseudepigrapha" since the term does not adequately characterize them in terms of what the authorial activity behind them was attempting to do; cf. Annette Yoshiko Reed, "Pseudepigraphy, Authorship, and the Reception of 'the Bible' in Late

seems not to have been a first-person account attributed to Enoch[6] (*contra* the view advanced by Milik based on his reading of 4Q206 2–3, subsequently designated 4Q206a 1–2[7]). Admittedly, it is possible that the *Book of Giants* was included within copies of other Enochic writings,[8] as was supposed by Milik.[9] However, that it represents the same literary genre in the strict sense is unlikely.[10] In the *Book of Giants* Enoch is never clearly portrayed as a 1st person narrator;[11] moreover, none of the *Book of Giants* materials unambiguously casts Enoch into a role of being the recipient of visions or dreams. If so, *the Book of Giants'* presentation of Enoch contrasts significantly, for example, with the *Book of Watchers*, as well as with the remaining sections of *1 Enoch*.

Secondly, and following from the last point, the *Book of Giants* distinguishes itself in the particular role it assigns to the patriarch. As just mentioned, Enoch is not the recipient of dreams, but instead functions in the narrative as a dream interpreter *par excellence* as he clarifies the meaning of the ominous visions given to the giants. To be sure, as in *Book of Watchers* (*1 En.* chs. 12–13), Enoch is requested by the fallen angels to act as a mediator to God on their behalf. But whereas he actually attempts to convey their petition for mercy (*1 En.* 13:1–10), in the *Book*

Antiquity", in eds. Lorenzo DiTommaso and Lucian Turcescu, *The Reception and the Interpretation of the Bible in Late Antiquity* (BAC 6; Leiden: Brill, 2008), pp. 467–490 (esp. 474–480); Hindy Najman, Eva Mroczek and Itamar Manoff, "How to Make Sense of Pseudonymous Attribution: The Cases of 4 Ezra and 2 Baruch", in ed. Matthias Henze, *Companion to Biblical Interpretation in Early Judaism* (Grand Rapids: Eerdmans, 2012), pp. 308–336; and Loren T. Stuckenbruck, "'Apocrypha' and 'Pseudepigrapha'", in eds. John J. Collins and Daniel C. Harlow, *Dictionary of Early Judaism* (Grand Rapids: Eerdmans, 2010), pp. 179–203.

[6] The adaptation of the story about the watchers, giants and Enoch in *Jubilees* is rendered in the 3rd person, though in the larger framework a 1st person narrative (i. e. the voice of the Angel of the Presence) is sustained as belonging to revelation given to Moses on Mt. Sinai. See Hindy Najman, e. g. in *Seconding Sinai: The Development of Mosaic Discourse in Second Temple Judaism* (JSJSup 77; Leiden / Boston: Brill, 2003).

[7] So Puech in DJD 31, pp. 111–113; cf. further Stuckenbruck, DJD 36, pp. 45–46.

[8] This is especially possible, for example, in the case of 4Q203 (4QEnGiants[a]), which was copied by the same hand as 4Q204 (4QEnoch[c]). However, an identical hand does not necessarily mean that 4Q203–204 formed part of the same manuscript. Cf. Michael A. Knibb, "The Book of Enoch or Books of Enoch?", in eds. Gabriele Boccaccini and John J. Collins, *The Early Enoch Literature* (JSJSup 121; Leiden / Boston: Brill, 2007), pp. 21–40 (here pp. 27–26) and fuller argumentation in Loren T. Stuckenbruck, "The Early Traditions Related to 1 Enoch: A Summary and Overview", in *The Early Enoch Literature*, pp. 43–61 (here pp. 48–49).

[9] Milik, *The Books of Enoch*, pp. 22, 178–179, and 310.

[10] Although, like the *Book of Giants*, the *Book of Watchers* at *1 En.* 6–11, 12–13, and 15–16 (as well as the introductory superscript in 1:1–2a) is not narrated in the 1st person. The 3rd person account reflects the use of source materials that have been incorporated into the 1st person Enochic framework of the *Book of Watchers* as a whole.

[11] I remain convinced by Devorah Dimant, "The Biography and the Books of Enoch", *VT* 33 (1983), pp. 14–29 (here p. 16 n. 8), who is critical of those who regard Milik's view that the *Book of Giants* was written as if compiled or composed by Enoch as an "unquestioned assumption". Although the 1st person in 4Q203 9 and 10 may be explained as a prayer that could be attributed to Enoch, it nevertheless would represent a micro-form within the larger 3rd person narrative of the work.

of Giants his relationship to the watchers and giants seems more distant. In fact, the fragments have him communicating with only one of the giants, *Mahaway*, who has to cross over a great desert to reach the ends of the earth in order to consult with him on the meaning of the giants' dreams (4Q530 7 ii). Thus the chain of mediation in the *Book of Giants* ends up being somewhat complex: God (or an angel) to Enoch to *Mahaway* (4Q530 7 ii) to the watchers (4Q203 8) or the giants (4Q530 2 ii + 6–12(?), line 23; 4Q530 7 ii 10).

Thirdly, and most significant for the discussion to follow, the author(s) of the *Book of Giants* cast the spotlight on the gigantic offspring of the watchers more intensely and in more detail than any other extant Jewish document written or copied during the Second Temple period.[12] Of course, its tradition-historical predecessor, the *Book of Watchers*, also shows an interest in these giants: there is mention there of their pre-diluvian activities (*1 En.* 7:2–5; 9:9), their post-diluvian existence as evil spirits (15:8–12; 16:1), and their ultimate destruction (10:9–15). The *Book of Giants* presupposes or contains all these elements and more. Similar to the *Book of Watchers*, the *Book of Giants* fragments refer to the watchers' fall from heaven (4Q531 1), they underscore the angels' and giants' powerlessness in the face of conflict with God's angels (4Q531 22), and they contain an announcement of their punishment (4Q203 7A and 8). But whereas the *Book of Watchers* at *1 Enoch* chapters 12–16 is concerned with the announcement of punishment to the watchers, much of the storyline in the *Book of Giants* revolves around how it was that the *giants* come to realize that they are doomed as well and cannot expect mercy for themselves. This shift of the spotlight from the disobedient angels to the giants is reflected, in particular, by an elaborate account of the giants' exploits and miscreant deeds before the time of the Flood (e. g., in 1Q23 9+14+15; 4Q206a 1; and 4Q532–533); also featured are their dream-visions of an ominous judgment (esp. 4Q530 2 ii + 6–12(?), lines 7–12 and 16–20) and their anxiety as they come to terms with God's wrath against them. While it is clear that the very fragmentary narrative of the *Book of Giants* cannot, in many ways, be properly understood or even reconstructed without reference to the *Book of Watchers* and (to a lesser extent) *Jubilees*, a more limited focus on the giants themselves is not fully explained on this account alone. Why, one may ask, have the giants been singled out for such attention? What was it about *them* that evoked a particular interest on the part of those who wrote, told, and retold the *Book of Giants*?

In seeking an answer to these questions, we find one clue in the formal means by which the book demonstrates its specific concern with the giants: in addition to

---

[12] One only needs to compare the version of the story in the *Book of Watchers* (at *1 En.* 6–16), which focuses much more on the watchers' predicament (chs. 12–16) and recounts the decree of divine judgment in relation to their point of view. The periodic mention of the giants in the *Book of Watchers* thus serves primarily to reinforce the transgression that the angels inaugurated; cf. esp. *1 En.* 10:7, 10; 12:4–6; 14:6–7; and 15:3–5. The giants' misdeeds are of course taken seriously (7:2–5; 9:9), though they are the consequence of the illicit sexual union between the angels and human women.

the mention of what are possibly a few previously unknown names of disobedient angels (cf. 4Q531 7),[13] it is only in the *Book of Giants* that any of the offspring of the watchers are actually identified with proper names. These names, some seven in number, are as follows:

Ahiram (אחירם; 4Q531 7.1);

'ADK. (cf. אדכ.[14]; 4Q203 3.3);

Mahaway (מהוי; 1Q23 27.2; 4Q203 2.4; 4Q530 2 ii + 8–12 (?), line 20; 4Q530 7 ii 6–7; 6Q8 1.2, 5);

'Ohyah (אוהיה; 1Q23 29.1; 4Q203 4.3; 7A 5; 4Q530 2 ii + 8–12 (?), lines 1 and 15; 12.2; 4Q531 17.9; 6Q8 1.2, 4);

Hahyah (ההיה; 4Q203 4.3; 7A 5);

Hobabis/š (חובבס/ש; 4Q203 3.3; 4Q530 2 ii + 6–12 (?); 6.2[15]); and

Gilgames/š (גלגמיס/ש; 4Q530 2 ii + 6–12 (?); 4Q531 22.12).

Taking these names as a point of departure, the present discussion shall inquire into the possible significance of the giants referred to in the *Book of Giants*. The discussion is two-fold: initially we probe the meaning of each name, before considering what can be observed in the texts regarding the character profile of each. The considerations to follow are based on clues taken from linguistic inferences, a reconstruction of the *Book of Giants* narrative, limited and cautious comparison with the later Manichaean *Book of Giants* fragments, and, finally, comparison with traditions from the Ancient Near East. Taken together, these indications may provide one background through which to understand better the development of demonology among Jewish apocalyptic circles during the last three centuries B. C. E.

---

[13] 4Q531 7.2–3 refers to *'Ana'el, Baraq'e[l], Na'am'el, R(a)[...]*, and *'Ammi'el*. The first two names, on line 2, are followed by a reference to what Puech has reconstructed as ולנ[פילין ("and to Ne]philim"), while the last three names on line 3, are followed on line 4 by a reference to "all these mighty men" (כול אלין גבריא). Though the context of the lacuna-ridden fragment does not directly inform us just who they are (whether watchers or giants), their theophoric character (with *-'el* endings) correspond to the forms of names assigned to the rebellious angels listed in *1 En.* 6:7; cf. Stuckenbruck, *The Book of Giants from Qumran*, p. 146. Thus unless evidence emerges to the contrary, I assume that these names did not designate giants, though the matter remains uncertain. In addition, it seems that Milik (*The Books of Enoch*, p. 313) has treated 'Azazel (see 4Q203 7A 6) as one of the giants because of his identity as a goat-man (in his view a mixed being as the other giants); though this interpretation of the name is possible, the designation more probably refers to one of the chief leaders of the watchers (called 'Asa'el in the Aramaic fragments of the *Book of Watchers*, but later 'Azazel in the Ethiopic (with approximations in that direction in the Greek tradition), perhaps under the influence of the scapegoat by that name in Lev. 16:8, 10, and 26.

[14] The name here remains uncertain despite the suggestions made by Puech, DJD 31, p. 32 n. 13, ארכז(י)], which requires an emendation of an unmistakable *daleth* to *reš*.

[15] It is so in this text, per the plausible suggestion and reading by Puech, DJD 31, p. 28.

B. Profiles of Individual Giants

B.1. An Uncertain Name

In the case of some of the giants, very little can be observed or even inferred with any confidence on the basis of the name and context. This paucity of information, holds in relation to the only partially visible name *'ADK.*[in 4Q203 3.3 (see n. 13), except that, due to its occurrence immediately following the name *Ḥobabiš* (on which see below), it is more likely the name of a giant than one belonging to either one of the rebellious angels or a human character.

B.2. Aḥiram

A little more may be said about the name *Aḥiram*, which carries the meaning "my brother is exalted". The name itself corresponds to the ancient king of Byblos, the port city in the northern Phoenician coast known during the second and first millennia B.C.E. for its export of cedar wood. A similar or identical name perhaps occurs in the fragmentary text of the later Middle Persian *Kawân* (= the Manichaean *Book of Giants*), according to which "*Ḥobabiš* robbed *'Aḥr.*[" (frg. *j*, line 24).[16] If the Manichaean text refers here to the same figure in the fragment from Qumran Cave 4 (4Q531 7.1), then the likelihood that the name belongs to a giant is strengthened. One similarity between the later Manichaean and earlier Jewish versions of the *Book of Giants* presents itself: both the context of 4Q531 7 and the *Kawân* fragment directly relate this figure (if the same one) to an event of violence among the giants, whether through internecine conflict (so the *Kawân* version) or through fighting with an angel or angels of God (cf. 4Q531 22.3–7, though the name does not occur in the text here). While in the *Kawân* text "*'Aḥr.* [" is the target of ill-treatment by *Ḥobabiš*, in 4Q531 7 *Aḥiram* occurs within a list of giants (and perhaps watchers) who have perished "by the sword" (line 5). The cause of the deaths in the 4Q531 fragment is, however, not explicitly given, though either infighting (cf. *1 En.* 7:5; 10:12; *Jub.* 5:9; 7:22–24a) and/or conflict with divine emissaries is possible (cf. e.g. 4Q531 22.3–7; *Jub.* 5:6–7).

B.3. Mahaway

The meaning of the name *Mahaway* (מהוי in the Dead Sea fragments; *Mahawai* in the Manichaean materials) is impossible to decipher with any confidence. Perhaps, however, the name includes a derivation from the Aramaic verb "to be" (הוי) in conjunction with a *mem* prefix. More important, however, is what can be said

---

[16] The text is published in transcription and translation by Walter B. Henning, "The Book of Giants", *BSOAS* 11 (1943–1946), pp. 52–74 (here pp. 57 and 60, respectively).

about this giant on the basis of the Qumran fragments. The broken text of 6Q8 1 records a conversation between *Mahaway* and another giant, *'Ohyah*. The text is fragmentary, but may be reconstructed enough to infer a narrative context. It seems that *Mahaway* has delivered a message to *'Ohyah* – it is not clear whether further giants have been addressed as well. *'Ohyah* responds to *Mahaway* by challenging his or his source's authority (line 3: "Who has shown you everything…?"). *Mahaway* replies by appealing to the fact that his father *Baraq'el*[17] (i. e. one of the watchers) was with him at the time (line 4). On line 6 the defense of *Mahaway* is apparently interrupted by words of *'Ohyah* who expresses his own disbelief at what his fellow giant has just communicated. This text thus represents what seems to have been an emerging conflict between *Mahaway*, on the one hand, and another giant (or other giants), on the other. Two of the Manichaean fragments, one from the Middle Persian *Kawân* and another from a Sogdian version of the *Book of Giants*, may preserve parallel texts to the one in 6Q8 1: they, respectively, record the name of *Mahaway*'s father, here called *Virogdad* – the name in Sogdian means "gift of lightning", which is etymologically related to *Baraq'el* ("lightning of God"). Moreover, the two Manichaean fragments refer to a conflict between *Sam* (the equivalent for *'Ohyah*) and *Mahawai* (who, as indicated above, is the equivalent for *Mahaway* in the Dead Sea fragments). The texts have been translated by Walter B. Henning as follows:

Sam said: "Blessed be … had [he?] seen this, he would not have died." Then *Shahmizad* [= the watcher *Shemihazah* in the Aram. Enoch texts] said to *Sam*, his [son]: "All that *Mahawai* …, is spoilt (?)." Thereupon he said to … "We are … until … and … that are in (?) the fiery hell (?) … As my father, *Virogdad*, was …" *Shahmizad* said: "It is true what he says. He says one of thousands. For one of thousands …" *Sam* thereupon began … *Mahawa*, too, in many places … until to that place … he might escape (?) and …

(Middle Persian *Kawân* frg. *c*, pp. 1–2, lines 4–22)[18]

… I shall see. Thereupon now S[ahm, the giant] was [very] angry, and laid hands on M[ahawai, the giant], with the intention: I shall … and kill [you]. Then … the other g[iants] … do not be afraid, for … [Sa]hm, the giant, will want to [kill] you, but I shall not let him … I myself shall damage … Thereupon *Mahawai*, the g[iant], was satisfied …

(Sogdian, pp. 1–2, lines 1–18)[19]

The conflict between *Mahaway* and *'Ohyah* seems to have arisen from the former's mediating role as bearer of a message. The fragmentary evidence allows one to infer that the *Book of Giants* contained an account of two journeys in which *Mahaway* travels to Enoch, in order to inquire about the meaning of dreams that the giants

---

[17] Spelled ברקאל (4Q203 1.2; here 6Q8 1.4), which corresponds to the spellin;g of the disobedient angel listed from *1 En.* 6:7 (4Q201 1 iii 8, the "ninth" angel in the list), and not to *Baraki'el* as given in *Jub.* 4:28. Only in Codex Panopolitanus to *1 En.* 6:7 is the pronunciation Βαρακιηλ (the equivalent to the pronunciation of the Eth. text in *Jub.*) attested for the angel.

[18] See Henning, "The Book of Giants", pp. 56–57 (text transcription) and 60 (translation).

[19] Henning, "The Book of Giants", pp. 65–66 (both transcription and translation).

have had. 4Q530 2 ii + 6–12 (?) and 7 ii (a narrative in two contiguous columns) relate the second of these journeys, one which follows two dream-visions given to *Hahyah* and *'Ohyah* and the giants' subsequent decision to send *Mahaway* once again to Enoch, the very one who can provide the right interpretation. Of special interest for us here is the text in 4Q530 7 ii 4: "as a whirlwind, and he (i. e. *Mahaway*) flew with his hands (i. e. wings) as [an] eag[le". The description of the giant as one who has wings with which to fly suggests that he is being regarded as a creature with characteristics of a bird. Indeed, in one of the Manichaean Uygur fragments published by Henning, references are likewise made to *Mahawai*'s "wings" in the context of that giant's journey to Enoch (cf. p. 2).[20] *Mahaway*'s features may be explained on the grounds that he is the offspring of a human mother, on the one hand, and especially of *Baraq'el* the disobedient watcher, on the other, from whom he may have derived his wings.

B.4. 'Ohyah and Hahyah

These two giants, prominent in the narrative, may be treated together, as they are referred to as brothers (4Q530 2 ii + 6–12 (?), line 15). They are the sons of *Shemihazah*[21] who, according to one of the traditions picked up in the *Book of Watchers*, was the chief of the rebellious angels (*1 En.* 6:3, 7; 9:7; cf. 10:11). Their names can be interpreted in two ways: (1) like *Mahaway*, the names of the brothers may be different forms related to the verb "to be" (but from the Hebrew היה, not Aram.); or, (2) given the ending יה-, their names might also be regarded as theophoric. The matter remains uncertain. If, however, there is any analogy with the names of many of the watchers (that e. g. carry -'el suffixes),[22] then there is reason to prefer the latter explanation.

It could be argued that the heart of the *Book of Giants* narrates the experiences of the giant siblings as they discover to their horror that they are going to be held accountable and punished for the atrocities they have committed.[23] The means

---

[20] See Henning, "The Book of Giants", p. 65. The Manichaean text describes what may have been the giant's *first* journey to Enoch; cf. Milik, *The Books of Enoch*, p. 307.

[21] So according to the Middle Persian *Kawân*, frg. *c*, line 6 and the *Midrash of Shemḥazai and 'Aza'el*.

[22] See Milik, *The Books of Enoch*, pp. 152–156; Michael A. Knibb, *The Ethiopic Book of Enoch; A New Edition in Light of the Aramaic Dead Sea Fragments* (2 vols.; Oxford: Clarendon Press, 1978), 2.69–76; Matthew Black, "The Twenty Angel Dekadarchs and 1 Enoch 6, 7 and 69, 2", *JJS* 33 (1982) pp. 227–235, and *idem*, *The Book of Enoch or 1 Enoch: A New English Edition* (SVTP 7; Leiden: Brill, 1985), pp. 118–124; and George W. E. Nickelsburg, *1 Enoch 1: A Commentary on the Book of 1 Enoch, Chapters 1–36; 81–108* (Hermeneia; Minneapolis: Fortress Press, 2001), pp. 179–181. Beyond the names of the watchers in *1 En.* 6:7 and 69:2, the *Book of Giants* from the Dead Sea materials mentions a number of theophoric names; cf. the names referred to in n. 13 above. Puech (DJD 31, p. 60) regards the name *'Ana'el* (4Q531 7.2: ענאל) as an equivalent to עננאל, the name of the "thirteenth" watcher listed in *1 En.* 6:7 (4Q201 1 iii 10).

[23] On this see Loren T. Stuckenbruck, "Sequencing the Fragments in the Qumran *Book of*

through which they learn of their irreversible fate is two-fold. First, they have dream-visions of which they have at least one pair (so 4Q530 2 ii + 6–12(?), lines 7–12 and 16–20, respectively). In the case of *'Ohyah*, there is evidence of his having had at least one more dream (4Q531 22.9–11; cf. in section B.6 below).[24] Second, Enoch, through the mediation of *Mahaway*, interprets the extant pair of the brothers' dreams (cf. 4Q530 7 ii). In another fragment, the incredulity expressed by *'Ohyah* towards *Mahaway*'s apparently foreboding message (6Q8 1) seems to contribute to the development of the plot, though precisely where each of the fragments belong in the narrative is uncertain. Nonetheless, enough text has survived to infer that the storyline unfolds as *'Ohyah* and his brother *Hahyah* initially refuse to acknowledge the message of punishment against them, but then learn, not least through Enoch's interpretation of their dreams, that there is nothing either of them (or any of the other giants) can do to escape the divine wrath that their dreams have envisioned.

The Qumran fragments of the *Book of Giants* do not provide any hints concerning the appearance of either of the giant brothers. The Middle Persian *Kawân* (frg. *k*, p. 1), however, mentions them in connection with "their nest (?)".[25] Thus, at least according to the later version, provided that Henning's translation is correct, *'Ohyah* and *Hahyah* are assumed to have animal features, perhaps characteristics of a bird.[26] If this is the case, they may have shared the kind of profile we have observed in relation to the winged *Mahaway*.

The two names that stand out among the *Book of Giants* fragments are *Ḥobabis/š* and *Gilgames/š*. They are presently discussed in turn.

B.5. *Ḥobabis/š*

This name occurs at least once, possibly twice among the Qumran fragments. In one instance the reading is incontestable (4Q203 3.3, חובבש), while in the other text the letters are less clear and require partial restoration (4Q530 2 ii + 6–12(?), line 2).[27] The text of 4Q203 3 is so fragmentary that hardly more than three words at the beginning of four lines on the right margin of a column are visible. The fragment contains what may derive from a discussion among the giants during time of their pre-diluvian activity. On line 4, one giant apparently asks another,

---

Giants: An Inquiry into the Structure and Purpose of an Early Jewish Composition", *JSP* 16 (1997), pp. 3–24.

[24] It is possible that *'Ohyah* has seen yet a further vision or visions; cf. the fragment in 2Q26 and its correspondences in content with the dream given to *'Aheyyâ* (= *'Ohyah*) in the *Midrash of Shemḥazai and 'Aza'el* (Oxford Bodleian Hebrew manuscript [1325 CE]), section 8. In addition, Puech (DJD 31, p. 93) reads 4Q531 46.1–2 as the beginning of a report about a vision by *'Ohyah*.

[25] So the translation of Henning, "The Book of Giants", p. 61.

[26] So also the inference by Milik, *The Books of Enoch*, p. 313.

[27] Puech (DJD 31, pp. 28–29, 32) reads and restores וח[ו]בבס, in which the first three visible letters (before and after the lacuna) cannot be recognized beyond traces.

"And what will you give me for k[illing ...]?" These few lines are consistent with the content preserved in the Middle Persian *Kawân* (frg. *j*, p. 1, lines 23–28):[28]

... *Virogdad* (= *Barak'el*) ... *Hobabiš* robbed *Ahr*. ... of ... -*naxtag*, his wife. Thereupon the giants began to kill each other and [to abduct their wives]. The creatures, too, began to kill each other.

If the reference to "killing" has been correctly restored in 4Q203 3.4 and if the term refers to activities of the giants among themselves, then the Manichaean fragment provides a parallel, not least as in both fragmentary texts the name *Hobabiš //* *Hobabiš* occurs as well. The relation between this activity and *Hobabiš*, however, is difficult to infer in the Qumran fragment, unless one appeals to the *Kawân* text, in which the giant functions as one of the named perpetrators of violence.

In the other, though less clear, instance of the giant's appearance in the text (4Q530 2 ii + 6–12 (?), line 2), the name is spelled with *samek* instead of *šin*; this corresponds to the orthography of the copyist behind the manuscript and is reflected, for example, in the comparable spelling in the same line for Gilgamesh (גלגמיס). If *Hobabis* is to be read here (וח[ו]בבס, in which the first two letters before and the one letter after the lacuna are in themselves difficult to certify), then the giant is depicted as uttering a howl or cry. The verb is to be read as אפחא (i. e. as "he roared" or "howled", though the form would have to be an otherwise unattested *'aph'el* of פחי, analogous to the related root פעי.[29] *Hobabis*, then, is given in the text to make a sound that is fitting for an animal.[30] The context suggests that the giant's cry comes in response to something 'Ohyah has communicated regarding what Gilgamesh had told him. Again, as in 4Q203 3 *Hobabis* plays a role in the context of the giants' interaction with one another. The roar is indicative of a negative reaction on his part to what 'Ohyah has just conveyed.

In his publication of the Manichaean fragments, Henning supposed that the name *Hobabiš* can be explained as a corrupted form from that of one of the fallen watchers mentioned in *1 Enoch* 6:7. *Hobabiš*, he thought, may be a variation of כוכבאל (4Q201 1 iii 7, 4Q204 1 ii 25), rendered in the Greek translations as Χωχαριηλ (Codex Panopolitanus) or as Χωβαβιηλ (Syncellus).[31] The name of the watcher, however, and the form *Hobabiš* should not be confused. As has now become clear, the derivation of the giant's name lies somewhere else.

---

[28] See Henning, "The Book of Giants", p. 60. The correspondence is primarily thematic and cannot be explained as an example of literary dependence on the version extant at Qumran for which insufficient text is preserved.

[29] So Puech, DJD 31, p. 32 and n. 16, against my suggestion to read אפחד i. e. "I shall fear" (Stuckenbruck, *The Book of Giants from Qumran*, p. 105), which does not make any sense if *Hobabis* is read just before.

[30] See esp. Marcus Jastrow, *Dictionary of the Targumim, the Talmud Babli and Yerushalmi, and the Midrashic Literature* (Philadelphia: Judaica Press, 1903, repr. New York: Judaica Press, 1971), p. 1202.

[31] Henning, "The Book of Giants", p. 60 n. 3.

Józef T. Milik was no doubt correct that *Ḥobabiš* (or, rather, the *Ḥobab-* part of the name) derives from a character in the *Gilgamesh Epic*. In the *Epic* the power-wielding and ferocious monster who guarded the Cedar Forest is called Humbaba (so in the Neo-Assyrian tradition; the Old Babylonian form is *Ḥuwawa*).[32] It is within the *Epic*, too, that this creature loses out in a fierce battle against Gilgamesh and his companion Enkidu as they seek to gain access to the Cedar Forest. The focus of the *Epic* on Humbaba's power and propensity to violence makes it thematically appropriate that his name be assigned to one of the gargantuan offspring of the watchers in the *Book of Giants*. Moreover, the name Humbaba also occurs frequently in Old Babylonian incantations materials (i. e. on seals and clay plaques) in which he functions as a demonic entity that is expected to exercise authority over other malevolent demons.[33] While it is thus clear that the figure behind the name *Ḥobabiš* has Babylonian roots, it is less apparent whether on this basis one can maintain that the *Book of Giants* is familiar with the *Gilgamesh Epic* itself.

However, the significance of the *Epic* in relation to *Ḥobabiš* requires that one consider a further point. According to the *Epic*, as mentioned above, Humbaba is associated with the Cedar Mountain. In the version preserved through the Old Babylonian Ishchali Tablet discovered in 1947 at Tel Harmal (18th cent. B. C. E.), the area that Ḥuwawa guards from trespassers includes "the peaks of Sirion (*sa-ri-a*) and Lebanon (*la-ab-na-am*)".[34] John Reeves has argued that this geographical location of Ḥuwawa corresponds to that mentioned in the *Book of Watchers* at *1 Enoch* 13:9, which locates the watchers "at Ubelseyael, ... between Lebanon and Senir", Senir referring to Mt. Hermon.[35] None of these place names (Lebanon and Senir) are extant among the Enoch Aramaic fragments, but the broken text of 4Q204 1 vi 5 to 13:9 reads: "I (Enoch) came] unto them and all of them (the watchers) were assembled together and sitting and c[rying ...]". the last word is only partly visible: only the first letter can be seen of what may be restored as א.[בלין] The weeping of the watchers thus reflects a wordplay on the place name to follow, as "Ubelseyael" may be the corrupted form of a place name.[36] Though Robert Henry Charles, followed by Knibb and Reeves, regarded the original place name as "Abilene" to the north, another clue may be provided by the text just preceding, 13:7, which locates Enoch "by the waters of Dan which is southwest of Hermon". Thus the place name

---

[32] Milik, *The Book of Giants from Qumran*, p. 313.

[33] On this, see conveniently Karel van der Toorn, "Humbaba", in eds. Karel van der Toorn, Bob Becking, and Pieter W. van der Horst, *Dictionary of Deities and Demons in the Bible* (Leiden: Brill, 1999, 2nd ed.), pp. 431–432 and the literature cited there.

[34] Ishchali Tablet, strophe 31. The references here as taken from Andrew George, *The Epic of Gilgamesh: The Babylonian Epic Poem and Other Texts in Akkadian and Sumerian* (New York: Barnes & Noble, 1999), p. 120. For further texts and translation, see Jeffrey Tigay, *The Evolution of the Gilgamesh Epic* (Philadelphia: University of Pennsylvania Press, 1982), pp. 32–33 and 93–95.

[35] Reeves, *Jewish Lore in Manichaean Cosmogony*, pp. 124 and 161 (n. 400).

[36] So Knibb, *The Ethiopic Book of Enoch*, 2:94.

may in fact have been Abel-Mayya or Abel-Men (אבל מיא/ן) in the Aramaic, which was located south, between Lebanon and Mt. Hermon.[37] If the location of the watchers and the giants in this region according to the *Book of Watchers* is assumed by the *Book of Giants*, then the geographical correspondence with the Ishchali Tablet of the *Gilgamesh Epic* may have provided stimulus for the author(s) of the *Book of Giants* to have included Humbaba "among his cast of characters".[38]

Excursus One: Mount Hermon and the Book of Giants

Alongside three quotations from the *Book of Watchers* preserved in Georgius Syncellus,[39] Milik drew attention to a fourth passage that claims to derive from "the book of Enoch concerning the watchers", but neither corresponds to any version of it nor to any part of *1 Enoch*.[40] Milik argued that, although the text does not overlap with any preserved part of the *Book of Giants*, it is in fact a quote from this work.

The argument, insofar as it is based on the passage's non-appearance in any other part of early Enochic tradition, does not carry much weight. More important, however, is a further consideration. The text announces a great judgment against Mt. Hermon for being the place upon which the watchers pledged themselves not to retreat from their plan to sire offspring through the women on earth. In addition, it contains an announcement, directed at the watchers – in the text they are called "sons of men", that their sons (i.e. the giants) "will be annihilated ... and die from the whole earth". The identification of this fragment quotation is uncertain. It is, however, consistent with the denunciation of the watchers found in 4Q203 8 i 3–15, as well as with a detail in 4Q203 11 that Milik suggests "should perhaps be placed below frg. 8, in other words 11 i = 7 ii, and 8 + 11 ii = 7 iii".[41] Not insignificant to note is that portion of text below the denunciation of the watchers in 4Q203 8 contains the words "and dew and fro[st", words that, if read correctly, correspond to what the same quotation relates about Mount Hermon: "There will descend on it neither cold, nor snow, *nor frost, nor dew*, unless they descend on it as a curse, until the great day of judgment." If Milik's attribution of the passage is correct, then the relation of at least some of the storyline

---

[37] I follow, therefore, the suggestion of Milik, "Le Testament de Lévi en araméen: fragment de la grotte 4 de Qumran", *RB* 62 (1955), p. 404 and *The Books of Enoch*, p. 196; see also Black, *The Book of Enoch or 1 Enoch*, p. 144 and Nickelsburg, *1 Enoch 1*, p. 250.

[38] So Reeves, *Jewish Lore in Manichaean Cosmogony*, p. 125. Significantly, Reeves catalogues evidence for the name Humbaba outside the cuneiform tradition in antiquity. The Manichaean fragments aside (which derived their use of the name from the *Book of Giants* itself), the name – taking the form Κομβαβος and being without parallel among ancient Greek documents – occurs in Lucian of Samosata's *de Dea Syria* 19–27 (2nd cent. CE), where it is given to the young man commissioned to protect a beautiful queen. In addition to the name here and function as guardian of this character, the story's location in and around Syria has convinced a number of scholars of a derivation from the *Gilgamesh Epic*; see Reeves, *Jewish Lore in Manichaean Cosmogony*, pp. 161–162 (n. 403) and Austin Morris Harmon, *Lucian* (8 vols.; LCL; Cambridge, Massachusetts: Harvard University Press, 1969), 4.378–379 (n. 1).

[39] For the publication of the Syncellus texts, see Alden A. Mosshammer, *Georgii Syncelli Ecloga chronographica* (Leipzig: Teubner, 1984) and William Adler and Paul Tuffin, *The Chronography of George Synkellos: A Byzantine Chronicle of Universal History from the Creation, Translated with Introduction and Notes* (Oxford: Oxford University Press, 2002).

[40] Milik, *The Books of Enoch*, pp. 317–320, with text and translation of this passage on p. 318.

[41] Milik, *The Books of Enoch*, p. 317.

in the *Book of Giants* to Mt. Hermon is reconcilable with the setting assigned to Humbaba in the *Gilgamesh Epic* and with the setting of the angels' binding oath to leave heaven in the *Book of Watchers*.[42]

Beyond the Ancient Near Eastern background for the inclusion of *Ḥobabiš* in the *Book of Giants*, Milik has argued that something further can be inferred from the name itself. Whereas *Ḥobab-* may reflect an association with the monster of the *Gilgamesh Epic*, the suffix *-iš* does not. And so Milik suggested that the last syllable may derive from the Hebrew איש ("man"), which, added to *Ḥobab*, results in a composite name. For the author(s) of the *Book of Giants* such a name would have signified the hybrid nature of the giant, who is part monster and part *human*.[43] If the name reflects the giant's composite form of existence, then the name *Ḥobabiš* is consistent with the hybridity we have been able to draw in relation to the giants *Mahaway*, *'Ohyah*, and *Hahyah*.[44] Milik's argument falters, however, because *šin* has been shown to be a common suffix for personal names of people among materials excavated from ancient Philistia.[45] Significantly, Nadav Na'aman and Ran Zadok have argued that the suffix constitutes evidence for *non-Semitic* people deported to Philistia by the Assyrians near the end of the 8th century B. C. E.[46] If these materials are taken into account, then Milik's interpretation becomes less plausible; the likelihood is greatly increased that names suffixed with *-(i)š* are not, in the first instance, to be derived from a Hebrew term. Nevertheless, if Na'aman and Zadok are correct, the evidence points in the direction of an eastern origin for the suffix, and this would at least be consistent with the notion of influence, whether directly or indirectly, from the east on the *Book of Giants*. Moreover, the spelling of the name with final *samek* in 4Q530 2 ii + 6–12 (?), line 2 renders a derivation from Hebrew איש unlikely.

---

[42] If in Syncellus the *Book of Watchers* and *Book of Giants* are preserved together, then their association with one another stands in contrast with the Ethiopic text traditions in which the Enoch traditions known thus far leave no trace of the *Book of Giants*.

[43] Milik, *The Books of Enoch*, p. 313.

[44] It is impossible to know whether the inclusion of *Humbaba* relates at all to the *Gilgamesh Epic*'s description of him as having "wings" (see e. g. the standard version at IV 159 and V 267).

[45] See two ostraca and a dedicatory inscription from the 7th cent. B. C. E. published, respectively, by Joseph Naveh, "Writing and Scripts in Seventh-Century BCE Philistia: The New Evidence from Tell Jemmeh", *IEJ* 35 (1985), pp. 8–21, esp. pp. 11–15 and 20–21 and Seymour Gitin, Trude Dothan, and Joseph Naveh, "A Royal Dedicatory Inscription from Ekron", *IEJ* 47 (1997), pp. 1–16. I am grateful to Hanan Eshel for referring me to this evidence.

[46] See esp. Nadav Na'aman and Ran Zadok, "Sargon II's Deportations to Israel and Philistia (716–708 B. C.)", *JCS* 40 (1988), pp. 36–46 (here pp. 40–42) and Nadav Na'aman, "Population Changes in Palestine Following Assyrian Deportations", *TA* 20 (1993), pp. 104–124 (here pp. 108–109).

B.6. *Gilgames/š*

As noted above, like *Ḥobabiš*, this name is spelled with the same final consonants *šin* and *samek*, in 4Q531 and 4Q530 respectively. However, as we have just discussed, nothing concerning the nature of *Gilgameš* can be inferred from the suffix ‎‫יש‬‎-. Again, the dual suffix seems to rule out a Hebrew etymology from ‎‫איש‬‎. Aside from knowing that in the *Book of Giants* this character is considered an offspring of disobedient angels and women on earth, can we learn anything further from the Dead Sea fragments? The materials do not offer any immediate clue for such information and, unfortunately, this name is not preserved among any of the Manichaean fragments published thus far. If one looks to the *Gilgamesh Epic*, however, a reason for an inclusion of a giant by this name emerges: the protagonist is at several points in the story described as part divine (two-thirds) and part human (one third).[47] Perhaps this mixed nature is part of what has motivated the author (s) to draw on the name, although there is no evidence in any of the extant versions of the *Epic* that animal features are assigned to the hero (analogous to what we have seen for several of the other giants discussed above). Furthermore, the gigantic stature of Gilgamesh may have furnished reason for his inclusion. His size (height?) is actually referred to in a fragmentary Hittite version of the *Epic* (dated to ca. 1500 B. C. E.) as "eleven cubits".[48]

Nevertheless, the notion of ancient ante-diluvian sages bearing animal (in addition to human) features is attested for the early 3rd century B. C. E., that is, not long before the composition of the *Book of Giants* during the first half of the 2nd century B. C. E.[49] The source for this motif is the Babylonian priest of Marduk, Berossos, as cited in his *History of Babylonia* preserved through Eusebius (*Chronicon*).[50] In the first book of the *History* Berossos refers to a certain Oannes, sea monster, cultural hero and ruler, who instructed human beings in writing, architecture, and agriculture. Of particular note is that this Oannes was part fish and part human;[51] in addition, his successors are also described as having been composed of human and ichthyomorphic characteristics.[52]

---

[47] Cf. the standard version, "He who saw the Deep", I 48–50; IX 51; and cf. X 268 ("built] from gods' flesh and human"); see Tigay, *The Evolution of the Gilgamesh Epic*, pp. 142 and 264, respectively.

[48] For the publication and translation of the Hittite fragments excavated at Bogazköy, see Johannes Friedrich, "Die hethitischen Bruchstücke des Gilgameš-Epos", *ZA* 39 (1930), pp. 1–82 (here pp. 3–4 for the text, and pp. 35–37 for the discussion.

[49] Concerning the issue of date and the date proposed here, see Stuckenbruck, *The Book of Giants from Qumran*, pp. 28–31 and *idem*, "The Sequencing of Fragments", p. 21 n. 63.

[50] Eusebius' *Chronicon* itself does not survive except in fragment quotations in Georgius Syncellus and in an Armenian translation; see Gerald Verbrugghe and John Moore Vickersham, *Berossos and Manetho, Introduced and Translated: Native Traditions in Mesopotamia and Egypt* (Ann Arbor: University of Michigan Press, 1996), here pp. 29–31.

[51] The text describes Oannes as follows: "... his whole body was that of a fish. And below the head of the fish, there was another head, and at the tail it had feet as those of a human, and his

Although the hybrid nature of Gilgamesh in the *Epic* does not necessarily lead to a conclusion that this ancient piece of literature has influenced the *Book of Giants* in some way, such a case may be strengthened when the possible function of *Gilgames/š* in the storyline is considered. My reconstruction of the narrative, based on the two fragmentary passages in the *Book of Giants* that mention this giant, suggests that the author(s) may have picked up at least one aspect of the *Epic*'s account. The last, partially legible lines of 4Q531 22 (lines 9–12) record words of *'Ohyah*, who expresses his own troubled state because of a dream-vision that he has had; he is, in fact, so anxious about the dream that he is unable to sleep (lines 9b–11).[53] Now, in the following line (12), the few visible words can be construed in various ways. The text, as edited and restored by Puech,[54] reads:

ואדין ג[א]לגמיש אמר [ח]ל[מכה] [ ] [של]ם

It is clear from the preceding lines that *'Ohyah* has been the speaker and that he is recounting a dream he has had to someone else, probably another giant (line 9: "according to this *'Ohyah* said to him, 'My dream troubled m[e...'"). It is, however, less clear to whom the words in line 12 can be ascribed. Assuming that *'Ohyah* is still the one speaking, I have suggested that *Gilgameš* is being addressed here in the vocative, so that the verb is in the imperative: "*Gi]lgameš*, tell your drea[m".[55] This reading of the text, which does not attempt to either render or translate the further letter traces at the left, suggests that the giants *'Ohyah* and *Gilgameš* are recounting their visions to one another, that is, that the latter is likewise a visionary, whose dream, about to be told, is not preserved. Puech, on the other hand, has interpreted the words as involving a change of subject and includes the letter traces just before the text breaks off entirely. In this construal *'Ohyah* is no longer the speaker, and the verb is perfect 3rd person singular: "Then *Gi]lgameš* said, 'Your dream is com[-plete (?) ...'".[56] On this reading, reference is being made to *'Ohyah*'s dream, about which *Gilgameš* is giving a comment.[57] Significant, in any case, is the association of

---

voice sounded like that of a human". For the Greek, see Felix Jacoby, *Die Fragmente der griechischen Historiker. Band 3: Geschichte von Staedten and Voelkern* (Leiden: Brill, 1958), no. 680 ("Beros(s)os von Babylon") F 1 (p. 369).

[52] On the widespread presentation of ante-diluvian sages (the *apkallu* or *adapu*) as half human and as bringers of culture into the world, see Milik, *The Books of Enoch*, p. 313, who, in turn, summarizes and refers to Rijkle Borger, "Die Beschwörungsserie *bit meseri* und die Himmelfahrt Henochs", *JNES* 33 (1974), pp. 183–196.

[53] For the text and translation, see Stuckenbruck, *The Book of Giants from Qumran*, pp. 162–164. It is important to note the text, especially at line 12, can be interpreted very differently; see e.g. Puech, DJD 31, pp. 74–78 and Goff, "Gilgamesh the Giant" (bibl. in n. 3 above), pp. 238–252.

[54] Puech, DJD 31, p. 74.

[55] Stuckenbruck, *The Book of Giants from Qumran*, pp. 166–167.

[56] Puech DJD 31, p. 75: "*Ensuite* Gi]lgamesh dit: 'Ton songe *accom[plit* (?) ...'".

[57] The construal of Puech is followed by Goff, "Gilgamesh the Giant", p. 242.

Gilgameš with a dream, if not his own, then certainly as one who is responding to the dream had by another giant.[58]

Leaving aside the theoretical ambiguity of line 12 in 4Q531 22, one may inquire about the context of the text immediately prior to 'Ohyah's recounting of his dream in lines 9–11. Since 'Ohyah is relating his vision to someone else (line 9), the occurrence of *Gilgameš* in line 12 in conversation with him (on Puech's reading) opens up the possibility that in line 9 *Gilgameš* is the one being spoken to.[59] Lines 3–7 stand spatially on their own, preceded and followed by a *vacat* in the latter half of line 2 and at the latter half of line 7. In these lines a figure tells of an unsuccessful battle that he has waged against "my accusers" (line 5, ולא [משכח אנה who "dwell [in] the [heavens] and reside in holy ... (עמן לאשתררה דבעלי דיני abodes" (line 6, דבשמי/א יתבין ובקדשיא אנון שרין ...) and are "stronger than I" (line 7, תקיפין מני).[60] Perhaps the *vacat* following the last cited phrase in line 7 led Milik to propose that the speaker is one of the fallen angels; accordingly, he suggested that the text may convey words in which *Shemiḥazah*, chief of the disobedient watchers and progenitor of 'Ohyah, tells of his prior defeat.[61] Moreover, a conflict with what appears to be heavenly (angelic) beings might indicate that the speaker was once of comparable rank. Matthew Goff, following the suggestion of Émile Puech,[62] argues that instead of the speaker being one of the watchers, it is possibly Gilgamesh himself who is describing his defeat at the hands of the angels. This reading of the text is plausible, not only because of this giant's presence in the text that follows (certainly in line 12, by inference in line 9), but also because of the content of lines 3–7 itself. The speaker, in referring to his foes' dwelling in the heavenly sphere – this construal does not depend entirely on the correctness of Puech's reconstruction of "heavens" in the lacuna – implies that his own location is not there, that is, on earth. While the location of a rebellious angel likewise no longer seems to be in heaven, the text suggests that the conflict described is not one that has resulted in an eviction from heaven, but is rather one that has taken place while the speaker was attempting to wage battle from his position from below. Such a scenario fits well with the involvement of a giant in such a battle. If the conflict in the text is indeed one waged unsuccessfully from earth against heavenly beings, then the story is reminiscent of the *gigantomachy* myth that circulated within Greek mythology during from the 7th century B.C.E. through to the Hellenistic and Graeco-Roman periods.[63]

---

[58] On Gilgamesh as a recipient of dreams in advance of his conflict with Humbaba in Tablet IV of the *Gilgamesh Epic*, see the discussion by Goff, "Gilgamesh the Giant", pp. 228–229.

[59] Puech, DJD 31, pp. 75 and 77.

[60] The text is cited as given by Puech (DJD 31, p. 74)

[61] Milik, *The Books of Enoch*, p. 307.

[62] Goff, "Gilgamesh the Giant", p. 242

[63] Despite the similarity in this respect, there are also many differences with the Greek myth, and a thorough comparison bears further investigation. In addition to being presented in architecture, sculpture and painted pottery from antiquity, the myth is recounted variously in Hesiod,

The involvement of *Gilgames/š* in the story as it relates to dream visions brings us to consider the second passage in which he occurs, 4Q530 2 ii + 6–12(?), lines 1–3. According to this text, as we have seen,'*Ohyah* reports to the other giants (including *Ḥobabis*, line 2) "what *Gilgames* said to him" (lines 1b–2a). It is not possible to certify that what '*Ohyah* reports has to do with what *Gilgameš* told him, either in 4Q531 22.3–7 (if the latter is the speaker in the text) or in the text missing at the bottom of 4Q531 22.12. But if one reads the 4Q530 text in this light, the report of a giant's defeat at the hands of (good) angelic beings would not be good news for the giants. After *Ḥobabis*'s roar in response, the text in line 2 goes on to say that "judgment('?) was spoken against him, and the guilty one (*Ḥobabis*?) cursed the princes".[64] While this scenario does look like a positive outcome for at least one giant, it is not clear from the narrative that the giants as a whole expect the same. At the beginning of the following line (3), the text reads: "and the giants rejoiced regarding it/him, and he returned and was cur[se]d [and raised a com]-plaint regarding it".[65] The text reflects a scenario in which not all giants are at once coming to terms with their guilt. One could speculate that what has been reported in relation to *Gilgames* was initially understood by the giants (except for *Ḥobabis*) as a reason not to fall into despair. Thus the scene is set for the giant siblings' ominous dreams (that of *Hahyah* in lines 4–12 and of '*Ohyah* in 15–20). These dreams are followed by the giants' commissioning of *Mahaway* to travel to Enoch (lines 20–24 and 7 ii 1–10a; for the second time!) in order to receive an interpretation (7 ii 10bff.) that, in turn, seals the giants' unavoidable fate.

Although the specific profile assigned to *Gilgames/š* in the *Book of Giants* can-not be sketched much beyond what we have just considered, the window of hope that the giants entertain for themselves – this motif is analogous to the rebellious angels' petition that they will be shown mercy in the *Book of Watchers* at *1 Enoch* 13:4–7 – may have some of its background in the storyline of the *Gilgamesh Epic*. As is well known, one of the main sections of the *Epic* is concerned with Gilga-mesh's search for immortality. After the death of his friend, Enkidu, Gilgamesh sets off in search of eternal life. In the end, however, even after he has consulted with Utnapishtim (who had been granted immortality following his survival of the great

---

Theogony, 617–819; Ovid, *Metamorphosis*, 1.151–162; and Pseudo-Apollodorus, *Bibliotheca* 1.6.1–2. For a summary, see Karl Kerényi, trans. Norman Cameron, *The Gods of the Greeks* (New York / London: Thames and Hudson, 1951), pp. 28–30.

[64] I acknowledge that, as the text is very difficult to read, even during a subsequent attempt with infrared lighting, I initially read "for us the Great One has cursed the princes" (לנא רבא לט לדרוניא; cf. *The Book of Giants from Qumran*, p. 105). Since there is insufficient space for the letters in this reading (including the requirement of smaller than usual space between the words) and in view of the remaining possibility that the vertical stroke (read as *lamed*) is actually from a *nun* of line 1 above, Puech's rendering is to be preferred (DJD 31, pp. 30 and 33): "Et le coupable maudit les princes."

[65] The text following "and he returned and" is unclear, and Puech's restoration in the lacuna ("cursed and raised a complaint") remains speculative, though it is plausible that the action still refer to that of *Ḥobabis*.

deluge), Gilgamesh realizes that his aspirations have been in vain. I suggest, therefore, that in addition to the cultural hero's hybrid nature, it is the motif of an *illusionary hope* not to be held accountable that underlies the development of the storyline in the *Book of Giants*. Thus, rather than just being a straightforward account that describes the oppressive and violent activities of the giants and their subsequent punishment, the *Book of Giants* propels the story forward by endowing it with a measure of suspense. Without gainsaying that this view, along with other readings, may depend on the reconstruction of the storyline and on several inferences, we are only left to speculate that the author(s) of the *Book of Giants* not only borrowed the name of *Gilgameš* from Ancient Near East mythology, but also identified him as a culpable giant who, as in the *Epic*, failed to gain what he hoped for. The fate of this giant in the story runs parallel to that of the other giants who discover, through dreams and reports of events, that their hope to go without punishment is illusory as well.

Milik singled out the inclusion of *Gilgameš* in the *Book of Giants* as remarkable in that this is "the only mention of Gilgamesh outside the cuneiform literature."[66] It is more accurate, however, to note that the occurrence of Gilgamesh (and of *Ḥobabiš*, for that matter) presupposes that these figures in the *Gilgamesh Epic* continued to be known during the Second Temple period. With respect to Gilgamesh, John Reeves has been able to cite important evidence. Though the name does not appear anywhere among other extant early Jewish compositions, it is known that the *Gilgamesh Epic* had continued to be copied by scribes as late as the 2nd or 1st centuries B. C. E.[67] Furthermore, the Greek naturalist Aelian, in his work *On Animals* 12.21 (ca. 200 C. E.), tells the story of a baby named Γίλγαμος, who escaped death and was raised by a gardener, eventually becoming the king of Babylon. Against Reeves, one might argue that it is not necessary to assume that the author(s) of the *Book of Giants* must have had access to the *Epic* through an Aramaic translation; there is no evidence to date that such a translation existed. All one can infer is the likelihood that the story was known at least in broad outline along with a few details from it, if not in written form, then at least through oral tradition.[68]

---

[66] Milik, *The Books of Enoch*, p. 313.

[67] See the material adduced by Reeves, *Jewish Lore in Manichaean Cosmogony*, pp. 120 and 158 (cf. n. 365). The tenor of Reeves' view is shared by an independent study published by Stephanie Dalley, "Gilgamesh in the Arabian Nights", *JRAS* 1 (1991), pp. 1–16, who argues that the *Book of Giants* as known at Qumran and *1 En.* (esp. the *Book of Watchers*) transmitted knowledge of the *Gilgamesh Epic* to the Manicheans through whom, in turn, the tradition would be picked up in *Arabian Nights* traditions.

[68] Karel van der Toorn, "Echoes of Gilgamesh in the Book of Qohelet?", in eds. W. H. van Soldt *et al.*, *Veenhof Anniversary Volume: Studies Presented to Klaas R. Veenhof on the Occasion of His Sixty-Fifth Birthday* (Leiden: Netherlands Institute for the Near East, 2001), pp. 503–514 (here p. 512), is correct to be cautious about the degree to which the *Gilgamesh Epic* in written form could have been known in Palestine by the last few centuries B. C. E. The discovery of a fragment of the *Epic* (overlapping with the content of Tablet VII of the standard version) at

Excursus Two: Was Atambiš a Giant in the Manichaean Book of Giants?

Reeves has attempted to argue that the name *Atambiš* in the Manichaean *Book of Giants* further reflects the influence of the *Epic of Gilgamesh*.[69] The name is not preserved among the Dead Sea materials, but, spelled *'tnbyš* in two Middle Persian *Kawân* fragments (frg. L and twice in M 5900),[70] it is thought to go back to or be modeled on the figure Utnapish-tim in the *Epic* (the standard version, Tablets X–XI). In the *Epic*, it is Utnapishtim who achieved immortality when he survived the flood sent by the gods against the earth. Reeves thus suggests that *Atambiš* in the Manichaean *Book of Giants* goes back to a now-lost part of the version of the book preserved at Qumran, according to which this character functioned as an anti- Noachic figure who, much in contrast to Noah (and in contrast with Utnapish-tim of the *Epic*), is destroyed as one of the giants.[71] The Great Flood, from which Noah and his family escape, destroys the mythological flood-hero. The author(s) of the *Book of Giants* have thus integrated the names of such "pagan actors" from the *Epic* into the storyline in order to communicate "a bold polemical thrust against the revered traditions of a rival cul-ture."[72]

In a summary and evaluation of Reeves' thesis, Ronald Huggins has agreed that *Atambiš* in the Manichaean *Book of Giants* corresponds to Utnapishtim in the *Epic of Gilgamesh*. However, rather than identifying *Atambiš* as one of the culpable giants, he has argued that here we are dealing with a more exemplary character: *Atambiš* (= Utnapishtim) functions in the Manichaean *Book of Giants* as the equivalent for the patriarch Enoch. Huggins focuses on Fragment "L" (page 1, verso, lines 1–7) as published and discussed by Werner Sunder-mann (see n. 69):

> Then *Sam* (= *'Ohyah*) said to the giants: "Come here that we may eat and be glad!" Because of sorrow they ate no bread. They went to sleep. *Mahawai* went to *Atambiš* (and) related everything. Again *Mahawai* came. *Sam* had a dream ...

Among the possible identifications of *Atambiš* – i. e. as a giant, a watcher, or Enoch – Hug-gins opts for Enoch, emphasizing the parallels between Utnapishtim of the *Epic of Gilgamesh*

Megiddo, which dates to the Late Bronze Age, does not provide a sufficient explanation. As part of his attempt to modify the supposition that Qoheleth has drawn directly on the *Epic* (e. g. at Qoh. 9:7–9 and 4:12), van der Toorn argues that the Megiddo fragment served training purposes only, that is, it reflected the need for rulers in Palestine to have "scribes with a training in cuneiform" in order to cope with the official language of diplomacy, Akkadian. In basic agreement with van der Toorn, I would nevertheless argue that knowledge of the *Epic* was not restricted to the mere use of names derived from it, but is reflected in the broad narrative of the *Book of Giants*, not simply where the figure of *Gilgames/š* himself is concerned.

[69] See John C. Reeves, "Utnapishtim in the Book of Giants?", *JBL* 112 (1993), pp. 110–115 (here p. 115).

[70] Published by Werner Sundermann, as M 5900 recto and as Fragment L page 1, verso line 5 in *Mittelpersische und partische kosmogonische und Parabeltexte* (Berliner Turfantexte 4; Berlin: Akademie-Verlag, 1973), p. 78 and "Ein weiteres Fragment aus Manis Gigantenbuch", in *Orienta-lia J. Duchesne-Guillemin emerito oblate* (Acta Iranica 23 and Second Series 9; Leiden: Brill, 1984), pp. 491–505 (here p. 497).

[71] Reeves, "Utnapishtim", p. 115. Reeves takes issue with the identification of *Atambiš* as one of the fallen angels proposed by Sundermann, *Mittelpersische und partische kosmogonische und Parabeltexte*, p. 78 n. 1, and in "Ein weiteres Fragment", p. 495 n. 19.

[72] Reeves, *Jewish Lore in Manichaean Cosmogony*, p. 126.

and Enoch: both are ante-diluvian, both found immortality without dying, both understood mysteries that they can also reveal, and both live at the ends of the world.

Huggins' identification of *Atambiš* with Enoch is weakened when one considers the use of them both in the Manichaean materials. If *Atambiš* is being equivocated with Enoch in Fragment L, then it would come as rather unexpected in a piece that on the recto at line 11 is supplied with a heading that introduces a new section of the book: "A copy of Enoch the scribe". Furthermore, the two occurrences of *Atambiš* in M 5900 locate him among the giants and watchers:

> And those three giants who were with *Atambiš* were slain ... And he came[?] before those wa[tch]ers and giants who were with him.

Enoch, on the other hand, however much he may have a predecessor in Utnapishtim of the *Epic*, is not so easily accessible to the giants; apparently only *Mahawai/y* (in both versions of the *Book of Giants*) is able to consult him; in fact, Fragment i (98) of the Middle Persian *Kawân* describes Enoch as being "veiled", "covered", "protected", and "moved out of sight" by the angels.[73] The resulting impression is that *Atambiš*, at least in the Manichaean *Book of Giants*, is one of Enoch's leading opponents, who is either one of the leaders among the giants or, as Sundermann originally proposed (see n. 70), a watcher. Again, if the suffix *–iš* provides any indication, the form of *Atambiš* coheres formally to names assigned to other giants considered above. If *Atambiš* is one of the giants in the *Book of Giants*, the fragmentary textual evidence does not permit anything further to be observed about his nature.

C. General Profile of the Giants from the Early Enochic Traditions

The "giants" (גבורין/א) in the *Book of Giants* for whom we have been able to draw a limited portrait have *inter alia* in common that they were not considered to be purely human in form. For *Mahaway*, *'Ohyah*, *Hahyah*, and *Hobabiš* one can infer a hybrid, animal-human, form of existence. Though Gilgamesh is portrayed in the *Epic* as part human and part divine, we do not know directly what sort of nature the author(s) of the *Book of Giants* thought or assumed he had. One can be relatively certain, nonetheless, that the *Gilgames/š* of the *Book of Giants* was regarded as only partly human, whether this means he was part human and part angel or, as the other giants we have considered, part human and part animal. With respect to the giants' composite forms, the *Book of Giants* – and, indeed, the whole early Enochic tradition – differs in viewpoint from the *Epic of Gilgamesh* and other ancient sources that refer to such hybrid figures: the early Enochic traditions hold that the giants, precisely *because they are composite creatures* (that is, because they are the products of a deplorable union between angels and human women), are *inherently* impure and corrupt.

As in the *Book of Watchers* (at *1 En.* 6–11 and 15–16), the *Book of Giants* regards the sexual union of the watchers with the women as an act of defilement (so 4Q531 1.1) that has violated the boundaries imposed by God upon the created

---

[73] Henning, "The Book of Giants", pp. 58 (text) and 62 (translation).

order.[74] Because their nature was inadmissible within the bounds of the created order, the giants' punishment will involve a reconfiguration of their mode of being. As I have argued elsewhere,[75] this reconfiguration may be implied in the text of 4Q531 19.2–3, in which (presumably) the giants acknowledge they are neither simply bones nor flesh and thus expect to be "blotted out" from their "form". For all the difficulty of interpreting such a fragmentary text, without recourse to the larger immediate narrative context, some altered form of existence is here being anticipated, a form that will come about when the giants have been "killed". The Dead Sea *Book of Giants* fragments attest how in the story some of the giants do perish through fighting among themselves (so 4Q203 3; 4Q531 7.4–5), though nothing is preserved that informs us explicitly about what happens to them then. We do not know, for instance, whether in the *Book of Giants* – as in *Jubilees* 5:8–9 – the deaths of giants through intramural conflict resulted in a continued existence as evil spirits that emerge from their dead bodies (cf. also *1 En.* 15:11–16:1). But what about those giants who have not yet died through such conflict? What is the form from which they are to be "blotted"? In order to acquire some perspective on these questions, it is appropriate to turn briefly to the *Book of Watchers* by which the *Book of Giants* may have been influenced at several places.[76]

In the *Book of Watchers*, although Noah is the only one who escapes the Flood (*1 En.* 10:1–3), the divine response to the complaints of the human dead (8:4–9:11; 10:4–15) results, at the first stage of tradition, in the giants' continuous punishment until the end (10:12–13). However, with additional material in *1 Enoch* chapters 12–16, the divine punishment does allow them to enter into a post-diluvian existence that impacts the world of human experience (esp. 15:3–16:3). To be sure, the giants do not as such escape, whether through infighting or the Flood; yet they are allowed to survive in an altered form, that is, as "evil spirits" (15:8–9). Out of the unsanctioned mixture that they represent (15:8–9) emerges a more one-dimensional spirit-form that, despite the suffering and errors it leads to among humans, stands under divine judgment.[77]

Since the spirits coming from the punished giants are ultimately products of a reprehensible union, they are irreversibly corrupt. In fact, according to the Greek Codex Panopolitanus to *1 Enoch* 10:9, they are called οἱ μαζήρεοι, that is, "bastards", a transliteration of a no longer extant Hebrew ממזרים or Aramaic ממזריא in that text.[78] And so, after the Flood, the giant spirits continue to engage in some of

---

[74] Cf. Archie T. Wright, *The Origin of Evil Spirits* (WUNT 2.198; Tübingen: Mohr Siebeck, 2005), pp. 118–136.

[75] See Chapter One above. See further Puech, DJD 31, pp. 71–72.

[76] Concerning the likelihood of such dependence, see Stuckenbruck, *The Book of Giants from Qumran*, pp. 24–25.

[77] See section C.2 in Chapter One above.

[78] Therefore, when 4Q510 1.5 mentions the רוחות ממזרים among a list of demonic entities, it is likely that we have to do with a reference to the spirits of the giants. So also 4Q511 35.7 and 48 +49.2–3; and 4Q444 2 i 4, in which they are also singled out among lists. A further reference to

the destructive activities that had characterized them before (15:11). In particular, they wish to bring affliction to humans (15:12), that is, to the offspring of Noah, perhaps because humans, and not they, have escaped the destruction with their bodies intact.[79]

D. Conclusion

In summarizing the discussion above, we may emphasize two points. First, if we are correct that the *Book of Giants* can portray the giants' composite existence by describing them as part human and part animal or angel, then what they lose after their "death" is the human part of their "form" (cf. 4Q531 19). In effect, they become "de-humanized" beings who, even more than before, have no appropriate place within the created order. Second, the appearance of names such as *Ḥobabis/š* and *Gilgames/š* among the cast of characters in the *Book of Giants* attests the knowledge of oral, perhaps even literary, traditions originating from Mesopotamia among learned circles of Judaism during the final centuries B.C.E. We do not know *how* the author(s) of the *Book of Giants* came to know any of these traditions. They may have been aware, respectively, of these characters' notoriously villainous and semi-divine status. Their names were taken up by the scribes and blended, in the case of Gilgamesh, into the narrative about wicked and hybrid giants who were thought to have flourished during pre-diluvian times when they brought chaos and suffering to the world. In this way, a subversive polemic was waged against non-Jewish traditions that were circulating in antiquity.

---

the ongoing demonic presence of the giants may be reconstructed in 11Q11 v 6 as part of an incantation formula: when the demon comes in the night, the formula requires that this malevolent being be addressed as "offspring of] humanity and (of) the seed of the ho[ly ones". In view of the discussion above about giants as hybrid creatures, it is interesting that this demon is described as having "horns" in its disembodied state (11Q11 v 7).

[79] On Noah as an anti-giant figure, see Chapter Three below.

Chapter Three

The Lamech Narrative in the *Genesis Apocryphon* (1QapGen) and *1 Enoch 106–107*: A Tradition-Historical Study of Two Ancient Accounts about Noah's Birth

A. Introduction

The parallels between the *Genesis Apocryphon* (1Q20) at columns ii 1 – v 27 and *1 Enoch* chapters 106–107 (*Birth of Noah*) have been noted since the early days when the Qumran Cave 1 materials were being published.[1] The purpose of the present discussion will be to inquire into how these two sources are related to one another. I have recently argued that, "in terms of overall length, it is more difficult to explain *Birth of Noah* as derived from the longer *Genesis Apocryphon* account since the omission of so many details in *1 Enoch* becomes hard to explain."[2] Even if this claim is largely correct, it would be misleading to assume that the *Birth of Noah* as a whole and on account of its relative brevity occupies a tradition-historically prior position in relation to its counterpart in the *Genesis Apocryphon*. Thus, inspired chiefly by Esther Eshel's recent claim for the latter work's antiquity in relation to the *Jubilees*,[3] I would like to examine the problem

---

[1] See e.g. Józef T. Milik, "'Livre de Noé' (Pl. XVI)" and "'Apocalypse de Lamech' (Pl. XVII)", in eds. Dominique Barthélemy and Józef T. Milik, *Qumran Cave I* (DJD 1; Oxford: Clarendon Press, 1955), pp. 84–86 and 86–87 (hereafter DJD 1), respectively, and Nahman Avigad and Yigael Yadin, *A Genesis Apocryphon: A Scroll from the Wilderness of Judaea* (Jerusalem: Magnes Press, 1956), pp. 16–19.

[2] Loren T. Stuckenbruck, *1 Enoch 91–108* (CEJL; Berlin: Walter de Gruyter, 2007), p. 613.

[3] Esther Eshel, "The *Imago Mundi* of the *Genesis Apocryphon*", in eds. Lynn R. LiDonnici and Andrea Lieber, *Heavenly Tablets: Interpretation, Identity and Tradition in Ancient Judaism* (JSJSup 119; Leiden/Boston: Brill, 2007), pp. 111–131 and *idem*, "The Aramaic Levi Document, the Genesis Apocryphon, and Jubilees: A Study of Shared Traditions", in eds. Gabriele Boccaccini and Giovanni Ibba, *Enoch and the Mosaic Torah: The Evidence of Jubilees* (Grand Rapids: Eerdmans 2009), pp. 82–98. For an earlier argument in favor of this position, see Cana Werman, "Qumran and the Book of Noah", in eds. Esther G. Chazon and Michael E. Stone, *Pseudepigraphic Perspectives: The Apocrypha and Pseudepigrapha in Light of the Dead Sea Scrolls* (STDJ 31; Leiden: Brill, 1999), 171–181 (here, pp. 172–177). Along these lines, a nuanced argument has been recently advanced by Daniel Machiela, *The Dead Sea Genesis Apocryphon (1Q20): A New Text and Translation, with Introduction and Special Treatment of Columns 13–17* (STDJ 79; Leiden: Brill, 2009), pp. 85–104 and Michael Segal, "The Literary Relationship between the Genesis Apocryphon and Jubilees: The Chronology of Abram and Sarai's Descent to Egypt", *Aramaic Studies* 8 (2010), pp. 71–88; see also Geza Vermes, "2. The Genesis Apocryphon from Qumran", in Emil Schürer, *The History of the Jewish People in the Age of Jesus Christ*, revd. Geza Vermes, Fergus Millar and

in more detail (esp. section C below) and consider how much my previous claim may stand in need of qualification.

B. 1Q19 and 1Q19*bis*, 4Q534–536, and *Genesis Apocryphon* vi 1–5

It is well known, however, that the *Genesis Apocryphon* and *1 Enoch* 106–107 are concerned with the birth of Noah and its immediate aftermath and that as such, they link thematically with at least two other fragmentary documents (see subsections B.1 and B.2 below) from the Dead Sea Scrolls which need to be taken into account. In addition, it is appropriate to mention a further passage from the *Genesis Apocryphon* (subsection B.3 below) that in the work is formally assigned to a different source, but offers a précis of Noah's childhood.

B.1. 1Q19 and 1Q19bis

The designations 1Q19 and 1Q19*bis* each represent a constellation of Hebrew fragments that, taken together, are interrelated. The former of these manuscripts was early on given the title "Livre de Noé" by Józef T. Milik.[4] This designation was not without justification. Although not one of this manuscripts' 21 fragments mentions Noah by name, several of them preserve details that are unmistakably

---

Martin Goodman (3 vols.; Edingurgh: T. & T. Clark, 1973–1987), 3:318–325. For a very different position, which argues strongly in favor of the dependence of the *Genesis Apocryphon* on *Jubilees*, see Joseph A. Fitzmyer, *The Genesis Apocryphon of Qumran Cave 1; A Commentary* (BibOr 18; Rome: Pontifical Biblical Institute, 1966, 1st ed.), p. 14 (a view retained in the 1971[2] and 2004[3] editions); Klaus Beyer, *Die aramäischen Texte vom Toten Meer* (Göttingen: Vandenhoeck & Ruprecht, 1984), p. 165; George W. E. Nickelsburg, "Patriarchs Who Worry about Their Wives", in eds. Jacob Neusner and Alan J. Avery-Peck, *George Nickelsburg in Perspective: An Ongoing Dialogue of Learning* (2 vols.; JSJSup 80; Leiden: Brill, 2003), pp. 200–212 (esp. p. 199 n. 45); Daniel K. Falk, *The Parabiblical Texts: Strategies for Extending the Scriptures among the Dead Sea Scrolls* (LSTS 63; London: T. & T. Clark International, 2007), pp. 26–106 (esp. pp. 97–100); William G. Loader, *Enoch, Levi, and Jubilees on Sexuality* (Grand Rapids: Eerdmans, 2007), pp. 71–77 (esp. p. 75); James Kugel, "Which is Older, *Jubilees* or the *Genesis Apocryphon*? Some Exegetical Considerations", in eds. Lawrence H. Schiffman, Adolfo D. Roitman, and Shani Tsoref, *The Dead Sea Scrolls and Contemporary Culture* (STDJ 93; Leiden / Boston: Brill, 2010), pp. 257–294. Moshe J. Bernstein, "Divine Titles and Epithets and the Sources of the Genesis Apocryphon", *JBL* 128 (2009), pp. 291–310.

[4] Milik, "'Livre de Noé' (Pl. XVI)", DJD 1, p. 84. Given the significant developments in research on early Enochic and Noahic traditions over the last fifty years, 1Q19 and 1Q19*bis* are in need of fresh study and re-editing. For an orientating discussion, see Dorothy M. Peters, *Noah Traditions and the Dead Sea Scrolls: Conversations and Controversies of Antiquity* (SBLEJL 26; Atlanta: Society of Biblical Literature, 2008), pp. 132–134 and in relation to fundamental palaeographical observations, see Claire Ruth Pfann, "A Note on 1Q19: The 'Book of Noah'", in eds. Michael E. Stone, Aryeh Amihay, and Vered Hillel, *Noah and His Book(s)* (SBLEJL 28; Atlanta: Society of Biblical Literature, 2010), pp. 71–76.

associated both with early Enoch tradition (from *1 En.* 6–11) and with the figure of Noah, including his birth (*1 En.* 106–107). These details[5] are as follows:

(A) In 1Q19 fragment 1, the text on lines 2–4 shows verbal echoes of the *Book of Watchers* at *1 Enoch* 8–9:

]*m* did greatly upon the earth, and[	2	cf. *1 En.* 8:2 or 9:1
]*t* his way upon the earth[	3	cf. *1 En.* 8:2 or 9:1; Gen. 6:12
]their(?) [cry] before God and[	4	cf. *1 En.* 8:4 or 9:2–3

(B) 1Q19*bis* (= 1Q19 fragment 2[6]) similarly overlaps with parts of *1 Enoch* 9:3–4, to which its content corresponds in sequence:

]*y* he[aven	1	cf. *1 En.* 9:3a
]our [ju]dgment bef[ore	2	cf. *1 En.* 9:3b
]and not under you [	3	
Rapha]el and Gabriel [	4	cf. *1 En.* 9:4a, but cf. Eth. 9:1
Lord of] lords and Migh[ty One of mighty ones	5	cf. *1 En.* 9:4b
] ages[	6	cf. *1 En.* 9:4c

(C) 1Q19 fragment 3 lines 3–5 refer to Noah's father, Lamech, and are reminiscent of several parts of the *Birth of Noah* in *1 Enoch* 106:

fir]stborn was born like the glorious ones [	3	cf. *1 En.* 106:5–6, 10, 12, 18
]his father, and when Lamech saw the[	4	cf. *1 En.* 106:4
] the rooms of the house like beams of the sun [	5	cf. *1 En.* 106:2b (Lat.), 5b, 10

(D) 1Q19 fragment 8 line 2 mentions "Methusela[h", Noah's grandfather (cf. *1 En.* 106:4, 8).

(E) The text in 1Q19 fragments 13+14 lines 1–3 is consistent with the story of Noah's birth, though its precise meaning is harder to determine[7]: the lines may be either the words which Noah spoke when he praised God at the moment of his birth (cf. *1 En.* 106:3, 11) or they describe the extraordinary qualities which his birth bespeak (cf. *1 En.* 106:2–5, 10–11).[8]

---

[5] The translations below are my own.

[6] No photograph was printed in DJD 1. The nomenclature is presumably to be explained on the (perhaps misleading) assumption that this fragment, along with 1Q19 1, relates to *1 En.* 9:1–4 and therefore should not be assigned to the same document.

[7] 1Q19 13+14.1–3:

]. because radiant(?) glory .[.....] to glory God in[	1
he] will be lifted up in glorious splendour, and honour[	2
]. he will be glorified among [	3

[8] If the text is concerned with the latter alternative, then 1Q19 may, unlike *1 En.* 106–107, take Noahic tradition in the direction of representing him as a divine agent; cf. Stuckenbruck, *1 Enoch 91–108*, p. 608.

The parallels adduced above to 1Q19 reinforce the links between *1 Enoch* 6–11 and Noahic tradition. These affinities between them accord with the suggestion of R. H. Charles that *1 Enoch* 6–11, which does not mention Enoch but instead refers to the figure of Noah (*1 En.* 10:1–3), derives from a now lost "Apocalypse" or "Book of Noah".[9]

B.2. 4Q534–536

The second document to consider is a group of texts represented by the partly overlapping manuscripts 4Q534–536.[10] Jean Starcky had originally thought that the special figure described in 4Q534 was the Messiah.[11] This assessment, however, has been overtaken by the view, initially argued by Joseph Fitzmyer,[12] that the text is actually concerned with the birth of Noah (4Q534 1 i 1–5, 10–11; 4Q535 3.1–6) and with Noah's extraordinary knowledge and wisdom (4Q534 1 i 4–8; 4Q535 2.3; 4Q536 2 i + 3.2–9, 12–13).[13] The lines that purportedly relate to Noah's birth and youth are as follows:

4Q534 1 i 1–5[14]

> of the hand[and] both his kn[e]es. [And on his head are strip]es of a mark. Red is   1
> [his] hair [and] (there are) moles on [his face(?)] *vacat*   2
> And (there are) small marks on his thighs, and [hair]s are different from one another,   3
> and knowledge will b[e] in his heart.
> In his boyhood he will be keen [and as] a [m]an who does not know anything until   4
> the time when
> [he] knows the three books. *vacat*   5

4Q534 1 i 10 (par. 4Q535 1 ii + 2.7)

> [...]his [th]oughts because he is the chosen one of God. His birth and the spirit   10
> of his breath
> [...]his [th]oughts will be eternal. *vacat*   11

---

[9] Robert Henry Charles, *The Book of Enoch or 1 Enoch* (Oxford: Clarendon Press, 1912), pp. 13–14.

[10] Edited by Émile Puech, "4QNaissance de Noé$^{a-c}$", in *idem, Qumrân Grotte 4 XXII. Textes araméens, Première Partie: 4Q529–549* (DJD 31; Oxford: Clarendon Press, 2001), pp. 118–170.

[11] See Jean Starcky, "Un texte messianique araméen de la grotte 4 de Qumrân", in *École des langues orientales anciennes de l'Institut Catholique de Paris. Mémorial du cinquantenaire 1914–1964* (Travaux de l'Institut Catholique de Paris 10; Paris: Bloud et Gay, 1964), pp. 51–66.

[12] So Joseph A. Fitzmyer, "The Aramaic 'Elect of God' Text from Qumran Cave 4", in *idem, Essays on the Semitic Background of the New Testament* (SBLSBS 5; Missoula, Montana: Scholars Press, 1979, repr. from 1965), pp. 127–160 (esp. pp. 158–159). For further bibliography and an excellent review of research, see Puech, "4QNaissance de Noé$^{a-c}$", pp. 118–127.

[13] Significant in the identification are the possible allusions to the Great Flood in 4Q534 1 i 10 + 2 ("waters will put to an end[") and to avoidance of death "in the days of evil" in 4Q536 2 ii 11.

[14] The translation and restorations below are based on Puech's edition.

4Q535 3.1–6 (par. 4Q536 1.1–3)

> [... (he)]. is born, and from evening they will be together [1
> [... fi]fth [hour] in the night (he) is born and comes forth comp[lete   2
> [...]weight (in) shekels of three hundred and fif[ty-(one)   3
> [...]the [da]ys he sleeps until half (4Q536: his) days are co[mplete   4
> [...] by day until the completion of [eight] y[ears   5
> [...] shall move from him [and] af[ter eight years   6

Especially important for the possible identity of Noah behind the text may be the phrase "and comes forth comp[lete" (ונפק של[ם]; cf. the *Birth of Noah* at *1 En.* 106:2–12). However, the absence in 4Q534–536 of any precise parallels to either *Birth of Noah* or the *Genesis Apocryphon* reflects, given the shared interest in birth features, the diversity Noahic traditions could take.[15] Though it is therefore difficult to assume that there existed a single "Book of Noah" into which many or most Noahic texts could be reconciled,[16] the details held in common by the *Birth of Noah* and the *Genesis Apocryphon* ii 1 – v 26 are sufficient to allow us to infer a source-critical relationship between at least these two sources (and, perhaps more distantly, with 1Q19). Before assessing what this relationship signifies in the conclusion below, I shall in the present discussion provide an overview of the texts along with a detailed comparison (section C below).

B.3. Genesis Apocryphon *vi 1–5*

The first person Lamech narrative about Noah's birth in the *Genesis Apocryphon* (ii 1 – v 26) is followed by a new section entitled "the book of the words of Noah" (1Q20 v 29). Hereafter, until the end of column xvii of 1Q20, we read a mostly first person account attributed to Noah. While no text is extant below this heading in column v, column vi opens in the middle of a sentence in which Noah mentions his own birth. 1Q20 vi 2–5 pertain to the period of Noah's youth, emphasizing Noah's wisdom and righteous character (lines 2–4) and referring to help he received "to warn me from the ..*yb* of deception which leads to darkness" (line 3). With respect to Noah's birth, it is line 1 is comes into view:

---

[15] This point, of course, depends on the correctness of the Noahic character of this material. For this reason, Devorah Dimant has urged caution against any foregone conclusion that 4Q534–536 refers to Noah's birth; see her review of Émile Puech's discussion of these manuscripts in DJD 31 in *DSD* 10 (2003), pp. 292–304 (here pp. 197–198). Similarly cautious is Peters, who, however, ventures a more wide ranging interpretation (*Noah Traditions in the Dead Sea Scrolls*, pp. 98–106): the characteristics presented in 4Q534–536 "may have been intended to apply to an entire lineage of exceptional people, chosen by God, through whom wisdom and esoteric knowledge were properly transmitted, from Enoch to Noah, Levi, and through to the wise and inspired teachers of the writer's day" (p. 106). There is little among the fragments themselves, however, which would indicate that the details apply to more than one figure. See further Aryeh Amihay and Daniel A. Machiela, "Traditions of the Birth of Noah", in eds. Michael E. Stone, Aryeh Amihay, and Vered Hillel, *Noah and His Book(s)* (SBLEJL 28; Atlanta: Society of Biblical Literature, 2010), pp. 53–70.

... from iniquity, and within the crucible of the one who was pregnant with me, I grew in righteousness. And when I came out from the womb of my mother, I was planted for righteousness.

By focusing on Noah's righteousness from conception, the text reinforces the divine purpose behind his origin. This concern with Noah's conception contrasts with Lamech's suspicion that his wife has been inseminated by a rebellious angel (1Q20 ii 1; see below).[17] In addition, the claim that Noah himself is a righteous planting – here it is expressed verbally – cannot be derived from the *Book of Watchers* at *1 Enoch* 10:3 in which the "righteous plant" refers to Noah's righteous descendants (cf. 10:15–16). A closer analogy might be provided in the *Book of Giants* at 6Q8 2, which probably refers to Noah's sons as "three shoots" and implies that Noah himself is a tree. If anything, the writer is pressing an already existing association between Noah and the plant metaphor back to the very moment of his beginning.

The subsequent emphasis on Noah's wisdom (line 3) as a feature of his character is elaborated in the remaining columns of the Noah story in the *Genesis Apocryphon*. In addition, it corresponds to the even more elaborate tradition of Noah as a sapient found in 4Q534–536.[18]

We see, then, that the plant metaphor for Noah is developed in the larger narrative of *Genesis Apocryphon*. In addition to 1Q20 vi 1, it is already expressed in the account of Noah's birth in 1Q20 ii, where Noah is referred to as "the planting of [this] fruit" (ii 15, ‏נצבת פריא[דן‎) and as "seed" (ii 15). This metaphorical language is, however, entirely absent from the Enochic *Birth of Noah* in *1 Enoch* 106–107.

C. *Genesis Apocryphon* (1Q20 ii – v 27) and *Birth of Noah*: An Overview and Comparison

As we have seen in section B.3 above, the Noahic material in the *Genesis Apocryphon* extends well beyond the first five columns (i. e. into 1Q20 vi – xvii). Significantly, it is the material *following* the story of Noah's birth that carries the heading,

---

[16] For an overview of the issues of the debate and bibliography, see Stuckenbruck, *1 Enoch 91–108*, pp. 608–611 (and esp. notes 1027–1028). In addition to *1 En.* chs. 6–11, chs. 106–107 and *Genesis Apocryphon* 1Q20 i – v 26, the texts most frequently discussed in relation to the problem of a "Book of Noah" include: *Book of Giants* (6Q8 2; cf. 2Q26 and 6Q26); *Animal Apocalypse* at *1 En.* 89:1–9; *Book of Dreams* at *1 En.* 83:1–84:6; *Similitudes* at *1 En.* 54:7–55:2, 60:1–10 and 24–25, 65:1–67:3, 67:4–68:5, 69:1–26; 1Q20=*Genesis Apocryphon* v 29 – xvii; *Jub.* 21:5–11; and *Aramaic Levi Document* (Grk. Athos Koutloumous 39, f. 206v ii 17–19).

[17] I. e. Noah was not a giant; for a discussion and bibliography, cf. Stuckenbruck, *1 Enoch 91–108*, pp. 633–635.

[18] Cf. 4Q534 1 i 4 (referring to his youth), 6 ("then he will be prudent [‏יערם‎] and know the pat[hs of sa]ges (with) seers to come to him on their knees"), and 7–8 ("with him will be counsel and pruden[ce, and] he will know the secrets of humanity and his wisdom will go to all the peoples, and he will know the secrets of all life").

at column v 29, "the book of the words of Noah" (כתב מלי נוח).[19] The text, therefore, formally distinguishes between the so-called "book of Noah" and its account of Noah's birth. With the exception of 1Q20 vi 1–5, the fragmentary text of columns vi through xvii, which relates primarily to the story of the Flood, does not exhibit any connection with *1 Enoch* 106–107.[20]

The account of Noah's birth in *Genesis Apocryphon* in ii 1 – v 26 is being summarized, noting the parallels with *Birth of Noah* in both the Greek (G) and Ethiopic (E) versions.[21] This account is presented from the perspective of Lamech, who speaks in the 1st person (so e. g. 1Q20 ii 3) while, on the other hand, *1 Enoch* 106–107 is told as the words of Enoch (106:1, 8–9, 12–13).

C.1. Lamech's Initial Reaction to His Child

The small amount of surviving text from 1Q20 i does not provide much of a narrative. The opening lines of column ii, however, recount Lamech's worry about his son, probably based on a description of his appearance at birth:

Behold, then I thought in my heart that the conception was from the Watchers or (that) the seed was from the Holy Ones or Nephil[im...]. /I was confused on account of this child. Then I, Lamech, was frightened and went to Bitenosh [my] wi[fe] (1Q20 ii 1–2)

This initial reaction of Lamech is followed by a lengthy quarrel between him and his wife regarding the identity of the boy's father (ii 3–18), with Bitenosh denying Lamech's suspicions and insisting instead that her husband was responsible for the pregnancy. In the end, Lamech consults his father Methuselah:

Then I, Lamech, ran to Methuselah my father, and [I] tol[d] him everything[... (ii 19)

The parallel in *1 Enoch* 106:4–6 reads in the Ethiopic and Greek versions, respectively, as follows:

(Eth.)	(Grk.)
[4] And Lamech his father was afraid of him and fled and came to his father Methuselah. [5] And he said to him, "I have fathered a strange son; his is not like a human being, and is like the children of the angels of hea-	[4] And Lamech was afraid of him and came to Methu[s]elah his father. [5] And he said [to] him, "A strange child of mine has been born, not li[k]e human beings, but (like) the children of the angels of heaven. And

---

[19] Thus "the book" is related to Noah by virtue of its being (pseudepigraphic) words attributed to Noah, not material about Noah *per se*. On this criterion the *Genesis Apocryphon*, 1Q20 i – v 27, would be a "book of Lamech", who acts as 1st person narrator.

[20] Instead, the details are shared more with various parts of *1 Enoch* and esp. *Book of Giants*. On the latter, see Daniel A. Machiela and Andrew B. Perrin, "That you may know everything with certainty: A New Reading in 4QEnGiants[b] ar (4Q530) and a literary connection between the Book of Giants and Genesis Apocryphon", *RevQ* 25 (2011), pp. 113–125.

[21] The translations are based on Stuckenbruck, *1 Enoch 91–108*, pp. 606–689, in which the underlying text-critical work (esp. Eth.) is provided.

ven. And his form (is) different, and his is not like us; and his eyes are as the rays of the sun; the face (is) glorious. [6] And it seems to me that he is not from me, but rather from the angels. And I fear, lest a marvel happen during his days on earth."

the form is diffe[r]ent, not like us. The eyes [are] as beams of the sun, and [his fa]ce is glori[ous]. [6] And I perceive that [he is] not from me, but from angels, and I am concerned about [hi]m, lest something happen during [h]is da[ys] on earth."

The texts of both *Genesis Apocryphon* and *Birth of Noah* share a basic storyline: Lamech is afraid and thinks that Noah is not his own child, but is of non-human origin instead. Despite this shared narrative, a number of differences in detail emerge. These distinguishing features in the parallel storylines are discussed in the following sections C.2–9 below.

C.2. Marital Altercation

Whereas in the *Birth of Noah* Lamech responds by consulting his father directly, *Genesis Apocryphon* narrates his reaction in two stages: firstly, he confronts his wife (1Q20 ii 3–18) and, secondly, then goes to Methuselah. The inclusion of the quarrel between husband and wife is without parallel in any other text. One could infer from Lamech's suspicions in *Birth of Noah* that he might not be the father (*1 En.* 106:6; cf. 106:12), and that he would have been upset with his wife. Thus a secondary expansion that offers the argument between them is certainly plausible.[22]

C.3. Lamech's Wife's Name

Closely related to this expansion is the fact that the anonymous wife of Lamech in *Birth of Noah* (*1 En.* 106:1) is given a proper name, Bitenosh, in *Genesis Apocryphon* (1Q20 ii 3, 8, 12). The significance of this point shall be discussed further below (see subsection C.4).

C.4. The Description of Lamech's Child

Lamech's fear is justified by an elaborate description of the child in the *Birth of Noah*. In 1Q20, however, only very little description is preserved, and that is found at a later, fragmentary part of the narrative (1Q20 v 12–13: "his face he lifted to me, and his eyes were shining as [the] su[n ...] / this boy fire, and he *l.*..["; cf. 1Q19 3.5 and *1 En.* 106:2b [Lat.], 5b, 10). There are two possible ways of explaining the occurrence of this text here: either Noah was originally described in the unpreserved parts of column i (though none of the very fragmentary text points in this direction) or there was no such description to begin with. Given that Lamech's

---

[22] The alternative possibility, i. e. that the *Birth of Noah* has omitted previously existing (and received) material about Lamech's altercation with Bitenosh, is harder to account for.

report to Methuselah in the *Birth of Noah* is already preceded by a narrative description of the event (cf. *1 En.* 106:2–3), it would not be surprising if it is the child's special features that in the *Genesis Apocryphon* give Lamech reason to worry. On the other hand, one is not to suppose that a purported portrayal of the child in 1Q20 column i would have been along the lines we encounter in *Birth of Noah*. The threefold repetition in the latter work of the description of the boy's appearance (*1 En.* 106:2–3, 4–5, 10–11), of which there is little trace in what remains from 1Q20 columns i–v, suggests that the narrative in *1 Enoch* 106–107, though shorter, has been subject to editorial shaping at this point. The argument of omission, however, may be applied the other way around: since it is unlikely that *Genesis Apocryphon* would have done away with the elaborate features of Noah given in *Birth of Noah*, the absence of these raises the possibility of whether such a depiction was in the tradition received by *Genesis Apocryphon* to begin with. At the very least, it may be questioned whether *Genesis Apocryphon* originally contained a *threefold* description of Lamech's son.

C.5. Designations for the Suspected Progenitor of Noah

The nomenclature for those beings suspected of fathering Noah differs between the texts. The terminology in *Birth of Noah*, for which no Aramaic text is extant, is more developed than in its counterpart. Here the rebellious watchers are referred to as "the angels of heaven" (*1 En.* 106:5, 12 – Eth. *malāʾekta samāy*, Grk. οἱ ἄγγελοι τοῦ οὐρανοῦ – possibly from Aram. or Heb. מלאכי (ה)שמיא) and "angels" (vv. 6, 12 – Eth. *malāʾekt*, Grk. οἱ ἄγγελοι). The designation "the angels of heaven", in its precise form, does not occur anywhere in the Hebrew Bible, Greek translations and the Dead Sea documents.[23] Something similar, however, occurs in several secondary manuscripts (A, D, E, F) to Genesis 6:2 (οἱ ἄγγελοι τοῦ θεοῦ) and, perhaps, in hybrid form in Codex Panopolitanus to *1 Enoch* 6:2 ("the angels, sons of heaven", οἱ ἄγγελοι υἱοὶ οὐρανοῦ; Eth. *malāʾekt weluda samāyāt*). In any case, the term "angels" became a neutral way of referring to heavenly beings that could be either bad or good (the aspect of which would be determined by the context). By contrast, the fallen angels in the corresponding passage in the *Genesis Apocryphon* are designated in three other ways: they are called (1) "holy ones" (קדישין, 1Q20 ii 1), a term that describes them again in 1Q20 vi 20;[24]

---

[23] In the New Testament, see only Mt. 24:36 (οἱ ἄγγελοι τοῦ θεοῦ par. Mk. 13:32 οἱ ἄγγελοι τοῦ οὐρανοῦ) where, however, the designation refers to obedient angelic beings aligned with "the Son" and "the Father".

[24] Cf. also 11Q11 v 6 if the reconstruction of the text as an address to a threatening spirit from a giant is correct: מי אתה [מ הילוד] אדם[ומזרע הקד]שי[ושי]ם ("Who are you, [oh offspring of] man and of the seed of the ho[ly] ones?"; cf. Florentino García Martínez and Eibert J. C. Tigchelaar, *The Dead Sea Scrolls Study Edition. Volume Two: 4Q274–11Q31* (Leiden / Boston / Köln: Brill, 1998), pp. 1202–1203. For other reconstructions, see Émile Puech, "Le deux derniers psaumes davidiques du ritual d'exorcisme 11QPsApᵃ IV,4-V,14", in eds. Devorah Dimant and Uri Rappa-

(2) "watchers" (עירין, 1Q20 ii 1, 15); and (3) "sons of heaven" (בני שמיא, 1Q20 ii 15; cf. LXX Gen. 6:2).[25]

The presence of a marital row in *Genesis Apocryphon* leaves the impression that we have to do with a secondary expansion of an originally shorter story. The additional material would have functioned to reinforce the vividness of the world within which Lamech's distress takes shape. To be sure, *Birth of Noah* in itself also seeks to make vivid the setting for Noah's birth, so that the implied reader is transported back into a key moment in ante-diluvian time and made to imagine – with the protagonists Lamech and Methuselah – that rebellious angels were (potentially) continuing to mate with women. If we compare this with the storyline in the *Book of Watchers*, the narrative reflects a development: whereas in *1 Enoch* 6–11 (and chapters 12–16) the "women" through whom the giant offspring are sired are simply referred to as "the daughters of men" whom the angels took "as wives" for themselves (*1 En.* 6:1–2; 7:1; cf. also *Jub.* 5:1; 7:21),[26] in *Birth of Noah* the woman in question is already a wife, that is, Lamech's wife (*1 En.* 106:1).[27] In *Genesis Apocryphon* the marital status of Noah's mother is highlighted, and the uncertainty of the times is stressed even more. In 1Q20 column ii, the dramatic effect of the story is augmented in at least two ways. First, Lamech's wife is given a proper name: Bitenosh (1Q20 ii 3, 8, 12 – בתאנש). This naming of the woman reflects what also happens in *Jubilees* (cf. e. g. 4:1–33; 12:9; 19:10–12)[28] in which,

---

port, *The Dead Sea Scrolls: Forty Years of Research* (STDJ 10; Leiden: Brill, 1992), pp. 64–89 (here p. 68) and Florentino García Martínez, "11Q11", in eds. Florentino García Martínez, Eibert J. C. Tigchelaar, and A. S. van der Woude, *Qumran Cave 11.II: 11Q2–18, 11Q20–30* (DJD 33; Oxford: Clarendon Press, 1998), pp. 198–201 (here p. 200).

[25] A further designation for the fallen angels might be "Nephilim" (1Q20 ii 1; cf. the pairing of "watchers" with "sons of heav[en" in ii 16), a designation normally used for their offspring, the giants; see further Stuckenbruck, *1 Enoch 91–108*, p. 639 n. 1076. On the growing conflation between the originally separate identities of Titans and *gigantes* in Greek mythology during the Hellenistic period, see Timothy Gantz, *Early Greek Myth: A Guide to Literary and Artistic Sources* (Baltimore / London: The Johns Hopkins University Press, 1993), pp. 4–56 and 45–54. However, even in 1Q20 ii 1 the term probably refers to the giants who could have been responsible for impregnating women as the fallen angels had initially done.

[26] The formulation "to take for themselves as wives" is reminiscent of language used in marriage contracts.

[27] This interpretation of the women as wives is taken up even more vividly in the later *T. Reub.* 5:1–6, the concern of which focuses on a claim that women are more susceptible to sexual impropriety (sic!). In such a context the fallen angels story becomes paradigmatic: because wives were responsible for tempting the angels to lust after them (by adorning themselves), husbands should ensure that they are kept in check; cf. Sir. 25:21–24.

[28] See Betsy Halpern-Amaru, "The First Woman, Wives, and Mothers in Jubilees", *JBL* 113 (1994), pp. 609–626, and *idem, The Empowerment of Women in the Book of Jubilees* (JSJSup 60; Leiden: Brill, 1999), esp. pp. 155 and 159 (for an explanation). In this respect, it is possible that *Jubilees* was influenced by traditions of the sort we find in *Genesis Apocryphon* though the influence could have moved in the other direction As we do not know where the latter work began or concluded, it is difficult to know whether *Jubilees* would have been attempting to carry out such naming in a more complete way.

incidentally, Lamech's wife is given the same name (*Jub.* 4:28, Eth. *betenos*) and is further described as the daughter of Baraki'il, who is Methuselah's brother. As has been observed,[29] hers is not just any name: it means "daughter of humankind" (a deliberate allusion to Gen. 6:2 and, no doubt, to *1 En.* 6:2). The vulnerability of Lamech's wife, then, is represented as typical of any such woman as imagined during that time.[30] In relation to *Birth of Noah*, for all its interest in etymologies of proper names (Lamech [Grk.], Jared, Noah),[31] it is remarkable that the name of Lamech's wife is not given. It is therefore difficult to imagine that the *Birth of Noah* was aware of *Genesis Apocryphon* (as Bitenosh would have served its etymologies well), while it is equally difficult to establish that *Genesis Apocryphon* has taken the name from a now lost version of *Birth of Noah*. It is therefore best to infer that both accounts have fashioned a common tradition in different ways, with the addition of Bitenosh's name (not in the underlying tradition) stemming from another tradition (such as one found in *Jub.* 4:28?) to which the writer had access.[32]

Second, as noted with respect to the text from the *Genesis Apocryphon* cited above (1Q20 ii 1), Lamech's suspicion may include the "Nephilim" as possible progenitors.[33] The term, of course, refers to the giant offspring of the rebellious watch-

---

[29] See esp. Klaus Beyer, *Die aramäischen Texte vom Toten Meer* (Göttingen: Vandenhoeck & Ruprecht, 1984), p. 167 and n. 2; James C. VanderKam, "The Birth of Noah", in ed. Zdzisław J. Kapera, *Intertestamental Essays in honour of Jósef Tadeusz Milik* (Qumranica Mogilanensia 6; Cracow: The Enigma Press, 1992), pp. 213–231 (here p. 217).

[30] The potential for confusion attributed to the period before the deluge may be further exemplified through the analogy between the name given to Betenos's father in *Jub.* 4:28 (Baraki'il) and that of one of the fallen angels mentioned several times in the early Enochic traditions (Baraqi'el; see *1 En.* 6:7 at 4QEn^a 1 iii 8 and Cod. Pan.; *Book of Giants* 1Q24 1.7; 4Q203 1.2; 4Q531 7.2; 6Q8 1.4 par. 1Q23 29.1). If Émile Puech is correct in assigning 4Q203 1.2 to the Noahic 4Q534–536 ("4Q530–533, 203 1. 4QLivre des Géants^b-e ar", in ed. *idem, Qumrân Grotte 4 XXII. Textes araméens, Première Partie: 4Q529–549* [DJD 31; Oxford: Clarendon Press, 2001], pp. 17–18), then it is possible – though there is no immediate evidence to support it – that the latter may also have shown a similar interest in the names.

[31] For an excellent discussion, see VanderKam, "The Birth of Noah", pp. 217–22 (bibl. in n. 29 above); see also Stuckenbruck, *1 Enoch 91–108*, pp. 620–621, 674–676, and 688.

[32] An onomatological connection between *Genesis Apocryphon* and *Jubilees* is further suggested by the name assigned in both documents to Noah's wife: *'Emzara* (1Q20 vi 7 – אמזרך; *Jub.* 4:33), which may be interpreted as "mother of the seed" (i.e. legitimate or righteous seed, in contrast to the illegitimate seed of the watchers). More than in *Jubilees*, the writer of *Genesis Apocryphon* integrates dynamically the meanings behind the names of the wives of Lamech and Noah – these would have been clear to ancient readers of the text – into the narrative. Is *Jubilees* aware of the more involved storyline of *Genesis Apocryphon* (without noting the latter's storyline), or has *Genesis Apocryphon* taken the womens' names in *Jubilees* and integrated them, with their etymological meanings in mind, into the story in service of establishing the contrast between the profiles of Noah and his family, on the one hand, and of the rebellious angels and their progeny, on the other? The appearance of these obviously etymological names in *Jubilees* suggests an awareness of an underlying tradition, while the embellished form in *Genesis Apocryphon* suggests the same. In this instance, then, it seems that there was a source behind both writings and that this source was a tradition they both received.

[33] So also Fitzmyer, *The Genesis Apocryphon from Qumran* (3rd ed.), p. 51. The Aram. text in 1Q20 ii 1 reads: מן עירין הריאתא ומן קדישין זרעא ומן נפילי[ן. The words can also be read and restored

ers;[34] of course, hardly any indication is given in the early Enoch traditions (including the *Book of Giants*) that the giants, in addition to the angels, were mating with women as well. However, such may be implied by the references to what is possibly several classes of giants in *Jubilees* 7:22 ("naphidim", "naphil", "Elyo"); moreover, in the later Syncellus Greek version to *1 Enoch* 7:1–2 the "great giants" (γίγαντας μεγάλους) are said to have begotten "the Naphilim" (Ναφηλειμ) to whom, in turn, were born "the Elioud" (Ελιουδ).[35] Whether or not there was any precedent in received tradition, the *Genesis Apocryphon* could have invited readers to imagine that the watchers' gargantuan offspring could, among all their oppressive activities, have been engaging in the procreation of further offspring.

The proper name for Lamech's wife and the nomenclature applied to the disobedient watchers may be reasonably regarded as expansive features in the *Genesis Apocryphon* text. However, is there any reason why the Enochic writer of *Birth of Noah*, if he knew *Genesis Apocryphon*, would have omitted Bitenosh, or is there any explanation for why this writer would not have found such a detail important? The very difficulty of answering these questions suggests that the comparative brevity of the *Birth of Noah* as a whole should not lead one to suppose that, in principle, the lengthier account in *Genesis Apocryphon* should be seen as secondary.[36]

Finally, the designations used to denote the fallen angels are less conventional in *Birth of Noah* than the vocabulary used in *Genesis Apocryphon*. If this is so, we may have reason to infer in relation to this detail, the latter reflects an early tradition that was either ignored by or not directly picked up by the *Birth of Noah*.

C.6. Lamech's Consultation with Methuselah

The altercation between Lamech and Bitenosh in *Genesis Apocryphon* concludes with the latter's categorical declaration of Lamech's fatherhood as she reminds her

---

so that the holy ones and nephilim are not synonymous: "from watchers is the pregnancy and from the holy ones is the seed, and [this boy belongs] to the nephil[im"; so Beyer, *Die aramäischen Texte vom Toten Meer*, p. 167 and George W. E. Nickelsburg, *1 Enoch 1* (Hermeneia: Minneapolis: Fortress Press, 2001), p. 544.

[34] See also 1Q20 vi 19; *1 En.* Sync. to 7:1–2; and the Aram. texts extant in *Book of Giants* at 4Q530 2 ii 6–12.6; 7 ii 8; 4Q531 1.2, 8; 7.2; 4Q532 2.3. Cf. further the Heb. texts in 11Q12 7.1 (to *Jub.* 7:22) and 1Q36 16.3.

[35] *Jub.* 7:22 reads: "They (sc. the rebellious angels) fathered (as their) sons the Nephi*l*im. They were all dissimilar (from one another) and would devour one another: the giant killed the Naphil; the Naphil killed the Elyo; the Elyo mankind; and the people their fellows"; I follow the translation of James C. VanderKam, *The Book of Jubilees* (CSCO 511 and Scriptores Aethiopici 88; Leuven: E. Peeters, 1989), here p. 47. The progression in the text does not make clear that each of these classes was directly sired by the watchers and may assume the possibility that giants carried on with their fathers' sexual activities by fathering further generations of (increasingly humanlike) creatures.

[36] This feature of *Genesis Apocryphon*'s tradition-historical priority is consistent with the discussion in C.3 above.

husband of the "pleasure" of their sexual union. This brings Lamech to his second port of call: his father Methuselah. The text reads as follows:

> Then I, Lamech, ran to Methuselah my father, and [I] tol[d] him everything [... Enoch] / his father, that he might learn with certainty the entire matter from him since he is beloved and a friend of [God, and among the holy ones (is)] / his lot divided; and they tell him everything. *vacat* (1Q20 ii 19–21)

The opening of 1Q20 ii 19 is reminiscent of *1 Enoch* 106:4 cited in section C.1 above. In addition, both texts have Lamech petition Methuselah to ask Enoch for a true interpretation of the matter. As 106:4–7 shows, in the *Birth of Noah* the conversation between Lamech and Methuselah is more developed; in addition, unlike the *Genesis Apocryphon*, Lamech relays a description of Noah's appearance to Methuselah. As this repetition forms part of the strategy of the author of the *Birth of Noah*, and since the absence of it in 1Q20 is hard to explain as an omission of such material, it is likely that this part of the *Genesis Apocryphon* account retains the tradition in an earlier form.

More elaborate in *Genesis Apocryphon*, however, are the credentials ascribed to Enoch. *1 Enoch* 106:7 has Lamech petition and declare to his father:

> "And now I beg of you, my father, that you go to Enoch our father and hear the truth from him, for his dwelling is with the angels."

The text says nothing more about Enoch other than that his abode is with the angels, leaving readers to infer that for this reason he would be ideally positioned to know something (from them) about the significance of the child. This inference is spelt out more fully in 1Q20, which has Lamech declare, in indirect speech, that the angels act as Enoch's informants (cf. *Jub.* 4:21; *Apocalypse of Weeks* at *1 En.* 93:2).[37]

C.7. Methuselah's Journey and Report to Enoch

In *Genesis Apocryphon* the fragmentary text breaks off before the end of column ii, and several lines are lost. The preserved text reads:

> And when Methusela[h] heard[...] / he ran to Enoch his father in order to learn from him the entire matter in truth ...[...] / his will, and he went to the higher level, to Parvain, and there he found Enoch [his father ...] / [And] he said to Enoch his father, "O, my father, and O, my lord, I have com[e] to you[...] / [wh]at I say to you. Do not be angry with me since I have come here to ...*k*[...]." / Frightening for you [...] (1Q20 ii 21–26)

If the last legible words on 1Q20 ii 26 ("frightening for you") are attributed to Enoch and not to Methuselah, then Methuselah's initial speech to Enoch breaks

---

[37] See Stefan Beyerle, *Die Gottesvorstellungen in der antik-jüdischen Apokalyptik* (JSJSup 103; Leiden / Boston: Brill, 2005), pp. 101–113 and Stuckenbruck, *1 Enoch 91–108*, pp. 81–82.

off on line 25 and is therefore considerably shorter than the corresponding text in the *Birth of Noah* at *1 Enoch* 106:8–12, even if one follows the Greek version:

(Eth.)

(Grk.)

⁸ And when Methuselah heard the words of his son, he came to me at the ends of the earth, for he had heard that I would be there. And he cried out, and I heard his voice, and I came to him and said to him, "Behold, I am here, my son, for you have come to me"

⁸

... he cam]e to me at the ends of the earth, where he [knew] I was then. And he said to me, "[My] father, hear my voice and come [to] me." And I heard his voice and I [ca] me to him and said, "Behold, I am here, child. Why have you come to me, child?"

⁹ And he answered me and said, "Because of a great desire I have come to you, and it is because of a troubling vision that I have come near."

⁹ And he answered, saying, "Because of a great worry I have come here, O father.

¹⁰ And now, my father, listen to me, for to my son Lamech there has been born a son, and neither his form nor his nature is like the nature of a human being. And his colour is whiter than snow an dis redder than a rose blossom; and the hair of his head is whiter than white wool, and his eyes are as the rays of the sun; and he opened his eyes and they illumined the entire house.

¹⁰ And now there has been born a child to Lamech my son, and his form and his image are ... whiter than snow and redder than a rose; and the hair of his head is whiter than white wool, and his eyes are like the beams of the sun.

¹¹ And he was taken from the hands of the midwife and opened his mouth and praise the Lord of heaven.

¹¹ And he arose from the hands of the midwife and opening his mouth he blessed the Lord of eternity.

¹² And his father Lamech was afraid and fled to me and did not believe that he came from him, but his image (is) from the angels of heaven. And behold, I have come to you, so that you may make known to me the truth."

¹² And my son Lamech was afraid and fled to me and does not believe that he is his son, but that (he is) from angels [...] the accuracy and the truth."

The description of the child that Methuselah presents to Enoch (*1 En.* 106:10–11) occurs here for the third time in the *Birth of Noah*. This description is surely secondary, and modelled on the first and second instances in the story (vv. 2–3 and 5–6). The shorter form of Methuselah's speech in 1Q20 may therefore be regarded as the more traditional and less expansionistic of the two accounts. In this case, the form of the tradition in *Genesis Apocryphon* would be the earlier one.

The motif of an intermediary travelling to Enoch in order to secure an interpretation for something seen also occurs in the *Book of Giants*. However, instead of a patriarch making such a journey, we find in the latter that the giant Mahaway acts as the go-between. According to the text in the *Book of Giants* at 4Q530 2 ii + 6–12(?), line 20 until 4Q530 7 ii 11, the giants send him to Enoch who is to interpret for them the meaning of the two dreams that two of their number, Hahyah and 'Ohyah, have had (4Q530 2 ii + 6–12(?), lines 4–11 and 15–20). If this account from the *Book of Giants* is read together with its counterparts in the *Genesis Apocryphon* and *Birth of Noah*, then Enoch is one who can be consulted not only by human characters associated with righteousness but also by the antediluvian gargantuan doers of wickedness. Whatever the particular circumstances of the consultation, Enoch's interpretations in all three instances relate to the same event (the Flood), by means of which God is to punish the giants and save humanity. I regard it possible that Mahaway's visit to Enoch in the *Book of Giants* derives some of its narrative effectiveness by presuming awareness among the audience that a member of Noah's family (Methuselah, his grandfather) has also consulted the patriarch. Significantly, as occurs in the *Birth of Noah* (*1 En.* 106:13–107:2), the *Book of Giants* displays an interest in Noah's rescue from the destruction of the Great Flood (cf. 6Q8 2).

It seems, furthermore, that the location of Enoch in *Genesis Apocryphon* is more analogous to that given in the *Book of Giants* than what one finds in *Birth of Noah*. Whereas the *Birth of Noah* is more austere in locating Enoch "at the ends of the earth" (Eth. *'aṣnāfa medr*; Grk. τὰ τέρματα τῆς γῆς),[38] both the accounts in *Genesis Apocryphon* and *Book of Giants* are more precise: according to the former, Methuselah goes "the length of the land, to Parvain" (לארכ מת לפרוין,[39] 1Q20 ii 23), and in the latter Mahaway travels across "the inhabited world, and passed over desolation, the great desert" (חלד וחלף לשהוין מדברא רבא, 4Q530 7 ii 5). This comparison can be interpreted in more than one way. On the one hand, the longer text regarding Enoch's whereabouts in *Genesis Apocryphon* could be thought to have expanded a slightly shorter one such as appears in the *Birth of Noah*; in this way, the *Genesis Apocryphon* implies that Enoch dwells on the other side of (and separate from) the part of earth inhabited by humans. Since this description is more specific than that in the *Birth of Noah*, the *Genesis Apocryphon* may preserve the location in an earlier form. On the other hand, it is possible, though less likely, that for this detail the *Birth of Noah* has conventionalized the more specific language in 1Q20 ii 23. A third possibility would be that, given the parallels between all three traditions, the *Birth of Noah* relates more closely to location ascribed to Enoch in the *Book of Giants*. The latter, which emphasizes even more than the *Birth of Noah* that Enoch dwells away from the inhabited world, is the more expansionistic of the two versions. It is not unlikely that the assumption in *Genesis Apocryphon* ii–v and *Birth of Noah* of dangers associated with the fallen angels and their progeny during antediluvian times suggests the reliance of both, not only on the storyline known through the *Book of Watchers*, but also on a form of that tradition shared with the

---

[38] This location may be influenced by Job 28:20–28 (esp. v. 24, the location there of divine wisdom responsible for the created order).

[39] I am grateful to Daniel Machiela for reminding me of this reading and translation of the text; see *idem*, *The Dead Sea Genesis Apocryphon* (bibl. in n. 3) p. 37. The alternative, read by Milik (*The Books of Enoch*, p. 41 and n. 4), has been לארכבת, i.e. "to the higher level", while similarly Florentino García Martínez and Eibert J.C. Tigchelaar (*The Dead Sea Scrolls Study Edition* [2 vols.; Leiden: Brill, 1998] 1:30–31) read לארקבת.

Book of Giants, though no one of these traditions can, as a whole, be dated earlier than the other.[40]

C.8. Enoch's Explanation to Methuselah

Enoch's interpretation of Noah's unusual birth occupies most, if not all, of the remainder of the parallel narratives. In 1Q20 Enoch's words begin in ii 27 and go all the way through v 23, while they are given at *1 Enoch* 106:13–107:2 in the *Birth of Noah*.[41] The account in 1Q20 is very fragmentary and therefore provides only a minimum of clues about the content of Enoch's message. Nevertheless, there is enough text to establish that some of the details and basic themes in the more expansive version of *Genesis Apocryphon* overlap with those of the *Birth of Noah*. These overlaps are as follows:

(a) Enoch rehearses events which, from Methuselah's point of view, will lead up to the Great Flood (1Q20 iii – iv; *1 En.* 106:13–17). These include the angelic rebellion "in the days of Jared" (4Q204 5 ii 17 frgt. *d*[42] to *1 En.* 106:13 par. 1Q20 iii 3).

(b) In all likelihood, both texts describe the divine response to the angels' disobedience in terms of the Flood that will destroy the whole earth (*1 En.* 106:15–17; 1Q20 iii 11–12?).

(c) Both texts contain phrases of emphasis. According to the Aramaic text of the *Birth of Noah*, Enoch declares that Lamech is "in truth" and "not falsely" Noah's father (*1 En.* 107:2 at 4Q204 5 ii 30: "... that this boy is in truth and not falsely his son", די עלימא דן ברה הואה בקשוט ולא בכדבין); this compares with the formula in 1Q20 iii 13, that "he is in truth and not falsely" (הואא בקשוט די לא בכדבין).

(d) The longer account devoted to Enoch's interpretation in the *Genesis Apocryphon* may be due to the possible repetition of a motif that both texts have in common: Enoch's instruction that Methuselah "go" – וכען אזל in 1Q20 iii 12 ("and now, go!") and ללמך ברך אזל אמר at v 10 ("to your son, Lamech, now go!").[43] In any event, the counterpart to the commission of Methuselah to

---

[40] These traditions are not to be confused with the earlier one preserved in the *Book of Watchers* (at *1 En.* 12–16), according to which Enoch is consulted as well as one whose location is among the "holy ones" and "watchers" (12:1–12). In this context, the rebellious angels ask Enoch to petition on their behalf for mercy. The divine pronouncement against the watchers in 15:1–16:3 states nothing about the Flood.

[41] For this passage, the text is not only preserved in Ethiopic and Greek (with a shorter version in Lat.), but also in fragmentary form through 4Q204 5 iii 17–22.

[42] Following the reading of Józef T. Milik, *The Books of Enoch. Aramaic Fragments from Qumrân Cave 4* (Oxford: Clarendon, 1976), pp. 209–211, though no photograph to frag. *d* was published by Milik on Plate XV.

[43] The longer account can also be accounted for through additional material in Enoch's final instructions to Methuselah that occupy 1Q20 v 2–3 (cf. *1 En.* 106:18–107:2).

return to Lamech by Enoch in the *Birth of Noah* (cf. *1 En.* 107:2) is much shorter, and incorporates the element noted in (c) above:

(Eth.)	(Grk.)
"And now go, my son, make known to your son Lamech that this son who has been born is truly his son and is not a lie."	And now run, O chil[d] and make known to Lamech your son that his boy[44] who has been born is truly, and not falsely, his child."

In one respect, it is doubtful that some material from Enoch's words to Methuselah in the *Birth of Noah* was taken over by the *Genesis Apocryphon*. In *Birth of Noah*, Enoch's prediction of the Flood (*1 En.* 106:13–17) and explanation of Noah's significance (106:18) to Methuselah is followed by a further prediction that the wicked will be destroyed and that the righteous will be saved in the eschatological future (106:19–107:1). This second prediction regarding the wicked, preserved in 4Q204 5 ii 25–28, draws an *Urzeit-Endzeit* analogy between the antediluvian events leading up to the Flood and eschatological events leading up to the final judgement. This Flood typology seems to be a secondary intrusion and reflects the effort of an early editor to embed the *Birth of Noah* more completely within the early Enochic traditions to which it was attached (see esp. *1 En.* 91:5–7; cf. 10:1–23).[45] By contrast, nothing preserved from the *Genesis Apocryphon* at 1Q20 columns i–v signals an interest in eschatological events. If the *Genesis Apocryphon* does not draw on Flood typology to describe the ultimate fate of the wicked and righteous, we would then have further reason to support the antiquity of its account about Noah's birth in comparison to *Birth of Noah*. While expansionist activity on the part of the writer of 1Q20 columns iii–v is likely and at least cannot be ruled out, *Genesis Apocryphon* is here to be regarded as at least as important a source for reconstructing the tradition as the *Birth of Noah*.

C.9. The Conclusion: Methuselah Brings Enoch's Message back to Lamech

The parallel passages in the texts are of similar length. The very fragmentary lines in 1Q20 v 24–27 read:

And when Methuselah heard /[...] / and with Lamech his son he spoke in secret [...] / And when I, Lamech, ..[ ]. [...] / see that he has brought forth from me m.. [...]

---

[44] Text: τὸ παιδίον τοῦτο, which adheres more precisely to the Aramaic דן עלימא (4Q204 5 ii 30) than the Ethiopic *ze-wald*.

[45] Significantly, in the manuscript 4Q204 5 i, the text of the *Birth of Noah* opens (5 i 24) immediately after the conclusion of the *Epistle of Enoch* (5 i 23, text relating to *1 En.* 105:2), with only a small amount of additional space between the lines to mark the shift between sections. If in 4Q204 the *Epistle* was preceded by the *Exhortation* in *1 En.* 91:1–10, 18–19 (as it is in 4Q212), then the argument that 106:19–107:1 was added in order to integrate the *Birth of Noah* into its acquired literary context is strengthened.

The counterpart to this text in the *Birth of Noah* (*1 En.* 107:3) overlaps in a few details with the above text. The Ethiopic and Greek recensions read:

(Eth.)	(Grk.)
And when Methuselah heard the word of his father Enoch – for in secret he had shown to him the whole matter – he returned and showed (it) to him and called the name of that son "Noah", for he will make the earth glad from all its destruction.	And when Methuselah heard the words of Enoch his father – for secretly he had shown (them) to him – <omitted text through homoioteleuton>[46] And his name was called "Noah", consoling the earth from the destruction.

A particular textual problem is opened up by the Aramaic text in 4Q204, which preserves no part of this verse. The end of the previous verse in *1 Enoch* 107:2 appears in the middle of line 30 (before a *vacat* broken off by a lacuna) at the bottom of column ii in 4Q204 5. On the manuscript, the text of 107:3 would have had to be copied on the next column, whether it began on line 30 or, following the *vacat*, appeared entirely on column iii.[47] Given the very small folds on the largest fragment on column ii, folds which show that the text is very near the end of the inside of the scroll, it is not entirely certain that there would have been sufficient space for text on the putative column iii to have been copied within a space as wide as column ii. The question, therefore, must remain open whether or not 4Q204 originally contained any text that corresponds to *1 Enoch* 107:3.[48]

Keeping the textual problem in mind, we may note two corresponding details between the *Genesis Apocryphon* at 1Q20 v 24–27 and the *Birth of Noah*: (1) the phrase "and when Methuselah heard" and (2) the secretive communication (though in the *Birth of Noah* the text qualifies Enoch's words to Methuselah, while in 1Q20 it refers to Methuselah's message from Enoch to Lamech). A noticeable difference, of course, is that in 1Q20 v 26 the form of a first person account by Lamech reasserts itself, while the *Birth of Noah* simply draws to a close in the form of a third person narrative that leaves the Enochic pseudepigraphal idiom behind altogether. If, however, the *Birth of Noah* originally came to an end at *1 Enoch* 107:2, then its conclusion is reconcilable with the pseudepigraphal form of the work.

D. Conclusion

The discussion above makes it possible to formulate a summary of how traditions about Noah's birth in *Genesis Apocryphon* and the *Birth of Noah* might be related. We have observed that there are sufficient overlaps in both narrative structure and

---

[46] Cf. Stuckenbruck, *1 Enoch 91–108*, p. 686.

[47] Milik's view was that the rest of line 30 was "probably left blank" so that the entire verse was copied on the last column of the scroll (*The Books of Enoch*, p. 217).

[48] See the discussion in Stuckenbruck, *1 Enoch 91–108*, p. 687.

linguistic detail to conclude that a genetic relationship between these texts existed in *some* form. Determining what kind of literary or tradition-historical link the shared traditions indicate is, however, not so easy, and any solution or hypothesis should attempt to take the complexity arising from the comparison above into account. This complexity is illustrated by the likelihood that sometimes one text, sometimes the other, preserves details, motifs or a form that more plausibly underlies the other.

First, the *Genesis Apocryphon* exhibits expansionist tendencies that appear to be secondary to the tradition it shares with the *Birth of Noah*. These expansions include:

– the addition of the marital row between Lamech and Bitenosh (1Q20 ii 3–18) and
– Enoch's longer instructions as he commissions Methuselah to "go" and return to Lamech (1Q20 iii 12, v 10; cf. *1 En.* 107:2).

Unless the *Birth of Noah* has omitted the marital row and simplified the double commissioning by Enoch into one, it is difficult to argue for its dependence at these points on the *Genesis Apocryphon*.

This observation could conceivably be supplemented by further instances of detail in 1Q20 that are indicative of secondary developments of tradition (in comparison with *Birth of Noah*):

– the naming of Lamech's wife (1Q20 ii 3, 8, 12) which, together with the naming of Noah's wife in 1Q20 vi 7, bears an implicit etymology and, related to this point,
– the embellishment in the description of ante-diluvian conditions through the reference to the "Nephilim" (1Q20 ii 1 and iii 20).

The former of these additional elements does not, however, imply that the *Birth of Noah* is uni-directionally prior to the *Genesis Apocryphon*. Though it is hard to account for why the *Birth of Noah* would have left such details out had they already been available, it remains possible that the *Genesis Apocryphon* has found them, not from its immediate source about Noah's birth, but from another tradition (cf. the names of the wives in *Jub.* 4:28, 33).

Second, one cannot overlook that the *Birth of Noah* also has expansionist tendencies of its own. These can be observed in:

– the three-fold description of Noah's appearance (*1 En.* 106:2–3, 5–6, 10–11);
– the material in *1 Enoch* 106:18–107:1 (probably editorial), which draws on a typology between the Great Flood and eschatological events; and
– in contrast to *Genesis Apocryphon*, an apparently greater interest in the etymologizing of the names of the male characters in the story.

Third, and following from these observations, we have noted that in a number of places the Noahic birth account in *Genesis Apocryphon* is more traditional, as seen in the following details:

- the designations used to describe the fallen angels ("watchers", "holy ones");
- the absence of interest in eschatology; and
- the description of Enoch's location on the other side of "the length of the land, in Parvain".

Taken together, these comparisons lead to the conclusion that, rather than assigning a one-sided tradition-historical priority to either *Genesis Apocryphon* or the *Birth of Noah* as a whole, both works can be said to have drawn on a shared skeletal storyline that their respective writers have embellished in very different ways. While the similarities between the documents suggest a genetic link between them, the differences indicate that either (a) this link was not known to the writers in written form (i.e. it was circulating orally) or that, in any case, (b) the tradition, though written, was not fixed. Finally, additional links – for example, to *Jubilees* and *Book of Giants* – indicate that from the early stages of its development, stories about Noah's birth were infused by a number of traditions circulating during the 2nd century B.C.E. that were also concerned with the ante-diluvian period.

Chapter Four

Demonic Beings and the Dead Sea Scrolls

A. Introduction

The discussion of this chapter focuses on offering some observations regarding "demonic"[1] beings in the Dead Sea Scrolls. This topic not only merits interest in itself, but also serves to bring a number of basic issues into focus. Any broad topical study among the Dead Sea Scrolls is not as straightforward as was often assumed by scholars at the time of their discovery among eleven caves 1947–1956. The rapid publication of numerous additional materials since the early 1990's have required scholars to reassess a number of issues once thought to be a matter of consensus. For example, although the authorship of many of the previously unknown Hebrew documents was frequently attributed by default to a movement of "Essenes" thought to have settled at Khirbet Qumran, there is some recognition that many of these documents do not show telltale or obvious signs of such an origin.[2] To the extent that it holds, such a view implies that the Dead Sea Scrolls, taken as a whole, may preserve a significant

---

[1] The term "demonic" or "demon" is here used as a general designation, though the Semitic equivalent for the noun שׁד (*šēd*) occurs in only six documents among the Dead Sea materials, six times in Hebrew (4Q386 1 iii 4; 4Q510 1.5; 11Q11 1.10; 2.3, 4; 5.12) and eight times in Aramaic manuscripts: 4Q196 14 i 5; = Tob. 6:15; 4Q196 14 i 12 = Tob. 6:18; 4Q197 4 i 13 = Tob. 6:9; 4Q197 4 ii 9 = Tob. 6:15; 4Q197 4 i 13 = Tob. 6:16; 4Q243 = 4QPsDan[a] 13.2 (par. 4Q244 = 4QPsDan[b] 12.2); and 4Q547 = 4QAmram[e] 3.1.

[2] This awareness is the product of numerous efforts to distinguish between "sectarian", "proto-sectarian" (e. g. *Damascus Document*), and "non-sectarian" documents among the scrolls. The most important of these discussions include Carol A. Newsom, "'Sectually Explicit' Literature from Qumran", in eds. William H. Propp, Baruch Halpern, and David Noel Freedman, *The Hebrew Bible and Its Interpreters* (Winona Lake: Eisenbrauns, 1990), pp. 167–187; Devorah Dimant, "The Qumran Manuscripts: Contents and Significance", in eds. Devorah Dimant and Lawrence H. Schiffman, *Time to Prepare the Way in the Wilderness* (STDJ 26; Leiden: Brill, 1995), pp. 23–58; Armin Lange and Hermann Lichtenberger, "Qumran. Die Textfunde von Qumran", in eds. Gerhard Müller *et al.*, *Theologische Realienzyklopädie* (36 vols.; Berlin: Walter de Gruyter, 1997), 28:45–65, 75–79; and the contributions by Lange and Charlotte Hempel in eds. J. Frey and H. Stegemann, *Qumran kontrovers* (Einblicke 6; Paderborn: Bonifatius, 2003), pp. 59–69 ("Kriterien essenischer Texte") and 71–85 ("Kriterien zur Bestimmung 'essenischer Verfasserschaft' von Qumrantexten"), respectively. Beyond these more brief discussions, scholars are currently attempting to delineate more nuanced views, especially among the Hebrew texts, regarding their relationship to discourse about "the Qumran Community" or "*Yaḥad*"; cf. e. g. Alison Schofield, *From Qumran to the Yaḥad: A New Paradigm of Textual Development for* The Community Rule (STDJ 77; Leiden / Boston: Brill, 2009) and John J. Collins, *Beyond the Qumran Community: The Sectarian Movement of the Dead Sea Scrolls* (Grand Rapids: Eerdmans, 2010).

number of works that reflect traditions which circulated more broadly in Hebrew and, of course, Aramaic speaking Judaism of the Eastern Mediterranean world.[3]

Lest one have the impression that "demonology" is ubiquitous in the Scrolls, it is important for us to note from the start that many of the texts have little or nothing specifically to say about the demonic beings. The absence of any explicit reference to the demonic world in the texts does not in each case have to be interpreted as an ideological avoidance of language when dealing with the question of evil. When demons are not expressly mentioned, this may simply have to do with the genre of a given work or with the one-sided purposes of a composition – e. g. a strict focus on topics such as heavenly liturgy (e. g. *Songs of the Sabbath Sacrifice, Non-Canonical Psalms, Barki Nafshi*), wisdom instruction (e. g. *4QInstruction, 4QMysteries*, Ben Sira), halakhic instruction (e. g. *4QMiqseh Ma'aseh ha-Torah*), visionary material (*New Jerusalem*), the interpretation or reconfiguration of sacred tradition (e. g. *Temple Scroll, Reworked Pentateuch, Tanḥumim, pesharim*), and the calendrical texts (see e. g. 4Q317, 319–326, 328–330, 334, 337).

Though recognizing the complex make-up of the Dead Sea materials, the following overview of the demonic world among the Scrolls nevertheless finds reason to make an attempt to be diachronic. Where relevant within each of the terms or categories taken up below, we begin with what may be regarded as earlier, often Aramaic, traditions that show little sign of having been produced by the Qumran community (*Yaḥad*) itself. There is a further group of texts, mostly in Hebrew, which likewise cannot be confidently assigned to authorship within the *Yaḥad*, but which to varying degrees seem to anticipate ideas found among some of the more "sectarian" texts. Finally, the discussion will consider Hebrew literature that can be associated with the *Yaḥad* itself. At the risk of being overly confident at "knowing too much", such an approach may allow us to discern possible lines of development in relation to ideas and practices, while trying not to assume that shifts in tradition necessarily signify a shift in social context.

In anticipation of the discussion to follow, one may strike a note of caution in relation to several points. First, with regard to social context, we may expect the texts as a whole to present us with a complex web of traditions that wove their way in and out of any number of pious Jewish groups whose relationship to each other cannot be easily discerned. Second, it should be clear that any developments or shifts one might infer from the Scrolls should not be confused with what was going on in all parts of Judaism generally during the Second Temple period. Many voices of Jewish writers, especially those who wrote in Greek, are not represented among any of the materials recovered among the Caves. Third, the ideas of each text need to be heard for themselves as much as possible without straining to fit or connect them to those of other documents when evidence for such is not available.

---

[3] This is to say nothing of the manuscripts preserving "biblical" writings (approximately 230 in number), which were of course not composed by the movement associated with the group living at Khirbet Qumran and that would eventually be given a place in the Hebrew Bible.

Fourth, it is possible, if not likely, that a number of logically incompatible ideas could have co-existed in a single, sociologically definable group. In other words, different ideas do not always have to be traced to different groups.

I am nevertheless convinced that certain developments regarding attitudes towards demonic powers can be upheld within the literature of the Dead Sea Scrolls and that some of these attitudes can be associated with groups that can be either broadly or narrowly profiled. One of the observable shifts in the character of tradition emerges, for example, between ideas and practices in unambiguous *Yaḥad* texts and those that do not so obviously reflect this connection. Moreover, to some degree, we shall notice a broad difference between traditions about demonic beings among the writings preserved in Aramaic, on the one hand, and those coming to us in Hebrew, on the other. The crucial period for these shifts will be around the middle of the 2nd century B. C. E., a period of major change not only in the way Jews were responding to incursions of Hellenistic culture under the Seleucids, but also in the way Jewish groups began to form while openly staking out cultural and religious claims in response to one another.

B. Demonic Origins in the Enochic Tradition and Its Early Influence

In the present section I can only briefly summarize what other publications – we note especially those of Philip Alexander,[4] Esther Eshel,[5] Archie Wright,[6] Kelley Coblentz Bautch,[7] Ida Fröhlich,[8] and myself[9] – have discussed in more detail.[10]

---

[4] See "'Wrestling against Wickedness in High Places': Magic in the Worldview of the Qumran Community", in eds. Stanley E. Porter and Craig A. Evans, *The Scrolls and the Scriptures: Qumran Fifty Years After* (JSPSup 26; Sheffield: Sheffield Academic Press, 1997), pp. 318–37; "The Demonology of the Dead Sea Scrolls", in eds. Peter W. Flint and James C. VanderKam, *The Dead Sea Scrolls After Fifty Years. Volume II: A Comprehensive Assessment* (Leiden/Boston/Köln: Brill, 1999), pp. 331–353 (here pp. 337–341).

[5] "Demonology in Palestine During the Second Temple Period" (Ph.D. Dissertation, Hebrew University, 1999 [mod. Heb.]), pp. 10–90 ("The Origin of the Evil Spirits"); "Genres of Magical Texts in the Dead Sea Scrolls", in eds. Armin Lange, Hermann Lichtenberger, and K. F. Diethard Römheld, *Die Dämonen – Demons. Die Dämonologie der israelitisch-jüdischen und frühchristlichen Literatur im Kontext ihrer Umwelt* (Tübingen: Mohr Siebeck, 2003), pp. 395–415.

[6] *The Origin of Evil Spirits* (WUNT 2.198; Tübingen: Mohr Siebeck, 2005), esp. pp. 96–177.

[7] "Putting Angels in Their Place: Developments in Second Temple Angelology", in eds. Miklós Kőszeghy, Gábor Buzási, and Károly Dobos, *"With Wisdom as a Robe": Studies in Honour of Ida Fröhlich* (Sheffield: Phoenix Press, 2009), pp. 174–188 and "Heavenly Beings Brought Low: A Study of Angels and the Netherworld", in eds. Friedrich Reiterer, Tobias Nicklas, and Karin Schöpflin, *The Concept of Celestial Beings. Origins, Development and Reception. Deuterocanonical and Cognate Literature Yearbook* (Berlin/New York: Walter de Gruyter, 2007), pp. 59–75.

[8] Among a number of publications, see Ida Fröhlich, "Evil in Second Temple Texts", in eds. Erkki Koskenniemi and Ida Fröhlich, *Evil and the Devil* (ISCO in LNTS 481; London: Bloomsbury, 2013), pp. 23–50.

[9] See chapters One and Two above.

[10] See further John J. Collins, *Seers, Sybils and Sages in Hellenistic-Roman Judaism* (Leiden/

Fragmentary Aramaic texts recovered from the Dead Sea caves, such as those belonging to *Book of Watchers* of *1 Enoch* and the very fragmentary *Book of Giants*, attribute the origin of evil to a club of rebellious angels and their offspring, the giants, who in these texts are held responsible for deteriorating conditions on earth before the Great Flood. The brief tradition from Genesis 6:1–4 is paralleled in the Enochic literature by a more elaborate scheme which blames disobedient angels (less so, human beings who are at most represented as complicit) for much of the sin and violence committed on the earth during ante-diluvian times. The Flood tradition, as well as internecine fighting amongst the giants, is then presented as the result of God's response to the catastrophic activities introduced by these beings (cf. *1 En.* 8:4–10:16; *Book of Giants* at 4Q530 2 ii + 6–12 (?)). The story-line of these early Enochic traditions is not only concerned with the very ancient past, but also serves to explain what the writers wished to emphasize about the continuing presence and effects of demonic evil in their own times (cf. *1 En.* 15:8–16:1).

At least two main purposes can be discerned in the telling of the story about fallen angels in *1 Enoch* chapters 6–16. First, the story functions as a way of condemning expressions of culture associated with foreign impositions, perhaps in the wake of the conquests of Alexander the Great and his successors.[11] Thus the rebellious angels are said to have introduced to humanity the making of weaponry, jewelry, techniques of beautification, and all kinds of "magical" arts (*1 En.* 7:3–5, 8:3). The reprehensible practices and instructions in *1 Enoch* 7–8 can be traced back to a tradition that emphasizes the role of ʿAsaʾel as the leader of the mutinous angels. In this way, the tradition "demonizes" expressions of culture that pose a threat to the religious identity of the author(s) and the pious community envisioned behind the text. Second, the story provides an etiology, or explanation, for the origin of demonic spirits (*1 En.* chs. 15–16). This etiology focuses primarily on the giants, the offspring of the angels who have breached the cosmic order by mating with the daughters of humanity. In this part of the tradition, the leadership of Shemiḥazah

New York/Köln: Brill, 1997), pp. 287–299 ("The Origins of Evil in Apocalyptic Judaism and the Dead Sea Scrolls"); W. John Lyons and Andrew M. Reimer, "The Demonic Virus and Qumran Studies: Some Preventative Measures," *DSD* 5 (1998), pp. 16–32; and Menahem Kister, "Demons, Theology and Abraham's Covenant (CD 16:4–6 and Related Texts)", in eds. Robert A. Kugler and Eileen M. Schuller, *The Dead Sea Scrolls at Fifty: Proceedings of the 1997 Society of Biblical Literature Qumran Section Meetings* (SBLEJL 15; Atlanta: Society of Biblical Literature, 1999), pp. 167–184.
[11] Some interpreters argue that the fallen angels and their gargantuan progeny simply refer to the Seleucid overlords in the wake of Alexander the Great's conquest of the Judea-Palestine or to an elite priesthood that did not observe purity regulations with regard to marriage and other practices; see e.g. George W. E. Nickelsburg, "Apocalyptic and Myth in 1 Enoch 6–11" *JBL* 96 (1977), pp. 383–405; idem, *1 Enoch 1* (Hermeneia; Minneapolis: Fortress Press, 2001), p. 170; and David Suter, "Fallen Angel, Fallen Priest", *HUCA* 50 (1979), pp. 115–135, who takes *1 En.* 10:9 as his point of departure (on this text, see below). An oversimplified and reductionistic reading that decodes the traditions in this way is, however, misleading (see below).

is more prominent. The deeds committed by the giants before the Flood include the agricultural enslavement of humanity to grow and produce food to satisfy their appetites, the killing of sea and land animals, the destruction of birds, and even cannibalism. Divine intervention against these giants comes about when (a) the giants turn against and kill one another; and (b) as apparently stressed in the *Book of Giants*, when the Flood destroys them.[12] Either way, it is significant that the giants are by nature half angel and half human, and as such are regarded as an illegitimate mixture of spheres that should have been kept separate (*1 En.* 15:8– 16:1; cf. 10:9, where they are called "bastards" – Cod. Pan. μαζηρους = *mamzerim*). Divine punishment thus only brought them physical death, after which they continued to have a disembodied existence as spirits. We may infer that, being jealous of humanity who have survived the cataclysm with their bodies intact, these spirits instinctively attempt to reclaim a corporal existence that they once had and so are especially inclined to afflict by attacking or entering the bodies of humans (15:12). Although only a partial punishment of evil, the Flood's significance is clear: God's decisive intervention in the past against the angels and especially the giants demonstrates that powers of evil in all their forms are, in effect, already defeated and that their final annihilation is assured (16:1). The implication of this is that measures to be taken against them in the present, such as exorcism or other methods of warding and staving them off (these are not expressly mentioned in the text), are to be regarded as temporary expedients which portend God's ultimate triumph.

A number of traditions that survive from antiquity adapt this Enochic etiology (not least some of the exorcism accounts preserved for us in Jesus tradition[13]), including several documents preserved among the Dead Sea Scrolls (see below).[14] However, despite the influence of the Enochic accounts, the names of the chief angelic perpetrators of evil are conspicuously absent outside the earliest Enoch tradition.[15] What does survive outside the Enoch tradition is a few references to the term "Nephilim", a designation applied to the angels' offspring on the basis of Genesis 6:4.[16] However, "Nephilim", if a proper name, does not designate any of

---

[12] It is less explicit in *1 En.* 10 that the Flood directly drowns or kills the giants, though their punishment occurs at the same time.

[13] See Chapter Nine below.

[14] See e. g. Alexander, "The Demonology of the Dead Sea Scrolls", pp. 344–350; Wright, *The Origin of Evil Spirits*, pp. 178–189.

[15] The *Book of Giants* aside, see of course the later *Book of Parables* at *1 En.* 69:2–12 in which a number of named rebellious angels is 26, among whom Shemiḥazah (69:2) but not ʿAsaʾel occurs; cf. George W. E. Nickelsburg and James C. VanderKam, *1 Enoch 2: A Commentary on the Book of 1 Enoch Chapters 37–82* (Hermeneia; Minneapolis: Fortress Press, 2012), pp. 297–303. Among the Scrolls themselves, see only the mention in 4Q180 1.7–8 of ʿAzazʾel (so, the approximate spelling of the chief angel's name in the later Ethiopic texts of *1 Enoch*; cf. 8:1 and Cod. Pan. to 6:7, Αζαλζηλ); see Wright, *The Origin of Evil Spirits*, pp. 107–114.

[16] So the Aramaic *Genesis Apocryphon* in 1Q20 ii 1 and vi 19, which is clearly influenced by the fallen angels story; *Jubilees* 5:1 (Heb.) in 11Q12 7.1 (where the Eth. text has "giants"); and 1Q36 16.3, a broken text difficult to interpret.

the giants individually, nor is there any mention of proper names for the giants as given in the *Book of Giants* to be found elsewhere in Second Temple literature,[17] that is, until we get to some early Christian[18] and the much later rabbinic,[19] Manichaean[20] and medieval Jewish sources.[21]

Nevertheless, the examples of Enochic influence on demonology among the Dead Sea texts are significant, not only with respect to specific details but also in the overarching eschatological framework within which they negotiate the persistence of and triumph over evil. The fragmentary Hebrew document which has been given the title *Songs of the Maskil* (4Q510–511 and 4Q444) lists at several points a series of malevolent beings whom the writer intends to frighten and terrify by means of his praises to God.[22] These beings are variously itemized as follows: "all spirits of the angels of destruction" (4Q510 1.5; cf. CD ii 6; 4QD^h 2.7; 1QS iv 12; 1QM xiii 12 par. 4Q495 2.4; – כול רוחי מלאכי חבל),[23] "spirits of *mamzerim*" (4Q510 1.5; 4Q511 35.7; cf. 48–49+51.2–3 and 4Q444 1–2+5.8[24] – רוחי ממזרים), "demons" (4Q510 1.5 – שדים),[25] Lilith (4Q510 1.5; 4Q511 10.1 – לילית),[26] howlers and hyenas (4Q510 1.5 – אחים] וציים),[27] and "those who strike suddenly in order to lead astray the spirit of understanding" (4Q510 1.6; 4Q511 10.2 – הפוגעים פתע פתאום לתעות רוח בינה). Though the occurrence of these beings in the lists derives from different backgrounds, it can at least be maintained with some confidence that the *mamzerim*, who as noted above are mentioned in *1 Enoch* 10:9, denote the disembodied spirits of the giants. These beings, though

---

[17] For a discussion of the etymologies and possible significance of these names, see Chapter Two above.

[18] Cf. *Test. Sol.* 5:3 and 17:1.

[19] So *b.Nid.* 61a; *Tg. Ps.-Jon.* to Deut. 2:2 and 3:11 (Sihon and Og); *b.Zebahim* 113; *b.Erub.* 30a, 48a; and *b.Yoma* 80b (Og).

[20] See Chapter Two above.

[21] Esp. the *Midrash of Shemhazai and 'Aza'el*; cf. Józef T. Milik, *The Books of Enoch. Aramaic Fragments from Qumrân Cave 4* (Oxford: Clarendon, 1976), pp. 321–330.

[22] A text related to 4Q444 and 4Q510–511 is the very fragmentary 8Q5, in which a writer, addressing God as "M]ighty One" in the 1st person, claims to "frighten and ad[jure" (אני מירא ומש]ביע, 1.1) beings whose designations are not preserved; cf. the discussion of Eshel, "Genres of Magical Texts", pp. 401–402. The status of another fragmentary manuscript, 6Q18, which praises God and mentions Belial, is even harder to establish.

[23] See section C.2 below.

[24] A further reference to *mamzerim* in 1QH^a xxiv 12 is isolated and without sufficient context to determine its precise meaning, i.e. whether it is a label applied to a class of sinners or functions as a designation for demonic beings *per se*.

[25] See section C.1 below.

[26] Cf. Isa. 34:14 for an occurrence of the term. The background is to be found in ANE texts in which it is mentioned alongside other demonic beings. See Manfred Hutter, "Lilith", in eds. Karl van der Toorn, Bob Becking, and Pieter W. van der Horst, *Dictionary of Deities and Demons in the Bible* (Leiden: Brill, 2nd ed.), pp. 520–521; and Christa Müller-Kessler, "Lilit(s) in der aramäisch-magischen Literatur der Spätantike", *AF* 28 (2001), pp. 338–352.

[27] These two terms are paired in Isa. 13:21, and occur together with שעירים, which in the Grk. version is translated with δαιμόνια. Significantly, in the Grk. version to Isa. 34:14, ציים, reconstructed here and likely reconstructed with אחים in 4Q511 10.2, is rendered by δαιμόνια.

considered operative during the present age (designed in *Songs of the Maskil* as "the age of the dominion of wickedness [ממשלת רשעה]"),[28] can be managed in the present in anticipation of their final punishment. The tension in the Enochic tradition between God's triumph over evil in the past (i. e. during the time of the Great Flood) and the complete annihilation of evil in the future has contributed to at least some of this.[29] In addition, it is possible that a demonic being denounced in an "in]cantation" (ל[חש) in 11Q11 (=11QapPs) reflects influence of the Enochic tradition. The being, addressed directly in the second person singular ("Who are you?", v 6), may be called "offspring from] Adam and from the seed of the ho[ly one]s" (הילוד מ[אדם ומזרע הקד]ושי[ם] , v 6).[30] If the restoration of this text is correct, then it may be taken as a reference to a demonic being whose nature is ultimately a *mixtum compositum* (a hybrid, i. e. angelic and human, creature) as is the case with the Enochic giants.[31]

The only other obvious place where the Enoch tradition's impact within the Dead Sea Scrolls can be observed with some confidence is the *Book of Jubilees*, originally composed in Hebrew. The evil spirits who afflict Noah's grandchildren following the Flood are identified as the spirits that emerged from the giants' bodies when they were destroyed (*Jub.* 10:5).[32] In *Jubilees* these spirits, however, come under the rule not of one of the named fallen angels from the *Book of Watchers* and *Book of Giants*, but under Mastema (see section D.4 below), whose origin in that work is not specified. As in the Enoch tradition, the evil spirits (specified as a tenth of their number cf. *Jub.* 10:9) are given temporary leave to afflict humanity. Their ultimate destruction, however, remains assured, and measures given to Noah to neutralize some of their malevolent effects function as temporary expedients in the meantime (cf. *Jub.* 10:10–14).

---

[28] See 4Q510 1.6–7 ("and you [viz. the demonic beings] have been placed in the age of the dominion of wickedness and in the periods of subjugation of the sons of ligh[t]..." (par. 4Q511 10.3–4). In the *Yaḥad* texts, this era is referred to as the time of "the dominion of Belial (ממשלת בליעל)" (e. g. 1QS i 18, 23–24; ii 19).

[29] See Loren T. Stuckenbruck, *1 Enoch 91–108* (CEJL; Berlin: Walter de Gruyter, 2007), pp. 94–95 (comment on *1 En.* 93:4c and related texts).

[30] For a discussion of the alternative reconstructions of the lacuna, see Wright, *The Origin of Evil Spirits*, p. 183–184 and n. 66.

[31] Another text in which an evil being who has entered into the human body is directly addressed and adjured is preserved in 4Q560 (two small fragments). Although the text shows no obvious influence of the Enochic tradition, its understanding of the relation of the demonic to the human body is consistent with it. See more in Chapter Nine below.

[32] This may be inferred from *Jub.* 5:8–9 and 10:1–6, passages which are conceptually influenced by *1 En.* 7:4; 10:9; 15:9. On the influence of the Enoch tradition on the understanding of evil and demonology in *Jubilees*, see Stuckenbruck, "The Book of Jubilees and the Origin of Evil", in eds. Gabriele Boccaccini and Giovanni Ibba, *Enoch and the Mosaic Torah* (Grand Rapids: Eerdmans, 2009), pp. 294–308 (here pp. 298–306). See also Chapter One above.

C. "Demons", "Spirits" and "Angels" in the Dead Sea Scrolls

It is outside the scope of the present discussion to examine all the references and allusions to demonic beings mentioned in the Dead Sea texts. In this section we shall focus on several general designations applied to such entities that occur in both the Aramaic and Hebrew texts and in different combinations. These are: (1) *šed* (שד, i. e. "demon"); (2) *ruaḥ* (רוח, in this context, "spirit"); and (3) *mal'ak* (מלאך, i. e. "angel").

C.1. "Demon" (šed)

The word *šed* is unambiguously preserved 14 times in six documents. Six of the occurrences are found in the Hebrew texts. In four of these six instances, the term is found in the above-mentioned small text of 11Q11,[33] which, as noted above, shows signs of having been influenced by the early Enochic tradition. In addition, there is one occurrence of the term in *Songs of the Maskil* (at 4Q510 1.5), where the plural form (*šedim*) is placed within a list of malevolent beings that includes the "spirits of the *mamzerim*" (see section B above). As 11Q11, the *Songs of the Maskil* shows signs of influence by the Enochic tradition. The only other reference to "demon" surfaces in a manuscript called *4QPseudo-Ezekiel* in 4Q386 1 iii 4, the context of which suggests that Babylon (cf. iii 1, 3) is being referred to as "a dwelling place of demons" (מדור שדים).[34] The manuscript contains no language that is characteristic of either the *Yaḥad* or of a community that is precisely defined other than "the children of Israel" (4Q386 1 i 3).

With respect to the far less numerous Aramaic materials from the Dead Sea, the term "demon" is preserved eight times among fragments from three documents. In five cases, all of which occur in the singular form, we have to do with the Book of Tobit (4Q196 14 i 5, 12; 4Q197 4 i 13, ii 9 and 13). Each of these references to a *šed* is found in the Book of Tobit chapter 6. In one of these texts, the term occurs as part of a recipe for getting rid of a demon, a recipe that originally circulated independently before being incorporated into the book (6:8).[35] In the other four instances, the term directly refers to Asmodaeus (Tob. 6:15–17), who in the story attempts to prevent Sarah from marrying by killing her previous seven husbands on her wedding nights and then threatens her divinely preordained marriage to Tobias. Significantly, in the later *Testament of Solomon* (which, in its present form, is Christian) Asmodaeus is identified as one of the giants, that is, as an offspring of a fallen angel and a human woman (*T. Sol.* 5:1–11, esp. v. 3).

---

[33] 11Q11 i 10; ii 3, 4; v 12 – the term is restored and may be an equivalent for the being who is denounced at the beginning of the song in v 6.

[34] For the only other attestation of the phrase, which is applied to Babylon, see Rev. 18:2: κατοικητήριον δαιμονίων.

[35] See further in Chapter Six below.

The second Aramaic document, which this time refers to "demons" in the plural (שׁדים), is designated *Pseudo-Daniel* in the overlapping texts of 4Q243 13.2 and 4Q244 12.2.[36] This overlapping text from two manuscripts claims that "the children of Israel preferred their presence (i. e. of other deities) to [the presence of God and sacr]ificed their children to demons of error".[37] By attributing such a practice to Jews, the text reflects an idea that is developed within the Enochic tradition and in the *Book of Jubilees* (see immediately below).

The term "demon" is not extant among the Dead Sea Scrolls Aramaic fragments corresponding to *1 Enoch*. However, in the *Book of Watchers* at *1 Enoch* 19:1, we have a reference to people offering sacrifice "to demons (Eth. mss. add: as gods) until the great (Eth. mss. add: day of) judgment" (Cod. Pan. – τοις δαιμονιοις μεχρι της μεγαλης κρισεως). Significantly, this activity of sacrificing to demons is blamed on the fallen angels' spirits who have led humans astray. This text, which may be a facile allusion to Gentile idolatry, influences the *Epistle of Enoch* at *1 Enoch* 99:7: the sinners "will worship evil spirits and demons and every (kind of) error" (so the Eth.; Grk. of the Chester-Beatty Michigan papyrus: "worship [phan]toms and demons [and abomina]tions and evi[l] spirits and all (kinds of) errors".[38] Here the motif of demon worship is more explicitly associated with idolatry. The text of the *Epistle* probably not only describes what Gentiles do but also, and especially, has in mind those whom the writer regards as faithless Jews.

The association of "demons" with idolatry, of course, may have been shaped by texts such as Deuteronomy 32:16–17 and Psalm 96 [95]:5 (where the Grk. δαιμονια corresponds to Heb. אלילים, "idols"). However, the accusation that other Jews are engaged in idol worship, as we find in both *Pseudo-Daniel* and the *Epistle of Enoch*, is more developed than in the biblical texts. The *Book of Jubilees* deals with the motif in much the same way as the *Epistle of Enoch*. Because the Gentiles can be labeled as those who "offer their sacrifices to the dead, and ... worship demons" (*Jub.* 22:17),[39] the force of attributing this to Jews who are disloyal to the covenant is not lost: God instructs Moses to write down the message of the book because, in the future, his posterity, as a consequence of serving the gods of the nations, will "sacrifice their children to demons and to every product (conceived by) their erring minds" (*Jub.* 1:11). The influence of "demons" on Israel is otherwise seen in the immediate aftermath of the Flood, when Noah petitions that his grandchildren be delivered from the "demons" (in this case, the disembodied spirits of the dead

---

[36] For the edition, see John J. Collins and Peter W. Flint, "4Q423 (4QpsDanᵃ)", in ed. James C. VanderKam, *Qumran Cave 4.XVII: Parabiblical Texts, Part 3* (DJD 22; Oxford: Clarendon Press, 1996), pp. 95–152 (combined text beginning on p. 132).

[37] See Bennie H. Reynolds, "What Are Demons of Error? The Meaning of שׁידי טעותא and Israelite Child Sacrifice", *RevQ* 88 (2007), pp. 593–613.

[38] For the text, translation, critical notes and commentary on the versions, see Stuckenbruck, *1 Enoch 91–108*, pp. 393–395 and 399–403.

[39] The English translation of *Jubilees*, here and below, is taken from James C. VanderKam, *The Book of Jubilees: Translated* (CSCO 511; Leuven: Peeters, 1989).

giants) who are leading them astray (10:1–14). Unfortunately, none of these texts from *Jubilees* are preserved amongst the Hebrew Dead Sea fragments.

Keeping in mind that we do not have – and never will have – access to all the materials originally deposited in the Qumran caves, we can only observe that, for the most part (except for the identification of Babylon as a "dwelling place of demons" in *4QPseudo-Ezekiel*),[40] those texts that refer to "demons" bear a certain affinity with different parts of the Enoch tradition. Furthermore, in no case does any document that uses the term for "demon" draw on language that is character-istic for the *Yaḥad* literature related to the Qumran Community.

C.2. "Spirit" (ruaḥ)

Unlike the term for "demons" – which can operate as a category or classification of beings on its own – the term "spirit", whether in the singular or plural, is never on its own applied to malevolent beings; it is always qualified through the addition of a further word. In particular, the references to malevolent beings as "spirits" (with the plur. form *rwḥwt or rwḥy* in the cstr.) abound.

Here, something can be made of the distinction between Aramaic and Hebrew literature. In the Aramaic texts, the term *ruaḥ*, when it is applied to an evil being, occurs only nine times. In these cases, it is *always* in the singular:

Genesis Apocryphon (1Q20 xx 16, 17, 20, 26, 28 – the afflicting spirit sent by God against Pharaoh Zoan king of Egypt);
Tobit 6:8 (at 4Q197 4 i 13 – "evil spirit" functions as a synonym for "demon");
4QTestJud ar (=4Q538) 1+2.4 (the "evil [s]pirit");
4QExorcism ar (=4Q560) 1 ii 5, 6 (the "spirit" which is adjured); and 4Q584 1 ("the [spir]it of wickedness").

In the Hebrew materials, however, the term, when used for malevolent power, occurs mostly in the plural. These instances are itemized below:

Damascus Document in CD xii 2 ("spirits of Belial" par. 4Q271 5 i 18);
Community Rule (*Serekh ha-Yaḥad* below) in 1QS iii 18, 24 (spirits of the lot of the Angel of Darkness);
War Scroll (*Serekh ha-Milḥamah* below) in 1QM xiii 2 and 4 (spirits of the lot of Belial);
Serekh ha-Milḥamah in 1QM xiii 11 (spirits of his [Belial's] lot, the angels of destruction);
Serekh ha-Milḥamah in 1QM xv 14 (spirits of wick[edness]);
Thanksgiving Hymns (*Hodayoth* below) in 1QHª iv 23 (perverted spirit rules over a human being);
Hodayoth in 1QHª xi 18 (spirits of the serpent);
Hodayoth in 1QHª xxiv 26 (spirits of *mamzerim*);

---

[40] A further exception may be the reference to *šed* in 4Q547 (= 4QAmramᵉ) 3.1, the fragmen-tary context of which is not sufficiently specific to suggest an Enochic background. A Mosaic con-text for the term is suggested by Robert Duke, *The Social Location of the* Visions of Amram *(4Q543–547)* (Studies in Biblical Literature 135; New York: Peter Lang, 2010), pp. 26–27. I am grateful to Blake Jurgens for consultation on *Visions of Amram*.

Hodayoth in 1QH^a xxv 6 (spirits of wickedness);
Hodayoth in 1QH^a xxv 8 (spirits of iniquity);
Hodayoth in 1QH^a 5.4 (spirits of wickedness);
Hodayoth in 1QH^a 5.6 (spirits of iniquity which lay waste for mourning);
1Q36 (spirits of transgression);
4QCatena A (=4Q177) 1–4.7 (spirits of Belial);
4Q177 12–13 i 9 (God's great hand will help them from all the spirits of [Belial]);
Songs of the Maskil in 4Q444 1–4 i+5.2 (spirits of dispute);
4Q444 1–4 i+5.4 (spirits of wickedness);
4Q444 1–4 i+5.8 ("spirits of the *m]amzerim*");
4Q449 1.3 (rule of the spirits of his [Belial's?] lot);
Serekh ha-Milḥamah in 4Q491 14–15.10 (spirits of [his] lot; no par. in 1QM);
Songs of the Maskil in 4Q510 1.5 (all the spirits of the angels of destruction);
Songs of the Maskil in 4Q510 1.5 (the spirits of the *mamzerim*, the demons, Lilith, howlers, jackals);
Songs of the Maskil in 4Q511 1.6 (spirits of wickedness);
Songs of the Maskil in 4Q511 15.5 (spirits of vanity-*ḥebalim*);
Songs of the Maskil in 4Q511 35.7 (spirits of the *mamzerim*);
Songs of the Maskil in 4Q511 43.6 (spirits of vanity-*ḥebel*);
Songs of the Maskil in 4Q511 48–49+51.2–3 ("spirits of] the *mamzerim*");
Songs of the Maskil in 4Q511 182.1 ("spirit]s of the *mamzeri[m*");
11QapPs (=11Q11) ii 3 ("sp]irits [ ] and demons");
11QMelchizedek (=11Q13) ii 12 (against Belial and the spirits of his lot); and
11Q13 ii 13 ("from the power of] Belial and from the power of all the s[pirits of his lot").

Among these instances, 29 are clearly readable in the texts, while four are reconstructed. Among them, there is only one instance of *ruaḥ* in the singular (1QH^a iv 23). While the examples listed here show an affinity with the Enochic tradition (cf. "spirits" of the giants in *1 En.* 15:8–16:1; recall the association of "spirits" in *Songs of the Maskil* with *mamzerim* and in 11Q11 with demonic hybrid beings), they demonstrate a growing association of the spirits with a figurehead called Belial who acts as their leader (see D.5 below). Moreover, the predominant occurrence of this connection in the *Damascus Document*, *Serekh ha-Yaḥad*, *Serekh ha-Milḥamah*, *Hodayoth*, and *4QCatena* (4Q177) suggests that this association with Belial flourished in a sectarian context,[41] while the connection of "spirits" with *mamzerim* did not.

Less clear is whether, as Philip Alexander has argued, "the angels of destruction" comprise a reference to the fallen angels and that their association with the "spirits" under Belial amounts to a demotion and subordination of them into a more clearly

---

[41] The *Treatise on the Two Spirits* in 1QS may not be a *Yaḥad* composition; see Jörg Frey, "Different Patterns of Dualistic Thought in the Qumran Library", in eds. Moshe Bernstein, Florentino García Martínez, John Kampen, *Legal Texts and Legal Issues* (STDJ 23; Leiden: Brill, 1997), pp. 275–335. Thus Belial does not occur in the *Treatise*, and the reference to "the spirits of his lot" in 1QS iii 24 has to do with the dominion of "the Angel of Darkness". Nevertheless, the phrases "spirits of his lot", "lot of" (1QS ii 4–5), and "dominion of" (1QS i 17, 23–24; ii 19) are overwhelmingly applied to Belial in the sectarian texts.

structured hierarchy with only Belial at the top;[42] after all, like Belial, such beings can be said to "rule over" humans (so the *Damascus Document* in CD xii 2 par. 4Q271 5 i 18).

Given the frequency of the plural form for "spirit" to denote evil beings in the Hebrew texts, it is instructive to note how the singular form is used in the Hebrew texts. The list above suggests that, in relation to demonic beings, we primarily have to do with plural forms, while a number of expressions in which the singular is used bear a different connotation: "spirit of perversity" (רוח עולה; 1QS iv 9 [par. 4Q257 5.7], 20), "promiscuous spirit" (רוח זנות; 1QS iv 10), "spirit of wickedness" (רוח רשעה/רשע; 1QS v 26), "spirit of impurity" (רוח נדה; 1QS iv 22), "spirit of disloyalty" (רוח נסוגה; 1QS viii 12 par. 4Q259 iii 3?), "perverse spirit" (רוח נעוה; 1QH^a viii 18; xi 22; xix 15), "spirit of error" (רוחהתועה; 1QH^a ix 24), "spirit of frenzy" (רוח עועיים; 1QH^a xiv 26; xv 8), "spirit of ruin" (רוח הוות; 1QH^a xv 14), "twisted spirit" (רוח נעולה; 1QH^a v 32), and "spirit of flesh"[43] (רוח בשר; 1QH^a iv 37; v 15, v 30; 4Q416 1.12 par. 4Q418 2+2a-c, line 4; 4Q417 1 i 17; 4Q418 81.2). These designations seem to function less as references to invasive spirits and more as ways to describe the human condition.

There are, however, a few exceptions to this. First, in the *Treatise on the Two Spirits*, the phrase "the spirits of truth and of deceit" does not refer to two collectives of opposing spirits, but rather to the two contrasting beings, each of which is individually called, respectively, the Prince of Lights (1QS iii 20) and the Angel of Darkness (iii 20–21) and to which are assigned further cohorts that cause the children of light to stumble (iii 24). Second, in the fragmentary text of *4QBerakoth* (= 4Q286) a curse is pronounced against "the ange[l] of the pit and [the] spiri[t of dest]ruction" (4Q286 7 ii 7), where the spirit (best reconstructed as sg.) stands at the head of the cohort of spirits just cursed in the text (4Q286 7 ii 3). Third, it is possible that in the *Songs of the Maskil* at 4Q444 1–4 i + 5.8, "the spirit of uncleanness" (רוח הטמעה) which is listed alongside the *mamzerim* is treated as a demonic being, perhaps even as a leading member of the fallen angels who, given a more generic designation, has been involved in the corruption of humanity (see *1 En.* 9:8; 15:4; and *Book of Giants* at 4Q531 1.1, "they [i. e. the fallen angels] defiled" [*'aṭmyw*]). Fourth, and following on the last example, the writer of a "prayer of deliverance" in 11Q5 petitions God, "do not let Satan/a satan or a spirit of uncleanness (רוח טמעה) have authority over me" (xix 15). The coupling of this

---

[42] Alexander, "The Demonology of the Dead Sea Scrolls", pp. 343–344.

[43] On this expression as a category for theological anthropology, see Jörg Frey, "Flesh and Spirit in the Palestinian Jewish Sapiential Tradition and in the Qumran Texts: An Inquiry into the Background of Pauline Usage", in *Wisdom Texts*, pp. 367–404 (here, pp. 385–97); see also Frey, "The Notion of 'Flesh' in 4QInstruction and the Background of Pauline Usage", in eds. Daniel Falk *et al.*, *Sapiential, Liturgical and Poetical Texts from Qumran: Proceedings of the Third Meeting of the International Organization for Qumran Studies, Oslo 1998* (STDJ 35; Leiden: Brill, 2000), pp. 197–226 and "Die paulinische Antithese von 'Fleisch' und 'Geist' und die palästinisch-jüdische Weisheitstradition", *ZNW* 90 (1999), pp. 45–77.

impure spirit with "satan" suggests that here the spirit may be treated as an external power that threatens the human being (see section D.3 below). These exceptional occurrences of the singular "spirit" in the Hebrew texts are revealing. Apart from possibly the occurrence in *4QBerakoth*, they are not found in an obviously *Yaḥad* or sectarian context, but reflect, instead, ideas that can be said to have developed out of Enoch tradition.

In this connection, it is instructive to consider the *Book of Jubilees* in Ethiopic texts which probably derive from an originally lost Hebrew text that did not survive among the Dead Sea materials. In *Jubilees*, with the exception of two texts (cf. *Jub.* 2:2; 15:32), the term "spirits" occurs almost always in a negative sense; this holds, for example, in 10:3, 5, 8, 11, 13; 11:5; 12:20; and 15:31–32. The narrative in *Jubilees* makes clear that, as in the early Enochic traditions, these "spirits" represent the afterlife of the giants who rule over the Gentiles (15:31–32), on the one hand, and who plague Noah's offspring (ch.'s 10–11), on the other. In the book, they are subordinate to a chief being called Mastema (10:8; cf. section D.4 below). Alongside this, the term "spirit" (Eth. *manfas*), when qualified by a further substantive, can apply to a top-ranked malevolent force. In his prayer near the beginning of the work, Moses petitions God not to let "the spirit of Beliar" rule over Israel so as to bring charges against them (1:20). This reference to a single spirit at the top is, when compared with the Enochic traditions, innovative. The combination of "spirits" derived from the giants and "*the* spirit of Belial" within the narrative world of *Jubilees* anticipates what will develop within the *Yaḥad* literature into a lack of any specific mention of the giants' spirits as well as the use of "spirit", as we have seen, in senses that depart from the Enoch tradition (i. e. as a description of the human condition, spirits of Belial).

C.3 *"Angel"* (*mal'ak*)

As with "spirit", this word, when referring to an evil power, never occurs as an absolute noun unless combined with other terms. For the malevolent use of this term, a similar picture emerges among the Hebrew texts that we have observed for "spirit": the predominant usage is plural, most often in combinations. The following expressions serve as examples:

"angels of enmity/Mastema" (מלאכי משטמה/א/ות) – *Pseudo-Jubilees* at 4Q225 2 ii 6; *Pseudo-Ezekiel* at 4Q387 2 iii 4, 4Q390 1.11 and 2 i 7);
"angels of destruction" (מלאכי חבל) – CD ii 6; 1QS iv 12; 1QM xiii 11; 4Q495 2.4?; 4Q510 1.5, "spirits of the angels of destructions"); and
"angels of his [Belial's] rule" (מלאכי ממשלתו) – 1QM i 15).

In one text, the so-called *Pesher of the Periods*, the plural form המלאכים ("the angels") denotes the disobedient beings who are mentioned together with 'Azaz'el and as having sired giants for themselves (4Q180 1.7–8).

There are also several occurrences in the Hebrew texts of the singular "angel": the *Treatise on the Two Spirits* ("the Angel of Darkness", 1QS iii 20–21), *Damascus Document* ("the angel of enmity/Mastema", CD xvi 6 pars. 4Q270 6 ii 18, 4Q271 4 ii 6), and *Serekh ha-Milḥamah* ("the angel of enmity/Mastema", 1QM xiii 11). Both *Damascus Document* and *Serekh ha-Milḥamah* use the plural and singular together in relation to the term enmity/Mastema. Within the Hebrew texts of the Dead Sea Scrolls, then, the introduction of the singular "angel", especially in combination with a further substantive or proper name, to designate an evil being is first preserved in proto-*Yaḥad* works such as the *Damascus Document* and perhaps within the editorial growth of *Serekh ha-Milḥamah*. The discussion below will have more to say about Mastema below (sections D.4 and 5).

Before we focus attention on "angel(s)" in the Aramaic texts, it is once again instructive to look at *Jubilees*. Significantly, in *Jubilees* there is little general use of this term for malevolent beings; when referring to demonic beings, the term "spirit", whether in the singular or plural, is the preferred designation. The word for "angel" (Eth. *malʾak*, Heb. מלאך, *malʾak*) is never employed in the singular for a heavenly being obedient to God. However, the plural "angels" (Eth. *malāʾekt*, Heb. מלאכים, *malāʾkim*) is made to designate the fallen angels twice. In *Jubilees* 4:15 they are called "the angels of the Lord" who "descended to earth to teach mankind and to do what is just and upright upon the earth", while in 5:1 they are called "his (i. e. God's) angels whom he had sent to the earth". In both these cases, however, the nomenclature reflects the tendency in *Jubilees* to apply the appellation to angels who are subordinate to God (which is expressly recognized as the fallen angels' original state).

Now the lean application of the term "angel" for an evil being in *Jubilees* is interesting when we note the complete absence of this usage among the preserved materials in Aramaic, among which each interpretable context has in view "angels" or an "angel" whether subordinate to God or acting on God's behalf (*Genesis Apocryphon* at 1Q20 xv 14; 4Q157 1 ii 3; Tobit at 4Q196 13.2, 17 i 5 and 4 i 5; *Aramaic Levi Document* at 4Q213a 2.18; 4Q529 1.1, 4; *Book of Giants* at 4Q531 47.1; *Visions of Amram* at 4Q543 2a-b.4 and 4Q545 1a i 9, 17; 4Q552 1.5; 4Q553 2 ii 1; 4Q557 2; and *Targum Job* at 11Q10 xxx 5). In the Enochic *Book of Watchers* no *single* disobedient heavenly being is actually referred to as an "angel", while the "sons of heaven" are collectively referred to as "angels" on a number of occasions (so *1 En.* 6:2, 8; 10:7; 19:1–2; 21:10; cf. *Birth of Noah* 106:5–6, 12, though in the *Epistle of Enoch* there is no reference to these beings). Thus, in avoiding the term "angel" for a demonic being, *Jubilees* follows what we know from the early Enoch tradition. In introducing a single figure at the top of the malevolent hierarchy, *Jubilees* adopts other terminology (see below).

Instead of "angel(s)", the main words used to designate rebellious or disobedient heavenly beings in the Aramaic literature (including the Enoch texts) are:

"watcher(s)" (עירין, *ʿirin* – extant in *Genesis Apocryphon* 1Q20 ii 1, 16; *Book of Watchers* at 4Q202 1 iv 6; 4Q204 1 vi 8; *Book of Giants* at 4Q203 7a.7; 7b i 4; 4Q531 1.1; 36.1?; 4Q532 2.7; and, more rarely,

"holy ones" (קדישין, *qadišin* – so *Genesis Apocryphon* 1Q20 ii 1; vi 20 and *Book of Watchers* at 4Q201 1 i 3).

The term "watcher" is picked up in *Jubilees* and in several of the Hebrew Dead Sea texts (*Damascus Document* in CD ii 18 par. 4Q266 2 ii 18 and *Pseudo-Jubilees* at 4Q227 2.4, which probably echoes terminology of the now lost Hebrew portions of *Jubilees* [cf. 4:15, 22; 7:21; 8:3; 10:5]). By contrast, the term "holy ones" is arguably only applied to the rebellious angels in 11Q11 v 6, a text which we have seen (section B above) is influenced by the Enoch tradition.

D. Chief Demonic Beings

Over against the Enoch tradition which, in its early received form, presented both Shemiḥazah and ʿAsaʾel as leaders of rebellious angels, many of the writings among the Dead Sea Scrolls draw demonic forces together under a single figure. It is not clear how much the widely divergent texts allow us to infer that any of the writers identified a figure designated by one name with a figure designated by another. Moreover, we cannot assume that when single figures are referred to, their designations always function as proper names rather than as descriptions. In what follows, I briefly outline the material and organize my observations around the names or designations that actually occur in the texts. Here I focus on the five main ones: (1) Melki-rešaʿ, (2) "the Angel of Darkness", (3) "S/satan", (4) Mastema, and (5) Belial.

D.1. Melki-rešaʿ

The designation (מלכי רשע), which means "king of wickedness", occurs twice as a proper name, once in an Aramaic source and once in a Hebrew text. In the Aramaic *Visions of Amram* (4Q544 2.13) Melki-rešaʿ is mentioned as one of two angelic beings striving against one another to have authority over the eponymous patriarch. His association in the passage with "darkness" and with its "deeds" is contrasted with the association of his counterpart (probably Melchizedek, meaning "king of righteousness") with "light" (4Q544 2.13–16). The oppositional framework within which Melki-rešaʿ participates is not one of a pre-determinism as is found in the *Treatise on the Two Spirits* (cf. 1QS iii 13 – iv 26).[44] Instead, it is

---

[44] For a summary of scholarship on the *Treatise*, see John R. Levison, "The Two Spirits in Qumran Theology", in ed. James H. Charlesworth, *The Bible and the Dead Sea Scrolls* (3 vols.; Waco, Texas: Baylor University Press, 2006), 2:169–194.

the patriarch, Amram himself, who is asked to choose between these opposing angels and to decide which one may have authority over him (see Section D.2 below).

In the Hebrew text of *4QCurses* (=4Q280) 1.2–7 Melki-rešaᶜ is addressed directly (in the 2ⁿᵈ pers. sg.) and expressly cursed in terms that are reminiscent of the denunciation in *Serekh ha-Yaḥad*, which is pronounced against "all the men of the lot of Belial" (1QS ii 5–9; see under Section D.5 below).

D.2. *"The Angel of Darkness"* (מלאך החשך)

The scholarly attention devoted to this figure is disproportionate to the two times he is mentioned in the Dead Sea Scrolls. This notice is due to the fact that this angelic being occurs in one of the earliest manuscripts to be discussed after the initial discovery of Cave 1 and because he is presented in the well-known *Treatise on the Two Spirits* (1QS iii 13 – iv 26) within the *Serekh ha-Yaḥad* as the negative counterpart to "the Prince of Lights" (iii 20, 21). The *Treatise on the Two Spirits* forms a discrete literary unit within the *Serekh*, though, misleadingly, has been regarded as the core or pinnacle of the Qumran Community's theological perspective.[45] Within the *Treatise*, the Angel of Darkness is further identified as the "spirit ... of deceit" (iii 18–19, רוח ... העולה), one of opposing "two spirits" placed within human beings until the eschatological time of visitation (iii 18). Parallels, of course, have been noted between the dualistic duo in the *Treatise* and that involving Melki-rešaᶜ in the *Visions of Amram*. For example, the opposition between both pairs of beings is expressed in cosmological terms of darkness and light. A fuller comparison, however, cannot be undertaken due to the fragmentary text of the *Visions of Amram*. Nevertheless, one difference does appear to lie in the existence, activities and outcome of the activities of the "two spirits" in the *Treatise*. Unlike the *Visions of Amram*, the respective influences of the spirits on humanity are from the start predetermined by "the God of knowledge" and, therefore, are unalterable (iii 13–16). By contrast, the selection of one angel or another by the patriarch in the *Visions of Amram* is less predeterministic and comes closer to the implicit exhortation underlying the description of virtues and vices in the *Treatise*, which are essentially polarizing categories that are correlated, respectively, to "the spirit of the sons of truth" (iv 2–8) and "the spirit of deceit" (iv 9–14).

Although the Angel of Darkness initially appears as an external force under the auspices of God the creator of all, the association of the "spirit of deceit" in 1QS iv with vices for which human beings are held responsible suggests a close association

---

[45] So e. g. James H. Charlesworth, "John the Baptizer and the Dead Sea Scrolls", in *The Bible and the Dead Sea Scrolls*, 3:1–35 (here, p. 11). This assumption is rightly questioned *inter alia* by Armin Lange, *Weisheit und Prädestination: Weisheitliche Urordnung und Prädestination in den Textfunden von Qumran* (STDJ 15; Leiden/New York: Brill, 1995), pp. 126–130 and Jörg Frey, "Different Patterns of Dualistic Thought" (see n. 41 above).

between such a figure and a notion of theological anthropology that renders the angel's influence as part of the human condition.[46] Until the eschatological visitation of God destroys all evil, it is taken for granted that an invasive force of evil persists to some degree within every human being.

D.3. "Satan" (שטן)

As is well known, the term *saṭan* means "accuser" or "one who brings charges against". There are five occurrence of the term in the Hebrew Dead Sea manuscripts and once among the Aramaic texts. In two, perhaps three of these instances, the word is preceded by the adjective meaning "all/every"; in combination with the negative, it is best translated "any" (כ(ו)ל שטן; cf. 1QHᵃ 4.6, 45.3; 1QSb i 8?). In the latter case we do not have to do with "Satan" as a proper name, but rather with the description of a figure who could also be a human adversary. The same may also be inferred from the negative which precedes it in *Words of the Luminaries* at 4Q504 1–2 iv 12: "and there is no satan or evil plague" (ואין שטן ופגע רע). *Jubilees* offers a similar picture: the apocalyptic passage in chapter 23 anticipates that in the end of days "there will be neither satan nor *any* evil who (or better: which) will destroy" (23:29). Here, the term *saṭan* generically denotes someone – anyone – who destroys by cutting short the life of human beings. Less clear is *Jubilees* 10:11: the angels of the presence are made to say that, "[a]ll the evil ones (i.e. the spirits from the giants) who were savage we tied up in the place of judgment, while we left a tenth of them to exercise power on the earth before the satan." Here, "the satan" refers to the chief of the evil spirits who has just previously been mentioned by name as "Mastema"; the expression, then, describes a function associated with Mastema rather than being a proper name in itself.

In the one remaining, fifth occurrence in the "Prayer of Deliverance" mentioned above (section C.2 above), *saṭan* may function as a proper noun. The petition for divine help, according to the text of 11Q5 xix 13–16, reads:

> Forgive my sin, YHWH, and cleanse me from my iniquity.
> Bestow upon me a spirit of faithfulness and knowledge.
> Do not allow me to stumble in transgression (בעויה).
> Do not let *saṭan* or a spirit of uncleanness have authority over me;
> Let neither rain nor evil purpose take hold of my bones.[47]

The interpretation of *saṭan* in the text may be brought into sharper relief when we consider it alongside the only other occurrence of the word among the Scrolls: the older *Aramaic Levi Document* at 4Q213a 1 i 10, which is also preserved in a much

---

[46] Thus cosmology and theological anthropology cannot easily be categorically distinguished in the texts.

[47] Translation my own.

later Greek manuscript from Mt. Athos (Athos Koutloumous no. 39) to the *Testament of Levi*. The text can be restored with some confidence as follows:[48]

> And do n]ot let have authority over me *any* satan [to lead me astray
> from your path.
> (ואל תשלט בי כל סטן [לתעני מן אורחכה)

In this text, the placement of "any" before *satan* makes it unlikely that a proper name is in view. Furthermore, both texts, as argued by Armin Lange, show a striking affinity to Psalm 119:33b: "and do not let any iniquity rule over me".[49] If the "Prayer of Deliverance" in 11Q5 is aware of these traditions, then the absence of *kol* may suggest a shift, so that a more specific malevolent being is now in view, one called "Satan". A move in this direction, though without involving the designation "Satan", is also at work in *Jubilees*. In chapter 1:19–20 of *Jubilees*, Moses pleads that God not deliver Israel "into the hand of their enemy, the gentiles, lest they rule over them" and that God "not let the spirit of Beliar rule over them to accuse them before you and ensnare them from every path of righteousness so that they might be destroyed from your face". As in the petition in the "Prayer of Deliverance" of 11Q5, this text in *Jubilees* contains no equivalent for *kol* ("any" with the negative); perhaps by analogy, an abstract term (such as "iniquity" from Ps. 119:33b) or a generic designation (such as "satan" from *Aramaic Levi Document*) has been replaced in *Jubilees* by "spirit of Beliar" whose activity involves bringing accusations against God's people. For similar adaptations of this tradition in *Jubilees*, one should note also Noah's prayer for his grandchildren in 10:3–6 ("do not let evil spirits rule over them" … "let them not rule over the spirits of the living" … "do not let them have power over the children of the righteous now and forever"); and Abraham's prayers in 12:19–20 ("save me from the hands of evil spirits which rule over the thought of the heart of man"), in 19:28 ("may the spirits of Mastema not rule over you and your descendants"), and in 15:30–32 (Israel, over whom God "made no angel or spirit rule").

D.4 and D.5 "Mastema" and "Belial"

Both terms are treated together in this section, as the texts provide evidence that they can be associated with one another and because neither word is necessarily a proper name. Both are only preserved among Hebrew texts of the Scrolls. Not counting *Jubilees*, the Hebrew scroll fragments of which do not preserve either term, the word *mastema* (משטמה/א) occurs 18 times, while *beliyaʿal* (בליעל) occurs 88 times. While *mastema* as a noun or substantive can denote "enmity" or "ani-

---

[48] For the presentation of these texts, see Henryk Drawnel, *An Aramaic Wisdom Text from Qumran* (JSJSup 86; Leiden/Boston: Brill, 2004), esp. pp. 98–101.

[49] Cf. Armin Lange, "Considerations Concerning the 'Spirit of Impurity' in Zech 13:2", in *Die Dämonen – Demons* (bibl. in n. 6), pp. 254–268 (here, p. 262).

mosity" in the abstract, *beliyaʿal* can often simply be translated as a noun meaning "worthlessness".

D.4. Masṭema

While there is little doubt that in *Jubilees* "Mastema" represents a proper name for the chief demonic power that has jurisdiction over a contingent of evil spirits (see below), the function of the term in a number of the Qumran texts as well as its relation to Belial is unclear. We cannot, for example, assume that Masṭema and Belial are but different names for the same figure, as the narrative world of *Jubilees* might lead one to infer (*Jub.* 1:19–20, Beliar; 10:5–6, Masṭema). For example, according to *4QBerakoth* in 4Q286, a curse is pronounced against Belial "in his inimical plan" (ב[חמ]שבת משטמתו), so that *masṭema* functions here as a feature of Belial's activity.[50]

A couple of interesting examples illustrate how both terms can appear alongside each other, with some ambiguity as to whether they refer to different beings. The fragmentary text from *Pseudo-Jubilees* at 4Q225 2 ii 14 reads:

"the Prince of A/an[im]osity (M/mastema), and Belial listened to["

The cited text does not preserve sufficient context for us to decide how the Prince of Animosity/Mastema and Belial are related; the activity (listening) of the latter figure, Belial, does not necessarily imply his subordination to the former.[51] In any case, it is not even clear that we should be comparing Mastema with Belial to begin with; the text could instead be drawing a comparison between the Prince (i. e. of Animosity or Mastema)[52] and Belial.

A final example occurs in the *Serekh ha-Milḥamah* in 1QM xiii 10–12. This text, formally part of a lengthy prayer, declares that God "made Belial for the pit, an angel of *masṭema*; and in dark[ness is] his [rule] and in his counsel is to bring wickedness and guilt about; and all the spirits of his lot are angels of destruction; they walk in the statutes of darkness." Here the equation, as Devorah Dimant rightly argues,[53] is not so much between Belial and Mastema, but rather between Belial and a "*Prince* of M/masṭema", where "M/masṭema" either characterizes the

---

[50] See the parallel expression 1QS iii 23, where a similar phrase – "and the times of their troubles are in his inimical dominion [משטמתו בממשלת]" – applies to the Angel of Darkness.

[51] See Devorah Dimant, "Between Qumran Sectarian and Non-Sectarian Texts: The Case of Belial and Mastema", in eds. Adolfo Roitman, Lawrence H. Schiffman and Shani Tsoref, *The Dead Sea Scrolls and Contemporary Culture* (STDJ 93; Leiden/Boston: Brill, 2010), pp. 235–256 (here p. 240).

[52] Linguistically, a parallel problem of choosing between "Prince Mastema" and "Prince of Mastema" presents itself in *Jubilees*; cf. *Jub.* 11:5, 11; 18:9, 12; 48:2, 9, 12, 15. However, the macro-context, in which Mastema is initially introduced as the chief of demonic beings and continues to act in the narrative, suggests that "Prince" is simply used here as a title; see below.

[53] Dimant, "Between Qumran Sectarian and non-Sectarian Texts". p. 240.

kind of angel that Belial is or is the proper name of the angel with whom Belial is being identified.

It is possible that in the *Damascus Document*, in which the expression "angel of *maṣṭema*" (מלאך המסטמה) occurs by itself, we may not have to do with a proper name such as "the angel of/from Mastema" (i. e. the angel under Mastema's jurisdiction) or with "the angel Mastema" (so that Mastema is identified as an angel). The text in CD xvi 2–5 (pars. in 4Q270 6 ii 18 and 4Q271 4 ii 6) reads:

"And the precise interpretation of their ages with regard to the blindness of Israel in all these things, behold, it is defined in the book of the divisions of the periods according to their jubilees and in their weeks. And on the day in which a man takes upon himself to return to the Torah of Moses, the Angel of Animosity/Mastema (מלאך המסטמה) will turn away from after him if he sustains his words. This is why Abraham circumcised himself on the day of his knowledge."

In this passage, the construction, in which *maṣṭema* is attached to the definite article as the *nomen rectum*, is telling; one would not expect a proper name to require an article "the". By analogy, in *Pseudo-Jubilees* at 4Q225 2 ii 6, the plural expression, "angels of Animosity" (מלאכי המסטמה) denotes those beings who were anticipating that Abraham would indeed sacrifice Isaac. The episode in this incomplete text is initiated by "the Prince of A[ni]mosity" (שר המ[ש]טמה), with whom these "angels of A/animosity" are aligned (the same form of the expression occurs also in 4Q225 2 ii 13–14), while in *Jubilees* itself the account mentions only the presence of the "Prince of Mastema" in this episode (*Jub.* 18:9). Essentially, the malevolent figures are the Prince (*sar*) and the angels (*mal'akim*), not M/mastema him- or by itself. If this is correct, then the three occurrences of the phrase *mal'ake ha-maṣṭemut* (מלאכי המסטמות) in *Pseudo-Ezekiel* (4Q387 2 iii 4, 4Q390 1.11 and 2 i 7), which are "angels of Animosity" (the form of the noun, *maṣṭemut*, is abstract) who rule over the disobedient of Israel, may be a variant that makes the linguistic possibility of an abstraction inherent in *ha-maṣṭema* more explicit.

Unfortunately, not a single text in *Jubilees* (in which *maṣṭema* occurs twelve times) is sufficiently preserved from the Scrolls for us to know whether *maṣṭema* was affixed to a definite article. The most frequent expression is "Prince of Mastema/ Animosity" or, better translated, "Prince Mastema" (*Jub.* 11:5, 11; 18:9, 12; 48:2, 9, 12, 15); as the context suggests, the Prince is to be identified with Mastema who is introduced as the leader of the spirits requesting permission for a tenth of their number to carry out their work after the Flood.[54] In this way, "prince" seems to be a title given to Mastema rather than the main designation itself. As such, Prince Mastema is written into the storyline: he is the initiator of the testing of Abraham to sacrifice Isaac (17:16; cf. 18:9, 12); he is the force behind an attempt to kill Moses (48:2–4, where Mastema encounters Moses, *contra* Exodus 4:24–26

---

[54] If the initial occurrence of "Maṣṭema" in *Jub.* 10 clearly functions as a proper name, the likelihood that this usage of the word occurs in the subsequent parts of the work is strengthened.

where it is YHWH [MT] or an "angel of the Lord" [LXX]); he is behind the work of Pharaoh's magicians to counteract Moses (48:9, 12); and he foments the Egyptians to pursue the Israelites in the wilderness (48:15–18). Finally, it is "all the forces of Mastema" which are sent to kill the first-born in the land of Egypt (49:2; cf. Exodus 12:29, according to which the subject of the verb "to strike" [הכה] is the Lord). In each of these passages where Prince Mastema is mentioned, the narrative makes clear that his activities only happen under the terms of allowance granted both him and his reduced entourage (10:8–9).

D.5. Belial

As the statistics indicate, Belial is by far the most frequent designation used for an evil being in the Dead Sea Scrolls. Like Mastema, there must have been a close connection between the figure and the meaning of the name, in this case "worthlessness". However, unlike Mastema, the word Belial never appears in a text affixed to the definite article, even in the position of *nomen rectum*. Therefore, phrases such as "dominion of Belial", "lot of Belial", "the army of Belial", "spirits of Belial", "congregation of Belial", "child" or "children of Belial" and "men of Belial" all suggest that in many cases at least we have to do with a term that has become a proper name. On the other hand, when "Belial" is preceded by *kol* ("any"), then we are dealing with the same linguistic phenomenon that we have observed in relation to *saṭan* (see 1QH^a xi 28, which refers to "the time of anger against any *belial*").

Most of the extant occurrences of Belial are to be found among the more "sectarian", that is, the proto-*Yaḥad* (i. e. *Damascus Document, Serekh ha-Milḥamah*) and *Yaḥad* documents (*Serekh ha-Yaḥad, Hodayoth*, pesharic interpretations, *Catena, Berakoth*, and *11QMelchizedek*). Belial (or rather, Beliar) occurs in *Jubilees* only twice (1:20 and 15:30–33), though in 1:20 it is in a prominent position as part of Moses' initial petition that future generations of Israel not be ruled by "the spirit of Beliar", while in 15:33 it is the unfaithful of Israel who are branded "the people of Beliar" (something not said of Mastema). It is possible, however, that in both these phrases we are dealing with *beliar* (derived from Belial) as a descriptive rather than as a proper noun. In this case, it would be the term "spirit" that personifies the designation. Whether Belial represents a proper noun or not among the more explicit *Yaḥad* writings, the activity of B/belial comes to be associated in the most immediate sense with that of faithless Jews (though it certainly would have included Gentiles as well).

The striking development here is, of course, that under the name "Belial" a number of the motifs associated with other malevolent beings found in the Aramaic and Hebrew texts are brought together. There are two important examples of this. First, Belial – and those errant Jews associated with Belial (1QS ii 11–18 pars. 4Q257 ii 1–7; 5Q11 1.2–6) – is denounced (cf. 1QS ii 4–10 par. 4Q256 ii 12 – iii 4), just as other malevolent beings are directly addressed and denounced in earlier apocalyptic literature.[55] There is a difference, however: in relation to Belial the curse formulae, which is more fixed and ritualized, is pronounced by a priestly figure or by the worshipping congregation. A second example that illustrates how language about Belial is indebted to earlier tradition relates to his rule or dominion in the present age (1QS i 23–24, ii 19; 1QM xiv 9–10 par. 4QMᵃ = 4Q491 8–10 i 6–7; cf. further 4Q177 3.8). This is, of course, a motif in the Enochic tradition in which the present – that is, the time between now and the eschatological visitation of God – demonic evil appears to hold sway. Like the Enochic tradition and those traditions which took it up, the texts hold unequivocally that Belial's dominion is temporary. Moreover, like the apocalyptic traditions, it is possible to manage or neutralize demonic power in anticipation of its final destruction. Again, however, there is a difference in the Belial texts: whereas the Enochic tradition itself could be compatible *inter alia* with the practice of exorcism, no such measures are appropriated against Belial. During the time of Belial's dominion, the Community's curses and blessings, based on Numbers 6:24–26, which petition for protection and according to *Serekh ha-Yaḥad* are to be spoken year after year (1QS ii 19), function as the predominant means (cf. 1QS i 16 – iii 11).[56] In other words, the chief power is cursed, not exorcized.

Traditions which are pivotal in receiving Enochic tradition and paving the way for the sectarian *Yaḥad* way of dealing with Belial may be seen in *Jubilees*, on the one hand, and *Songs of the Maskil*, on the other. The *Book of Jubilees* presents demonic activity under the leadership of Mastema as an inevitable characteristic of this age until the final judgment (ch. 10). Thus, in *Jubilees* not only do angels reveal remedies to Noah (and his progeny) for warding off or neutralizing the effects of evil spirits (*Jub.* 10:10–13), the patriarchs – Moses (1:19–20), Noah (10:1–6), and Abraham (12:19–20) – are made to utter prayers of deliverance against them. There is no formal denunciation or curse against any of the malevolent powers. In *Songs of the Maskil*, the language of dominion by evil powers in the present age comes closer to later Belial texts, without actually pronouncing curses against the demonic beings themselves (at least this is absence among the extant texts). In one of the songs, the sage initially declares the splendor of God's radiance

"in order to terrify and fr[ighten] all the spirits of the angels of destruction, and the bastard spirits, demons, Lilith, owls and [jackals ...] and those who strike suddenly to lead astray the

---

[55] As against the fallen Watchers who have corrupted the earth, who are denounced with the formula "you will have peace" (*1 En.* 12:5 Cod. Pan. – "there is no peace for you", with 3ʳᵈ pers. in Eth.; 13:1 – against ʿAsaʾel, Cod. Pan. Azael, Eth. Azazel; and 16:4; cf. also *Book of Giants* at 1Q24 8.2 and 4Q203 13.3) which not only influences pronouncements against the human wicked in *1 En.* 5:4 and in the *Epistle of Enoch* (98:11, 16; 99:13; 101:3; 102:3; 103:8), but also carries over into formulae that adapt the language of the Aaronic blessing in Numbers 6:24–26; see 4Q480 2.2 (a curse against Melki-rešaʿ). For other denunciations of the demonic in the Scrolls, see 4Q410 1.5, 4Q511 3.5 (against demonic spirits), and 11Q11 v.

[56] See similarly the *Sereh ha-Milḥamah* at 1QM xiv 9–10 par. 4Q491=4QMᵃ 8–10 i 6–7 and *4QCatena A* at 4Q177 iii 8.

spirit of understanding and to cause their hearts to shudder." (4Q510 1.4–6a par. 4Q511 10.1–3a)

This proclamation of divine majesty, which Armin Lange has described as a "hymnic exorcism",[57] is then followed by an address to "righteous ones" in which the sage states:

You have been put in a time of the dominion [of] wickedness and in the eras of the humiliation of the sons of lig[ht] in the guilt of the times of those plagued by iniquities, not for an eternal destruction, [but] for the era of the humiliation of transgression. Rejoice, O righteous ones, in the God of wonder. My psalms (are) for the upright ones. (4Q510 1.6b–8; par. 4Q511 10.3b–6)

The *Maskil*'s declarations about God, told in the 3rd person (i. e. not in the form of a 2nd person prayer addressed to God), are presumed to be potent enough to diminish or counteract demonic powers that are at work in the present order of things ("the dominion [of] wickedness"). While the text does not furnish a prayer for divine protection against these demons, it reflects a framework that holds two concurrent things in tension: (1) the existence of a community of those who are unambiguously "righteous" and "upright"; and (2) the characterization of the present age as "a time of the dominion [of] wickedness". Analogous to the pronouncement of a benediction in the yearly covenant renewal ceremony in *Serekh ha-Yaḥad* (cols. i 18 – iii 12) is the song addressed by the *Maskil* to those who are righteous, functioning as an expedient measure that neutralizes the threats associated with the power of Belial until the present age of wickedness is brought to an end.

The pronouncements against Belial and his lot bring together and merge several evolving features that in their specificity are partly lost, yet whose conceptual framework is preserved within a new form. The eschatological framework – it is found in the Enochic pronouncements of doom against the disobedient angels, the prayers for deliverance we have observed in other texts, exorcisms, and hymnic forms of protection – is retained in the way the *Yaḥad* treats Belial. However, the various means of dealing with evil known in the other texts are replaced by curses against Belial that adapt language from the Aaronic blessing (Num. 6:24–27) and should be understood in relation to the larger context of covenant blessings and curses found in Deuteronomy (cf. Deut. chs. 28–30).

E. Conclusion

Our survey of language used for the demonic world in the Dead Sea Scrolls yields several conclusions. First, the texts, especially the earlier ones in Aramaic, apply a wide variety of terms to designate beings in the demonic world: "demon", "spirit",

---

[57] See Lange, "The Essene Position on Magic and Divination", *Legal Texts and Legal Issues*, pp. 377–435 (here, pp. 383, 402–403, 430–433), who also applies this classification to *Genesis Apocryphon* at 1QapGen xx 12–18, *Jub.* 10:1–14; and 12:16–21.

"angel", "watcher", and even "holy ones". In addition, in at least the Enochic trad-itions of the *Book of Watchers* and *Book of Giants*, a range of demonic beings – leaders and sub-leaders of the fallen angels and, in the case of the *Book of Giants*, their offspring – are referred to with proper names, nomenclature to which, no doubt, some significance was attached. A corollary to the diversity of terms and use of proper names is an interest in these texts for different classes of evil beings. Here, mostly in the Aramaic literature, we have early representatives of a tradition, to be more fully developed at a later period, which itemized and classified malevo-lent powers and dealt with them in accordance with their particular functions and characteristics (so *1 En.* 15:8–16:1; 69:2–12; Asmodaeus in Tobit; 4Q560; 11Q11; and 4Q510–511; see also Mk. 9:29 ["this kind (of demon)"], the later demonic classes in the *Testament of Solomon*, *Sefer ha-Razim*, and the much later incantation bowls).

Second, this review has also highlighted some distinctions that can be made within the literature. An overall shift in thought and approach can be discerned if we distinguish between (a) Aramaic documents and (b) literature composed in Hebrew. Allowing for instances of occasional overlap and genetic development, this shift in language corresponds to the further difference between (a) earlier non-*Yaḥad* and (b) later *Yaḥad* literature.

Third, the most important witnesses to the shifts between earlier and later trends can be found in three works composed in Hebrew: *Jubilees*, *Treatise on the Two Spirits*, and *Songs of the Maskil*. The authors who composed each of these writings represented a pivotal phase that anticipated subsequent developments. They gathered up and reformulated ideas from the literature and traditions they inherited and recast them in ways that were eventually incorporated into the litur-gical life of the Qumran Community.

Fourth, "demons" and other lower-class beings tended to attract responses that regarded them as powers to be "managed" or "relocated" by various means. The afflictions, illnesses, other evils, and human sins they were thought to have caused could be effectively dealt with or at least addressed with confidence through a series of methods such as exorcism, prayer, recitation of hymns, and other acts of piety. The matter was different for a chief of demons – for example, Mastema, Belial, Satan, the Angel of Darkness, or Melki-resha᷉. To the extent that they were per-ceived as demonic beings who are active in the cosmos, these figures, catapulted into a position of prominence (whether they were chiefs of other demons or sim-ply organizing principles that represented evil as a whole), are not managed or neutralized in the same way. The *Yaḥad*, for example, resorted to the formal reciting of curses in their liturgy. However, whether by small-scale activities or community liturgy, the means undertaken to deal with the demonic functioned as "temporary expedients" in recognition that the evil powers that malign human dignity and distract from faithfulness to God will indeed come to an end.

Fifth and finally, the present review of demonology in the Dead Sea Scrolls lays the groundwork for drawing a series of distinctions that are crucial to understanding and interpreting the demonic world as it is dealt with in the New Testament and in early Christian literature. These are threefold and overlapping: (1) the distinction between the nature of evil (which distorts the cosmos as created by God) and humanity (whose essential dignity within the created order remains intact); (ii) the distinction between the present "era of wickedness" (in which evil can never be extinguished and persists as a reality) and the eschatological annihilation of evil; and, in practical terms, (iii) the distinction between matters of "salvation" (to draw on the Christian sense of the term) and "the management of evil powers". It remains for further studies to work out the theological implications coming from each of these points.[58]

---

[58] These points are explored in Chapter Nine below.

Chapter Five

Early Enochic and Daniel Traditions in the Dead Sea Scrolls

A. Introduction

It is well known that the Dead Sea discoveries include manuscript fragments that correspond to previously known works reflecting an apocalyptic world view such as the Book of Daniel,[1] the *Book of Jubilees*,[2] and *1 Enoch*.[3] The location of these materials among the eleven Caves near Khirbet Qumran has, in turn, raised questions concerning their relationship to apocalyptic traditions composed during the early to mid-2nd century B.C.E., not least with respect to how formative they were for the group that collected and copied many of them. In particular, attention has

---

[1] Eight copies of Daniel were found in Caves 1, 4, and 6: (a) 1Q71–72, published initially by Dominic Barthélemy in Barthélemy and Józef T. Milik, *Qumrân Cave 1* (DJD 1; Oxford: Clarendon Press, 1955), pp. 150–151; (b) 6Q7pap, published by Maurice Baillet, in Baillet, Józef T. Milik, and Roland de Vaux, *Les 'Petites Grottes' de Qumran: Exploration de la falaise, Les grottes 2Q, 3Q, 5Q, 6Q, 7Q, à 10Q, Le rouleau de cuivre* (DJD 3; Oxford: Clarendon Press, 1962), pp. 114–116; and (c) 4Q112–116, published preliminarily by Eugene Ulrich in "Daniel Manuscripts from Qumran. Part 1" and "Daniel Manuscripts from Qumran. Part 2", *BASOR* 268 (1987), pp. 17–37, and *BASOR* 274 (1989), pp. 3–26, respectively; and by Stephen J. Pfann, "4QDaniel[d] 4Q115: A Preliminary Edition with Critical Notes", *RevQ* 17 (1996), pp. 37–71. For Ulrich's critical edition of the Cave 4 manuscripts, see Eugene Ulrich *et al.*, *Qumran Cave 4. XI: Psalms to Chronicles* (DJD 16; Oxford: Clarendon Press, 2000), pp. 239–289 + Plates XXIX–XXVII.

[2] There are no less than fourteen copies of *Jubilees* among the eleven Caves near Qumran. Certain identifications include the following: (a) 1Q17–18, perhaps one manuscript, edited by Józef T. Milik, in DJD 1, pp. 82–84; (b) 2Q19–20 and 3Q5, published by Maurice Baillet in DJD 3, pp. 77–79 and 96–98; (c) 4Q216–224, published by James C. VanderKam and Józef T. Milik in *Qumran Cave 4. VIII: Parabiblical Texts, Part 1* (DJD 13; Oxford: Clarendon Press, 1994), pp. 1–140 (4Q223–224 are perhaps one manuscript); and (d) 11Q12 in Florentino García Martínez and Eibert J.C. Tigchelaar, *Qumran Cave 11. II: 11Q2–18, 11Q20–31* (DJD 23; Oxford: Clarendon Press, 1998), pp. 207–220.

[3] Corresponding to the different works collected in *1 Enoch* (except for the *Book of Parables*, chs. 37–71 and the appendix in ch. 108), there are at least 13 manuscripts published, though incompletely, by Józef T. Milik, *The Books of Enoch: Aramaic Fragments from Qumrân Cave 4* (Oxford: Clarendon Press, 1976): 1Q19 (frgs. 1, 3, and 8) and 4Q201–212. If the broader category of Enochic literature or tradition is considered, then the *Book of Giants* should be included. The relevant scroll fragments for the *Book of Giants* are 1Q23–24, 2Q26, 4Q206a, 4Q530–533, and 6Q8; these are published by Loren T. Stuckenbruck, in eds. Stephen J. Pfann *et al.*, *Qumran Cave 4. XXVI: Cryptic Texts, and Miscellanea, Part 1* (DJD 36; Oxford: Clarendon Press, 2000), pp. 3–94 + Plates I–II (1Q23–24; 2Q26; 6Q8; 4Q203; 4Q206 2–3=4Q206a) and Émile Puech, in ed. *idem*, *Qumrân Grotte 4. XXII: Textes araméens, Première Partie 4Q529–549* (DJD 31; Oxford: Clarendon Press, 2001), pp. 9–115 (4Q530–533) + Plates I–VI.

turned to the origin of the community of Qumran, the *Yaḥad*. Did this group actually originate from an apocalyptic movement (sometimes termed "pre-Essene") whose adherents produced writings such as Daniel, *Jubilees*, and some of the early Enochic literature? This possibility has been argued, for instance, by Martin Hengel, along with a contingent of scholars. *Jubilees*, they have maintained, was itself a product of the "early" Essene movement, while the origins of this group ultimately go back to the "Hasidaeans" who generated Daniel, the *Apocalypse of Weeks* (i. e. *1 En.* 93:1–10; 91:11–17), the *Book of Dreams* (*1 En.* 83–90, including the *Animal Apocalypse* in chs. 85–90), and the *Exhortation* and *Epistle of Enoch* (*1 En.* 91:1–10, 18–19; 92; 93:11–105:2).[4]

Other scholars, however, have taken a different view. While it is generally accepted that, for example, Daniel and the early Enochic writings broadly share an apocalyptic milieu, John Collins, among others, has maintained that while such tradition-historical continuity may explain why the Qumran community could be influenced by both Danielic and Enochic traditions, such connections should in no way be taken to mean that there is significant social continuity between them.[5]

---

[4] See Martin Hengel, *Judaism and Hellenism* (Philadelphia: Fortress Press, 1974), pp. 175–218, who argued that both the Essenes and the Pharisees emerged as splinter groups from these "Hasidaeans" (cf. 1 Macc. 2:42; 7:13; 2 Macc. 14:6). Hengel identifies this group with the "wise ones" mentioned in Dan. 11:33–35 and 12:3 (here: "bringers of understanding", משכילים), as well as with the "lambs who began to open their eyes" in the *Animal Apocalypse* at *1 En.* 90:6 and the "chosen righteous ones" in the *Apocalypse of Weeks* at *1 En.* 93:10. Since his understanding of the "Hasidaeans" is not limited to texts that specifically refer to them, Hengel's definition ends up being very broad; the term becomes virtually indistinguishable from any apocalyptic movement. This equivalence does not take adequate account of the diversity of apocalyptic responses to the Maccabean crisis. While essentially adopting the same view, Florentino García Martínez has pushed the "Essene movement" even further back to "the close of the 3rd century BCE. or the beginnings of the 2nd century BCE"; cf. *idem*, "The Origins of the Essene Movement and of the Qumran Sect", in Florentino García Martínez and Julio Trebolle Barrera, *The People of the Dead Sea Scrolls: Their Writings, Beliefs and Practices* (Leiden: Brill, 1993), pp. 77–96 (here p. 91). See also Frank Moore Cross, *The Ancient Library of Qumran* (The Biblical Seminar 30; Sheffield: Sheffield Academic Press, 1995, 2nd ed.), p. 104. While attempts to fit the designations for groups into a broader scheme of social and religious movements have been valuable, the hesitation to apply nomenclature such as "Essene" to texts in which such terminology does not appear is justified. Hence more recent research has focused on developing a more differentiating and nuanced approach to *Yaḥad* among the scrolls; cf. Torleif Elgvin, "The *Yaḥad* is more than Qumran", in ed. Gabriele Boccaccini, *Enoch and Qumran Origins: New Light on a Forgotten Connection* (Grand Rapids: Eerdmans, 2005), pp. 273–279; Alison Schofield, *From Qumran to the Yaḥad: A New Paradigm of Textual Development for the Community Rule* (STDJ 77; Leiden / Boston: Brill, 2009); and John J. Collins, *Beyond the Qumran Community: Sectarian Movement of the Dead Sea Scrolls* (Grand Rapids: Eerdmans, 2010).

[5] Note, e. g., John J. Collins, *Apocalypticism in the Dead Sea Scrolls* (New York / London: Routledge, 1997), pp. 12–29 and 153–154; now *idem, Beyond the Qumran Community*, pp. 40–45 and 51. See esp. also the views of Philip Davies, "*Hasidim* in the Maccabean Period", *JJS* 28 (1977), pp. 127–140 and George W. E. Nickelsburg, e. g. in "Social Aspects of Palestinian Jewish Apocalypticism", in ed. David Hellholm, *Apocalypticism in the Mediterranean World and the Near East* (Tübingen: Mohr-Siebeck, 1989, 2nd ed.), pp. 641–654.

While the view represented by Collins reflects an appropriate degree of caution, the recognition of basic differences between the Book of Daniel and the early Enochic works should not be taken for granted. Indeed, the complexity of their relationship is made apparent by the preservation of manuscript fragments among the materials from the Dead Sea that do not correspond to anything in either Daniel or *1 Enoch*, yet which preserve an overlap of traditions contained in both. Such similarities of tradition, which are explored below, have been identified among the "pseudo-Danielic" literature (4Q243–245) and may arguably be found in one of the visions of judgment attributed to a giant's dream vision in a manuscript belonging to the *Book of Giants* (4Q530). How is such evidence to be explained? According to Gabriele Boccaccini – who assumes the dependence of 4Q243–245 on Daniel – the pseudo-Danielic materials represent a reading of Daniel in light of the Enochic *Animal Apocalypse* by "[t]hose who collected the Dead Sea Scrolls". Like *Jubilees*, then, the merging of these different apocalyptic traditions – the Danielic traditions being Torah-centered and adopting a positive view towards the Second Temple, while the Enochic tradition virtually ignores the Sinai covenant (except *1 En.* 93:5) and regards the Second Temple as run by a corrupt priesthood – is best understood as a development subsequent or secondary to the composition of the apocalypses themselves.

In the present chapter, we focus on sources found among the Qumran caves in which the Danielic and Enochic apocalyptic traditions overlap (4Q243–245; 4Q530), and consider what these signify concerning the tradition-historical relationship between the Danielic and Enochic *corpora*, especially since the mythic story of disobedient angelic beings known through the latter seems on the surface to play no role whatsoever in Daniel. More specifically, it is to be asked whether any of these extant materials are best thought to presuppose knowledge of either Daniel or Enochic tradition. To the extent that some knowledge of these traditions is the case, the form of apocalyptic traditions the materials contain may be thought to represent a subsequent development inspired by previously composed works of presumably independent provenience. If, however, the convergences suggest more fluid traditions during the early 2nd century B.C.E., whether formulated before or alongside the Book of Daniel, then it becomes possible to interpret them along different lines from those suggested by, for instance, Boccaccini. The present consideration of these pseudo-Danielic and giants materials will also allow for a brief analysis of those portions of Daniel and *1 Enoch* that are tradition-historically similar, but not extant among the Scrolls (i.e., Dan. 7:9–14; *Book of Watchers* at *1 En.* 14:9–25; and *Animal Apocalypse* at *1 En.* 90:13–27).[6]

---

[6] A thorough study of these and other overlaps of tradition in Danielic and early Enochic literature has not yet been a proper focus of study. Such an analysis would not only include the texts discussed below, but also the following traditions: the use of the number "seventy" in Dan. 9:24–27 (cf. *1 En.* 10:12; 89:58; 90:22, 25); the mention of a "flood" in Dan. 9:26 (cf. e.g. *1 En.* 102:2; 89:1–9; 106:15–17); and the mode of existence for the righteous in the afterlife in Dan.

B. The Pseudo-Danielic Fragments (4Q243–245)

B.1. 4QPseudo-Daniel^{a–b} (4Q243–244)

The very fragmentary remains of these manuscripts, which consist of 40 and 13 fragments respectively, were re-edited in the *edition princeps* by John Collins and Peter Flint in 1996.[7] Since they preserve overlapping texts (so 4Q243 frg. 13 and 4Q244 frg. 12), there is little doubt that the two manuscripts belong to the same document.[8] Although these manuscript remains have often been studied together with those of 4Q245 since Józef T. Milik's early discussion (1956),[9] it is appropriate that here we discuss them separately (see section B.1 on 4Q245 below).

The fragments as a whole show an interest in major persons and events in the sacred tradition of Israel. They recount Israel's history in the past and, from the point of view of the real author, apparently contain a prediction of future eschatological events. While there are notable differences in detail among these minute fragments, on the one hand, and in Daniel, on the other (see below), several extant words and phrases confirm that these materials have a Danielic character. These commonalities are five-fold:

(1) the occurrence five times of the proper name "Daniel" (4Q243 frgs. 1, 2, 5 and 4Q244 frgs. 1, 4);
(2) the narrative setting at the court of a foreign king (so 4Q243 frgs. 1–3, 5–6 and 4Q244 frgs. 1–4; cf. Dan. chs. 2–6);
(3) mention of the name "Belshazzar" (4Q243 frg. 2; cf. Dan. 5:1–2, 9, 22, 29–30);
(4) the inclusion of eschatological prophecy (as likely in 4Q243 frgs. 16, 24–26, 33; cf. Dan. 7:15–27; 8:25; 9:24–27; 11:40–12:3); and
(5) an emphasis on the exile as the result of Israel's sins (4Q243 frg. 13 + 4Q244 frg. 12; cf. Dan. 9:4–19).

Less certain, however, are further elements based on questionable readings that Milik took as evidence leaving one with "l'impression que l'ouvrage … est postérieur à *Daniel*."[10] For instance, he argued that 4Q243 16.1 mentions a period of "seventy years" (cf. Dan. 9:2, 20–27); moreover, line 4 refers, according to Milik's

---

12:1–3 (cf. *1 En.* 104:2); on the latter, see Loren T. Stuckenbruck, *1 Enoch 91–108* (CEJL; Berlin: Walter de Gruyter, 2007), pp. 561–577.

[7] In *Parabiblical Texts, Part 3* (DJD 22; Oxford: Oxford University Press, 1996), pp. 95–151 + Plates VII–IX. See also Collins' thorough study, *"Pseudo-Daniel* Revisited", in *RevQ* 17 (1996), pp. 111–150. For the texts and discussion, see also the article by Peter W. Flint, "The Daniel Tradition at Qumran", in eds. John J. Collins and Peter W. Flint, *The Book of Daniel: Composition and Reception* (VTSup 83.2; Leiden / Boston / Köln: Brill, 2001), pp. 329–367.

[8] See Collins and Flint, DJD 22, p. 142. The shared phrases and words correspond exactly in spelling and sequence, and are consistent with their physical placement on the lines of the respective fragments.

[9] See Milik, "'Prière de Nabonide' et autres écrits d'un cycle de Daniel: Fragments araméens de Qumrân 4", *RB* 63 (1956), pp. 411–415.

[10] Milik, "'Prière de Nabonide' et autres écrits d'un cycle de Daniel", p. 415.

reconstruction, to a "fi[rst] kingdom" (cf. Dan. 2:26–45; 7:3–8, 17–24; 8:22), a detail which he surmised belonged to part of a four-kingdom scheme.[11] Milik's readings and construal have been taken a further step by Émile Puech and Florentino García Martínez, who both take for granted that 4Q243–244 (as well as 4Q245) drew their inspiration directly from the book of Daniel.[12] However, as Collins and Flint have correctly noted, a look at the photographic plates shows just how far from being clear Milik's readings of 4Q243 frg. 16 actually are. Though possible, these readings cannot be confirmed; but even if they turn out to be correct, it is still by no means certain that they reflect any reliance on Daniel.[13]

To be sure, some knowledge of the book of Daniel among the 4Q243–244 fragments is not impossible. At the same time, none of the common features listed under (1) through (5) above warrant the conclusion that the book of Daniel had tradition-historical priority *vis-à-vis* the manuscript fragments. Again, as Collins and Flint have cautioned,[14] the names "Daniel" and "Belshazzar" could simply have derived from a common tradition; in addition, the royal court setting is neither unique to the Daniel tradition among the biblical writings,[15] nor to "non-biblical" Dead Sea manuscripts.[16] Furthermore, the notion of eschatological prophecy (see below), found in many biblical and early Jewish writings, cannot confirm any special relationship with the book of Daniel itself. Finally, the view of the exile as punishment for the sins of Israel is likewise widespread, and so provides a tenuous basis on which to posit a dependence of the text in these fragments on

---

[11] Milik, "'Prière de Nabonide' et autres écrits d'un cycle de Daniel", p. 413. Only ‏קד‎[is visible; another possible restoration, suggested by Collins and Flint, is "holy" (‏קד]ישתא‎)–so DJD 22, pp. 108–109 (see pp. 150–151 for problems posed by Milik's restoration).

[12] So Puech, *La croyance des Esséniens en la vie future: immortalité, resurrection, vie éternelle* (Paris: Gabalda, 1993), pp. 568–570; idem, "Messianism, Resurrection, and Eschatology at Qumran and in the New Testament", in eds. Eugene Ulrich and James C. VanderKam, *The Community of the Renewed Covenant: The Notre Dame Symposium on the Dead Sea Scrolls* (CJA 10; Notre Dame, IN: University of Notre Dame Press, 1994), pp. 247–248. See also Florentino García Martínez, "4QPseudo Daniel Aramaic and the Pseudo-Danielic Literature", in *idem, Qumran and Apocalyptic: Studies on the Aramaic Texts from Qumran* (STDJ 9; Leiden: Brill, 1992), pp. 137–149.

[13] For Milik ("'Prière de Nabonide' et autres écrits d'un cycle de Daniel", p. 415) 4Q243 frgs. 19 and 21 are significant for determining the date of composition. Frg. 21.2 contains the Hellenistic name in Heb. transliteration: ‏בלכרוס‎, which Milik identified as a possible reference to Alexander Balas, who set himself up as the successor of Antiochus Epiphanes. This identification with the Greek name Βαλας remains unverifiable (so also Collins and Flint in DJD 22, pp. 137 and 150). Milik's further restoration and identification of the incomplete ‏רהוס‎ in 4Q243 19.2 with the Seleucid ruler Demetrius is problematic: in 4Q169 3+4 i 2 this name is restored ‏דמי[תרוס‎, i. e. without the *he* between *reš* and *waw*. Moreover, Puech's suggestion that the letters refer to "Darius" is equally untenable (see the spelling ‏דריוש‎ in Dan. 6:1–2, 26, 29; 9:1; 11:1 and wherever the name occurs among the Dead Sea materials (e. g., *4QProto-Esther* [= 4Q550] lines 5–6).

[14] DJD 22, pp. 134–136.

[15] See, for instance, the Joseph story in Gen. 39–41 and the book of Esther.

[16] So esp. the Aramaic texts of *4QPrayer of Nabonidus* (=4Q242), the so-called "proto-Esther" document (4Q550), and possibly in 4Q246 col. i.

Daniel. By contrast, the overlapping and combined texts in 4Q243 frg. 13 and 4Q244 frg. 12[17] seem to regard the exile as the result of God's anger at the Israelites who were "sacri]ficing their children to the demons of error" (cf. Ps. 106:37, 40: "they sacrifice their sons and their daughters to demons [לשדים, τοῖς δαιμονίοις]"),[18] whereas in Daniel the sins of Israel are more generally attributed to Israel's transgression of the Torah (Dan. 9:11). In fact, more than Daniel, the motif of sacrificing to demonic beings in 4Q243–244 comes closer to the early Enochic tradition and to *Jubilees*. Though *1 Enoch* does not refer to the sacrificing of children (so that Ps. 106:37 remains in view), it is the Enochic and not the Danielic tradition that refers twice to the giving of sacrifice or worship to demonic beings. The first text is the *Book of Watchers* at *1 Enoch* 19:1, according to which sacrificing to "demons" is blamed on the spirits of the disobedient angels as they "lead people astray" (πλανήσει αὐτούς; Eth. *yāsehtewwomu*). While it is likely here that the text has practices of idolatry among Gentiles in view, the other Enochic text, the *Epistle of Enoch* at *1 Enoch* 99:7, attributes – like 4Q243–244 – such activity to disobedient Jews, who are designated as "sinners". The *Epistle* states that they "will worship evil spirits and demons and every (kind of) error (*ṭā'ot*)" (Eth.; the Grk. reads "worship [phan]toms and demons [and abomina]tions and evi[l] spirits and all (kinds of) errors [πάσαις ταῖς πλάναις]").[19] In *Jubilees* 1:11 the allusion to Psalm 106:37 is unmistakable, and the language overlaps almost identically with that of 4Q243–244: "they will sacrifice their children to demons". Additionally, the text also refers to "the error of their hearts". The resulting impression for the *4QPseudo Daniel* fragments is that they are not merely receiving tradition from Daniel but, at this point, are negotiating traditions that are conveyed through apocalyptic texts in which demonology expressly plays a role in the recasting of sacred history.

4QPseudo Daniel also shares other features with the Enochic tradition. These elements include the following: First, in contrast to Daniel, those who are righteous are designated as "the elect" who "will be gathered together" (4Q243 24.2; cf. the *Apocalypse of Weeks* at *1 En.* 93:10 and *Animal Apocalypse* at *1 En.* 90:33). Second, and in development of the point raised in the previous paragraph, though more broadly, the presence of the demonic is written into the sacred history of Israel (4Q243 frg. 13 + 4Q244 frg. 12; cf. *Book of Watchers* at *1 En.* chs. 6–8;

---

[17] See Collins and Flint, DJD 22, p. 142.

[18] Concerning the influence of Ps. 106 see Klaus Beyer, *Die aramäischen Texte vom Toten Meer. Ergänzungsband* (Göttingen: Vandenhoeck & Ruprecht, 1994), pp. 105 and 107 (hereafter *ATTM Ergänzungsband*). The association of the straying Israelites with "demons of error" is consistent with the tone elsewhere in 4Q243; see frg. 24.1–2, in which a group that has been "led astray" is distinguished from "the elect" who "will be gathered".

[19] See, however, the quotation in Tertullian, *de Idolotria* 4, which does not mention "error/s". For the text, translation, critical notes and commentary on these versions, see Stuckenbruck, *1 Enoch 91–108*, pp. 393–395 and 399–403. The early association between demons and idolatry also occurs among 2nd cent. writings in *Jub.* 1:11 and 22:17–18.

15–16; the *Animal Apocalypse* at *1 En.* 86:1–6; 88:1–3; 89:59–90:25, which refers to the "stars" and "the seventy shepherds").[20] Third, and unlike Daniel, 4Q243–244 show a strong interest in pre-exilic events in Israel's sacred history. This last point merits further comment.

Although the evidence is fragmentary, the perspective on biblical history in 4Q243–244 differs significantly from that of Daniel's account. The period of history with which the book of Daniel is concerned spans from the exile until the time of Antiochus Epiphanes. This history is presented in the form of *vaticinium ex eventu* from the perspective of the real author, while most, if not all, of it lies in the future for the ostensible 6th century B.C.E. author, Daniel.[21] The pseudo-Danielic fragments, however, are not only concerned with post-exilic times (including the Hellenistic period), but they also, as does the Enochic *Animal Apocalypse*, cover sacred history from the primeval and patriarchal periods. Several fragments, which reflect this perspective, may be assigned to an account of the primeval, diluvian, and early post-diluvian history. The texts mention "Enoch" (4Q243 9.1), "Noah" and "the Flood" (4Q244 8.2–3), "Mount Lubar" (4Q244 8.3),[22] and "the h[igh?] tower" (likely an allusion to the tower in Babel, Gen. 11:1–9; 4Q243 10.2; 4Q244 9.2).[23] Given the likelihood that the history in 4Q243–244 is being recounted by and attributed to Daniel himself, not all events covered in the narrative context are, strictly speaking, *vaticinia ex eventu*. While Collins and Flint find precedent for this combination of past with "future" accounts in *Jubilees*,[24] the closest analogy for such a structure is to be found in the *Animal Apocalypse*. The

---

[20] The view of 4Q243–244 thus seems to correspond more closely to the thought world of the *Animal Apocalypse* than with that of the *Book of Watchers*. The latter, along with the *Book of Giants*, develops the tradition of sin being introduced into the world by the disobedient watchers led by Shemiḥazah and ʿAsaʾel. In contrast, the *Animal Apocalypse* emphasizes that the sad state of affairs in the world is the result of human sin that existed before the angels' rebellion (*1 En.* 85:4–5) and results in Israel's misfortunes following the exile (so *1 En.* 89:59–90:25); the "seventy shepherds" only react indirectly to the Israelites' misdeeds by allowing her enemies, represented by wild animals, to punish them; a similar role is played by "Belial" and "the angels of destruction" in 4Q390 1.9–11 and 2 i 4, 6–7.

[21] So similarly 4Q390 which focuses on "future" events from the perspective of Moses.

[22] Mt. Lubar is also mentioned in the *Book of Giants* at 6Q8 26.1. However, the relation to Enochic tradition in 4Q244 8 is not exclusive, since this mountain is designated as the place where the ark came to rest in *Jub.* 5:28 and 7:1. Moreover, according to the *Genesis Apocryphon* at 1Q20 xii 13 Noah planted a vineyard there.

[23] This tower, designated by מגדלא, is identified with the Babel tower by Milik, "'Prière de Nabonide' et autres écrits d'un cycle de Daniel", p. 412. If Milik is correct, the inclusion of the event related to the tower would be suitable for a literary setting in the royal court of the king of Babel, Nebuchadnezzar.

[24] So in DJD 22, p. 135, where Collins and Flint draw attention to the retelling of primeval and patriarchal biblical history (i. e., Gen. 1 until the giving of the Torah in Exod. 20) from Moses' perspective on Mt. Sinai, in combination with the eschatological sections in chs. 1 and 23. However, Collins and Flint recognize that the parallels only exist in terms of content; *Jubilees* as a whole is not structured as a survey of past history that leads to an ostensible future and beyond to eschatological events.

Enochic author's account in *1 Enoch* 85–86 begins with Adam and the fallen "stars", events in the narrative from Enoch's past, before covering the biblical story and eschatological events that lie in Enoch's future. In 4Q243–244, the mention of "Enoch" from before the Flood, the interest in early biblical history as an ostensible future, and the apparent literary pattern and setting all suggest that here we have an blending of Danielic and Enoch traditions that takes a form found in neither Daniel nor in the *Animal Apocalypse*.

If either the book of Daniel or Enochic tradition (esp. the *Animal Apocalypse*) have wielded any influence on the pseudo-Daniel materials, as is frequently supposed, then their respective forms and emphases have been significantly neutralized. Neither Daniel nor early Enoch tradition can be said to have gained an "upper hand" in having shaped the content of 4Q243–244, the fragments of which instead put on display a cross-fertilization between intellectual traditions associated with both Daniel and Enoch. These traditions would have been in a state of flux, not only after but perhaps also before and during the Maccabean crisis.

B.2. 4QPseudo-Daniel^b (4Q245)

Milik initially treated this manuscript together with 4Q243–244 as part of one composition,[25] a position since followed by a number of others.[26] Features that might favor the identification of 4Q245 as belonging to the same document as 4Q243–244 include the following: (1) the occurrence of the name "Daniel" (4Q245 1 i 3); (2) the inclusion of a list of names of priests given in chronological order (1 i 5–10); (3) a reference to "Qahat" (קהת, 1 i 5; cf.].רק at 4Q243 28.1); and (4) a similar emphasis on the wicked who "have gone astray" (4Q245 2.3; cf. 4Q243 24.1).

Features (1) and (3), however, are not decisive. Moreover, the list of priests' names in (2) – from the very beginning of the priesthood (Qahat) until at least the time of "Simon" in the 2nd century B.C.E. – followed by the chronological list of kings (lines 11–12, including "David" and "Solomon") are difficult to fit into the sacred history as found in 4Q243–244.[27]

Dependence of 4Q245 on the book of Daniel has also found scholarly support. Besides the occurrence of the prophet's name "Daniel" (1 ii 3), the connection to

---

[25] Milik, "'Prière de Nabonide' et autres écrits d'un cycle de Daniel", pp. 411–415.

[26] So esp. Alfred Mertens, *Das Buch Daniel im Lichte der Texte vom Toten Meer* (SBM 12; Stuttgart: Echter, 1971), pp. 43–46 (though regarding 4Q245 as a different work or recension, he nevertheless arranges 4Q243–245 together); García Martínez, "4QPseudo Daniel", pp. 137–140; Robert Eisenman and Michael O. Wise, *The Dead Sea Scrolls Uncovered* (Shaftsbury, UK: Element, 1992), pp. 64–68; Puech, *La Croyance des Esséniens*, p. 568; Beyer, *ATTM Ergänzungsband*, pp. 105–107; and Collins and Flint, "4Q245 (4QpsDan^c)", pp. 153–164.

[27] So argued by Collins and Flint, in DJD 22, p. 155.

Daniel is based on a purported allusion to resurrection (Dan. 12:2) in the expression יקומון, "they shall arise" (4Q245 2.4).[28] In Daniel, however, the Hebrew term used is יקיצו, "they will awake", which refers to the lot of both the righteous (eternal life) and the wicked (eternal contempt). Moreover, the subject of the verb in 4Q245 is not as clear as in Daniel. Flint stresses that – unlike Daniel 12:2, in which both the righteous and the wicked will awake – in 4Q245 it is only the righteous who shall "arise" and "return" (1 ii 5), not those who live "in blindness and have gone astray" (1 ii 3).[29] In the face of the lacunae, however, the precise context of the verb remains uncertain. In any case, the mention of a subsequent return in 4Q245 1 ii 5 suggests how problematic it is to infer a technical term for some form of post-mortem resuscitation as in Daniel 12:1–3.[30]

There is thus no firm evidence that details in 4Q245 are to be traced back to the book of Daniel in any way. The use of "blindness" and "going astray" as metaphors to describe the wicked does not occur in Daniel at all, while both are abundantly attested in the Hebrew Bible.[31] It is perhaps significant in this respect that these metaphors are combined in the *Animal Apocalypse* (cf. *1 En.* 89:32–33, 54) and that the vision goes on to refer to the "dim-sightedness" and "blindness" of the unfaithful Israelite "sheep" (e. g., *1 En.* 89:74; 90:7, 26).

This convergence of metaphors (excepting the "sheep" imagery) is, among Jewish documents composed before the mid-2nd century B. C. E., shared only with the *Animal Apocalypse*. While this commonality does not necessarily mean that the writer of 4Q245 has actually borrowed his description of the wicked directly from the *Animal Apocalypse*, it is possible that, as in the case of 4Q243–244, these materials preserve the early stages of an intellectual tradition in which the tradition-historical boundaries between Danielic and the Enochic literature from the 2nd century B. C. E. were still fluid.

---

[28] So García Martínez, "4QPseudo Daniel", p. 146 and Puech, *La Croyance des Esséniens*, p. 569 n. 12.

[29] See Peter W. Flint, "4Qpseudo-Daniel ar^c (4Q245) and the Restoration of the Priesthood", *RevQ* 17 (1996), pp. 137–150 (here p. 148).

[30] A reading of the text in light of Isa. 26:14 and 19 is, for this reason, misleading. Moreover, Flint argues convincingly ("4Qpseudo-Daniel ar^c (4Q245)", p. 148) that the wicked mentioned in line 3 (those who lived in "blindness and have gone astray") are hardly in "a post-resurrection condition".

[31] Yet it is significant that among the biblical writings these metaphors *do not occur together*: "blindness" (עור) in Deut. 27:18; 28:28–29: Isa. 59:10; Zeph. 1:17; Lam. 4:14; and "going astray" (סרר, תעה) in Ps. 58:4; 119:176; Prov. 7:5; Isa. 53:6; Ezek. 14:11; 14:10, 15; 48:11; Hos. 4:16. So also CD at i 9, 14–15; ii 6, 13, 16; iii 1, 4, 14; and iv 1.

C. The Book of Giants

C.1. 4QBook of Giants[b] (4Q530 2 ii + 6–12(?) lines 15b–20)[32]

Although fragments belonging to the *Book of Giants* among the Dead Sea materials were known after Milik's publication of some of them in 1971 and 1976,[33] they have yet to figure properly in discussions of the early Enochic literature.[34] For instance, while frequent comparisons are made between the throne vision of Daniel 7:9–14 and that in the *Book of Watchers* (in *1 En.* 14:8–25), the more immediate background of Daniel 7 in relation to the *Book of Giants* (as preserved in 4Q530) and the implications of such a discussion have been insufficiently recognized.[35] There are several reasons for this. Firstly, until the photographs of the unpublished materials from Cave 4 were made generally accessible in 1991–1993,[36] no scholar outside the official editorial team had been given the opportunity to study the partially shrunken and damaged fragments of 4Q530 2 ii + 6–12(?),[37] the script of which is unusual among the Dead Sea manuscripts.[38] Second,

---

[32] For a fuller treatment of this passage, see Loren T. Stuckenbruck, *The Book of Giants from Qumran* (TSAJ 63; Tübingen: Mohr Siebeck, 1997), pp. 119–123 and *idem*, "The Throne-Theophany of the Book of Giants: Some New Light on the Background of Daniel 7", in eds. Stanley E. Porter and Craig A. Evans, *The Scrolls and the Scriptures* (JSPSup 26; Sheffield: Sheffield Academic Press, 1997), pp. 211–220.

[33] See Józef T. Milik, "Turfan et Qumran: Livre des géants juif et manichéen", in eds. Gerd Jeremias, Heinz-Wolfgang Kuhn and Hartmut Stegemann, *Tradition und Glaube. Das frühe Christentum in seiner Umwelt* (Göttingen: Vandenhoeck & Ruprecht, 1971), pp. 117–127 and idem, *The Books of Enoch*, pp. 4, 6–7, 57–58, 230, 236–238, and 298–339.

[34] The description of the *Book of Giants* as an Enochic work is warranted by the crucial role as interpreter *par excellence* given to Enoch in the work (see Stuckenbruck, *The Book of Giants from Qumran*, pp. 25–27, 116–119, and 124–27), by the apparent reliance of the work on the *Book of Watchers* (ibid., pp. 24–25), and by the real, though not certain possibility that 4QEnoch[c] (=4Q204) and 4QEnGiants[a] (=4Q203) were copied by the same scribe, if not as part of the same manuscript.

[35] See now, however, two recent discussions that attempt to include the *Book of Giants* within the discussion of Dan. 7 and to interact with my thesis, see Ryan E. Stokes, "The Throne Visions of Daniel 7, 1 Enoch 14, and the Qumran Book of Giants: An Analysis of Their Literary Relationship", *DSD* 15 (2008), pp. 340–358 and Jonathan R. Trotter, "The Tradition of the Throne Vision in the Second Temple Period: Daniel 7:9–10, 1 Enoch 14:18–23, and the Book of Giants (4Q530)", *RevQ* 99 (2012), pp. 451–466.

[36] Photographic collections that included 4Q530 were published by Robert H. Eisenman and James M. Robinson, *A Facsimile Edition of the Dead Sea Scrolls* (2 vols.; Washington D.C.: Biblical Archeological Society, 1991), Plates 80, 302, 887, and 1516; and by Emanuel Tov with the collaboration of Stephen J. Pfann, in *The Dead Sea Scrolls on Microfiche. A Comprehensive Facsimile Edition of the Texts from the Judaean Desert, Companion Volume* (Leiden: Brill and IDC, 1993), PAM photographs 40.620, 41.444, 42.496, and 43.568.

[37] The first to do so was Beyer, *ATTM Ergänzungsband*, pp. 120–121.

[38] Frank Moore Cross described the script of 4Q530, which he at the time designated "4QPs.-Enoch", as "an unusual semicursive" to be dated between 100 and 50 B.C.E.; see Frank Moore Cross, "The Development of Jewish Scripts", in ed. G. Ernest Wright, *The Bible and the Ancient Near East: Essays in Honor of William Foxwell Albright* (New York: Doubleday, 1961), pp. 133–202 (here p. 149).

while Milik offered readings for 4Q530 in his edition of the Enochic fragments, he did so without any accompanying photographs and did not include any readings for the passage in question: lines 17–19 of fragment 2 ii + 6–12 (?). Third, and most important for purposes of the present discussion, Milik merely summarized the content of these lines by stating that they preserve a description of divine judgment "s'inspire de Dan 7:9–10".[39] Whereas Klaus Beyer and John C. Reeves adopted a more cautious approach by referring to no more than a similarity between lines 17–19 and the throne-theophany of Daniel 7:9–10,[40] Florentino García Martínez reasoned that if Milik's claim of literary dependence of the *Book of Giants* on Daniel 7 is correct, then one may suppose that it was composed earlier "by the middle of the second century BCE".[41] A comparative analysis, however, provides every reason to reach a conclusion that runs counter to the impression left by Milik's initial comments on the passage. In addition, we are now placed in a better position to consider the tradition-historical relationship between Daniel and Enochic visions of judgment.

Before offering several observations, we present the passage from 4Q530 2 ii + 6–12 (?), lines 15b–20 in a comparative table with Daniel 7:9–10, 28 below. Two further visions, details of which occasionally overlap with one or both of these texts, though in a less sustained way, are also taken into consideration: *Book of Watchers* (*1 En.* 14:8–25) and the *Animal Apocalypse* (*1 En.* 90:14–27)–these are provided in the middle column labeled *BW/AA* (see next page).

The text from the *Book of Giants* occurs in a column that relates two dream visions seen by the giant brothers 'Ohyah and Hahyah, who in the broader storyline are identified as the sons of the disobedient angel Shemiḥazah. Similar to the *Book of Watchers*, the narrative is an elaboration of the biblical tradition, according to which these giants are the offspring of "the sons of God" and "daughters of humanity". Whereas in the biblical tradition the Great Flood occurs as punishment resulting from the increase of human sin on earth (Gen. 6:3, 5–7), the Enochic traditions in the *Book of Watchers* (*1 En.* 6:1–16:3) and the *Book of Giants* regard the Flood as God's response to the catastrophic events brought into the world by the disobedience of the angels and the giants' overwhelming oppression of humanity (*1 En.* 7:3–4; 8:4; 9:9–10). In 4Q530 2 ii + 6–12(?), the giant brothers' dreams function as visions that underscore that they will not escape punishment for their deeds, for which they will be held accountable and, indeed, punished decisively. It is the figure of Enoch who interprets these dreams for them (4Q530 2 ii + 6–12(?), lines 21–23 and 7 ii). In the earlier part of 4Q530 2 ii + 6–12(?), lines

---

[39] Milik, *The Books of Enoch*, p. 303. So also in Milik, "Turfan et Qumran: Livre des géants juif et manichéen", p. 122.

[40] Beyer, *Die aramäischen Texte vom Toten Meer* (Göttingen: Vandenhoeck & Ruprecht, 1984), p. 264 n. 1 and Reeves, *Jewish Lore in Manichean Cosmogony. Studies in the Book of Giants Traditions* (MHUC 14; Cincinnati: Hebrew Union College, 1992), p. 92.

[41] García Martínez, "The Book of Giants", in *idem, Qumran and Apocalyptic* (bibl. in n. 12 above), pp. 97–115, esp. p. 104.

Book of Giants (4Q530 2 ii + 6–12(?), lines 15b–20)	BW/AA (1 En.)	Daniel 7:9–10, 28
(15b–16a) I too saw something amazing during this night:	(90:20) I saw until	(9a) I was looking until (cf. 4Q530 2 ii + 6–12, line 9)
(16b) [Be]hold, the Ruler of the Heavens descended to the earth	(90:20) pleasant land	
(17a) and *thrones were erected* (וכרסון רמיו)	(90:20) a throne was constructed	(9b) *thrones were set up* (כרסון רמיו)
(17b) and the Great Holy One *sat d[own* (י]ת[ב)	(14:20) the Great Glory *sat* on it	(9c) the Ancient of Days *sat down* (יתב)
	(90:20) the Lord of the sheep *sat* on it	
	(14:20) *his clothing* like the appearance of the sun and *whiter* than much snow	(9d) *his clothing* (was) like snow-white
		(9e) and the hair of his head (was) like white wool
	(14:17) its floor was *of fire*	(9f) his throne (was) flames *of fire*
	(14:18) *its wheels* were like the shining sun	(9g) *its wheels* (were) a burning fire
	(14:19) from under the throne *came forth* rivers of flaming fire	(10) a river of fire flowed and *went forth* from before it (see 10c)
(17c) *a hundred hu]ndred* (were) *serving him* (לה משמשין)		
(17d–18a) *a thousand thousands* [(were) worshipping?] him (ל]ה [אלף אלפין)		(10c) *a thousand thousands served him* (אלף אלפים ישמשונה)
(18b) a]ll *stood [be]fore him* (ק]דמוה[י קימין) [	(14:22) *a myriad myriads stood before him*	(10d) *a myriad myriads stood before him* (יקומון)
(18–d) *and behold* (ואר[ו)		
[book]s *were opened* (וספרין פתיחו) and judgment (דין) was spoken	(90:17) he opened those *books*	(10e) *the court* (דינא) sat down
(18d–19a) and the judgment of (די]ן) [the Great One] (was) wr]itten [in a book] and (was) sealed in an inscription [	(90:24) and judgment took place	(10f) *and books were opened* (וספרין פתיחו)
(19b)] for every living being and (all) flesh and upon [	(90:20) and he took all the sealed books	
(20) here is the end of the dream (אנתה סוף חלמא דן)		(28) here is the end of the matter (עד כה סופא די מלתא)

7–12) Hahyah tells his fellow giants about an ominous vision he has had, while the throne-scene of judgment in lines 16b–20 is told by 'Ohyah. Daniel 7, of course, does not mention anything about either the giants or rebellious angels. Here, the *Book of Giants* broadly fits into the early Enoch tradition, in which the visions related to judgment are concerned with the divine punishment of the fallen angels; in the *Book of Watchers* the throne vision culminates in a divine pronouncement of punishment against the angels and their progeny (*1 En.* chs. 15–16) and in the *Animal Apocalypse* the judgment is not only carried out against the inimical oppressors of Israel but also against the "seventy shepherds" who have functioned as disobedient angelic beings in the storyline (cf. *1 En.* 89:59–67).

The number of correspondences between the passages in 4Q530 and Daniel 7 makes a tradition-historical connection among them likely. These correspondences are as follows: First, they open and conclude with similar formulae (4Q530 2 ii + 6–12(?), line 16 [cf. also line 9] and Dan. 7:9; and 4Q530 line 20 and Dan. 7:28). Second, in addition to some conjunctions and pronominal suffixes, both passages share at least eight vocabulary words (*throne, sit down, serve, thousand, book, before, arise/stand, open*). Third and significantly, many of the shared lexical items are preserved in the same grammatical form: *thrones* in the absolute plural; *sat down* in the G perfect 3rd person singular; *books* in the absolute plural; *were opened* (in the G passive perfect 3rd person plural); *before him* as a preposition with 3rd person pronominal suffix; and *thousand thousands* in the absolute singular and plural.[42] Fourth, the parallel phrases *all* occur in the same relative sequence (cf. 4Q530 2 ii + 6–12(?), lines 17a, b, c-d, 18b, c corresponding to Dan. 7:9b, c, 10c-d, f). Fifth and finally, among the five parallel phrases the individual parts also occur in the same sequence. This correspondence cannot be observed in the parallel passages in either the *Book of Watchers* or *Animal Apocalypse*.

Despite the extent of these parallels, it is less certain how the texts are to be conceived in relation to one another. Nevertheless, Milik's assumption that the tradition in Daniel 7 served as a *Vorlage* for the *Book of Giants* text is not the only possible construal. It is important in the present context to consider a number of further alternatives: (1) the text in Daniel depends directly on the Enochic *Book of Giants* (opposite to Milik's view); (2) the *Book of Giants* is adapted from a tradition more faithfully preserved in the book of Daniel; (3) Daniel derives from a tradition more faithfully preserved in the *Book of Giants*; (4) Daniel betrays an awareness of a broader range of Enochic tradition, not only what is preserved in the *Book of Giants*, but also of the throne-room vision in the *Book of Watchers*.

Given the differences between the passages it is unlikely that the author(s) of the *Book of Giants* depended on Daniel, whether directly or indirectly, in any form. A comparative analysis, which goes beyond the two passages to include *1*

---

[42] In addition, we may note the G passive perfect equivalents רמיו (Dan. 7:9b) and יחיטו 4)Q530 2 ii + 6–12(?), line 17a), and the correspondence between יקומון (Dan. 7:10d) and הוא קאמין (4Q530 2 ii + 6–12(?), 18b).

Enoch 14:8–25 and 90:13–27,[43] provides some clues about how the throne-theophanic tradition in the book of Daniel may have developed. Most obviously, the differences include the following features:

(1) The visions are seen by different figures who are righteous (so in Daniel; similarly the Enochic seer in *1 En.* 14 and 90). In the *Book of Giants*, on the other hand, the visionary is a culpable figure, one of the giants. This difference relates closely to another incongruity, namely, that unlike the visions in the *Book of Watchers* and Daniel, the *Book of Giants* texts offer no description of the enthroned divine figure. The latter may not have wished a vision of the divine, in a strict detailed sense, to be attributed to an evil character.

(2) The subject of the theophany is variously designated: "the Ruler of the Heavens" (*Book of Giants*, line 16b), "the Great Holy One" (*Book of Giants*, line 17b and *1 En.* 14:1), "the Great Glory" (*1 En.* 14:20), "the Lord of the sheep" (*1 En.* 90:20), and "Ancient of Days" (Dan. 7:9).

(3) The giant's vision in 4Q530 restricts the court session to being in the presence of "the Great Holy One" (though the text can speak of "thrones"), similar to the vision in *1 Enoch* 14, in which no court is held apart from God (v. 23a). In Daniel, on the other hand, both God (v. 9c) and the heavenly court (v. 10e) seat themselves.

(4) Similar to the theophany of the *Book of Watchers* (*1 En.* 14) the Danielic text implies that divine judgment occurs in heaven, whereas in both the *Book of Giants* (line 16b) and the *Animal Apocalypse* (*1 En.* 90:20 – "a pleasant land") it takes place on earth. The *Book of Giants* expressly states that it is on earth where the thrones are erected, and it is here to where "the Ruler of the Heavens" has descended.[44]

(5) The number of worshipers differs: while the *Book of Giants* refers to only "hundreds" and "thousands" (lines 17c, d), Daniel speaks of "thousands" and "myriad myriads" (v. 10c, d) and the *Book of Watchers* similarly mentions "a myriad myriads" (*1 En.* 14:23).

(6) Daniel's vision of judgment is targeted against the mythic "beast", which represents the contemporary historical figure of Antiochus Epiphanes (Dan. 7:11–12). The vision in the *Book of Giants*, however, is concerned with the punishment of the disobedient angels and their offspring, a judgment that occurs provisionally through the Great Flood and that will be consummate in the eschatological judgment.[45] Whereas Enoch's vision in the *Book of Watchers* (*1 En.* 14) is a prelude to divine judgment against the fallen angels and the giants (*1 En.* 16:1), the punishment scene in the *Animal Apocalypse* focuses on the final destruction of both evil angelic forces ("stars", "seventy shepherds") and those whom the author considers disobedient Jews (*1 En.* 90:24–27).

(7) The vision in the *Book of Giants*, similar to *1 Enoch* 14, makes no reference to an intermediary, that is, a figure between God and the visionary who acts on God's behalf. By contrast, in Daniel 7 "one like a son of man" becomes involved in the description of

---

[43] The throne visions in the *Book of Parables* (esp. *1 En.* 46 and 71) need not be considered here since they are late (late 1st cent. B.C.E. at the earliest) and therefore do not throw light on the background of Daniel, but rather demonstrate the influence of Dan. 7.

[44] The *Animal Apocalypse* states nothing about how "the Lord of the Sheep" reached the "pleasant land"; his throne is simply constructed there.

[45] I see no reason to specify a particular socio-historical or political reality behind the giants in the *Book of Giants*, such as vicissitudes of Seleucid rule in Judaea leading to and during the Maccabean Revolt. The allusion to such reality is indirect, insofar as it draws on the story of the rebellious angels in the *Book of Watchers* which, in turn, took shape in the aftermath of Alexander the Great's conquests during the late 4th and early-mid 3rd centuries B.C.E.

divine judgment (7:13–14). Another Enochic tradition in the *Animal Apocalypse*, however, provides a much closer analogy in this respect to the book of Daniel. Here a humanlike angelic figure, which is identified as "one of those seven snow-white ones" (*1 En.* 90:22), participates in the judgment as a court scribe who has recorded the deeds of the wicked seventy shepherds in a book (90:14, 17, 20, 22).[46]

What may be inferred about the relation of Daniel 7 to Enochic tradition, both to the *Book of Giants*, in the first instance, and to the overall tradition in the second? With respect to the former, three points are clear. First, if the comparison is isolated to Daniel 7:10e-f and 4Q530 2 ii + 6–12 (?), lines 18c–19, it emerges that, although the *Book of Giants* transmits a longer pronouncement of divine judgment, 'Ohyah's vision is *not* to be regarded as an expansion of Daniel 7:10.[47] Rather, the elaboration of the divine decree in the *Book of Giants* can be explained as the author's particular concern with the assurance that God's judgment against the giants is irreversible and final. This difference in relative length between the passages, however, raises the possibility that both texts drew on a common tradition, which in this case the *Book of Giants* has adapted to its own interests. That this would happen is not unusual, and it is perhaps worth noting that in the *Animal Apocalypse* the pronouncement is likewise found in a more elaborate form (*1 En.* 90:24–27).

Second, the giant's vision is, in its structure and theology, not as complicated as the better-developed and more intricate one in Daniel 7. It may well be that the author of Daniel 7 has adapted his tradition to include details about the appearance of both the seated figure (v. 9d-e) and the divine throne (vv. 9f–10b). These details reflect not only the formative importance of Ezekiel 1 for the author, but also, its relationship to the features of the divine figure of Enoch's vision in the *Book of Watchers* (esp. *1 En.* 14:17–22, as noted in the synopsis above). Although it is possible that the *Book of Giants* removed such details from a received tradition in order to avoid attributing such visionary speculation to a culpable giant, it seems more likely that Daniel 7 has added such traditional material. In addition, the appearance of "one like a son of man" in Daniel 7:13 is paralleled by a development in the contemporary Enochic tradition of the *Animal Apocalypse*: the humanlike angel-scribe assists "the Lord of the sheep" within the context of eschatological judgment. This parallel leaves the impression that the details in Daniel

---

[46] The differences between Daniel and the *Animal Apocalypse* are numerous: the angelic figure in the latter identifies the angelic figure who comes to the ram's (i. e., Judas Maccabeus') aid in the battle against the Seleucid forces (*1 En.* 90:14; cf. 2 Macc. 11:6–12), while Daniel's figure is not identified with any known historical personage. On the historical allusion see Milik, *The Books of Enoch*, p. 44 and Patrick A. Tiller, *A Commentary on the Animal Apocalypse of 1 Enoch* (SBLEJL 4; Atlanta: Scholars Press, 1993), pp. 65–78, who argues that *1 En.* 90:13b–14 may have been added after the rest of the vision, in order to take the battle into account. If so, an originally mythic figure has been associated with a contemporary event.

[47] Concerning its significance in the context of the early to mid-2nd cent. B. C. E., see Stuckenbruck, *The Book of Giants from Qumran*, pp. 31–40.

7:9–13 concerning the divine figure, the heavenly throne, and the "son of man" – all of which are absent in the *Book of Giants* – are at least to some extent indebted to or paralleled by different elements within the early Enochic tradition.[48]

A third inference is, in my view, decisive about the direction in which the throne-theophany developed. In the *Book of Giants* (lines 17c–18a) the worshipers, as already noted, are numbered in the "hundreds" and "thousands", while in Daniel (7:10c-d) they are given as "thousands" and "a myriad myriads". If a tendency towards inflating numbers is a viable criterion for determining the way a tradition grows, then it is more likely that the "hundreds" and "thousands" preserved in the *Book of Giants* have been transformed into the "thousands" and "a myriad myriads" in Daniel (which may be expanding *1 En.* 14:22) than the other way around.

Though it is difficult simply to maintain that Daniel borrowed the vision directly from the *Book of Giants*, the above considerations make it plausible to think that the latter work has preserved the throne-theophany in an earlier form. The parallels between the passages show not only how indebted the book of Daniel is at this point to one strand of Enochic tradition (*Book of Giants*) for the basic language and structure of the vision, but also how much Daniel's redaction of this tradition was shaped by other Enochic traditions, whether they were already established (the *Book of Watchers*) or were in the process of developing (*Animal Apocalypse*).

D. Conclusion

The evidence considered in the discussion above demonstrates how precarious it is to assume that convergences between Danielic and Enochic traditions are to be interpreted in each instance as developments subsequent to the composition of Daniel. If anything, the opposite is true. During the years leading up to and during the Maccabean crisis, apocalyptic traditions associated with the ante-diluvian Enoch and exilic Daniel were fluid enough for the Danielic tradition, whether in 4Q243–4Q245 or in the book of Daniel itself, to incorporate and adapt ideas found in writings associated with Enoch. If, as Boccaccini suggests, Daniel and the early Enoch literature (i. e., the *Book of Watchers* and *Animal Apocalypse*) were composed by opposing parties,[49] it must be stressed in view of the materials reviewed here that they drew on at least some common traditions not thought by

---

[48] There is no evidence that the text of Daniel 7 has influenced the wording of the Ethiopic tradition as found in either *1 En.* ch. 14 or 90.

[49] Gabriele Boccaccini, *Beyond the Essene Hypothesis: The Parting of the Ways between Enochic and Qumran Judaism* (Grand Rapids: Eerdmans, 1997), pp. 81–86, has argued that the following issues divided a Danielic from an Enochic circle (as attested in the *Animal Apocalypse*): the origin of evil, the importance of the Mosaic Torah, the manner of resistance to the Seleucids, and the legitimacy of the Temple in Jerusalem.

the writers to be incompatible. As in the *Animal Apocalypse*, the pseudo-Danielic materials could combine an apparent interest in ante-diluvian history with an emphasis on human accountability for sin. Moreover, as in the *Book of Watchers*, the *Animal Apocalypse*, and the *Book of Giants*, the book of Daniel could draw on visions of divine judgment, and, comparable to the *Animal Apocalypse*, could specifically relate eschatological judgment of the wicked to contemporary events. These similarities, and indeed even substantial verbal overlaps of tradition, allow for the possibility that the author of Daniel 7 knew the early Enochic traditions well enough to draw on and then adapt them for his own purposes. Nowhere is this clearer than in the throne-theophany itself. However, as much as Daniel's party may have differentiated itself during the Maccabean crisis from an Enochic group, the respective intellectual traditions remained in sufficiently close contact for Enoch to have continued to inform the visions and ideas contained in the Danielic literature.

Chapter Six

The Book of Tobit and the Problem of "Magic"

During the final three centuries before the Common Era, the legitimacy of using "magico-medical"[1] cures against illness seems to have been a matter of debate among Jewish circles.[2] Accordingly, the literature from this period offers fundamentally different perspectives that subsequently had implications for praxis. The present discussion takes the Book of Tobit as the point of departure. As will become clear in relation to the topic at hand, it is difficult simply to speak of Tobit "as a book", that is, as a single text to which readers can attribute a particular line of thought. Accordingly, I would like to offer some observations on how differences observed among the recensions of Tobit throw light on the character of the cures to the predicaments faced by Tobit and Sarah in the narrative. After briefly delineating the basic positions regarding medicines and doctors espoused by Jewish writers during the Second Temple period, I shall attempt to present the views to be found in the Book of Tobit by drawing attention to the significance of differences between the ancient versions of the story.

---

[1] For reasons that will become clear in the discussion of Tobit below, it is important that the categories of "medicine" and "magic" not be neatly distinguished from one another. Scholars and students of antiquity have gone to considerable lengths in their attempts to define what "magic" is in contrast, for example, to "religion"; see David E. Aune, "Magic in Early Christianity", in ed. Wolfgang Haase, *Aufstieg und Niedergang der römischen Welt* II.23.2 (Berlin / New York: Walter de Gruyter, 1980), pp. 1507–1557, who therefore attempts to define "magic" sociologically, while subordinating the conceptual dimension which he terms "goal-oriented practices with virtually guaranteed results" (p. 1515). However, rather than trying to define what magic is from the "outside" of a given passage from antiquity (the "etic" approach), it is important that one attempt to listen to what such a text itself may have to say about its author's particular conception of the problem (the "emic" approach), which may in turn have varied from that of other writers. In the present discussion on Tobit, this is what I shall venture to do. For a still useful treatment of "etic" and "emic" approaches in the study of magic from antiquity, see Susan R. Garrett, *The Demise of the Devil* (Minneapolis: Fortress Press, 1989), pp. 27–36.

[2] For a treatment of this debate, within the context of the Jewish literature covered in this chapter and the wider world of classical antiquity, see Maria Chrysovergi's forthcoming monograph, *Attitudes towards the Use of Medicine in Jewish Literature from the Third and Second Centuries BCE* (JSJSup; Leiden: Brill, 2014).

1. Early Jewish Traditions Opposed to the Use of Medicines

On the one side, there was considerable suspicion towards the application of medicines and, along with it, the practice of consulting physicians. This view could be derived from the basic notion in Exodus 15:26, according to which *God* is declared to be Israel's physician: כי אני יהוה רפאך.[3] A logical extension of this conviction was the widespread belief that sickness and other misfortunes experienced by people are ultimately the result of human wrongdoing and transgression, that is, that bad circumstances are at least ideally mitigated or altogether removed through the appropriation of divine forgiveness and mercy.

Such a framework for understanding illness surfaces in both the Hebrew Bible and early Jewish sources. Among the Jewish scriptures, there are passages that attest that disease could be interpreted as being the result of divine punishment for a misdeed.[4] The assumption of such texts is that the cure or restoration to wholeness can only appropriately come from God (Ex. 15:26; 23:25; Deut. 7:15; 1 Kgs. 13:6; 2 Chr. 7:14; Ps. 41:3 and 103:3). Consequently, resorting to doctors would be considered unacceptable, as this could be thought to encroach upon a divine prerogative.[5] For example, the author of 2 Chronicles 16:12, in contrast to the earlier parallel version in 1 Kings 15:23, deems it reprehensible that Asa the king of Judah, when struck with a malady in his feet, sought the help of doctors without relying on the Lord.[6]

---

[3] See the Septuagint tradition: ἐγὼ γάρ εἰμι κύριος ὁ ἰώμενός σε; cf. similarly Deut. 32:39; Job 5:17–18. Concerning the development of this idea, which crystalized in the post-exilic period, see Norbert Lohfink, "'Ich bin Jahwe, dein Arzt' (Ex 15,26). Gott, Gesellschaft und menschliche Gesundheit in einer nachexilischen Pentateuchbearbeitung (Ex 15,25b.26)", in *idem et al.*, *"Ich will euer Gott werden". Beispiele biblischen Redens von Gott* (SB 100; Stuttgart: Verlag Katholisches Bibelwerk, 1981), pp. 11–73 and esp. Herbert Niehr, "JHWH als Arzt. Herkunft und Geschichte einer alttestamentlichen Gottesprädikation", *BZ* 35 (1991), pp. 3–17. See further Bernd Kollmann, "Göttliche Offenbarung magisch-pharmakologischer Heilkunst im Buch Tobit", *ZAW* 106 (1994), pp. 289–299 (here pp. 289–291) and his monograph, *Jesus und die Christen als Wundertäter. Studien zu Magie, Medizin und Schamanismus in Antike und Christentum* (FRLANT 170; Göttingen: Vandenhoeck & Ruprecht, 1996), esp. pp. 118–173.

[4] See for instance the following passages: (a) Num. 12:4–15, according to which Miriam is struck with leprosy for having criticized Moses; (b) Deut. 28:22, 27, 35 (cf. 28:61; 29:22), a catalogue of afflictions to come upon Israel because of her disobedience to the covenant; (c) 1 Kgs. 13:4–6, which relates that Jeroboam's hand withered because of his wickedness and that later it is restored through the prophet; (d) 2 Chr. 21:18, in which Jehoram is struck by God with a disease for his idolatrous activities (v. 11); and (e) 2 Chr. 26:16–21, which regards the leprosy of Uzziah the king of Judah as divine punishment for presumptuously assuming a priestly role by administering the burning of incense. It is this view that exacerbated the problem of suffering addressed in the book of Job.

[5] So, e.g., the later m.Qid. 4:14: טוב שברופאים לגיהנם ("the best of the doctors is for Gehinnom!"). See on this emerging attitude the overview by Howard Clark Kee, "Medicine and Healing", in ed. David Noel Freedman, *Anchor Bible Dictionary* (6 vols.; Garden City, New York: Doubleday, 1992), 4:660–662 and Sussman Munter, "Medicine", in eds. Cecil Roth and Geoffrey Wigodor, *Encyclopaedia Judaica* (16 vols.; New York: Keter, 1971), 11:1178–1185.

[6] The Masoretic Tradition: וגם בחליו לא דרש את יהוה כי ברפאם ("and even in his disease he did not seek the help of YHWH but through physicians"; LXX: καὶ ἐν τῇ μαλακίᾳ αὐτοῦ οὐκ ἐζήτησεν

These texts reflect the rejection of medical techniques and practices that were more widespread among the Babylonian, Egyptian, and Hellenistic cultures contiguous to Judaism during post-exilic antiquity.

Among some of the Dead Sea documents, a very similar view is preserved.[7] In the Aramaic text of *4QPrayer of Nabonidus* (4Q242), Nabonidus the king, after being punished by God for his haughtiness with bad sores, is healed when he receives divine forgiveness of his sin through the mediation of a "sojourner" (4Q242 1–3.4–5).[8] The *Genesis Apocryphon* (1Q20) recasts the story of Abraham's sojourn in Egypt (cf. Gen. ch. 20) by having an spirit sent by "the Most High" afflict Pharaoh and his household with bodily sores, in order to convince Pharaoh to return Sarah to Abraham. In the account, it is God who is called upon to act as healer through Abraham's prayer that is accompanied by the laying on of hands (1Q20 xx 12–16, 28–29).[9] Although these texts refer to human intermediaries and, to a certain extent, to particular actions on their part, the authors of these passages leave no indication that they regarded the immediate source of healing to be anyone other than God.

Such a perspective is consistent with the categorical rejection of the use of magico-medical cures in the early Enochic tradition, the *Book of Watchers* at *1 Enoch* chapters 7 and 8. According to *1 Enoch* 7:1, and in contrast to Genesis 6:1–4, the rebellious watchers, who are held responsible for introducing evil into the world, instruct the earthly women they chose in the use of medicines (Cod. Pan. – φαρμακεῖαι; 4QEnoch[a] = 4Q201 iii 15 has חרשה), incantations (Cod. Pan. – ἐπαοιδαί), and the cutting of roots to make medicinal herbs (Cod. Pan. – ῥιζοτό-μιαι). In chapter 8 the watcher tradition associated with ʿAsaʾel (Gr., Eth. – ʿAza-zʾel) also refers to reprehensible instructions, but within a more elaborate list that includes instruments of violence, techniques of beautification, and astrological methods of divination (vv. 1–2). In verse 3 the Greek translation (consistent with the Aram. fragment of 4QEnoch[b] = 4Q202 1 iii 1–6) ascribes the teaching on

---

κύριον ἀλλὰ τοὺς ἰατρούς). Significantly, the Syriac Peshitta altogether omits this criticism of Asa. See further Job 13:4 and Jer. 46:11 (cf. 8:22; 51:8).

[7] Uniformity on this point cannot be expected. Not clear is the position of the difficult so-called "skin disease" text of 4Q266 (4QDamascus Document[a]) 6 i 5–13 and parallels (4Q269 7; 4Q272 1 i–ii; and 4Q273 4 ii): a condition of ringworm, referred to in Lev. 13:33, is attributed to a "spirit" and subjected to a priest's examination, to determine whether the condition has been healed. It could be argued, however, that the priest is not acting as a physician and that the text assumes that God is the one who heals the condition described.

[8] The source of healing does not depend on whether the mediator is read גיר (as here) or גזר ("exorcist").

[9] See Armin Lange, "1QGenAp XIX₁₀-XX₁₂ as Paradigm of the Wisdom Didactive Narra-tive", in eds. Heinz-Josef Fabry, Armin Lange and Hermann Lichtenberger, *Qumranstudien. Vor-träge und Beiträge der Teilnehmer des Qumranseminars auf dem internationalen Treffen der Society of Biblical Literature, Münster, 25.-26. Juli 1993* (Schriften des Institutum Judaicum Delitzschia-num 4; Göttingen: Vandenhoeck & Ruprecht, 1996), pp. 197–198. Lange correctly argues that it is the prayer of Abraham (a "hymnic exorcism", as in *Jub.* 10:3–6 and 12:19–20) and not the laying on of hands as such, which results in Pharaoh's healing.

cutting of roots and the casting of spells to Shemiḥazah, while according to the Aramaic evidence Hermoni taught the undoing of incantations, sorcery (כשפו), magic (חרתמו), and such knowledge (תושין).[10] The rejection of medicinal cures is reinforced by their association with practices involving incantations that may have involved the risk of misusing the holy name of God. The implication is that those who use these cures will be judged together with the fallen angels whose culpability derives in part from the kind of knowledge they have disseminated through their instructions to humankind (*1 En.* 9:8b; 16:3).

2. The Legitimation of Medicine in Second Temple Judaism

As is well known, during the late 3rd through 1st centuries B. C. E. some Jews were attempting to find theological justification for medico-magical cures, the application of which was on the rise on account of the influences of surrounding, in particular Hellenistic, cultures. In contrast to the Enoch tradition, the author of Wisdom of Solomon (1st cent. B. C. E.) considers the knowledge of, among other things, various plants "and the powers of roots" to be *God*-given (Wisd. 7:15–16:20). This perspective is even more pronounced and argued theologically in the early 2nd century B. C. E. composition of Ben Sira, which focuses on the legitimacy of medicines and doctors. According to the Greek tradition in Sirach 37:27–38:15, the use of medication and the consultation of physicians is justifiable on the basis of a creation theology. Since "the Lord created medicines (designated φάρμακα) from the earth, the sensible man (ἀνὴρ φρόνιμος) will not despise them" (Sir. 38:4). Since "the Lord created" (ἔκτισεν κύριος) the physician (ἰατρός), the author (so, if we follow the Hebrew texts from Masada) goes so far as to conclude that "the one who sins against his Maker" will at the same time be the one who is "defiant towards the physician" (38:15). Both prayer to God (38:9) and seeking help from a doctor – especially from one who prays (38:14) – are regarded as complementary activities (*contra* 2 Chr. 16:12). Thus, there is no inherent contradiction between a doctor's use of medicines and the belief in God who is the healer *par excellence* (so 38:9–11; v. 9: "pray to the Lord and he will heal you", εὖξαι κυρίῳ καὶ αὐτὸς ἰάσεταί σε).

In the *Book of Jubilees* we encounter a tradition in which medical-herbal cures are justified on a very different basis. Here the role of an angelic intermediary is crucial, as the kind of tradition known through the *Book of Watchers* is reconfigured. Like the Enochic tradition, the author of *Jubilees* regarded rebellious angels as the source of reprehensible practices among humanity. Specifically, as in *1 Enoch* 8, these practices include divination through the observation of heavenly bodies (*Jub.* 8:3).[11] However, the *Jubilees* approach to the tradition differs markedly from

---

[10] A precise meaning for each of these Aramaic terms is difficult to establish.

[11] See also *Jub.* 12:17–20; this teaching of the fallen angels is passed on through an inscribed stone discovered by the post-diluvian Cainan, son of Arpachshad.

the *Book of Watchers* in two main ways. First, the angelic rebellion does not occur in heaven but takes place on earth to where God sent the angels. Second, and more important, nothing is said in *Jubilees* about any instructions concerning cures by the wayward angels. Instead, the knowledge of herbal medicine is taught through one of the good angels (10:10, 13). This instruction is given to Noah who has prayed to God that his children might be delivered from the evil spirits who have been corrupting his progeny following the Great Flood (10:1–6). God's response to Noah's petition is to have the angels banish the spirits to a place of judgment. But after Mastema, the chief of the evil spirits, pleads with God, a tenth of the spirits are allowed to remain on earth. It is in order to combat the afflictions brought about by these spirits that the angels are told to inform Noah how to effect cures by means of herbs from the earth (10:10–13). Thus, the medicinal use of herbs according to *Jubilees* is sanctioned not only on the basis that it is revealed through good angels but also because it is applied to counter the malevolent activity of evil spirits. Whereas in the *Book of Watchers* medicines are categorically attributed to the disobedient angels who beget giants (who are identified as the "evil spirits"; cf. *1 En.* 15:8–11), in *Jubilees* this same knowledge is revealed in order to be used against those (same) spirits that cause harm.

3. The Medico-Magical Cures in the Book of Tobit

An analogy to the justification offered in *Jubilees* for the use of medicine has been observed in the Book of Tobit: magico-medical cures are admissible on condition that they are knowledge revealed through an angel sent by God.[12] The cures in Tobit are, of course, two-fold since they are brought to bear on the problems of two protagonists in the storyline, Tobit and Sarah. They involve, on the one hand, a fish's heart and liver and, on the other, the same fish's gall. In a detailed study of "magisch-pharmakologische Heilkunst" in Tobit, Bernd Kollmann[13] has argued that the book distinguishes between the nature of these cures since they are used to treat two essentially different kinds of illness. First, there is *Tobit's blindness which has a natural cause*, that is, the condition is the result of white films that have formed when sparrow droppings fall on his eyes (Tob. 2:10). Such a problem, argues Kollmann, would therefore have required a *rational medical procedure* that in the story is provided by the gall of the fish. Despite its straightforwardness, the treatment could not be implemented by anyone, such as a physician, and so, the

---

[12] So esp. Kollmann, "Heilkunst im Buch Tobit", pp. 298–299 n. 27 (bibl. in n. 3 above) and Armin Lange, "The Essene Position on Magic and Divination", in eds. Moshe Bernstein, Florentino García Martínez, and John Kampen, *Legal Texts and Legal Issues. Proceedings of the Second Meeting of the International Organization for Qumran Studies, Cambridge 1995, Published in Honour of Joseph M. Baumgarten* (STDJ 23; Leiden: Brill, 1997), pp. 384–385.

[13] Kollmann, "Heilkunst im Buch Tobit", esp. pp. 291–297.

doctors consulted by Tobit serve only to worsen his condition (2:10). Instead, the application of the gall to cure Tobit's blindness belongs in the category of divine knowledge revealed by God through the angel Raphael. The second problem addressed is *Sarah's loss of seven bridegrooms because of the activity of the demon Asmodaeus* (3:7–8) at a point penultimate to marital consummation. Kollmann maintains that, given the demonic cause for Sarah's misfortune, the cure is to be effected in the story by *less rational, magical means*: the fish's heart and liver are burned to produce a pungent odor intended to drive the malevolent demon away. In other words, there is no reasonable or logical connection between the problem and the cure used to address it.

Although no exact parallel exists in ancient sources for burning the organs of a fish to expel demonic power, no one has yet doubted that this technique has a "magical" character (cf. Tob. 6:17, esp. the long recension of Codex Sinaiticus). The preservation of several documents from antiquity demonstrates, for instance, how widespread the notion was of driving out demons through foul-smelling sub-stances.[14] According to Kollmann, this "magical" solution is essentially different from the "medical" approach exemplified in the use of the fish's gall. As for the latter, Kollmann is able to cite its medical use in antiquity for a condition of λευ-κώματα ("white scales"), a *terminus technicus* for a bad case of the swelling of mem-branes over the iris (Grk. οὐλή; Lat. *cicatrix*) resulting from a wound (so Galen, Pedanius Dioscorides, and Pliny).[15] Although the problems of Sarah and Tobit are resolved by means of the same fish through knowledge revealed by the angel Raphael, the methods are categorically distinguishable.

For all the excellence of Kollmann's thoroughgoing study of the background for interpreting the cures effected in the Book of Tobit, his reading of the story is nevertheless flawed by his exclusive focus on the shorter recension that is repre-sented above all in the Greek codices Vaticanus (B) and Alexandrinus (A) and is largely followed by the Vulgate. In a brief note, Kollmann explains his approach to the text of Tobit: "Zitiert wird Tobit im folgenden nach der Edition von R. Han-hart ... und zwar in der von BA überlieferten, dem ausschmückenden Text des Sinaiticus vorzuziehenden Rezension".[16] I would like to show that Kollmann's view of the text, upon which his interpretation of "magic" and "medicine" in Tobit is based, is highly suspect. He completely neglects the longer recension of Sinaiti-

---

[14] Perhaps the most well-known example remains Josephus' report in *Antiquities* 8.47 about Eleazar the Jewish exorcist who is said to have used a ring with a root to extract a demon through the nostrils of a possessed man. See further Josephus, *Bellum* 7.185; *Papyri Graecae Magicae* (2. vols.; collection edited by Karl Preisendanz *et al.*; Stuttgart: Teubner, 1973–1974, 2nd ed.) Ms. no. XIII, lines 242–244; *Pesiqta Rabbati* 14:14; and Justin Martyr, *Dialogue with Trypho* 85.3.

[15] On these sources, see Kollmann's excellent review, "Heilkunst im Buch Tobit", pp. 293–297.

[16] Kollmann, "Heilkunst im Buch Tobit", pp. 290–291 n. 5; in the English translation: "Tobit will be cited in the following according to the edition of Robert Hanhart ... specifically the recen-sion transmitted in BA, which is to be preferred to the embellished text of Sinaiticus."

cus, which is not only reflected in the Old Latin version, but also now has its closest correspondences in the Aramaic and Hebrew manuscript fragments from Qumran Cave 4 (4Q196–199 Aram. and 4Q200 Heb.). As a result, his distinction between "magic" and "medicine" fails to consider what may have been a "conversation" about the legitimacy of magic or medicine that took place, not so much *between* different early Jewish writings, but in this case *within the creative transmission and rewriting* of the Book of Tobit itself.

As the history of research on the text of Tobit during the 19th and 20th centuries has shown, determining a more original of the several recensions of the book has been fraught with difficulty.[17] During the 19th century a number of scholars argued that the longer recension was a reworking of the shorter one.[18] This text-critical judgment was based, quite naturally, on the assumption that a shorter text would more likely have been expanded in time through changes and additions than have been the result of a reduction from a longer one. Such a premise has continued to govern the more recent work of Paul Deselaers (1982),[19] Heinrich Gross (1987),[20] and, as referred to above, Kollmann (1994). There has, however, been an increasing tendency to regard the shorter, not the longer, recension as the more secondary of the two.[21] The study and publication of the Tobit fragments from Qumran Cave 4 by Józef T. Milik (1966)[22] and especially the official edition in the *Discoveries in the Judaean Desert* series published by Joseph A. Fitzmyer[23] have furnished sufficient evidence for the existence of a Semitic version which, with very few exceptions,[24]

---

[17] See the overview by Paul Deselaers, *Das Buch Tobit. Studien zu seiner Entstehung, Komposition und Theologie* (OBO 43; Freiburg, Schweiz/Göttingen: Universitätsverlag/Vandenhoeck & Ruprecht, 1982), pp. 16–20; Carey A. Moore, "Scholarly Issues in the Book of Tobit Before Qumran and After: An Assessment", *JSP* 5 (1989), pp. 65–81 and *idem*, *Tobit. A New Translation with Introduction and Commentary* (AB 40A; Garden City: Doubleday, 1996), pp. 53–64.

[18] See Moore, *Tobit*, p. 56 and n. 144, who refers to studies by Fritzsche, Hilgenfeld, Nöldeke, Grimm, Plath, Löhr, and Müller. Unfortunately, Moore does not give sufficient consideration to the status of the third Greek recension in scholarly discussion; this recension, though independent, preserves a text that shares similarities with the other two recensions. See the important recent study by Stuart Weeks, "Some Neglected Texts of Tobit: the Third Greek Version", in ed. Mark Bredin, *Studies in the Book of Tobit: A Multidisciplinary Approach* (LSTS 55; London/New York: T. & T. Clark, 2006), pp. 12–42.

[19] Deselaers, *Das Buch Tobit*; see esp. pp. 19–20 for his presentation of this position.

[20] Heinrich Gross, *Tobit und Judit* (NEBAT 19; Würzburg: Echter Verlag, 1987), pp. 5–7.

[21] Moore, *Tobit*, p. 56, lists among early representatives of this view Nestle (1899), Simpson (1913), Zimmermann (1958), and Thomas (1972), singling out Simpson and Thomas with particular approval.

[22] Józef T. Milik, "La patrie de Tobie", *RB* 73 (1966), pp. 322–330.

[23] Joseph A. Fitzmyer, "4Q196 (4QTob[a] ar)", "4Q197 (4QTob[b] ar)", "4Q198 (4QTob[c] ar)", "4Q199 (4QTob[d] ar)" and "4Q200 (4QTob[e] hebr)", in eds. Magen Broshi *et al.*, *Qumran Cave 4 XIV. Parabiblical Texts, Part 2* (DJD 19; Oxford: Clarendon Press, 1995), pp. 1–76 (and Plates I–IX); cf. also *idem*, "The Aramaic and Hebrew Fragments of Tobit from Cave 4", *CBQ* 57 (1995), pp. 655–675 and *Tobit* (CEJL; Berlin: Walter de Gruyter, 2003).

[24] These exceptions–see a few examples thereof given by Moore, *Tobit*, p. 57–need to be scrutinized for possible correspondences to the Third Greek recension. With the aim *inter alia* of tak-

comes closest to the text of Codex Sinaiticus and to the Old Latin version. Significant here is that this is especially true for the passages in Tobit that are concerned
with the use of the fish's liver and heart, on the one hand, and its gall, on the other.

Without assuming that the version of Sinaiticus should in every case be thought
of to preserve a more original text than either Vaticanus or Alexandrinus, a comparison reveals differences in two main areas. The first main digression lies in the
use of the term φάρμακον in Sinaiticus. Whereas in Tobit 6:4 the shorter recension
has the angel instruct Tobias, Tobit's son, to "[c]ut open the fish, take the heart
and the liver and the gall and arrange (them) exactly", the longer recension reads:
"Cut open the fish and remove the gall and the heart and its liver and keep them
with you, and take out the entrails, for the gall and the heart and its liver are useful
medicine (φάρμακον)".[25] Furthermore, in 6:7 Tobias is made to ask the angel:

Vaticanus, Alexandrinus	Sinaiticus
What is	What *medicine* (φάρμακον)[26] is
the liver	in the heart
and the heart	and the liver
and the gall	of the fish,
of the fish?	and in the gall?

Here the main difference between the recensions, beyond the sequence of phrases,
is the use of the term φάρμακον in the longer Greek version (similarly, the Latin
recensions). This distinguishing feature clearly corresponds to the Dead Sea text
in the Aramaic 4Q197 4 i 12: מה סם בלבב נונא ("what is the *medicine* in the heart
of the fish?"). In addition, it is likely that this text may be reconstructed for
4Q196 13.2.

Finally, twice more, in Tobit 11:8 and 11:11 the term φάρμακον, absent from
Vaticanus and Alexandrinus, occurs in Sinaiticus to describe the function of the
fish's gall through which Tobit's blindness is healed. The parallel texts are given
below, with the underlined words having no correspondence in the other version:

---

ing the position of the Third recension seriously, Stuart Weeks, Simon Gathercole and I have
published synopsis of texts of Tobit in the horizontal presentation that includes it alongside the
other two Greek recensions, Dead Sea fragments, Old Latin and Vulgate manuscripts, the Syriac
Peshitta and medieval Aramaic and Hebrew versions; see *The Book of Tobit: Texts from the Principal Ancient and Medieval Traditions* (FoSub 3; Berlin: Walter de Gruyter, 2004).

[25] καὶ εἶπεν αὐτῷ ὁ ἄγγελος ἀνάσχισον τὸν ἰχθὺν καὶ ἔξελε τὴν χολὴν καὶ τὴν καρδίαν καὶ τὸ ἧπαρ
αὐτοῦ καὶ ἀπόθες αὐτὰ μετὰ σαυτοῦ καὶ τὰ ἔγκατα ἔκβαλε ἔστιν γὰρ εἰς φάρμακον χρήσιμον ἡ χολὴ καὶ
ἡ καρδία καὶ τὸ ἧπαρ αὐτοῦ. The Old Latin, which preserves a similar recension, reflects a slightly
shorter text at the end of the verse: *sunt enim necessaria haec ad medicamenta utilia*, i. e. "for these
are necessary, useful for medicine" (so Codex Regius 3564; similarly, though with different wording, the Alcalà Bible, Codex Reginensis 7, and even Codex Amiatinus of the Vulgate).

[26] The Old Latin Regius 3564, Alcalà Bible, and Amiantinus have *remedium*, while Reginensis
7 has *medicamentum*.

Vaticanus, Alexandrinus	*Sinaiticus*
[8]You, therefore,	[8]
apply	Rub
the gall	the gall of the fish
into his eyes,	into his eyes,
and taking hold	and the medicine (φάρμακον)[27]
it will penetrate	will shrink
and drive out	and peel off
the white scales,	the white scales from his eyes
and he will see you.	and your father will look up and see the light.
...	...
[11]And he took hold of	[11]And Tobiah went up to
his father	him,
and rubbed	with the gall of the fish in his hand and he blew[28]
the gall	
upon the eyes	into his eyes
of his father	and he took hold of him
saying,	and said,
"Take courage, father!"	"Take courage, father!"
	And he put the medicine (φάρμακον)[29] on him, and it took effect

Though a correspondence to φάρμακον is not preserved in the fragmentary Hebrew text of 4Q200, the Dead Sea fragments, despite preserving a somewhat slightly shorter text than Sinaiticus, nevertheless agree more with the longer than with the shorter version.

A second difference between the recensions can be observed in Tobit 6:8: The angel instructs Tobias on what to do with the heart and liver. The recensions agree that the burning of these organs "before a man or a woman" being attacked by "a demon or an evil spirit" will guarantee protection against the danger posed by the demon. Notably, however, Raphael's assurance of success is more emphatic in the longer version: "... and every attack will flee from him and they will not remain with him for ever".[30] This text again corresponds to the fragmentary texts of 4Q196 13.4 ([ו]יסחר[ו] [א]ל[ל].[) and 4Q197 4 i 14: לעלם [ו]יסחרו[ן] סחרתהו [לא). The formulaic guarantee in the longer recension underscores that the procedure is not only intended to work in the case of Asmodaeus's lethal activity against Sarah in

---

[27] The Old Latin Regius 3564 and Alcalà Bible translate *medicamentum*, while the Vulgate, in contrast to Tob. 6:4 and 7 (see n. 24 above), preserves no equivalent.

[28] This part of the text is extant in the Hebrew text of 4Q200: ... ורת הדג בידו ונפוץ [בעיניו ומר] (5.2). The blowing procedure is, as in Tob. 6:9, omitted in the short recension. It is not clear whether this blowing is intended to activate the gall ointment or, as also possible, to have some effect on an assumed demonic source of the problem (cf. Moore, *Tobit*, pp. 202 and 263). Since the demon is only identified in relation to Sarah's problem, the former alternative seems the more likely.

[29] See n. 25 above.

[30] Sinaiticus: καὶ φεύξεται ἀπ᾽ αὐτοῦ πᾶν ἀπάντημα καὶ οὐ μὴ μείνωσιν μετ᾽ αὐτοῦ εἰς τὸν αἰῶνα. Vaticanus and Alexandrinus simply have "and he/she will no longer be attacked".

the storyline, but is also expected to be potent *in any situation* of demonic attack, whether the victim be a man or a woman. It seems likely, therefore, that Raphael's instruction in Sinaiticus preserves a recipe that has been inserted into the story, a recipe not unlike those for ridding oneself of unwanted demons found in ancient magical texts (cf. esp. *Papyri Graecae Magicae* XIII, 242–244).

Because of the neglect of the longer recension, Kollmann's analysis does not take any of these differences between the recensions into account. A careful reading of the recensions, along with a comparison with the Dead Sea Aramaic and Hebrew fragments (where possible), reveals versions that diverge in the degree to which magico-medical vocabulary is deemed appropriate for describing the cures revealed by Raphael. The evidence for the text from Qumran Cave 4 supports the likelihood that the version that identifies *all three fish organs* as φάρμακον is to be preferred as the more original. Although it remains unclear whether the shorter recension already existed in Aramaic and/or Hebrew, there are grounds to suppose that the Vaticanus and Alexandrinus texts, along with their corresponding versions, while retaining the essential elements of the storyline, have nevertheless excised some words that had allowed for unwanted "magico-medical" associations in the story.[31] Indeed, the longer recension in chapters 6 and 8 creates a logical difficulty in Codex Sinaiticus when one considers the text of 2:10, according to which Tobit describes how in vain he consulted doctors (ἰατροὺς) in hopes of finding a cure through their medicines (φάρμακα). That is, in Sinaiticus some φάρμακα are rejected as impotent and even harmful in their effects,[32] while others that are revealed through an angel commissioned by God provide the essential resolution in the story. Given the different views expressed in related traditions among some Jews during the Second Temple period (see sections 2 and 3 above), the application of the same language for both reprehensible and acceptable activity may have been regarded as problematic or even as inconsistent by some later scribal editors.

Conclusions

How, in the end, does a reconsideration of the longer recension of Tobit affect the presentation of cures in the narrative? In contrast to Kollmann, who on the basis

---

[31] This observation in relation to the omission of medical terminology in the shorter recension was already made by David Capell Simpson, "The Chief Recensions of the Book of Tobit", *JTS* 14 (1913), pp. 516–530, esp. p. 519; cf. Moore, *Tobit*, p. 131.

[32] That is, the doctors in Sinaiticus to Tob. 2:10 are made the cause of Tobit's blindness. According to the Old Latin version in Codes Regius 3564, Alcalà Bible, and Codex Reginensis 7, the point seems to be stressed even more, as the medicines of the doctors are derogatorily associated with "magic"; the text of Regius 3564, for example, reads: *et ibam caucus ad medicos ut curare, et quanto mihi medicamenta imponebant, tanto magis excaecabantur oculi mei maculis, donec perexcaecatus sum* ("I went for advice to doctors in order to be cured, and when the medicines were unable to help me, my eyes were blinded by such magic, so that I was thoroughly blinded.").

of codices Vaticanus and Alexandrinus alone, forges a clear-cut distinction between the magic of the heart and liver and the medicine of the gall, Codex Sinaiticus – indeed, supported by the fragmentary Dead Sea fragments and Old Latin texts of Tobit – lumps these together under the same category (φάρμακον, Aram. סם). If one inquires into what the author of Tobit considers magic/medicine to be and not to be, it is meaningless to differentiate between these putative categories, as proposed by Kollmann. Instead, for the recension in and underlying Sinaiticus and the Old Latin tradition, both acts of healing are simply that, and the label φάρμακον, undergirded by revelation, is taken up in the Greek text to lend them legitimacy. The cures revealed to Tobias by God's angel are, therefore, not more or less medical or more or less magical than the cures and ointment that the physicians in Tobit 2:10 apply without success (even, in the longer recension, inflicting more damage on Tobit and being the very cause of his becoming completely blind). The difference between right and wrong does not lie in the appropriateness or impropriety of the means itself; rather, the means – whatever the procedure may involve – is simply justified on the basis of divine sanction.[33]

As in *Jubilees*, an allowance is made for cures that can be attributed to knowledge revealed by an emissary of God. It is clear that this justification not only serves the interests of the narrative, but also implies that the author(s) may have been attempting to make room for a practice with which the readers would already have been familiar.[34] The shorter recension has toned such language down; by removing a label sometimes open to controversy in Jewish tradition (cf. Sir. 38 and *1 En.* 7–8), the shorter recension has produced a more innocuous text. If such a shift through the reworking of the tradition took place, then the shorter recension may reflect a mild hesitation to apply medico-magical language to a practice that it otherwise affirms. In this way, the shorter and longer recensions of Tobit betray different theological concerns that are reflected by their respective usage of terminology.

While it is precarious at the outset to assume that differences between the versions are going to have a theological explanation, I hope here at least to have shown how the Tobit recensions' respective attitudes towards the use of descriptive terms for cures are based on different views regarding the propriety of φάρμακα, views that are variously represented by those who produced the recensions for the same Jewish document. A study of the versions, then, opens for us a window into a "conversation" that extended beyond the time of composition itself into the period during which Tobit was being copied and re-edited.

---

[33] Though the character Tobias in the story does not know the identity of 'Azariah as God's angel Raphael, this is made known to the reader at an early stage of the narrative (Tob. 3:16–17).

[34] This would be likely if, for instance, the recipe in Tob. 6:8 has been imported into the story and reflects known practices (see section 3 above).

Chapter Seven

To What Extent Did Philo's Treatment of Enoch and the Giants Presuppose Knowledge of Enochic and Other Sources Preserved in the Dead Sea Scrolls?

In his work *De gigantibus* Philo's treatment of Genesis 6:1–4 broaches several themes familiar to us through Jewish apocalyptic and sapiential literature composed before his time, that is, from the late 4th century until the late 2nd century B.C.E. The aim of this discussion is to focus on two areas of comparability between Philo, who composed his works in Greek, and the early apocalyptic and wisdom traditions written in Aramaic and Hebrew. These two areas are: (1) how these sources handled the story about the "sons of God", "daughters of humanity", and their gigantic offspring and, following from this, (2) the extent to which Philo's statements relating to human nature bear any similarity with reflections on human nature in some of the Dead Sea documents. In the end, we are concerned with whether or not Philo can be shown to have had any tradition-historical contact with apocalyptic (in particular, the Enochic traditions) and sapiential sources preserved in materials found among the Dead Sea manuscripts.

Before we venture into the comparison at hand, a brief note on the treatment of "Enoch" in Philo is in order. Philo's view of the pre-diluvian patriarch contrasts markedly from the Enoch we meet in the *1 Enoch* literature and related traditions that refer to him (esp. the *Book of Giants* and *Jubilees*). This difference relates to Philo's paradigmatic use of Enoch, whose name he interprets in relation to the Hebrew word חן (*ḥn*) followed by a pronominal suffix *-k*, thus meaning "your favor/grace" (χάρις σου, *Conf.* 123; *Post.* 35–36,[1] 41; κεχαρισμένος, "gifted one" *Abr.* 17). This explanation of the name is due to Philo's wish to present Enoch as an example of "repentance" (μετάνοια), that is, as "one who changed from the worse life to the better" (*Abr.* 17).[2] The transference of Enoch (Gen. 5:25 Masoretic Tradition – "and Enoch was not, for God took him"), which some traditions took as a euphemism for his death (so *Targum Onqelos*) and which other traditions understood as a reference to his ascension without death (e.g. *1 En.* 12:1–2; 71:1–4, 5–16; *Targum Pseudo-Jonathan*, *Targum Neofiti*; cf. *Jub.* 4:23–25),

---

[1] Though the "Enoch" in this passage is the one mentioned in Gen. 4:17 as the son of Cain, not the Enoch of 5:18, the descendent of Seth.

[2] The English translation of Philo is cited according to *Philo in Ten Volumes (and Two Supplementary Volumes)*, by F. H. Colson, G. H. Whitaker (and R. Marcus) (LCL; London: Heinemann, 1929–1962).

implies for Philo a "turning and changing" (μετάθεσις ... καὶ μεταβολήν, *Abr.* 18). That is, in Enoch there was an "old reprehensible life" (τὸν ἀρχαῖον καὶ ἐπίληπτον ... βίον) that had to be blotted out (*Abr.* 19): he passed "from ignorance to instruction, from folly to sound sense, from cowardice to courage, from impiety to piety, ... from voluptuousness to self-control, from vaingloriousness to simplicity" (*Abr.* 24).[3]

Philo thus distinguishes Enoch, a repentant one,[4] from Noah, whose name he interprets as "rest" or "just" (ἀνάπαυσις ... δίκαιος, *Abr.* 27; cf. *Leg.* 3.77–78[5]) and who became "perfect" (τέλειος, *Abr.* 34), since "repentance" (μετάνοια) comes up second behind "perfection" (τελειότης, *Abr.* 26). By way of contrast, we may point out that there is not a hint amongst Enochic and related traditions that the patriarch was anything other than righteous his entire life. Thus with respect to Enoch's early life, Philo's exegesis or source of information has little in common with the apocalyptic tradition that so idealized him. Is one, therefore, to infer that Philo must not have been aware of any further ideas associated with the patriarch as transmitted in apocalyptic writings extant in Hebrew and Aramaic sources? Our consideration of Philo's "giants" in his *De gigantibus* suggests that a categorically negative answer to this question is misleading.

The treatise *De gigantibus* is best known for Philo's distinction between three types of people: those who are (1) earth-born; (2) heaven-born; and (3) God-born (*De gig.* 60–61). He formulates this classification of humans while discussing the reference to "giants" (γίγαντες) in Genesis 6:4. Dismissing that the biblical text should in any way be associated with "the myths of the poets" (*De gig.* 58 and 60 – perhaps an allusion to Hesiod's *Theogony*), Philo adopts a more widespread criticism of mythological accounts of religion known among the Greek philosophers (e. g. Xenophon, Plato;[6] cf. Herodotus' Prologue to *Hist.* and *passim*) and taken over to some degree by contemporary Jewish thinkers (e. g. Josephus, *Ant.* 1.15). In this way, Philo departs from much of the Jewish literature (apocalyptic and sapiential) that regarded Genesis 6:1–4 as a *real story*, that is, as one about rebellious angelic beings, human daughters, and evil progeny. As Peder Borgen has rightly argued, Philo's critical statements about myth suggest his awareness of a

---

[3] For a brief discussion, see also James C. VanderKam, *Enoch: A Man for All Generations* (Columbia: University of South Carolina Press, 1995), pp. 150–151.

[4] With this caricature, Philo may know the tradition in Ben Sira 44:16, according to which Enoch is described as "an example of repentance for all generations" (ὑπόδειγμα μετανοίας ταῖς γενεαῖς), even though his being "taken from the earth" in 49:14 (ἀνελήμφθη ἀπὸ τῆς γῆς) leaves ambiguous whether nor not he died.

[5] In this passage, Philo incorporates some of the language applied to Enoch to Noah himself, saying however that the latter recognizes the "gift / grace of God", though not as one who has rested "from sinful and unrighteous acts" (ἀδικημάτων καὶ ἁμαρτημάτων). This presentation of Noah contrasts, of course, with what *Abr.* 17 relates about Enoch as one who repented.

[6] On the early development of this critique of "myths", see Wolfgang Rösler, "Die Entdeckung der Fiktionalität in der Antike", *Poetica* 12 (1980), pp. 283–319.

"misconception on the side of some persons".[7] To be sure, Philo does seem to draw on a text that refers to ἄγγελοι instead of the reading "sons of God" (Gen. 6:2);[8] as such these "angels" correspond to what "the philosophers" also have designated as "demons" and "souls" (*De gig.* 6). However, whereas the philosophers have directed their interest towards discarnate, incorporeal beings, Philo, in his reading of Genesis 6, wishes his emphasis to fall on how this all relates to human experience. To this extent, Philo's approach to the passage, as elsewhere in his writings, is allegorical (see *Somn.* 1.102): the earth-born are those people who indulge in bodily pleasures (τῶν σώματος ἡδονῶν); the heaven-born are lovers of learning such as the arts and knowledge and those in whom the mind (νοῦς), which is heavenly in nature, is primarily active; the God-born, on the other hand, have little at all to do with the visible world, as they are "priests and prophets who have refused to accept membership in the commonwealth of the world and to become citizens therein" and rise wholly above the realm of sense-perception in their existence. In light of this classification, the "angels" and "giants" of Genesis 6, who are not clearly distinguished from one another, function as a negative foil: they signify those "souls" which have abandoned themselves to the gratification of and seduction by bodily appetites. They would seem to belong among the earth-born.

A closer reading, however, suggests that Philo's exegetical reading of Genesis 6 is not simply concerned with different types of people, who at any given time are acting within one of the three groups of humans. Philo's treatise functions as exhortation; it implies that his explanation for the story about the giants should inspire people to orient themselves around the incorporeal world of ideas. Human experience, for Philo, is more complex than his own classification allows. His implied readers are not simply of one sort or another. Indeed, "the bad and the good", he maintains, "are knit in a twin existence" and may even be "equally matched in times and numbers" (*De gig.* 56–57). Each person, on account of having a body, has to negotiate between the good and the bad;[9] as such, humans are "compound beings" (cf. *De gig.* 62).[10] Thus the person's "soul", which can be tempted to go astray, is not to be diverted by the love-lures of pleasure (ἡδονή), but rather to "gaze upon virtue (ἀρετή)", thus mitigating the potentially compromising effects of living in the body.

---

[7] Peder Borgen, *Philo of Alexandria. An Exegete for His Time* (NovTSup 86; Leiden: Brill, 1997), p. 106. Philo's statement, "it is no myth at all about giants that he sets before us" (60), firmly echoes his earlier warning in *De gigantibus* 7, "Let no one suppose that what is here said is a myth", which implies his knowledge of those who treat the story as such.

[8] The reading of ἄγγελοι in Gen. 6:2 is, in addition to Codex Alexandrinus, widely shared; cf. the edition of John William Wevers, *Genesis* (SVTG 1; Göttingen: Vandenhoeck & Ruprecht, 1974), p. 108.

[9] On the basis of *De gig.* 4, one might infer that Philo coordinates the good and the bad, respectively, with the masculine and feminine parts among humanity.

[10] On humanity's composite or mixed nature (the rational and irrational), see esp. *QE* 2.33 and, further, *Her.* 167, 232; *Cong.* 26.

Philo's description of humans as having a compound existence is analogous to what he reads in Genesis 6 about the giants. However, the situation for humans and giants is not entirely the same. Whereas "giants" represent the complete absorption of souls into an existence dominated by somatic appetites, humans whose minds or souls focus on virtue can actually temper the pleasures of the body; for such people, a mixed nature does not ultimately have to be detrimental.[11] The difference between humans and giants emerges more clearly if we take the *Quaestiones et solutiones in Genesim* into account (1.92). In answer to the question on Genesis 6:4, "Why were the giants born from angels and women?", the text draws attention to the giants' excessive body size and specifies that "their creation was a mixture of two things, of angels and mortal women". Whereas "the substance of angels is spiritual", they are capable of imitating "the forms of men" and can thus "know" women sexually and so produce offspring. The giants, then, are the embodiment of what happens when "parental (masculine) virtue" has been absorbed into "maternal depravity" (cf. a similar disregard for the feminine in *De gig.* 4–5); one gains the impression here that for Philo, "giants" exemplify a mixture gone irretrievably wrong, while humans do not, in principle, have to be so far down the path. The analogy between giants and humans emerges only when humans, who in the text can be designated as "bodies", have become "wicked and evil".

Of the three categories of humans, Philo focuses on the God-born and the earth-born, and less so the heaven-born. This interest may imply that Philo thinks his readers are struggling with existence somewhere in between. Philo provides examples of both. Abraham starts out as "a man of heaven", that is, he corresponds at this stage of his life to the "heaven-born" soul.[12] This state is reflected by the patriarch's initial name, "Abram", which Philo interprets to mean "uplifted father", in whom the mind (νοῦς) is oriented towards "the upper world of heaven" (*De gig.* 62; cf. *Leg.* 3.83; *Mut.* 66; *Abr.* 82; *QG* 3.4; and *Cher.* 4). However, the change of

---

[11] Commenting on *De gig.*, Lionel R. Wickham infers, "That human bodies and immaterial spirits should intermingle is, for Philo, not an unnatural controversion of divine ordinances; human beings simply *are* earthly flesh and immaterial, pre-existent spirit"; cf. Wickham, "The Sons of God and the Daughters of Men: Genesis VI 2 in Early Christian Exegesis", in eds. James Barr *et al.*, *Language and Meaning: Studies in Hebrew Language and Biblical Exegesis* (OtSt 19; Leiden: Brill, 1974), pp. 135–147 (here p. 142).

[12] Abraham's former association with astrology (ἀστρονομία) as a Chaldaean may be the reason why Philo chooses him as an example of one who is "heaven-born". Philo declares elsewhere (*Abr.* 68–71; cf. *Migr.* 184–191; *QG* 3.1; *Virt.* 212, and *Her.* 96–99) that the Chaldaeans' interest in the movements of the stars was a focus on the visible, rather than the invisible, world. By distancing Abraham from any claim that he was the founder of astronomy (emphasizing the Chaldaean interest therein instead), Philo may have been at odds with earlier claims of the 2nd cent. B.C.E. that positively credited Abraham as a founder of astronomy (Artapanos, in Eusebius, *Praep. Ev.* 9.18.1 and Pseudo-Eupolemus, in *Praep. Ev.* 9.17.2–9 and 9.18.2); cf. Christian Noack, *Gottesbewußtsein. Exegetische Studien zur Soteriologie und Mystik bei Philo von Alexandria* (WUNT 2.116; Tübingen: Mohr Siebeck, 2000), pp. 43–47. A similar distancing of Abraham from prognostication of heavenly bodies is found in *Jub.* 12:17–20, in which this activity is associated with the influence of evil spirits.

the patriarch's name to "Abraham" signals an even further movement upward, away from the interest in celestial prognostications that for Philo characterized the Chaldaeans from whence Abraham came.[13] Taking the biblical text of Genesis 17:1–5 as his point of departure, Philo associates the name change to Abraham with God's declaration to Abraham that "I am your God; walk before me according to my pleasure, and show yourself blameless" (Gen. 17:1). Philo reasons that in the text God becomes Abraham's God in a special sense, so that he becomes "a man of God". His new name, accordingly, is taken to mean "the elect father of sound", that is, "the good man's reasoning" (*De gig.* 64; cf. *Cher.* 7; *Mut.* 66; *Abr.* 82; and *QG* 3.43). Whatever the etymology behind the name,[14] Philo's point is that in Abraham reason, which has God as its only owner, guides speech in such a way that the person can swerve neither to the right nor to the left. Abraham, then, functions as an example of one who successfully negotiates the bad by remaining on the good, that is, the King's way without distraction.

By contrast, Philo refers to Nimrod as an example of those "children of the earth" who "have turned the steps of the mind out of the path of reason and transmuted it into the lifeless and inert (ἄψυχος καὶ ἀκίνητος) nature of the flesh" (*De gig.* 66). Citing the description of Nimrod in Genesis 10:8 ("he began to be a *giant* in those days"), Philo credits Nimrod as having been the initiator of the desertion of the mind from reason to the flesh. (Indeed, for Philo, the name "Nimrod" means "desertion", αὐτομόλησις[15]). Nimrod stands for those in whom the neutral, heavenly mind (νοῦς), also referred to as the soul (ψυχή), descends into a state that is overwhelmed by the flesh. Nimrod is further credited as the founder of the Babylonian kingdom, so that he is connected more directly than in the biblical story with the tower of Babel. In light of Genesis 6:1–4, the designation "Babylon", understood as "alteration" or "change" (*De gig.* 66; cf. *Conf.* 1), links up with and corresponds to the downward fall made by "the angels" and is manifested in the abandonment to fleshly existence by the "giants". Nimrod, in effect, is an example of opposition to God, a point made explicitly in *Quaestiones et solutiones in Genesim* 1.82 in which Philo presents his interpretation as "the truth of the story about the giants and Titans".[16]

---

[13] Samuel Sandmel, *Philo's Place in Judaism. A Study of Conceptions of Abraham in Jewish Literature* (Cincinnati: Hebrew Union College Press, 1956), pp. 144–145 n. 213 finds an exception for this in *Leg.* 3.83–84, according to which "Abram" is favorably regarded. However, while the interpretation in this passage is indeed more positive in tone than the other passages, Philo still associates "Abram" with a state when "the mind ... turning away from what is base ... explores what is divine (τὸ θεῖον)," no longer able to "continue to entertain the principles it imbibed originally, but in its desire to improve itself seeks to change its abode for a better one".

[14] On the possibility that Abraham reflects the combination *ab* (father) and *b-r-r* (select) + *ha* + *am(on)* (noise), see Lester L. Grabbe, *Etymology in Early Jewish Interpretation. The Hebrew Names in Philo* (Brown Judaic Studies 118; Atlanta: Scholars Press, 1988), pp. 126–127.

[15] This meaning is probably derived, in turn, from an etymology that derives נמרד from the verbal root מרד, i. e. "to rebel" (as in *b.Pes.* 94b).

[16] This passage further, and enigmatically, states that the name "Nimrod" is to be translated as "Ethiopian"; concerning the problem, see Grabbe, *Etymology*, p. 130.

Philo's examples of the God-born and earthly-born are intended to strengthen his view that Genesis 6 is not ultimately a mythological narrative about different beings, heavenly and earthly, but rather is concerned with the situation humans find themselves in, by mere fact of a bodily existence. Humanity "by nature" is not, however, defined as a "body" or "flesh", but rather, as "soul" or "mind". It is this core of the human being that has to negotiate between what is fleshly, on the one hand, and what is heavenly, on the other. For Philo, of course, it is bad for the mind to be fused with or dragged down by the flesh, a condition which the giants represent. Thus the possibility exists that Philo's theological anthropology was shaped by an essentially bipartite soul (rational and irrational, respectively; cf. *Her.* 167, 232; *Cong.* 26; *QE* 2.33) as reflected in many parts of Plato's *Timaeus* (61c7; 65a5; 69c7, d5, e1; 72d4).[17]

Despite his allegorizing exegesis, Philo interprets Genesis 6:1–4 in *De gigantibus* in a way that is comparable, if not similar, to what other Second Temple period interpreters had to say. This is readily apparent if one compares Philo's categorically negative branding of "the angels" and "the giants" with the early Enochic traditions that largely blame the rebellious watchers for the bad state the world has got into (*1 En.* 6–16, 86–88; *Jub.* 5:3–11, 7:21–25; cf. 10:4–7; and the *Book of Giants*). The same attitude – whether this be in relation to the fallen angels, their giant offspring, or both – is reflected in numerous other early Jewish writings which insist that, for reason of the evil they caused, they were held to account and punished by God (Sir. 16:7; Wisd. 14:6; *Sib. Or.* 2.227–232; 3 Macc. 2:4; *3 Bar.* 4:10; CD ii 19–20; *4QExhortation Based on the Flood* = 4Q370 i 6). While this element of Philo's understanding is not surprising, his use of Abraham and Nimrod, respectively as positive and negative illustrations in relation to the "giants", suggests that he may have been aware of some traditions against which the early Enochic writings were formulated.

First, we note that Philo's description of Abraham serves, after all, as a foil for "the giants". Though Abraham's relation to giants is not a theme broached by the Enochic (or any other) apocalyptic sources,[18] it does occur in the euhemeristic source commonly called "Pseudo-Eupolemus". According to the second of Eusebius' citations of Pseudo-Eupolemus (fragment 2), the learned Abraham's lineage is traced back to the ante-diluvian giants.[19] Though the giants are additionally described as known for their "impiety" (ἀσέβεια), their connection with Abraham does not imply an altogether negative view. We may thus ask: Does Philo betray

---

[17] As argued by David Runia, *Philo of Alexandria and the* Timaeus *of Plato* (Philosophia Antiqua 44; Leiden: Brill, 1986), pp. 299–311.

[18] If anything, the earlier sources, which denied an embodied existence to the giants after the Flood, were more immediately concerned with contrasting the giants form the figure of Noah; so, for example, in the *Genesis Apocryphon* at 1Q20 ii–iii and *1 En.* 106–107.

[19] For the Greek text and brief commentary, see Carl R. Holladay, *Fragments from Hellenistic Jewish Authors. Volume 1: Historians* (Texts and Translations 20; Pseudepigrapha Series 10; Chico, California: Scholars Press, 1983), pp. 170–187.

the knowledge of a tradition that relates Abraham to the giants and, if so, is he by way of deliberate contrast attempting to distance Abraham from them categorically? Of course, it could be argued that Abraham is so commonly understood as an ideal patriarch from whom Israel derives her identity as God's elect people so that, once the giants of Genesis 6:4 are interpreted negatively, it becomes a necessity that he be cast as one who is of an entirely different character and nature. Significantly, it is only in Pseudo-Eupolemus and Philo that both Abraham and the giants are connected within the context of the same work. It may be that Philo's description of Abraham in *De gigantibus* is more a function of what he says about Abraham in his other writings, namely, that his status as one who is "heaven-born" fits with his orientation towards "the upper world of heaven", as Philo implies elsewhere (see above). Nevertheless, the bringing together of Abraham and the fallen angel story, including the giants, assumes a prior association. Like the apocalyptic literature, that holds Noah at a distance from the giants, so also Philo, albeit as part of his own attempt to say something about the vicissitudes of human existence, adopts a comparable strategy in relation to Abraham.

Second, Philo's description of Nimrod assumes a biblical story-line that regards the "giants" referred to in Genesis 6:4 as having somehow survived the Flood. Though Philo himself does not seem concerned with the chronology of the narrative, we may nevertheless ask what kind of narrative his statements presuppose. Here, instead of a contrast, we meet up with a view that corresponds with the same Pseudo-Eupolemus source just mentioned. Fragment 2 (Eusebius, *Praep. Ev.* 9.18.2) not only links Abraham back to the giants, but also tells of a certain Belos who, having escaped death, came to dwell in Babylon, where he built a tower to live in. The allusion here to Genesis 11:1–10 and the tower of Babel is unmistakable. Furthermore, it is hard to ignore the possibility that the text, which attempts to coordinate biblical with Hellenistic culture heroes of antiquity, is in some way alluding to Nimrod. The other fragment commonly associated with Pseudo-Eupolemus (frg. 1, *Praep. Ev.* 9.17.2–3) also connects "giants" with the building of a tower. These giants, who are said to have founded Babylon "were saved from the Flood". Now, Philo's association of the ante-diluvian "giants" with the post-diluvian "giant" Nimrod would, one may argue, have been suggested by the occurrence of the term γίγας in his Greek translation of Genesis 6:4 (in the plural) and 10:8 (in the singular). Though Philo does not seem to have been interested in shaping his exegesis in relation to questions of biblical chronology *per se*, his singling out of Nimrod as an example of a wayward "giant" suggests, I think, an awareness on his part of a tradition that also linked him with the "giants" of Genesis 6:4.

If Philo knew the tradition of Pseudo-Eupolemus at all, we may assume that he used it discriminatingly: on the one hand, unlike that tradition, he distances Abraham altogether from giants (and, in doing so, he follows the general direction that would been taken by many other Jewish traditions of his); on the other hand, like that tradition, he assumes a narrative that associates the post-diluvian Nimrod with the ante-diluvian giants. While this does not leave us in a position to postulate any dependence on early Jewish apocalyptic traditions as such, these cursory observations place Philo within a web of debate that already, during the 2nd century B.C.E., had been concerned with the nature and function of the biblical giants.[20]

The possible relation of Philonic exegesis to Enochic tradition is strengthened if we take into account what both relate about the nature of the giants. Like Philo, especially in the passage at *Quaestiones et solutione in Genesim* (1.92), the author of the *Book of Watchers* at *1 Enoch* 15–16 had a particular scorn for the offspring of the fallen angels and women of the earth: they are *mala mixta*, embodying a coming together of separate realms, "spiritual" and "somatic", which in principle were meant to be kept distinct. In comparing Philo with the apocalyptic tradition, one should keep in mind his way of distinguishing between human nature and "giants": the giants represent what humans become when they abandon the spiritual existence in the mind or soul for that of the flesh, just as humans may rise above the *soma* to participate in what is incorporeal. Humans, as the "giants", may be composite beings, but they are not, *sui generis*, a *bad* mixture. Similarly, the Enochic giants are irreversibly evil; because they are an unsanctioned mixture of angelic spirit and human flesh, their doom is assured. The Enochic tradition does not go further to reflect for us about human nature. If anything, however, and unlike Philo, the apocalyptic texts assume that human beings are endowed with bodies, and there is no indication that their "souls" are immortal in any sense. His view of human nature notwithstanding, Philo's way of understanding the giants comes closer to that of the *Book of Watchers* than to any other extant early Jewish text. Tempting as this hypothesis is, I am not yet convinced that there existed a direct link between Philo and apocalyptic tradition, since other writers who may have shared views about the giants with either Philo or the *Book of Watchers* have not provided sufficient details to allow more precise comparisons to be made. If, however, we suppose that Philo was at least aware of a view, circulated in his day, that the antediluvian giants were a *bad mixture*, then we are not far from the Enochic literature's mythical world of fallen angels, giants, and humans. If we speculate, furthermore, about where or in what context Philo may have encountered such a view about the giants, then an acquaintance with the apocalyptic tradition, which, though composed in either Hebrew or, more probably Aramaic, may already have been rendered into Greek by or during the 1st century C.E., cannot be dismissed out of hand.

What are the implications of the present discussion of "the giants" in Philo and the Enochic tradition for an understanding of human nature during the Second Temple period? We note, with the study of Archie Wright, that the early Enochic traditions and Philo have very different approaches to the question of human na-

---

[20] See Chapter One, sections B and C.

ture in their considerations of the giants. Whereas the *Book of Watchers* and *Jubilees* regard the spirit-residue of the giants after their punishment as an external threat to human beings, Philo thinks of giants as internal irrational vices with which humans must contend by reason of their fleshly existence.[21] What precisely are these gargantuan vices for Philo? Because they are encountered within the human being, are they necessarily *part of human nature* itself, so that the term "giants", on one level, is simply a metaphorical way of talking about discord that occurs within humans when they are overwhelmed by "pleasures relating to the body" (*De gig.* 34)? Philo's language is difficult to systematize on this point. However, without taking anything away from human accountability before God, Philo can maintain in *De opificio mundi* (160) that pleasure (ἡδονή) "makes use of myriads of champions and defenders who have taken up for her care and defense"; and, in *De gigantibus* itself (35), Philo can exhort his readers by saying, "Welcoming the friendly frugality of virtue rather than the things which belong to the body, let us destroy (καταλύωμεν) the vast and innumerable crowd of merciless foes". It is thus possible that Philo wants it both ways: on the one hand, vices are indelibly part of what human beings are, because they are souls that have acquired bodies; on the other hand, vices can be forces to be gotten rid of or managed. In either case, Philo thinks that, although good and bad coexist in a person, the good is far more powerful (*De gig.* 57); it is for this that Abraham provides a supreme example (62–64).

Philo's reflections on human nature, as just considered, may seem remote from the realm of Jewish apocalyptic and sapiential ideas composed in Hebrew and Aramaic. Having noted a superficial similarity with the *Book of Watchers*, however, we can observe that the account he gives of internal and external forces of good and bad in *De gigantibus* is not altogether unlike what we encounter in some statements within the *Two Spirits Treatise* (hereafter *Treatise*) incorporated into the *Serekh ha-Yaḥad* (1QS) at iii 13 – iv 26.

The similarities between Philo and the *Treatise* may be listed as follows: (1) For both Philo and the *Treatise*, human nature is composite. The *Treatise* (at 1QS iv 15–18) maintains that God has apportioned the deeds of humans

in equal measure (בד ובד) until the last time and has put eternal enmity between their divisions; abhorrence of truth are the deeds of injustice, and abhorrence of injustice are all the ways of truth. There is a violent conflict concerning all their judgments since they cannot walk together.

As we have seen, Philo holds that *the bad and the good, since they exist within us as inseparable entities, may be equally matched in times and numbers* (*De gig.* 56). Philo may have picked up an existing Jewish anthropology (humans as τῆς μικτῆς καὶ συνθέτου φύσεως, *Her.* 183), and, if David Runia's analysis is correct, may have

---

[21] Archie T. Wright, *The Origin of Evil Spirits* (WUNT 2.198; Tübingen: Mohr Siebeck, 2005), p. 214.

dressed it up through the influence of Plato's *Timaeus*.[22] (2) For both Philo and the *Treatise*, the power of the good outweighs that of the bad, and both refer to this in terms of the potential within human beings. Thus according to both it is possible for some people to be more successful than others in overcoming what is bad. However, whereas Philo may deem it possible for the mind to gaze on virtue and overcome the passions associated with the body (even in this life), the *Treatise*, while implying that people are going to attain different levels of purity, appeals to a time of divine visitation for the ultimate solution: the conflict between powers in the human beings will continue in principle until the end when "God will finish off (להתם) every spirit of injustice" from the innermost parts of human flesh, "cleansing it by the spirit of holiness from all deeds of wickedness" (1QS iv 20–21). (3) Similar to Philo's discussion of vices, the *Treatise* is not always clear about whether language about "the spirit of injustice" is a metaphorical way of referring to human activity in and of itself or to an external, invasive power. This would be especially true of the virtue and vice lists in 1QS iv 2–14, in which the spirits of truth and iniquity are, respectively, coordinated with a number of activities. (4) Broadly speaking, Philo and the *Treatise* deal with human nature in a rich and complex manner and, as such, stand apart from the wide range of Jewish traditions that come down to us from the Second Temple period.[23] As is well known, many texts, both amongst the Dead Sea materials and related sapiential and apocalyptic writings limit their discourse about human beings to bifurcatory *social* classifications. By distinguishing between "the righteous" on the one side and "the wicked" on the other, these materials adopt language that treats humans as acting *wholly* one way or the other at any given moment. Philo and some of the Dead Sea texts, however, reflect an anthropology that explores the conflict between wickedness and righteousness, between good and bad, within and in relation to human beings themselves.

Profound differences, however, remain: (1) Whereas the *Treatise* conceives of a list of virtues and vices (1QS iv 2–8 and 9–14, respectively), for Philo, in *De gigantibus*, virtue (ἀρετή) is in the singular, while vices are multiple, just as "the daughters of the earth began to be many" (*De gig.* 1, 18, 26–27, 53; cf. also *Conf.* 15).[24] (2) For Philo, the term "flesh" (σάρξ), which in *De gigantibus* arises from his treatment of Genesis 6:3 and Leviticus 18:6, operates as a negative category, as it is that which obstructs divine wisdom from flowering in the soul (19, 29, 32–36).[25]

---

[22] Runia, *Philo of Alexandria and the* Timaeus *of Plato*, pp. 406–411 and 527.

[23] Possible, though slight, exceptions to this may be Ben Sira and *Musar le-Mevin*; see Loren Stuckenbruck, "The Interiorization of Dualism in the Human Being in Second Temple Judaism: The Treatise on the Two Spirits (1QS iii 13 – iv 26) in its Tradition-Historical Context", in eds. Eric Myers, Armin Lange and Randall Styers, *Light Against Darkness: Dualism in Ancient Mediterranean Religion and the Contemporary World* (JAJSup 1; Göttingen: Vandenhoeck & Ruprecht, 2010), pp. 159–184.

[24] See, however, Philo's *Virt.*, in which ἀρεταί ("virtues") are treated in the plural.

[25] I am hesitant, therefore, to agree with Jörg Frey's influential study, e.g. in "Die paulinische

On the other hand, in the *Treatise* the term for "flesh", *baśar* (בשר), though infused by the spirit of iniquity, is an inextricable part of human nature; the spirit of iniquity will not be dislodged from this "flesh" in its innermost parts until the time of God's visitation (1QS iv 20).

Our comparison between Philo's *De gigantibus* and early Enochic traditions, on the one hand, and with the *Two Spirits Treatise*, on the other, suggest how much Philo's own work could weld together traditions – not necessarily genetically linked – into his own flexible web of ideas. While the fallen angels traditions in the early Enoch literature did not openly reflect very much on what the story about the giants has to do with human nature, neither did the *Two Spirits Treatise* attempt to integrate, beyond faint echoes, its cosmic, psychological, ethical, and anthropological oppositions into the watcher tradition. Philo, in bringing these ideas together, albeit in an almost idiosyncratic way, provides at least a place to start when we reflect on the implications of early apocalyptic tradition for its reception in a very different context. While Martin Hengel, for example, has famously emphasized the Hellenization of Judaea-Palestine during the first century,[26] our comparisons at least raise the possibility that Hebrew and Aramaic traditions – whether by means of oral tradition, translation, or as transmitted written traditions – could have been exerting an influence, profound or not, in the other direction, even among Alexandrian Jewry of the 1st century C. E.

Antithese von 'Fleisch' und 'Geist' und die palästinisch-jüdische Weisheitstradition", *ZNW* 90 (1999), pp. 45–7 that Philo, though emphasizing σῶμα far more than σάρξ, does not provide as relevant a Jewish background for the Pauline "flesh"–"spirit" antithesis (cf. Rom. 8:5–8; Gal. 5:3, 17, 19) as a number of texts from the Dead Sea (e. g. 4Q418 81.1–2; 4Q416 1.10–13; 4Q417 1 i 15–18; 1QS v 23–24 par. 4Q261 1.2–6 and 4Q258 ii 2–4; cf. also 1QS vi 17, 22 par. 4Q258 ii 8 and vii 20–21, 4Q259 ii 4 and viii 19, and 4Q258 vii 3 and 1QS ix 3, 14–15, 18 par. 4Q259 iii 10).

[26] Martin Hengel, e. g. in *The "Hellenization" of Judaea in the First Century after Christ* (London: SCM Press, 1989).

Chapter Eight

Conflicting Stories: The Spirit Origin of Jesus' Birth

Introduction: Posing the Question

Independent interpreters of texts considered sacred usually agree on few things. One point, however, that has found wide agreement among scholars who study the New Testament is the following: the birth of Jesus, though told in different versions in the gospels according to Matthew and Luke, was surrounded by unusual circumstances. The Gospel of Matthew chapter 1 illustrates this problematic beginning for Jesus clearly: Mary becomes pregnant and although the reader is informed that the pregnancy was "from the Holy Spirit" (1:18), from the point of view of Joseph, Mary's conception has happened by unexplained means. After worrying about what to do (1:19), Joseph is told in a dream by "an angel of the Lord" that the origin of this pregnancy is "the Holy Spirit" (Mt. 1:20). Socially, a pregnancy before husband and wife came together, especially if it had not come about from the man who was to become the husband, was unacceptable. Since pregnancy was in effect proof that the woman was no longer a virgin, the situation could even be dangerous for the woman (Deut. 22:20–21), especially if she did not cry for help as she was being violated by another man (Deut. 22:23–27). Given the location of this predicament in a story filled with significance for "Christian origins", it is not surprising that many exegetes, theologians and historians have devoted a great deal of attention to the narratives about Jesus' birth, not least in order to account for the unusual features of the story. A large array of often overlapping approaches have been adopted,[1] as the story is read, for example, through the lens of systematic theology,[2] of historical theology,[3] of reception his-

---

[1] For works that adopt several of the perspectives mentioned below, though in very different ways, see Jane Schaberg, *The Illegitimacy of Jesus: A Feminist Theological Interpretation of the Infancy Narratives* (San Francisco: Harper & Row, 1987, expanded ed. in 2006); Raymond E. Brown, *The Birth of the Messiah: A Commentary on the Infancy Narratives in the Gospels of Matthew and Luke* (ABRL; Garden City: Doubleday, 1993); Beverly Roberts Gaventa, *Mary: Glimpses of the Mother of Jesus* (Columbia, South Carolina: University of South Carolina Press, 1995); and Edwin D. Freed, *The Stories of Jesus' Birth: A Critical Introduction* (The Biblical Seminar 72; Sheffield: Academic Press, 2001); Robert J. Miller, *Born Divine: The Birth of Jesus and Other Sons of God* (Santa Rosa, CA: Polebridge Press, 2003); and Andrew T. Lincoln, *Born of a Virgin? Reconceiving Jesus in the Bible, Tradition, and Theology* (London: SPCK, 2013).

[2] John Macquarrie, *Mary for All Christians* (Edinburgh: T. & T. Clark, 2001, 2nd ed.).

[3] For example, see Brian E. Daley, "The Word and His Flesh: Human Weakness and the Iden-

tory,[4] of narrative-literary analysis,[5] of exegesis,[6] of the interpretation of Israel's scriptures,[7] of the socio-political context,[8] of a hermeneutic of suspicion,[9] of feminist criticism,[10] and of biblicist fundamentalism.[11] Recognizing that several of these approaches do not exclude the use of another, we shall take a look at a neglected part of the ancient debate about the origins of Jesus' birth. The broad question we pose here is: *what was at stake as people wondered what actually happened when Jesus was conceived?*

---

tity of Jesus in Patristic Christology", in eds. Beverly Roberts Gaventa and Richard B. Hays, *Seeking the Identity of Jesus: A Pilgrimage* (Grand Rapids: Eerdmans, 2008), pp. 251–269.

[4] An aspect that, e. g., Ulrich Luz has included in his commentary, *Matthew 1–7: A Commentary*, trans. Wilhelm C. Linss (Edinburgh: T. & T. Clark, 1989), pp. 111–151. See also Tord Fornberg, "The Annunciation: A Study in Reception History, the New Testament", in eds. Morgens Müller and Henrik Tronier, *The New Testament as Reception* (JSNTSup 30; Sheffield: Academic Press, 2002), pp. 157–180.

[5] See esp. Laurence Cantwell, "The Parentage of Jesus: Mt. 1:18–21", *NovT* 24 (1982), pp. 304–315; Robert C. Tannehill, *The Narrative Unity of Luke-Acts: A Literary Interpretation. Volume One: the Gospel According to Luke* (Philadelphia: Fortress Press, 1986), pp. 20–26; Jack Dean Kingsbury, *Matthew as Story* (Philadelphia: Fortress Press, 1988, 2nd ed.), pp. 49–55; Gaventa, *Mary: Glimpses of the Mother of Jesus*, esp. pp. 30–42 and 50–68; Warren Carter, *Matthew: Storyteller, Interpreter, Evangelist* (Peabody, Mass.: Hendrickson, 2004), pp. 109–133; David T. Landry, "Narrative Logic in the Annunciation to Mary. Luke 1:26–38", *JBL* 114 (1995), 65–79; already Paul S. Minear, "Luke's Use of the Birth Stories", in eds. Leander E. Keck and J. Louis Martyn, *Studies in Luke-Acts* (Philadelphia: Fortress Press, 1980, repr. 1966), pp. 111–130, who argued that the birth stories inaugurate a series of motifs that are sustained throughout the gospel and Acts.

[6] Esp. Joseph A. Fitzmyer, *The Gospel According to Luke* (2 vols.; AB 28–28A; Garden City: Doubleday, 1981–1985), 1:287–448; Joel B. Green, *The Gospel of Luke* (NICNT; Grand Rapids: Eerdmans, 1997), pp. 49–158 (esp. pp. 82–92).

[7] See e. g. for the birth narrative in the Gospel of Luke, Robert Alter, "How Convention Helps Us Read: The Case of the Biblical Annunciation's Type-Scene", *Prooftexts* 3 (1983), pp. 115–130; Edgar Conrad, "The Annunciation of Birth and the Birth of the Messiah", *CBQ* 47 (1985), pp. 656–668; Joel B. Green, "The Problem of a Beginning: Israel's Scriptures in Luke 1–2", *BBR* 4 (1994), pp. 61–86; Ulrike Mittmann-Richert, *Der Sühnetod des Gottesknechts* (WUNT 220; Tübingen: Mohr Siebeck, 2008), pp. 297–312 (esp. pp. 298–305). In relation to Matthew's Gospel, see Charles Thomas Davis, "Tradition and Redaction in Matthew 1:18–2:23", *JBL* 90 (1971), pp. 404–421; W. Barnes Tatum, "The Origin of Jesus Messiah (Matt 1:1, 18a). Matthew's Use of the Infancy Traditions", *JBL* 96 (1977), pp. 523–535; James M. Hamilton, "'The Virgin Will Conceive': Typological Fulfilment in Matthew 1:18–23", in eds. Daniel M. Gurtner and John Nolland, *Built upon the Rock: Studies in the Gospel of Matthew* (Grand Rapids: Eerdmans, 2008), pp. 187–206.

[8] Richard A. Horsley, *The Liberation of Christmas: The Infancy Narratives in Social Context* (New York: Crossroad, 1989).

[9] Esp. those who emphasize that the infancy stories conceal what, historically, was actually an illegitimate conception; see esp. John Shelby Spong, *Born of a Woman: A Bishop Rethinks the Birth of Jesus* (San Francisco: HarperSanFrancisco, 1992); Schaberg, *The Illegitimacy of Jesus.*

[10] See e. g. Elaine M. Wainwright, *Towards a Feminist Critical Reading of the Gospel according to Matthew* (BZNW 60; Berlin: Walter de Gruyter, 1991), pp. 171–175; see further Jane Schaberg, "Feminist Interpretations of the Infancy Narrative of Matthew", *Journal of Feminist Studies in Religion* 13 (1997), pp. 35–62.

[11] So the well known apologetic work by John Gresham Machen, *The Virgin Birth of Christ* (New York: Harper & Row, 1932).

During the first century C. E. and late antiquity, three main views concerning what actually happened in relation to the conception and birth of Jesus have come down to us. They are as follows. First, there was a view, especially widespread among Jesus' followers, that he was conceived "out of the Holy Spirit" (Mt. 1:18, 20; cf. further *Protoevangelium Jacobi* 14:2; 19:1). This came to be the traditional conviction that is sanctioned by most church confessions; it functioned – and still functions today – as a way to underscore and support the faith claim that Jesus was "divine" at birth, or at least that he is the Son of God.[12] Second, many thought that Jesus was an illegitimate child, born as the result of shameful sexual relations.[13] In this vein, it was thought that Mary may have become pregnant through a sexually immoral way,[14] whether she had been raped or had engaged in sexual relations with, for example, a Roman soldier. This was one of the views adopted by those who were voicing opposition to the initially emerging and then more established Christian movement (so Celsus [cf. Origen, *c. Celsum* 1.28 and 32]; *b.Talmud*; *Toledoth Yeshu*).[15] Third, a perspective that is not widespread but can be detected in the text, one could imagine that Jesus' father was in fact Joseph (cf. Cod. Sin. Syriacus reading of Mt. 1:16: "Joseph, to whom Mary the virgin became pregnant, begat Jesus who was called Christ"; see Jn. 1:45; Mt. 13:55 pars. Lk. 4:22, Jn. 6:42; *Ab. Zar.* 3b[16]), though such a conception occurred before he took Mary as wife (which is explicitly denied in Mt. 1:25; cf. 1:18).[17] Within this scenario one is to imagine that the story in Matthew was attempting to remove or cover up the embarrassment of Joseph having sired Jesus before the customary time.[18]

---

[12] The assumption that the Holy Spirit's role in Jesus' birth is linked to the question of his "divinity" (which, in turn, is derived from the emphasis on Jesus as Son of God) is widespread. See Ferdinand Hahn, *The Titles of Jesus in Christology: Their History in Early Christianity*, trans. Harold Knight and George Ogg (London: Lutterworth, 1969), pp. 295–304; Robert H. Gundry, *Matthew: A Commentary on his Literary and Theological Art* (Grand Rapids: Eerdmans, 1982), p. 20; John P. Meier, *A Marginal Jew: Rethinking the Historical Jesus* (4 vols.; New York: Doubleday, 1991), 1:205–252 (here p. 230); Donald A. Hagner, *Matthew 1–13* (WBC 33A; Dallas: Word Books, 1993), pp. 17–18; and Armand Puig i Tàrrech, *Jesus: A Biography* (Waco: Baylor University Press, 2011), pp. 160–161.

[13] See Schaberg, *The Illegitimacy of Jesus* and the overview of the claim in Meier, *A Marginal Jew: Rethinking the Historical Jesus*, 1:222–229.

[14] In Jn. 8:41, the Jews' statement to Jesus that "we were not born out of sexual immorality (ἡμεῖς ἐκ πορνείας οὐ γεγεννήμεθα); we have one father, God", indirectly questions the legitimacy of Jesus' origins.

[15] See Peter Schäfer, *Jesus in the Talmud* (Princeton: Princeton University Press, 2007), esp. pp. 15–24, 48, 56, and 95–130.

[16] While it is possible that in the gospel traditions the rhetorical question people ask about Jesus being "the son of Joseph" reflects a view that they reject, in *Ab. Zar.* this is precisely the story that is espoused.

[17] Schäfer, *Jesus in the Talmud*, pp. 21–22. For the sake of argument, had Joseph fathered Jesus after Mary more formally became his wife, there would have been no need to create a story that problematized Jesus' paternity.

[18] See Geza Vermes, *Jesus the Jew: A Historian's Reading of the Gospels* (Philadelphia: Fortress Press, 1973), pp. 215–218. In this case, Mary's claim in response to the angel's annunciation not to

To be sure, there were different reasons for each of these versions, reasons that reflect and correspond to the conflicting opinions that were circulating about the legitimacy of Jesus' activity. Of course, many of those who claimed that Jesus was born "of the Holy Spirit" in this way thought they were declaring something about Jesus' divine origins. Beyond this, however, they were also making a statement about what they believed in relation to Jesus' activity. To claim that Jesus came from the Holy Spirit was also to underscore that the power behind his healings, his exorcisms, and his teaching was God-given; in this way, what Jesus did and said was being re-enforced and sanctioned. Thus to maintain that Jesus was born "of the Holy Spirit" could, for example, have been one way to proclaim that Jesus is God's Messiah, an anointed royal figure whose eventual rule will subjugate the nations of the earth to Israel (Rev. 2:27, 12:5, 19:15; cf. Ps. 2:9; *Pss. Sol.* 17:24–25).[19] Accordingly, whatever his actual origins may have been, his birth must be portrayed as having been greater than that of Roman emperors as well as of others for whom honorable births, sometimes even divine origins, were being claimed.[20]

On the other hand, there were those who rejected Jesus' ministry, regarded him as a messianic pretender, or considered him politically and religiously dangerous.[21] Such critics of Jesus, of his disciples, and of emerging communities of his devotees would not have agreed with the emphasis in the Matthean and Lukan narratives that his birth stood under sanction of the God of Israel. Jesus' unusual birth should for them be presented more negatively; the unknown or strange circumstances surrounding Mary's pregnancy provided opponents a real opportunity to throw a spin that made Jesus (and, by inference, his followers) targets of social shame.

The stories of births in antiquity frequently functioned to honor well-known figures who were regarded as exemplary or, conversely, to cast those thought to be notoriously evil in a negative light.[22] In other words, such stories were bound up

---

have known a man (Lk. 1:34 – "how will this come about, since I do not know a man?") would be read as a denial of both this possibility and the claim that a man other than Joseph was Jesus' father.

[19] The combination of messianic identity with the work of God's "spirit" found support during the Second Temple period through widespread interpretation of Isa. 11:1–5 (v. 1 – "there shall go forth a shoot from the stump of Jesse, and a branch from its roots shall bear fruit", v. 2 – "the Spirit of the Lord shall rest upon him", v. 4 – "with his breath he will slay the wicked"); cf. *Pss. Sol.* 17:24, 35; *2 Bar.* 40:2; cf. *1 En.* 62:2–3; 4Q285 7.4; CD ii 12; 4Q270 2 ii 14; 4Q534 3 i 6–10.

[20] Cf. Miller, *Born Divine.*

[21] Evidence for such attitudes in the sources has, for example, been emphasized in the politicizing reconstructions of Jesus' activity by Samuel G. F. Brandon, *Jesus and the Zealots: A Study of the Political Factor in Primitive Christianity* (Manchester: Manchester University Press, 1967) and Ed P. Sanders, *Jesus and Judaism* (Philadelphia: Fortress Press, 1985).

[22] See Suetonius, *Divus Augustus* 2–6 (the birth and parentage is contested against the claims of Marcus Antonius); *Tiberius* 2–5 (different accounts compared); *Caius Caligula* 8 (different accounts compared); *Divus Claudius* 2 (but see the account of the suspicious birth of Claudius' father, Drusus, in 1); *Nero* 6 (note the interest in his ancestral heritage in 2–5); *Galba* (2–4, emphasis on his noble origin in 2); *Otho* 2 (interest in his ancestral heritage in 1); *Vittelius* 3 (interest in his contested ancestral heritage in 1–2); *Divus Vespanianus* 1 (ancestral heritage in 2);

with honoring and shaming, especially where groups of supporters and opponents of a personage were contesting his or her legacy. Unlike biographies today, which are constructed around events that illustrate the development of a character, in antiquity "biographies" of an individual were much more likely simply to adopt a view (i. e., whether that person was exemplary or not) and, as necessary, they superimposed this view onto his or her major life events.[23] Thus, the manner of birth and death of acclaimed, notorious or controversial figures quickly – if not from the very start of being told – became a matter of propaganda; the judgment of their character was simply replayed in *how* one related what happened concerning the *way* such figures were said to have been born or died. To state, for example, that Jesus was sired by a Roman soldier (some traditions name him "Pandera" or "Panthera", traceable to a deliberate subversion of the Greek word for virgin, "parthenos"/παρθένος)[24] was tantamount to saying that Jesus, by his very nature, was opposed to his own people; in this way, and on a profound level, Jesus is ultimately presented as an ally of the Roman oppressors of the Jews. Either way, Jesus' parentage – especially his paternal origin – was vulnerable to controversy, and it is precisely here where much of the debate took shape.[25]

The reasons for this or that view all show how difficult it is to subject the story of Jesus' birth to "historical analysis", if by that we are inquiring into "what originally happened". No one in antiquity could refer to this event without considerable social and religious investment; not surprisingly, much the same can be said about scholarly views voiced today. Therefore, if one poses a historical question at all, the issue is where and how to frame it. If we leave the event itself to one side, one investigation can focus on ancient ideas that lead to a better understanding of the social and ideological locations in which the varied and fractious discourse about Jesus' beginnings arose. For the interpretation of the gospel accounts in particular, one may properly focus on the mythological framework within which a claim about Jesus as the "Son of God" or as born "of the Holy Spirit" could have taken shape.

Divus Titus 1; *Domitianus* 1. See also Plutarch, *Life of Alexander* 2–3 (Alexander's birth accompanied by a sign, the serpent with his mother signifying his divine origin); *Lives of the Noble Greeks and Romans, Theseus* (2–3). See further Miller, *Born Divine: The Births of Jesus & Other Sons of God*, pp. 133–153.

[23] See esp. the monograph studies by Charles H. Talbert, *What is a Gospel? The Genre of the Canonical Gospels* (Philadelphia: Fortress Press, 1977); Dirk Frickenschmidt, *Evangelium als Biographie: Die vier Evangelien im Rahmen antiker Erzählkunst* (TANZ 22; Tübingen: Mohr Siebeck, 1997); and Richard A. Burridge, *What are the Gospels? A Comparison with Graeco-Roman Biography* (Grand Rapids: Eerdmans, 2004, 2nd ed.).

[24] Cf. Schäfer, *Jesus in the Talmud*, for a critical evaluation of the rabbinic and later Jewish evidence of this version of Jesus' birth.

[25] It is possible that this concern lies behind the language applied in the debate in John's Gospel between Jesus and "the Jews" regarding their respective *fatherly* origins (Jn. 8:39–59). There is no existing tradition that attempts to throw doubt on Mary having been Jesus' mother.

Now it has been assumed that opponents of the early Christian movement would have tried to demythologize the account, that is, they would have wished to undermine Jesus by asserting through their own versions of the birth story – whether this involved Jesus being fathered by a soldier or even by Joseph – that he was not only merely human but also an undignified one at that. I would like to argue, however, that one circulated version about Jesus' conception has not been given sufficient attention, namely, that Jesus ultimately originated from the devil who was understood as a chief rebellious angelic being. In what follows, I shall elaborate the logic behind this myth, while linking it to two further hypotheses. The first hypothesis is that the earliest versions of Jesus' birth, which circulated well before the stories in Matthew and Luke took shape, did not originally mention the "Holy Spirit" as playing a direct role in Mary's pregnancy.[26] The second hypothesis, which follows from the first, is that the "Holy Spirit" was added to an older tradition about Jesus' birth in order to refute the charge that Jesus' parentage involved an evil angel or the devil. To be as clear as possible in our considerations, I propose that we first discuss the earliest reconstructable tradition about Jesus' birth, that we then consider the counter-claims that were being raised by Jesus' opponents, and, finally, that we ask how the birth narratives may have developed in response to these accusations.

Jesus' Conception: pre-Gospel Tradition

The earliest recoverable account of Jesus' birth was already steeped in and shaped by traditional language; it was probably told at an early stage in a manner reminiscent of several annunciation narratives preserved for us through the Hebrew Bible,[27] having to do with the births of Ishmael (Gen. 16:7–12, announced by an "angel of the Lord" – מלאך יהוה, ἄγγελος κυρίου), the patriarch Isaac (Gen. 17:19; 18:9–15), the prophet Samuel (1 Sam. 1:3–20), and Samson (Jdg. 13:2–25). In the story of Samson, similar to the accounts about John the Baptizer and Jesus in Luke 1:5–20 and 1:26–38, it is an "angel" or "angel of the Lord" (מלאך יהוה, ἄγγελος κυρίου: Jdg. 13:3, 13, 15–18, 20–21; cf. Lk. 1:11, then simply "the angel" in 1:13, 18–19, 26, 30, 34–35, 38) who announces the birth of a special son through appearances, first to the wife of Menoah (Jdg. 13:3–5, 9) and then to Menoah

---

[26] This has nothing to do with affirming or denying the theological convictions of many Christians about the Holy Spirit's involvement; it is simply to argue that earliest traditions probably did not describe Jesus' birth in this way.

[27] Cf. Rudolf Bultmann, *History of the Synoptic Tradition*, trans. John Marsh (London / New York / Hagerstown / San Francisco: Harper & Row, 1963, revd. ed.), pp. 291–292 (and n. 2 for further references). For Bultmann the Jewish tradition provided the source behind the birth narratives (esp. Mt.), while the tradition, as it reached the gospels themselves, had been transformed by "Hellenism, where the idea of a king or a hero from a virgin by the godhead was widespread".

himself (13:11–20). The angel specifies to the wife that she will conceive and bear a son (Jdg. 13:3; cf. Lk. 1:31) and that he will be a Nazirite and deliver Israel from the hand of the Philistines (Jdg. 13:4, 7; cf. Mt. 1:21). The angel also instructs both the mother and her husband that she is to observe dietary restrictions, including that she not eat anything "unclean" (Jdg. 13:7, 14). The narrative goes on to claim repeatedly that "the Spirit of Adonai (YHWH)" was active in Samson's life (רוח יהוה, πνεῦμα κυρίου: 13:25; 14:6; 15:14; cf. Lk. 1:15 for John – "and he shall be filled with the Holy Spirit" καὶ πνεύματος ἁγίου πλησθήσεται – and 4:14 for Jesus), implying a connection between God's activity and a claim about Samson's cultic purity channelled to him through his mother.

The model of an angelic annunciation informed the descriptions of both the birth of John the Baptizer and that of Jesus in Luke 1. At the same time, the Lukan birth narrative uses both accounts to distinguish clearly between John and Jesus. Raymond Brown has, for example, attempted to show that the parallels between these birth stories serve to emphasize that Jesus is greater than John.[28] Like the Hebrew Bible stories, the former account about the birth of John the Baptist involves a woman who is (a) barren at first and who, (b) with her husband, is elderly (Lk. 1:7). In addition, the work of the Spirit, as we have seen above, relates to the person's later activity (so Samson and John the Baptizer). In the case of Mary, on the other hand, we have to do with a young woman for whom barrenness is not a problem, and the Spirit's involvement is claimed in relation to the conception itself (Lk. 1:35; cf. Mt. 1:18, 20). Despite these differences, common to each of these stories, especially to the birth of Samson and to Jesus, is the avoidance of language that states *explicitly* that the birth announced by the angel occurs as the result of sexual relations.[29] Those who told these stories probably assumed that these births came about through normal procreative activity, though in the stories themselves they wished to underline the beneficent role of God in the event. However, absence of any specific or euphemistic mention of sex following the announcements by angels would have furnished a useful form, at least initially, through which to communicate the birth of the special person. This form, as far as Jesus' birth is concerned, is followed more closely by the Gospel of Luke; in Luke 1:26–38 the angel "Gabriel" (a name that literally means "man of God" – angelic beings in Jewish antiquity are invariably represented as male) appears to Mary and announces the birth and its importance (1:30–33):

Do not be afraid, Mary; you have found favor with God. You will be with child and give birth to a son, and you are to give him the name Jesus. He will be great and will be called the Son of the Most High. The Lord God will give him the throne of his father David, and he will reign over the house of Jacob forever; his kingdom will never end.

---

[28] Brown, *The Birth of the Messiah*, pp. 300–301; Green, *The Gospel of Luke*, p. 83 (a comparative table); and esp. Freed, *The Stories of Jesus' Birth*, pp. 114–115.

[29] Andrew T. Lincoln, "Luke and Jesus' Conception: A Case of Double Paternity", *JBL* 132 (2013), pp. 639–658 (here pp. 651–652).

Though the significance of Jesus, in continuity with tradition in the Hebrew Bible, may at first have been underscored along conventional lines, the gathering of traditional material around him, including traditions about controversies between Jesus and contemporary Jews who opposed him, ensured that a story patterned after an angelic annunciation would soon undergo change. In fact, it may well be that the shift from an angelic annunciation to something more directly concerned with the nature of Jesus' person happened almost immediately.[30] After all, both birth narratives preserved for us in the New Testament (Matthew and Luke) take such a further step; they emphasize that Jesus' origin is bound up with the activity of the God of Israel and underscore this claim by attributing a role in the birth to the Holy Spirit.

Despite the tradition common to Matthew and Luke, nothing compels us to suppose that the Holy Spirit was a progenerative agent for Jesus' conception in the earliest form of the birth narratives.[31] This is reflected in the earliest formal mentions of Jesus' birth, which were made by Paul in his letters to the Galatians and Romans. In the former, Paul states that, "God sent forth his Son, born of a woman, born under the law" (4:4). This remark specifies that God had something to do with the advent of Jesus, without, however, specifically linking God's activity with the birth itself. Moreover, the text, which is formulated very concisely, makes no mention of the Spirit or Holy Spirit. Writing his letter to the Romans around 56 C. E., however, Paul asserts near the beginning something about Jesus' birth in which he no doubt borrows from earlier Jewish-Christian tradition.[32] According to Romans 1:3–4, Jesus is described as:

... the Son who came into being *out of the seed of David according to the flesh*, who was *raised (as) the Son of God in power according to the Spirit of holiness* out of the resurrection of the dead, Jesus Christ our Lord.

Here "the Spirit of holiness" (πνεῦμα ἁγιωσύνης), which is reminiscent of Hebrew tradition (רוח הקודש) is, unlike the infancy narratives of the gospels, not linked to the birth of Jesus itself; instead, Jesus' origin is "out of the seed of David according to the flesh" (ἐκ σπέρματος Δαυὶδ κατὰ σάρκα; cf. also the later 2 Tim. 2:8). As

---

[30] This shift in the growth of tradition towards Jesus' divinity ("the Son of the Most High") does not entirely leave behind the notion of his human parentage ("his father David"); cf. Lincoln, "Luke and Jesus' Conception" (bibl. in n. 30).

[31] Indeed, the casual references to Jesus' parentage in Mk. 6:1–6 (esp. v. 3) and Jn. 6:42 do not assume more than that Jesus, important as he was, had a normal birth; cf. Jürgen Becker, *Jesus of Nazareth*, trans. James E. Crouch (Berlin: Walter de Gruyter, 1998), pp. 21–22.

[32] See *inter alia* Charles E. B. Cranfield, *The Epistle to the Romans* (2 vols.; ICC; Edinburgh: T. & T. Clark, 1975), 1:57–65; Otto Michel, *Der Brief an die Römer* (KDKNT 4; Göttingen: Vandenhoeck & Ruprecht, 1978, 5th ed.), pp. 72–73; Ernst Käsemann, *Commentary on Romans*, trans. Geoffrey W. Bromiley (Grand Rapids: Eerdmans, 1980), pp. 10–14; James D. G. Dunn, *Romans 1–8* (WBC 38A; Dallas: Word, 1988), pp. 10–15; Joseph A. Fitzmyer, *Romans* (AB 33; New York: Doubleday, 1992), pp. 229–230; Robert Jewett, *Romans* (Hermeneia; Minneapolis: Fortress Press, 2007), pp. 98–103.

many commentators have noted, the language used here is uncharacteristic of Paul and, in its conciseness, draws on an earlier formulation that would have circulated, for example, in the early community of Jesus' Jewish followers. Instead of being related to the birth, the Spirit is associated with the claim that Jesus was resurrected after his death; whereas Jesus' birth betrayed an ancestry that "according to the flesh" goes back to David, his status as Son of God is linked to the resurrection event in which the Spirit of holiness functioned as the divine agent. The role of the Spirit is thus understood to be that of life-giving power that overcomes death of the mortal body (as also in Rom. 8:12; cf. Gen. 1:2, in which "the Spirit of God" is presented as an active creative force). Though neither Galatians 4:4 nor Romans 1:3–4 actually deny the Spirit a role in Jesus' birth, the non-mention of the Spirit in Paul contrasts markedly from the emphasis on or at least mention of the Holy Spirit in the gospel narratives. All this lends further weight to the possibility that, at least in these Jewish Christian traditions, the Spirit did not feature as an essential component in relation to the birth of Jesus.

So, because of what Matthew and Luke share in common (despite their differences) – the unusual circumstances of Mary, the supportive role of a prominent angel, and the involvement of the Holy Spirit – we may infer that it was not long (indeed, well before the gospel birth narratives took their present shape) before the agency of the Holy Spirit was added to an angelic annunciation. The question we may ask is *why*? Why would the early devotees of Jesus who began to tell and retell the story of Jesus' birth require, in an unprecedented manner, that the tradition involve the Holy Spirit in Jesus' birth? After all, if they were wishing to assert something like Jesus' divinity, there would have been other ways of doing so, for which mentioning the "Holy Spirit" was unnecessary.[33] One possible answer to this question may be brought under the following four points.

The Holy Spirit and Jesus' Birth

First, *there were accusations that Jesus' deeds were performed by demonic power, that is, by an evil or unclean spirit.* According to Mark's Gospel chapter 3 (cf. vv. 22–

---

[33] As, for example, is the case with the Prologue in the Gospel of John (1:1–14). Brown, *The Birth of the Messiah*, pp. 311–316, follows a generally held scheme of development in early Christology when he argues that, historically, the Spirit's involvement was moved back from the time of Jesus' resurrection (cf. Rom. 1:3–4) to the time of Jesus' baptism (Lk. 3:22; cf. Mk. 1:10–11 // Mt. 3:16–17; cf. Acts 10:37–38), which, in time, was pushed further back to encompass Jesus' very birth (esp. Lk. 1:35). Whereas the first two events draw on the Davidic royal ideology in Ps. 2:7 ("today I have begotten you"), there is no hint of adoption (i.e., of *becoming* Son of God) in the birth story, which speaks of the Holy Spirit as "overshadowing" Mary (Lk. 1:35). Brown's explanation of how earlier Christological formulations are applied to Jesus' conception can be entertained as plausible, though it does not address why it is that, unlike Lk. 3:22, Acts 10:37–38 and Rom. 1:3–4, the birth narratives preserve the tradition that delineates the Spirit as "holy" (see below).

30), the experts in the law "were saying" (ἔλεγον) – the form of the verb (in the impf.) denotes that this occurred not once, but repeatedly – that Jesus is carrying out his activity in alliance with Beelzebul: "he has Beelzebul and by the ruler of demons he is casting out demons" (v. 22). In an attached saying, Jesus declares that all sins will be forgiven people except for one: sinning against the "Holy Spirit" (3:28–29). The narrative, in a parenthetic comment (3:30), goes on to explain that Jesus had made this statement (in reply to the accusations) "because they were saying (again ἔλεγον), 'He has an *unclean* spirit (πνεῦμα ἀκάθαρτον ἔχει).'" The narrative in Mark's Gospel does not in itself provide an answer to the charge of Jesus operating under an unclean spirit's influence (i. e., of Beelzebul) beyond the logical argument that Satan, if Jesus were on his side, would surely not act in opposition to himself (3:23 – "can Satan cast out Satan?").[34] There is no need to imagine that Jesus' opponents would have been convinced by such an argument; those among Jesus' devotees who transmitted tradition about him knew this kind of debate and would have been aware that simply to counter an accusation with a counter-accusation (Jesus' word against the word of his opponents, as happens in Jn. 8:39–47) would not be sufficient in the eyes of some in order to underline Jesus' alliance with God. Moreover, it is likely that Jesus' opponents would not have found Jesus' words a convincing response to their accusation.[35] How, then, does one defend Jesus by re-enforcing the conviction that Jesus was pious and so not under the influence of demons? Though the debate about collusion with Satan surfaces in Mark chapter 3 (see parallels in Mt. 12:24–27 and Lk. 11:15–19), it is ultimately a larger issue. Jesus' activities were under suspicion for other reasons: for example, his sharing table fellowship with "sinners" (Mt. 9:10–11; 11:19; Mk. 2:15–16; Lk. 5:30; 7:34, 37; 15:1–2; 19:7) and his and his disciples' improper or, at best, casual observance of the Sabbath (Mt. 12:1–12; Mk. 2:23–3:4; Lk. 6:1–9; 13:14–16; 14:1–5) would easily have been associated with ritual impurity.

The association of "Satan" with an "an unclean spirit" in Mark 3 reflects prior tradition, as found in the prayer of deliverance in 11Q5 column xix – "Do not let Satan or an unclean spirit rule over me." One (perhaps obvious) way for Jesus' followers to respond to accusations about his halakhic impropriety would have been to associate him in every possible way with that which is a holy, not unclean (or evil), spirit. Admittedly, neither the Gospel of Matthew nor that of Luke, in their parallels to Mark 3:22–30, attach Mark's explanation that Jesus was responding to the charge of having an "unclean spirit" (cf. Mt. 12:22–32; Lk. 11:14–20). However, it was certainly important for those rising to Jesus' defence, at an early stage, to associate the activity of Jesus with a pure spirit as opposed to an unclean

---

[34] The audience will, of course, already be aware of the Spirit coming upon Jesus at his baptism (Mk. 1:10–11); however, that Spirit is not specifically referred to as "holy".

[35] That Jesus' exorcisms could have resulted in the perception of him as dangerous, is also reflected in the witnesses of the Gerasene demoniac episode, due to fear of what happened, wishing Jesus to leave their region (Mk. 5:16–17 pars. Mt. 8:33–34, Lk. 8:36–37).

one and to do so in the form of a story. So, in the development of tradition, part of the answer to the question raised within Mark's Gospel can be found in the Gospels of Matthew and Luke in the storyline provided at the very outset. Jesus not only performed deeds and spoke by the Holy Spirit,[36] he was also *conceived* of the Holy Spirit. If the story is told in this way, Jesus' very being, from inception, makes it impossible that he (or those who follow him) should collude with Satan in any way. The need to insist that Jesus did what was clean led to the claim that he himself was clean at the very start.

Second, *Jesus' birth by the Holy Spirit takes shape as part of an early argument which emphasizes that Jesus' origin cannot be linked with an unclean spirit.* The divine sanctioning of Jesus' activity is re-enforced by a portrait regarding his origin. The use of a birth narrative to counter or address debates about the propriety or impropriety of a person's deeds draws on a widely held assumption in that there is a link between activities attributed to a wonder-worker and the nature of his/her origin in antiquity.[37] It was only natural when someone did unusual things, such as miraculous deeds, to ask where this person came from. One example occurs in Mark 6:1–6: when Jesus is doing miracles in Galilee, the people ask (v. 3), "Is this not the son of Mary (v. 3; some mss. include the reading, 'the son of the carpenter' as in Mt. 13:55[38])?" A further example suggests itself in John 1:46, according to which Nathanael's comment regarding Jesus, "Can anything good come from Nazareth?", expresses grounds for suspecting his character. Just as Jesus' identity as the son of Mary (or further, of a carpenter) and his Galilean identity affected popular opinion concerning his legitimacy, so too the question of the manner and origin of his birth regulated opinion concerning the identity of this worker of wonders.

---

[36] See Mk. 1:8 pars. Mt. 3:11, Lk. 3:16, Jn. 1:33; Mk. 1:12 par. Mt. 4:1; Lk. 10:21; Mt. 12:28; Jn. 5:9–10, 16, 18; 7:22–23; 9:14, 16.

[37] Note Origen (*c. Cels.* 1.28–37), who quotes the detractor of Christianity, Celsus, as drawing on a Jewish man's argument that Jesus' birth was the result of an act of adultery on Mary's part, so that Jesus is rendered illegitimate (28; cf. *b. Shabbat* 104b, *b. Sanhedrin* 67a). Significantly, the debate is not really about the birth itself, but takes its point of departure in what Celsus, the Jewish man, and Origen believed regarding the validity of Jesus' (and his disciples') activities. See also *Life of Apollonius* (of Tyana) by his admirer Philostratus, who claims that Apollonius' birth was accompanied by a series of miraculous signs to underscore his legitimacy as a philosopher and wonder worker (1.4–17). Birth accounts, of course, played an important role in sanctioning or undermining the character of debated figures, as repeatedly illustrated in Suetonius' *Lives of the Caesars* and Plutarch's *Lives of the Noble Greeks and Romans* (cf. n. 22 above).

[38] The most important witness to this reading of Mk. 6:3 is the 3rd cent. 𝔓[45], though it is probably an accommodation to Mt. 13:55 (cf. also Lk. 4:22). The Matthean text could, in light of this discussion, be understood as a charge that problematizes Jesus in terms of his origins, i.e. someone with a father who is merely a carpenter should neither be able to teach as he does in the synagogue nor accomplish these miracles. For a different explanation that argues that the reading "son of a carpenter" attempts to distance Jesus from the class of his father and so to undergird his authority, for example, as a teacher, see Chris Keith, *Jesus Against the Scribal Elite* (Grand Rapids: Baker Academic, 2014), pp. 50–56.

Third, *among Second Temple Jewish traditions that come down to us, there was a mythological framework within which the idea of Jesus' demonic origin could be imagined.* What might such a tradition have looked like? During the Second Temple period, a growing number of accounts were told about the way evil and, with it, sin were introduced into the world. These were not actually concerned with the origin of evil *per se*, but rather were stories making claims about beginnings in order to enjoin certain kinds of social behavior or to offer perspectives in the face of sociopolitical and religious upheaval. Among such stories, there was an increasing emphasis that sin was introduced into the world involving the agency of Adam (4 Ez. 7:116–125, *2 Bar.* 54:15, 19; Rom. 5:12), Eve (*Book of Parables* in *1 En.* 69:6–7; Ben Sira 25:21–26; *2 En.* 30:16–17; 2 Cor. 11:3; 1 Tim. 2:8–15), women in general (*T. Reub.* 5:1–6; cf. *1 En.* 8:1 Grk. Syncellus), or humans in general (*Epistle of Enoch* at *1 En.* 98:4–6; Jas. 1:13–16). Sometimes, the role of Adam or Eve was combined, of course, with the notion of coming under the influence of a demonic figure, whether an evil angel (*Book of Parables* at *1 En.* 69:6–7) or an overarching malevolent being at the top (2 Cor. 11:3; *Vit. Ad. et Ev.* 12:1–16:3); sometimes a particular activity is blamed for evil, such as idolatry (Wisd. Sol. 14:27–31), the wearing of jewellery or use of beautification techniques (1 Tim. 2:8–15; *T. Reub.* 5:1–6; cf. Sir. 25:21–26), or one's own appetite (Jas. 1:13–16); sometimes, texts simply mention "the devil" (Wisd. Sol. 2:21–24) or a demonic being such as "the Angel of Darkness" (1QS iii 20–23). These "origins" were often combined with one another in various forms, so that we cannot posit any existing master or systematized narrative that was emerging within Jewish tradition at the turn of the Common Era. Arguably, one of the popular stories, which circulated in Jewish apocalyptic tradition, had to do with what is conventionally called "the fallen angels" (cf. esp. *Book of Watchers* in *1 En.* chs. 6–11; *Book of Giants*; cf. *Jub.* 5:1–8; 10:1–11). This story located itself and took shape in relation to tradition familiar to us from Genesis 6:1–4. In this brief and unusual passage of the Hebrew Bible, which occurs just before God sends the Great Flood during the days of Noah, beings called "sons of God" are said to have been attracted to the beautiful women among the humans who had been multiplying on the face of the earth (Gen. 6:1–2). These "sons of God" – soon to be called "angels" (so Philo, *De gig.*; Cod. Alex.) and "watchers" (*1 En.*) by, respectively, Jewish translators into Greek and Jewish authors of literature composed before the 1st century C. E. – sired a race of large men called "Nephilim" (נפילים) or "giants" (גבורים) through these women. Although the text of Genesis itself does not say anything so obviously negative about either these "sons of God" or the "giants" they sired – the giants, in Genesis 6:4 are even called "men of repute" (אנשי השם) – Jewish apocalyptic tradition went to great lengths to ensure that they would be categorically branded as bad.[39] According to the early Enoch tradition found in the *Book of Watchers*

---

[39] This would be to counter construals of the tradition that traced the ancestry of Noah and

(*1 En.* 7–8), the rebellious angels not only introduced objectionable practices into the world such as the making of weaponry, cosmetics, and jewelry, as well as the use of herbal medicines, astrology and related activities, but they and their off-spring the giants also were the primary and most immediate reason why God took action to punish evil during the time of the Great Flood. In particular, the "giants" were singled out as bad for two reasons: (1) they were thought to have oppressed human beings and the rest of the created order (vegetation and animal species) to the brink of extinction; and (2) they were half angel and half human and thus embodied within their nature a forbidden mixture of heavenly and earthly spheres which should be kept separate (cf. *1 En.* 15:8–11). Being such an unsanctioned mix, they were "unclean" creatures without a legitimate place within the created order.[40] Divine punishment came in response to the cries and com-plaints of the souls of people who had suffered mercilessly on account of the giants (*1 En.* 8:4). God's response was to punish the angels and the giants, while humans – represented by Noah and his family – were saved and could live on. Since the giants had been half angel and half human, only the flesh side of their existence was destroyed. After the Flood, then, they could be allowed to exist in the form of spirits, disembodied from the flesh that they had once inhabited. We can infer from the traditions that these spirits were therefore jealous of human beings, who survived the Flood's destruction with their bodies intact. Thus, the giants' spirits were thought to be responsible for making life miserable for people through every kind of affliction, not least through attempting to enter into their bodies, that is, into a kind of embodied existence that they knew before they were punished (*1 En.* 15–16; *Jub.* 10). Now this "story" functioned, among other things, as an explanation for some Jews during the Second Temple period for the existence of demons as well as the rationale behind why demons were thought to be so intent on *entering* into the bodies of humans. Jesus' ministry of exorcism, which focuses on *expelling* or *driving out* demons from people's bodies, is ulti-mately to be understood against this background,[41] and there are vestiges of a tradition that even explicitly identify demons as the disembodied giants directly (*Test. Sol.*; 11Q11 v). In addition, some of the fallen angels themselves could be thought to be evil spirits (see *1 En.* 19:1), and there was a growing tradition that conflated these bad angels with the giants.

Now to those who were familiar with rebellious angels from Jewish apocalyptic tradition, the claim that Jesus' birth was of the "Holy Spirit" may have been heard

---

even Abraham to the giants (Pseudo-Eupolemus fragments; cf. also the suspicion that Noah was a giant in the *Genesis Apocryphon* [1Q20] col. ii and the *Birth of Noah* in *1 En.* chs. 106–107); see chapters One and Three above.

[40] In *1 En.* 10:9, the Greek text of Cod. Pan. reads τοὺς μεζηρέους = Heb. ממזרים "bastards"; the term is taken up among the Dead Sea materials within the expression "spirits of the bastards", רוחי ממזרים, who are probably the spirits that come from the giants who had been disembodied after the time of the Flood).

[41] See the more detailed discussion in Chapter Nine below.

in a particular way. The Gospels of Matthew and Luke and those devotees of Jesus from whom the gospels received the birth stories would have wanted to ensure that Jesus' birth, mysterious and open to suspicion as it was, *cannot in any way be linked with a popular myth about women being impregnated by prominent, disobedient angelic beings*. Any hint or suspicion of such an origin of Jesus, as implied by those opposed to Jesus' ministry, should not be allowed to fester.

The possibility of such a tradition playing a role in the background at early stages of the tradition about Jesus' birth is raised if one recognizes that during the Second Temple period the association between evil angelic beings and unusual circumstances surrounding the birth of a righteous figure did not circulate infrequently.[42] We may note three examples, two of which are interrelated and are concerned with the figure of Noah who, of course, lived before, during, and after the days of the Great Flood. In the texts cited below, writers wrote about Noah's birth while contemplating what it would have meant for the event to have taken place during the time before the Flood. In this way they "historicized" the myth of the rebellious angels, as Noah's conception and birth were coordinated with the time when the "sons of God" were siring the giants (Gen. 6:1–4).

The first of the two texts about Noah's birth are found in the fragmentary text from the early extant columns of the Aramaic *Genesis Apocryphon* (1Q20), a document likely composed during the 2nd century B. C. E. and the copy of which, on palaeographical grounds, can be dated to around the turn of the Common Era.[43] In the storyline, the wife of Noah's father Lamech, falls pregnant. Significantly, she is named Bitenosh (1Q20 ii 2, בתאנש), which suggestively means "daughter of man", no doubt an allusion to Genesis 6:2, according to which the "daughters of Adam" (Heb. בנות האדם) were impregnated by the sons of God. Lamech, speaking in the 1st person at the beginning of column ii, notices something unusual. Because of the missing text at the end of column i, however, we do not know whether it was the pregnancy itself that raised his suspicion[44] or, as in the parallel text of

---

[42] The first scholar, as far as I know, to note a possible connection between the rebellious angels tradition and the birth narratives of Matthew and Luke was Vermes, *Jesus the Jew*, pp. 214 and 265 (n. 106). In addition, see the discussion by George W. E. Nickelsburg, "Patriarchs Who Worry about their Wives: A Haggadic Tendency in the Genesis Apocryphon", in eds. Michael E. Stone and Esther G. Chazon, *Biblical Perspectives: Early Use and Interpretation of the Bible in Light of the Dead Sea Scrolls. Proceedings of the First International Symposium of the Orion Center for the Study of the Dead Sea Scrolls and Associated Literature, 12–14 May 1996* (STDJ 28; Leiden: Brill, 1998), pp. 137–158. While recognizing the significance of the adjective "holy" as attached to both angelic beings (even rebellious ones) and to the "spirit" in the birth narratives, neither Vermes nor Nickelsburg develop the point in relation to Jesus' ministry as suggested here.

[43] The time of composition and the palaeographical dating should not be confused. Fitzmyer's dating of the *Genesis Apocryphon* to the 1st cent. C. E. is, in any case, much too late. See the recent discussion by Daniel A. Machiela, *The Dead Sea Genesis Apocryphon (1Q20): A New Text and Translation, with Introduction and Special Treatment of Columns 13–17* (STDJ 79; Leiden: Brill, 2009), pp. 134–142.

[44] In this case it would presumably have been on account of Bitenosh's unusually large size.

1 Enoch 106:5–6 (see below), it was the appearance of Noah at his birth. Lamech suspects that his wife has been impregnated by "the Watchers" or that "the seed was from the holy ones or Nephil[im".[45] The circumstances around Noah's conception, in other words, are linked to the fallen angels tradition and Lamech worries that Noah is a giant or perhaps even one of their offspring.[46] Thinking that his wife has had sexual intercourse with one of these beings, Lamech asks his wife about the matter; in response, she tries to remind her husband of her sexual pleasure (1Q20 ii 9, 14 – עדינתי) that led to the pregnancy. Continuing to worry, Lamech relates the situation to his father Methuselah, who, in turn, travels to Enoch, who lives far away in "Parvain", to ask for an explanation (1Q20 ii 19–26). Enoch explains that, in fact, the child is not the product of a wayward angel, but rather has been sired by Lamech himself (1Q20 v 3–4: "n[ot] from the sons of / heaven but from Lamech your son"). And so, the irregularity surrounding the child illustrates the purposes of God and has nothing whatsoever to do with the activity of a malevolent power.

A parallel account to that of the *Genesis Apocryphon*, again extant among fragmentary Aramaic remains (4QEnoch^c = 4Q204 5 i–ii)[47] but fully preserved in later corresponding Ethiopic and Greek versions in the *Birth of Noah* at *1 Enoch* 106–107.[48] Here, Lamech again is suspicious that his wife (who this time is not named) has been made pregnant by one of the "angels of heaven" (οἱ ἄγγελοι τοῦ οὐρανοῦ, Eth. *malā'ekta samāy*; *1 En.* 106:5, 6, 12). More clearly than in the *Genesis Apocryphon*, Lamech's worry has to do with Noah's unusual appearance and activity at the moment of his birth. Upon seeing Noah, Lamech declares:

"I have begotten a strange son: He is not like an (ordinary) human being, but looks like the children of the angels of heaven to me;[49] his form is different, and he is not like us. His eyes are like the rays of the sun, and his face glorious. It does not seem to me that he is of me, but of angels ... his image is (from) the angels of heaven." (*1 En.* 106:5–6, 12)

Again, Lamech asks his father Methuselah to consult Enoch. Enoch announces that, in effect, Noah's appearance indicates that God is doing something extraordinary for the sake of humanity during that catastrophic time when angels are having sex with women and fathering giants who corrupt the earth (*1 En.* 106:13–

---

[45] For a closer reading of this passage, see Chapter Three sections C.1 to C.4 above and n. 33 for possible readings of this text. It is worth noting here, however, that the term "holy" (Aram. קדיש, Heb. קדוש) could refer to the rebellious angels as well as to the obedient ones; in addition to 1Q20 ii 1, see vi 20, the *Book of Watchers* at 4Q201 1 i 3, and 11Q11 v 6.

[46] That it was thought that the giants were also siring during the time before the Flood is reflected in *1 En.* 7:1–2 (Grk. Syncellus) and *Jub.* 7:22.

[47] See Józef T. Milik, *The Books of Enoch. Aramaic Fragments from Qumrân Cave 4* (Oxford: Clarendon, 1976), pp. 217–225 and 353–355 and Plates XVI–XVII.

[48] For a more thoroughgoing discussion of the Eth., Grk. and shorter Lat. versions of the text, see Loren T. Stuckenbruck, *1 Enoch 91–108* (CEJL; Berlin / New York: Walter de Gruyter, 2007), pp. 606–689, from which also the translation is taken.

[49] I. e., Lamech thinks Noah may be one of the giants.

17). Noah functions, then, as an anti-giant figure;[50] he is God's answer to what the rebellious angels have been doing. Noah's wondrous appearance is a sign that God has the situation under control and, through Noah, will save and guarantee the survival of humanity in the coming cataclysm (106:16, 18; the passive "saved" denoting God's activity). Significantly, the text goes on, as it stands, to draw a parallel between the time of the Flood and eschatological time when, after a period of increasing evil, the audience of the text can expect the salvific activity of God to win out when "a generation of righteousness" arises (106:18–107:1).

It is important to note here that, despite the parallels to the gospel birth narratives, there is no hint that Lamech's wife is in either case a virgin or, perhaps more significantly, that Noah is being presented as an active agent whose own activity brings God's purposes about. Much more, in the Enochic *Birth of Noah*, the figure of Noah, especially his name, symbolizes what *God* does to rescue humanity during the time of the Flood.[51]

A third text, whose ultimate origin and date is disputed, is concerned with the unusual birth of Melchizedek, which is claimed to have taken place just before the Flood. The tradition is preserved in *2 Enoch* chapters 71–72 and is only preserved in Old Church Slavonic (the earliest of which is dated to the 14th cent.). The passage, which is extant through at least two, perhaps up to four recensions,[52] is unstable, making it difficult to secure the text[53] and, even given that, to posit traditions early enough to be considered for a meaningful comparison with the birth narratives of the gospels, especially that of Luke. The story, however, preserves several remarkable features, which furnish a basis for comparison with both the Hebrew Bible and Second Temple stories, on the one hand, and with those of the gospels, on the other. Like the former texts, the mother of Melchizedek, Sopanima, who is the wife of "Nir" the brother of "Noe", is old and barren (*2 En.* 71:1–2). Like the gospels, however, a sexual abstinence (in relation to the birth itself) is maintained. This abstinence is emphasized in relation to the father, Nir, who has lived in this state since assuming priestly office (71:2). Interestingly, Nir is declared to have been sexually abstinent once he had assumed his priestly office (72:2). While nothing is explicitly stated in the text traditions that an evil angel has made

---

[50] See the discussion in Chapter One, section C above on early Enochic responses to the tradition, preserved in the Pseudo-Eupolemus fragments, that present Noah as one of the giants.

[51] As correctly argued by James C. VanderKam, "The Birth of Noah", in ed. Zdzislaw J. Kapera, *Intertestamental Essays in honour of Jósef Tadeusz Milik* (Qumranica Mogilanensia, 6; Cracow: The Enigma Press, 1992), pp. 213–31.

[52] For an excellent summary of these issues, see the contributions by Christfried Böttrich, "The 'Book of the Secrets of Enoch' (2En) Between Jewish Origin and Christian Transmission. An Overview" and Grant Macaskill, "Manuscripts, Recensions, and Original Language", in eds. Andrei A. Orlov and Gabriele Boccaccini, *New Perspectives on 2 Enoch: No Longer Slavonic Only* (SJS 4; Leiden/Boston: Brill, 2011), pp. 37–68 and 83–102, respectively.

[53] The recently published edition by Grant Macaskill is therefore a welcome contribution: *The Slavonic Texts of 2 Enoch* (SJS 6; Leiden/Boston: Brill, 2013).

Sopanima pregnant, the father does suspect that something indecent and miraculous has taken place: the pregnancy is inappropriate because he himself was not involved (i. e., through sexual intercourse between husband and wife), and the pregnancy is miraculous because the narrator of the story declares that *no normal sexual relations have taken place* (cf. 71:2). The child, who is turned over to Nir's care after the mother's death (cf. 72:3), is the product of a creative act of God. When informed by the Lord through a dream about the unprecedented significance that Melchizedek will have as a priest, Nir declares, "Blessed be the Lord, the God of my fathers, who has not condemned my priesthood and the priesthood of my fathers, because by his word he has created a great priest in the womb of Sopanima my wife" (71:30).[54] While further aspects in *2 Enoch* chapters 71–72 may be compared with both the gospels and early Jewish traditions,[55] these details, which are shared among the different recensions, again focus on a suspicious pregnancy that is assigned to the time just preceding the Flood. It is possible that here, the grounds for Nir's suspicion in the text would have derived from Enochic tradition, according to which the angels were impregnating women during this time.

Now it is *not* the intention here to claim that the New Testament gospels show signs of a "massive cover-up" of a mythical tradition that attributed Mary's pregnancy to the sexual activity of an "angel", whether a righteous one (Gabriel) or an evil, unclean one (i. e., one of the rebellious angels). The reason to bring these stories into the conversation is rather to raise plausibility for the claim that one tradition that eventually flowed into the birth narratives of the gospels was concerned with refuting charges that Jesus' activity and his being reflect an alliance with the demonic (cf. Mk. 3:22–30 and parallels). Around the turn of the Common Era, Jewish traditions circulated that could make the parlance possible to imagine in relation to the origin of figures, who are crucial for the unfolding of God's purposes, from a rebellious angel. Indeed, such language could be exploited when questions were raised about the legitimacy of Jesus' controversial and therefore debatable activities. Questions, guided by suspicion, could be posed. To ask, rhetorically, "Where did Jesus get his ability to teach and to do these deeds from?" and "Where is Jesus himself ultimately from?" (cf. Mk. 6:1–3; Mt. 12:53–56) was to bring

---

[54] The citation is adapted from Francis I. Andersen, "2 (Slavonic Apocalypse of) Enoch", in ed. James H. Charlesworth, *The Old Testament Pseudepigrapha* (2 vols.; Garden City: Doubleday, 1983), 1:37. The storyline does not seem interested in offering any details beyond this declaration. In addition, some matters that would attract attention are not developed, Unlike the gospels, there is no mention of a "spirit", Sopanima is not portrayed as a virgin, the involvement of a named angel in the story (whether Michael in the J recension or Gabriel in the A recension) is probably secondary, and no attempt is made to have blame rest on Nir for having hit his wife before she dies and gives birth to the child (*2 En.* 71:8–9).

[55] The most important contribution along these lines thus far is the study by Christfried Böttrich, "Die vergessene Geburtsgeschichte. Mt 1–2/Lk 1–2 und die wunderbare Geburt des Melchizedek in slHen 71–72", in eds. Hermann Lichtenberger and Gerbern S. Oegema, *Jüdische Schriften in ihrem antik-jüdischen und urchristlichen Kontext* (Jüdische Schriften aus hellenistisch-römischer Zeit 1; Gütersloh: Gütersloher Verlagshaus, 2002), pp. 222–248 (esp. pp. 241–244).

together two interwoven issues; to pose and answer the one question was to pose and answer the other.

Fourth, *the addition of the "holy" Spirit to the birth narrative tradition in a form that would eventually be adapted in the gospels suggests that the role of an angel in the annunciation to Joseph and Mary, respectively, was not, in contrast to stories known from the Hebrew Bible, found adequate enough to underscore the singularity of Jesus' significance.* Indeed, the involvement of the "holy" Spirit moves the spotlight of the story away from the role of the angel himself; moreover, we have seen that in Luke 1, the role of the Spirit functions as a way of marking out Jesus as superior to John the Baptizer. However, there is more to be said: the addition of the holy Spirit would have functioned as a corrective against a probable misconception that ancient readers and hearers familiar with Jewish apocalyptic traditions may have had some basis for inferring: namely, that the angel himself might have been involved in some way with the impregnation of Mary.[56] Emphasis on a creative act through the Spirit shifted the tradition away from possible sexual overtones that an angelic annunciation might otherwise imply. Thus the role of Gabriel ("man of God") in Luke 1 remains within the more conventional storyline assigned to angelic figures known in the Jewish scriptures: he merely announces the conception and the birth, and is the first to declare what the significance of the child will be.

Conclusion

It is possible that a claim circulated that Mary, Jesus' mother, had been made pregnant through an evil or unclean spirit, whether directly or implicitly if it was thought that Jesus was an illegitimate child. Even before the gospel traditions in the New Testament took shape, Jesus' followers would have attempted to counteract such a charge with a claim of their own: Jesus' activities were not only in accord with halakhic piety, but his purity was also endemic to his very being. To declare that Jesus was born of the holy Spirit was, therefore, not simply a matter of stating the obvious, nor was the claim initially concerned with emphasizing Jesus' divinity. Rather, the account of Jesus' origins in relation to the Spirit first emerged within a context within which Jesus was seen as a controversial figure, whose activities and instructions, while taking place in an unmistakably Jewish context, could not be easily domesticated or pigeonholed by his contemporaries.

The accounts of Jesus' conception and birth in the gospels of Matthew and Luke functioned in a number of ways: to secure his lineage within Israel's sacred story (more specifically, the line of Davidic kingship), to present him as the Messiah whose coming had been part of God's plan all along, and to underscore his

---

[56] This is indeed the suspicion attributed to Joseph about what happened to Mary in the much later *Protoevangelium of James* 14–15.

superiority to other figures known from Jewish tradition and in the Graeco-Roman world for whom special births were being claimed. Early on, however, the holy Spirit had been introduced into the rapidly developing tradition to safeguard – at least to the apparent satisfaction of Jesus' adherents and devotees – that there was nothing illegitimate about Jesus at all. Jesus may have been controversial, but to them he was entirely "clean". He may have contravened a few religious sensibilities of some Jewish contemporaries, but his followers ensured that accounts about his birth should serve their conviction that from the beginning he was a fully sanctioned agent of God.

Chapter Nine

The Human Being and Demonic Invasion: Therapeutic Models in Ancient Jewish and Christian Texts

Introduction

The expression "mental health" is used today to refer to a state or degree of well-being while, in negative terms, it is sometimes understood as a state in which mental illness or disorder is absent.[1] On the one hand, mental wellness ideally involves the ability to adapt to new situations, to engage in appropriate social behaviour, to handle conflicts and to make considered decisions. On the other hand, discourse about mental illness or mental disorders draws attention to a bewildering variety of problems and, increasingly, to a wide range of diagnoses that characterize a dysfunctional mind. Conditions associated with mental illness have included some of the following designations:[2] psychosis, depression, attention deficit disorder, agoraphobia, paranoia, bulimia, bi-polar disorder, Alzheimer's Disease, Asperger's Syndrome, autism, a diverse set of learning disabilities and all sorts of addictions. These and similar conditions have been regarded as disorders that impact clinical, developmental, personal and psychosocial dimensions of an individual's life and, as is increasingly recognized, often end up affecting the psychological and physical well-being of those affected. The above-named disorders, which themselves are fluid and complex, present issues which, however they are classified, affect people in all parts of the globe. Moreover, they illustrate how difficult it can be to define a particular form of "mental illness" with precision.

If one turns to the Gospel traditions in the New Testament, the closest analogy to what today passes for mental illness and its treatment may be found, respectively, in the dire circumstances in individuals that are ascribed to the destructive

---

[1] This is not to imply that mental health is merely the absence of mental illness. It is thus appropriate to draw attention to the often cited definition of the World Health Organization for mental health in 2001: "... a state of wellbeing in which the individual realizes his or her own abilities, can cope with the normal stresses of life, can work productively and fruitfully, and is able to make a contribution to his or her community". See the World Health Organization Factsheet no. 220 (2010; accessed 15 October 2013 at http://www.who.int/mediacentre/factsheets/fs220/en) and further *The World Health Organization Report 2001: Mental Health: New Understanding, New Hope* (Geneva: The World Health Organization, 2001), pp. 3–4.

[2] See e.g. *Diagnostic and Statistic Manual of Mental Disorders* (Washington D.C.: American Psychiatric Association, 2000 4th ed.).

activity of demons and in Jesus' effective handling of them.[3] One of the most obvious comparisons has to do with social arrangement: on the one side of the equation there is the specialist exorcist and psychotherapist, while on the other side there is the suffering patient. In addition, those being treated, whether through exorcism or psychotherapy, are thought to live with harmful conditions that call for relief. We have already noted a number of possible diagnoses related to mental disorders in the previous paragraph. Turning to the Synoptic Gospels composed nearly two millennia ago, we observe that a number of detrimental states or symptoms are attributed to demonic beings.[4] When expressly mentioned, demons can be said to convulse (Mk. 1:16; 9:20; Lk. 9:39, 42), seize (Mk. 9:18; Lk. 9:39), throw down (Mk. 9:18; Lk. 4:35; cf. Mt. 17:15; Mk. 3:11, Lk. 8:28), trouble (Lk. 6:18), isolate (Mk. 5:3; Lk. 8:27, 29), strike dumb (Mk. 9:17, 25; Mt. 9:32–33; 12:22; Lk. 11:14), make deaf (Mk. 9:25), inflict bodily harm on (Mt. 17:15; Mk. 5:5; 9:22), make naked (Lk. 8:27; cf. Mk. 5:15 par. Lk. 8:35), incapacitate (cf. Mk. 7:30), render ritually unclean (Mk. 1:23, 26, 27; 3:11, 30; 5:2, 8, 13; 6:7; 7:25; 9:25; Mt. 10:1; 12:43; Lk. 4:33, 36; 6:18; 8:29; 11:24) and generally worsen the state of their victims (Mt. 12:45 par. Lk. 11:26). These texts assume that a proper or ideal response to the conditions described involves the removal or mitigation of demonic activity, just as mental illness is thus classified because it is a condition in need of treatment.

That said, the analogy between ancient exorcism and contemporary psychotherapy is a very complex one, and those who look for discontinuity between the two need not reach far. References to demonic entities in accounts of Jesus' activity reflected a way of looking at the world that is very different from that adopted by many therapists today who seek to help their patients. For example, demonic attribution posits the invasive ontological existence of *another* being, while strategies devised to deal with mental disorders in the modern sciences are more inclined to focus on issues that reside within the individual him- or herself.[5] Correspondingly,

---

[3] Stephen A. Diamond, *Anger, Madness, and the Daimonic* (Albany: State University of New York Press, 1996) and *idem*, "The Devil Inside: Psychotherapy, Exorcism, and Demonic Possession" (dated 2012; see www.psychologytoday.com/blog/ evil-deeds/ 201201/ the-devil-inside-psychotherapy-exorcism-and-demonic-possession, accessed 15 October 2013).

[4] Concerning the terminology used in the Gospel traditions, see below, under the section "God, Demons and Humans in the Jesus Tradition".

[5] It should be acknowledged that both academics and practitioners in the fields of psychology and psychiatry frequently engage in discourse about "demons" as well. Here the term, especially under the influence of Sigmund Freud, is metaphorical and is made to refer to conditions *of the individual* to be treated. See Freud, *Totem and Taboo: Resemblances Between the Psychic Lives of Savages and Neurotics*, trans. by James Stracey (London: Routledge, 1950, repr. from 1913), pp. 18–74 ("Taboo and Emotion Ambivalence", esp. p. 65) and 75–99 ("Animism, Magic, and the Omnipotence of Thoughts", esp. p. 92); Alfred Ribi, *Demons of the Inner World: Understanding Our Hidden Complexes*, transl. by M. Kohn (Boston: Shambhala, 1990); Frans Ilkka Mäyrä, *Demonic Texts and Textual Demons* (Tampere: Tampere University Press, 1999), esp. pp. 51–80 ("The Demonic in the Self"); and Russell Harris, "Embracing Your Demons: An Overview of Acceptance and Commitment Therapy", *Psychotherapy in Australia* 12 (2006), pp. 2–8.

whereas the former is more likely to take the victimization of the person as a point of departure, the latter is more likely to stress a person's agency in his or her return to wellbeing. To make matters even more complicated, the differences between language of the Gospels and that adopted by psychotherapists are not always clear-cut: a number of texts in the Gospels move discourse about demons in a metaphorical direction,[6] while psychotherapists can use the term "demons" – or "daimons" – to denote something real (i.e., destructive mental states within a person).[7] Finally, we may note that the Gospel accounts make relatively little attempt to "get to the bottom" of problems of individuals being treated by Jesus and thus tend to streamline and simplify their diagnoses (e.g., as ontologically demonic or as physical illness, without showing an interest in distinguishing clearly between the two), while, by contrast and as intimated in the opening paragraph above, mental health sciences today have developed a discourse that works with a wide range classifications in the process of treating patients.

There is thus no doubt that for many Christian interpreters of biblical writings – in the present case, we are considering the Gospels – the recognition of demonic influence within human beings brings with it a hermeneutical challenge. How does one relate a religiously "normative" tradition to problems that in many parts of the world today are discussed or dealt with on other terms? Forging links between contemporary illnesses and demon-induced maladies encountered by the Jesus of the Gospel tradition within the context of the ancient world is fraught with difficulty. This discontinuity is, for example, seen by those psychiatrists who, regardless of their religious or non-religious affiliations, regard "Jesus" and religion as factors that actually contribute to mental illness rather than being resources for therapeutic treatment.[8]

Is it fair, then, to ask what, if anything, we can learn from Jesus' activity in relation to mental illness, especially since what Jesus did involved dealing straightforwardly with the demonic while we have many more alternative diagnoses at our disposal? In an effort to read the Gospels constructively, notwithstanding these and other difficulties, I would like to suggest in what follows that a meaningful conversation is indeed possible, especially if one recognizes the important role ancient Jewish apocalyptic tradition played in shaping the theological contours of Jesus traditions in the New Testament.

---

[6] The most notable example of this is the Gerasene demoniac episode, in which the demoniac presence is called "Legion" (Mk. 5:1–20 pars. Mt. 8:28–34 and Lk. 8:26–39).

[7] See the bibl. n. 5 above.

[8] So Sam Harris, *The End of Faith* (New York: W. W. Norton, 2004) and Christopher Hitchens, *God is not Great: How Religion Poisons Everything* (New York: Warner, 2007).

Coming to Terms with Jesus' Exorcisms: Contemporary Interpretation

Before addressing the activity of Jesus within the Synoptic Gospels and his Jewish context directly, we may find it helpful to note how many interpreters have attempted, on hermeneutical grounds, to make contemporary sense of what the Gospels state about Jesus' confrontations with the demonic world. One option, followed by many Christians in the developing and western world (among them, for example, Pentecostals), has simply been to "take the Gospels at their word": if Jesus dealt with problems by exorcizing demons, then the worldview that accompanies what Jesus did must be true as well, even if it needs to be qualified.[9] Problems people face today can thus also reflect the existence of demonic powers. This perspective finds something normative in the worldview behind Jesus' exorcistic activity, coming as it does from "Scripture", so that the Church should be able to factor it into life and practice.

Other interpreters, especially those who take analytical methods developed in the West as their point of departure, find it difficult to adopt straightforwardly the worldview of Jesus' time and therefore prefer symbolic interpretations of Jesus' exorcisms.[10] Accordingly, scholars of ancient Christianity, theologians, priests and pastors in the church often look for ways to make such texts easier for contemporary readers to access. In this vein, readings of Jesus' exorcisms have gone in several directions, and sometimes several of these views are held at the same time. Before offering a perspective that I think is often overlooked, I would like to mention some of the more common ways Jesus' exorcisms have been and are being understood.

---

[9] See the widely disseminated books by Donald Basham, *Deliver Us from Evil* (Washington Depot, CT: Chosen Books, 1972, repr. 2005); Francis MacNutt, *Healing* (New York: Bantam Books and Ave Maria Press, 1974), esp. pp. 189–210 ("On Deliverance and Exorcism") and *idem*, *Deliverance from Evil Spirits: A Practical Manual*, Grand Rapids: Chosen Books, 1995, repr. 2009). A more recent exegetical attempt to give place within New Testament theology for the notion of exorcisms as deliverance from the demonic has been offered by Richard H. Bell, *Deliver Us from Evil: Interpreting the Redemption from the Power of Satan in New Testament Theology* (WUNT 216; Tübingen: Mohr Siebeck, 2007), who uses the notion of myth to forge a link between Jesus' exorcisms, on the one hand, and the notion of salvation from the realm of Satan in Pauline tradition, on the other. Much in contrast to Bell's approach, the present discussion focuses on the constructive contribution of Jewish tradition to the theological context of exorcism.

[10] Many think it necessary to explain how Jesus could have expelled demons, almost as if it was an embarrassing aspect of his activity. A frequent response to Jesus' exorcisms assumes that one is obliged to find or retain something normative that does not rest on the exorcisms *as such*: since there are many people today (i.e., in the "enlightened West") who do not believe in the existence of demons, one is to regard Jesus' activity as an exorcist as an accommodation to beliefs at the time, an accommodation that no longer needs to be made. So, e.g., Edward Langton, *Essentials of Demonology. A Study of Jewish and Christian Doctrine: Its Origin and Development* (London: Epworth Press, 1949), esp. pp. 147–183 and 219–225; and Stuart Y. Blanch, *Encounters with Jesus* (The Jesus Library; London: Hodder and Stoughton, 1998), pp. 56–66.

One way of construing Jesus' demonic encounters is to think of demons as metaphors for political oppression. This perspective emphasizes that Jesus was actively engaged, on a symbolic and profound level, in a war of resistance against the economic and political domination of Rome. Getting rid of demons was, on Jesus' part, a way to subvert the control of Rome and proclaim boldly the over-arching reality of another kingdom, that of God. Thus, for example, the successful exorcism of "Legion" from the Gerasene demoniac (cf. Mk. 5:1–20; pars. Mt. 8:28–34, Lk. 8:26–39) reflects the conviction that in Jesus' ministry God's rule manifests itself so strongly that it can vanquish the military might of Rome.[11]

Second and closely related to the interpretation just mentioned, the expulsion of demonic beings by Jesus is taken to be concerned with portraying Jesus as the one who fulfils the ultimate hopes of the covenant people of Israel. In such a series of small-scale episodes, Jesus is acting out a much grander narrative: by ridding people of evil spirits, he puts God's restorative power for Israel on display, so that, free from enslavement and oppression, Israel can become the covenant faithful people they were meant to be.[12]

Third, Jesus' exorcisms are sometimes taken as evidence that, in very general terms, establishes that Jesus was acting as a Jew. His exorcisms can be compared with the activities of a number of Jewish miracle-workers who, like Jesus and according to tradition, were based in Galilee. This comparison means that Jesus was simply been doing the kind of thing that a Galilean "charismatic" *ḥasid* would have done.[13]

---

[11] As argued, for example, by, Samson Eitrem, *Some Notes on the Demonology in the New Testament* (Symbolae osloenses Fasc. Supplet 20, Oslo: Universitetsforlaget, 1966, 2nd ed.), p. 70; Richard A. Horsley, *Jesus and the Spiral of Violence: Popular Jewish Resistance in Roman Palestine* (San Francisco: Harper & Row, 1987), pp. 184–190; Ched Myers, *Binding the Strong Man: A Political Reading of Mark's Story of Jesus* (Maryknoll, NY: Orbis, 1988), pp. 191–194; Hermann C. Waetjen, *A Reordering of Power: A Sociopolitical Reading of Mark's Gospel* (Minneapolis: Augsburg Fortress Press, 1989), pp. 81–3, 113–119; John Dominic Crossan, *The Historical Jesus: The Life of a Mediterranean Jewish Peasant* (San Francisco: HarperSanFrancisco, 1991), pp. 313–318; Amanda Witmer, *Jesus the Galilean Exorcist: His Exorcisms in Social and Political Context* (LNTS 459 and LHSS 10; London: T & T Clark, 2012); and Cheryl S. Pero, *Liberation from Empire: Demonic Possession and Exorcism in the Gospel of Mark* (SBL 150; New York: Peter Lang, 2013). Both Witmer and Pero, however, attempt to recognize the multi-dimensional levels on which the exorcism episodes are recounted in the Gospel of Mark.

[12] Cf. Nicholas T. Wright, *Jesus and the Victory of God* (London: SPCK, 1996), pp. 193–197 and 226–229: Referring to Jesus' logion in Lk. 11:20/Mt. 12:28 ("if by the finger of God I cast out demons, then the kingdom of God has come upon you"), Wright concludes that Jesus' exorcisms are "clear signs" that the God of Israel is beginning to defeat the enemy that has "held Israel captive" (p. 228).

[13] Geza Vermes, *Jesus the Jew: A Historian's Reading of the Gospels* (Philadelphia: Fortress Press, 1973), pp. 58–82; Marcus Borg, *A New Vision* (San Francisco: Harper & Row, 1988), esp. pp. 30–32 and Bart D. Ehrman, *Jesus: Apocalyptic Prophet of the New Millennium* (Oxford: Oxford University Press, 1999), pp. 197–198. Morton Smith, *Jesus the Magician*, (London: Gollancz, 1978), adopted a similar approach, though he pressed his presentation of Jesus into the category of "magician". Crossan, *The Historical Jesus*, pp. 142–158, takes up a position that med-

Fourth, and in a different sense, many use a comparison of Jesus' activities with those of contemporary healers and exorcists to emphasize how much Jesus is different and is essentially without meaningful parallel in his contemporary world. It is held that this "uniqueness" of Jesus holds true whether comparisons are drawn with sources from the Ancient Near East, with non-Jewish and non-Christian pagan sources, or with Second Temple Jewish literature.[14] Driven by prior theological convictions centered around Christology, interpreters who adopt this position focus on the character of Jesus' exorcisms as miraculous. The exorcisms are to be read alongside the stories of Jesus' healing and nature miracles as interventionary acts of God. There was no equal to what Jesus did. The result of this approach is to render Jesus' activity *itself* as remote, while symbolic interpretations (see especially the first two described above and the fifth and sixth immediately below) are made to bridge the gap between the accounts and contemporary experience.

Fifth, exorcisms could also be interpreted as symbolic in relation to individuals themselves. They are, in effect, stories that signify how Jesus' proclamation of God's rule agitates for a more just society; Jesus' ministry is essentially a matter of re-integrating marginalized or excluded people into the life and activity of social and religious institutions. Jesus' exorcisms have to do with those who on account of illness or some condition were without social honour, dispossessed of dignity and, within the Jewish context, ritually "unclean". The effect of an exorcism on afflicted and unclean individuals is their full inclusion within the worshiping community.[15]

Sixth, exorcisms are sometimes comprehended as stories, again in a symbolic sense, about the salvation of people who are, on a profound level, delivered from evil and its effects. This soteriological interpretation is bound up with an understanding of Jesus as the essential way to salvation. When Jesus' disciples perform

---

iates between the views of Vermes and Smith, arguing that traditions about the originally "magical" Ḥoni and Ḥanina were eventually domesticated by the time we meet them in the literature in which they are first mentioned (e. g., m. Taʿan. 3.8 and t. Taʿan. 2.13).

[14] See Graham H. Twelftree, *Jesus the Exorcist: A Contribution to the Study of the Historical Jesus* (Peabody, MA: Hendrickson, 1993), e. g. pp. 157–174, for whom Jesus stands out as different in the connection he established between his own expulsion of demons and the dawning rule of God. See further *idem*, *In the Name of Jesus: Exorcism Among Early Christians* (Grand Rapids: Baker Academic, 2007); Hartmut Stegemann, *The Library of Qumran: On the Essenes, Qumran, John the Baptist, and Jesus* (Grand Rapids and Leiden: Eerdmans and Brill, 1998), pp. 237–238; Eric Eve, *The Jewish Context of Jesus' Miracles* (JSNTSup 231; Sheffield: Academic Press, 2002); and Thomas Söding, "'Wenn ich mit dem Finger Gottes die Dämonen austreibe ...' (Lk 11,20): Die Exorzismen im Rahmen der Basileia-Verkündigung Jesu", in eds. Armin Lange, Hermann Lichtenberger and K. F. Diethard Römheld, *Die Dämonen – Demons* (Tübingen: Mohr Siebeck, 2003), pp. 519–549.

[15] E. g., Stephen J. Patterson, *The God of Jesus: The Historical Jesus and the Search for Meaning* (Harrisburg: Trinity Press International, 1998), pp. 69–73; Ehrman, *Jesus: Apocalyptic Prophet*, pp. 187–188; Todd E. Klutz, "The Grammar of Exorcism in the Ancient Mediterranean World", in eds. Carey C. Newman, James R. Davila and Gladys S. Lewis, *The Jewish Roots of Christological Monotheism* (JSJSup 63; Leiden / Boston / Köln: Brill, 1999), pp. 156–165; cf. also John Dominic Crossan, *Jesus: A Revolutionary Biography* (San Francisco: HarperSanFrancisco, 1994), pp. 81–82.

exorcisms, they do so in Jesus' name and so continue that ministry of salvation through Jesus to others. Exorcisms show how Jesus' ministry brings about God's salvation within a world that is otherwise hostile to God.[16]

Seventh, and a less symbolic interpretation, exorcism (and healing) stories in the Gospels illustrate that Jesus was "a physician before his time". With remarkable success, he was in effect able to treat people with mental disorders, which sometimes manifested themselves through physical symptoms or illness. Thus language about demons was actually a way to talk about psychosomatic, mental illness. Jesus brought wholeness and hope to the mind, with the result that physical symptoms could be alleviated.[17]

Good reasons have been put forward for each of the interpretations just described. Indeed, it would be a mistake, in looking for alternative readings, to eclipse them entirely. However, they each lose some of their force to the extent that they make Jesus' exorcisms illustrate *something else* than what they claim to be: Jesus dealing with people who suffer from invasive demonic control. Without disavowing the symbolic or metaphorical reading of Jesus' exorcisms, the argument that follows below shall attempt to move in a somewhat different direction.

An attempt to focus on Jesus' activity as confrontation with the demonic may meet with resistance among interpreters who are shaped by modernist sensibilities. I hope, nonetheless, that by focusing on the demonic world in the Gospels *per se*, we find ourselves in a better position to recover some additional, yet fundamental insights. For ancient readers of the Gospels the metaphorical and symbolic power of stories about the defeat of demonic evil (so interpretations 1–2 and 5–6 above) gain their force if they could assume that Jesus of Galilee had actually been effective in dealing with individuals in the way the Gospel accounts claimed. If one does not reach too quickly for several of the sociological, political, psychological or even theological interpretations outlined above, it may be possible to hear what some of the Gospel traditions in their portrait of Jesus convey about several basic issues. These issues may be formulated through the following questions: What is the

---

[16] So, for example, Bent Noack, *SATANÁS und SOTERÍA: Untersuchungen zur neutestamentlichen Dämonologie* (Copenhagen: G. E. C. Gads Forlag, 1948).

[17] See Donald Capps, *Jesus the Village Psychiatrist* (Louisville / London: Westminster John Knox Press, 2008); J. Harold Ellens, "Biblical Miracles and Psychological Process: Jesus as Psychotherapist", in ed. J. Harold Ellens, *Miracles: God, Science, and Psychology in the Paranormal* (Westport, CT: Praeger, 2008), pp. 1–14; and, in another vein, Justin Meggitt, "The historical Jesus and healing: Jesus' miracles in psychosocial context", in ed. Fraser Watts, *Spiritual Healing. Scientific and Religious Perspectives* (Cambridge: Cambridge University Press, 2011), pp. 17–43. Meggitt, rather than attempting a psychosomatic reading, models his interpretation after the function of a "placebo" in medical practice and emphasizes the role of both faith (in Jesus) and self-healing (human agency) in the Gospel healing and exorcism narratives. Aside from the general points made below, the difficulty with these psychologically oriented interpretations of problems suffered by people in Jesus' day is that, while looking for language to describe what may have actually been the case, they attempt to recover what is inaccessible and, more importantly, do not adequately seek to understand what was happening in the framework and terms set by the ancient sources themselves.

power and nature of evil itself? How do the harmful effects of evil manifest themselves in people? What is the place of human beings within the created order? Within what larger framework of time and space does conflict with evil occur? And, what role might a faith perspective have in coping with the stubborn persistence of evils that intrude into life and cannot be fixed?

One reason why Jesus' exorcisms are considered problematic within some religious circles has to do with the following question: Many ask, "Can or should exorcisms be performed today and, if so, what can be learned for this purpose from the New Testament Gospels?" This question misses the point; it is misguided because it looks for something normative in a particular worldview. It is precisely a response of "No!" to this question that has led to some of the interpretations we have reviewed above. On the other hand, for those who would answer the question with a "Yes!" (that exorcism is a valid religious practice for today) there is the burden of coming up with a "right" diagnosis.[18] A diagnosis that includes an ontological demonic element more often than not stands in tension with approaches to illnesses adopted in medical professions shaped by western education. Despite the stark contrast between these positions, however, it is possible that advocates of exorcism as a legitimate practice and those who *a priori* have no place for it have something to learn from one another. Indeed, the question about the validity or non-validity of exorcism can be replaced by a more germane one: What fundamental *perspective* on demonic power, on the human being and on Jesus' activity in relation to people do exorcism passages of the Gospels convey? What understanding of the world and God's activity within the world can one reasonably discern?

This refocus of the issues put us in a position to reconsider the conflict between Jesus the exorcist and the demonic world. After reviewing the Gospel traditions briefly, I shall focus on selected passages that may contribute to a fresh reading of Jesus' exorcisms.

Jesus' Ministry against the Demonic: An Overview

References in the Synoptic Gospels for the practice of exorcism are not wanting. In fact, the presentation of activity that expels demons is preserved among each of the main literary sources both in and behind the Gospels.[19]

---

[18] See the different approaches by Basham, *Deliver Us from Evil* (cf. n. 9); MacNutt, *Deliverance from Evil Spirits* (cf. n. 9); and the more thoroughgoing treatment by John C. Thomas, *The Devil, Disease and Deliverance: Origins of Illness in New Testament Thought* (JPTS 13; Sheffield: Sheffield Academic Press, 1998).

[19] The categories set forth here do not strictly follow the "four source hypothesis", though omissions of references to exorcisms within parallel passages in some literary relationship are noted. The presentation below, which does not presume a particular direction in literary dependence, bears the advantage of reflecting the proclivities of each Gospel while noting where the parallel pericopae occur.

- *tradition in Mark alone* – two times

Mark 3:13–15 (omitted in par. Lk. 6:12–13) – Jesus' commissioning of his disciples,
Mark 6:13 (omitted in par. Lk. 9:6) – summary of the disciples' deeds;

- *tradition shared by Mark and Matthew* – once

Mark 7:24–30 par. Matthew 15:21–28 – the Syrophoenician woman;

- *tradition shared by Mark and Luke* – three times

Mark 1:23–28 par. Luke 4:33–37 – exorcism of a man in the synagogue,
Mark 3:11–12 par. Luke 6:18 – summary of Jesus' deeds at the sea,
Mark 9:38–41 par. Luke 9:49–50 – the "strange" exorcist;

- *tradition shared by Mark with Matthew and Luke* – five times

Mark 1:32–34 pars. Matthew 8:16–17 and Luke 4:40–41 – summary of Jesus' activity,
Mark 3:22–27, pars. Matthew 12:24–30 and Luke 11:15–23 (perhaps an overlap of Mk.
and "Q") – accusation of Jesus' collusion with Beelzebul,
Mark 5:1–20 pars. Matthew 8:28–34 and Luke 8:26–39 – exorcism of the Gerasene
man (two men in Matthew),
Mark 6:7 pars. Matthew 10:1 and Luke 9:1 – Jesus' commissioning of his disciples,
Mark 9:14–29 pars. Matthew 17:14–21 and Luke 9:37–43 – exorcism of a boy;

- *tradition in Matthew alone* – three times

Matthew 7:21–23 (omitted in pars. in Lk. 6:46 and 13:25–27) – saying about inauthen-
tic followers of Jesus,
Matthew 9:32–34 – exorcism of a mute man,
Matthew 10:7–8 (omitted in par. Lk. 10:9) – Jesus' commission of his disciples;

- *tradition in Luke alone* – four times

Luke 7:18–23 (omitted in par. Mt. 11:2–6) – Jesus' response to John the Baptist,
Luke 10:17–20 (cf. Mk.'s longer ending, 16:17–18) – the return of the 70 disciples,
Luke 13:10–17 – exorcism of a crippled woman in the synagogue,
Luke 13:32 – summary of Jesus' activity; and

- *tradition shared only by Matthew and Luke* – two times

Matthew 12:22–23 par. Luke 11:14 – exorcism of a blind and mute man,
Matthew 12:43–45 par. Luke 11:24–26 – return of an evil spirit.

This listing is, in the first instance, revealing. It provides evidence for the multiple
attestation of the exorcism tradition in the Synoptic Gospels, not only in relation to
a documentary hypothesis (if one accepts categories such as the "triple tradition",
"Q", "special Matthew", "special Luke"), but also in relation to identifiable tendencies of the gospels each of which alone refers to the tradition at particular points.

A look at these passages as a whole allows us to make several further observations. Firstly, exorcistic activity in the Gospels is preserved in different forms. Far
more than simply being the subject matter of Jesus' encounters in narrative form,
exorcisms are referred to in a number of Jesus sayings as well as among more gen-

eral summaries of Jesus' or his disciples' activity. Secondly, it is significant that successful exorcisms in the Synoptic Gospels are not only attributed to Jesus alone. Not only are exorcisms performed by Jesus' disciples (Mk. 6:7, 13–15; Mt. 10:1, 7–8; Lk. 9:1; 10:17–20),[20] they are also a condonable activity practiced by those who are not among Jesus' immediate followers. This is, for instance, the case with the so-called "strange" exorcist mentioned in Mark 9:38–41 (par. Lk. 9:49–50) as well as with Jesus' rhetorical question which assumes that his Jewish contemporaries were likewise able to exorcise demons (Mt. 12:27 par. Lk. 11:19: "by whom do your sons cast out?"). The latter episode, which is tucked away in a passage that focuses on Jesus' response to an accusation that questioned the source of his power, admits that an analogy exists between the exorcisms of Jesus and those performed by the "sons" of his interlocutors (the "Pharisees" in Matthew and "scribes" in Luke). In other words, Jesus' encounters with the demonic world are located by the Synoptic Gospels within a religious climate in which exorcisms were considered a legitimate, if not effective way to combat evil. According to the Gospels, Jesus, as an exorcist, participated in a worldview in which exorcism makes sense. For all the wish of the Gospel writers to accentuate Jesus' prowess and expertise in this area, this portrait of Jesus would have shared some fundamental assumptions with his contemporaries on how such activity works and what it signifies for both practitioners and those deemed to be under demonic sway. Thirdly, both the multiple attestation in the Gospels and their recognition of exorcism as an effective practice among non-devotees of Jesus strengthen the likelihood that we are dealing with the shared preservation of an early tradition that may have been circulating during the time of Jesus' ministry. Whether or not they identified with the Jesus movement, a wide number of contemporaries believed that Jesus engaged in open conflict with demonic beings. However much individual pericopae, especially the exorcism episodes, were shaped by conventional oral and literary forms, there is no reason to doubt that any reconstruction of Jesus' life and ministry that does not include the claim that he expelled evil spirits omits something essential. Likewise, since each of the Gospel writers wished to emphasize the unprecedented magnitude of Jesus' life, teaching and ministry,[21] there is no compelling reason why a post-Easter community would have generated stories that acknowledged the performance of exorcisms by his contemporaries.

Both on the level of their respective presentations and in the traditions they variously preserve, the Synoptic Gospels leave us with a portrait of Jesus who, as a

---

[20] See, however, the lack of success to exorcise by the disciples in Mk. 9:18 par. Lk. 9:40 and Mk. 9:28–29 par. Mt. 17:19–20. This presentation of the disciples' inability makes Jesus as the expert exorcist stand out in sharp relief.

[21] So e. g., Mk. 1:22; 1:27b (par. Lk. 4:36); 2:12b; 4:41 (pars. Mt. 8:27 and Lk. 8:25); Mt. 7:29; 9:33; Lk. 5:26. Of these texts, the depiction of Jesus' superior ability in performing exorcisms occurs in Mk. 1:27b (par. Lk. 4:36) and Mt. 9:33.

pious Jew of his time, believed he was effectively able to confront and gain control over demonic power.[22]

God, Demons and Humans in the Jesus Tradition

Within the Gospel traditions about Jesus' exorcisms, three features stand out with regularity. They add up to a worldview that integrates God's activity, the nature of evil, and the nature of humanity.

First, we note that Jesus' exorcisms are associated with the beginning of God's rule. As acts of power, they manifest and proclaim the royal power of the God of Israel. In addition to his healing miracles, Jesus regarded his expulsion of demons from people as concrete demonstrations that God's rule is breaking into this world, dispossessing evil forces from the foothold they have on people in the present age. However, none of the exorcism *stories* in the Gospels actually affirms the connection between what Jesus was doing, on the one hand, and God's kingship or rule, on the other. For this link the Gospels steer our attention to the sayings of Jesus.

In this respect, most scholarly attention has focused on the "Q" tradition in Luke 11:20 (par. Mt. 12:28). According to the Lucan version Jesus claims, "But if by the finger of God I cast out demons, then God's rule has come upon you."[23] The saying assumes that a vacuum that arises within a person dispossessed of

---

[22] Though I would advocate for the plausibility of the exorcism tradition as a feature of the earliest Jesus traditions, the significance of the argument in this chapter does not depend on such an assertion. In relation to the determination of tradition being traceable back to the time of Jesus, the criterion of multiple attestations in this case plays an important role. For a discussion that *inter alia* stresses the importance of multiple attestations as a criterion, see William R. Telford, *The Theology of the Gospel of Mark* (New Testament Theology; Cambridge, UK / New York: Cambridge University Press, 1999), pp. 88–103. – Here the study is limited to the Synoptic Gospels precisely because the Gospel of John does not preserve any account of an exorcism performed by Jesus. This does not mean, however, that the Fourth Gospel completely ignores this aspect of the Jesus tradition; traces of it are, instead, reconfigured to reinforce characteristic Johannine interests: (a) The language of casting out (ἐκβάλλειν) of demonic power is taken up in Jn. 12:31, according to which Jesus' death is the event which marks the decisive defeat of "the ruler of this world"; (b) The accusations of "having a demon" which in the Synoptic Gospels are linked to the performance of exorcisms (cf. Mk. 3:22–30 par. Mt. 12:24–32, Lk. 11:15–23) and also involve John the Baptizer (Mt. 11:18; Lk. 7:33) are more widespread in John (7:20; 8:48–49, 52; 10:20–21), where they are made to function as labels in order to exercise social control over religious threat from opponents. The motif of "having a demon" is thus reminiscent of, and perhaps grew out of, accusations surrounding Jesus' exorcistic activity as attested in the Synoptic Gospels. For an excellent discussion of the absence of exorcisms in the Johannine tradition, see Ronald A. Piper, "The Absence of Exorcisms in the Fourth Gospel", in eds. David G. Horrell and Christopher M. Tuckett, *Christology, Controversy, and Community: New Testament Essays in Honour of David R. Catchpole* (NovTSup 99; Leiden / Boston / Köln: Brill, 2000), pp. 252–278.

[23] Instead of "the finger of God" Matthew's version has "the Spirit of God", a phrase that reflects editorial interests (cf. Mt. 12:18, 32). Thus, despite the allusion here to Exod. 8:9, Luke's wording is to be preferred.

demonic power is filled by the protective power of God's rule. For those who have been exorcized, Jesus' ministry signals the beginning of a process of deliverance. Similarly, Jesus' declaration upon the return of the seventy disciples in Luke 10:18 that he "saw Satan fall from heaven like lightning" is offered as an explanation of why the disciples could be portrayed as successful exorcists.[24] Exorcisms result from a power struggle in which demonic power is being overcome.

Though the link between exorcisms and God's rule may be traced back to early tradition about Jesus,[25] how unique a link is it? Is Graham Twelftree correct, for instance, when he concludes that "it was Jesus himself who made this connection between exorcism and eschatology", as if such a link had no real precedent in Jesus' environment?[26] Was Hartmut Stegemann, similar to Twelftree, correct when he concluded that the notion that God's reign is beginning to vanquish Satan's rule is to be found "neither in the Qumran texts nor in other Jewish literature, at least where these surely stem from pre-Christian times"?[27] I will attempt to address this claim below.

Second, we note that in the Gospels "demons" always refer to evil or unclean spirits. Another feature belonging to the tradition about Jesus has to do with the consistent presentation of "demons" as evil powers. In the Synoptic Gospels the following designations occur, sometimes as a single term and sometimes in combination with one or more qualifying adjectives:

(a) "demon" – δαίμων or δαιμόνιον (Mk. 1:34 *bis*, 39; 3:15, 22; 6:13; 7:26, 29, 30; 9:38; Mt. 7:22; 9:33, 34; 10:8; 11:18; 12:24 *bis*, 27, 28; 17:13; Lk. 4:33, 35, 41; 7:33; 8:2, 27, 30, 33, 35, 38; 9:1, 42, 49; 10:17; 11:14 *bis*, 15 *bis*, 18, 19, 20; 13:32)

(b) "evil spirit" – πνεῦμα πονηρόν (Lk. 7:21; 8:2; cf. Acts 19:12, 13, 15, 16)[28]

---

[24] See Jürgen Becker, *Jesus of Nazareth*, translated by James E. Crouch (New York: Walter de Gruyter, 1998), pp. 107–110.

[25] The historicity of this or that episode of exorcism attributed to Jesus is less important than the more general point that it played a vital role in demonstrating his proclamation of God's kingship. On this see John P. Meier, *A Marginal Jew: Rethinking the Historical Jesus. Volume 2: Mentor, Message, and Miracles* (ABRL; New York: Doubleday, 2001), pp. 646–648.

[26] So Twelftree, *Jesus the Exorcist*, p. 220. Wright, *Jesus and the Victory of God*, p. 195, advocates a similar point of view: "The exorcisms are especially interesting, in that they formed a part neither of the regular Old Testament predictions, nor of first-century Jewish expectations, concerning healing and deliverance associated with the coming of the kingdom; nor were they a major focus of the life and work of the early church. They therefore stand out, by the criterion of dissimilarity, as being part of a battle in which Jesus alone was engaged."

[27] See Stegemann, *The Library from Qumran*, p. 233. Throughout his chapter on "Jesus" (*ibid.*, pp. 228–257), Stegemann draws too categorical a distinction between Jesus and his Jewish context. As far as exorcism in relation to God's rule is concerned, he stresses differences in technique and methods between Jesus and his contemporaries, but fails to consider the wider theme of God's rule in relation to the defeat of evil in Second Temple texts; see Chapter Eleven below.

[28] The restricted distribution of the expression within Luke-Acts suggests that this expression is a Lucanism.

(c) "unclean spirit" – ἀκάθαρτον πνεῦμα (Mk. 1:23, 26, 27; 3:11, 30; 5:2, 8, 13; 6:7; 7:25; 9:25; Mt. 10:1; 12:43 [Q]; Lk. 4:36; 6:18; 8:29; 11:24 [Q])

(d) "spirit of an unclean demon" – πνεῦμα δαιμονίου ἀκαθάρτου (Lk. 4:33 [cf. Mk. 1:23])

(e) "spirit of weakness" – πνεῦμα … ἀσθενείας (Lk. 13:11)

(f) "dumb" or "deaf-and-dumb spirit" – πνεῦμα ἄλαλον (Mk. 9:17), ἄλαλον καὶ κωφὸν πνεῦμα (Mk. 9:25)

(g) "spirit" – πνεῦμα (Mt. 8:16; 9:20; Lk. 9:31 [cf. Mk. 9:17], 38)

Three points are noteworthy from this list of terms. First, in the Gospel narratives, the expressions "demon" and "unclean spirit" are used interchangeably (cf. Mt. 10:1, 8; Mk. 3:22, 30; Lk. 8:27, 29). To be impure was to have a demon and to have a demon was to be impure.[29] While this might signify that exorcism functioned as a means of reintegrating someone "impure" into society, the function of exorcisms, in the first instance, related to the wellbeing of individuals.[30]

Second, it is well known that in the ancient world outside of Judaism and Christianity, the term δαίμων was, on the whole, a neutral expression. It referred to intermediary beings capable of having beneficial as well as harmful effects on humans.[31] However, in the Gospels – indeed, in the New Testament as a whole – the related term δαιμόνιον acquires a categorically negative meaning.[32]

---

[29] See Klutz, "The Grammar of Exorcism in the Ancient Mediterranean World", p. 161, who refers to such a symbiosis as the "demonization of impurity".

[30] As we shall see below, this becomes clear when *1 En.* chs. 6–16 and its early influence are taken into consideration. This point contrasts with the emphasis of David W. Suter, "Fallen Angel, Fallen Priest: The Problem of Family Purity in 1 Enoch", *HUCA* 50 (1979), pp. 115–135, for whom the myth of rebellious angels who breed illegitimate offspring through women functions as a protest against priests who were thought to be falling prey to reprehensible incursions of Hellenistic culture. For a critique of Suter, see Archie T. Wright, *The Origin of Evil Spirits: The Reception of Genesis 6:1–4 in Early Jewish Literature* (WUNT 2.98; Tübingen: Mohr Siebeck, 2005), pp. 46–47.

[31] To be sure, there are occasional instances in which δαίμων or a related verb denotes inimical powers as, for example, in the Hippocratic school's criticism of those who think they (δυσμενέες δαίμονες) lie behind illnesses such as epileptic seizures ("the sacred disease") and related conditions (so *On the Ailments of Young Women* 8:466); Plutarch's view that the notion of "evil demons" (φαῦλοι δαίμονες) derives from Heracleon, Plato, Xenocrates, Chrysippus and Democritus (*Def. orac.* 419A); and the vilifying rhetoric used by orators in Athenian law courts (e. g., Aeschines, *In Ctesiphontem* 157; Dinarchos, *In Demosthenem* 91; Isocrates, *Areopagiticus* 73). However much *daimones* could be regarded as harmful to humans, their malevolence was not addressed by means of exorcistic practices in Greek and Roman culture. On their essential neutrality in early folk traditions, Homeric and post-Homeric literature, the philosophical literature (esp. Plato), Neopythagorean thought, Philo, Plutarch, Lucian, Apuleius and Philostratus (on Apollonius of Tyana), see Frederick E. Brenk, "In the Light of the Moon: Demonology in the Early Imperial Period", in ed. Wolfgang Haase, *Aufstieg und Niedergang der römischen Welt* II.16.3 (Berlin: Walter de Gruyter, 1986), pp. 2068–2145; Eric Sorensen, *Possession and Exorcism in the New Testament and Early Christianity* (WUNT 2.157, Tübingen: Mohr Siebeck, 2002), pp. 75–117; and Lars Albinus, "The Greek δαίμων between Mythos and Logos", in *Die Dämonen – Demons* (bibl. in n. 14), pp. 425–446.

[32] See Sorensen, *Possession and Exorcism in the New Testament and Early Christianity*, p. 121.

The third point to note is the remarkable distribution and frequency of the designation "unclean spirit". As far as I am able to ascertain, this expression is without parallel in non-Jewish literature from pre-Christian times. Here, at least as far as the Synoptic Gospels are concerned, we find ourselves on unmistakably Jewish soil with which Jesus and those who spoke and wrote about him would have been familiar. This language extends back to Zechariah 13:2, where in an association with idolatry, the "unclean spirit" (רוח הטמאה, τὸ πνεῦμα τὸ ἀκάθαρτον) describes Judah and Jerusalem in an imperilled state of religious unfaithfulness; correspondingly, the removal of this spirit by God is envisioned on a national scale. The next references, preserved among the Dead Sea Scrolls, bring us closer to the climate of the Gospels in that a "spirit of uncleanness" pertains to a state of being from which *individuals* seek deliverance or relief (cf. 11Q5 xix 15; 4Q444 1 i 8; 1QS iv 22; perhaps also 4Q458 2 i 5).[33] The expression here suggests that the effect of the bad spirit is to make its victim ritually unclean and therefore unable to participate in the religious life of Israel. While the origins of such spirits can be contemplated by considering the larger context of the Dead Sea Scrolls and their reception of Enochic tradition (see Excursus B below), the Gospels offer very little information about what it is that made the exorcized spirits unclean;[34] instead, the impurity of such spirits is taken for granted and, in addition, it is assumed that the effects of such spirits is injurious to human wellbeing.

Third, we note that demonic possession in the Synoptic Gospels invariably involves entry into the human body. Despite the many passages in the Gospels that refer to the exorcisms of Jesus, his disciples and others in the Gospels, there is an extraordinary uniformity when it comes to the way demons are described in relation to their human victims. Almost all the texts portray exorcism as a *disembodiment* of spirits: they are "cast *out*" (ἐκβάλλειν) of the victims they have possessed.[35] The image of exit from within is reinforced by the notion of evil spirits either "entering" (εἰσέρχομαι)[36] into individual human beings or "departing" (ἐξέρχεσθαι)[37] from them. Underlying this language is the twin-assumption that people can be victi-

---

[33] See Philip S. Alexander, "The Demonology of the Dead Sea Scrolls", in eds. Peter W. Flint and James C. VanderKam, *The Dead Sea Scrolls After Fifty Years: A Comprehensive Assessment* (2 vols.; Leiden: Brill, 1998–1999), 2:331–353 (here pp. 349–350); Armin Lange, "Considerations Concerning the 'Spirit of Impurity' in Zech 13:2", in *Die Dämonen – Demons*, pp. 254–268; and Clinton Wahlen, *Jesus and the Impurity of Spirits in the Synoptic Gospels* (WUNT 2.185; Tübingen: Mohr Siebeck, 2004), pp. 41–47.

[34] The accounts of the exorcisms of the Gerasene demoniac (Mk. 5:1–20 and parallels) and the possessed boy (Mk. 9:14–29 and parallels) include descriptions of the harm inflicted by the unclean spirit on their victims without, however, indulging in any explanation of how these spirits became impure to begin with.

[35] So in Mk. 1:34, 39; 3:15, 22, 23; 6:13; 9:18, 28; Mt. 7:2; 8:16, 31; 9:33, 34; 10:1, 8; 12:24, 26, 27 *bis*, 28; 17:19; Lk. 9:40, 49; 11:14, 15, 18, 19 *bis*, 20; 13:32.

[36] Mk. 3:27; 5:12, 13; 9:25; Mt. 12:29; Lk. 8:30, 32, 33; 22:3.

[37] Mk. 5:13; 7:29, 30; Mt. 12:43 (Q); Lk. 8:2, 33; 11:14, 24 (Q).

mized by demons when the demons inhabit their bodies and that such affliction occurs when the inner equilibrium of a person is out of balance.

Among the sayings of Jesus, this understanding of exit and entry is most clear in a passage from a tradition shared by Matthew and Luke (Mt. 12:43–45 par. Lk. 11:24–26) often referred to as "the return of the spirit". The less redacted version, which is found in Luke,[38] reads as follows:

(24) When an unclean spirit departs (ἐξέλθῃ) from a person, it passes through dry places seeking rest; and when it does not find (it), it says, "I will return to house from whence I left". (25) And it goes and finds it swept and put in order. (26) Then it goes and takes seven other spirits more evil than itself and they enter and dwell there. And the last state of that person is worse than the first.

This Jesus saying simply concludes with a warning (v. 26b) without any accompanying exhortation. In its present form, this *logion* is remarkably open about the danger that, we may assume, follows an exorcism: the "last state" is not presented as a potential condition, but rather as what can be expected to happen if, presumably, further measures are not undertaken. The scenario depicted here is that of an exorcism that is ultimately ineffectual; no attempt is made in the saying to specify whether the exorcist could be Jesus, one of his disciples or others exorcizing in Jesus' name. For this reason a number of interpreters regard this tradition as one which neither Jesus' disciples nor the early church would have been likely to create; the thrust of the saying, especially in the Lucan version, is counter-intuitive to the portrait provided in the Gospels of Jesus whose exorcisms would more ideally have been portrayed as successful.[39] If this saying can be traced back to Jesus, it is significant that, consistent with the exorcism stories, Jesus presupposes that the human body can serve both as a demon's "house" (v. 24b,[40] cf. the metaphorical use of "house" in Mk. 3:25, 27//Mt. 12:25, 29) and as the natural place to which it can return (v. 26a).

The uniformity of demonic corporeal indwelling in the Synoptic Gospels stands out, given that it is relatively rare in Jewish sources that pre-date the New Testament writings.[41] Far more widespread in Greco-Roman antiquity is language that

---

[38] At the end of the pericope Matthew (12:45) adds a comparison that awkwardly makes the saying refer to the "perverse generation" at the end-time.

[39] Wright, *The Origin of Evil Spirits*, pp. 455–456.

[40] The metaphorical use of "house" corresponds to Mk. 3:25, 27 (cf. Mt. 12:25, 29), though has gotten lost in its Lucan redaction at 11:17. This further strengthens Luke's preservation of a tradition that ultimately derives from another source.

[41] Meier overstates the matter when he asserts that "demonic possession as well as obsession became a frequent theme in the Jewish literature of the intertestamental (*sic!*) period"; see Meier, *A Marginal Jew. Volume 2*, p. 405. The instances that Meier cites as evidence (i. e., *Genesis Apocryphon* and *4QPrayer of Nabodinus*) relate more to what he calls "obsession" than to "possession" in the strict sense. Meier cites with approval (*A Marginal Jew. Volume 2*, p. 460 n. 30) the conclusion of Jonathan M. Hull, *Hellenistic Magic and the Synoptic Tradition* (SBT 2.28; London: SCM Press, 1974), pp. 62–63, that despite considerable evidence for exorcism in the Ancient Near East before the Common Era, actual stories of such encounters remain relatively rare.

depicts demonic activity more in terms of affliction or attack rather than as entry *per se*.[42]

Excursus A: Jewish Sources, Demonic Affliction and Demonic Embodiment

The distinction between demonic attack and demonic entry introduces to us a semantic problem. Thus, before noting a few analogies in Jewish sources for demonic possession, we may draw attention to several texts that have sometimes been misleadingly understood as references to "possession" in the strict sense. First, in the Book of Tobit, there are the fatal attacks by the demon Asmodaeus against the seven would-be husbands of Sarah, as well as the threat this poses for Tobias (Tob. 3:8; 6:8, 14–15; 8:2). Here the means undertaken to gain control of the demon (i. e., the smoking of a fish's heart and liver) are protective and do not formally amount to any expulsion from a body. Second, there is the well-known account in the Aramaic document *Genesis Apocryphon* (1Q20 xx 16–29) which relates to the biblical story of Abraham and Sarah in Egypt (Gen. 12:10–20). Although Pharaoh and his household are made to suffer physical sores from a plaguing spirit, the trouble is described more in terms of an affliction (as in Gen. 12:17) than as possession. In line with this, the evil spirit, when Abram lays his hands on Hyrqanosh,[43] is not so much "expelled" or "driven out" as it is "banished" or "driven away" (אתגער, line 29).[44] A third example can be observed in the fragmentary *Apocryphal Psalms* text from Qumran Cave 11 (11Q11), which includes a version of Psalm 91 in the final column vi. The psalms of the text, one of which is called an "[in]cantation" (11Q11 v 4: ל[חש]),[45] were a collection of short pieces to be sung or recited for the purpose of warding off demonic attacks. Again, there is no evidence that the demonic powers in view are being thought to "possess" the human body.[46] The same is true in a fourth document which has come to be called *Songs of the Maskil* (4Q510–511; 4Q444); in the text, the *Maskil*'s proclamation in praise of the splendour of God's radiance is intended "to frighten and terrify" malevolent powers who might strike without warning to lead people astray (4Q510 1.4–6 par. 4Q511 10.1–3; 4Q511 8.4; 35.6–9; 48+49+51 ii 2–3).[47] Fifth

---

[42] It remains possible that writers thought demons could inhabit bodies, while not choosing to depict demonic affliction in precisely this way. However, it is conspicuous that the language of corporeal habitation that characterizes the Gospel traditions is not as widespread as one might be led to assume.

[43] See Eve, *The Jewish Context of Jesus' Miracles*, pp. 177–182.

[44] For a similar use of the verb גער, without any concern for the interiority of evil within humans, see the Hebrew *War Rule* at 1QM xiv 10: "you (i. e. God) have driven away from [us] the spirits of [de]struction".

[45] According to 11Q11 v 4–5, this incantation may be "spoken at any time to the heavens when a demon comes to you during the night".

[46] Michael O. Wise, Martin G. Abegg, and Edward M. Cook, *The Dead Sea Scrolls* (London: Harper Collins 1996), p. 454; Florentino García Martínez and Eibert J. C. Tigchelaar, *The Dead Sea Scrolls Study Edition* (2 vols.; Leiden: Brill, 1999) 2:1179, 1203; and Armin Lange, "The Essene Position on Magic and Divination", in eds. Moshe Bernstein, Florentino García Martínez and John Kampen, *Legal Texts & Legal Issues: Proceedings of the Second Meeting of the International Organization for Qumran Studies, Cambridge, 1995: Published in Honour of Joseph M. Baumgarten* (STDJ 23; Leiden: Brill, 1997), pp. 377–435 (here pp. 379–384 and 431–433).

[47] Though at times casually referring to "exorcism", Bilhah Nitzan, *Qumran Prayer and Religious Poetry* (STDJ 12; Leiden: Brill, 1994), pp. 227–272 (here p. 238) has emphasized the apotropaic function of 4Q510–511 and designated them broadly as a variety of "anti-demonic songs".

and finally, it is the "afflicted" (i. e., not necessarily the "possessed") for whom David is said in 11Q5 xxvii 9–10 to have composed four songs.[48]

Less clear in distinguishing between affliction and possession is the text of *Jubilees* 10:7–14. According to this passage, the angels of the presence give instructions to Noah on how, for example, to use herbs to combat the malevolent effects of the remaining evil spirits (a tenth of their original number) who, following the Great Flood, were allowed to engage in seductive activities and to cause illnesses. It is not clear whether the text assumes that the revealed herbal remedies have exorcistic effects (in dealing with physical ailments within the body), are prophylactic and simply ward the evil spirits, or – as most likely the case – both.

There are, in any case, only a few Jewish sources outside the New Testament and composed before the end of the first century C. E. which, analogous to the Synoptic Gospels, communicate demonic effects in terms of the inhabitation of demons within the human body. Perhaps the most well known instance of an exorcism is the story of "a certain Eleazar" recounted by Josephus who illustrates the continuing potency of exorcistic cures attributed to Solomon (*Ant.* 8.42–49).[49]

Three other examples from the Dead Sea Scrolls may offer further evidence for the embodiment of evil power. The first of these comes to us from the *Damascus Document*, a portion of which is unattested among the later materials recovered from the Geniza of the Ezra Synagogue in Cairo: 4Q266 = 4QD[a] 6 i 5–7 (with more fragmentary parallels in 4Q269 = 4QD[d] 7; 4Q272 = 4QD[g] 1 i–ii; and 4Q273 = 4QD[h] 4 ii).[50] The text describes with precision a condition located "under the hair" (4Q266 6 i 7 + 4Q272 1 i 15) attributed to a spirit that has "entered the head or the beard, taking hold of the blood vessels" (4Q266 6 i 6–7) and has rendered the person "unclean" (4Q266 6 i 11).[51] As the text focuses on the establishment by a priest of when the diseased person is cured, no procedure of dealing with the spirit (such as exorcism, prayer or purification ritual) is described in the text. The cure is deemed to have taken effect when the priest can observe (a) that there are no further living hairs beyond the dead ones after seven days (4Q266 6 i 11–12); (b) that the artery is filled with blood again (line 12); and (c) that the "spirit of life" ascends and descends in it (line 12). While it seems that the cure is effected by the removal of the disease-causing spirit, the text implies that the "spirit of life" can either co-exist with it or replaces it within the person once the malevolent spirit is gone. I find it plausible, then, to regard this text as an instance of "possession", though perhaps a softer expression such as "habitation" is preferable.

A second text to note occurs within the *Treatise of the Two Spirits* preserved within the *Community Rule* at 1QS iii 13 – iv 26. At first glance it might not seem clear that the *Treatise* refers to "possession". After all, in 1QS iv 9–12 "the spirit of deceit" (רוח עולה, line 9) is co-ordinated with or thought to underlie a number of vices; moreover, according to the

---

[48] Within the collections of psalms in 11Q5 as a whole, it is important to note that the twin notions of exorcism, on the one hand, and possession, on the other, are not necessarily absent by virtue of not being explicitly mentioned. For language that comes closer to that of exorcism, see e. g. the petition (or perhaps self-exorcism?) in the prayer for deliverance in 11Q5 xix 15–16, especially if both parts of the petition are to be read as synonymously parallel: "Do not let Satan rule over me, nor an unclean spirit; let neither pain nor evil inclination take possession of my bones."

[49] H. St. John Thackeray and Ralph Marcus, *Josephus. Jewish Antiquities V: Books V–VIII* (LCL 281; Cambridge, MA: Harvard University Press. 1938), pp. 594–595.

[50] See Joseph M. Baumgarten, in *Qumran Cave 4 XIII: The Damascus Document (4Q266–273)* (DJD 18; Oxford: Clarendon Press 1996), pp. 52–53.

[51] See further Joseph M. Baumgarten, "The 4Q Zadokite Fragments on Skin Disease", *JJS* 41 (1990), pp. 153–165.

text, the influence of this spirit leads to "abundance of afflictions" (רוב נגועים) brought about by "all the angels of destruction" (מלאכי חבל כול, line 12) for those who fall sway to its rule. Though the precise relation of this spirit of deceit to human beings is not apparent, towards the end of the *Treatise* such a notion becomes clear: at the appointed time of divine judgment, the deeds of humans will be purified from all wrongdoing, and God will "finish off every spirit of deceit from the inward parts of his (the human's) flesh" (1QS iv 20–21 – להתם כול רוח עולה מתכמי בשרו) – an act further described in the following phrase as a cleansing from every wicked deed through the spirit of holiness. The *Treatise* thus portrays eschatological judgment in terms of a global exorcism (cf. Jn. 12:31) that is anthropologically focused: anything that remains from the spirit of deceit within humanity will be completely annihilated. In the present age, the spirit of deceit indwells human beings, though not alone; the text declares that both "the spirits of truth and deceit contend (against one another) in the hearts of man" (1QS iv 23: יריבו רוחי אמת ועול בלבב גבר) in an attempt to control a person's actions. The language of possession does not occur and the habitation of the spirit of deceit is not exclusive; nonetheless, such a spirit, insofar as it is pitched in conflict with the spirit of truth, manifests itself within the human being as the cause of reprehensible deeds and attitudes (1QS iv 9–11).

Whereas the last two texts only approximate the idea of possession as we meet up with it in the New Testament Gospels, a third offers the clearest example thereof among the Dead Sea materials. The source in question consists of two small Aramaic fragments bearing the numerical designation 4Q560.[52] The incompletely preserved text refers to male and female poisonous beings that invade the human body and its parts: they gain "[e]ntry into the flesh" (1 i 3: עלל בבשרא[) where, presumably, their activities become the cause of "iniquity and guilt", on the one hand, and of "fever, chills, and fire of the heart", on the other (1 i 4: ועריה ואשת לבב עואן ופשע אשא).[53] Column ii of the fragment (lines 5–6) preserves the beginning of an adjuration formula in which a malevolent spirit is directly addressed by an exorcist ("I, O spirit, adjure" – [אנה רוח מומה, and "I adjure you, O spirit" –] אומיתך רוחא, respectively) who by such means is to bring the spirit (along with its effects) under control. To be sure, the text does not explicitly refer to an act of expulsion; however, one may infer that the formula to be recited by the practitioner was intended to reverse that which has occurred when the spirit has invaded the body.

While the last three examples do not provide evidence for practices that immediately underlie episodes recorded in the Gospels, they do preserve language that conceives of demonic influence in terms of corporeal invasion or habitation. On the basis of the texts reviewed

---

[52] Émile Puech, "560: 4QLivre magique ar" in idem, *Qumrân Grotte 4 XXVII: Textes Araméens Deuxième Partie. 4Q550–4Q575a, 4Q580–4Q587 et Appendices* (DJD 37; Oxford: Clarendon Press, 2009), pp. 291–302; see also Douglas L. Penney and Michael O. Wise, "By the Power of Beelzebub: An Aramaic Incantation Formula from Qumran (4Q560)", *JBL* 113 (1994), pp. 627–650; Joseph Naveh, "Fragments of an Aramaic Magic Book from Qumran", *IEJ* 48 (1998), pp. 252–261; and Klaus Beyer, *Die aramäischen Texte vom Toten Meer. Band 2* (Göttingen: Vandenhoeck & Ruprecht 2005), p. 168.

[53] Following the interpretation of Puech, "560: 4QLivre magique ar", p. 298 *contra* Penney and Wise, "By the Power of Beelzebub", pp. 631–632 and 640, who are too quick to assign the phrase "iniquity and guilt" to a citation of Exod. 34:7 and Num. 14:18 (which contain the Heb. cognates ופשע). In addition, as initially suggested Naveh, "Fragments of an Aramaic Magic Book", pp. 256–257 and followed by Puech ("560: 4QLivre magique ar", pp. 296, 299), the text at 1 i 5 refers to demonic entry "into the tooth" (בשנא), while Penney and Wise read the expression as denoting a time during which the demonic attack can take place, i.e. "during sleep".

thus far, we may at least conclude that they enhance the plausibility of the theological anthropology assumed in the Synoptic Gospels within a Jewish setting.

The Synoptic Gospels draw together the motif of God's reign as king, the belief that *daimones* are evil and unclean, and the view that they affect humans by gaining entry into their bodies. Taken together, these three points can be understood to reflect what the Jesus tradition thought exorcisms (especially those of Jesus) signified, how demons affect the human body and what is going on when they are expelled. This puts us in a better position to ask how the ministry attributed to Jesus participates in the worldview of his Jewish environment and what an understanding of Jesus in relation to Jewish tradition may have to tell us about demonic discourse, on the one hand, and ultimately mental health, on the other.

The Demonic in Apocalyptic Perspective

It is at this point where we can recognize the value of bringing early Enochic traditions – especially the *Book of Watchers* (*1 En.* 1–36), the *Book of Giants* and the *Book of Dreams* (*1 En.* 83–90) – into the conversation. These texts, composed by pious Jews during the 3rd and 2nd centuries B. C. E., have become the focus of increasing attention during the last several decades for a number of reasons, including what their respective authors had to say about the introduction of evil into the world.[54] In these texts, which in turn influenced many others, discourse about the origins of evil focused on rebellious angelic beings who, related to "the sons of God" in Genesis 6:2, are blamed for having disseminated unacceptable knowledge

---

[54] Since the seminal research between the 1970s and 2000 (see Chapter One n. 1 above), a significant number of studies have focused on the significance of the fallen angels myth within Second Temple Judaism and in relation to the New Testament. In addition to numerous articles published in journals such as *Dead Sea Discoveries, Journal of Biblical Literature, Henoch, Revue de Qumran,* and *Journal for the Study of the Pseudepigrapha,* a representation of these studies may be found in the following works published since 2000: David R. Jackson, *Enochic Judaism: Three Defining Paradigm Exemplars* (LSTS 49; London: T & T Clark Intl., 2004); eds. Christoph Auffarth and Loren T. Stuckenbruck, *The Fall of the Angels* (TBN 6; Leiden: Brill, 2004); Siam Bhayro, *The Shemihaza and Asael Narrative of 1 Enoch: Introduction, Text, Translation and Commentary with Reference to Ancient Near Eastern and Biblical Antecedents* (AOAT 322; Münster: Ugarit-Verlag, 2005); Annette Yoshiko Reed, *Fallen Angels and the History of Judaism and Christianity: The Reception of Enochic Literature,* Cambridge and New York: Cambridge University Press, 2005); Wright, *The Origin of Evil Spirits*; and eds. Gabriele Boccaccini and Giovanni Ibba, *Enoch and the Mosaic Torah: The Evidence of Jubilees,* (Grand Rapids: Eerdmans, 2009); cf. further Chapter Four notes 4–10. Though none of the Discoveries in the Judean Desert series volumes have as yet presented the materials relating to *1 Enoch* together in edited form, the *Book of Giants* fragments constitute an exception; see Loren T. Stuckenbruck, *Qumran Cave 4 XXVI. Cryptic Texts and Miscellanea, Part 1* (DJD 36; Oxford: Clarendon Press, 2000), pp. 8–94 (on 1Q23, 1Q24, 4Q203, and 6Q8) and Émile Puech, *Qumrân Grotte 4 XXII. Textes araméens, Première Partie: 4Q529–549* (DJD 31; Oxford: Clarendon Press, 2001), pp. 9–115 (on 4Q530, 4Q531, 4Q532, 4Q533, 4Q203 1, and 4Q206a,).

and practices to humanity and, through the women of the earth, produced a large race of "mighty men" (or "giants"; cf. Grk. to Gen. 6:4) who enslaved humans and brought destruction to the natural world during the days before the Great Flood.

Unlike Genesis 6 to 9, the early Enochic traditions draw heavily on an interpretation of the Great Flood as a decisive act of divine punishment carried out in response to the evils committed by the fallen angels and their giant offspring. Significantly, motifs and imagery associated with the Flood[55] contribute to the way the Enochic authors attempted to describe God's ultimate triumph over and annihilation of evil. Perhaps the most influential form of this tradition is preserved in the *Book of Watchers* which, as a whole, dates to the third century B. C. E. The earliest extant copy of *Book of Watchers*, 4Q201,[56] already combines the once separate strands of tradition in *1 Enoch* chapters 6–11 and 12–16.[57] The resulting narrative, if one reads chapters 6–16 as a unit, focuses on the reprehensible instructions given to humanity during the period before the Flood by the wayward angelic beings (*1 En.* 7:1; 8:3; 9:6–8a; 13:2b; cf. Eth. to 16:3), as well as on the violent activities of their progeny, the giants, who correspond to the "mighty men" and "Nephilim" in Genesis 6:4. In contrast to Genesis 6, which makes no direct mention of the giants' involvement in the events leading up to the Flood, the giants in the *Book of Watchers* are prominent among those who are held accountable for the increase of oppression and suffering on the earth (*1 En.* 7:3–6; 9:1, 9–10). So, it is in response to the cries of the giants' human victims (8:4–9:3; cf. 7:6) that divine judgment is set in motion (ch. 10). The giants are then punished through either infighting among themselves (7:5; 10:9, 12)[58] or, though less clearly, through the Great Flood (10:15; *Jub.* 7:21–25).[59]

The emphasis placed by the *Book of Watchers* and, subsequently, the *Book of Giants* on divine judgment of the giant offspring of the rebellious angels was not simply based on the violence and oppressiveness of their deeds. More fundamentally, there was something inherently wrong with the very form of their existence. According to one strand of the narrative associated with the angel Shemiḥazah, the giants were the product of the illicit sexual union between the angels as heavenly beings and the human women as earthly beings (*1 En.* 6:1–4; 7:1–2; 9:7–8; 10:9,

---

[55] See *1 En.* 10; 83–84; 91:5–10; 93:1–3 and 93:12–15; 106:13–107:1; *Book of Giants* at 4Q530 2 ii + 6–7 + 8–12, lines 4–20.

[56] See Józef T. Milik, *The Books of Enoch: Aramaic Fragments of Qumrân Cave 4* (Oxford: Clarendon Press 1976), pp. 140–141.

[57] Carol A. Newsom, "The Development of 1 Enoch 6–19: Cosmology and Judgment", *CBQ* 42 (1980), pp. 310–329.

[58] See also *Jub.* 5:9; 7:22; and the *Book of Giants* at 6Q8 1 and 4Q531 7.

[59] Within the early Enochic tradition, punishment of the giants through the deluge is clearest in the *Animal Apocalypse* at *1 En.* 89:5. In service of paradigmatic interests, the Flood soon became the primary, if not only, means for the giants' destruction in Second Temple literature from the second century on. So esp. *4QExhortation Based on the Flood* (= 4Q370) i 6; *Damascus Document* (CD ii 19–20); Sir. 16:7(?); Wisd. Sol. 14:6; *3 Macc.* 2:4; and *3 Bar.* 4:10.

11; 15:3–7, 12; cf. *Book of Giants* at 4Q531 1). In *1 Enoch* 15:3–7, the main reason why this union is so objectionable is given: the giants are a mixture of spirit and body that derives from acts of defilement in which beings, angels and humans, assigned to essentially separate spheres in the cosmos (i. e., heaven and earth), had come together. By definition, then, the giants embodied a violation of the created order (15:4, 9–10; cf. *Jub.* 7:21). As the offspring of such an illegitimate union, they were neither fully angel nor fully human.[60] Hence, they are called "bastards" in *1 Enoch* 10:9 (Cod. Panopolitanus reads τοὺς μαζηρέους, a transliteration from Heb. or Aram. ממזריא/ם). They are misfits and have no proper place.

Both the *Book of Watchers* and the *Book of Giants* make it clear that through an act of divine intervention the giants had to be categorically and decisively held accountable.[61] Nonetheless, although the giants are not spared, neither is it the case that they are completely annihilated; though not escaping divine wrath, they end up surviving in a radically altered state: they are "evil spirits" (*1 En.* 15:8–9). The preserved textual witnesses to *1 Enoch* 15 do not state how this alteration of existence has occurred, but it is possible to reconstruct an etiology[62] behind the existence of demons based on 15:3–16:3 and the *Book of Giants* that may have been elaborating on parts of *1 Enoch* 10. When the giants came under God's judgment, their physical nature was destroyed while their spirits or souls emerged from their dead bodies. In this disembodied state, they continue to exist until the final triumph of God at the end of history as we know it (16:1). After the Great Flood they engage in the sorts of activities that they had previously done. In particular, as before, they wished to afflict human beings (15:12). Why? We may infer that they were jealous of humanity who had managed to escape the deluge with their bodies intact. *The spirits who came from the giants, then, are misfits and have no sanctioned place within the created order. It is this kind of being that lies behind the physical and mental afflictions that people suffer* (*1 En.* 15:12–16:1a).

Excursus B: The Giants' Spirits as Demonic Beings in Second Temple Judaism and Early Christianity

This storyline explains how it is that the giants could become identified as demons, not only among the Dead Sea Scrolls but also at a later stage. Among the Dead Sea materials several references to demonic beings reflect the direct influence of the Enochic tradition and have the giants' post-diluvian existence in view. According to *Songs of the Maskil* at 4Q510 1.5 the expression "spirits of the bastards" (ממזרים רוחות) occurs within a longer catalogue of malevolent forces. This also avails in the same document at 4Q511 35.7; 48+49+51 ii 2–3 and at 4Q444 2 i 4 where they are beings who need to be brought under control by the hymns directed by the Maskil to God.[63] Furthermore, in the above mentioned *Apocryphal Psalms*

---

[60] See Chapter Two above and Wright, *The Origin of Evil Spirits*, pp. 143–151.

[61] See Chapter One.

[62] An etiology is understood here as a story that explains how what is experienced has come about.

[63] Lange, "The Essene Position on Magic and Divination", pp. 383, 402–403 and 430–433; see also Chapter Two.

text (section D.3), at 11Q11 v 6, the demon visiting during the night is, if the text is correctly restored, addressed as "offspring of] Adam and seed of the ho[ly] ones".[64] This explanation of demons as disembodied spirits emanating from the giant offspring of the fallen angels continues in later Christian literature, picked up in *Testament of Solomon* (5:3; 17:1), the *Pseudo-Clementine Homilies* (8:12–18; giants designated as "bastards" and "demons"), Tertullian's *Apology* (22), Lactantius' *Institutes* (2:15) and Commodianus' *Instructions* (3).[65]

Jewish Apocalyptic Perspective and the Gospel Traditions: What this Means for Understanding Mental Illness

Before stating what our consideration of the Gospels and Jewish traditions can contribute constructively to understanding pastoral implications of Jesus' ministry, I think it appropriate to acknowledge a couple of points for the sake of caution. We acknowledge, first, that none of the Enochic traditions contains any of the more technical language such as "kingdom of God" which in the Gospels plays such a prominent role in Jesus' proclamation and which, as we have seen, is related to Jesus' exorcism ministry. Second, not a single instance among the Gospels openly identifies a demon as a giant living in a post-diluvian state of existence. Nevertheless, what might the early Enochic traditions and the trajectory of development they set within the Dead Sea documents (see Excursus A and B) contribute to what Jesus the exorcist is seen to accomplish in the lives of people according to the Synoptic Gospels?

In relation to a better understanding of the ministry of Jesus in the Gospel tradition, the story of the giants could function in a number of ways. *First*, although it is hard to show that the origin of bodiless giants was conscious to the Gospel writers themselves, *the story does help to explain why it is that demons were so intent on entering the bodies of human beings.* Demonic entry is understood as an attempt to recover a form of existence the giants had lost and to make humans suffer since, as a species, they came through the Great Flood unscathed. When present inside of humans, these spirits interfered with and upset the balance of humans whom God had created to have a body and spirit of their own.

Second, the story serves to locate the problem of demonic evil within an apocalyptic-eschatological framework. On the one hand, the giants' punishment during the period of the Flood is regarded as a decisive, indeed definitive, act of God in the past.

---

[64] For the expression "holy ones" as referring to the fallen angels, see Chapter Four section C.3 above.

[65] James C. VanderKam, "1 Enoch, Enochic Motifs, and Enoch in Early Christian Literature", in eds. James C. VanderKam and William R. Adler, *The Jewish Apocalyptic Heritage in Early Christianity* (CRINT III.4; Assen: Van Gorcum and Minneapolis: Fortress Press, 1996), pp. 33–101 and Annette Yoshiko Reed, "The Trickery of the Fallen Angels and the Demonic Mimesis of the Divine: Aetiology, Demonology, and Polemics in the Writings of Justin Martyr", *JECS* 2 (2004), pp. 141–171.

On the other hand, although the giants were allowed to survive after the Flood as disembodied spirits, their newly altered state as spirits was accompanied by a consciousness on their part that they are powers that have already, in essence, been defeated. Thus, even the demonic world knows that it is fighting a battle that it will ultimately lose. The Flood is portrayed and retold as a proleptic episode out of the sacred past. Accordingly, imagery from the Flood narrative is adapted in *1 Enoch* 10, as the text looks forward to an eschatological judgment when evil will be destroyed once and for all (10:13–11:2). In the meantime – that is, between the time God's rule became manifest in the Flood and the time when evil will be eradicated – is an age during which evil spirits that came from the giants can operate under restriction (cf. *Jub.* 10:7–9), knowing their time to wreak havoc on humanity is limited (*1 En.* 16:1; *Jub.* 10:7–9; see Mt. 8:29 – "have you come to torment us before the time?" [pars. Mk. 5:7, Lk. 8:28]; cf. also Mk. 1:24 par. Lk. 4:34 – "have you come to destroy us?"; and Jas. 2:19 – "even the demons believe and tremble"). In this sense the Gospels present us with a world order which, as in Jewish apocalyptic tradition, temporarily falls under "the dominion of wickedness"[66] or, similarly, "the dominion of Satan" (cf. Mt. 4:8 par. Lk. 4:5–6; Lk. 22:31–32; Mt. 12:26 par. Lk. 11:17–18; cf. also Jn. 12:31; 14:30; 16:11).[67] Jewish contemporaries of Jesus who undertook means to curb the influence of demons could, against such a background, proceed with a certain measure of confidence. In relation to the discourse about the demonic world, then, Jesus does not so much introduce the notion of an eschatological tension between the "already" and "not yet" as much as he intensifies it through his ministry.

Third, God's act of delivering humanity and God's punishment of evil at the time of the Flood are associated with royal power (cf. Ps. 29:10). The divine response happens following complaints of murdered souls in which the archangels address God *inter alia* as "King of kings" (*1 En.* 9:4).[68]

Fourth, in view of the framework outlined here, one may then well ask: what do the Gospel stories of exorcisms performed by Jesus and others think happens to

---

[66] Among the Dead Sea materials, see esp. 4Q510 1.6–7 par. 4Q511 10.3–4.

[67] Cf. 1QS i 23–24, ii 19; 1QM xiv 9–10 par. 4QMa = 4Q491 8–10 i 6–7; 4Q177=4QCatena A iii 8; 4Q390 2 i 4.

[68] Moreover, if it is correct to read one of the *Book of Giants* fragments (4Q203 9) as a petition (by Enoch?) that God intervene to punish the fallen angels and giants, then the reference "your great rule" (מלכות רבותכה) in the prayer suggests that God's kingship was being understood to have manifested itself in the past in the deluge (cf. also *1 En.* 9:4–11). Indeed, Enoch's petition in the *Book of Dreams* (*1 En.* 84:2–6), which also appeals to God's kingship, anticipates – and is followed by – the punishment of ante-diluvian evil. The presence of royal power in curbing or dealing with the effects of demonic power may be also implied in the *Songs of the Maskil* mentioned in Excursus A above. The writer of the songs holds two convictions in tension: a belief that one now lives during a time of "a dominion of wickedness" during which "the sons of light" can be expected to suffer and be "plagued by iniquities", and a belief that despite this the threats posed by such evil powers, which are temporary in any case, can be neutralized until the present age is brought to an end (cf. 4Q510 1.6b–8 par. 4Q511 10.3b–6).

demonic powers when they have been expelled? *Those who understood themselves to live in a world inhabited by demons would not have thought exorcism is a matter of extermination or of total destruction.* Through exorcism, *spiritual forces are not destroyed, they are relocated.* This is the view affirmed in Luke 11:24–26 (par. Mt. 12:43–45; cf. the section above under "God, Demons and Humans in the Jesus Tradition") and is presumed by all the accounts of Jesus' confrontation with malevolent spirits. Even the Gerasene demoniac episode provides another case in point, with its two-stage exorcism that builds on the presumption (articulated by "Legion" in Mk. 5:12, "send us into the swine so that we may enter into them") that this is what customarily happens.[69] Therefore, despite the story's attempt to highlight the distinct authority with which Jesus takes control over the situation, the drowning of two thousand swine indwelt by the spirits (5:13) does not mark the end of those spirits (so Mk. 5:13 par. Lk. 8:33; *contra* Mt. 8:32). Whatever early storylines of this tradition may have contained, on the level of the Markan narrative, the drowning signifies the end of demonic power on this person, though an eschatological act of complete subjugation lies ahead.[70] The same applies to Jesus' expulsion of a father's son plagued since childhood by a demon in Mark 9:14–29. Notably, Jesus' address to the demon includes the command "Do not enter him again!" (9:25). Again, however, the conclusion of this episode underscores the effectiveness of the exorcism itself, rather than claiming anything about the destruction of the demon (cf. Tob. 6:8; 8:3). Moreover, it reflects a view that "possession" can be momentary or sporadic as well as sustained.

Fifth, and following from the last point, the "return of the spirit" saying in Luke 11:24–26 acknowledged, as we have seen, that *exorcized powers can return and do so in such a way that the person's condition is worse than before.* This reflects an outlook that evil power, once extricated from the human body, needs to be kept at bay, negotiated, or managed in order for the person to remain in an improved state of being. *Being exorcised is not a static condition, but is a mode of being within a fluid life process.* If this is so, then Jesus' exorcisms are not simply to be understood as "miracles" in a remote or unusual sense. It is important to say this, since many mental health professionals think that the Bible presents us with a worldview that is essentially irrelevant to today. Jesus is imagined as one who offered "quick or sudden solutions" for people's problems. *Our evidence in the Gospels, informed by the Enoch tradition, paints a much more realistic portrait of life. People suffering from problems we might refer to today as mental illnesses were being helped, and we are not to assume that cures were automatically permanent.* Exorcism – and we may include

---

[69] See Matthias Konradt, *Israel, Kirche und die Völker im Matthäusevangelium* (WUNT 215; Tübingen: Mohr Siebeck, 2007), pp. 60–61 and bibl. in n. 240.

[70] Cf. Lamar Williamson, *Mark* (NTL; Louisville, KY: Westminster John Knox Press, 2009), p. 104. Significantly, in Luke's version (8:31) what the demons beg of Jesus is that he not send them "into the abyss", a reference to the temporary holding place until their final destruction (cf. *1 En.* 10:4–5; 88:1; *Jub.* 10:5; cf. 2 Pet. 2:4).

healing (whether through medicine or prayer or both) – is, even in Jesus' ministry, *a temporary expedient*. From the perspective of the Gospel tradition, it illustrates that the physical, spiritual, and mental problems that beset people are evils that, under the eyes of faith, have already been defeated. From the perspective of the Gospel tradition, exorcism also illustrates that such problems cannot simply be wished away. It is in this respect that the world of the psychiatrist – even one who is not a Jew or Christian – is not so completely remote. Psychiatrists and psychologists rely on their patients to have hope that they can improve; equally, they know that even with medication mental illness does not simply vanish into thin air. For too long the mental health profession and the world of the Gospels have been held apart when, in reality, they are not so completely disconnected.

Sixth and finally, *the very idea that exorcism is needed at all is not actually built around an understanding of a person as someone invaded by evil*. The Enochic tradition and a number of texts that drew upon it regarded demonic powers as inherently out of place in and alien to the world as God has set it up to be.[71] *The notion of possession, instead of undermining the dignity of this or that individual, could actually have functioned to preserve it*. Whatever their problems, *humans are not presented as "metaphysically evil", but are seen to remain integral to the created order*. This is fundamental to both the Enoch tradition and the ministry of Jesus.

Conclusion

The Synoptic Gospels underline the success of Jesus as one whose power is superior to that of demonic powers in the present age (Mt. 9:34 par. earlier form of the tradition in Lk. 11:14; Mk. 1:27; cf. Mk. 5:20). Jesus' prominence as an exorcist *par excellence* is also reflected in the effectiveness attributed to the use of his "name" by others (Mt. 7:22; Mk. 9:38; Lk. 9:49; 10:17).[72] There is every reason to think, then, that the presentation of Jesus in the Gospels stressed the "miraculous" character of his deeds.

At the same time, the counter-demonic maneuvers described in the Gospels fit logically into the framework of an apocalyptic worldview that Jesus shared with some, if not many, of his pious Jewish contemporaries. Our consideration of the Second Temple context may provide one way of getting past the hermeneutical conundrum associated with Jesus' exorcisms. In parts of our contemporary world, readers of the Gospels have stressed the dramatic, spectacular character with which

---

[71] Loren T. Stuckenbruck, "The Eschatological Worship by the Nations: An Inquiry into the Early Enoch Tradition", in eds. Károly Dániel Dobos and Miklós Kőszeghy, *Wisdom Like a Robe: Festschrift in Honour of Ida Fröhlich* (Sheffield: Sheffield Phoenix Press, 2009), pp. 191–208.

[72] The scope for successful exorcisms in Acts 19:13–16 is implicitly narrowed to Jesus' followers, though the sons of Sceva are presented as having wrongly assumed that their use of Jesus' name would be effective.

the descriptions of these episodes are invested in the text. While such a reading rightly picks up on the significance being attached to the person of Jesus, it may serve to make Jesus more remote or bifurcate readers around the misleading question of whether or not there is a place at all in religious communities today for such or similar activity. By contrast, we have attempted here to refocus the problem to being one that is primarily *a matter of perspective*. It is possible to regard a hermeneutically, cosmologically and sociologically controversial part of Jesus' activity in combating demonic forces not only as miracle (with its attendant symbolic interpretations) but also as – perhaps surprisingly so – a realistic approach, informed by his Jewish context. Read more specifically in relation to an apocalyptic worldview, the accounts of exorcisms performed by Jesus and others, for all their "success" as depicted in the Gospels, presuppose the recognition of two things: that (1) however one treats it, evil is a persistent reality that cannot be conveniently ignored or removed from human experience; and that (2) from a standpoint of faith, the wholeness of individual and collective humanity is assured through anticipation of God's ultimate victory which can, though not necessarily, be already experienced in this life.

Against this background, the notion of having a mental disorder, therefore, should not be regarded as "taboo". In the community of faith, whether one attributes problems to the demonic or to chemical imbalance, the suffering person, created in the image of God, has an undeniable dignity that is to be cultivated and preserved. Those standing in a Christian or Jewish tradition might not be able to "get rid" of or do away with problems in others or within themselves. The above discussion, however, gives place to exorcisms in the Gospels alongside other practices – these include petitionary prayer, community support, the worshipping life of the assembled church or synagogue – through which it is possible to gain perspective on the sometimes irretrievable sufferings people face. The confession and proclamation that evil has already in principle been overcome opens up a vision for the value of personhood that signals hope that there is restoration to come.

Chapter Ten

The Need for Protection from the Evil One and John's Gospel

A. Introduction: Language for "Evil" in the Fourth Gospel

There are many today who maintain that there is a strong socio-rhetorical component to language about evil in the Gospel of John and the Johannine Epistles. This has been recognized by many for several decades, especially since the influential studies of Wayne Meeks,[1] Raymond Brown,[2] and J. Louis Martyn.[3] Within such a framework, conditioned as it is by the interaction between groups, the use of an adjective such as "evil" (φαῦλος Jn. 3:20, 5:29; πονηρός 3:19, 7:7)[4] and especially more unambiguously personifying expressions of "having a demon" (ἔχειν δαιμόνιον; cf. Jn. 7:20; 8:48–49, 52; 10:20–21), "you are from the father the devil" (ὑμεῖς ἐκ τοῦ πατρὸς τοῦ διαβόλου ἐστέ; Jn. 8:44) or simply "the devil" (διάβολος; Jn. 6:70, cf. 13:2 – referring to Judas) are ultimately products of polemical perception. To a certain degree, the use of negative labels for detractors also holds for language in the Fourth Gospel about "the world" as well (ὁ κόσμος), though references to this term are not so one-sided, such that the text assumes an ability on the part of an audience to discern the difference between "world" as an arena of God's activity within the created order (1:9–10, 29; 3:16–17, 19; 4:42; 6:14, 33, 51; 8:12, 26; 9:5; 10:36; 11:27; 12:46–47; 16:28; 17:21–23; 18:37) and as an unwelcoming or even inimical force represented by anything that, in principle, is opposed to God's purposes and is incapable of understanding God's activity through Jesus the Son (esp. Jn. 1:10 [3rd occurrence]; 7:4, 7[5]; 13:1; 14:17, 19, 22, 27; 15:18–19; 16:8, 20, 33; 17:6, 9, 11, 14–16, 18, 25).

---

[1] See "The Man from Heaven and Johannine Sectarianism", *JBL* 91 (1972), pp. 44–72 (esp. pp. 67–69).

[2] Especially *The Gospel According to John* (AB 29–30; Garden City: Doubleday, 1979) and *The Community of the Beloved Disciple* (New York: Paulist Press, 1979).

[3] So *The Gospel of John in Christian History* (New York: Paulist Press, 1978) and *History and Theology in the Fourth Gospel* (Louisville: Westminster John Knox, 2003, 3rd ed. [1st ed. 1968]).

[4] The adjectives here are, except for πονηρός in Jn. 17:15 (see below), always made to characterize "deeds".

[5] Significantly, the plural adjective πονηρά describes the "works" or "deeds" (ἔργα) associated with the world. Such works are diametrically opposed to ἔργα in all other instances of Jn. where they refer to the allied activities of God and the Son (3:19–21; 5:20, 36; 6:28; 7:3; 9:3–4; 10:25, 32, 37–38; 14:10–12; 15:24) which Jesus' followers emulate and participate in (6:28; 14:12).

Another framework within which language about evil in the Fourth Gospel has been interpreted sometimes goes under the category of what is called "realized eschatology".[6] The categorical statement in the Gospel by Jesus that "I have conquered the world" (16:33 – ἐγὼ νενίκηκα τὸν κόσμον; cf. 1:5), taken in tandem with the uncompromising claims the Johannine Jesus makes about himself and about what he expects of those who adhere and are obedient to him, presupposes that the audience are to imagine themselves as participants in an existence that reflects such a reality. Through identification with the Son, believers place themselves on the side of a victory that has already, in effect, taken place.

Given these rhetorical-sociological and realized eschatological dimensions for interpreting the language of evil in the Fourth Gospel, is there anything in the Johannine tradition that stands outside of this? Is there anything that suggests the lines are not firmly drawn between the emerging Johannine community and others or between the present state of entrenched ideological certainty and a reality that is yet to be? Since I am not simply asking whether or not the Johannine tradition has any room for eschatology,[7] it may help to formulate the problem another way, that is, in relation to the persistence of evil: is there anything eschatological or even "apocalyptic" when it comes to the way evil is dealt with in the text? In one sense, one may be able to answer this question rather easily: after all, for John, as in Jewish apocalyptic writings, there remains an eschatological judgment in which the wicked will be punished and the righteous rewarded (esp. 5:28–29; see further 3:36; 6:54, 57–58; 11:24–27; 12:48[8]; 14:2–4, 15–24; 16:16–33).[9]

However, what about the way evil is expressly combated? Posing the question this way is appropriate on at least three counts. First, there is a general consideration: the notion of realized eschatology, to the extent that it applies to the Fourth

---

[6] See, famously, Charles H. Dodd, *The Interpretation of the Fourth Gospel* (Cambridge: Cambridge University Press, 1965) and Rudolf Bultmann, *The Gospel of John: A Commentary*, trans. George R. Beasley-Murray, Rupert W. N. Hoare and John K. Riches (Philadelphia: Westminster, 1976).

[7] For strong criticisms of Bultmann's demythologization project in interpreting John's Gospel which, at the same time, stress the presence of a Johannine future eschatology, see especially Udo Schnelle, "Die Abschiedsreden im Johannesevangelium", *ZNW* 80 (1989), pp. 64–79 and Jörg Frey, *Die johanneische Eschatologie* (3 vols.; WUNT 2.96, 110, 116; Tübingen: Mohr Siebeck, 1997), esp. 1:119–150.

[8] Here Jesus claims that "on the last day the word I have spoken will judge him (i. e., the one who rejects Jesus)". While this initially appears to be an extraordinary claim, it is the kind of claim that is sustained in the Enochic writer of the *Epistle of Enoch* whose words are not simply denunciatory, but are intended to function as formal testimony at the time of judgment (cf. *1 En.* 96:4, 7; 97:2–7; 99:3, 16; 103:4; 104:1). See Loren T. Stuckenbruck, *1 Enoch 91–108* (CEJL; Berlin/New York: Walter de Gruyter, 2007), p. 216 and *idem*, "The Epistle of Enoch: Genre and Authorial Presentation", *DSD* 17/2 (2010), pp. 387–417, here p. 417: "In terms of function, the work, which inscribes the 'memory' of human deeds (94:8; 96:4, 7; 97:2, 7; 99:3, 16; 103:4; cf. 103:15), imparts irreversible testimony (enhanced by exhortations, disclosure formulae) that guarantees the outcome of eschatological judgment."

[9] For a significant attempt to restore eschatology as a cardinal theme in the Fourth Gospel, see Frey, *Die johanneische Eschatologie* (bibl. in n. 7 above).

Gospel, represents the ideal for a community's self-understanding that includes the hedging of itself off from other groups, especially those with which it is most immediately in tension. In all this, the resulting question would remain: how does one negotiate the undeniable continuing reality of evil wherever it exists, even within the Johannine community? If in the present world the "already" (cf. 16:33) is a reality that determines and defines socio-religious identity, what does one do with experience that does not fit into or reflect this? An ideal self-perception, whether embraced by a religious community or individuals, still has to reckon with the very means by which counter-experiences are to be interpreted and navigated. Second, not all the vocabulary regarding personified evil in the Fourth Gospel can be reduced sociologically to sectarian and theologically to realized eschatological frames of reference. Nor is evil simply, in my view, a matter of "ethics". We may note here a designation such as "the evil one" in Jesus' prayer at John 17:15 (see on this below) and the several references to "the ruler of this world" in John 12:31, 14:30 (with "*the* world") and 16:11. Third, a reconsideration of evil in the Gospel of John, when placed in conversation with Second Temple Jewish traditions, should caution us from drawing on too narrow a conception of "apocalyptic". Since the influential studies on genre and "apocalypse" in the late 1970's and 1980's,[10] many scholars have made it their business to broaden the scope of what one means by "apocalyptic" beyond eschatology to, for example, include sapiential and cosmological dimensions as well. My own developing view is that even the provision of a conceptual place for wisdom in apocalyptic thought does not go far enough, and I hope that the consideration of evil in the Fourth Gospel will help to make this more apparent.

B. The Problem: The Need for Protection from "the Evil One"

In dealing with a neglected dimension of evil in the Fourth Gospel, I would like to take Jesus' prayer in John 17:15 as a point of departure:[11]

"I am not asking you to take them out of the world, but to keep them from the evil one."

---

[10] See the contributions to ed. David Hellholm, *Apocalypticism in the Mediterranean World and the Near East: Proceedings of the International Colloquium on Apocalypticism, Uppsala, August 12–17, 1979* (Tübingen: Mohr Siebeck, 1989, 2nd ed.); John J. Collins, "Introduction: Towards the Morphology of a Genre", in ed. *idem, Apocalypse: The Morphology of a Genre* (Semeia 14; Missoula, Montana: Scholars Press, 1979), pp. 1–20 and *idem, The Apocalyptic Imagination* (Grand Rapids: Eerdmans, 1998, 2nd ed.), pp. 2–11, esp. pp. 4–9.

[11] A substantial part of the following argument draws on my earlier study, "'Protect them from the Evil One' (John 17:15): Light from the Dead Sea Scrolls", in eds. Mary L. Coloe and Tom Thatcher, *John, Qumran and the Dead Sea Scrolls: Sixty Years of Discovery and Debate* (SBLEJL 32; Atlanta: Society of Biblical literature, 2011), pp. 139–160.

There are, at first glance, several observations we may wish to make: First, we note that the Greek expression behind what I have translated as "the evil one" is ambiguous. Being in the genitive case, τοῦ πονηροῦ could be either masculine or neuter. The latter sense is *prima facie* a viable option. In general terms, to render the expression as a moral state of being accords more easily with modernist sensibilities (in avoiding a personified reading); it also occurs within a prayer of Jesus that emphasizes love and unity among Jesus' disciples and followers (17:11, 21–23, 26); and, finally, it is the same term which, in an unambiguous neuter form, describes the "works" of the world (cf. n. 6 above).[12] There are, however, reasons to steer the perspective in the other, more personifying direction. In 17:12 Jesus refers to "the son of destruction" as the only one whom he did not keep among those God gave to him. This designation is a reference to Judas Iscariot whose activity to betray Jesus occurs when "Satan entered him" (13:27 – εἰσῆλθεν εἰς ἐκεῖνον ὁ Σατανᾶς); if, as is likely, Jesus' loss of the "son of destruction" alludes back to the story of Judas as presented in the Fourth Gospel, Jesus' prayer assumes the existence of an extra-human force in the world that attempts to distract those who belong to the Son (cf. 17:11, 13).[13] This context, in turn, makes it more plausible to read Jesus' prayer in conversation with traditions about prayer preserved for us in Second Temple Jewish texts (as below).[14]

---

[12] Several scholars, appealing to such reasoning, have adopted this interpretation; see Marie-Joseph Lagrange, *Évangile selon Saint Jean* (Études Bibliques; Paris: J. Gabalda, 1936, 5th ed.), p. 447; Klaus Wengst, *Das Johannesevangelium* (2 vols.; TKNT; Stuttgart: Kohlhammer, 2001), 2:185; and Udo Schnelle, *Das Evangelium nach Johannes* (THNT 4; Leipzig: Evangelische Verlagsanstalt, 2004, 3rd ed.), p. 282. Cf. also Rudolf Bultmann, *Das Evangelium des Johannes* (2 vols.; KEKNT; Göttingen: Vandenhoeck & Ruprecht, 1950), 2:389, for whom the precise sense of the expression "ist sachlich gleichgültig".

[13] Those who have supported this position on exegetical grounds include: George H. C. MacGregor, *The Gospel of John* (MNTC; London: Hodder and Stoughton, 1942), p. 319; William Hendriksen, *Exposition of the Gospel According to John* (Grand Rapids: Baker Academic, 2002, repr. 1952), p. 360; Joseph N. Sanders, *The Gospel According to Saint John* (London: Adam and Charles Black, 1968), pp. 374–375; John Marsh, *Saint John* (Westminster Pelican Commentaries; Philadelphia: Penguin Books, 1978), p. 567; Leon Morris, *The Gospel According to John* (NICNT; Grand Rapids: Eerdmans, 1971), p. 730; Rudolf Schnackenburg, *Das Johannesevangelium* (3 vols.; HTKNT 4; Freiburg/Basel/Vienna: Herder, 1975), 3:209; Juan Mateos and Juan Barreto, *El Evangelio de Juan* (vol. 4; Madrid: Ediciones Cristiandad, 1982, 2nd ed.), p. 720; Jürgen Becker, *Das Evangelium nach Johannes* (2 vols.; ÖTK 412; Gütersloh: Gerd Mohn/Echter Verlag, 1984), 2:523–524; Charles Kingsley Barrett, *Das Evangelium nach Johannes*, trans. Hans Bold (KEK; Göttingen: Vandenhoeck & Ruprecht, 1990), p. 493; Donald A. Carson, *The Gospel According to John* (Pillar New Testament Commentary; Grand Rapids: Eerdmans, 1991), p. 565; Francis J. Maloney, *The Gospel of John* (SP 4; Collegeville, Minnesota: The Liturgical Press, 1998), p. 471; Andreas J. Köstenberger, *John* (BECNT; Grand Rapids: Baker Academic, 2004), p. 465; Andrew T. Lincoln, *The Gospel According to Saint John* (Black NT Commentaries; Peabody, Massachusetts: Hendrikson, 2005), pp. 437–438; Hartwig Thyen, *Das Johannesevangelium* (HNT 6; Tübingen: Mohr Siebeck, 2005), pp. 695–696; and Jean Zumstein, *L'Évangile selon Saint Jean* (2 vols.; CNT 4b; Geneva: Labor et Fides, 2007), p. 177 and n. 26.

[14] This approach to Jesus' petition in Jn. 17:15 holds more promise than one that focuses on proximity between the Fourth Gospel and Gnostic traditions. See n. 20 below.

The second observation to make is that the prayer is a petition for protection uttered by Jesus on behalf of those who are his disciples and, arguably, that the prayer is concerned with his later followers in the Johannine community. To be sure, the verb in the petition is not φυλάσσειν ("to guard, protect"), but rather τηρεῖν ("to keep") with which it is interchangeable in the Gospel.[15] As we shall see below, τηρεῖν has its background in the Hebrew term שׁמר (though in the Aaronic blessing of Num. 6:24 the available Grk. translation reads φυλάξαι σε). We may ask, simply, for all the so-called realized eschatology at work in the Gospel, why does it remain that the Jesus of this Gospel might have found it necessary to ask that, in contrast to what happened to Judas, his followers be protected from demonic power (if we may call it that)?

Third, the term "world" bears a largely negative connotation both here and throughout the prayer. Despite being allied to the evil one, however, it is not treated as the same; though the world "hates" Jesus' disciples (17:14), it is still considered a place within which they must remain while seeking protection from the evil one who dwells there too. The association between the world and the evil one has to do with cosmology and control. The world is the arena of existence for Jesus' adherents, and the evil one has dominion over it. Thus the main challenge for the believing community in the Johannine perspective is less to escape and relocate out of world's way but, much more, to live in defiance of the grip on power attributed to demonic evil in this world (17:15). This possibility throws up a possible link between the petition being uttered by Jesus and the designation "the ruler of this world" which has occurred several times in the preceding chapters (12:31; 14:30; 16:11). These references to a being who is deemed to be in control of the present world order occur in words of Jesus that have the defeat of evil in view. In words to the disciples, Jesus has declared, "Now is the judgment of this world; now the ruler of this world will be driven out" (12:31); "I will no longer talk much with you, for the ruler of the world is coming" (14:30); and the advocate (i. e. the Spirit) will prove the world wrong "about judgment, because the ruler of this world has been condemned" (16:11).

Here we return once again to the question: in view of Jesus' assurance that he has overcome the ruler of this world (cf. 16:33), what is the function of a prayer for protection? Before addressing the function of Jesus' prayer, I would like to set the stage for drawing on petitionary prayers for protection as they occur in Jewish apocalyptic traditions, especially from those writings preserved among the Dead Sea Scrolls. For the significance of Jewish tradition for John 17:15 to be appreciated, however, two preliminary points require attention: (i) the expression ὁ ἄρχων τοῦ κόσμου in both the wider and Johannine contexts (section C) and (ii) a more detailed summary of Jesus' prayer in John 17 (section D).

---

[15] For φυλάσσειν in the sense of "keep" in the Fourth Gospel, see 12:25 and 47, and for τηρεῖν in the sense of "protect", see 17:11 and the present text of v. 15.

C. The Ruler of this World in the Fourth Gospel

The designation "ruler" (ἄρχων), of course, referred in Greek antiquity to a high official, a person with civic authority or to a military commander. In relation to the non-physical world, Plato made mention of ἄρχοντες in his *Laws* as beings to whom God has given authority over circumscribed areas of the cosmos (*Nom.* 903b). The term also occurs in the Greek text traditions to Daniel, where it refers to the prominent otherworldly beings – Michael ("the first of the rulers", Dan. 10:13 OG, Th), "the ruler of the Persians" (10:13, 20 Th), "the ruler of the Greeks" (10:21 Th) – who are made to function as protectors of the nations. In this context, the angel Michael assumes such a duty on behalf of Israel.[16] In and of itself the expression "the ruler of this world" is unique in John's Gospel, though it picks up on the notion of one with authority over beings who are inimical to God's purposes, a notion widespread in Jewish apocalyptic tradition.[17] This emphasis on one who acts as an organizing power over those who oppose God and God's people also reflects something not developed in Jewish tradition by means of any of the other personalizing designations for evil such as "the devil" or "demon".[18] As Jutta Leonhardt-Balzer has observed, neither of these designations serve in the Fourth Gospel to denote God's overarching opponent.[19] The devil (ὁ διάβολος) is presented not so much as one who acts on its own but through people who oppose Jesus. Activity that opposes Jesus comes from the devil and is described through the metaphor of parentage; Jesus accuses his Jewish detractors in John 8:37–45 of being "from your father the devil" as a way to explain why it is that they reject him. Jesus can even say directly to his own disciples, "one of you *is* a devil" (6:70–71), by which he refers to Judas who would betray him. "Being the devil" will, in John 13:2 (see also references to Satan's entry into Judas in 13:27 and Lk. 22:3), be re-expressed in terms of Satan putting "into his heart in order that Judas Simeon Iscariot might betray" Jesus. Similarly, Jesus is accused of having a "demon" because his teaching and activity make no sense to others (7:20 – to the crowd; 8:48, 49, 52 – to the Jews; 10:20 – some Jews, though in 10:21 other Jews dispute this). This emphasis is picked up in 1 John, in which the devil is held

---

[16] See the useful overview of these sources in Jutta Leonhardt-Balzer, "Gestalten des Bösen im frühen Christentum", in eds. Jörg Frey and Michael Becker, *Apokalyptik und Qumran* (Einblicke 10; Paderborn: Bonifatius, 2007), pp. 203–235.

[17] See Loren Stuckenbruck, "Demonic Beings and the Dead Sea Scrolls", in ed. J. Harold Ellens, *Explaining Evil. Volume 1: Definitions and Development* (Santa Barbara, CA: Praegers Publishers, 2011), pp. 121–144 and Chapter Four above.

[18] On the other hand, for the use of "Satan" as an adversary against God's people and as a chief over an array of demonic spirits, see *Jub.* 10:11 (cf. also 11Q5 xix 13–16, though the relation of "Satan" to any other entities is not specified. These texts are discussed in more detail below).

[19] Cf. Leonhardt-Balzer, "Gestalten des Bösen im frühen Christentum", pp. 221–225, for an excellent introductory discussion of evil in the Fourth Gospel.

accountable for all human sin and is thus characterized as the one who "sins from the beginning" (1 Jn. 3:8, 10)

However, the close alignment between demonic and human activity is not ultimately a matter of collapsing the two. Judas' betrayal is, after all, attributed to the *invasive* force of Satan in his heart (Jn. 13:2); and the charges that Jesus has a demon (8:48–49, 52) presuppose the suspicion, however rhetorical, that a power inimical to God's purposes has gotten hold of Jesus, even as Jesus is referring to his death (7:19–20) and is being credited with healing those who are blind (10:21). If such language cannot be reduced to metaphor, then the "the ruler of this world" appropriately functions as an overarching designation for a power that controls impulses which on a profound level contravenes what Jesus declares about himself. In contrast to the terms "devil" or "demon" and perhaps even "Satan" – these terms surface in specific instances of oppositional activity that occurs in particular groups or human beings – the designation "the ruler of this world" is more comprehensive and wide-ranging. Without referring specifically to "the ruler", Jesus declares in John 7:7 that the world hates him since he testifies that its works are evil (cf. also 15:18–16:4). As such, "the world" is personified as an organic conduit for such works. To refer, then, to "the ruler of this world" is to acknowledge that there is a coherent, organizing power behind these deeds and that this organizing power is characteristic of the present world order that comes under its sway.[20]

In one respect, Jesus' announcement of his death in the Fourth Gospel heralds the judgment over "this world". In John 12:20–33 Jesus' death is the time, "the hour", for his glorification (12:23, 27–28). In the text Jesus declares also that *now* "the ruler of this world" *will* be cast out. This combination of present (now) and future (will) in connection with Jesus' death is striking. Jesus' death marks a defeat, though not fully realized, over demonic evil. In John 14:30–31, Jesus announces that "the ruler of this world is coming", yet declares that it "does not have anything in me, so that the world may know that I love the Father, even as the Father has commanded me". Again this is a pronouncement of both the simultaneous presence and powerlessness of "the ruler of the world". Although the ruler of this world plays an essential role in bringing Jesus' death about, Jesus affirms that this "rule" is not in fact displaying any real power over Jesus. Accordingly, the advocate,

---

[20] This is in my view not to be confused with the beings called "*archons*" who in Gnostic literature from the Nag Hammadi corpus are credited with creating humanity and are custodians of the cosmos in its material state; see e.g. *The Hypostasis of the Archons* (NHC II, 4); *On the Origin of the World* [NHC II, 5; 97.24–127.17 and the fragmentary texts in XII,2; 50.25–34 and British Library Or. 4926]; and *Apocryphon of John* [NHC II 1.1–32.9 = IV 1.1–49.28]). Most instances of the term *archon* in this corpus are in the plural, while the singular is reserved for Yaldabaoth, the chief *archon* among them. The Gospel of John, on the other hand, does not pluralize its discourse about evil beings, staying instead with the singular (whether πονηρός, δαιμόνιον, διάβολος, or ἄρχων). While the Johannine tradition may have functioned as one tributary for such a worldview, the Gnostic framework itself does not offer the best point of departure for determining the origin of the ideas the Fourth Gospel inherited.

the Spirit, reveals the truth about Jesus to the disciples who remain in the world and reveals the condemnation under which "the ruler of this world" already stands (16:8–11). Thus mention of "the ruler of this world" is closely bound up with the notion that he already stands under divine judgment, for example, as exposed through Jesus' death.

If by means of Jesus' death "the ruler of this world" is rendered powerless, one may ask: what kind of defeat is this? Is it a complete removal of that force which coordinates opposition against God, Jesus, and the Johannine community? Does the exorcistic language of "casting out" (14:30), of being rendered powerless, or of being already judged or condemned bear a finality that leaves little else to be done? In the narrative world of the Fourth Gospel the answer would be "yes" and "no". Insofar as the answer is "yes", Jesus' death is definitive and, in the Fourth Gospel, functions in *principle* as that which ring-fences or circumscribes the devil's activity as no longer determinative for human existence in the context of faithfulness to God. Much of John's language about evil takes this conviction as its point of departure. That the answer, somehow, can likewise be "no" is reflected by the fact that Jesus utters petitions for those who will come after him, culminating in their need for divine protection from the evil one (17:15).

D. The Prayer of Jesus in John Chapter 17 and Its Petitionary Character

Jesus' prayer in John 17 is elaborate and can be subdivided into four parts:
(1) a series of declarative statements about Jesus' and the disciples' special position and faithfulness in relation to God (17:1–8);
(2) petitions for Jesus' disciples (17:9–19);
(3) a petition for those who come to faith through the disciples' ministry (17:20–23); and
(4) statements that resume and build on selected elements of the prayer (17:24–26).

Limiting our observations to Jesus' petition for his disciples in 17:9–19, we note several points of emphasis:

(a) Jesus underlines the enmity or tension between his disciples and "the world". This tension manifests itself in the hate the world shows the disciples (v. 14). Jesus' petition unambiguously takes the side of the disciples: he does not pray for the world, but for those whom God has given him (v. 9). Despite the sharp distinction between the disciples and the world, however, Jesus does not seek to resolve this tension by requesting that God remove the disciples from the world (v. 15).

(b) Formally, in 17:9–19, Jesus presents God with three petitions. The first occurs in verses 9–13: God – who is addressed as "holy Father" – is asked to "keep (τήρησον) them (i. e. the disciples) in your name which you have given to me" (v. 11). The basis for this request is provided by Jesus, who himself has "kept" (ἐτήρουν) the disciples "in your name which you have given me" (v. 12). The notion of "keeping" is formulated in terms of protection by Jesus, who has guarded (ἐφύλαξα) his disciples so that none of them would be lost.[21] Initially, the petition is concerned with unity among Jesus' disciples: "in order that they may be one" (v. 11), a petition which is also brought to bear on later believers (vv. 20–23). At this point, it is not clear from the petition what the protection is supposed to be from. Implied, however, is the perception of a danger that threatens to splinter the community for whom Jesus is praying. Second, in verses 14–16, Jesus prays again for God to "keep" (ἵνα τηρήσῃς). Here, there is no doubt that Jesus is asking for protection: "that you keep them from the evil one" (v. 15). The reason why protection is requested lies, as we have seen, in a tension between Jesus' followers and "the world". Because Jesus is not of the world, those whose unity he has maintained are not from the world (v. 16) which has "hated them" (v. 14). Despite this perceived alienation and enmity, Jesus' words refuse to contemplate removal (v. 15); the protection he requests assumes, instead, that the cosmos as presently constituted for the disciples involves an open clash or conflict with "the evil one" who is "the ruler of this world". As in the first request of verse 11, God's protection is bound up with protection by Jesus, who in 14:30 has already declared that "the ruler of the world has no power over me". Thus the protection is required if Jesus' adherents are living in an age dominated by "the evil one". The third petition of Jesus, in verses 17–19, is a request that God sanctify or make his disciples holy (ἁγίασον αὐτούς). Again, as in the first and second petitions of chapter 17, the request is linked with Jesus' own definitive activity: because he has sanctified himself or rendered himself pure for the disciples' sake, they themselves can also be sanctified.

(c) Each of Jesus' petitions to God is a genuine supplication, that is, none merely borrows a petitionary formula in order to accomplish something else. However, because the very basis for the divine response to these requests is already to be found in Jesus' activity, these petitions are replete with statements about him in relation to both God and his followers: One the one hand, Jesus is *the one* sent by God (vv. 3, 21, 23, 25); he is *the one* entrusted by God with the divine name (vv. 6, 12, 26); he is *the one* who is being glorified by God (vv. 1, 5, 10, 22, 24); and he and God are "one" (vv. 11, 22). On the other hand, the unity between Jesus and God (vv. 11, 22 – "just as we are one") and Jesus' origin in God rather than in the world are determinative for Jesus' followers who are aligned with him. Alignment with Jesus makes it possible for his followers to be "one" amongst themselves and, in their mutual belonging to God through Jesus, to be in tension with "the world" (v. 14).

---

[21] This protection by Jesus echoes the shepherd imagery applied to him in Jn. 10:7–16, though there the protection attributed to him is implied.

The proclamations in chapter 17 – so much of the language attempts to shore up Jesus' and his followers' identity – cannot hide the petitionary force of Jesus' prayer. We have been noting that the designation "the ruler of this world" is of particular relevance here; Jesus asks for protection from the evil one precisely because of the existing, *ongoing* hostility between the disciples and the world. The defeat of this inimical ruler may be assured in Jesus' death to be a reality, at least in principle, though it is incomplete. The Fourth Gospel presents Jesus' death as that event which provides the assurance of the evil one's essential powerlessness while acknowledging, nonetheless, that the complete destruction of this force lies in the eschatological future.

Several considerations suggest that Jesus' petition in John 17:15 has been shaped by tradition. First, as noted, "the evil one" as a designation for the devil occurs only here in the Fourth Gospel and thus seems uncharacteristic of the writer's language which otherwise may have been expected to refer here to "the ruler of this world". Second, the phrase "that you may keep them from the evil one" is reminiscent of language found in the Matthean version of the Lord's Prayer (Mt. 6:13 – "but deliver us from the evil one")[22] and in one Pauline writer's declaration about God's faithfulness in 2 Thessalonians 3:3 ("for faithful is the Lord, who will strengthen you and guard you from the evil one").[23] Third, the verb "keep" (τηρεῖν), which in verses 11–12 of John 17 is treated as a synonym for "protect, guard", may be an echo of the Aaronic blessing of Numbers 6:24: "may the Lord bless you and keep you" (MT; Grk. εὐλογήσαι σε κύριος καὶ φυλάξαι σε).

The main difference between the New Testament texts just mentioned and the Aaronic blessing lies in the absence of any reference in the latter to "the evil one". Admittedly, the Aaronic blessing simply concludes with the object of the verb ("you") without specifying what it is that Israel is to be kept or protected from. To be sure, in two adaptations of the Aaronic blessing in the Hebrew Bible, "evil" is added to the equation: (1) 1 Chronicles 4:10 – "Jabez called on the God of

---

[22] In the Matthean context of the Sermon on the Mount, the personified meaning of the expression is strengthened by the less ambiguous references to "the evil one" in Mt. 5:37; 13:19, 38.

[23] While it is possible to construe the phrase as an abstract reference to "evil", the foregoing mention of "the lawless one" in 2 Thess. 2:8 strengthens the case for a personified meaning here. In 2 Tim. 4:18, on the other hand, the deutero-Pauline writer – though possibly alluding to the Lord's Prayer – is not directly concerned with an evil being when he declares that "the Lord will rescue me from every evil work (NRSV: attack!) (ἀπὸ παντὸς ἔργου πονηροῦ) and save me for his heavenly kingdom". – Beyond its semantic overlap with φυλάσσειν, the term "keep" (τηρεῖν) operates in the Fourth Gospel with a double function: Being "kept" or protected by God from adversity (whether "the evil one", wickedness, or adversity) varies directly with "keeping" God's words or commands; this not only avails in Jn. (cf. 17:11 with 17:6 and 12:47; 14:15, 21, 23–24; 15:10, 20), but also in Rev. (cf. 3:10 with 1:3; 3:8, 10; 12:17; 14:12; 22:7, 9). In addition to further references given by Bultmann, *The Gospel of John: A Commentary*, pp. 301–302 n. 5, see *j.Peah* 16b:
אם שמרתם דברי תורה אני משמר אתכם מן המזיקין
("if you keep the words of the Torah, I will protect you from the demons")
In this formulation the motif of protection from the demonic represents a much earlier tradition that is explored below.

Israel, saying 'Oh that you would bless me and enlarge my border and that your hand would be with me, and that you would *keep me from evil* and harm!'" (so MT; the Grk. presupposes a very different text); (2) Psalm 121:7 – "The Lord will keep you from all evil; he will keep your life" (NRSV; MT and Grk. agree). In neither of these cases, however, do the texts suggest anything about protection from an "evil one". The same seems to be the case in the later 2 Maccabees 1:25, according to which God is addressed as one who rescues Israel "from all evil" and in Wisdom of Solomon 16:8 ("you persuaded our enemies that it is you who delivers from all evil").

Beyond the Matthean version of the Lord's Prayer and 2 Thessalonians, is there anything which may help one explain the background to the petition for protection from personified evil, and what light this might shed on a Johannine perspective in relation to the defeat yet persistent reality of demonic evil? What might such a background tell us, more specifically, about the theological framework in which Jesus' petitions in John 17 are formulated? In the following section, we shall explore some petitions, arguing that our closest link between the Aaronic blessing and its adaptations, on the one hand, and the narrative world of John 17 and the Johannine understanding of "the ruler of this world", on the other, lies in sources preserved in the Dead Sea Scrolls and related literature.

E: The Gospel of John in Context:
Protection from Demonic Power in an Age of Evil in Second Temple Jewish Tradition

Petitions to God for help in the Hebrew Bible and the Greek translations are attested in abundance.[24] Despite this, in line with the few passages we have already considered, there is no single instance in the Hebrew Bible in which God is specifically invoked for deliverance against another deity. That being said, prayers seeking divine protection from harm or help in neutralizing the effects of demonic power do begin to surface in literature from the Second Temple period.

---

[24] Such prayers request divine help in relation to one's own shortcomings (Ps. 27:12; 39:8; 51:14; 79:9); from dangers coming from opponents or enemies (so e. g., Gen. 32:11; Jos. 2:13; Jdg. 10:15; 1 Sam. 12:10; 2 Kgs. 21:14; 1 Chr. 6:36; 16:35; Ps. 6:4; 17:13; 22:20; 25:20; 31:1–2; 31:15; 40:13; 43:1; 59:1–2; 69:14, 18; 70:1; 71:2, 4; 82:4; 116:4; 119:134, 170; 120:2; 140:1; 142:6; 143:9; 144:7, 11; Isa. 44:17); or from premature death or an unwanted afterlife (e. g., Job 33:24 and 28). The material in this section is also discussed in Loren Stuckenbruck, "Pleas for Deliverance from the Demonic in Early Jewish Texts", in eds. Robert Hayward and Brad Embry, *Studies in Jewish Prayer* (JSSSup 17; Oxford: Oxford University Press, 2005), pp. 55–78 and "Deliverance Prayers and Hymns in Early Jewish Documents", in eds. Gerbern S. Oegema and Ian Henderson, *The Changing Face of Judaism and Christianity* (Gütersloh: Gerd Mohn, 2005), pp. 146–165.

E.1. Serekh ha-Yaḥad

Representative of this development is an adaptation of the Aaronic blessing within the Qumran community's covenant renewal ceremony, which according to the *Serek ha-Yaḥad* was to take place year by year (1QS ii 19; the ceremony as a whole is described in 1QS i 16 – iii 12). After an opening confession of wrongdoing and affirmation of divine favour by the community (i 23 – ii 1a), the liturgy is organised into a short series of blessings to be pronounced by the priests on "all the men of the lot of God" (ii 1b–4) and two longer series of curses pronounced by the Levites against "all the men of the lot of Belial" (ii 14–17). The language of both the blessings and curses, though reflecting contemporary concerns of the community, relies heavily on the Aaronic blessing. In particular, the benediction in Numbers 6:24, "May the Lord bless you and keep you" (יברכך יהוה וישמרך; Grk. εὐλογήσαι σε κύριος καὶ φυλάξαι σε) is reformulated in 1QS ii 2–3 in terms of contrasting activities of God, thus avoiding the possible implication that the verbs "bless" and "keep" are synonymous or complementary: "May he bless you with everything good, and may he keep you from every evil" (מכול רע יברככה בכול טוב וישמורכה). While in comparison to 1 Chronicles 4:10 and Psalm 121:7 (or even 2 Macc. 1:25 and Wis. 16:8), the reformulation does not seem to mark much of a conceptual shift from the Aaronic blessing, the larger context makes clear that the blessing is concerned with divine protection from Belial.[25] As the text following the liturgy suggests, it is precisely because the community knows itself to be living during a time of Belial's rule that the ceremony is necessary: "they shall do thus year by year all the days of the dominion of Belial" (1QS ii 19). Indeed, the ceremony counteracts the reality of life "during the dominion of Belial" because it is a time when it is possible for members to stray from the covenant on account of "fear or dread or testing" (1QS i 17–18); likewise, the opening confession of sins is expressly understood as a measure to be taken by the community "during the dominion of Belial" (1QS i 23–24). The expanded benediction that God "keep you from every evil", therefore, ultimately has protection from demonic power that causes transgression in view. The repetition of the ceremony during the era when Belial exercises dominion implies that there will be a time when it is no longer necessary (cf. 1QS iv 19–21).

---

[25] In this respect, the text's appropriation of Numbers 6:24 is on a trajectory that leads to the version preserved in Targum Pseudo-Jonathan: יברכינך ייי בכל עיסקך ויטרינך מן לילי ומזייעי ובני טיהררי ובני צפרירי ומזיקי וטלני ("may YYY bless you in all your undertaking, and may he guard you from the night demon, the vile demons, the children of the noon demons, the children of the morning demons, injurious and shadowy beings"); cf. Robert Hayward, "The Priestly Blessing in Targum Pseudo-Jonathan", *JSP* 19 (1999), pp. 81–101.

E.2. Serekh ha-Milḥamah

A similar perspective is reflected in other Dead Sea documents which, however, do not as explicitly formulate a need for divine protection as part of a blessing or petition. This is, for example, the case in *Sereh ha-Milḥamah*[26] where the sons of light declare that "during the dominion of Belial ... you (God) have driven away from [us] his (Belial's) [de]struction, [and when the me]n of his dominion [acted wickedly] you have kept (or: protected) the soul of your redeemed ones (שמרתה נפש פרותכה)" (1QM xiv 9–10 par. 4Q491=4QMᵃ 8–10 i 6–7; cf. further 1Q177=4QCatena A iii 8).

E.3. Songs of the Maskil

Of special note here is the document *Songs of the Maskil*, preserved in fragments of 4Q444, 4Q510 and 4Q511. In one of the songs, the sage initially declares the splendour of God's radiance

in order to terrify and fr[ighten] all the spirits of the angels of destruction, and the bastard spirits, demons, Lilith, owls and [jackals ...] and those who strike suddenly to lead astray the spirit of understanding and to cause their hearts to shudder. (4Q510 1.4–6a par. 4Q511 10.1–3a)

This proclamation of divine majesty, which Armin Lange has described as a "hymnic exorcism",[27] is then followed by an address to "righteous ones" in which the sage states:

You have been put in a time of the dominion [of] wickedness and in the eras of the humiliation of the sons of lig[ht] in the guilt of the times of those plagued by iniquities, not for an eternal destruction, [but] for the era of the humiliation of transgression. Rejoice, O righteous ones, in the God of wonder. My psalms (are) for the upright ones (4Q510 1.6b–8; par. 4Q511 10.3b–6).

The *Maskil*'s declarations about God, told in the 3ʳᵈ person (i.e., not in the 2ⁿᵈ person in the form of prayer addressed to God), are regarded as potent enough to diminish or counteract demonic powers which are at work in the present order of

---

[26] Thus in the *Two Spirits Treatise*, the Angel of Darkness, who has complete dominion over the sons of iniquity, is made out to be the influence behind the sins, iniquities, guilty deeds and transgressions of the sons of light (1QS iii 21–24); see further 1QS iv 19: "then truth shall go forth forever (in the) world, for it has been corrupted in paths of wickedness during the dominion of iniquity...".

[27] See Armin Lange, "The Essene Position on Magic and Divination", in eds. Moshe Bernstein, Florentino García Martínez and John Kampen, *Legal Texts and Legal Issues. Proceedings of the Second Meeting of the International Organization for Qumran Studies, Published in Honour of Joseph M. Baumgarten* (STDJ 23; Leiden/New York/Köln, 1997), pp. 383, 402–403, and 430–433. Lange also applies this classification to 1QapGen xx 12–18, *Jub.* 10:1–14; 12:16–21. On the problem of categorising the passage from 1QapGen in this way, see Stuckenbruck, "Pleas for Deliverance from the Demonic in Early Jewish Texts", pp. 60–62 (bibl. in n. 24).

things ("the dominion [of] wickedness"). While the text does not furnish a prayer for divine protection against these demons, it reflects a framework that holds two concurrent things in tension: (1) there is a community of those who are unambiguously "righteous" and "upright" and (2) the present is essentially "a time of the dominion [of] wickedness". Analogous to the pronouncement of a benediction in the yearly covenant renewal ceremony in *Sereh ha-Yaḥad*, the song to the righteous functions as an expedient measure that neutralises the threats associated with demonic powers until the present age of wickedness is brought to an end.

Significantly, the documents just considered are arguably sectarian. The hostility between the group behind the writings and other groups may have been felt to such an extent that the world order, as a whole, could not be portrayed as anything other than inimical. This notion, however, of an eschatological tension between divine activity already being realised in a specially elect community and ongoing demonic activity was not entirely unique to the community associated with Qumran. Several prayers come down to us in documents preserved among the texts recovered from the Qumran caves that do not show any obvious signs of having been composed by or for the *Yaḥad*. Before returning to the Fourth Gospel, we may briefly review prayers for protection from the demonic preserved in Qumran fragments from a "Prayer of Deliverance" (11Q5 xix), the *Aramaic Levi Document* (4Q213a=4QTLevi^a 1 i 10 par. *Jub.* 1:19–20), the *Book of Jubilees* 10:3–6 and 12:19–20, and the Book of Tobit.[28]

E.4. Prayer of Deliverance (11Q5 col. xix)

The text, which is also extant through two of the six fragments belonging to 11Q6, comes to us as part of a larger manuscript that consists of psalmic texts known through the Hebrew Bible, other hymnic compositions, and a text that attributes a series of compositions to David.[29] Since both 11Q5 and 11Q6 are copied in Herodian hands, they provide evidence for the prayer at the turn of the Common Era, though the compilation itself is surely earlier.[30] The piece, significantly, is

---

[28] For a fuller treatment of these and other texts, see Loren T. Stuckenbruck, "Deliverance Prayers and Hymns in Early Jewish Documents", pp. 146–165 (bibl. in n. 24 above).

[29] For a description of the contents of the six fragments of 11Q5, see James A. Sanders, *The Psalms Scroll of Qumrân Cave 11 (11QPs^a)* (DJD 4; Oxford: Clarendon Press, 1996), p. 5. See further Peter W. Flint, *The Dead Sea Psalms Scrolls and the Book of Psalms* (STDJ 17; Leiden: Brill, 1997), p. 190. According to J. van der Ploeg, 11Q6 is an exact copy of 11Q5; cf. idem, "Fragments d'un manuscrit de Paumes de Qumran (11QPs^b)", *RB* 74 (1967), pp. 408–413. It is possible, in addition, that 4Q87 (= 4QPs^e) is a copy of the same collection; see Flint, *The Dead Sea Psalms Scrolls*, pp. 160–164.

[30] Lange argues for a date as early as the first half of the 2nd century B.C.E.; see "Die Endgestalt des protomasoretischen Psalters und die Toraweisheit: Zur Bedeutung der nichtessenischen Weisheitstexte aus Qumran für die Auslegung des protomasoretischen Psalters", in ed. Erich Zenger, *Der Psalter in Judentum und Christentum* (HBS 18; Freiburg: Herder, 1998), p. 108. If the

composed as a prayer *per se*, showing – perhaps as in 1QS i–ii and the *Maskil* songs of 4Q510–511 – that we are safe to assume that the text consists of words actually in use during the Second Temple period.

Of the originally 24 or 25 verses of the prayer,[31] some 18 lines of 20 verses are preserved. In the opening extant lines of 11Q5 xix (ll. 1–5), the writer declares that only living creatures can praise God, implying that God should therefore spare him from death (cf. Isa. 38:18–19 and Ps. 6:4–5). In the next section (ll. 5–12), the writer proclaims YHWH's faithfulness based on his own experience, and for this he offers YHWH praise. This praise of divine activity introduces a plea for forgiveness and purification from iniquity (ll. 13–14), in place of which the one praying seeks to be given a "spirit of faith and knowledge" so as not to be dishonoured in iniquity. The petition culminates in lines 15–16 as follows:

אל תשלט בי שטן ורוח טמאה מכאוב ויצר רע אל ירשו עצמי

Do not let rule (or: have power) over me a satan (or: Satan) or an unclean spirit;
and may an evil inclination not take possession of my bones.

The first thing to notice is that the petition seeks divine help not to come under the rule or power of a demonic being. Here, that being which would have sway over the one praying is designated as both "a satan" and "an unclean spirit". The latter expression may be an echo of Zechariah 13:2.[32] However, in the present context it may refer to a disembodied spirit, that is, to a being whose origin lies in the illegitimate sexual union between the rebellious angels and the daughters of men which resulted in the birth of the pre-diluvian giants.[33] If the Enochic background, known to us through the *Book of Watchers* (*1 En.* chs. 10 and 15–16) and the *Book of Giants*, lies in the background, the prayer presupposes a wider narrative that negotiates God's decisive intervention against evil in the past (i. e., through the Flood and other acts of punishment) and the final destruction or eradication of evil in the future. The petition is therefore one that expresses confidence in God's

---

treatment of *Aramaic Levi Document* below is correct, however, this prayer may be even go back to the 3rd cent. B. C. E.

[31] Sanders, *The Psalms Scroll*, p. 76 argues that the psalm probably began on the previous column xviii; regarding the end of the prayer, see James A. Sanders with James H. Charlesworth and Henry W. L. Rietz, "Non-Masoretic Psalms", in ed. James H. Charlesworth PTSDSS Project, vol. 4a: *Pseudepigraphic and Non-Masoretic Psalms and Prayers* (Tübingen: Mohr Siebeck and Louisville: Westminster John Knox, 1997), p. 193 (hereafter PTSDSS).

[32] See Armin Lange, "Considerations Concerning the 'Spirit of Impurity' in Zech 13:2", in eds. Armin Lange, Hermann Lichtenberger, and K. F. Diethard Römheld, *Die Dämonen – Demons. Die Dämonologie der israelitisch-jüdischen und frühchristlichen Literatur im Kontext ihrer Umwelt* (Tübingen: Mohr Siebeck, 2003), pp. 254–255.

[33] For discussions of a wider network of related references in *1 Enoch* (esp. chs. 10, 15–16) and the Dead Sea materials (*inter alia* of *Book of Giants*, 4Q444; 4Q510–511; and 11Q11) see e.g. Philip S. Alexander, "The Demonology of the Dead Sea Scrolls", in eds. Peter W. Flint and James C. VanderKam, *The Dead Sea Scrolls after Fifty Years. A Comprehensive Assessment* (2 vols.; Leiden: Brill, 1999), 1:331–353 and Chapter One section C above.

control over the demonic (i. e., "do not allow…" *hiph.* vb. + "satan" and "unclean spirit" as dir. obj.'s), while recognising the very real possibility that such power still leaves its mark in the present. As for the former designation, "satan", it is not clear whether the writer has a chief demonic ruler in view (i. e., "Satan", as translated by Sanders and in PTSDSS[34]) or uses the term functionally to refer to a being that plays an adversarial role. Its juxtaposition with "unclean spirit" may suggest that "satan" is not a proper name (see below on the *Aramaic Levi Document* prayer).[35] What is clear, nonetheless, is that the use of the term reflects a development that has gone well beyond its use in the Hebrew Bible where it denotes an angelic being that is subservient to God (cf. Num. 22:22, 32; Ps. 109:6; even Job 1–2 and Zech. 3:1–2) or functions as a general designation for one's enemies (1 Kgs. 11:23, 25; Ps. 71:13; 109:20, 29). In the "Prayer of Deliverance" of 11Q5 "satan" refers generally to an angelic being whose activity in seeking to rule over the human being runs counter to what the petitioner regards as the divine will.

Though further observations about the petition will be made below when we consider the parallel prayer text in *Aramaic Levi Document*, a more general point about the compilation of psalms in which this petition is found should be made. Whereas James Sanders argued in his edition of the scroll that the compilation in 11QPs[a] was produced by the Qumran community,[36] Peter Flint has emphasized that the absence of peculiarly Qumranic expressions and the presence of calendrical affinities with those groups within which the early Enochic works and *Jubilees* were composed suggest that this collection probably predates the formation of the Qumran community and thus enjoyed a wider circulation.[37] If Flint is correct and if the "Prayer of Deliverance" was in the psalmic compilation, then it is likely that its petition that YHWH act on behalf of the pious petitioner to disempower 'a satan' and 'an impure spirit' from ruling over him was probably not a single prayer written by and for an individual. It would have enjoyed some degree of circulation, and we are perhaps to imagine that it was written as a model prayer for the pious to recite. This view is strengthened by our consideration of the following text.

---

[34] See n. 31.

[35] This would, then, be in contrast with *Jub.* 10:11, in which "Satan" is the named equivalent for Mastema as the ruler of demons on the earth; cf. also *Test. Dan* 5:6.

[36] Sanders, *The Psalms Scroll*, p. 158, designated it the "Qumran Psalter".

[37] See the discussion by Flint in *Dead Sea Psalms Scrolls*, pp. 198–200. While continuing to underscore the consistency between the ideas in the scroll and those of the Qumran community, Sanders has more recently adopted a less narrow view about its origins, arguing that the compilation was acquired by the community; see James A. Sanders, "Psalm 154 Revisited", in eds. Georg Braulik, Walter Gross, and Sean McEvenue, *Biblische Theologie und gesellschaftlicher Wandel. Festschrift für Norbert Lohfink S. J.* (Freiburg: Herder, 1993), pp. 301–302.

E.5. Aramaic Levi Document

The text in question (4Q213a=4QTLevi[a] 1 i 10) was initially published by Michael E. Stone and Jonas C. Greenfield,[38] and has been dated by Józef T. Milik to the late 2nd-early 1st century B. C. E.[39] However, the document itself was likely composed during the 3rd or perhaps even the late 4th century B. C. E.[40] Since the wording of the Aramaic text corresponds closely to that of the more complete Greek manuscript from Mt. Athos (Athos Koutloumous no. 39, at *Testament of Levi* 2:3), the latter may be used to reconstruct many of the lacunae in 4Q213a.[41]

The text with which we are concerned is part of a prayer spoken by the patriarch Levi just before he is granted a vision of heaven (cf. 4Q213a 1 ii 14–18) and commissioned to become a priest (cf. the later *T. Levi* 2:5–4:6).[42] After Levi makes preparations through cleansing and gestures (4Q213a 1 i 6–10), a text of his prayer is given (Grk. vv. 5–19; Aram. 1 i 10–ii 10). The prayer, according to Robert Kugler, may be loosely structured as follows: (a) In verses 6–9 (Grk.; Aram. 1 i 10–16) Levi prays that God would purify him from evil and wickedness, show him the holy spirit, and endow him with counsel, wisdom, knowledge and strength, in order that he might find favor before God and give God praise; (b) in verse 10 (Grk.; Aram. 1 i 17) the patriarch petitions that God protect him from evil; and (c) in verses 11–19 (Grk.; Aram. 1 i 18–ii 10) the patriarch formulates a series of requests that resume themes touched upon during the earlier part of the prayer (a), namely, that God cleanse and shelter Levi from evil (Grk. vv. 12 and 14), that wickedness be destroyed from the earth (Grk. v. 13), and that Levi and his descendants be placed in God's service for all generations (Grk. v. 18; 4Q213a 1 ii 8–9). The wording in the petition for protection in 4Q213a 1 i 17 is remark-

---

[38] Initially in "The Prayer of Levi", *JBL* 112 (1993), pp. 247–266 (with photograph) and then in eds. George Brooke et al., *Qumran Cave 4. XVII: Parabiblical Texts, Part 3* (DJD 22; Oxford: Clarendon Press, 1996), pp. 25–36 and Plate II.

[39] So Józef T. Milik, "Le Testament de Lévi en araméen", *Revue Biblique* 62 (1955), pp. 398–408.

[40] See esp. the thorough discussion and considerations offered by Henryk Drawnel, *An Aramaic Wisdom Text from Qumran* (JSJSup 86; Leiden and Boston: Brill, 2004), pp. 63–75 (the early Hellenistic period). Other recent treatments have dated the work to the 3rd and late 3rd to early 2nd century B.C.E.; so, respectively, Robert Kugler, *From Patriarch to Priest. The Levi-Priestly Tradition from Aramaic Levi to Testament of Levi* (SBLEJL 9; Atlanta: Scholars Press, 1996), pp. 131–38 and Jonas C. Greenfield, Michael E. Stone and Esther Eshel, *The Aramaic Levi Document* (SVTP 19; Leiden/Boston: Brill, 2004), pp. 19–22.

[41] So e.g. Stone and Greenfield, "The Prayer of Levi", 257–58 (Aramaic and Greek texts, respectively, from which the citations here are taken); cf. Drawnel, *An Aramaic Wisdom Text from Qumran*, esp. pp. 99 and 101.

[42] Unless otherwise indicted, my present comments follow the line numeration from 4Q213a, rather than the versification derived from the Greek text. However, the content is partially reconstructed by referring to the Greek, as in the eclectic translation of Stone and Greenfield, "The Prayer of Levi", pp. 259–260.

ably close to that of the text from 11Q5 discussed above; with the help of the Greek, it reads as follows:

וא[ל תשלט בי כל שטן [לאטעני מן ארחך

"And do n]ot let rule (or: have power) over me any satan [to lead me astray from your path."

καὶ μὴ κατίσχυσῃς με πᾶς σατανᾶς πλανῆσαι με ἀπὸ τῆς ὁδοῦ σου

"And may no satan rule (or: have power) over me to lead me astray from your path."

The context suggests that the petition here is concerned with demonic threat. Earlier in the prayer, Levi has asked that God "turn away" (4Q213a 1 i 7 רחא, Grk. ἀπόστρεψον) to a distance "the unrighteous spirit (Grk. τὸ πνεῦμα τὸ ἄδικον) and evil thoughts and fornication and hubris". He then asks, instead, to be shown "the holy spirit (Grk. τὸ πνεῦμα τὸ ἅγιον) and counsel and wisdom and knowledge and strength". Moreover, in a further petition not extant in the Aramaic but preserved in the Greek (v. 12), Levi asks for protection as follows: "and let your shelter of power shelter me from every evil (ἀπὸ παντὸς κακοῦ)". Thus, in seeking protection from overpowerment from "any satan", the writer – as argued above for 11Q5 – is referring to a being belonging to a category of demonic power[43] rather than to a primary power of evil who is called "Satan". This is even clearer here than in 11Q5 with the addition of "any" (כל).

Given the similarity between the petitions in 4Q213a and 11Q5, is there any genetic link? The parallel is strikingly similar to the text that comes down to us in Psalm 119:33b: ואל תשלט בי כל און ("and do not allow any iniquity to rule/have power over me", Grk. καὶ μὴ κατακυριευσάτω μου πᾶσα ἀνομία "may no iniquity rule over me"). It is possible, therefore, that both texts, rather than being directly interdependent in one direction or another, draw on a "common interpretation" of Psalm 119.[44] This view, if correct, (a) underscores that the writers of these texts and of the underlying tradition were personifying traditional references to evil; and (b) suggests that such a reinterpretation of biblical prayer was more generally widespread than the evidence preserved in 4Q213a and 11Q5 alone. Lange, however, has argued against a dependence of either text on Psalm 119 and, instead, reasons as follows for a literary dependence between the two documents: (1) it is unlikely that both 4Q213a and 11Q5 column xix would have independently substituted the term "iniquity" of the Psalm with "Satan"; and (2) both texts exhibit "extensive parallels in demonic thought".[45] More significantly, Lange admits that there is a parallel between the petition in 11Q5 xix and *Jubilees*

---

[43] See Stone and Greenfield, "The Prayer of Levi", p. 262, who draw attention to the use of the same expression ("every satan") in 1QH[a] isolated frg.'s 4 and 45.

[44] So David Flusser, "Qumrân and Jewish 'Apotropaic' Prayers", *IEJ* 16 (1966), pp. 196–197; Kugler, *From Patriarch to Priest*, p. 73; Stone and Greenfield, "The Prayer of Levi", p. 263.

[45] Lange, "Spirit of Impurity", p. 262. In favour of literary dependence, Lange argues that one would have expected the Aramaic verb in 4Q213a מלך rather than the cognate שלט; this point is not persuasive; cf. Klaus Beyer, *Die aramäischen Texte vom Toten Meer* (Göttingen: Vandenhoeck & Ruprecht, 1984), pp. 709–710 and *idem*, *Die aramäischen Texte vom Toten Meer. Ergänzungsband* (Göttingen: Vandenhoeck & Ruprecht, 1994), p. 422.

1:19–20,[46] in which Moses pleads that God not deliver Israel "into the control of the nations with the result that they rule over them lest they make them sin against you" and that "*the spirit of Beliar not rule them so as to bring charges against them* before you *and to trap them* away from every proper path so that they may be destroyed from your presence".[47] The text also shares language with the petition in *Aramaic Levi Document* which, however, lacks the specificity of "Satan" (= the spirit of Beliar in *Jub.*) as the inimical demonic power. The wording in *Jubilees* 1:20, as in the "Prayer of Deliverance", has no equivalent for כל and the mention of 'satan' has been replaced by the more proper name in the designation 'the spirit of Beliar' and reformulated as a verb that describes the activity of the demonic Beliar as an accuser of God's people.

These considerations suggest that both Levi's prayer in *Aramaic Levi Document* and Moses' intercession in *Jubilees* 1:20 reflect the influence of a tradition that is extant through the "Prayer of Deliverance". If this is the case, however, their common concern with the bestowal of a "holy spirit" in the context of the petition (cf. *Aramaic Levi Document* Grk. v. 8; *Jub.* 1:21), suggests that the underlying tradition was not entirely in line with the petition as preserved in 11Q5. Moreover, if the text of Psalm 119:133 is lurking in the background, by the time of *Jubilees*, at least, it lies well behind, and we may infer that the petition for protection from demonic power was beginning to acquire a life of its own. If this is correct, then we may offer two observations: First, the writers of these texts have adapted the generally formulated prayer text to suit the purposes of their narrative, doing so in different ways. Whereas the author of *Jubilees* has transformed the ambiguous "satan", perhaps from 11Q5, into a proper name Beliar while retaining his adversarial function, the author of the prayer of Levi retains "satan" as a type of demonic being that poses a threat. Second, the existence of the deliverance prayer in 11Q5 demonstrates that the attestation of the petitions for deliverance within larger narratives that have shaped them (i. e., in 4Q213a and *Jub.* 1), does not mean they bear no relation to religious practice. In fact, if the underlying tradition to *Aramaic Levi Document* and *Jubilees* was independent from the petition in 11Q5, then we have to deal with a more widespread prayer than has previously been recognised.

In other words, in 4Q213a and *Jubilees* 1 we do not have prayers formulated in order to enhance a given storyline so much as an independently circulating petition against demonic power which, due to its popularity, has been narrativized, that is, adapted into literary settings. The adaptability of the petitionary prayer for protection is illustrated by two further passages in *Jubilees*. Though none of the passages from *Jubilees* discussed here are preserved amongst the fragments of at least fifteen

---

[46] Beyer, *Die aramäischen Texte, Ergänzungsband,* p. 262 n. 38.

[47] The translation is that of James C. VanderKam, *The Book of Jubilees* (CSCO 511 and Scriptores Aethiopici 88; Leuven: Peeters, 1989), p. 5.

manuscripts of this work among the Dead Sea scrolls, it is the discovery of these materials which gives the considerations here firmer footing when it comes to describing the use of petitionary prayer during the Second Temple period.

E.6. Jubilees 10:3–6

This text contains a prayer formulated as the words of Noah spoken after the Great Flood (10:1–2). This prayer comes at the request of Noah's sons, who complain that Noah's grandchildren were being led astray, being blinded and being killed by "demons". In response, Noah utters a petition to curb the activities of evil spirits. The text of the prayer is as follows:

(v. 3) ... God of the spirits which are in all flesh,
　　　　who has acted mercifully with me and saved me and my sons
　　　　　　from the water of the Flood
　　　　and did not let me perish as you did the children of perdition,
　　　　　　because great was your grace upon me,
　　　　　　and great was your mercy upon my soul.
　　　　Let your grace be lifted up upon my sons,
　　　　and *do not let the evil spirits rule* over them,
　　　　　　lest they destroy them from the earth.
(v. 4) But bless me and my sons.
　　　　And let us grow and increase and fill the earth.
(v. 5) And you know that which your Watchers, the fathers of these spirits, did in my days
　　　　and also these spirits who are alive.
　　　　Shut them up and take them to the place of judgment.
　　　　And do not let them cause corruption among the sons of your servant,
　　　　O my God,
　　　　because they are cruel and were created to destroy.
(v. 6) And *let them not rule over* the spirits of the living
　　　　because you alone know their judgement.
　　　　And *do not let them have power over the children of the righteous now and forever.*[48]

Formally, the prayer has a two-fold structure. First, it opens with a declaration of all that God has done on behalf of Noah and his sons to save them from the destruction of the deluge (v. 3). Thus the prayer initially assumes a posture of thanksgiving and praise. The second, more extensive, part of the prayer contains a petition in two parts: (1) Noah asks God to bless him and his sons in order that they might "grow and increase and fill the earth" (cf. Gen. 9:1, 7).[49] (2) As almost

---

[48] Here I follow the translation by Orvil S. Wintermute in ed. James H. Charlesworth, *The Old Testament Pseudepigrapha* (2 vols.; Garden City, New York: Doubleday, 1983–1985), 2:75–76, because it structures Noah's prayer into stichs (italics my own).

[49] Cf. the MT: "God blessed Noah and his sons, and said to them, 'Be fruitful and multiply, and fill the earth.'" In terms of intertextuality, Noah's prayer in *Jub.* makes God's act of blessing Noah the object of the petition. Significantly, no such command is given in *Jub.* to the first humans (see Gen. 1:28a). This implies that the demons pose an obstacle to the carrying out of

a prerequisite for such a blessing, Noah asks God to punish "the spirits", the off-spring of the fallen angels (v. 5). Because of their destructive activities towards humankind, the prayer asks that the spirits be consigned to a place of judgement. Then, in verse 6, the petition concludes with two reformulations of the initial peti-tion for protection in verse 3, a formula reminiscent of *Jubilees* 1:20, "let not them (i. e. the evil spirits) rule over the spirits of the living" and "do not let them have power over the children of the righteous now and forever".[50]

With respect to its specific content, the petition has been recast to reflect the preceding and following narrative in *Jubilees*. The evil spirits referred to are those of the giant offspring of the Watchers and the women they deceived (v. 5; see 5:1–11 and 7:21–24). Though they began as creatures with human flesh (v. 3; cf. 5:8), they became spirits when they killed one another. And so, after the deluge,[51] Noah's descendants (i. e. his grandchildren) are being threatened by the activities of these impure spirits who are now called "demons" (v. 2). As for the narrative following Noah's prayer: it describes God's response to the petition. God directs the angels to bind all of the demons (10:7). However, the divine judgement is not achieved with finality. Mastema, the chief of these punished spirits and mentioned here for the first time in *Jubilees*, begs God to permit him to exercise his (rightful) authority, given that the greatness of human sin is inevitable (v. 8). God responds by having nine-tenths of the spirits consigned to the place of judgement below (v. 9) while a limited number (one tenth) may carry out Mastema's orders (cf. v. 9). In the end, Noah is taught various herbal remedies through which the afflic-tions brought about by the evil spirits on his offspring could be curbed or at least kept in check (v. 12).

In its position between the ante-diluvian catastrophes and the deluge, on the one hand, and the containment and punishment of malevolent forces, on the other hand, the prayer comes at a pivotal point in the storyline. Because of Noah's great piety, his prayer functions to set on course the temporary position of evil spirits until the eschatological judgement. God's response to his petition ensures that from now on, the evil that is manifest on earth represents an essentially defeated power whose activity has already been subjected to a preliminary judgement. This strong link to the literary context means that the prayer is here really conceived as

---

God's command to "be fruitful and multiply" after the Flood; cf. James C. VanderKam, "The Demons in the Book of Jubilees", in *Die Dämonen – Demons* (bibl. in n. 31), pp. 339–364 (here p. 343).

[50] This petition is also similar to texts in *Aramaic Levi Document* and 11Q5 xix mentioned above.

[51] Similar to the *Book of Watchers* (*1 En.* 1–36; esp. chs. 6–16), the role of the Flood as divine punishment against the rebellious angels and their progeny in *Jubilees* is unclear; whereas the *Book of Giants* seems to have given the deluge a more prominent role in this respect, *1 En.* 6–16 and *Jub.* give the impression that when they describe the remaining demonic activity following God's initial judgement against the fallen angels and giants, they have post-diluvian times in view; cf. Chapter One section D.

Noah's prayer, and in its present form does not draw on a prayer that could have been uttered by just anyone. Thus the wording of the petition that God punish the demonic spirits is "narrativized", that is, it takes into account what the author believed were the specific circumstances faced by the patriarch after the Great Flood. However, this is not merely a prayer *composed ad hoc*; the petition that God not permit evil spirits to have power over those who are pious, as we have seen, in use outside the text. It is likely that early readers of *Jubilees* would have been familiar with such a prayer and would have recognised it as it is put into the mouths of Moses in 1:20 and of Noah in 10:3–6.

Not only would ancient readers have recognised the petition for protection, the content of the prayer itself widens the horizon beyond that of Noah and his grand-children to embrace the implied readers of the author's own time. Two details in the prayer suggest this. First, at the end of the prayer, the plea to curtail the spirits' power no longer simply refers specifically to Noah's grandchildren. Though "the sons of your servant" could refer to Noah's immediate family, the mention of "the spirits of the living" and, in particular, "the children of the righteous *henceforth and forever*" opens the horizon to include all those who are pious after the time of Noah until the very end. In this sense, then, Noah's prayer is also a plea for protection on behalf of all righteous ones who come after him, and readers would have understood themselves to be included in this protection.[52] Second, the brief and conventional form of the conclusion to the petition presupposes a certain familiarity with this sort of prayer among the readers. To attribute a petition which readers perhaps knew amongst themselves to Noah not only anchors their prayer within a pivotal point of the covenant story of Israel, but also strengthens their confidence in the effectiveness of their prayers for protection against demonic powers: though they lie behind the afflictions and iniquities suffered and carried by God's people, evil spirits are but defeated powers whose complete destruction is assured.

E.7. Jubilees 12:19–20

In *Jubilees* yet a third figure is made to offer a petition for protection: Abram, whose prayer is given in 12:19–20:

(v. 19) ... My God, my God, God most High,
You alone are my God.
You have created everything;
Everything that was and has been is the product of your hands.
You and your lordship I have chosen.

(v. 20) *Save me from the power of the evil spirits,*
who rule the thoughts of people's minds.
May they not mislead me from following you, my God.

---

[52] The same may be implied by Moses' intercessory prayer in *Jub.* 1:19–20.

Do establish *me and my posterity*
May we not go astray from now until eternity.[53]

Abram's petition shares the two-fold structure observed above for 10:3–6. In the first part, the prayer extols God as the only God, and the one who has created all things (v. 19). In the second part, the petition asks for rescue from the rule of evil spirits who would lead humankind astray from showing exclusive devotion to God.[54]

Again, as in the case of Noah's prayer in *Jubilees* 10, it is important to consider Abram's prayer in relation to its immediate literary context. Abram is made to utter his petition just prior to receiving God's promise that he and his descendants will be given a land. The petition, then, associates the promise of the land to Abram with God's power over evil, on behalf of Abram and his descendants. Earlier in the narrative, the path to the story about Abram is laid in chapter 11. After the Flood, Noah's descendants became involved in violent and oppressive activities (v. 2); indeed, they had begun to make idols and thus were coming under the influence of those evil spirits which, under Mastema's rule, were being allowed to lead people astray to commit sin and acts of impurity (vv. 4–5). The introduction of Abram into the narrative, beginning with 11:14, marks a shift in the midst of this post-diluvian corruption among humanity. Abram, at an early age, offers prayers during this time "to the creator of all" and thus demonstrates the rejection of his father's worship of idols (11:16; 12:2–8, 12–14). At one point, Abram even tells his father, Terah, not to worship idols fashioned by human hands, but rather "the God of heaven" who has "created everything by his word" (12:3–4). Therefore, Abram's prayer in 12:19–20, in its focus on God as creator (v. 19), expresses an objection to post-diluvian idolatry behind which lay the activities of malevolent demonic beings. As in the prayer of Noah, Abram's proclamation of God as "creator" shows how embedded the petition is within the storyline.

If one links the first part of Abram's prayer back to the account of growing post-diluvian evil, it is possible to find the rationale for the petition to counteract the "evil spirits" in the second part. The reason for the mention of "evil spirits", however, need be neither so remote nor so implicit. As Lange rightly argues, since the prayer occurs while Abram is gazing at the stars by night (12:16), these spirits must be the stars linked with "astrology".[55] Abram, after all, recognises that it is wrong for him to prognosticate on the basis of the stars; this even includes the weather – for example, whether or not it will rain – as the making of such predictions distracts from the conviction that meteorological events are to be left in

---

[53] The text given follows the translation of VanderKam, *The Book of Jubilees*, p. 72 (italics my own).

[54] As 4Q213a, the prayer in *Jub.* 1:20 and 12:20 refers to demonic activity as "leading astray", a motif that occurs in the narrative before Noah's prayer in 10:3. The "Prayer of Deliverance" in 11Q5, however, makes no mention of this.

[55] Lange, "The Essene Position on Magic and Divination", p. 383.

God's control. In sitting alone at night, Abram thus finds himself resisting the temptation to adopt the instruction about "the omens of the sun and moon and stars within all the signs of heaven", which in the story has been attributed to the fallen angels and which has been re-discovered after the deluge by Noah's great-grandson, Cainan, who "sinned" because of it (8:1–4).

Yet, why does the nomenclature of "evil spirits" occur in the prayer rather than a more direct reference to the heavenly bodies which Abram has just seen? Although the "evil spirits" which originated in the giants are featured in the periods associated with Enoch and Noah, they are nowhere explicitly mentioned in the early part of Abram's story; moreover, though the connection between demonic spirits and idols is mentioned in 11:4–5, the link is not explicitly made here.

Nonetheless, in the subsequent part of the Abraham narrative in *Jubilees*, several passages are illuminating: the angel's explanation of the significance of the law of circumcision (15:30–32); the account about the sacrifice of Isaac (17:15–18:19); and the blessings pronounced by Abraham over Jacob (esp. 19:27–29). In 15:30–32, the angel's instruction to Abraham about circumcision is explained as a means by which God rules over his people Israel, over whom "he made no angel or spirit rule" (v. 32). The rest of the nations, by contrast, are ruled by spirits who lead them astray (v. 31). The link already made in 11:4–5 between evil spirits and the worship of idols (cf. 22:16)[56] suggests that Abram's petition in chapter 12 for the establishment of his "seed" is one that is ultimately answered when God separates Israel from the nations of the earth to become the people he will protect (15:32). In 17:15–18:19, "Mastema" is identified as the one who sought to distract Abraham from obedience to God in the sacrifice of Isaac (17:16; 18:12). In 19:28, Abraham pronounces a blessing over Jacob: "may the spirit of Mastema not rule over you or over your seed in order to remove you from following the Lord who is your God henceforth and forever...". Abraham's story thus exemplifies how his prayer for deliverance from the rule of "evil spirits" is answered: His obedience to God thwarts Mastema's plan to test his character; and God's separation of Israel as his elect people is God's response to Abram's prayer of deliverance (and perhaps also the prayers of Moses and Noah).

---

[56] For the association of idolatry among the Gentiles with the influence of demonic powers, Deut. 32:16–17 played a formative role: "They made him [God] jealous with strange gods (בזרים, ἐπ' ἀλλοτρίοις), with abhorrent things (בתועבת, ἐν βδελύγμασιν) they provoked him. They sacrificed to demons (יזבחו לשדים, ἔθυσαν δαιμονίοις), to deities they had never known, to new ones recently arrived, whom your ancestors had not feared" (NSRV). In the Hebrew Bible, the equation of demons and idols is more explicitly made in the Greek translation to Psalm 96[95]:5a: "For all the gods of the nations are demons" (δαιμόνια; Heb. אלילים "idols"); cf. also Psalm 106[105]:37 and Isaiah 65:11. *1 En.* 19:1 picks up this association during the 3rd cent. B. C. E., followed in the 2nd cent. B. C. E. by *Jub.* (1:11 as well as at 22:16–18) and *Epistle of Enoch* (*1 En.* 99:7). After this, the idea becomes more widespread: see 4Q243 13.2 par. 4Q244 12.2, "demons of error" שידי טעותא; *T. Jud.* 23:1; *T. Job* 3:6; *Sib. Or.* 8.47, 381–394 and Frg. 1.20–22; 1 Bar. 4:7; 1 Cor. 10:20; Rev. 9:20; cf. Gal. 4:8; *Ep. Barn.* 16:7; Ignatius *Magn.* 3:1 [long rec.]).

For all the connections between Abram's prayer in chapter 12 and the narrative, the subject matter of the petition itself remains conventional – that is, it is formulated in a way that is not fully bound into the literary context. The petition for deliverance from the rule of "evil spirits" (rather than, simply, from the rule of Mastema, as the story bears out) is formulated in general terms. As such, it is a petition by the pious that expresses the desire to stay away from idolatry. Moreover, similar to Noah's petition at 10:6, Abram's plea is concerned with all his progeny "forever", which includes the implied readers of the story. With perhaps the exception of the Abram-specific phrase "me and my seed forever", the prayer itself could be uttered by any of Abram's seed, i. e., those whom the author regards as pious.

Regarding *Jubilees*, we may, in summary, note that the language of petition for protection from demonic evil occurs in a number of texts: 1:20, 10:3–6, 12:19–20, 15:30–32, and 19:28. As we have been able to note on the basis of 11Q5 xix and the *Aramaic Levi Document*, the recurrence of such language in *Jubilees* picks up on a prayer formula that circulated prior to and independently from the setting within which the communication between its writer(s) and implied readers took shape. In *Jubilees*, to a greater degree than in *Aramaic Levi Document*, a more widely known petition is placed in the mouths of patriarchs to whom formulations are attributed that include the community in relation to whom the work was composed.

F. From Jewish Tradition to Jesus' Petitions in John 17: Conclusion

In our review of Second Temple Jewish literature preserved in the Dead Sea Scrolls, we have discovered several things that may have an impact on the way one reads Jesus' petitions for his disciples and later followers in John 17. First, analogous to John 17, each of our Jewish traditions construes prayer for protection in relation to demonic power, something which marks a development beyond prayers conveyed through the Hebrew Bible. Second, the texts we have looked at are not merely literary; they reflect a piety which in at least some Jewish circles was expressed through the offering of prayers for divine protection from the personified forms of evil (cf. 11Q5 xix). Third, such petitions were adaptable. They could be narrativized into stories involving ideal figures from Israel's ancient past (*Aramaic Levi Document*; *Jubilees*). Thus patriarchs would not only be presented as practitioners of the piety familiar to those who read about them, but also would be made to formulate petitions which sought God's protection for their descendants. In such cases – we have found reason to observe this in *Jubilees* chapters 1, 10, 12, 15 and 19 – readers would have been able to recognize themselves as addressed in the unfolding storyline. Fourth, the petitions for divine help against malevolent power were based on a twinfold assumption that (a) the present age is under the dominion of evil (i. e., it is ruled by Belial/r, Mastema, or evil spirits; cf. *Serekh ha-Yaḥad* with the *Two Spirits Treatise*, *Sereh ha-Milḥamah* and *Songs of the Maskil*) and (b) the powers which hold sway are essentially defeated and await certain eschatological destruction (*1 En.* 10, 15–16; *Jubilees, Serekh ha-Yaḥad* with the *Two Spirits Treatise*).

These texts contribute to our understanding of Jesus' prayer in the Fourth Gospel in at least three ways.

First, according to John's Gospel "the world", which is under the dominion of "the ruler of the world", is completely opposed to Jesus and his followers because they are not of the world. While the hostility between the present age of wickedness and a future age of restoration has long been known through Second Temple period literature produced by apocalyptic circles, some of the Dead Sea materials express this tension in language that comes close to what one meets in John's Gospel.

Second, the confidence expressed in the early Jewish petitionary prayers considered here – based on definitive acts of God in the past and the certain eschatological defeat of demonic power in the future – is re-framed in John's Gospel around Jesus' death through which the world is already judged. Though the inimical world order holds sway, its days are numbered, and it already stands condemned.

Third and finally, the petitions in search of protection are formulated in the recognition that in the meantime a community which considers itself especially elect needs divine help in order to ward off the unabating influences of evil power. Such prayers would have been known to the pious, whether they were those who recited the "Prayer of Deliverance" preserved in 11Q5 xix or members of the Matthean and similar communities who prayed to be delivered from "the evil one" in the Lord's Prayer (Mt. 6:13; cf. 2 Thess. 3:3). If such a petition was known to implied readers of the Johannine community, then it is not without significance that in John's Gospel the petition that God protect Jesus' disciples "from the evil one" is placed on the lips of Jesus. In doing this, the writer of the prayer in John 17 would have been providing readers something that we have witnessed in some texts of the Gospel's Jewish predecessors: *a prayer which readers may already have been reciting for themselves has been strengthened by having it spoken by the very one in and through whom their religiosity is determined.* Therefore, just as the patriarchs' petitions against demonic evil are formulated as prayers for their descendants and spiritual heirs, so also Jesus' petition is concerned with his "descendants." And so, the disciples and "those who believe in me (sc. Jesus) through their word" in the Johannine community find themselves covered in the Johannine text by the force of Jesus' petition.

G. Post-scriptum

I have one final note for reflection on "apocalyptic" which I find necessary to sketch as we consider the theme of evil in relation to the Fourth Gospel. So much of the scholarly discussion of an apocalyptic world view (as well as on "apocalypse" as a literary genre) during the 19th and 20th centuries has been dominated by a model oriented around the future. Jewish apocalyptic writers, it is made out, had a view of the world conceived in two stages, one about the present as an era of evil and the other as a future time when, after divine judgment, all evil will be held to account as a new world order is established. This way of understanding apocalyptic thought – based primarily on readings of documents such as Daniel, the Apocalypse of John, 4 Ezra and *2 Baruch* – has served New Testament scholars as a convenient way not only to characterize the novelty associated with the (Jewish) historical Jesus, but also to throw light on adaptations of Jewish tradition in Pauline theology. The emphasis on Jewish apocalyptic eschatology as a background that Jesus and Paul took over and ultimately subverted, while recognizing in principle the importance of Second Temple literature for the interpretation of early Christian traditions, does not go far enough in ascertaining the extent of that indebtedness.

Of course, scholarly work on Jewish apocalyptic in conversation with the New Testament is included in other dimensions. For some scholars Jewish apocalyptic thought has provided a platform for understanding Jesus within a "thoroughgoing eschatology", a view that amounts to an attempt to take Jesus' place within apocalyptic Jewish ideology (as one who focused on the future) seriously.[57] For other scholars, Jesus' activity, both as the Synoptic Gospels present it and in the way Jesus may have understood his mission, God's rule has broken into this world in a definitive way so that "history" could no longer be the same.[58] Scholars have, of

---

[57] So the well-known work of Albert Schweitzer, *The Quest of the Historical Jesus: From Reimarus to Wrede*, translated by William Montgomery (London: Black, 1954, 3rd ed.). For a more recent take-up of this perspective, see Dale C. Allison, "A Plea for Thoroughgoing Eschatology", *JBL* 113 (1994), pp. 651–668 and *Jesus of Nazareth: Millenarian Prophet* (Minneapolis: Fortress Press, 1998), whose argument is formulated against the "unapocalyptic" reconstruction of Jesus put forth by members contributing to the Jesus Seminar (esp. Marcus Borg, John Dominic Crossan, Burton Mack); on the latter, see Robert W. Funk and Roy W. Hoover, *The Five Gospels: The Search for the Authentic Words of Jesus* (New York / Toronto: Macmillan, 1993), pp. 34–38 and 137.

[58] See e.g. Charles H. Dodd, *The Founder of Christianity* (New York: Macmillan, 1970); Norman Perrin, *Jesus and the Language of the Kingdom: Symbol and Metaphor in New Testament Interpretation* (Philadelphia: Fortress Press, 1976), p. 204; James D. G. Dunn, *Jesus and the Spirit: A Study of the Religious and Charismatic Experience of Jesus and the First Christians as Reflected in the New Testament* (London: SCM Press, 1975), pp. 41–67 and *idem, Christianity in the Making, Volume I: Jesus Remembered* (Grand Rapids: Eerdmans, 2003), pp. 478–484; Thomas P. Rausch, *Who Is Jesus? An Introduction to Christology* (Collegeville, Minnesota: Liturgical Press, 2003), pp. 77–93. – A similar move is frequently made to underscore the distinctiveness of Pauline theology. Influential advocates of such an understanding of Paul have included Werner Kümmel, "Paulus", in *idem, Heilsgeschehen und Geschichte: Gesammelte Aufsätze 1933–1964* (Marburg: Elwert,

course, observed the shortcomings of such a one-dimensional future orientation of Jewish apocalyptic; after all, the earliest recoverable apocalypses seem just as interested in a spatial understanding of the world made possible through revealed knowledge as in the conversion of the present into a future cosmos.[59] In addition, some apocalyptic writers demonstrated a concern with divine activity as a constant that shaped the unfolding story of Israel in order to understand and evaluate the present.[60] Finally, an influential way of understanding the temporal dimension of apocalyptic thought has been the correspondence in apocalyptic literature between *Urzeit* and *Endzeit*, a framework construed as a means to re-enforce eschatology[61] – here the primordial past is understood to have served as a repository of images and symbols that helped apocalyptic writers to imagine the future.

The study above has hinted, however, at another, much neglected dimension, one that is not only overlooked by New Testament scholars but also by those who specialize in Second Temple literature.[62] In addition to helping to describe deteriorating conditions in the world and how the God of Israel will inaugurate a new age, language about the *Urzeit* also functioned, when adopted, to provide a basis that the faithful can be confident about the future: God's activity in defeating evil is not only a matter to be hoped for in the future, for the object of hope has its correlative in the *sacred past* (e. g., at the time of the Great Flood, or at the time of

---

1965), pp. 439–456; Ernst Käsemann, e. g. in *Commentary on Romans*, translated by Geoffrey W. Bromiley (Grand Rapids: Eerdmans, 1980), pp. 139–159 (on Rom. 5:12–21); Johan C. Beker, *Paul the Apostle: The Triumph of God in Life and Thought* (Edinburgh: T. & T. Clark, 1989); and James D. G. Dunn, e. g. in *Jesus and the Spirit*, p. 308 ("[t]he most characteristic feature of Christian experience") and *The Theology of St. Paul the Apostle* (Grand Rapids: Eerdmans, 1998), pp. 461–498 (esp. pp. 462–477); cf. recently Thomas R. Schreiner, *New Testament Theology: Magnifying God in Christ* (Grand Rapids: Baker Academic, 2008). For a more thorough discussion of the problem in relation to Pauline theology, see Chapter Twelve below.

[59] So the often-repeated definition in the publications by John J. Collins cited in n. 8 above. In addition, the critique by Christopher Rowland of the one-dimensionally eschatological reading of Jewish apocalyptic literature remains valuable; see *idem, The Open Heaven: A Study of Apocalyptic in Judaism and Early Christianity* (New York: Crossroad, 1982), pp. 9–72.

[60] So esp. Nicholas T. Wright, *The Climax of the Covenant: Paul and the Law in Pauline Theology* (Edinburgh: T. & T. Clark, 1991) and *Jesus and the Victory of God* (London: SPCK, 1996) and *passim*.

[61] The most important 3rd and 2nd cent. B. C. E. documents which draw on this correspondence between beginning and end include the Enochic *Book of Watchers* (*1 En.* 1–36), the *Book of Dreams* (*1 En.* 83–84 and 85–90), *Apocalypse of Weeks* (*1 En.* 93:1–10 and 91:11–17), *Exhortation* (*1 En.* 91:1–10, 18–19), *Birth of Noah* (*1 En.* 106–107), *Book of Parables* (*1 En.* 37–71), *Book of Giants* and *Jubilees*. Except for the *Book of Parables*, the impact of the perspectives upheld by these works in Second Temple literature (including writings among the Dead Sea Scrolls and Jewish literature composed in Greek) was significant.

[62] A fine overview of recent scholarship on Jewish "apocalyptic" thought and literature and its implications for New Testament scholarship is offered by Jörg Frey, "Die Apokalyptik als Herausforderung der neutestamentlichen Wissenschaft. Zum Problem: Jesus und die Apokalyptik", in eds. Michael Becker and Markus Öhler, *Apokalyptik als Herausforderung neutestamentlicher Theologie* (WUNT 2.214; Tübingen: Mohr Siebeck, 2006), pp. 23–94, though without pointing out the particular suggestion being made here.

other definitive moments in Israel's history), a past that guarantees an outcome in which evil has no place (*1 En.* 10; 15–16; 91:5–10; 106:13–107:1; *Jub.* 5–10; *Book of Giants* at 4Q530 2 ii + 6–12 (?), lines 4–20). Thus, in essence, evil, however dominant or overwhelming it may seem to be in the present, is but a defeated power whose time is marked. Since God's rule has asserted itself in the cosmos on a global scale, the present "era of wickedness" is no time of waiting or despair. One can, even now, proceed confidently enough to deal with demonic power, knowing that, although it cannot be gotten rid of altogether before the ultimate end of things, it is nevertheless possible to address, contain or circumscribe its effects. While these reflections range broadly in scope, one may nevertheless ask: how remote is the world of the Fourth Gospel from Jewish apocalyptic tradition in this respect?

Chapter Eleven

The "Cleansing" of the Gentiles:
Background for the Rationale behind the Apostles' Decree

The Question

Most readings and interpretations of the Jerusalem council and apostles' decree in Acts 15 have focused on historical and literary-contextual matters: (a) the chronology and issues debated within the Jewish Christian community of Acts as they compare to those recorded in chapter 11 and in Galatians 2 (Paul's account of his visit to Jerusalem)[1] and (b) the stipulations enjoined in the apostolic decree on Gentile believers (Acts 15:20–21 – the degree to which, based on Lev. 17–18, they are Noahide in character and play a role in the Luke-Acts narrative as a whole or in Pauline thought).[2] Less sustained attention has centered on grounds for why the Gentiles are to be counted among the people of God in 15:8–9, no doubt because this theme in Acts 15 is usually regarded as a throwback to the events already narrated in Acts 10–11.[3] The reason for the Gentiles' acceptance, presented as the words of Peter, is given in the text of 15:8–9 as follows:

---

[1] On the much discussed question of whether Acts ch. 11 or the Council in Acts ch. 15 corresponds to Luke's version of events reported by Paul in Gal. 2, see James D. G. Dunn, *Christianity in the Making. Volume 2: Beginning from Jerusalem* (Grand Rapids: Eerdmans, 2009), pp. 416–494.

[2] See e. g. Matthias Klinghardt, *Gesetz und Volk Gottes. Das lukanische Verständnis des Gesetzes* (WUNT 2.32; Tübingen: Mohr Siebeck, 1988), pp. 181–189; Luke Timothy Johnson, *The Acts of the Apostles* (SP 5; Collegeville, Minnesota: Liturgical Press, 1992), pp. 266–267 and 272–273; Markus Bockmuehl, *Jewish Law in Gentile Churches: Halakhah and the Beginning of Christian Public Ethics* (Edinburgh: T. & T. Clark, 2000), pp. 161–173; Hilary Le Cornu and Joseph Shulam, *A Commentary on the Jewish Roots of Acts* (Jerusalem: Academon, 2003), pp. 835–837; and Charles H. Talbert, *Reading Acts. A Literary and Theological Commentary* (Macon: Smyth & Helwys, 2005), pp. 131–133.

[3] This is the case with most commentators; so, for example, Édouard Barde, *Commentaire sur les Acts des Apôtres* (Lausanne: Bridel, 1905), p. 311; Johann Evangelist Belser, *Die Apostelgeschichte* (Münster: Aschendorff, 1910, 3rd ed.), p. 191; Gerhard Krodel, *Acts* (Minneapolis: Augsburg Publishing, 1986), p. 277; Hans Conzelmann, *Acts of the Apostles*, translated by James Limburg, A. Thomas Kraabel, and Donald H. Juel (Hermeneia; Philadelphia: Fortress Press, 1987), pp. 116–117; Gerd Lüdemann, *Early Christianity According to the Traditions in Acts. A Commentary*, trans. John Bowden (Minneapolis: Fortress Press, 1989), pp. 167–168; French L. Arrington, *The Acts of the Apostles. An Introduction and Commentary* (Peabody, Massachusetts: Hendrickson, 1988), p. 153; Frederick F. Bruce, *The Acts of the Apostles* (Grand Rapids: Eerdmans, 1990 3rd ed.), p. 336; John Polhill, *Acts* (Nashville: Abingdon Press, 1992), pp. 326–327; Jacob Jervell, *Die Apostelgeschichte*

(8) And God, who knows the human heart (καρδιογνώστης), testified to them by giving them the Holy Spirit, just as (he did) to us; (9) and in cleansing their hearts (καθαρίσας τὰς καρδίας αὐτῶν) by faith he has made no distinction between them and us.

Though Peter's words are in some measure a repetition of what he has reported in Jerusalem in Acts 11 (11:15 – the giving of the Holy Spirit; cf. also 10:44–45), here they express something essentially new[4]: the Gentiles' *hearts* have been cleansed or purified by God, who is a *"heart knower"*. Of course, here the cleansing of hearts is closely linked to the giving of the *Holy* Spirit; that is, the presence of the Holy Spirit among Gentiles renders them pure because something that is impure has been removed: "what God has made clean, you must not render profane" (ἃ ὁ θεὸς ἐκαθάρισεν, σὺ μὴ κοίνου; cf. 10:15).

Now the question arises: Where does the author of Acts get the idea of cleansing the Gentiles' hearts from? Is this simply the product of a literary dynamic, that is, is it a matter of drawing inference from the narrative in Acts 10–11?[5] Does it reflect the influence of other early Christian traditions?[6] Even if we answer either or both of the last two questions in the affirmative, the question still remains how this motif functions within the Jerusalem debate as it now stands in the text.

When we look to the larger context of Luke-Acts and beyond, we may note that language about the "heart" plays an important role in drawing attention to the area within which a person's religious status is determined, whether it be good or bad. The most important examples for this are found in Luke 6:45 ("The good person out of the good treasure of the heart produces good, and the evil person out of evil treasure produces evil; for it is out of the abundance of the heart that the mouth speaks" NRSV[7]; cf. par. Mt. 12:34–35); 8:15 (the explanation of the sower parable: "... that in the good soil, these are the ones who, when they hear the word,

---

(KEK 3; Göttingen: Vandenhoeck & Ruprecht, 1998), pp. 391–392; and J. Bradley Chance, *Acts* (Macon: Smyth & Helwys, 2007), pp. 251–252.

[4] See Jürgen Roloff, *Apostelgeschichte* (NTD 5; Göttingen: Vandenhoeck & Ruprecht, 1981), pp. 230–231; Charles K. Barrett, *The Acts of the Apostles* (2 vols.; ICC; Edinburgh: T. & T. Clark, 1994 and 1998), pp. 716–717; and esp. *idem, Acts. A Shorter Commentary* (Edinburgh: T. & T. Clark, 2002), p. 229 on Acts 15:9 "Cleansing, an image not frequently used in Acts, occurs in the Cornelius story (10:15; 11:9) but in a different sense. There, Peter must not hesitate to approach those whom God has cleansed; here, cleansing results from the faith with which Cornelius and others respond to the word."

[5] So e.g. Mikeal C. Parsons, *Acts* (Grand Rapids: Eerdmans, 2008), p. 211: "At this point Peter is forced to make explicit the implications of the Cornelius episode: 'he cleansed their hearts (as well as ours)' (15,9)."

[6] For example, the phrase "by faith" in 15:9 (τῇ πίστει) and the emphasis that there is no distinction between Jewish and Gentile Christians has led some to think Luke has "Paulinized" Peter's speech; see Walter Schmithals, *Die Apostelgeschichte des Lukas* (ZBK 3/2; Zürich: Theologischer Verlag, 1982), pp. 137–138 and Charles l'Éplattenier, *Livre des Actes: Commentaire pastorale* (Paris / Outremont: Centurion and Novalis, 1994), pp. 160–161 (appealing to Gal. 3:28 and 1 Cor. 12:13); cf. Lüdemann, *Early Christianity*, pp. 167–168.

[7] All biblical citations, unless otherwise indicated, are taken from the New Revised Standard Version.

hold it fast in an honest and good heart, and bear fruit with patient endurance"[8]); 12:34 ("For where your treasure is, there will our heart be also"; par. Mt. 6:21); and Acts 5:3–4 (Peter's words to Annanias, "Why has Satan filled your heart ... How is it that you have contrived this deed in your heart?"); 7:51 (disobedient Jews are "uncircumcised in heart and ears, forever opposing the Holy Spirit"); 8:21 (Simon Magus is told by Peter, "your heart is not right before God"); and 16:14 (Lydia's conversion: "the Lord opened her heart to listen eagerly to what was said by Paul"). If we look in the rest of the writings of the New Testament, we can see a similar emphasis: for example, Matthew 5:8 ("blessed are the pure in heart"); 5:28 (the one who lusts after a woman commits adultery "in his heart"); 11:29 (Jesus is "humble in heart"); Mark 7:21 ("it is from within, from the human heart, that evil intentions come"; intensified in Mt. 15:18–19) and 11:23 ("if you do not doubt in your heart"); Romans 2:29 ("real circumcision is a matter of the heart"); 6:17 (referring to the obedience of the Gentiles "from the heart"); 10:9–10 (having faith in the heart); 1 Corinthians 4:5 (the purposes of the heart will be disclosed when the Lord comes); Ephesians 6:6 ("as slaves of Christ, doing the will of God from the heart"); 1 Timothy 1:5 ("love that comes from a pure heart"); 2 Timothy 2:22 ("those who call on the Lord with a pure heart"); Hebrews 10:22 ("let us approach with a true heart in full assurance of faith, with our hearts sprinkled clean from an evil conscience and our bodies washed with pure water"); and 1 Peter 1:22 ("love one another deeply from the heart"). These passages, and others, regard the "heart" as the innermost part of the human being, the place where decisive activity takes place. What happens there is an index that reflects a person's integrity and, as such, it is where divine guidance or, alternatively, evil influence holds sway. In short, the heart is the place of interiorized reality and, when applied to the purification of cleansing of the Gentiles by the Holy Spirit, it provides the essential rationale within the Luke-Acts narrative for drawing (or re-drawing) the socio-religious boundaries between Jews and Gentiles within the faith community. In other words, it is not so much *faith* – whether taken as divine activity or as a human posture before God – that provides the *warrant* or grounds for putting Gentiles on an equal footing with Jewish Christians within the church as Acts presents it, but rather what faith brings: interiorized cleansing.

So, while the emphasis on the heart in Acts 15:8–9 resonates with early Christian tradition, is it this alone that explains how Gentiles could be understood as having been purified in the heart? The importance of this question relates to the specific purpose of Acts 15: how is it that Gentile believers can be admitted into and regarded as the people of God in a way that Jewish believers would not be reasonably expected to have had an argument against? Peter's speech, even beyond Acts 11:16–17, assumes that there is no more persuasive argument than an interior

---

[8] The Matthean parable of the sower uses "heart" with a different emphasis: in 13:19 it is less the place within the human being out of which faithfulness is expressed than it is an area vulnerable to the evil one's influence.

cleansing of Gentiles which, as *fait accompli*, matches what the Jewish believers had been given at Pentecost (15:8; cf. 11:15). If in this context the argument of Gentile cleansing was to be credible, however, would it have been sufficient for the writer to have simply drawn on a tradition that had already circulated amongst other early Christian communities, especially when something so fundamental as the redrawing of socio-religious boundaries was at stake? At such a crucial moment in the account, it is reasonable to suppose that the writer's presentation of events had to go beyond something that could be taken for granted. The narrative itself demands a form of reasoning that would not only make sense, by hindsight, of the success of the Gentile mission, but would also have shown continuity with Jewish traditions that circulated and were being received during the Second Temple period. A look at such formative ancient Jewish traditions will be offered below; as such, it will serve as a caution against the assumption that for Luke, at least, a criticism is not so much being leveled against an exterior or legalistic Jewish form of piety (e. g., circumcision, dietary regulations) that is opposed to interior religiosity (e. g., heart, faith). Instead, Luke – as some of his contemporary writers (cf. the texts cited in the previous paragraph) – draws on and remaps, on a fundamental level, a configuration of the human being to which sources from the Second Temple period attest.

The following discussion will explore Jewish traditions that may have provided a larger backdrop to Peter's extraordinary claim that Gentiles have been cleansed (culturally purified) in Acts 15:8–9. First, however, it is appropriate to summarize briefly what traditions in the Hebrew Bible have to say about the ultimate status of the nations. Then, although the traditions in apocalyptic and sapiential literature are numerous, I will focus on two texts that to me seem especially important to place in conversation with the Peter's claim.

The Nations in the Hebrew Bible

Given the way the privileged status of Israel as the people of God was considered within a broader socio-religious context, the authors of a number of passages in the Hebrew Bible express the view that the remaining nations of the earth will ultimately worship Israel's God. These texts are primarily motivated by a conviction that what happens to Israel – whether it be exile, restoration, or voluntary life in the Diaspora – forms the centerpiece of God's design for the world as a whole.[9] In the traditions, which themselves are complex and cannot be properly explored here,[10] the future

---

[9] This point is generally recognized; see e. g. Nicholas T. Wright, *The New Testament and the People of God* (London: SPCK, 1992), p. 268, who states that "the fate of the nations was inexorably and irreversibly bound up with that of Israel".

[10] See now the recent discussion in Aaron Sherwood, *Paul and the Restoration of Humanity in Light of Ancient Jewish Traditions* (AJEC 82; Leiden: Brill, 2013), pp. 29–147.

response of non-Israelite nations of the earth to the God of Israel was described in a number of ways. The texts express the hope that the nations will

- come to Jerusalem in order to be instructed and to "walk in his (God's) paths" (Isa. 2:3; Mic. 4:2);
- bring gifts and their wealth to Jerusalem (Isa. 18:7; 45:14; 60:5, 11; Hag. 2:7; Zech. 14:14);
- supplicate or make petition to God (Isa. 19:22; Zech. 8:21–22);
- become subservient to Israel (Isa. 45:14; 49:22–23; 60:10, 12);
- come to recognize that the God of Israel is unique, that is, greater than all other gods (Isa. 45:14–15; 49:6, 26; 66:18; Ps. 102:15; Mal. 1:11);
- come to recognize the special status that Israel holds among the nations of the earth (Zech. 8:23; cf. Isa. 60:3; 62:2; 64:2);
- worship God in Jerusalem (Isa. 66:23; Zech. 14:16–19; Ps. 22:27; 86:9);
- praise God for God's justice and mercy (Ps 67:3–4; 117:1); and
- "turn" to God (Ps. 22:27; cf. Zech. 2:15).

Even this brief summary allows one to make several preliminary observations, especially if asking why the motif of the nations' eventual worship or recognition of God was considered so important. The first point to note is that the articulation of such a hope was a way to reinforce the supremacy of Israel's faith. This conviction emerges logically from the basic conviction that Israel is the elect people of a God who, at the same time, is Creator of the cosmos. However nationalistic or ethnic the expressions of Israel's faith may be (though under the premise that the covenant is divinely initiated), God is held to be at work throughout the world in a way that affects the other nations which, though not elect, nevertheless are subject to God's rule as well (e.g., Ps. 22:28; 47:8; 86:9). Against such a background, the inclusion of Gentiles in Acts within the apostolic mission, inaugurated through Peter and carried through more strategically by Paul and his companions, can be understood as a development of this ideology, which now combines God's rule over the nations along with *their* election as well.

Second, the worship of God by the nations (esp. Isa. 66:23; Zech. 14:16–19; Ps. 22:27; 86:9) reflects the hope that Israel's sufferings, associated with peoples who now serve other deities, will be eliminated. Despite Israel's lowly state (e.g., during the exile when away from the Land), the acknowledgment of Israel's God by the nations will demonstrate that they – and not Israel – should be the ones who are subservient (see esp. Isa. 60). After Luke chapters 1–2 (cf. 1:50–55 and 68–75), the reversal of Israel's sufferings is not retained as a major theme in Luke-Acts.[11]

---

[11] That Luke-Acts, after Lk. 1:50–55 and 1:68–75, does not make more of the elimination of Israel's sufferings in the *eschatological* future is related to the introduction of Gentiles into the equation and, therefore, to the shift of terms on which Israel's restoration is conceived, especially in the speeches of Acts (cf. perhaps only 3:20–21; 15:11, 16).

Third, Jerusalem (and the Temple) is and remains the unmatched location of the divine presence. In the proper order of things, when Israel is restored from her dispersion among the other nations to worship in the place where God is ritually present, the nations will finally recognize the futility of their deities and follow in tow (e. g., Jer. 16:19). While the Acts narrative marks a shift of emphasis in mission from Jews to Gentiles, as exemplified in the activities of Paul, Jerusalem nevertheless remains an ideological center that, in principle, functions as the starting point for God's activity after Jesus' ascension (Acts 1:8).

It is not clear, however, that any of the passages from the Hebrew Bible listed above (including Ps. 22:27) refer to a "conversion" of the nations in the way it is represented in Acts. This is especially the case if we define the term "conversion" as a complete transfer to Judaism (as, for example, through circumcision). To be sure, the texts could imagine that the nations can receive instruction, be governed by God's justice and mercy, and even that they will "walk in his paths" (Isa. 2:3; Mic. 4:2). Yet in the passages noted here they remain without a special covenant; they do not enjoy the status of being "elect" or "chosen"; "righteousness" is never associated with them; and, as far as the Temple cult is concerned, their participation is only indirect (through the offering of their wealth, their submission to Israel or compliance). Furthermore, and perhaps significantly, nothing is said in any of these texts about circumcision being part of what is ultimately envisioned for the nations; this lack of mention may have made it possible to conceive of a Gentile inclusion – if that were going to be considered at all – without, *at some level*, having specifically to involve circumcision in view. Finally, no passage in the Hebrew Bible has anything to say about a *cleansing of the Gentiles*, and certainly *nothing about a change or turning around of their "heart"*. If anything – and very obviously so – throughout the Hebrew Bible, the language of cleansing relates almost exclusively to Israel (e. g., Ezek. 36:25, 33; 37:23; Zech. 13:1–2), with several passages relating this theme to the "heart" (Ps. 51:10; Jer. 4:14; cf. Sir. 38:10).[12]

1 Enoch 10:20–22: the Worship of God by All Humanity

One passage worth looking at in some detail is from the *Book of Watchers* in *1 Enoch* 10:16–22, especially verses 20–22 in which God gives the archangel Michael

---

[12] On "heart" and purification in the Hebrew Bible, see esp. Thomas Krüger, "Das menschliche Herz und die Weisung Gottes", in eds. Thomas Krüger and Reinhard G. Kratz, *Rezeption und Auslegung im Alten Testament und in seinem Umfeld* (OBO 153; Freiburg/Göttingen: Universitätsverlag Fribourg and Vandenhoeck & Ruprecht, 1997), pp. 65–92; on developments of the motif among the Dead Sea Scrolls, see Loren T. Stuckenbruck, "The 'Heart' in the Dead Sea Scrolls: Negotiating between the Problem of Hypocrisy and Conflict within the Human Being", in eds. Armin Lange, Emanuel Tov and Matthias Weigold, *The Dead Sea Scrolls in Context: Integrating the Dead Sea Scrolls in the Study of Ancient Texts, Languages, and Cultures* (2 vols.; VTSup 140; Leiden/Boston: Brill, 2011), 1:237–253.

instructions after the Great Flood. The texts, translated respectively from the Ethiopic and Greek versions (as the Dead Sea Scroll fragment preserves only a small part of the text from v. 21), are as follows:

Ethiopic[13]

[20] And you, cleanse the earth
from every form of violence,
and from every sort of oppression,
and from all sin,
and from all wickedness,
and from every impure act
that has been committed on the earth.
Destroy them from the earth!
[21] And all children of men
will become righteous,[15]
and all the nations shall worship me
and bless me,
and all shall bow down[16] to me.
[22] And the earth will be cleansed
from all defilement, and from all sin,
and from all torment, and from all pain.
And I will never again bring about (a
    Flood) on it, from generation to gen-
    eration and forever.

Greek[14]

[20] And you, cleanse the earth
from all uncleanness[17]
and from all wickedness,
and from all sin
and ungodliness,
and wipe out all unclean acts
that have been committed[18] on the earth

[21] And all the peoples will be serving[19]
and blessing[20] me
and worshipping.[21]

[22] And the whole earth will be cleansed
from every blemish, and from all uncleanness,
and wrath and torment.
And I will never again send upon them (a
    Flood) for all generations of eternity.

Before we consider in some detail the remarkable association in this passage of all the nations with a divine act of purification, it is important to take the immediate literary setting of this passage into account: *1 Enoch* chapters 6–11, a discrete unit and one of the oldest subsections within the *Book of Watchers* (chs. 1–36). Unlike most of *1 Enoch*, these chapters do not mention the ancient patriarch Enoch at all and so are not presented as a vision in his name. Instead, chapters 6–11 come closer to focusing on the figure of Noah[22] and are presented in a 3rd person narra-

---

[13] The translation here takes EMML 7584 of the earlier recension as the point of departure. Concerning some variants from the other first recension manuscripts, see Michael A. Knibb, *The Ethiopic Book of Enoch* (2 vols.; Oxford: Clarendon Press, 1978), 1:39–40.

[14] The Aram (4QEnoch^a = 4Q201 1 vi 3) reads יׄ[תקשטון ("will become just") *contra* the Grk.

[15] Aram. (4QEnoch^a = 4Q201 1 vi 4) has]ירמ[ת]ח[("and will bow [itself] down").

[16] Based on Codex Panopolitanus; see the edition by Matthew Black in *Apocalypsis Henochi Graece* (PVTG 3; Leiden: Brill, 1970).

[17] Cod. Pan.: καθάρισόν ... ἀπὸ πάσης ἀκαθαρσίας.

[18] Cod. Pan.: τὰς ἀκαθαρσίας τὰς γινομένας.

[19] Cod. Pan.: λατρεύοντες.

[20] Cod. Pan.: εὐλογοῦντες.

[21] Cod. Pan.: προσκυνοῦντες.

[22] The brief address to "the son of Lamech" at the beginning of *1 En.* 10 (vv. 1–3) has led scholars to suggest that the acquired form of chapters 6–11 was Noahic in character; see esp. Robert H. Charles, *The Book of Enoch or 1 Enoch* (Oxford: Clarendon Press, 1912), pp. 13–14, who regarded this part of the *Book of Watchers* as a "fragment" from a now lost "Apocalypse" or

tive which, in turn, may be a conflation of several distinguishable traditions.[23] The unit thus variously elaborates a story such as or similar to Genesis 6–9 about "the sons of God" and "the daughters of men", their gargantuan progeny (*1 En.* 6:1– 7:2; Gen. 6:1–4), the growing evil and violence on earth (*1 En.* 7:2–9:11; cf. Gen. 6:5–12), the incarceration of the angels and punishment of their offspring (*1 En.* 10:4–15), and a veiled narrative of the Flood and use of imagery thereof to depict eschatological destruction and reward (*1 En.* 10:16–11:2; cf. Gen. 6:5–9:17).

The Noahic character of *1 Enoch* 10–11 picks up on the patriarch Noah's significance for the theme of a new beginning for humanity after divine punishment has taken its course. That the figure of Noah, and not Enoch, is the one who represents a new humanity that survives through a crisis is not surprising. In Genesis the mating of "the sons of God" with women on earth serves as a prelude to the Great Flood narrative and its aftermath in which Noah is the main protagonist, while the few verses mentioning Enoch (Gen. 5:21–24) have been left behind. Moreover, written traditions that focus on the figure of Noah circulated as constituent parts of several other sources that date back to at least the 2nd century B. C. E. Two of these works are concerned with the birth of Noah: *Genesis Apocryphon* (= 1Q20 ii 1 – v 26) and the *Birth of Noah* in *1 Enoch* (106:1–107:3). In addition, another writing, the *Book of Giants*, composed during the first half of the 2nd century B. C. E., displays an interest in Noah's escape from the Flood, thus standing in contrast with the destruction and punishment of the giants at that time (cf. 6Q8 2).[24] The euhemeristic tradition preserved in the Pseudo-Eupolemus

---

"Book of Noah". However, the existence of such a "Book of Noah", whether or not *1 En.* 6–11 is drawn into the discussion, remains disputed; for a convenient summary of the problem, see Loren T. Stuckenbruck, *1 Enoch 91–108* (CEJL; Berlin: Walter de Gruyter, 2007), pp. 610–611 (and ns. 1027–1028).

[23] So Paul Hanson, "Rebellion in Heaven, Azazel, and euheremistic Heroes in 1 Enoch 6–11", *JBL* 96 (1977), pp. 195–233; George W. E. Nickelsburg, "Apocalyptic and Myth in 1 Enoch 6–11", *JBL* 96 (1977), pp. 383–405; John J. Collins, "Methodological Issues in the Study of 1 Enoch. Reflections on the Articles of P. D. Hanson and G. W. Nickelsburg", in SBLSP 1978 (Missoula, Mont.: Scholars Press, 1978), pp. 315–322; Devorah Dimant, "1 Enoch 6–11. A Methodological Perspective", in SBLSP 1978, pp. 323–339; Carol A. Newsom, "The Development of 1 Enoch 6–19. Cosmology and Judgment", *CBQ* 42 (1980), pp. 310–329 (here p. 313); and George W. E. Nickelsburg, *1 Enoch 1* (Hermeneia; Minneapolis: Fortress Press, 2001), pp. 171–172. For a helpful summary of this discussion, see Archie T. Wright, *The Origin of Evil Spirits* (WUNT 2.198; Tübingen: Mohr Siebeck, 2005), pp. 29–47.

[24] Interestingly, whereas Noah emerges as the one whose fate stands in stark contrast with that of the giants, the *Book of Giants* refers to Enoch as the authoritative interpreter of ominous dreams given to the giants about their own and their angelic progenitors' punishment. The *Book of Giants*, then, is Enochic at least in this sense, though it is not clear how well it would have fit into the small but growing collection of Enoch works already emerging among the Dead Sea materials (esp. 4Q203/204, 4Q205, 4Q206, and 4Q212). Although one of the manuscripts of the book (4Q203, designated 4QEnGiants[a]) was thought by Milik to form part of a *1 Enoch* manuscript (4Q204, i. e. 4QEnoch[c]) – it preserves parts of the *Book of Watchers*, *Animal Apocalypse*, *Epistle of Enoch*, and *Birth of Noah* – it was not composed to form part of a corpus in which Enoch is speaking in the 1st person; instead, like *1 En.* chs. 6–11, the *Book of Giants* is not an Enochic pseudepigraphon.

fragments (Eusebius, *Praep. Ev.* 9.17.1–9 and 9.18.2) forges a genetic link between Noah and even Abraham, on the one hand, and the giants, on the other. As we have seen (see Chapter One section C), the Jewish apocalyptic writings mentioned above deny this connection categorically.[25] With the Noahic background in view, the *Book of Giants* joins *1 Enoch* 10 in picking up the tradition that describes future bliss in terms of unprecedented fertility in the created order as a whole (cf. 1Q23 1+6+22 with *1 En.* 10:17–19). Significantly, there is no indication in either text that the fertility is restricted to either a community that the authors may have represented or to Israel more generally; the eschatological future envisions what is to happen to the world as a whole.

In *1 Enoch* 10:1–3 the Noahic story is introduced at the beginning of the divine response to the complaints – these are conveyed to God by a quartet of angelic agents (*1 En.* 9:1–3) – raised by those who had been murdered because of the violent injustices they had suffered on account of the giants (*1 En.* 8:4–9:11). God's message to Noah, which Ariel an angel (Sariel – cf. 9:1; or Uriel – Sync.) mediates, declares three things: (1) that a destruction of "the whole earth" through a Flood is imminent (10:2); (2) that Noah is to be instructed on how to survive this cataclysm (10:1, 3); and (3) that from Noah a "plant" (so the Eth.; Grk. has σπέρμα "seed") will be established "for all generations of eternity" (10:3).

Readers familiar with the biblical storyline might at this point expect a retelling of the Flood (Gen. 6:5–8:22). The writer or compiler of the tradition, however, is doing more than reconfiguring and recounting events from the antediluvian period. The narrative is drawing an analogy between the Noahic period, on the one hand, and the writer's present and imminent future, on the other. The extent of this analogy is not immediately clear. While the Noahic storyline in *1 Enoch* 10:1–3 is not entirely lost – indeed, motifs related to the Genesis Noah account intermittently recur later in the chapter (esp. from v. 14) – what follows in 10:4–13 focuses instead on the punishments carried out against the main evildoers of the text: ʿAsaʾel (10:4–6 – he is bound, thrown into darkness, and is to be burnt with fire at the time of the Great Judgment), the giants (10:9–10 – they are condemned to annihilate one another), and "Shemiḥazah and his companions" (10:11–13 – they are bound for seventy generations and confined to a prison where in the end they will undergo fiery torment). These acts of divine judgment, which are, respectively carried out by the angels Raphael, Gabriel and Michael, deal directly with the demonic world against which the souls of the murdered humans have complained (8:4–9:2). By having the same quartet of angels carry out divine commands in chapter 10 (vv. 1, 4, 9, 11) which had conveyed the human souls' appeals for justice

---

Contrast Milik, *The Books of Enoch*, pp. 178 and 310 with Stuckenbruck, *1 Enoch 91*, pp. 11–12 (and bibl. in ns. 31 and 36).

[25] See further Stuckenbruck, *1 Enoch 91–108*, pp. 633–641 and 648–655 (on *1 En.* 106:4–7 and 106:9–12, respectively).

to heaven in chapter 9 (vv. 4–11), the narrative in its received form has inseparably woven the story of Noah, the emblem of new humanity after the Great Flood, into the fabric of the fallen angels tradition.

Both the "plant" to come from Noah "for eternity" (*1 En.* 10:3) and the final judgment against the rebellious angels (10:5–6, 12–13) demonstrate that the story correlates Noah's time with eschatological time. *Urzeit* and *Endzeit* converge, so that what happens in the first era to Noah has its counterpart in the final era to come. Thus the story about fallen angels at the beginning of chapter 6 is relevant to how the writer(s) conceived of the future, and vice-versa. Significantly, *the scope of this correlation involves all humanity.* The text of this part of the *Book of Watchers* opens with a statement about the mass of humanity – "the sons of men" and "the daughters of men" (6:1–2) – with whom the rebellious angels intermingle and who are overwhelmed by the angels' breach of the cosmic order. Through Noah this humanity's survival through the time of divine reckoning and punishment of evil is assured. Given the correspondence between the period of the Flood and that of the end time, it is not surprising that in 10:20–22 all humanity will be found to worship God.

The path to this end is not, however, straightforward. The condemnation of the Watchers and the slaughter of their offspring (10:14–15) – events inaugurated with the announcement of the Flood[26] and brought to its inevitable conclusion at the end – is in force during an intervening time characterized by the appearance of "the plant of truth and righteousness" (10:16). Though this second mention of a "plant" alludes to the "plant" associated with Noah's offspring in 10:3, it does so here in a narrower sense.

Who or what is this "plant of truth and righteousness" in the text? Here the narrative is not yet concerned with post-Noahic humanity as a whole, but rather with those who are obedient to the covenant, that is, a community with whom the Jewish writer(s) would have identified. It is important to note that this community is characterized by "works of righteousness" (so the Eth.; omitted in the Grk. through homoioteleuton[27]). As such, the plant consists of those who, presumably like Noah during the Flood, will "escape" when "all iniquity" and *"every evil work"* are destroyed (10:16; cf. also the *Birth of Noah* at *1 En.* 107:1). Read in relation to the story about the fallen angels, the text draws an analogy between the destruction and eternal punishment of the angels and giants (10:9–14) and the destruction of iniquitous *activities* among human beings. Given the demonic origin of evil presented in chapters 6–11, *punishment is not anticipated for human beings as a species;*

---

[26] The Flood does not itself constitute the punishment of either the Watchers or giants. Instead, imagery from the Deluge relates to the theme of Noah's escape (10:3), the destruction and elimination of iniquity and impurity from the earth (10:16–20, 22), and to the escape of the righteous from the eschatological cataclysm (10:17).

[27] See Nickelsburg, *1 Enoch 1*, p. 218, who notes with Milik (*The Books of Enoch*, p. 189) that the longer reading is also supported by the Aramaic text in 4QEnoch[c] 1 v 1.

instead the text brings into focus the reprehensible deeds and knowledge that they have learned from the angels (7:3–5; 8:1–3).

The stress on the culpability of the rebellious angels and the giants is thus nuanced. On the one hand, humans too are held responsible for the evils in which they have participated on earth. On the other hand, the narrative's focus on their *activities* introduces a distinction between human beings who are part of the created order and the deeds that they commit. This, in turn, may be closely related to the text's remarkably open stance towards what can be ultimately hoped for in relation to humanity as a whole in future time.

I am therefore hesitant to regard the "fallen angels" and "giants" simply as decipherable metaphors for either the Diadochi[28] or wayward priests during the late 4th or early 3rd century B. C. E.[29] While the former explanation of angels and giants as the Diadochi provides a plausible setting for Jewish resistance to unwelcome influences of Hellenistic culture in the wake of Alexander the Great's conquests in the Eastern Mediterranean world, *1 Enoch* chapters 6–11 operate on a more profound level: demonic forces are not only at work behind those human beings who have engaged in oppressive and culturally reprehensible activity, they even lie *behind* those who have introduced them in the first place. For all its rejection of aberrant culture and of the oppression that comes through it (through socio-political powers), the story's *essentially mythic character* lends it an openness that holds the existence of a community of obedient Jews in tension with the existence of a humanity who, though largely aligned with the demonic world, are nevertheless regarded as having been created by God and, as such, have not *in themselves*[30] set the world down the wrong path. By contrast, the angels have breached the boundaries that distinguish the heavenly from the earthly sphere (implied here and explicated in *1 En.* 15:7–10); while it is the giants who are a hybrid combination of spheres that ought to have remained separate.[31] The fundamental distinction between *human nature* (which is not an illegitimate joining of spirit and body) and the demonic world (which by its very nature is a perversion of the created order) keeps humanity as a whole within the purview of God's redemptive purpose.

But this does not do away with a distinction between "the plant of truth and righteousness" (10:16 – covenant loyal Jews) and "all the children of men" (10:21). The former – these consist of "the righteous ones" who will "escape" the punishment of the Watchers – are promised a limitless period of reproductive and agri-

---

[28] So e. g. Nickelsburg, "Apocalyptic and Myth in 1 Enoch 6–11", pp. 383–405 and *1 Enoch 1*, p. 170.

[29] See the influential article by David W. Suter, "Fallen Angel, Fallen Priest", *HUCA* 50 (1979), pp. 115–135, who takes as his point of departure the reference in *1 En.* 10:9 to "bastards" (interpreted as the offspring of illegitimate marriages between Jerusalem priests and ineligible women and reflecting the incursion of Hellenistic culture).

[30] This focus follows from the distinction between humans and their deeds and from the destruction of the latter (*1 En.* 10:16, 20).

[31] See Chapter Two above and Wright, *The Origin of Evil Spirits*, pp. 146–151.

cultural activity (10:17–19) that reverses the annihilation and oppression suffered in the time before the Flood (7:3–5). The extant Ethiopic and Greek texts do not spell out that this bliss will include all humanity, nor do any of the recensions specify precisely how the special "plant" is related to the rest of humankind. However, the arena of what "the righteous" will enjoy is "all the earth". While the idea of a new beginning evokes the Noahic covenant following the Flood (Gen. 9:1–17; cf. the allusion to Gen. 9:11 in *1 En.* 10:22), the passage draws conceptually on the language of Isaiah 65:17–25 and 66:22–23. Both these Isaianic texts refer to God's creation of a "new heaven and earth", the former passage associating it with images of fertility (cf. *1 En.* 10:17–19; 11:1) and the latter anticipating a world order in which "all flesh" (Isa. 66:23: כל בשר; Grk. πᾶσα σάρξ) will "worship God" (66:23; cf. *1 En.* 10:21).

Nevertheless, in several respects the text traditions of *1 Enoch* 10 differ from the antecedent traditions in Isaiah 65 and 66. First, they place Isaianic eschatological expectation within a Noahic framework. Hope for a new cosmos that accompanies faithful Israel's redemption is informed by a reading of tradition as preserved in Genesis 6 that addresses the cosmic dimension of evil. Second, and following from this, *it also projects the activity of divine redemption onto the world stage.* Therefore, whatever its precise status, "the plant of truth and righteousness" in 10:16 *must of necessity be linked up with the entirety of humanity that has also been subjected to demonic power.* Third, unlike Isaiah, the extant texts nowhere specify that the eschatological worship of God will take place in Jerusalem. To be sure, the Greek Codex Panopolitanus cited above may imply participation in the cult when it declares that all humanity will "serve" (λατρεύοντες) God, and there is no attempt to reject Jerusalem as the center of worship. However, the complete lack of emphasis on Jerusalem is conspicuous and contrasts with the biblical traditions that anticipate that *Jerusalem* is where the Gentiles' acknowledgment and worship of Israel's God will take place.[32]

How is it that the worship of God by all humanity will come about? As noted above, the passage in *1 Enoch* 10:14–11:2 does not draw a direct line of continuity between "the plant of truth and righteousness" and the deliverance of humanity from destruction; "the righteous" do not function as agents of deliverance, that is, they do not testify or bear witness to anything that results in the conversion of the nations (*contra* what will later be emphasized in the *Epistle of Enoch* in *1 En.* 105:1–2[33]). Instead, to the extent that the Isaianic paradigm is operative, the eschatological activity of the nations will take place as part of the establishment of a new world order after divine eradication of all "uncleanness" and godless activities from the earth. For this "new beginning" of humanity in the coming era (10:22), the period after the Flood (Gen. 9:1–17) serves as a prototype.

---

[32] Interestingly, the Eth. mss. traditions all read here the verb *yāmelleku* (lit. "to be subject to"), which has no obvious cultic connotation.

[33] See Stuckenbruck, *1 Enoch 91–108*, pp. 600–603.

To summarize thus far: In *1 Enoch* chapter 10 an inclusion of the nations within a world being cleansed from "purity" and "defilement" builds on a setting constructed out of the biblical Noah narrative. The narrative, which underscores the impure character of evil and takes primordial history as its point of departure, begins and ends with a concern for the situation of humanity as a whole, while providing crucial signposts for divine redemptive activity along the way (the deliverance of Noah, the escape of "the plant of truth and righteousness" from destruction, and the definitive punishment of evil powers). Even more profoundly, the motif of the nations' worship of God moves beyond biblical antecedents in its fundamental distinction between the essentially integrated nature of humanity as God's creation and the breach of cosmological order brought about by the rebellious angels and embodied by the giants. The destruction of evil *activity* by the Flood, a type that anticipates eschatological bliss and judgment, could therefore be carried through without doing away with the human race itself. Given the Noahic setting and conditions for a new, eschatological start in place, the conclusion to chapters 6–11 comes as no surprise.

Significantly, if we read the tradition within the context of the 3rd century B.C.E., the text was not simply placing blame for cultural, military and social upheavals on Alexander the Great's successors and those who spread and supported their influence. The "demonic" could not, and should not, be decoded in this reductionist way. Instead, while linking cultural and religious incursions with disobedient angelic powers that have fallen to earth from heaven, the Jewish author(s) of *1 Enoch* chapters 6–11 held out for the restoration of humanity. The stage occupied by these chapters was also that of a growing historiographical consciousness that euhemeristically attempted to place local traditions within a larger framework that forged connections with and between other cultures (so, e.g., Berossus' *History of Babylonia*; the Pseudo-Eupolemus fragments noted above), and to it they made a contribution that took ancient Jewish tradition (i.e., as in Gen. chs. 6–9) as the essential starting point.

The Enochic Tradition and Acts

The conversion of Gentiles deliberated in Jerusalem in Acts chapters 10–11 and 15 does not, of course, make any specific reference to the Noahic Flood, nor is there any discernible echo therein of the tradition about the rebellious angels as it comes to us in the early Enochic literature However, several points are of note. In contrast to the Hebrew Bible, *1 Enoch* 10 seems to include all of humanity (i.e., Gentiles as well as Jews) in the cleansing of the earth. While one could argue that the verb "to cleanse" in 10:20 and 10:22 is a euphemism for the destruction of evil humanity (which, for example, is associated with imagery taken from the Great Flood), a further point suggests that the matter is not so straightforward: the text, as even several others in the later early Enochic traditions (*Apocalypse of Weeks* in *1 En.* 91:14; *Exhortation* at 91:9–10), is at pains to distinguish between humanity *per se* and the deeds they do. This distinction between human beings and their activities is important: the text emphasizes that their *works* were destroyed or cleansed, not humanity itself. By "works", the text here may have referred to either *activities* or to *things that their activities have produced*, such as idols (cf. 91:9[34]).

The regulations enjoined on the Gentiles in the apostolic decree in Acts 15:20–21 include what some interpreters continue to regard as Noachide commandments, that is, commandments to which God holds all of humanity accountable (cf. Gen. 9) as opposed to commandments that are specifically enjoined on Israel, who are God's covenant people in the narrower sense. Among the regulations is the prohibition against involvement with idolatry (Acts 15:20–21). The significance of *1 Enoch* as a conceptual bridge to Acts 15 may therefore consists in two points: (1) The Gentiles, who as humans are a sanctioned part of the created order, will be cleansed *from their works*, that is, from the impurities with which they have been engaged. In other words, they will be in a position to worship God because their iniquitous activities (deemed, for example, by Enochic authors to be idolatrous) will have been done away with, just as happened in Noah's Flood long ago. (2) That Gentiles could be cleansed is held up as a distinct possibility; excised from their "works", they will constitute a renewed humanity (presumably alongside faithful Jews; cf. *Jub.* 5:12). The Enochic tradition at this point probably presupposes a well-worked out theological anthropology that understands human beings as God's creation at the core; they therefore have a symbolic – and actual – place in the final outcome of God's design for the world. Against and within this framework the cleansing of the Gentiles' hearts in Acts 15:9 becomes more explicable, as well as does the injunction in the apostolic decree that the now cleansed Gentile Christians (who therefore do not require circumcision) should stay away from food offered to idols. The instructions to Gentile Christians, then, do not simply take shape due to the vicissitudes of pragmatic decision-making, but rather are the outgrowth of a theological anthropology that can be discerned in the Second Temple texts being considered here.

From the perspective of Acts the cleansing of Gentiles is imagined as an event not anticipated for the future (as in *1 En.* 10), but as one that is already in process of being realized. In this respect, the claim of Peter that their hearts have been purified by the Holy Spirit assumes the opening of the speech attributed to Peter in Acts chapter 2, namely, which stresses the pouring out of the Holy Spirit on "all flesh" as an event that will take place "in these last days" (Acts 2:17; cf. Joel 2:28, in which there is no clear inauguration of an eschatological time).[35]

---

[34] Cf. Nickelsburg, *1 Enoch 1*, pp. 413–415 and Stuckenbruck, *1 Enoch 91–108*, pp. 178–180.

[35] This difference between Acts 2:17 and the Joel passage (2:28–31) does not provide a warrant for maintaining that the essential difference between *1 En.* 10 and Acts lies in the latter's inaugurated eschatology; see Chapter Twelve below.

The Treatise on the Two Spirits (1QS iii 13 – iv 26)

Another work, which is ultimately concerned with humanity as a whole and that has implications for the interpretation of Acts 15, is found embedded within the *Serekh ha-Yaḥad* or *Community Rule* preserved among the Dead Sea documents. Before dealing with the matter at hand, we should consider one important caveat, given the huge amount of attention the *Treatise* within the *Community Rule* has received since the initial discoveries of the Dead Sea Scrolls in November 1947. Despite the literary setting in which it is preserved, the *Treatise* should not be read in its original form as the product of a group that lived in isolation and shut itself off from others.[36] Study in recent years has demonstrated that the famous theological treatise preserved in *Serekh ha-Yaḥad* at 1QS columns iii 13 – iv 26 was not a masterpiece composed from within the Qumran community for the Qumran community and thus does not formally summarize or immediately reflect that group's ideology.[37] In this connection two subsidiary observations are also

---

[36] For example, the introduction of the piece as written "for the *Maskil*" (למשכיל, 1QS iii 13) and its interest in "the sons of light" may reflect editorial adjustments that sought to accommodate the more narrowly drawn social boundaries of the *Yaḥad* as reflected in the acquired literary setting of the document (cf. 1QS cols. i – xi); cf. the works cited in n. 38 below. Despite recognition that the *Treatise* departs formally from the remaining sections of the *Community Rule*, the assumption that it reflects the pinnacle of Qumran theology is reflected in most of the early overviews of "Qumran" literature; for example, see Alfred R. C. Leaney, *The Rule of Qumran and Its Meaning. Introduction, Translation, and Commentary* (Philadelphia: Fortress Press, 1966), esp. p. 143; George W. E. Nickelsburg, *Jewish Literature Between the Bible and the Mishnah* (Philadelphia: Fortress Press, 2005, 2nd ed.), pp. 132–137; Emil Schürer, *The History of the Jewish People in the Age of Jesus Christ*, rev. Geza Vermes, Fergus Millar, and Martin Goodman (III/1; Edinburgh: T. & T. Clark, 1986), pp. 381–386; Devorah Dimant, "Qumran Sectarian Literature", in ed. Michael E. Stone, *Jewish Writings of the Second Temple Period* (CRINT II.2; Assen/Philadelphia: Gorcum and Fortress Press, 1984), pp. 483–550 (here pp. 497–502 and 533–536); Michael A. Knibb, *The Qumran Community* (Commentaries on Writings of the Jewish and Christian World 2; Cambridge: Cambridge University Press, 1987), pp. 93–103; and as recently as Claude Coulot, "L'instruction sur les deux espirits (1QS III,13-IV,26)", *RSR* 82 (2008), pp. 147–160. It is on this basis that Jerome Murphy-O'Connor argued that the *Treatise* is the last, and theologically the most profound, layer of the *Community Rule*; see Murphy O'Connor, "La genèse littéraire de la Règle de la Communauté", *RB* 76 (1969), pp. 528–549 and, later, Jean Pouilly, *Le Règle de la Communauté. Son evolution littéraire* (Cahiers de la Revue Biblique 17; Paris: J. Gabalda, 1976).

[37] See Armin Lange, *Weisheit und Prädestination. Weisheitliche Urordnung und Prädestination in den Textfunden von Qumran* (STDJ 18; Leiden: Brill, 1995), pp. 121–170; Jörg Frey, "Different Patterns of Dualistic Thought in the Qumran Library: Reflections on Their Background and History", in eds. Moshe Bernstein, Florentino García Martínez, and John Kampen, *Legal Texts & Legal Issues. Proceedings of the Second Meeting of the International Organization for Qumran Studies, Published in Honour of Joseph M. Baumgarten* (STDJ 23; Leiden/New York/Köln: Brill, 1997), pp. 275–335 (here pp. 279–280); Armin Lange and Hermann Lichtenberger, "Qumran", in *Theologische Realenzyklopädie. Bd. 28* (Berlin: Walter de Gruyter, 1997), pp. 45–79; and Hartmut Stegemann, *The Library from Qumran. On the Essenes, Qumran, John the Baptist, and Jesus* (Leiden/Grand Rapids: Brill and Eerdmans, 1998), pp. 108–110. For an important study that attempts to take seriously both the originally independent existence of much of the *Treatise* while accounting for its integration into the *Community Rule*, see Charlotte Hempel, "The Treatise on

relevant. Firstly, among the twelve further manuscripts of the *Community Rule*, a small portion of the *Treatise* is preserved on two fragments of one manuscript, 4QS^c (= 4Q257), while there is no evidence that it was included in any of the other manuscripts of the work.[38] The physical evidence, therefore, may be enough at least to question the prominence of the *Treatise* for the *Yaḥad*. Secondly, the essential features, including the polarizing antitheses of the *Treatise*, are expressed with vocabulary and ideas that come closer to those found in other sapiential compositions than what it shares with the literature that more unambiguously derives from the Qumran community.[39]

It is appropriate, therefore, to interpret the *Treatise on the Two Spirits* as a document in its own right rather than, in content, simply as an extension of its immediate literary context. In and of itself, the *Treatise* is less concerned with socio-religious boundaries that can be physically marked between the righteous, on the one hand, and the wicked, on the other. Instead of being located in a "sectarian" community, it focuses ultimately – to be sure, from a pious Jewish perspective – on conditions that impact on *humanity as a whole*. While different levels of binary opposites are interwoven in the *Treatise*,[40] its structure progresses from one of these levels of contrast to another. This progression may be briefly outlined as follows: after the lengthy superscript (1QS iii 13–15a) and a brief hymn about creation (iii 15b–18), the first exposition is concerned with two spirits, also designated "the Prince of Light" and "the Angel of Darkness" (iii 18 – iv 1). This portrait of cosmic opposition[41] is followed by a classification, in the vein of ethical contrasts, of vices and virtues that characterize two sorts of spirits, "the spirit of the sons of truth" (1QS iv 6) and "the spirit of iniquity" (iv 9). The third exposition is then concerned with human activities as they reflect the influence on human nature by the two spirits referred to in column iii (iv 15–26). In the end, these contrasts – operative in the cosmic, ethical, and anthropological spheres – are inextricably bound up with and modify one another. Whereas the ethical antithesis could stand on its own as a social classification of human beings, the interrelation between the cosmological and anthropological oppositions demonstrates that the *Treatise* is

---

the *Two Spirits* and the Literary History of the *Rule of the Community*", in ed. Geza Xeravits, *Dualism in Qumran* (LSTS 76; London: T. & T. Clark International, 2010), pp. 102–120.

[38] Sarianna Metso, *The Textual Development of the Qumran Community Rule* (STDJ 27; Leiden: Brill, 1997), p. 106 notes that a fragment of 4QS^h (= 4Q262) that cannot easily be placed preserves themes that remind of the *Treatise*, though no link to the *Treatise* in its extant form in 1QS can be verified.

[39] See the bibl. cited in n. 37 above.

[40] See esp. the still very useful analysis by Hermann Lichtenberger, *Studien zum Menschenbild in den Texten der Qumrangemeinde* (SUNT 15; Göttingen: Vandenhoeck & Ruprecht, 1980), pp. 123–142.

[41] The language is not completely "dualistic". For example, whereas the text refers to a group of spirits that comprise the entourage of the Angel of Darkness and cause the sons of light to stumble, no contrasting host of beings is associated with "the Angel of his Truth" who, with "the God of Israel" comes to their aid (1QS iii 24–25).

informed by a more complex frame of understanding which reflects on the position of humanity itself. To appreciate how the *Treatise* opens its purview so widely, we look briefly at ways it has absorbed and transformed contemporary traditions.

Each of the antitheses in the *Treatise on the Two Spirits* finds at least some precedent in the Jewish literature composed during the 3rd and 2nd centuries B. C. E. First, in the *cosmic sphere* (1QS iii 18 – iv 1), the predetermined opposition between two angels with separate dominions over light and darkness crystallizes and intensifies an existing presentation of God as found in Ben Sira. According to Ben Sira God has structured the universe from the beginning to consist of pairs, both good and bad (Sir. 33:10–15; 42:24–25), pairs that, unlike the *Treatise*, are not personified.

The personification of dualistic cosmological powers can be observed, however, in both the Aramaic *Vision of Amram* (4Q543–547, 4Q548?)[42] and the *Serekh ha-Milhamah* or *War Rule*. In *Vision of Amram* two angels who together have authority over all humanity are in conflict with one another to gain control over the patriarch. The angel associated with darkness carries the name "Melki-resha'", while no name is extant for the other who speaks with the patriarch and is associated with light (cf. 4Q544 1.10–14). Since the patriarch is apparently asked to choose between the two (4Q544 1.12), the document does not seem to envisage the simultaneous influence of both powers. The patriarch, just as humanity as a whole (who are divided into "sons of light" and "sons of darkness"[43]), exists in only one sphere or another, and, unlike the *Treatise*, both opposing angelic powers are not projected onto good and bad activities of the human being. A similar framework is adopted in the *War Rule* (as preserved in 1QM), which envisions an eschatological conflict pitting "the sons of light" against "the sons of darkness". The contrast between the cosmic powers is, however, not consistently worked through. On one level, analogous to "the Prince of Lights" in the *Treatise*, Michael "the mighty angel", perhaps also called "the Prince of Light" (1QM xiii 10), can appear as the implied opponent of Belial, "the commander of the dominion of wickedness" (1QM xvii 5b–8a).[44] On another level and unlike the *Treatise*, how-

---

[42] On the fragments see Paul J. Kobelski, *Melchizedeq and Melchireša'* (CBQMS 10; Washington D. C.: Catholic University of America Press, 1981) and their publication by Émile Puech in *Qumran Cave 4. XXII. Textes araméens, première partie: 4Q529–549* (DJD 31; Oxford: Clarendon Press, 2001). In addition, see the *Testament of Qahat* (4Q542) in which such oppositions may be attested as well, though less clearly evidenced due to the document's fragmentary state of preservation: "sons of wickedness" (frg. 1 ii 8 – this expression may imply the designation "sons of truth/ righteousness") and the mention of "light" and "darkness" (frg. 2.11–12); see esp. Émile Puech, "Le Testament de Qahat en araméen de la grotte (4QTQah)", *RevQ* 15 (1991), pp. 23–54.

[43] See 4Q544 3.1 and 4Q548 1.9–15. On the contrasting divisions of humanity in 4Q548, see Joseph Verheyden, "The Fate of the Righteous and the Cursed at Qumran and in the Gospel of Matthew", in ed. Florentino García Martínez, *Wisdom and Apocalypticism in the Dead Sea Scrolls and in the Biblical Tradition* (BETL 168; Leuven: Peeters, 2003), pp. 427–449 (here pp. 433–439).

[44] Concerning Michael's ambiguous position as the opponent to Belial in the *War Rule*, which

ever, Belial's opponent is none other than God, so that both have their "lot" (e. g., God – 1QM xiii 5; xvii 7; Belial xiii 2, 4, 11–12) and are, by contrast, cursed (Belial) and blessed (God), respectively (xiii 4, 7). Just as in the *Visions of Amram*, however, the *War Rule* does not project any of these contrasts onto human nature or onto the lot of any individual.[45]

Second, in the *sphere of behavior* (1QS iv 2–14), the catalogue of vices and virtues in the *Treatise* adapts the widespread oppositional pattern that is variously encountered in Ben Sira, *Epistle of Enoch* (*1 En.* 92:1–4; 93:11–105:2), and *Musar le-Mevin* (1Q26; 4Q415–418; 4Q418a; 4Q423).[46] The designations used by the *Treatise* correspond to contrasts expressed along ethical lines, similar to those used in *Visions of Amram* and the *War Rule*. Those considered righteous are called "sons of truth" (1QS iv 6), "sons of light" (iii 25), and "sons of righteousness" (iii 20, 22). Indeed, it is an instruction for such that the *Treatise* was composed, much like the *Musar le Mevin* is addressed to one who understands. The opposite group is called "sons of perversity" (1QS iii 21).[47] This socio-ethical opposition is coordinated with cosmology through the contrasting expressions "paths of light" and "paths of darkness" (iii 20–21) that are described in detail among the virtues and vices.

In particular, the *Treatise*'s focus on the influence of two spirits within the human being means that a clear-cut classification of human beings themselves in the present into two completely distinguishable groups cannot be fully transparent (1QS iv 15–26). The admission that "the sons of light" can stumble (iii 24) is developed into an understanding of the human "heart" (iv 23) as a place of conflict between "divisions" that God has appointed until the end (iv 15–20a). Here it is deeds, not the human being, that are as a whole assigned to one or the other of the two divisions. Humans each have an "inheritance", whether "great or small" (from one of the two divisions) and, therefore, the righteous are capable of straying while the wicked are implicitly capable of being faithful. A comparison with Ben Sira and *1 Enoch* 91–105 illustrates this point. Ben Sira admits that someone can be on "two paths" at once (Sir. 2:12), but does not pursue the implications of this possibility for a theological anthropology; life on both paths at once represents, instead, the condition of "sinners", as is also the case of those who according to the Enochic

---

is reflected in the editorial activity of its copyists, see esp. Jean Duhaime, "Dualistic Reworking in the Scrolls from Qumran", *CBQ* 49 (1987), pp. 32–56 (here pp. 43–46).

[45] The same holds for 11Q13 (= 11QMelchizedek), which may reflect the influence of ideas found in *Vision of Amram*: Melchizedek is portrayed as being in charge over those belonging to "his lot" in the battle against Beliar.

[46] This Hebrew composition did not become available for study until the early 1990's and was officially published in the DJD series in 1999; cf. eds. John Strugnell and Daniel J. Harrington, *Qumran Cave 4. XXIV. Sapiential Texts, Part 2: 4QInstruction (Musar le Mevin): 4Q415ff. with a Re-edition of 1Q26* (DJD 34; Oxford: Clarendon Press, 1999).

[47] Interestingly, the designation "sons of darkness" does not occur in the *Treatise* which, instead, refers to "the spirits of darkness" (iii 25, in the phrase "the spirits of light and of darkness") who come under the dominion of "the Angel of Darkness". It is these who "make the sons of light stumble" (iii 24).

Exhortation are called "double-hearted" (*1 En.* 91:4; cf. Sir. 1:28). Any goodness, then, on the part of sinners is for Ben Sira only apparent; if good behavior manifests itself at all in a "sinner's" life, it is to be explained in terms of hypocrisy or as involving a wrong understanding of goodness to begin with (such as a reliance on wealth). Much in contrast, the duality of paths within a human being is *interiorized* in the *Treatise*, which in the first instance seems to focus on what happens *within* "the sons of righteousness". Here, a double life (so to speak) is not so much the aberrant way of "sinners", but is the essential make-up or composition of human nature itself; the *Treatise*, after all, lays claim to knowledge in relation to "all the sons of men" (iii 13). Whenever goodness occurs, whether within "the sons of righteousness" or "of perversity", it is real, just as badness, whenever it occurs, is real among these groups as well.[48] *All human beings, whether socially on the inside or outside of the righteous community, comprise the battleground wherein the conflict between opposing spirits is carried out.* In the *Treatise*, then, the boundaries between wickedness and righteousness are not ultimately physically or socially delineated. The possible charge of hypocrisy against sinners (who claim to be righteous, yet

---

[48] An analogous interiorization of the contrast between light and darkness may be found in the zodiacal physiognomic texts of 4Q186 and 4Q561, composed in Hebrew and Aramaic, respectively. The very fragmentary remains of 4Q186 and 4Q561 allow for the observation that they describe in detail the physical features of a human being (or, more accurately, a type of human being), features that are coordinated with the precise configuration of stars at the moment of a person's birth. The parts of lightness and darkness add up to a total of nine parts, the odd number being a deliberate way to ensure that the parts will not be equally distributed between the two spheres. Each person, though implicitly capable of doing both good and bad, is ultimately dominated by either light or darkness. This portrait is consistent with 1QS iv 15b–16 ("... every performance of their deeds is in their divisions, according to the inheritance of the man, whether much or little, for all times of the ages") and iv 24b–25a ("... and according to the inheritance of the man in the truth, he will be righteous and thus hate injustice; and according to this share in the lot of injustice, he will be wicked in it and thus abhor the truth, for in equal parts God has established them until the determined time and the making of something new"). – There are, however, differences between the physiognomic texts and the *Treatise*. The former, for example, do not contain any language that points towards an "equal" distribution of light and darkness in the cosmos; it is merely assumed that they co-exist and, together, constitute a human being's nine parts; see further Lichtenberger, *Studien zum Menschenbild in den Texten der Qumrangemeinde*, pp. 147–148. In addition, the comparison should be qualified by the differences in function between the texts. Whereas the *Treatise* functions as a reflection that explains human behavior in the world and coordinates it with the created order itself, it is less clear how the physiognomic texts were used. In a rigorous study of these materials in the context of the ancient world, Mladen Popović has argued that the zodiacal physiognomies functioned not so much to describe human nature as such, but were used to determine the extent to which a person's composition, based on a predetermined state derived from the time of birth, was either acceptable to a community or represented a "demonic" threat; see Popović, *Reading the Human Body: Physiognomics and Astrology in the Dead Sea Scrolls and Hellenistic-Early Roman Period Judaism* (STDJ 67; Leiden/Boston, 2007), esp. pp. 172–239. While there is no explicit demonic language in the physiognomies (other than several references to the measure of a person's "spirit" being in light or darkness; cf. 4Q186 1 ii 7, 1 iii 6, and 2 i 6; no clear reading of this in 4Q561), Popović's interpretation does suggest a stronger link to the yearly evaluation of "spirits" referred to in the *Serekh ha-Yaḥad* (1QS v 23–24; 4Q258 ii 2–4).

behave wickedly), found in documents like Ben Sira and *1 Enoch* chapters 91–105, is absent here. In the *Treatise*, such a view yields to a dualizing framework that explains inconsistent or irreconcilable activity as an inevitability for the human being.

For all its polarizing terminology, the *Treatise* formulates a nuanced understanding of what the righteous community is. Were the cosmic distinction between light and darkness simply a projection of clear boundary markers based on contrasting sets of behavior, then the designations "sons of righteousness" and "sons of perversity" would be functioning as descriptive socio-religious categories. These groups would consist of those who come, respectively, under the dominions of the Prince of Lights and the Angel of Darkness. The *Treatise*, in its present form, resists such a scheme. With other Jewish writings, the *Treatise* shares the view that the righteous can and do fail. This admission is explained in terms of an eschatological framework, according to which the present age, before the time of God's visitation to destroy evil, is one of uncertainty, not least for the elect community.[49] While the exhortational character of the *Treatise* does not make uncertainty a matter of emphasis, the logic of its argument recognizes that "the sons of righteousness" remain within a state of experiencing sin, iniquity and guilt (1QS iii 22).

Now, in principle, given the basis of the instruction of the *Treatise* in a theology of *creation*, the stated experience of sin, iniquity and guilt applies to Jew and non-Jew alike. The opposition between one kind of spirit and another (between a "spirit of truth" in iv 23 and a "spirit of perversity" and "uncleanness" in iv 20 and 22–23) is played out both within the cosmos as a whole and within the *heart* of every human being. When God brings an end to evil at the eschatological time of visitation, the "spirit of injustice" within the person will be removed from "the innermost framework of human flesh" to be replaced by purity and "the spirit of truth" (iv 18–21). The "flesh" itself re-emerges cleansed and purified from divine judgment.[50] If anything, then, one could argue that it is the "flesh" as much as the "heart" of the human being that is the essential place where divine purification takes place.

Given the spirit-embattled state within all human beings in the present age, how are the groups of the righteous and the wicked to be defined? The *Treatise* retains the notion of group identity in the present on the basis of an ethical distinction; the sons of light still remain sons of light precisely because they are helped by the God of Israel and "the Angel of Truth" (1QS iii 24–25). But the writer is also deeply aware that experience does not match the straightforward divisions of

---

[49] Lichtenberger, *Studien zum Menschenbild in den Texten der Qumrangemeinde*, p. 191, observes a parallel between the occasional slain among "the sons of light" by the forces of Belial (cf. 1QM xvi 15; xvii 1; 4Q491 10 ii 11) and the failings held possible for "the sons of light" in 1QS iii 21–25. This holds true, unless 1QS iii 21–25 anticipates the reflections on human nature presented later in the *Treatise* at iv 15–26.

[50] Hence there is no categorical opposition in the *Treatise* between "spirit" and "flesh".

the world into two realms of influence, realms that are socially expressed in the bounded existence of a righteous community. The reflections here on human nature are not satisfied with characterizing the experience of the righteous as one of awareness of sins and the subsequent seeking of forgiveness when they occur.[51] The dualistic language, interiorized into the human being, attempts to take ambiguities that run counter to socio-religious boundaries seriously; from this vantage point there is no essential difference between Jew and Gentile. It might be thought that the zodiacal physiognomic texts of 4Q186 and 4Q561 provide an analogy to this, since the nine parts of a person are each assigned to either a "house of light" or a "house of darkness" according to the time of birth.[52] However, these texts do not place their combination of anthropological and cosmic oppositions within an ethical frame of reference. Thus the great theological contribution of the *Treatise of the Two Spirits* in the *Community Rule* consists in the way it merges cosmic, anthropological and ethical contrasts, allowing them to modify the one-sided force of the other without ignoring the ambiguities of human experience. But these dimensions do more than modify one another: taken together, they reflect a temporary reality that will be wiped away at the appointed time of God's visitation when, with the ending of injustice, the conflict between the two spirits will cease to exist. This end is formulated in 1QS iv 20–21 as follows:

Then God, by his truth, will purge (יברר) *all the deeds of man*; he will refine (יזקק) for himself the human frame, *by putting an end to every spirit of iniquity out of the innermost parts of/ his flesh, by cleaning him with a spirit of holiness from every wicked deed* (ולטהרו ברוח קודש עלילות מכול רשעה).

What sort of community does the *Treatise* presuppose? It would be difficult to imagine that the contrasting categories in the work were originally formulated for a group merely undergoing a socio-religious crisis of identity in which one group is reflecting on how and why it contrasts from other groups. Likewise, it seems hard to posit a social setting of poverty behind the document. Rather, the *Treatise* presupposes an established, though not necessarily "sectarian", community that indulges in the kind of reflection that takes a certain degree of vulnerability for granted. The text does not emerge from those who are "fighting" to protect their group's identity over against either the challenges of other groups or the threat of cosmic invasions from darkness. Much more, the *Treatise* offers instruction to a community that has had a history of ups and downs and that has had the sort of longevity and social stability that allows for contemplation at such depth.

If the *Treatise* was not composed by or for the *Yaḥad*, we may nevertheless note that, within the literary context of the *Community Rule* from Cave 1, it has

---

[51] This is much in contrast with Ben Sira, which emphasizes the forgiveness of sins as a regular part of the life of the righteous; cf. Sir. 1:21; 2:11; 3:3, 30; 4:26 ("do not be ashamed to confess your sins"); 17:25; 18:21, 27; 20:3; 21:1; 28:2, 4–5; and 39:5; cf. also 23:11.

[52] See n. 48 above.

acquired a function analogous to the purpose for which it may have originally been composed. Unlike the following block of materials in the document (from 1QS v 1 – x 5), contrastive language of social and physical separation between people, the good and the bad, is absent. The relation of the *Treatise* to the preceding material in 1QS i 1 – iii 12 seems closer. In these early columns of 1QS strong cosmic boundaries between insiders and outsiders are erected, formulized through a liturgy that curses those who belong to Belial's lot (ii 5–9). Despite these boundaries, which seem to draw special lines around the community, the section allows for the possibility that someone who finds himself within the community may falsely bless himself "in his heart, saying 'Peace be with me'" (ii 13). The text says that such a person's spirit is to be destroyed and that he is to go without forgiveness (ii 14–15); he is no different from those who belong to Belial's lot (ii 17), and, just as those on the outside of the community, he is to become under the community's curse (ii 18; cf. ii 10). This is as far as the Qumran community could go *in terms of the group's own experience*. Here the problem of sin among members of the community is described within the framework of hypocrisy, that is, the person should know better than to "bless himself" if he has done something wrong. However, in venturing into the private experience of the individual, the compilers of this stage of the document were entering into vulnerable territory of the unknown that is marked by a degree of uncertainty, despite all efforts otherwise to draw socially definable perimeters that correspond to light and darkness. That such may not have been acceptable to contemplate for all members of the community is suggested by the absence of this opening section of 1QS in those manuscripts that begin with material parallel to 1QS column v (4Q258; 4Q261).

Dualistic structure of thought played an important role in crystallizing the identities of groups who saw themselves in religious conflict with either the conventionally wicked or with specific (other religious) opponents. It goes without saying that the same occurred between pious Jews and Gentiles, the latter of whom could be categorically dismissed as "sinners". Most often – though with significant exceptions – Jewish literature from the Second Temple period expressed itself in relation to the ethical distinction between good and bad. Less often, but not uncommon, is an arrangement of the world in cosmic terms that contrast God and/or a prominent angelic being (e.g., "the Prince of Lights", Melchizedek, Michael) with Belial or a prominent angelic leader (e.g., Melki-resha' or "the Angel of Darkness"). The least common among oppositional categories in Second Temple literature has to do with the interior dimensions of human nature. To be sure, documents such as Ben Sira and even the *Musar le-Mevin* show some concern for what a person is on the inside, but they do not work out their main ideas at this level. The *Treatise*, however, does explore the interiority of human nature *per se*, and initially may have arisen within a relatively stable social context. Its theological anthropology, which envisions the human being as the battleground between cosmic forces, interiorizes a socio-religious conflict that cannot be circumscribed by either physical or even socially well-defined boundaries. The *Treatise* was able to provide a theological framework that takes discrepancy between religious ideology and the failings of lived experienced into account, and within the *Community Rule* the *Yaḥad* adopted this tradition and applied it to themselves as they began to negotiate the possibility of evil among their ranks (ii 11–18).

The depth of reflection preserved in the *Treatise* suggests that, within a creation theology, the working out of the divine plan is, in principle, not far removed from Gentiles. Though unlike *1 Enoch* 10 Gentiles are not explicitly mentioned in the text, its concern with "every" human being (iii 13; iv 15–16, 20) includes them within both the actual and potential gambit of God's activity. Like *1 Enoch* 10, however, the *Treatise* demonstrates a particular focus on *deeds* as visibly constitutive of either faithfulness or disloyalty to God. No human being is completely iniquitous, on the one hand, or wholly righteous, on the other; rather, each person is a mixture of both. The arena in which this mixture of opposing forces is played out is "the heart of man" (1QS iv 23). Despite the compositeness in each human being, the *Treatise* essentially reflects the same theological anthropology as the *Book of Watchers* of *1 Enoch* 10, insofar as it draws a distinction between the person and the "works" or "deeds" the person does. At the time of God's visitation the iniquitous works will all be destroyed as God cleanses the innermost parts of the human "flesh" (which is closely related to the heart). In effect, this amounts to a cleansing of the heart, a purification that will restore human beings to their originally intended design, which is called "the glory of Adam" (iv 23). Though the *Treatise* has often been read and interpreted as a "sectarian" document that took shape within such a context, it provides a reflection that includes *humanity as a whole* and, accordingly, adopts a discourse that addresses *interiority* as the essential location where divine activity takes place. This understanding of the human being in relation to God is latent in the Enochic tradition, which does not reflect on the inner dimensions of human existence.[53]

In terms of the point last mentioned, the *Treatise on the Two Spirits* articulates something that neither the writings in the Hebrew Bible nor even the Enoch traditions offer. Cleansing and purification in the ultimate sense essentially take place in the innermost part of a person, and it is out of this innermost self that deeds or activities follow. The eschatological cleansing will mean that iniquitous deeds are destroyed; the text assumes that the degree of alignment with these deeds determines whether or not a given human being will also be destroyed (or rescued) in the process.

---

[53] This does not mean, however, that such a theological anthropology is not implied in the Enochic tradition; see Wright, *The Origin of Evil Spirits*, pp. 160–165 and Chapter Nine above.

Conclusion

The cleansing of the deeds or works of humanity as described in *1 Enoch* 10 and the *Treatise on the Two Spirits* is eschatological. If deeds are destroyed or cleansed away and removed, then those activities that remain reflect the resulting state of purity. Against such a background, Peter's speech in Acts 15 would have an audience that comprehended the mission to Gentiles as an event within the "last days" that heralds the eschaton and that goes hand-in-glove with the restoration of Israel and the giving of the Holy Spirit which purifies the heart (cf. 1QS iv 20–22). Once it is understood that the Holy Spirit has been interiorized within Gentiles, the socially bounded existence between Israel and the Gentiles cannot be maintained as before; the language about the Holy Spirit is not simply a general way of referring to divine activity, but is at the same time in at least Acts 10–11 and 15 the reflex of a theological anthropology in which the innermost part of the human being – who as such is indelibly part of the created order – takes center stage. It is here where effective divine activity resides; it is here where the essential distinctions between purity and impurity are regulated; and it is here, in the "heart", which is only known to God (Acts 15:8), where authentic transformation takes place.

This ideology, which we have observed by looking at two theologically significant writings from the Second Temple period, makes room for Gentile inclusion. Socio-religious boundaries previously taken for granted do not in themselves determine who will ultimately belong to the people of God. This is what Acts, in regarding the giving of the Holy Spirit as the beginning of a new era ("the last days", 2:17), has the Jewish Christians recognize as they deliberate on what to do regarding the Gentile mission. I do not, however, think that the writer of Acts reflected or held a theological anthropology that distinguishes between the interior of human beings and the works that they do (cf. Acts 5:32; 9:36; 26:20). Nonetheless, if the material in Acts 15:8–9 derives from a source in which Jewish Christians were debating the status of believing Gentiles, then it is perhaps such a prioritization of the interior of humanity that could, on terms known within Jewish tradition, lead to grounds for admitting Gentiles whose cleansing could then be expected to be made manifest through regulations to avoid impurity as enjoined in 15:20–21. Why, then, should any regulations be required from Gentiles? It is so on account of the close relationship that traditions have forged between purity and deeds – conversely between impurity and iniquitous deeds or works. If impurity is manifest through certain human activities, then the avoidance of these will establish this purity through observable deeds as well. What *1 Enoch* and the *Treatise* anticipate eschatologically has, according to Acts 10–11 and 15, now come to pass. The interpretation of the present as a time in which divine activity is taking hold on all people, whether Jew or Gentile, is the only real way in which Acts at this point has reconfigured tradition in a different direction.

Chapter Twelve

Posturing "Apocalyptic" in Pauline Theology: How Much Contrast to Jewish Tradition?

1. Introduction

In the discussion to follow, we focus on a problem whose significance is often taken for granted in Pauline studies: How is the "apocalyptic" dimension of Paul's thought related to Jewish tradition?[1] To what extent can the theological shape of the apostle's ideas be traced back to or be conceptualized within a Jewish matrix of tradition that developed from the time of Alexander the Great down to the 1st century C. E.? Of course, answering such a question depends on definitions; what *is* "apocalyptic" to begin with, and how much can we meaningfully invest in this term? These questions have come into play in treatments of several (often overlapping) themes in Paul's undisputed letters: the Torah,[2] messianic language and

---

[1] Early on, it was Albert Schweitzer who posed and adopted the category of "apocalyptic" (in the sense of its focus on eschatology and mystical participationism distinguishable from Rabbinic Judaism) as the essential way to understand Paul's thought; cf. *idem, The Mysticism of the Apostle Paul*, trans. William Montgomery (Baltimore, Md: Johns Hopkins Press, 1998, repr. from 1931). Schweitzer's influential discussion, however, could not endure since "apocalyptic" for him was a function of Hellenistic Diaspora Judaism. The view that Jesus' death could not be "apocalyptic" – a term reserved for the future – resulted in what has been called "consistent eschatology", i. e., consistent with Jewish apocalyptic eschatology. This view, which emphasized the coming of a future messianic age in line with Jewish expectation, was picked up by Martin Werner in his *The Formation of Christian Dogmas: An Historical Study of Its Problem*, trans. Samuel G. F. Brandon (London: A. & C. Black, 1957, from German 1941) and has left traces in the thought of Johan Christiaan Beker (on whom see below).

[2] See variously Ed P. Sanders, *Paul, the Law, and the Jewish People* (Philadelphia: Fortress Press, 1983); Lloyd Gaston, *Paul and the Torah* (Vancouver: University of British Columbia Press, 1987); Christoph Heil, *Die Ablehnung der Speisegebote durch Paulus: Zur Frage nach der Stellung des Apostels zum Gesetz* (BBB 96; Weilheim: Beltz Athenäum, 1996); ed. James D. G. Dunn, *Paul and the Mosaic Law.* (Grand Rapids: Eerdmans, 2001); eds. Donald A. Carson, Peter T. O'Brien, and Mark A. Seifried, *Justification and Variegated Nomism* (2 vols.; WUNT 2.140, 181; Tübingen: Mohr Siebeck, 2001 and 2004); Stephan K. Davis, *The Antithesis of the Ages: Paul's Reconfiguration of Torah* (CBQMS 33; Washington DC: The Catholic Biblical Association of America, 2002); James D. G. Dunn, *The New Perspective on Paul* (Grand Rapids: Eerdmans, 2008); Roland Bergmaier, *Gerechtigkeit, Gesetz und Glaube bei Paulus: Der judenchristliche Heidenapostel im Streit um das Gesetz und Seine Werke* (BTS 115; Neukirchen-Vluyn: Neukirchener Verlag, 2010); Mark D. Nanos, e. g., in "Paul's Relationship to Torah in Light of His Strategy 'to Become Everything to Everyone' (1 Corinthians 9:19–22)", in eds. Reimund Bieringer and Didier Pollefeyt, *Paul and Judaism: Crosscurrents in Pauline Exegesis and the Study of Jewish-Christian Relations* (London / New York: T & T Clark International and Continuum, 2012), pp. 106–140.

ideas,[3] eschatology,[4] cosmology,[5] attitudes towards Gentiles,[6] covenant,[7] the interpretation of sacred traditions[8] and theological anthropology.[9] In examining these areas of Pauline thought, one may ask whether or not the apostle Paul could have known this or that tradition or thematic complex and whether or not he may have

[3] See L. Joseph Kreitzer, *Jesus and God in Paul's Eschatology* (JSNTSup 19; Sheffield: JSOT Press, 1987); Magnus Zetterholm, "Paul and the missing Messiah," in ed. *idem, The Messiah in Early Judaism and Christianity* (Minneapolis: Fortress Press, 2007), pp. 33–55; and see recently James A. Waddell, *The Messiah: A Comparative Study of the Enochic Son of Man and the Pauline Kyrios* (JCTLS 10; London: T & T Clark, 2011) and Matthew V. Novenson, *Christ among the Messiahs: Christ Language in Paul and Messiah Language in Ancient Judaism* (Oxford: Oxford University Press, 2012).

[4] Franzjosef Froitzheim, *Christologie und Eschatologie bei Paulus* (FB 35; Würzburg: Echter Verlage, 1979); Andrew T. Lincoln, *Paradise Now and Not Yet: Studies in the Role of the Heavenly Dimension in Paul's Thought with Special Reference to His Eschatology* (SNTSMS 43; Cambridge / New York: Cambridge University Press, 1981); Kreitzer, *Jesus and God in Paul's Eschatology* (cf. n. 3); Martinus C. de Boer, *The Defeat of Death: Apocalyptic Eschatology in 1 Corinthians and Romans 5* (JSNTSup 22; Sheffield: JSOT Press, 1988); C. Marvin Pate, *The End of the Age Has Come: The Theology of Paul* (Grand Rapids: Zondervan, 1995); Allan J. McNicol, *Jesus' Directions for the Future: A Source and Redaction-History Study of the Use of the Eschatological Traditions in Paul and in the Synoptic Accounts of Jesus' Last Eschatological Discourse* (Macon: Mercer Press, 1996); Robert S. Smith, *Justification and Eschatology: A Dialogue with "the New Perspective on Paul"* (RTRSup 1; Doncaster, Australia: Reformed Theological Review, 2001); Joseph Plevnik, *What are They Saying about Paul and the End Time?* (New York: Paulist Press, 2009, revd. ed. from 1986).

[5] Edward Adams, *Constructing the World: A Study in Paul's Cosmological Language* (Edinburgh: T. & T. Clark, 2000). For a more recent study that compares Rom. 8:19–22 with motifs associated with creation in Jewish apocalyptic literature, see Harry Alan Hahne, *The Corruption and Redemption of Creation* (LNTS 336; London: T. & T. Clark, 2006), esp. pp. 210–226.

[6] Cf. Don B. Garlington, *Faith, Obedience, and Perseverance: Aspects of Paul's Letter to the Romans* (WUNT 2.79; Tübingen: Mohr Siebeck, 1994); Francis Watson, *Paul, Judaism, and the Gentiles: Beyond the New Perspective* (Grand Rapids: Eerdmans, 2007); Aaron Sherwood, *Paul and the Restoration of Humanity in Light of Ancient Jewish Traditions* (AJEC 82; Leiden: Brill, 2013).

[7] See, e. g., Bruce W. Longenecker, *Eschatology and the Covenant: A Comparison of 4 Ezra and Romans 1–11* (JSNTSup 57; Sheffield: JSOT Press, 1991); Nicholas T. Wright, *The Climax of the Covenant* (Edinburgh: T. & T. Clark, 1991); Kari Kuula, *The Law, the Covenant, and God's Plan* (Publications of the Finnish Exegetical Society 72; Göttingen: Vandenhoeck & Ruprecht, 1999); A. Andrew Das, *Paul, the Law, and the Covenant* (Peabody, Mass.: Hendrickson, 2001); eds. Florian Wilk and J. Ross Wagner, *Between Gospel and Election: Explorations in the Interpretation of Romans 9–11* (WUNT 257; Tübingen: Mohr Siebeck, 2010).

[8] Cf. David B. Capes, *Old Testament Yahweh Texts in Paul's Christology* (WUNT 2.47; Tübingen: Mohr Siebeck, 1992); J. Ross Wagner, *Heralds of the Good News: Isaiah and Paul "in Concert" in the Letter to the Romans* (NovTSup 102; Leiden / Boston: Brill, 2002); eds. Stanley E. Porter and Christopher D. Stanley, *As It Is Written: Studying Paul's Use of Scripture* (SBLSymS 50; Atlanta: Society of Biblical Literature, 2008); ed. Christopher D. Stanley, *Paul and Scripture: Extending the Conversation* (SBLECL 9; Atlanta: Scholars Press, 2012).

[9] Timo Laato, *Paulus und Judentum: Anthropologische Erwägungen* (Åbo: Åbo Akademis Förlag, 1991); Hermann Lichtenberger, *Das Ich Adams und das Ich der Menschheit: Studien zum Menschenbild in Römer 7* (WUNT 164; Tübingen: Mohr Siebeck, 2004); George H. van Kooten, *Paul's Anthropology in Context: The Image of God, Assimilation to God, and Tripartite Man in Ancient Judaism, Ancient Philosophy and Early Christianity* (WUNT 232; Tübingen: Mohr Siebeck, 2008); Troels Engberg-Pedersen, *Cosmology and the Self in the Apostle Paul: The Material Spirit* (Oxford: Oxford University Press, 2010); and Christian Dietzfelbinger, *Sohn: Skizzen zur Christologie und Anthropologie des Paulus* (BTS 188; Neukirchen-Vluyn: Neukirchener Verlag, 2011).

drawn directly on, significantly modified, or attempted to counter it altogether. Quite understandably, the crucial differences between Paul and the contemporary Jewish traditions with which his thought is compared are time and again exposed and identified by scholars, especially as the Christological point of departure in Paul's argument is recognized.

The broader question is, of course, the nature of Paul's religion. To put the problem dialectically: Was Paul's thought "Christian" in the sense that he, perhaps inspired by Jesus tradition itself, can be regarded as having placed the theological terrain of the fledgling Jesus movement on a course that essentially broke with its mother religion? Or, for all their particularity, is it possible to locate and interpret Paul's theological ideas within a complex Jewish theological framework, a framework that enabled the apostle to make sense of how the God who called Israel in the wilderness and gave them the Torah could be seen to have acted anew in the death and resurrection of Jesus? In any given comparison between Jewish tradition and Paul's writings, one way of responding to such a question has been to focus on minutiae in which texts of the one are placed alongside texts of the other to ascertain concretely where the similarities and differences lie.[10] Another way, however, remains vital, albeit difficult to get at: This is to consider the *structures* of Pauline thought, not so much by identifying straightforwardly certain traditions that the apostle may or may not have used, but, more profoundly, by discerning whether or not a *framework* in which he articulated his "gospel" marked something essentially new. It is primarily within the latter frame of questioning that discourse about Jewish "apocalyptic" in relation to early Christian notions, including that of Paul, has primarily taken shape.

Here, in considering "apocalyptic" as a feature of Paul's theology, we are aware of the vast amount of scholarly attention devoted to this topic, especially with regard to the organization and understanding of time. While it is taken as axiomatic that Paul was interested in time and that the organization of time for him was shaped by his conviction that Jesus' death and resurrection represented a definitive moment (of God's activity) in history, how clear is it that this amounted to a paradigmatic shift or even departure from Judaism, as many argue or assume? In my opinion, the often uncontested notion that Paul's understanding of time represents a significant if not novel modification of Jewish tradition is in need of a corrective, or at least a marked degree of nuancing. In this particular area much of Pauline scholarship has adopted well-worn paths of research concerning how Jews during the Second Temple period, especially those associated with an "apocalyptic"

---

[10] For examples of this, see Herbert Braun, *Qumran und das Neue Testament* (2 vols.; Tübingen: Mohr Siebeck, 1966), vol. 1, pp. 169–240 and vol. 2, pp. 165–180; Heinz-Wolfgang Kuhn, "The Impact of Selected Qumran Texts on the Understanding of Pauline Theology," in ed. James H. Charlesworth, *The Bible and the Dead Sea Scrolls. The Second Princeton Symposium on Judaism and Christian Origins. Volume 3: The Scrolls and Christian Origins* (Waco, Texas: Baylor University Press, 2006), pp. 153–185.

perspective, regarded the unfolding of time. On the other hand, some who have engaged in close readings of the sources may find themselves rethinking the issue in another way.[11]

2. The "Two Ages" of Jewish Tradition and Pauline Scholarship

If we ask specialists in Pauline theology from the last fifty years how time is structured, we may not be surprised to encounter more than one answer. Nevertheless, there has been a remarkable convergence in relation to Paul's understanding of time as it can be compared with Jewish tradition. This convergence, however, has less to do with what is being claimed for Paul himself than with the way Jewish apocalyptic thinking against or upon which Paul's thought is understood has been portrayed. Drawing mostly on the scholarly work of influential studies of ancient Jewish "apocalyptic" writings,[12] literature on Paul has regarded a "doctrine of the two ages", in which one age *follows* or *succeeds* upon the other, as the essential Jewish framework with which Paul's gospel was engaged.[13] The two ages Paul is seen to have modified consists, respectively, of the present age and the future, eschatological age to come. The former is a time marked by evil manifested through suffering and wrongdoing within the created order; the latter envisions the establish-

---

[11] A welcome case in point is the nuanced discussion of the eschatology of *2 Baruch* in the recent monograph by Matthias Henze, *Jewish Apocalypticism in Late First Century Israel* (TSAJ 142; Tübingen: Mohr Siebeck, 2011), esp. ch. 6. Other studies that have attempted to rethink aspects of time in Second Temple sources in ways related to, though distinguishable from, the approach taken here are Grant Macaskill, *Revealed Wisdom and Inaugurated Eschatology in Ancient Judaism and Early Christianity* (JSJSup 115; Leiden / Boston: Brill, 2007) and Jill Hicks-Keeton, "Already/Not Yet: Eschatological Tension in the Book of Tobit", *JBL* 132 (2013), pp. 97–117.

[12] So, for example, Robert Henry Charles, *Eschatology. The Doctrine of a Future Life in Israel, Judaism, and Christianity: A Critical History* (New York: Schocken Books, 1963 repr.); H. H. Rowley, *The Relevance of Apocalyptic: A Study of Jewish and Christian Apocalypses from Daniel to Revelation* (New York/London: Lutterworth, 1963); Philipp Vielhauer, "Apocalyptic' and 'Apocalyptic in Early Christianity", revd. by Georg Strecker, in Edgar Hennecke and William Schneemelcher, *New Testament Apocrypha* (2 vols. Louisville: Westminster John Knox Press, 1990–1992), vol. 2, pp. 581–600 and 608–642 respectively (originally published in 1964); D. S. Russell, *The Method and Message of Jewish Apocalyptic* (London/ Philadelphia: Westminster Press, 1964); Paul D. Hanson, *The Dawn of Apocalyptic: The Historical and Sociological Roots of Jewish Apocalyptic Eschatology* (Philadelphia: Fortress Press, 1979, revised ed.). In his important history of scholarship on apocalyptic thought, Johann Michael Schmidt, "apokalyptische Äonenlehre" recurs as a feature that characterizes much of research of apocalyptic between 1870 and 1947; *idem, Die jüdische Apokalyptik: Die Geschichte ihrer Erforschung von den Anfängen bis zu den Textfunden von Qumran* (Neukirchen-Vluyn: Neukirchener Verlag, 1969), pp. 157–317.

[13] In addition to the works discussed below, see Earl M. Caudill, "The Two-Age Doctrine in Paul: A Study of Pauline Apocalyptic" (Ph.D. Dissertation, Vanderbilt University, 1972); Kreitzer, *Jesus and God in Paul's Eschatology*; Barry R. Matlock, *Unveiling the Apocalyptic Paul: Paul's Interpreters and the Rhetoric of Criticism* (JSNTSup 127; Sheffield: Sheffield Academic Press, 1996); Scott M. Lewis, *What Are They Saying about New Testament Apocalyptic?* (New York: Paulist Press, 2004), pp. 38–52 (chapter on "Paul's Apocalyptic Gospel").

ment of divine rule that will wipe out evil and put to right all wrongs and injustices in line with God's purposes for the created order. Of course, it has been recognised that construals of time in Second Temple Jewish literature cannot be simplified into such a bipartite scheme.[14] It has been noted, for example, that the age to come could be understood in some sense as a return to primordial time and would thus not merely manifest itself as an unprecedented future age.[15] Moreover, some Pauline scholars have observed that several texts depict the future *within the present world order* as the unfolding of a series of events, usually catastrophic and some-times with the advent of a messianic figure, which will herald the conclusion of this age in anticipation of that divine act that will inaugurate the eschaton.[16]

Now there is no need to question the existence of the notion of a distinction between a present age and a future world order ordained by God in Jewish apoca-lyptic and related literature. There is also no need to question whether this under-standing of time can be nuanced in the ways just mentioned. However, it is helpful to discuss two points: (i) what it means to talk about the way Paul has appro-priated such an outlook and, in view of this, (ii) whether, in fact, more can be said about how some Jewish writers – here, we note the Enochic tradition and its take-up in related literature extant in the Dead Sea materials – could think about time.

First, we look at what the positing of two aeons as the major way of under-standing Jewish apocalyptic thought has meant for several influential Pauline inter-preters: (A) Ernst Käsemann,[17] (B) Johan Christiaan Beker,[18] (C) J. Louis Mar-

---

[14] See already John J. Collins, "Apocalyptic Eschatology as the Transcendence of Death", *CBQ* 36 (1974), pp. 21–43, who questioned the casually used formulations of "a definitive end" and "the distinction of two periods" as central features of apocalyptic eschatology. Aside from a further possibility to be discussed below, we can note periodization of history (including the periodization of the eschaton) and the progression of time through cycles. Though none of the alternatives do away with a notion of the present world versus a future world, they suggest that the movement from one to another could be conceived in complex ways.

[15] See, for example, George W. E. Nickelsburg, "Eschatology, Early Jewish", in David Noel Freedman, *Anchor Bible Dictionary* (6 vols.; Garden City, New York: Doubleday, 1992), vol. 2, pp. 579–594.

[16] See W. D. Davies, *Paul and Rabbinic Judaism* (Philadelphia: Fortress Press, 1980, 4th ed.), esp. pp. 285–320. This, of course, is consistent with the influential "Systematic Presentation" of Messianism found in Emil Schürer, *The history of the Jewish people in the age of Jesus Christ*, revised and edited by Geza Vermes, Fergus Millar and Matthew Black (3 vols.; Edinburgh: T. & T. Clark, 1979), vol. 2, pp. 514–547 (in organization of content, essentially unchanged from Schürer's two-volume work originally published in 1890–1896).

[17] See, e. g., his "The Beginnings of Christian Theology", in *idem, New Testament Questions of Today* (Philadelphia: Fortress Press, 1969, repr. from 1960), pp. 82–107. This essay is foundational for the perspective Käsemann worked out in his *Commentary on Romans*, translated by Geoffrey W. Bromiley (Grand Rapids: Eerdmans, 1980, 4th ed.).

[18] *Paul the Apostle: The Triumph of God in Life and Thought* (Philadelphia: Fortress Press, 1984) and *The Triumph of God: The Essence of Paul's Thought*, trans. Loren Stuckenbruck (Min-neapolis: Fortress Press, 1990).

[19] Cf. "Epistemology at the Turn of the Ages: 2 Corinthians 5.16", in eds. William R. Farmer, Charles F. D. Moule, and Richard R. Niebuhr, *Christian History and Interpretation: Studies Pre-sented to John Knox* (Cambridge: Cambridge University Press, 1967), pp. 269–287, repr. in *idem*,

tyn,[19] and (D) James D. G. Dunn.[20] Acknowledging the risk of oversimplifying the differences between these scholars and the nuanced arguments each has brought to their readings of Paul,[21] I think it is possible to identify a common thread among them in relation to the apocalyptic undercurrent which shaped their work. In sketching this, I shall be less concerned with what Jewish traditions influenced these New Testament scholars than with the assumptions they have made regarding what these traditions *could not* have included.

2.A. Ernst Käsemann

Ernst Käsemann's views on "the righteousness of God" in Paul as the invading power of God[22] and his claim that "Apocalyptic was the mother of all Christian theology" are well known. Lying in the background to these claims is "the apocalyptic ideal of the two aeons", which Paul presupposed.[23] Exegetically, Paul's adaptation of this scheme is vividly illustrated in Romans 5:12–21, in which Adam and Christ are antithetically juxtaposed. Whereas Jewish apocalyptic consigned "salvation" to the future, the advent of Christ and, in particular, Christ's death makes it possible for this to be realized in the present "obedience of those who are waiting for this moment, who hear and accept the prophetic proclamation of the standards of the Last Judgment and pass it on to the whole world".[24] What in Jewish apocalyptic is remote, is already underway. Paul's reception of the two aeons schema involved a serious modification of "the dominant Jewish view", resulting in a new form of apocalyptic, which has to do with a distinctive worldview capable of speaking about "eschatological salvation" and "life" in the present.[25] Instead of a Jewish scheme, which contrasted between primordial time (Adam and the sin and death that passed through him to all humans in the present) and the end-time (the final judgment), the present age of death is in Paul's view confronted by Christ, who is "the author and representative of the new aeon". In other words, for Paul "the end-time has already begun".[26]

Theological Issues in the Letters of Paul (Edinburgh: T & T Clark, 1997), pp. 87–110. These studies shaped the framework adopted by Martyn in *Galatians: A New Translation and Commentary* (AB 33A; New Haven: Yale University Press, 2010, repr. from 1997).

[20] See, e. g., *The Theology of Paul the Apostle* (Grand Rapids: Eerdmans, 1998).

[21] See Matlock, *Unveiling the Apocalyptic Paul*, for a fuller engagement with these (especially Käsemann) and others' ways of placing "apocalyptic" in service of constructing Pauline theology, though the critical approach taken here shall move in a different direction.

[22] See "The Righteousness of God in Paul", in *New Testament Questions of Today*, pp. 168–182 (bibl. n. 16; article repr. from 1961).

[23] Käsemann, *Romans*, p. 92 (comment on Rom. 3:21–26).

[24] "The Beginnings of Christian Theology", p. 105.

[25] *Romans*, p. 142.

[26] This understanding of time picked up Oscar Cullmann's description of early Christian thought as life between a "D-Day" (the event of the cross that was a decisive battle) and a "Victory Day" (the future when the new age comes into force); cf. Cullmann, *Christ and Time*, trans. Floyd

For Käsemann it is appropriate to speak about "Jewish apocalyptic" in relation to Paul's theology in two ways: it is a perspective that (i) remains nourished by eschatology (so that Paul's modifications of this stand out in the sharpest relief); and (ii) views the cosmos as a place in which divine power, the power not anticipated by Jews until the eschaton, as having broken into the world. The present, then, is one of conflict between the power that comes with the gospel and death that is shared by humanity. Käsemann did not allow the logic of an antithetical typology of Adam and Christ to be determinative for Paul; the advent of Christ did not do away with the ongoing power of death in this world. Against what Käsemann refers to as "the Hellenistic enthusiasts" of Corinth, Paul's thought retained an eschatological edge. Christ inaugurated the end-time, but the ultimate conclusion of things remains outstanding (so that Paul can refer to "the present evil aeon" in Gal. 1:4), a reality that could be placed in service of "primitive Christian paraenesis"[27] and would do so for Paul. The "universal realization" of the advent of life through Christ (Rom. 5:12–21) is now (Rom. 6:1–11) a summons for Christians "to confirm in their personal life the change of aeons that has been effected".[28] Käsemann acknowledges in principle the complexity of Jewish apocalyptic thought; however, Paul's language draws from the eschaton into the present the conflict between death and life in a way that, presumably, did not have any real precedent in existing Jewish paradigms. Käsemann did not explicitly claim that Paul's adaptation of Jewish apocalyptic eschatology (as Käsemann understood it) was not anticipated, perhaps because it is precisely this aspect of Paul's indebtedness to Jewish tradition that shaped the distinctive of his theology. However, inasmuch as Paul worked out the significance of Christ in relation to his Jewish heritage, what distinguishes Käsemann's Paul from Jewish apocalyptic thought is nothing less than radical and, indeed, innovative in terms of the history of religions.

2.B. Johann Christiaan Beker

J. Christiaan Beker's work on Paul drew from Käsemann the significance of "apocalyptic" as a key to understanding the theology of the apostle. He too accepted that Paul had shifted the tone of Jewish apocalyptic thought, so that the "Christ event" (i. e., the view of both Jesus' death and resurrection as a coherent act of God) could function as a proleptic event that anticipates God's ultimate triumph over sin and death. The Christ event in Paul's gospel lent the eschaton a certitude that has no equal in Jewish tradition. Therefore, it "is the apocalyptic turning point

---

V. Filson (Philadelphia: Westminster Press, 1964, revised ed., from the German publication of 1946), pp. 83–84; see further, Conzelmann, *Die Mitte der Zeit: Studien zur Theologie Lukas* (BHT 19; Tübingen: Mohr Siebeck, 1964, 5th ed.).

[27] *Romans*, p. 142; "The Beginnings of Christian Theology", p. 105.
[28] *Romans*, p. 159.

of history".[29] Unlike Käsemann, however, Beker gave more emphasis to the eschaton in Paul's thought as the time of God's definitive triumph over evil. In this sense, Beker understood himself as engaging in a theological reading that could take seriously the presence of ongoing evil in the lives of Christians, thus toning down the ethical imperative that had emerged from Käsemann's more conflict-orientated interpretation. Indeed, "[t]he death and resurrection of *Christ in their apocalyptic setting* constitute the core of Paul's thought"[30] and "signify that the cross is God's judgment of the world and that the resurrection is the beginning of the ontological renewal of creation that will come to completion in God's new age".[31] Despite Beker's difference in emphasis from that of Käsemann, his understanding of apocalyptic thought in Jewish tradition remains much the same: it divided time into two ages, and represented a distinction that Paul deliberately blurred in order to allow the significance of the Christ event in Paul's recent past to play a teleological role in the divine schema. Still, though Beker's reading allows for Paul's thought to approximate Jewish apocalyptic eschatology more than many other Pauline interpreters would permit, Beker could not escape the view that Paul's gospel was shaped by an impulse, a frame of thinking, that could not be more fully described by sustaining a *constructive* conversation with Second Temple literature.

2.C. J. Louis Martyn

Käsemann and Beker's understanding of "apocalyptic" in Paul, while drawing heavily on its eschatological component, nevertheless reflects a use of the term which, when applied casually, begins to take on a life of its own. Apocalyptic in Käsemann could thus refer to a worldview in which powers are in conflict, while for Beker it denoted a view of the world in which hope has a key role to play, especially since the complexities of suffering, sin and death are neither being vanquished nor necessarily find any tangible reckoning. J. Louis Martyn's understanding of "apocalyptic" takes the matter one step further; for him it operates as a key to epistemology. Rather than allowing the term simply to denote the eschatological future, Martyn draws on the fundamental meaning behind the word ("to reveal" or "uncover") to emphasize the recognition of a (divine) disclosure that pertains to *both* the present age and the age to come; the perception of the one necessarily involves a perception of the other. Hence, if history as Paul knew it is to be brought to end by God, it is because the present world order is being comprehended as essentially "evil" (Gal. 1:4). "Apocalyptic" is thus "the conviction that God has now given to the elect true perception both of present developments (the real world) and of a wondrous transformation in the near future"; it involves "a new way of knowing both present and future".[32]

---

[29] *Paul the Apostle*, p. 205.

[30] *Paul the Apostle*, p. 207 (emphasis my own).

[31] *Paul the Apostle*, p. 211.

[32] "Apocalyptic Antinomies in the Letter to the Galatians", in *Theological Issues in the Letters*

It follows for Martyn that the revelatory solution in Paul's thought, if it is to be a solution at all, does not lie in the future (as with Jewish apocalyptic) but rather in the present. Therefore, it is possible for the death of Jesus to be regarded as a moment of divine unveiling that confronts and, in turn, unmasks the world as it now exists. This frame of understanding provided Martyn with a way to present Paul's thought as a whole and, in particular, could help explain why, in contrast to Beker, he could read a letter like Galatians, with its Christo-centric orientation, as no less fundamentally apocalyptic than the other writings of the apostle.[33] Thus even less so than for either Käsemann or Beker, Martyn's approach to apocalyptic does not obligate the interpreter to find any essential continuity with comparable or contrasting Jewish paradigms. Once God has disclosed God's self in the Christ event as a new way of knowing, all else that came before becomes functionally irrelevant, not only for Paul but even for Paul's interpreters. Such an epistemology, a way of knowing that involves divine disclosure within the bounds of the created order as we know it, may arguably be a way of construing the thinking of Paul, but does this also have to mean that Jewish writers did not think about divine disclosure in any analogous way?

2.D. James D. G. Dunn

James D. G. Dunn is the last interpreter of Paul to whom we draw attention. Perhaps more than any of those whose readings of Paul are described above, Dunn has attempted to bring Jewish tradition into direct conversation with what he says about Paul. This is true in particular when it comes to his view of "the works of the law" which in several publications he regards as an expression that had currency amongst Jews in relation to practices that set them apart from Gentiles.[34] What, however, of the function of Jewish apocalyptic thought in the way Dunn reads Paul? Of the several areas he covers, it is in the sixth chapter of his *Theology of Paul the Apostle* entitled "The Process of Salvation" that his discussion of the two ages in Judaism and Paul's thought is most explicit.[35] The chapter opens with a sub-chapter (paragraph 18), the title of which – "The eschatological tension" –

---

of Paul, pp. 111–123 (here p. 123); *Galatians: A New Translation with Introduction and Commentary*, pp. 97–105.

[33] For a sensitive treatment of eschatology in Paul that largely adheres to Martyn's reading, see Martinus C. de Boer, "Paul and Apocalyptic Eschatology", in ed. John J. Collins, *The Encyclopedia of Apocalypticism. Volume 1: The Origins of Apocalypticism in Judaism and Christianity* (New York/London: Continuum, 2000), pp. 345–383. See also the earlier essay by Richard Sturm, "Defining the Word 'Apocalyptic': A Problem in Biblical Criticism", in eds. Joel Marcus and Marion L. Soards (JSNTSup 24; Sheffield: JSOT Press, 1989), pp. 17–48.

[34] See, e.g., Dunn, *Romans 1–8* (WBC 38A; Dallas, Texas: Word Books, 1988), pp. 183–194 (on Rom. 3:27–31) and *idem, The Theology of Paul*, pp. 354–379.

[35] *The Theology of Paul the Apostle*, pp. 461–498.

sums up the particular emphasis in Paul's modification of Jewish apocalyptic theology.[36]

Before we address what Dunn identifies as the Jewish tradition behind Paul, it is helpful first to observe that it is more the context of Pauline scholarship that immediately determines the position Dunn articulates rather than his engagement with the Second Temple Jewish literature itself. Over against readers for whom Pauline "justification by faith" translates into God's gracious, unmerited pronouncement of "righteousness" upon individuals,[37] Dunn stresses that soteriology, rather than being a given, denotes a lifetime *process* in which persons of faith negotiate between the power of the Spirit in their lives and the inevitable failures and sufferings that will always accompany them. This "eschatological tension" is known not just by anyone, but is emblazoned on the consciousness of believers whose participation in the power of the gospel exposes the problems that beset the human being in this age. Now Dunn presupposes, along with most interpreters of Paul, a Jewish schema of two ages in relation to which the particularity of the apostle's thought can be understood. Dunn takes for granted the view that Paul has modified this schema by noting a provisional transition from the present age to the age to come in the *parousia* of Christ; being "in Christ" is language that describes the position of believers who participate in this transition. This existence in a new state of being is not, however, what makes Paul different. The realism of Paul's view of life did not permit him to indulge in the "already" of the Christ event (in contrast, for example, to the "strong" in Corinth). Neither could Paul retain an eschatology that he had espoused before his apostolic call:

> ... the distinctive feature of Paul's theology ... is *not* the eschatology, but the *tension* which his revised eschatology sets up. Eschatological hope was a common feature of Paul's religious heritage. But an eschatology split in this way between such a decisive "already" and yet still a "not yet" was a new departure. ... Paul's gospel was eschatological not because of what he still hoped would happen, but because of what he believed had already happened.[38]

The old and new ages overlap. The old, present aeon extends from Adam until the age to come; during this time death, sin, and suffering remain undeniable realities. The new, future aeon is no longer entirely consigned to the future (as in Jewish tradition), but has had its beginning in Christ (especially his resurrection) in such a definitive way that the future reality of judgment is guaranteed. The resulting overlap is the time in-between; that is, it defines life "in Christ" and extends from the Christ event until the eschatological judgment that inaugurates the creation of a new cosmos.

---

[36] This is illustrated by Dunn's charts in *The Theology of Paul the Apostle*, pp. 464–465 and p. 475.

[37] See, e. g., Peter Stuhlmacher, *Paul's Letter to the Romans*, trans. Scott J. Hafemann (Louisville: Westminster John Knox, 1994), pp. 114–116, to which Dunn responds in *The Theology of Paul the Apostle*, pp. 474–475 ns. 62–63.

[38] *The Theology of Paul the Apostle*, p. 465.

Dunn's understanding of the way Jewish apocalyptic influenced and was modified by Paul exemplifies what, for all their different emphases, is also true for the other interpreters we have considered here. Taking as the point of departure his conviction about God's defining act in the death and resurrection of Jesus, the apostle is considered to have radically modified the notion of two successive ages. This modification represents not only Paul's particular contribution to early theologies that were emerging among followers of and adherents to Jesus, but is also an innovation that is specifically "Christian" and, by implication, is unimaginable for Second Temple Jewish apocalyptic tradition. The point here is not to determine which of the construals reviewed above is the more probable way to take account of Paul's thought. Instead, the task here is to reflect on whether or not a myopic focus on Pauline theology has resulted in a reductionistic reading of what some Jewish writers could articulate about the impact of God's past activity in creation on space and time of the present age as well as on the imminent yet essentially different age to come. If we recognise the obvious specificity surrounding claims made about the significance of the Christ event, would one be correct to infer that Jewish tradition could *not* have envisaged definitive activity against evil in the past on the part of Israel's God that, at the same time, functions as a guarantee of divine triumph in the future?

3. Models of Eschatology in Second Temple "Apocalyptic" Thought

Thus far the present discussion has indulged in using the term "apocalyptic" rather casually. This is in large part due to the frequently imprecise application of the word by the Pauline scholars we have reviewed. It is impossible within the space of this contribution to sketch in detail how problematic this expression has been for those attempting to offer a definition, not only in relation to a purported literary genre called "apocalypse" but also with regard to the adjective "apocalyptic" itself.[39] A very brief overview, however, can help us locate just where the problem lies with simplistic paradigms such as the two-age scheme attributed to Jewish traditions, which were both antecedent and contemporary to the time of Paul.

As is well known, much of the scholarly discussion of an apocalyptic world-view (as well as of "apocalypse" as a literary genre) was dominated during the 19th and 20th centuries by a model oriented around the future, conceived as divine judgment

---

[39] After his thorough review of 20th century scholarship on Paul, Matlock joins a chorus of those who question the casual use of "apocalyptic" and counsel, where possible, against the use of the term at all; so Matlock, *Unveiling the Apocalyptic Paul*, pp. 247–316. The critique, however justified, draws us to focus more specifically on literature and texts that contain terms which, whether as verbs or substantives, communicate something about divine "disclosure" or "revelation" to humanity.

that will eradicate irresolvable evils in the present world.[40] This understanding of apocalyptic thought has served New Testament scholarship as a convenient way not only to describe, for example, theological accents in the historical Jesus that mark a shift away from Judaism (so, especially in the thought of C. H. Dodd[41]) but also – as we have seen here – to identify and elaborate on distinctive features of Paul's thought. As we have noted among the scholars reviewed above, comparison with borrowings from Jewish tradition (sometimes simplistically received) both helped explain Pauline ideas as they are and have encouraged attempts to describe what marks them out as distinctive. In relation to Jesus, some scholars have found a two-age framework to provide a platform for understanding Jesus within a "thoroughgoing eschatology" (in contrast, e. g., to Dodd), a view that amounts to an attempt to take Jesus' place within apocalyptic Jewish ideology (as one who focused on the future) seriously.[42] For other scholars, it is in Jesus' activity, both in how the Synoptic Gospels present him and perhaps even in the way Jesus understood himself, that God's rule is seen as breaking into this world in a definitive way, a moment after which "history" could no longer be the same.[43] If

---

[40] Such a framework assumed a certain prominence of ways to read works such as Daniel, John's Apocalypse, 4 Ezra and 2 Baruch. However, it remains uncertain whether each of these writings can be pressed into this scheme in a simplistic way. For a recent sensitive consideration of vocabulary regarding time in *2 Baruch*, see Henze, *Jewish Apocalypticism in Late First Century Israel*, esp. pp. 253–320, who concludes, "… the past that is remembered in *2Bar* is not simply the paradigmatic past that becomes the basis for mapping out the utopian future, as if the *eschaton* meant a return to the idealized origins. The past is the time when the *eschaton* began – by remembering the past, Baruch remembers the future" (pp. 318–319).

[41] See Charles H. Dodd, *The Parables of the Kingdom* (London: Nisbet, 1936, 3rd ed.); *Apostolic Preaching and its Developments* (London: Hodder and Stoughton, 1936); and *History and the Gospel* (London: Hodder and Stoughton, 1964, revd. from 1938).

[42] So the well-known work of Albert Schweitzer, *The Quest of the Historical Jesus: From Reimarus to Wrede*, translated by W. Montgomery (London: Black, 1954, 3rd ed.). For a more recent take-up of this perspective, see Dale C. Allison, "A Plea for Thoroughgoing Eschatology", *JBL* 113 (1994), pp. 651–668 and *Jesus of Nazareth: Millenarian Prophet* (Minneapolis: Fortress Press, 1998), whose argument is formulated against the "unapocalyptic" reconstruction of Jesus put forth by members contributing to the Jesus Seminar (esp. Marcus Borg, John Dominic Crossan and Burton Mack); on the latter, see Robert W. Funk and Roy W. Hoover, *The Five Gospels: The Search for the Authentic Words of Jesus* (New York and Toronto: Macmillan, 1993), pp. 34 38 and 137.

[43] See, e. g., Charles H. Dodd, in addition to the works mentioned in n. 41, in *The Founder of Christianity* (New York: Macmillan, 1970); cf. further Norman Perrin, *Jesus and the Language of the Kingdom: Symbol and Metaphor in New Testament Interpretation* (Philadelphia: Fortress Press, 1976), p. 204; James D. G. Dunn, *Jesus and the Spirit: A Study of the Religious and Charismatic Experience of Jesus and the First Christians as Reflected in the New Testament* (London: SCM Press, 1975), pp. 41–67 and idem, *Christianity in the Making, Volume I: Jesus Remembered* (Grand Rapids: Eerdmans, 2003), pp. 478–484; and Thomas P. Rausch, *Who Is Jesus? An Introduction to Christology* (Collegeville, Minnesota: Liturgical Press, 2003), pp. 77–93. – A similar move is frequently made to underscore the distinctiveness of Pauline theology. Influential advocates of such an understanding of Paul have included Werner Kümmel, "Paulus", in idem, *Heilsgeschehen und Geschichte: Gesammelte Aufsätze 1933–1964* (Marburg: Elwert, 1965), pp. 439–456; Ernst Käsemann, e. g. in *Commentary on Romans*, trans. by Geoffrey W. Bromiley (Grand Rapids: Eerdmans, 1980), pp. 139–159 (on

we shift the focus to Paul, the Christ event marks God's breaking into the confines of history to alter perception of reality at a fundamental level.

Scholarship has, of course, observed the shortcomings of a one-dimensional future orientation of Jewish apocalyptic thought, especially since the earliest recoverable apocalypses seem just as interested in a spatial understanding of the world made possible through revealed knowledge and in the disclosure of esoteric wisdom as in the anticipated transformation of the present into a future cosmos.[44] Along the lines of esoteric revelation, the advent of Jesus, including his death, could make certain sense for Paul (cf. Rom. 3:21–26; 1 Cor. 1:18–2:16).

While the sapiential and cosmological dimensions of apocalyptic thought have enriched the way some have reflected theologically on the significance and impact of the Christ event, the temporal framework within Jewish tradition has not received adequate attention, specifically as it relates to what Pauline theologies have assumed about it. Beyond contrasting present and future reality, some writers of apocalyptic texts demonstrated a concern with divine activity as a constant that shaped the unfolding story of Israel as a way of understanding and posing questions about the present.[45] Furthermore, an influential way of understanding the temporal dimension of apocalyptic thought has been the correspondence found in some of the writings between *Urzeit* and *Endzeit*, a framework construed as a means to reinforce eschatology[46]: here various moments out of the primordial past

---

Rom. 5:12–21); Johan C. Beker, *Paul the Apostle: The Triumph of God in Life and Thought* (Edinburgh: T. & T. Clark, 1989); and James D. G. Dunn, e. g. in *Jesus and the Spirit*, p. 308 ("[t]he most characteristic feature of Christian experience") and *The Theology of St. Paul the Apostle* (Grand Rapids: Eerdmans, 1998), pp. 461–498 (esp. pp. 462–477); cf. recently Thomas R. Schreiner, *New Testament Theology: Magnifying God in Christ* (Grand Rapids: Baker, 2008).

[44] So the often repeated definition by John J. Collins, "Introduction: Towards the Morphology of a Genre", in ed. *idem*, *Apocalypse: The Morphology of a Genre* (Semeia 14; Missoula, Montana: Scholars Press, 1979), pp. 1–19 (here p. 9) and *The Apocalyptic Imagination* (Grand Rapids and Cambridge: Eerdmans, 1998), pp. 2–11, esp. pp. 4–9. Here, the critique by Christopher Rowland of the one-dimensionally eschatological reading of Jewish apocalyptic literature, if somewhat one-sided, remains valuable; see idem, *The Open Heaven: A Study of Apocalyptic in Judaism and Early Christianity* (New York: Crossroad, 1982), pp. 9–72. The disclosure of esoteric wisdom as emphasized by Rowland has not gone lost, for example, on de Boer, "Paul and Apocalyptic Eschatology", pp. 352–354 (with several points of critique) and Matlock, *Unveiling the Apocalyptic Paul*, esp. pp. 258–262 and 282–287.

[45] So esp. the so-called "historical apocalypses" (*Animal Apocalypse* of *1 En.* 85–90; *Apocalypse of Weeks*, *1 En.* 93:1–10 and 91:11–17; *4 Ezra*, cf. ch. 14). This perspective is underscored by Nicholas T. Wright, *The Climax of the Covenant: Christ and the Law in Pauline Theology* (Edinburgh: T & T Clark, 1991), for whom the Sin-Exile-Return framework enables a reading that regards Paul's gospel as formulated to exhort Israel to return from a present state of being in "spiritual exile". Wright handles Jesus tradition similarly in *Jesus and the Victory of God* (London: SPCK, 1996), esp. pp. 193–197 and 226–229; referring to Jesus' logion in Lk. 11:20/Mt. 12:28 ("if by the finger of God I cast out demons, then the kingdom of God has come upon you"), Wright concludes that Jesus' exorcisms are "clear signs" that the God of Israel is beginning to defeat the enemy that has "held Israel captive" (here, p. 228).

[46] The most important 3rd and 2nd century B. C. E. documents which draw on this correspondence between beginning and end include the Enochic *Book of Watchers* (*1 En.* 1–36), the *Dream*

served as a repository of images, symbols and motifs that helped apocalyptic writers to imagine the future. Paradisical existence, once lost, will be restored (Rev. 2:7); a messianic "white bull" concludes a story that began with an Adamic "white bull" (Animal Apocalypse, *1 En.* 85 and 90; cf. Rom. 5:12–21); eschatological judgment draws on imagery from the Great Flood (*1 En.* 10; 84; 91; 106–107); and Noah's rescue prefigures the salvation of God's people at the end of history.

A basis for a reconfiguring of primordial images, however, is not all that the sacred past has to offer. And so, *within the framework of temporality, there is another emphasis that has been neglected, not only by New Testament scholars but also by specialists in ancient Jewish apocalyptic literature.*[47] In addition to helping to describe deteriorating conditions in the world and how the God of Israel will inaugurate a new age, language about the *Urzeit* also functioned to provide *a basis for being confident about such an outcome*: God's definitive activity is not only a matter for the future; rather, it is God's invasive presence to defeat evil *in the past* (e. g., at the time of the Great Flood) that guarantees its annihilation in the future (*1 En.* 10; 15–16; 91:5–10; 106:13–107:1; *Jub.* 5–10; *Book of Giants* at 4Q530 2 ii + 6–12 (?), lines 4–20). Thus, in essence, evil, however rampant and overwhelming in the present age, *is but a defeated power whose time is marked*. Divine victory in the sacred past could even be understood as an expression of God's royal power (*1 En.* 84:2–6; *Book of Giants* at 4Q203 9 and 10; cf. the angels' address of God as "king of kings" in *1 En.* 9). Since God's rule has asserted itself in the cosmos on a global scale (e. g., through the Great Flood or, so Exod. 15, in the Song of the Red Sea that celebrates the rescue of Israel from inimical destruction), the "present era" is then a time when those who are pious can proceed with some confidence in dealing with the effects of demonic power, knowing that although it cannot be gotten rid of altogether before the ultimate end of things, it is nevertheless possible to address, curtail or manage its effects. This understanding of sacred past and imminent future was not simply a matter of charting how time works; it was a way of defining what it means to be God's people in the present and it could manifest itself in terms of a theological anthropology that negotiated the relentless uncertainties of life with the certainty of victory under the covenant. In its influential retelling of the story from creation until the Israelites' freedom from bondage in

---

Visions (*1 En.* 83–84 and 85–90), *Apocalypse of Weeks* (*1 En.* 93:1–10 and 91:11–17), *Exhortation* (*1 En.* 91:1–10, 18–19), *Birth of Noah* (*1 En.* 106–107), *Book of Parables* (*1 En.* 37–71 though of later date), *Book of Giants* and *Jubilees*. Except for the Similitudes, the impact of the perspectives upheld by these works in Second Temple literature (including writings among the Dead Sea Scrolls and Jewish literature composed in Greek) was significant.

[47] For an excellent overview of recent scholarship on Jewish "apocalyptic" thought and literature and its implications for New Testament scholarship, see Jörg Frey, "Die Apokalyptik als Herausforderung der neutestamentlichen Wissenschaft. Zum Problem: Jesus und die Apokalyptik", in eds. Michael Becker and Markus Öhler, *Apokalyptik als Herausforderung neutestamentlicher Theologie* (WUNT 2.214; Tübingen: Mohr Siebeck, 2006), pp. 23–94, though Frey does not press towards the emphasis of the present discussion.

Egypt, the *Book of Jubilees*, composed during around the middle of the 2nd century
B.C.E., describes the condition of humankind after their rescue from the Great
Flood. Here (so *Jub.* 5:12) God is said to have given human beings a new and
righteous nature, in order that with their whole being they never again sin and
live righteously. The remaining narrative of the book confirms time and again
that sinning among Jews does take place and that forces of evil continue to be
effective among God's people. However, both this new nature and the defeated
condition of demonic powers (*Jub.* 10) continue to be manifest in the story; they
anticipate the final result, namely, the destruction of all evil and with it, the fulfilment of God's original design for those who are among the elect.

The "already" principle of evil's defeat and the "not yet" of its manifest destruction was an existing framework that Paul could take for granted. Though the overlap between the present and future age is occasioned for Paul by a recent break-
through in history, we would not be mistaken to think that there were pious Jews
who understood themselves as living in an eschatological tension, inspired by confidence of concrete moments of divine activity in the past and present. *It is simply
misleading, if not wrong, to infer, with several Pauline scholars, that such religiosity is
merely the domain of early adherents of Jesus, not least Paul.*

One storyline that guaranteed the establishment of God's eschatological rule in
the cosmos has been briefly mentioned above. Motifs traceable to the Great Flood
are discernible, for example, in references to the "bastard" spirits in the Dead Sea
materials (so 4Q510 1.4–8 par. 4Q511 10.1–6); these *mamzerim*, spirits that were
thought to have emanated from the giants whose physical bodies had been
destroyed in the Flood (cf. *1 En.* 10:9), are powers of the present age. The present
age in which they are thought to be operative is described in the *Songs of the Maskil*
as follows:

> ... *a time of the dominion [of] wickedness* and in *the eras of the humiliation of the sons of lig[ht]*
> in the guilt of *the times of those plagued by iniquities*, not for an eternal destruction, [but] for
> the era of the humiliation of transgression (4Q510 1.6b–7 par. 4Q511 10.4–5)

In the document, it is by declaring the splendor of God's radiance and in the accla-
mation of God's power that the activities of a catalogue of malevolent forces can be
curbed. The *Maskil*'s declarations about God, told in the third person, are here
regarded as sufficiently potent to diminish or counteract demonic powers which are
at work in the present order of things. Although the text does not furnish a prayer
for divine protection against these demons, it does work within a framework that
holds two concurrent things in tension: (a) the existence of a community of those
who are unambiguously "righteous" and "upright", and (b) the characterization of
the present age as "a time of the dominion [of] wickedness" (בקץ ממשל[ת] / רשעה).
The *Maskil*'s song about God, addressed to those whom the writer considers to be
righteous, functions in itself as an expedient measure that neutralizes threats associated with demonic powers until the present age of wickedness is brought to an end.

This is, of course, not the only way powers in the present age are dealt with. In some of the more explicitly community-orientated and *Yaḥad* texts, curses are pronounced again against a chief angel (cf. *4QBerakoh* at 4Q286 7 ii 3, 7) and Belial (*Serekh ha-Yaḥad* at 1QS i 16–iii 12; cf. *Serekh ha-Milḥamah* at 1QM xiv 9–10 par. 4Q491=4QMᵃ 8–10 i 6–7 and *4QCatena A* at 4Q177 3.8). In other words, the chief power is cursed, not exorcised. The pronouncements against Belial and his lot bring together and merge several evolving features that in their specificity are partly lost, yet whose conceptual framework is preserved within a new form. The eschatological framework found in earlier Enochic pronouncements of doom against the fallen angels, exorcisms (11Q11, 4Q560) and hymns of protection, is retained in the community's treatment of a chief figure at the top. In the *Serekh ha-Yaḥad*, curses against Belial adapt language from the Aaronic blessing (Num. 6:24–27) and should be understood in relation to the larger context of covenant blessings and curses found in Deuteronomy (cf. Deut. 28–30). If we may read the liturgy near the beginning of 1QS in tandem with the hymn at the end (1QS x–xi), the way of dealing with Belial presupposes the community's present communion in the present with "the sons of heaven" (cf. 1QS xi 6–8); already in "the council of the flesh" God has granted them a participation in an eternal possession. Traditions that are pivotal in receiving Enochic tradition and paving the way for the *Yaḥad*'s way of dealing with Belial may be seen not only in the *Songs of the Maskil*, as we have just seen, but also in *Jubilees*. The *Book of Jubilees* presents demonic activity under the leadership of Mastema as an inevitable characteristic of this age until the final judgment (ch. 10). Thus, in *Jubilees* not only do angels reveal remedies to Noah (and his progeny) for the warding off or neutralizing the effects of evil spirits (*Jub.* 10:10–13), but also the patriarchs – Moses (1:19–20), Noah (10:1–6), and Abraham (12:19–20) – are made to utter potent prayers of deliverance against them (cf. also 11Q5 xix). There is no formal denunciation or curse against any of the malevolent powers. The Torah both frames and takes its place among these means of guiding Jewish communities along the paths of faithful obedience in anticipation of an end whose outcome is already known. The present is shaped by both an eschatological past and a future that loops back as an *inclusio* to bring God's activity in history to its proper end.

4. Conclusion

In sketching briefly the eschatological tension discernible among some of the Dead Sea Scrolls and related literature as they relate to malevolent powers, we have not come upon traditions that can, I think, be simplistically said to have influenced Paul directly. However, we are, in fact, dealing with traditions that run counter to the impression a number of Pauline theologians, who, in all their enthusiasm to recover the theological genius of Paul, leave their readers to infer about apocalyptic

Jewish thought. Significantly, demonic powers, however conceived (i. e., whether they are a group or groups of "spirits" or a chief demonic being at the top), are not thought to be destroyed so much as they can be managed by pious Jews who already could understand themselves as living in a time between God's proleptic establishment of control over evil and the effective defeat of it at the end. To be sure, the Christ event was a *novum*; but was it one that, in terms of religious history, broke through to an understanding of time that had not previously existed in Jewish tradition? What I have attempted to describe suggests that Paul's way of interpreting the significance of Jesus in time was not a flight from Jewish apocalyptic tradition. It was rooted less in an attempt to correct a Jewish apocalyptic idea of the "two ages" than it was indebted to the theological tensions known to and experienced by pious Jews as they negotiated convictions about the past with their expectations of the future.

Chapter Thirteen

Why Should Women Cover Their Heads Because of the Angels?
(1 Corinthians 11:10)

A. Introduction

The interpretation of 1 Corinthians 11:2–16 remains one of the more baffling problems of exegesis for contemporary scholars, clergy and laity. Not least problematic has been the view of some that this passage seems to represent a contradiction within Paul's thought. Whereas this passage presupposes that there are women in Corinth who pray and prophesy aloud during worship (11:5),[1] Paul admonishes in the same letter at 14:34 that "women should be silent in the churches". This possible contradiction is exacerbated by the fact that in both passages Paul appeals beyond his own views to common practice among the churches: On the one hand, concerning the suggestion that women should not cover their heads, he states, "we have no such custom, and neither do the churches of God" (11:16) while, on the other hand, concerning the silence of women, he emphasizes that "as in all the churches of God, let women be silent in the churches" (14:34).[2]

Thus, whatever one makes of 1 Corinthians 11:2–16, the problem, how Paul's statements fit into the literary context of the letter as a whole, is difficult to ignore. This is also true of smaller bits of the passage. Although different points are raised by Paul that seek to convince readers about the merits of women wearing head coverings in worship, it is not always clear how these are interrelated or, accordingly, to what extent they comprise an overarching coherent argument. This is nowhere more true than in 11:10. While the dictum of interpreting within the literary context may seem rather axiomatic, it is a point that bears mention here: in relation to 11:2–16, the reference to angels does not, at first glance, seem to add very much to Paul's reasons about women having long hair or wearing head cover-

---

[1] The text: "And every woman who prays or prophesies with the head uncovered shames her head."

[2] It should be noted that the practices referred to in both passages are different. The appeal to common practice in 1 Cor. 14 is more directly concerned with silencing women from speaking in "the churches", whereas in 1 Cor. 11 the reference to custom among congregations has to do with whether or not women wear veils or head coverings. This recognition of different contexts of argument might initially seem to be a plausible way of resolving the contradiction. However, the prophesying of women, which is taken for granted in 11:5, is excluded in 14:34. Thus, unless one adopts a text- or source-critical solution, one should not be too quick in attempting to resolve the material incongruity between the texts.

ings. Indeed, were the phrase διὰ τοὺς ἀγγέλους ("because of the angels") in 11:10b to be omitted from the text, the argument would proceed smoothly from 11:10a to 11:11–12 without anything being missed. Nevertheless, in view of the fact that "angels" are given as one reason among others within a passage replete with problems for interpretation, it is initially appropriate to consider two aspects of 11:2– 16: first, the discussion below will look at several interpretive difficulties in order to draw some preliminary decisions that provide a profile for an exegetical approach; second, the present discussion will contextualize 11:10 by drawing brief attention to other reasons assembled by Paul in support of his insistence that women, while they pray or prophesy, adjust their appearance as it relates to the head.

B. Problem Areas for Interpretation

B.1. Inconsistency

This logical tension between 1 Corinthians 11:2/3–16 and 14:33b–36 is resolved by a number of exegetes who argue that one or the other passage is an interpolation.[3] With respect to 11:2/3–16 in particular, such a later insertion is supposed to have been carried through by either Paul himself (Earle Ellis[4]) or by a pseudo-Pauline disciple (see Alfred Loisy,[5] William O. Walker,[6] Lamar Cope[7] and Garry W.

---

[3] More than in the case of 11:2–16, a number of scholars treat 14:33b–36 as a post-Pauline gloss, despite the absence of text-critical evidence to the contrary; so esp. Johannes Leipholdt, *Die Frau in der antiken Welt und im Urchristentum* (Gütersloh: Gerd Mohn, 1962), pp. 125–126; Charles Kingsley Barrett, *A Commentary on the First Epistle to the Corinthians* (New York: Harper and Row, 1968), pp. 330–333; Robin Scroggs, *The Text and the Times. New Testament Essays for Today* (Minneapolis: Fortress Press, 1993), p. 71; Gerhard Dautzenberg, *Urchristliche Prophetie: Ihre Erforschung, ihre Voraussetzung im Judentum und ihre Struktur im ersten Korintherbrief* (Stuttgart: Kohlhammer, 1975), pp. 257–273, and "Zur Stellung der Frauen in den paulinischen Gemeinden", in eds. Gerhard Dautzenberg, Helmut Merklein and Karlheinz Müller, *Die Frau im Urchristentum* (Quaestiones Disputatae 25; Freiburg im Breisgau: Herder, 1983), pp. 182–224. In addition to the contradiction between this passage and 11:2–16, further considerations have been identified: (a) 14:33b–36 intrudes into the context of 1 Corinthians 14 which is concerned with regulating prophetic activity; (b) the appeal in 14:34 to the law as the authoritarian basis for behavior is difficult to reconcile with Paul; and (c) its content is congruent with that of the deutero-Pauline 1 Tim 2:11–12 ("Let a woman learn in quiet [and] in all submission; that is [δε] I do not permit a woman to teach or to have authority over a man, but to be in quiet.").

[4] Earle E. Ellis, "Traditions in 1 Corinthians: For Martin Hengel on His Sixtieth Birthday", *NTS* 32 (1986), pp. 492–494: Paul himself or through instruction has inserted an "oral or written" tradition (i. e., 1 Cor. 11:2–16) "into an initial secretarial draft or into the completed roll or codex before the letter was sent to Corinth."

[5] Alfred Loisy, *Remarques sur la littérature épistolaire du Nouveau Testament* (Paris: Nourry, 1935), pp. 60–62: 1 Cor. 11:3–16 interrupts the flow of Paul's argument between 11:2 and 11:17 and, therefore, must have been added by another hand.

[6] Walker posits an insertion of 11:3–16, which was a combination of three post-Pauline sources; see William O. Walker, "1 Corinthians 11.2–16 and Paul's Views Regarding Women", *JBL* 94 (1975), pp. 94–110; "The 'Theology of Woman's Place' and the 'Paulinist' Tradition",

Trompf[8]). It is true that 11:17 ("In instructing you in this, I do not praise you") can be read as if following immediately upon 11:2 ("I praise you because you remember me in every way and [because] you hold fast to the traditions just as I transmitted [them] to you."). This solution, however, does not have any external (that is, text- or source-critical) evidence to support it.[9] Moreover, it is possible in my opinion to explore seriously the ways in which 11:2–16 presupposes or reflects content in the remainder of the epistle, a possibility which is not so easy in the case of 14:33b–36.[10]

B.2. Incomplete Knowledge about the Corinthian Situation

The passage 11:2–16 raises another, more general, exegetical difficulty: If one takes for granted that it stems from the apostle, what is the relationship between what Paul states and what was actually going on in the church at Corinth? This issue raises further questions: What can be said about the particular situation with which Paul is concerned? What did Paul know about what was happening in Corinth and how did he find out? Can one assume that what was reported to Paul, whether orally or through a letter from Corinth, accurately reflected the situation

---

Sem 28 (1983), pp. 101–112; "The Vocabulary of 1 Corinthians 11.3–16: Pauline or Non-Pauline?", *JSNT* 35 (1989), pp. 75–88 and esp. pp. 83–84, n.3.

[7] Lamar Cope, "1 Cor 11,2–16: One Step Further", *JBL* 97 (1978), pp. 435–436. Unlike Walker, Cope attributes 11:2 to Paul.

[8] Garry W. Trompf, "On Attitudes toward Women in Paul and Paulinist Literature: 1 Cor 11:3–16 and Its Context", *CBQ* 42 (1980), pp. 196–215.

[9] See the convincing arguments against the hypothesis by Walker in Jerome Murphy-O'Connor, "The Non-Pauline Character of 1 Cor 11,2–16?", *JBL* 95 (1976), pp. 615–621, and "Sex and Logic in 1 Corinthians 11:2–16", *CBQ* 42 (1980), pp. 482–500.

[10] The consideration of 14:33b–36 as a marginal note added by Paul between the initial draft and the sending of the letter has been suggested by Earle E. Ellis, "The Silenced Wives of Corinth (1 Cor 14,34–5)", in eds. Eldon J. Epp and Gordon D. Fee, *New Testament Textual Criticism: Its Significance for Exegesis,* (Oxford: Clarendon Press, 1981), pp. 213–220, followed by Stephen C. Barton, in "Paul's Sense of Place: An Anthropological Approach to Community Formation in Corinth", *NTS* 32 (1986), pp. 225–246. In support of the Pauline origin of the passage, Barton appeals to a coherence between 14:33b–36 and other parts of 1 Corinthians in the following areas: (a) the appeal to what the law says (14:34; see 9:8–9 and 14:21) and (b) the appeal to a distinction between private (οἶκος, "house") and public (ἐκκλησία, "assembly") in correcting behavior (14:35; see 11:17–34). However, Barton goes on to explain the incongruity of the "shame" of a woman speaking in the ἐκκλησία with 11:2–16 by stating that, unlike the former, the latter passage is concerned with "divinely inspired" speech (p. 231). The excellence of Barton's discussion aside, his explanation is unsatisfactory for the reason that, in a context in which Paul is concerned with prophecy, the writer of the text shows no attempt to qualify the categorical silence enjoined upon women. Likewise unsatisfactory is the attempt to reconcile 14:34–35 with the rest of 1 Corinthians by Elisabeth Schüssler-Fiorenza, *In Memory of Her: A Feminist Theological Reconstruction of Christian Origins* (London: SCM Press, 1983), pp. 228–229, who argues that 14:34–36 refers specifically to wives, while 11:2–16 is concerned with the activities of "pneumatic" women who can be devoted to the affairs of the Lord (see 7:32–35). Again, the text itself in 14:34–36 presupposes no such distinction.

there, so that historical judgments on the Corinthian situation should be cautious about assuming too much? Finally, how much of the passage reflects practices in Corinth, so that every statement of Paul may be mirror-read into similar or opposite opinions at Corinth,[11] and how much of it represents a persuasive sort of rhetoric which seeks to undermine views not yet held among those being addressed?[12] While hardly anyone today disputes that a situation at Corinth lies behind the multilayered arguments concerning the need for women to wear head coverings or to have long hair, one still may wish to consider just *which* of Paul's statements on this matter reflects the Corinthian context to which Paul was responding.[13]

B.3. Background in Contemporary Social Customs

A further obstacle to understanding the passage has received considerable attention, namely, the extent to which Paul's position and the position he seeks to correct (even in relation to angels) reflect contemporary social practices and tradition-historical sources from Jewish and classical antiquity as they relate to conventions among males and females with regard to the cutting of hair, hair styles and head

---

[11] For readings that tend to reflect this approach, see those of Antoinette Clark Wire, *The Corinthian Women Prophets: A Reconstruction through Paul's Rhetoric* (Minneapolis: Fortress Press, 1990), pp. 116–134; and Lee Ann Jervis, "'But I Want You to Know…' Paul's Midrashic Intertextual Response to the Corinthian Worshipers (1 Cor 11:2–16)", *JBL* 112 (1993), pp. 231–246.

[12] Unlike other sections of the epistle, 11:2–16 is not introduced by the phrase περὶ δὲ (*peri de*, "therefore") as in 7:1, 25; 8:1; 12:1; although this phrase, on the basis of 7:1, has been taken as an indicator that Paul is responding to problems he has learned about through written correspondence, the absence thereof does not, conversely, mean that Paul has therefore gleaned his *information* about the situation orally. See esp. Margaret M. Mitchell, *Paul and the Rhetoric of Reconciliation: An Exegetical Investigation of the Language and Composition of 1 Corinthians* (HUT 28; Tübingen: Mohr Siebeck, 1991), p. 261 and n. 214; and Ben Witherington, *Conflict and Community in Corinth: A Socio-Rhetorical Commentary on 1 and 2 Corinthians* (Grand Rapids: Eerdmans, 1995), p. 231.

[13] This matter is in part exemplified by Paul's statements about men. A number of interpreters have argued that Paul's reference in 11:4 to men who pray or prophesy with their heads covered is merely a hypothetical problem, meaning that it is a rhetorical construct marshaled in support of Paul's criticism of women who pray or prophesy without head coverings; so esp. Johannes Weiss, *Der erste Korintherbrief* (KEK 5; Göttingen: Vandenhoeck & Ruprecht, 1910, 9th ed.), p. 271; Archibald Robertson and Alfred Plummer, *A Critical and Exegetical Commentary on the First Epistle of St Paul to the Corinthians* (ICC; Edinburgh: T & T Clark, 1914, 2nd ed.), p. 229; Frederick F. Bruce, *1 and 2 Corinthians* (London: Butler and Tanner, 1971), p. 104; and Gordon D. Fee, *The First Epistle to the Corinthians* (Grand Rapids: Eerdmans, 1987), pp. 507–508. For a contrasting view, see esp. Richard F. Oster, "When Men Wore Veils to Worship: The Historical Context of 1 Corinthians 11.4", *NTS* 34 (1988), pp. 481–505 (esp. pp. 483–484 and 505) and "Use, Misuse, and Neglect of Archaeological Evidence", *ZNW* 72 (1990), pp. 52–73 (esp. pp. 67–69). With respect to women, most scholars have assumed that Paul is dealing with a real problem in the Corinthian congregation; however, see Susan T. Foh, *Women and the Word of God: A Response to Biblical Feminism* (Grand Rapids: Baker Academic, 1979), p. 106: "The possibility that 1 Corinthians 11.2–16 was not intended to correct an actual wrong must be noted."

coverings. Can any satisfactory "fit" be found between what Paul commends to the Corinthians and sources that describe practices among various groups in the Mediterranean world? Moreover, is there any straightforward correspondence with biblical tradition, contemporary Jewish interpretation of sacred tradition, and Second Temple literature?

With respect to the Greco-Roman context, attempts to provide some illumination have proven helpful, though perhaps they have invariably run into difficulties. Both the literary and archaeological evidence from Mediterranean antiquity – even when it relates to first-century Corinth – does not produce the sort of "perfect match" that fully clarifies either the statements of Paul or the problem he is purportedly addressing.[14]

Excursus: Head Coverings, Hairstyle, Corinth, and Mediterranean Antiquity

Cynthia L. Thompson's thoroughgoing investigation of excavated marble statues, small clay statuettes and numismatic materials from Corinth, which were produced by different social strata from the 1st century B. C. E. until the mid-2nd century C. E. is difficult to relate to Paul's statements insofar as they pertain to head coverings. If anything, this evidence provides some background to the coiffure of women, namely, Paul's assumption that women should have long hair (11:6) and that such hair, when it is styled on the head, may be appropriately described with the Greek term περιβόλαιον ("wrapping," 11:15).[15] For the notion of head coverings itself, concerning which the archaeological remains of Corinth provide almost no evidence, we have to turn to literary sources. Pausanius (*Descriptions of Greece*, Elis I.20.2–3) notes that priestesses, in the context of singing in the temple of Eileithyia when worshiping the deity Sosipolis, had to cover their heads and faces in a "white veil" (2nd cent. C. E.). According to Apuleius (*Metamorphoses* 11.10), women participating in the cult of Isis near Corinth "had their hair anointed and their heads covered with bright linen, but the men had their crowns shaven and shining bright" (2nd cent. C. E.). It is also known more generally that women, according to Roman custom, were known to have veiled their heads when offering sacrifices (so Varro, *de Lingua Latina* 5.29.130[16]; see also Juvenal, *Saturnalia* 6.390–392), though here one should observe that, in contrast to Paul, these practices were not regarded as ways of distinguishing women from men.[17] Thompson herself concludes that

---

[14] Despite the optimism of Oster, "Veils", pp. 481–505, the earlier remark by Joseph A. Fitzmyer in "A Feature of Qumran Angelology and 1 Cor. 11:10", in *idem, Essays on the Semitic Background of the New Testament* (SBLSBS 5; Missoula, MT: SBL and Scholars Press, 1974), p. 188, n. 1, still holds: "Though many details about the wearing of the veil in antiquity, both by Jewish and Greek women, have been preserved for us, none of them bears directly on the problem of the church in Corinth. We do not know the exact nature nor the origin of the abuse Paul was trying to handle."

[15] Thompson, "Hairstyles, Head coverings, and St. Paul: Portraits from Roman Corinth", *BA* 51 (1988), pp. 99–115, here p. 112. Schüssler-Fiorenza, *In Memory of Her*, p. 227, is surely correct that Paul's reference to hair as a wrapping suggests that he is not concerned in Corinth with a Jewish custom.

[16] Varro's note on the Roman *ritus* avails despite his strained etymological derivation for the term *rita* ("veil"). See further Mary Beard, "The Sexual Status of Vestal Virgins", *Journal of Roman Studies* 70 (1980), pp. 12–27 (here pp. 16 and 21).

[17] See Oster, "Veils."

Apuleius's description of the Isis cult must have referred to a special circumstance rather than to general practice in Roman society, while Plutarch's statements on Roman women going about in public with their hair covered while the men do not (*Roman Questions* 14)[18] are more speculative than derived from strict observation. The correspondence to Paul's view, especially in the case of the Isis and Sosipolis cults, is noteworthy, while the literary witnesses to the disheveled hair of the maenads in the cults of Dionysos, Cybele, the Delphian Pythia, and the Sibyl[19] correspond more, by contrast, to the behavior Paul is criticizing.

At least two points can be learned from this variegated evidence. First, with the possible exception of Plutarch's comments on Roman custom, the use of head coverings in a cultic context does not refer back to or pick up on a general practice; rather, it is function-specific. Thus we are not to imagine that Paul was requiring women to cover their heads in contexts other than when they were praying or prophesying in the context of gathered worship. Second, the custom of abandoning any head coverings in worship as a mark of true prophecy among some contemporary cults (e. g. the maenads mentioned above) may clarify why such a practice could have been adopted among the Corinthians, while the practice described by Apuleius in relation to the Isis cult shows that there could have been a similar precedent for the practice enjoined by Paul. Therefore, just because Paul is addressing a specifically "Christian" context of worship does not mean he would necessarily have wished to distinguish practices of the Corinthian believing community from those known among other religious cults. He is concerned, in the end, with customary practice in an unambiguously religious setting.

More significant (and problematic) is, on the one hand, the distinctive theological reasoning that Paul used to support his view and, on the other hand, the fact that he wished to use this reasoning as a mark of gender distinction. For the latter, and of course in relation to the role of "angels" in Paul's discussion, it becomes necessary to explore the backgrounds in biblical and contemporary Jewish traditions.

B.4. Problematic Terms

If we focus on the translation and interpretation of particular words and phrases, several difficulties arise. First, there is the difficulty of translating the term κεφαλή ("head") in 11:3–5:

... the head of every man is Christ, and the head of the woman is man, and the head of Christ is God. Every man who prays or prophesies while having (a covering) on the head shames [with his head covered dishonors] his head. And every woman who prays or prophesies without covering her head shames [with her head uncovered dishonors] her head.

---

[18] The passage is in Plutarch's *Moralia* 267 A–B. This custom is not in itself the focus of Plutarch's comments. His description of practice, instead, occurs while he inquires as to why, during funerals, sons cover their heads while daughters do not, reasoning that such a custom is intended to contrast from what is usually done in public.

[19] On the conventions associated with these cults, see Richard and Catherine Clark Kroeger, "An Inquiry into Evidence of Maenadism in the Corinthian Congregation", *SBLSP 1978* (2 vols.; Missoula: Scholars Press, 1978), vol. 2, pp. 331–346. See esp. Juvenal, *Saturnalia* 6.314–316.

The word is intended as a metaphor, but in what sense? Does it mean "origin" or "source"?[20] Or does it mean "lordship" or "superiority"? Whichever meaning one chooses, two points should be mentioned at this stage: (1) Paul is using the term to draw a distinction in some sense between God, Christ, male, and female (in *which* sense precisely remains to be seen); in other words, an understanding of its meaning cannot move far away from the notion of social and, indeed, cosmic hierarchy.[21] The next point is (2) that the behavior inferred by Paul on the basis of this term is closely bound up with "glory" (11:8–9,15; see 15:40–41), on the one hand, and with "shame" or "dishonor" (11:4–5,14), on the other. The question, for our purposes, will be to ask against which framework the distinctions of order and of behavior can best be understood.

That Paul is using a pun with respect to κεφαλή is reflected in his literal use of the term in the phrase κατὰ κεφαλῆς ἔχων ("having on the head"): to have on the head means for Paul to honor one's head. Concerning the meaning of "having on the head", however, interpretations are divided. Does the phrase, as used in 11:4, refer to a man who "has *something* [a head covering] on his head", as conventionally understood, or, as Murphy-O'Connor has for example argued, does the expression merely refer to a man who has long hair? By extension, does the term "to be covered" (κατακαλύπτω) allude to a piece of clothing or, again with Murphy-O'Connor, does it denote long hair?[22] The likelihood that Paul's language includes something on the head, rather than simply referring to hair itself, is strengthened by Plutarch's use of the phrase κατὰ κεφαλῆς in a similar way.[23]

I think that Paul's reference to hair "as a wrapper" (ἀντὶ περιβολαίου) in 11:15 is not a straightforward identification of what he is *ultimately* advocating, but should rather be understood *as a comparison*. Since in 11:5–6 Paul can associate being bareheaded with being without covering (ἀκατακάλυπτος), he leaves it to his read-

---

[20] So, early on, Stephen Bedale, "The Meaning of *Kephale* in the Pauline Epistles", *JTS* 5 (1954), pp. 211–215; Bruce, *1 and 2 Corinthians*, p. 103; Barrett, *Commentary on First Corinthians*, p. 248; Scroggs, "Paul and the Eschatological Women", p. 89 and n. 41; Murphy-O'Connor, "Sex and Logic", pp. 491–492. Schüssler-Fiorenza, *In Memory of Her*, p. 229, also adopts this interpretation, while allowing the term to denote a descending hierarchy, though in the sense that "each preceding member ... establishes the other's being."

[21] See esp. Jorunn Økland, *Women in Their Place: Paul and the Corinthian Discourse of Gender and Sanctuary Space* (JSNTSup 269; London: T & T Clark International, 2004), pp. 174–177.

[22] See Murphy-O'Connor, "1 Corinthians 11:2–16 Once Again", *CBQ* 50 (1988), pp. 268–269. Murphy-O'Connor thus translates the phrase ἀντὶ περιβολαίου in 11:15 to mean "as a wrapper" instead of "in place/instead of a wrapper." Moreover, on the basis of 11:6 Murphy-O'Connor regards "being covered" as Paul's way in the passage to denote a woman's long (uncut) hair.

[23] So Witherington, *Conflict and Community in Corinth*, p. 233, who appeals to Plutarch's *Regum* 200F; *Roman Questions* 267C; *Pyrrhus* 399B; *Pompey* 640C; *Caesar* 739D; *Lives of Ten Orators* 842B. However, one should note that these examples include the verb "to have" with an object, usually τὸ ἱμάτιον ("garment" or "piece of clothing"). Hence the importance of the cumulative weight added by the other reasons given here. For a further, though more one-sided argument that Paul is concerned with veiling and not hairstyle, see Annie Jaubert, "La voile des femmes (1 Cor. xi.2–16)", *NTS* 18 (1972), pp. 419–430.

ers to infer that having long hair should, as a matter of course, be accompanied by head covering. Furthermore – and this point should be stressed – a reference on the part of Paul to a piece of clothing seems apparent, since the context of "praying or prophesying" in worship is specified. Paul is not concerned here with how men and women *generally* carry themselves, that is, whether at all times they have short or long hair; thus a hairstyle (that is, styling the hair on the head as a wrapping) for the sake of a public mode of participation in worship would have been less practicable than the use of veils or a symbolic covering of the head, which would have more clearly signaled *the difference of context*. Thus, in both 11:4 and 11:13 the criticisms leveled against men and women being respectively covered ("having on the head", v. 4) and uncovered (v. 13) are *linked to their appearance while "praying"* (and prophesying, v. 4).[24]

Finally, and perhaps most disputed of all, is the question of how to understand the term ἐξουσία ("authority") in 11:10a. Since this term occurs just prior to mention of "the angels," it merits some comment. When the text says that "a woman ought to have ἐξουσία on/over the head," interpretations have been varied; analogous to "having on the κεφαλή," the translation of the phrase with ἐξουσία is not straightforward.

I have to admit that it is difficult to decide among the primary interpretations (both new and traditional); they include the following: (1) The phrase is made to refer to a woman's having "power," "control," or "authority" over her own activity when she prophesies or prays. Paul would thus be admitting that woman has the authority to "prophesy or pray" in the context of worship.[25] Along similar lines, (2) the phrase is related to the woman's "freedom" or "right" to choose to do what she wishes with her head.[26] This interpretation attempts to locate what Paul says here in relation to other parts of 1 Corinthians in which Paul, using ἐξουσία to refer to one's "freedom" or "right," mentions that, theoretically, a man is not under constraint to marry (7:37), that one may eat meat sacrificed to idols (8:9), and that an apostle ought to be supported (9:17–18). Problematic for this explanation is

---

[24] Significantly, only in 1 Cor. 11:4 and 13 is activity in worship (praying and prophesying) specified at all.

[25] In this connection two articles are most often referred to: Morna D. Hooker, "Authority on Her Head: An Examination of 1 Cor. XL10", *NTS* 10 (1963–1964), pp. 410–416; and Werner Foerster, "ἐξουσία", in *TDNT* 2:562–574. See further Barrett, *Commentary on First Corinthians*, p. 255; Jaubert, "La voile des femmes", pp. 428–430; Richard N. Longenecker, *New Testament Social Ethics for Today* (Grand Rapids: Eerdmans, 1984), p. 82. This view for 1 Cor. 11:10a is also what has been advocated by George Brooke, who argues that "customary decorum", whether a veil or braided hair, marks a woman's authority; cf. "Between Qumran and Corinth: Embroidered Allusions to Women's Authority", in ed. James Davila, *The Dead Sea Scrolls as Background to Parabiblical Judaism and Early Christianity* (STDJ 46; Leiden / Boston: Brill, 2003), pp. 157–176 (here p. 171).

[26] See Alan Padget, "Paul on Women in Church: The Contradiction of Coiffure in 1 Cor 11,2–16", *JSNT* 20 (1984), pp. 69–86, esp. p. 78; and Fee, *The First Epistle to the Corinthians*, p. 520.

that "having ἐξουσία over the head" in 11:10 is not a construction that takes this form[27] in the other instances. If either of the two options just mentioned avails here, it remains doubtful that it is the *only* meaning in play. It has to be remembered that Paul regards this ἐξουσία as an "obligation" (he uses the verb ὀφείλω, "ought"), that is, as a constraint rather than simply as a "right".

(3) A very different sort of explanation has been proposed, among others, by Joseph A. Fitzmyer: the use of ἐξουσία may itself mean "head covering" or "veil". Following the lead of Gerhard Kittel, Fitzmyer appeals to the Aramaic word שלטוניה, which in the *Talmud Yerushalmi* carries the meaning "head ornament" or "veil".[28] Since the root of this word, שלט, commonly means "to have power/ dominion over," the term ἐξουσία may be understood as its Greek equivalent. And so, Paul's vocabulary either derives from a simple mistranslation or, better, reflects a "popular etymology" that no longer betrays knowledge of the Aramaic word.[29] It is, of course, possible that the apostle himself knew such an etymology. However, the translation or identification of ἐξουσία as "veil" seems unnecessarily specific. Furthermore, I doubt whether the Corinthian recipients of this letter may be expected to have understood the term, which is illuminated through an Aramaic background, as an equivalent for "veil"! Without further explanation (one that is not provided in the text), the addressees would not have been able to comprehend such a nuance.

(4) The term ἐξουσία has in the past been frequently understood as a "magical power" possessed by the veiled or covered woman, there to protect her against the invasion of evil spirits or angels. This view would imply that, at least for Paul, women belong to "the more vulnerable sex" and, unlike men, need a head covering, even if only a symbolic one, to protect them, especially during times when they are vulnerable, such as when they pray or prophesy in ecstasy. Fitzmyer, among others, has rejected this view because he has found no evidence from antiquity which attests that such a protective function was accorded to a woman's veil. However, as will become clear below, such a conclusion is too dismissive.

C. Summary and the Nature of Gender Equality in Paul

The foregoing discussion brings us to the point of addressing the problem of the phrase "on account of the angels". In doing so, it is important not to forget the

---

[27] The closest analogy is in 1 Cor. 7:37. The phrase refers to a man's freedom *not* to touch his virgin, and not to the freedom to do so. In 11:10, however, ἐξουσία is related to an obligation.

[28] Fitzmyer, "A Feature of Qumran Angelology and the Angels of 1 Cor 11:10", pp. 193–194; see further Foerster, "ἐξουσία", p. 574.

[29] Along these lines, it is thought that the textual variant κάλυμμα ("veil"), *velamen* in some Lat. mss., in place of ἐξουσία and Origen's explanatory addition of κάλυμμα καὶ before the word when discussing the text (in a Lat. translation: *velamen et*) demonstrate a straightforward equivalence between "veil" and ἐξουσία.

perspectives reached thus far. For the sake of clarity, the views I adopt as a basis for the ensuing discussion may be summarized as follows: (1) 1 Corinthians 11:2–16 is Pauline. (2) The statements of Paul in the passage are not ultimately concerned with the question of hairstyles; Paul does not make any attempt to distinguish between head covering through hair or a piece of clothing, and it is likely that he regarded both as functioning in the same way. The essential point for Paul is that, *when exercising a prophetic role in the context of worship* (in contrast to her general or public appearance, a woman's head should be covered [11:5, 10, and 15]). (3) Although in 11:4, 7, Paul refers to men who do not wear head coverings, the thrust of the argument as a whole is directed towards the behavior of women. (4) The various interpretations of a woman's having ἐξουσία on the head are not all mutually exclusive. In fact, the text itself seems to reflect the ambiguous status of the woman: on the one hand, she may possess "authority" over what she does; on the other hand, since women are being asked to participate in exercising constraint over their own activity "on account of the angels," the notion of protection, and perhaps by extension subjugation, is not far away.

It is true that in 11:11–12 – in some ways a theological highpoint within the argument – Paul underlines the interdependence between women and men. Does this language of mutuality, however, transfer into "equality" in practice? Although the statements of Paul in verses 11–12 acknowledge equality between the sexes "in the Lord" and although elsewhere in his correspondence Paul can cite baptismal tradition that there is "neither male nor female" (so Gal. 3:28), what this principle signifies in reality is another matter (even in Gal. 3:28 the masculine form is used to denote male and female oneness). We know, for instance, from the *Gospel of Thomas* (Logion 114)[30] and *Joseph and Aseneth* (14:15–15:2)[31] that "androgyny" did not have to denote an equality that respects the woman's dignity *as a woman* but rather accepts equality on the grounds that she be virtually regarded as a male. By contrast Paul, of course, refuses in 11:2–16 to blend the distinctions between women and men. Nevertheless, we may learn, especially from *Gospel of Thomas,* that one ought not assume that notions of gender unification, in this case gender mutuality, are going to mean equality in practical terms. In other words, Paul might not have understood equality or even mutuality in a straightforward manner.[32]

---

[30] This often cited text may be translated from the Coptic as follows: "Simon Peter said to him, 'Let Mary depart from us, because women are unworthy of this life.' Jesus said, 'Behold, I shall lead her, in order that I may make her a male, so that she may also become a living spirit, being like you males. For every woman who makes herself a male shall enter into the kingdom of heaven.'"

[31] The virgin Aseneth's full preparedness for conversion to Judaism is signified by the removal of her head covering (at the angel's behest) which renders the appearance of her head "as that of a young man" (*Jos. Asen.* 15:1).

[32] See especially Wayne Meeks, "The Image of the Androgyne: Some Uses of a Symbol in Earliest Christianity", *History of Religions* 13 (1974), pp. 165–208; and Dennis R. MacDonald, "Corinthian Veils and Gnostic Androgynes", in ed. Karen L. King, *Images of the Feminine Gnosticism*

D. Paul's Arguments for Head "Covering"

As observed above, the expression κατὰ κεφαλῆς ἔχων (11:4, 10) looks like a throw-away, enigmatic comment that is unnecessary to the flow of the argument. Paul does not bother to explain it or to connect it to the immediate context with any transparency. In this sense, the phrase stands out in contrast with at least five other reasons given by Paul, reasons which more readily reinforce one another through notions of order, scriptural exegesis, "nature," and common practice among the Christian congregations. The fact that Paul produces not one, but a string of arguments in order to convince women to cover their heads, signals the particular importance he attached to this practice in relation to the worshiping assembly. Herewith, we briefly consider these other arguments, which are found in 11:3–9 and 11:13–16.

First, Paul appeals to the status of women in the hierarchical order of the cosmos (11:3–5a, 7). It is hard to escape the conclusion that the term κεφαλή, regardless of whether or not it is to be translated as "origin" or "source," denotes a pecking order of relationships within the cosmic order: God (the head of), Christ (the head of), man (the head of), woman. This hierarchy is reinforced in 11:7, where "Christ" is left out of the equation: the terms εἰκών ("image") and δόξα ("glory") are both directly applied to the man in relation to God, while the woman's δόξα is merely conceived in relation to the man.[33] For Paul, this essential difference between man and woman is to manifest itself in the matter of head coverings, with the man being without any at all and the woman having to cover herself. If this cosmological classification is disturbed by the woman, she brings shame upon her head (11:5), that is, upon her superior (the man), just as a man who crosses the boundaries of propriety by covering his head brings shame upon his head (11:4, presumably this is Christ). Given the introduction of κεφαλή in 11:3 to denote superiority, 11:4–5 cannot be read as activity which brings shame upon one's *self*. The language – that is, to "shame his/her head" – means instead that one dishonors the one who is next up or immediately above in the cosmic scale. The notion of

---

(Philadelphia: Fortress Press, 1988), pp. 276–292, who demonstrates how widespread male hierarchy within androgyny was among the gnostic sources (e. g., the *Apocryphon of John*); see further the excellent overview of the notion of "unequal androgyny" by Dale B. Martin, *The Corinthian Body* (New Haven: Yale University Press, 1995), pp. 230–232. Against Schüssler-Fiorenza *(In Memory of Her*, pp. 211–213), who attempts to rescue the *Gospel of Thomas* (and thus Paul) from gender-related notions of inequality, it seems rather that the notion of practical inequity in Paul (as may have been assumed by Paul in Gal. 3:28) ought not be dismissed too quickly, that is, merely on the grounds that gnostic beliefs cannot be shown to have influenced the behavior of the Corinthian women. The issue is more one of latent male attitudes than of tradition- and religious-historical influences.

[33] This argument assumes the "image" language of Gen. 1:27, which is being interpreted through the point of view of Gen. 2. See Gen. 5:1–3, in which both male and female are described as created, though unlike Gen. 1:27, the term "image" is reserved for "Adam", which is the name given to both of them.

shame characterizes activity which is in breach of the cosmic order. The metaphorical use of κεφαλή as "leader" or "ruler" (Hebrew ראש),[34] in combination with the literal meaning "head," results in a semantic wordplay: the appropriate treatment of one's head in terms of covering or not covering shows respect towards one's head, that is, towards one's distinct place in the divine order. This wordplay implies that the order imposed upon the world involves boundaries of distinction that should not be violated.

Second, as we have discussed, for the sake of the argument, Paul equates a woman's uncovered head with her having no hair at all. Strictly speaking, this argument makes no sense, because it is not based on observation; it builds, rather, on a sense of shame which Paul assumes his readers in Corinth would share towards the notion of female bareheadedness (11:6a).[35] The identification of an uncovered with a shorn head enables Paul to transfer the shame associated with being without hair to the practice of not covering the head.

Third, Paul's argument appeals to the chronological order of creation: woman was created from man, not vice-versa (11:8–9). This is clearly based, not on Genesis 1:26 – according to which "male and female" were created together – but on the creation story in Genesis 2,[36] in which a discernible sequence of time elapsed between the creation of Adam and the formation of the woman.

Fourth, Paul appeals to "nature" (φύσις, 11:14). Perhaps this argument is in some way related to the social shame Paul associates with a woman's bareheadedness in 11:6. Paul presumes that the Corinthians will agree with him that it is inappropriate, on grounds of nature itself, for a man to have long hair inasmuch as it is appropriate for a woman to have long hair. Granting that this view is shared by the Corinthians, Paul assumes further that they will conclude that long hair (in worship, that is) is to be accompanied by a head covering. Long hair is to be covered and short hair is not.[37] The logic of the argument also works in the other direction: since men should not wear a head covering in worship, they should not have long hair; if women should be covered (as Paul thinks should be the case), they should have long hair.

---

[34] For the Heb. term in the generic sense of "ruler", see Deut. 1:13 and Isa. 29:10; in the context of Israel, as "leaders", see Exod. 6:14, 25; 18:25; Num. 1:4, 16; 7:2; 8:12; 10:4; 13:3; 17:3; 25:4, 15; 30:1; Deut. 1:15; 5:23; 28:13, 44; 33:5, 21; Jos. 11:10; 14:1; 19:51; 21:1; 22:21; 23:2; 24:1; Jdg. 7:25; 10:18; 11:8, 9, 11; 1 Sam. 15:17; 1 Kgs. 8:1; 1 Chr. 5:24; 7:2, 4, 7, 9, 11, 40; 8:6, 10, 13, 28; 9:13; 12:32; 29:11; 2 Chr. 5:2; 28:12; and Ps. 18:43. Among the Dead Sea materials, see esp. lQSa *(Rule of the Congregation)* i 16, 23, and 25.

[35] See *Test. of Job* 23:8–10 and esp. 24:9–10, in which Job's wife shows her shame by having her hair cut.

[36] A similar adaptation of Gen. 2 seems to be operative in the fragmentary text of 4Q415 (= *4QInstruction*) 2 ii 1–9; see eds. John Strugnell and Daniel J. Harrington, *Qumran Cave 4 XXIV: Sapiential Texts, Part 2* (DJD 34; Oxford: Clarendon, 1999), pp. 47–48 (text and translation).

[37] See *Jos. Asen.* 15:1: The angelic humanlike figure tells Aseneth to remove her veil because her head "is like that of a young man"; i. e., because she has short hair, a veil is not deemed necessary.

Fifth, in 11:16 Paul cuts his own argument short by admitting that the problem is a contentious matter. Nevertheless, he stresses that anyone who would disagree with his present instruction contravenes uniform practice "in the churches of God". Paul thus appeals to "custom", that is, he claims that "we" have no other practice either. Is Paul referring to congregations under his own apostolic influence ("we") and, beyond that, to all the remaining congregations as well? It is not clear. Whatever the case, Paul's rhetoric is constructed in such a way as to emphasize that those among the Corinthians who would resist his instruction regarding head coverings risk isolating themselves from what is being practiced elsewhere in the fledgling movement.

E. Why, then, "on account of the angels"?

As we have observed, the angels are not as such integrated into the flow of the argument in 11:2–16. Therefore, the possible explanations are, by necessity, drawn from inferences based on the immediate context (in particular, 11:2–9), the epistle as a whole, traditions about angelic beings in early Jewish documents and, more broadly, Greco-Roman antiquity. In terms of a debate concerning which specific background throws the best light on what Paul consciously thought when he mentioned the angels, little has been said which may be called "decisive". Thus, in addition, we may need to consider the proper worldview – that is, the realm of what Paul may have assumed – against which an interpretation can be most satisfactorily pieced together. We need to be open to the possibility, therefore, that not all of the conventional alternative interpretations proposed are mutually exclusive; perhaps, moreover, the questions for which the alternative proposals provide an answer need to be rethought.

The four main interpretations of "the angels," whether offered in the distant or recent past, are as follows:

First, a number of interpreters have continued to maintain that *Paul was simply referring to human* ἄγγελοι.[38] Jerome Murphy-O'Connor, in support of this view, appeals to 1 Corinthians 10:32 and 14:23. In 10:32, just prior to this passage, Paul exhorts the Corinthians in general to "be without trouble to Jews, Gentiles, and to the church of God," while in 14:23, in addressing disorderly conduct in worship fomented by speaking in tongues, he warns that "ordinary people or unbelievers" would regard them as crazy. From these texts Murphy-O'Connor argues, that "Paul would be concerned that practices in Corinth should not shock envoys from other churches".[39]

---

[38] So, John Lightfoot, in *Horae Hebraicae et Talmudicae* (6 vols.; Cambridge: John Field, 1658–1678), 4:238; more recently, Padget, "Paul on Women in Church", p. 81; and Murphy-O'Connor, "1 Corinthians 11:2–16 Once Again", pp. 271–272.

[39] Murphy-O'Connor, p. 271–272.

This approach to the angels in 11:10 is very weak. Although the term ἄγγελοι can refer to a non-celestial human being several times in the writings of the New Testament (so Mt. 11:10; Lk. 7:24; 9:52; Jas. 2:25; and, as some argue, the "angels" of the seven churches in Rev. 2–3), it nowhere clearly refers to such in the Pauline or even deutero-Pauline corpus.[40] Furthermore, although 10:32 does refer to contact between the Corinthian Christians and others, it does not specify a context of worship. Finally, in 14:23 those whom Paul envisions as observers of the Corinthians' worship are not Murphy-O'Connor's "envoys from other churches," but rather ἰδιῶται ("untrained") *and* ἄπιστοι ("unbelievers")! Thus, while not entirely impossible, the notion that women are to wear head coverings on account of visiting humans as ἄγγελοι is highly unlikely.

Second, an interpretation which often regards "the angels" in 11:10 as unequivocally "good" or at least "obedient"; they are *guardians of the created order*. Within the immediate context, as we have seen, Paul draws on the biblical tradition from Genesis 2 to assert the chronological priority of man over woman (11:8–9; see 11:3). If the creation story is in view, it could be argued that a mention of "angels" in 11:10 would not be out of place. Indeed, according to some exegetical traditions, angels were considered to have been active participants with God in the creation of humanity. According to Philo, in Genesis (1:26) God is speaking to the angels when God says, "let us make man" *(Opif.* 72–76; see *Conf.* 171–182; *Fug.* 65–70; *Mut.* 27–34).[41] The tradition in *Targum Pseudo-Jonathan* to Gen 1:26 is thus probably dependent on an older tradition when it specifies that "let us" refers to "the angels who minister before him and who were created on the second day of the creation of the world". Such participation of angels in creation is presupposed among the *4QInstruction* manuscripts, in which two types of humanity are distinguished (4Q417 1 i 15–18): on the one hand, there is "Enosh" (אנוש), a spiritual people (עם רוח, 1.16) whose created form corresponds to "the pattern of the holy ones" (כתבנית קדושים, 1.17); on the other hand, there are the "children of Seth" (1.15) who presumably do not have the capacity to discern between good and evil (1.18).[42] Unquestionably, Paul is concerned with maintaining distinctions within

---

[40] Gal. 4:14 does, admittedly, come close. However, Paul uses the expression ἄγγελον θεοῦ there as a hypothetical (not real) description of himself to emphasize the exemplary hospitality of the Galatians towards him ("you welcomed me as [though I were] an angel of God, as Christ Jesus"). The thrust of the statement, which extends the comparison to include Christ, suggests that Paul is thinking of a strictly nonhuman, divine messenger.

[41] Philo's purpose for involving angels (identified as "heavenly bodies" created on the fourth day) in the creation of humanity is to account for the duality of voluntary and involuntary dimensions of human nature. Whereas heavenly bodies possess a mind (but only unto themselves) and plants and animals are without mind and reason, only humans have the capacity to participate willingly in evil. The role of angels in creation of humanity, therefore, serves to distance the utter goodness and transcendence of God from responsibility for being the originator of evil.

[42] On the analysis of this passage, I am indebted to Benjamin G. Wold; see *Women, Men, and Angels: The Qumran Wisdom Document* Musar LeMevin *and Its Allusions to Genesis Creation Traditions* (WUNT 2.201; Tübingen: Mohr Siebeck, 2005), esp. chapter 4.

divine order, both in 11:2–16 and in 1 Corinthians as a whole (see Paul's reference to the distinct δόξα of "heavenly" as opposed to "earthly" bodies and, more specifically, among the heavenly bodies themselves in 15:40–41). Angels guard this order – here the distinction between man and woman – and, presumably, would take offence at a practice which violates this order as set forth in verses 3 and 8–9.[43] A difficulty with this interpretation is that, surprisingly, there is hardly an instance in early or rabbinic Jewish tradition in which angelic beings are specifically assigned such a role,[44] to say nothing about what such guardian angels would have had to do with the management of either a woman's coiffure or head covering. This is not to deny that the mention of angels in 11:10 in some way relates to cosmic order; indeed, the reverse seems to be the case. However, in what sense?

Third, we are brought a step further by the proposal of Fitzmyer, who has drawn attention to a number of texts from the Dead Sea documents concerned with the notion *of the angels' presence in the congregation of the community*.[45] In his initial publication, Fitzmyer was only able to refer to four texts, according to which purity in the community is demanded because of the presence of the angels (*1QM* = *1QSerekh ha-Milḥamah* vii 6; 1QSa = *1QRule of the Congregation* ii 8–9; 4Q174 = *4QFlorilegium* 1 i 3–4; see *CD* = *Damascus Document* xv 15–17); since then, further materials overlapping with the previously known documents have come to light which echo this motif (4Q491 = *4QMᵃ* 1–3.10; *4QDᵃ* = 4Q266 8 i 6–9).[46] In terms of form, these texts provide a list, inspired by Leviticus 21:18–23,

---

[43] Those adopting this view include James Moffatt, *The First Epistle of Paul to the Corinthians* (London: Hodder and Stoughton, 1947), p. 152; Fitzmyer, "A Feature of Qumran Angelology and 1 Cor 11:10", p. 197 ns. 36–37; and Charles H. Talbert, *Reading Corinthians: A Literary and Theological Commentary on 1 and 2 Corinthians* (New York: Crossroad, 1987), p. 69. This view has provided an attractive option for those who interpret Paul's emphasis on man's chronological priority over woman in creation as a concession to the old order (i. e., of the law), of which angels are guardians. – A different way of relating the function of angelic beings to creation has been maintained by those who regard them as guardians of the "old" order, presumably as they are often regarded as having acted as mediators in the giving of the law (Gal 3:19; see Acts 7:53; Heb 2:2; *Jub.*. 1:27, 29; 2:1 *passim*; *Apoc. Mos.* introduction; and Josephus, *Ant.* 15.136). Paul is negotiating between the eschatological (see 11:11–12) and the old order (11:8–9) and instructs women to wear head coverings either (a) as a concession to the old (or even pagan) order itself or (b) in order to show that they have the authority (see 11:10a) to transcend the old order to which she was once subjected. For the position of (a), see George B. Caird, *Principalities and Powers* (Oxford: Clarendon Press, 1956), pp. 15–22; and T. W. Manson, *On Paul and John* (SBT 38; London: SCM, 1963), pp. 19–20; in relation to (b), see Hooker, "Authority on Her Head", pp. 412–413; and Scroggs, "Paul and the Eschatological Women", p. 91, n. 46.

[44] I am in agreement with Jaubert, "La voile des femmes", p. 427, who emphasizes that there are no sources from antiquity that support this interpretation.

[45] Fitzmyer, "A Feature of Qumran Angelology in 1 Cor 11:10".

[46] For convenient access to the Hebrew texts of these Dead Sea documents and to corresponding English translations, see Florentino Garcia Martinez and Eibert J. C. Tigchelaar, *The Dead Sea Scrolls Study Edition* (2 vols.; Grand Rapids: Eerdmans, 2000, lightly reworked edition from the 1997–1998 publication).

of categories of *men*[47] who are not allowed to participate in the community, whether it be in the eschatological war (as in the *War Rule*) or the worshiping, eschatological assembly (as in the *Rule of the Congregation, Damascus Document,* and *Florilegium*). Of particular interest, notes Fitzmyer, is the explanatory formula "for the angels of holiness shall be with" (כי מלאכי קודש עם) of which the construction διὰ plus the accusative τοὺς ἀγγέλους in 1 Corinthians 11:10 is reminiscent.[48] Taken together, the texts strengthen the view that the presence of angels was considered to have significant ramifications for the observance of purity regulations in the Qumran community.[49]

One could develop Fitzmyer's ideas further. These Qumran texts, in turn, reflect the belief, more widely attested among the Dead Sea documents, that the community (and, possibly other communities as well) related its self-understanding to the presence of angels in their midst.[50] For instance, in *11QBerakhoth* the presence of God and of God's holy angels in the community is given as the reason (ii 14) for the community's enjoyment of favorable weather, good harvest, and protection from a variety of mortal and unclean dangers (ii 7–14); for this function the angels present in the community can even be "blessed" alongside God (ii, lines 4– 6).[51] Among the *Songs of the Sabbath Sacrifice*, extant mostly through the Cave 4

---

[47] Only in 1QM vii 3–4 does the category of women occur: "no young male or woman (אשה) shall enter into their camps when they go out from Jerusalem to go to war until their return."

[48] Fitzmyer, "A Feature of Qumran Angelology in 1 Cor 11:10".

[49] Those who have shared or followed Fitzmyer's interpretation of 1 Cor. 11:10 include the following: Henry J. Cadbury, "A Qumran Parallel to Paul", *HTR* 51 (1958), pp. 1–2; and Jervis, "But I Want You to Know...", pp. 231–246 (here p. 244, n. 53).

[50] See esp. 1QS xi 8; 1QSb iii 6; iv 26; 1QH^a iii 21–23; vi 13; xi 11–14; 2.10, 14; 5.3; 7.11; 10.6–7; 1QM i 14–15; xii 1–2, 4–5, 7–9; xiii 10; xvii 6; 1Q36; 4Q181 1.3–4; 4Q400 ii 5–7; 4Q491 24.4; 4Q511 2 i 7–8; 8.9; 11Q14 ii 13–14. On the significance of these texts, see the studies by Bergil Gärtner, *The Temple and the Community* (SNTSMS 1; Cambridge: Cambridge University Press, 1965); Peter von der Osten-Sacken, *Gott und Belial* (SUNT 6; Gottingen: Vandenhoeck & Ruprecht, 1969), pp. 222–232; Heinz-Wolfgang Kuhn, *Enderwartung und Gegenwärtiges Heil* (SUNT 4; Göttingen: Vandenhoeck & Ruprecht, 1966), pp. 66–73; Hermann Lichtenberger, *Studien zum Menschenbild in Texten der Qumrangemeinde* (SUNT 15; Göttingen: Vandenhoeck & Ruprecht, 1980), esp. pp. 224–227; and Loren T. Stuckenbruck, *Angel Veneration and Christology,* (WUNT 2.70; Tübingen: Mohr Siebeck, 1995), pp. 150–163. As the composition of the sapiential document *Instruction* extant among materials from Caves 1 and 4 cannot be assigned to the Qumran community itself, the following texts which coordinate the life of the faithful community with angelic beings are of special interest: 4Q417 1 ii 15–18//4Q418 43.11–14; 55.8–12; 69.10–14; 81.4–5.

[51] Column ii in *11QBerakhoth* overlaps in content with 4Q285 1.1–10 and, therefore, Martin G. Abegg has argued that it preserves a portion of the *War Scroll*; see "Messianic Hope and 4Q285: A Reassessment", *JBL* 113 (1994), pp. 81–91; and, further, Philip S. Alexander and Geza Vermes, "4QSefer ha-Milḥamah", in eds. Stephen Pfann *et al.*, *Qumran Cave 4. XXVI: Cryptic Texts and Miscellanea, Part 1* (DJD 36; Oxford: Clarendon Press, 2000), pp. 231–232 and 241– 243. The blessing formula of this text, in which the blessing of God precedes the blessing of the angels, shows that the Book of Tobit, at 11:14–15 (where the same occurs), draws on a traditional formula (both recensions; Cod. Sinaiticus preserves a more elaborate form); see further 4Q418 81.1–5.

manuscripts from Qumran (4Q400–407; see 11Q17 and the Masada manuscript), the community describes the heavenly worship of the angels; the members of this community are said to stand in awe of the privilege they have to participate in this angelic cultus (4Q400 ii 5–7). Angelic worship is thus described as exemplary, and this inspires the human community to declare about the angelic *elim*: "they are honored among all the camps of the *elohim* and revered by human councils". Clearly, the presence of angels in the community was related not only to its members' general sense of well-being, but also represented a form of cultic worship to which the community aspired. We may infer, therefore, that the inclusion of angels into the reason for drawing clear boundaries between the clean and unclean takes for granted that they convey the holiness of God in the community.

When we return to 1 Corinthians 11, we may consider how the Dead Sea materials could be thought to provide a background. Of course, one glaring difference that comparison reveals is the presence of women in the Christian worshiping community. The Dead Sea documents do not envisage women as full participants in the present, heavenly, or even eschatological *cultus*. To the extent that Christian men and women, especially those of Jewish descent, fell heir to such traditions, they would have been aware of the new status given to the woman in the post-resurrection era, when circumcision – from which women had been excluded by definition – no longer functioned as a requirement for full admission into the participation in worship. One does not have to argue much further to show how this new perspective would have led to a reconfiguration of male-female relationships; thus Paul could write in 11:11: "neither is woman without man nor man without woman in the Lord". Paul would have instructed the women of the congregation to cover themselves, in accordance with the woman's secondary appearance in the order of creation and because her δόξα *is different from* that given to men. Fitzmyer explains, in analogy to the Dead Sea texts, that the unveiled woman would have been perceived by the angels as a "bodily defect" to be excluded from the assembly.[52] The covering would, then, be a way for compensating for this deficiency, especially so in the presence of holy angels, with whom an exemplary, heavenly, and pure worship of God is associated. Presumably the Corinthians, not least the women who prayed and prophesied in the assembly, would have been familiar with such an ideal: they would have understood themselves to be worshipers of God alongside the angels (13:1,[53] in which Paul may be subordinating such a perception to an ἀγάπη-ethic). Thus, in 11:10 Paul would be seen to advocate head

---

[52] Fitzmyer, "A Feature of Qumran Angelology in 1 Cor 11:10", pp. 56–57.

[53] See, e. g., Schüssler-Fiorenza, *In Memory of Her, p.* 228; and Judith M. Gundry-Volf, "Paul on Women and Gender: A Comparison with Early Jewish Views", in ed. Richard N. Longenecker, *The Road from Damascus: The Impact of Paul's Conversion on His Life, Thought, and Ministry* (Grand Rapids: Eerdmans, 1997), pp. 184–212, esp. p. 205, where 13:1 is taken to suggest that the angels of 11:10 are those who were understood to mediate "gifts of inspiration".

coverings for women out of respect for the angels with whom the congregations' members understand themselves to be worshiping God.

Appealing to a number of the Dead Sea Scrolls texts mentioned above, Cecilia Wassen has more recently argued for a similar approach, by regarding the angels in 11:10 as beings in whose presence respect is to be shown. Significantly, however, she departs from Fitzmyer's interpretation of the unveiled woman as being the functional equivalent for a bodily defect and emphasizes instead that a woman's head covering would have been intended to make her look more like a male.[54]

This picture is coherent, even inspiring. It even attempts to situate Paul's reference to the angels within the context of 1 Corinthians as a letter and, to some extent, the situation in Corinth. It is also compatible with the notion of angelic guardians of the created order.[55] Fitzmyer is convincing, furthermore, in showing that Paul is concerned with maintaining "holiness" and "purity" in the worshiping community and that "the angels" in 11:10 have something to do with this. However, there are several problems with this approach if it is adopted to the exclusion of other possibilities. First, it presupposes that Paul would have imagined that physical defects are sufficient reason for exclusion from the Christian community, since women are, on argument, being instructed to cover their heads on account of their association with other defects which, according to Leviticus 21:18–23 and the Dead Sea materials, are inadmissible to the cult.[56] Secondly, and more of a difficulty, the tradition-historical background invoked by Fitzmyer does not directly bear on the presence or activity of *women* in the religious community.[57] One could, of course, argue that Paul is simply applying a tradition to a situation which, by its very nature, is essentially different (where the inclusion of women in the worshiping community is more or less being taken for granted); this argument, however, carries weight to the extent that there are no other traditions which more directly relate women to angelic beings. Thirdly, Fitzmyer – as indeed many interpreters of this passage[58] – feels constrained to decide whether the angels are "good"

---

[54] Cecilia Wassen, "'Because of the Angels': Reading 1 Cor 11:2–16 in Light of Angelology in the Dead Sea Scrolls", in eds. Armin Lange, Emanuel Tov, and Matthias Weigold, *The Dead Sea Scrolls in Context: Integrating the Study of the Dead Sea Scrolls in Ancient Texts, Languages, and Cultures* (SVTP 140; Leiden / Boston: Brill, 2011), 2:735–754 (here p. 753, referring in addition to *Jos. and Asen.* 15:1 in support identifying the underlying issue in 1 Cor. 11 as "the uneasiness over the appearance of women in the presence of angels".

[55] See the reference to Fitzmyer in n. 28 above.

[56] Similarly, see the criticism by Murphy-O'Connor, "Sex and Logic in 1 Cor 11:2–16", p. 497 and n. 57.

[57] In this respect, Wassen's discussion (bibl. in n. 54 above), which takes the language about women in the Dead Sea materials into account, is more updated.

[58] So, Jean Héring, *The First Epistle of Saint Paul to the Corinthians*, trans. Arthur W. Heth-cote and Philip J. Allcock (London: Epworth, 1962), pp. 106–108; Hooker, "Authority on Her Head", p. 412; Barrett, *Commentary on the First Epistle to the Corinthians*, pp. 253–254; Schüssler-Fiorenza, *In Memory of Her*, p. 228; Fee, *The First Epistle to the Corinthians*, p. 521; Talbert, *Reading Corinthians*, p. 69; Jacques Winandy, "Un curieux *casus pendens*: 1 Corinthiens 11.10 et

or "bad"; for reasons I wish yet to specify, the need to reach such a decision sets up a false dichotomy.[59] The question should not be to what kind of angels Paul is referring, but rather what kind of worldview, whether conscious or not to Paul and his readers, would have made it possible to regard the covering of the female head in a highly charged religious context such a necessity. Our asking this question reveals the greatest difficulty of all in Fitzmyer's thesis: it relies wholly on analogy and does not help to account for the head covering (and by women!) in and of itself. Rather than taking "angels" as a logical point of departure, discussions should actually reconsider the question about veiling and head covering in antiquity.

The point last mentioned brings us to a *fourth* explanation, which I regard as tenable despite the fact that variations of it have been so categorically dismissed by a number of scholars: *the head coverings were intended to be prophylactic*. While this reason may seem to assume that "the angels" to which Paul refers must therefore be "bad", this is not a necessary inference. The more important question is what social functions could be attributed to the veiling or covering of a woman's head in antiquity – whether this involved a covering up of the woman's face, a covering of the top of the head itself, or a smaller covering represents a symbolic covering of the whole. How, moreover, do any of these functions bear upon the importance Paul attaches to women covering themselves while they are prophesying? In asking these questions, we are not necessarily looking for a theological intentionality on the part of Paul, but rather we wish to consider predominant assumptions which accompanied the use of a head covering in relation to women.[60]

Although the wearing of head coverings among men in antiquity was not uncommon, the practice among women carried with it strong sexual connotations. Apparel was, of course, one way of marking the differences – or, better, boundaries – between the sexes, that is, to keep gender categories distinct. Of course, we are not in a position to generalize about Greco-Roman antiquity, as practices must have varied according to time period, place and social context.[61] When, however,

---

son interprétation", *NTS* 38 (1992), pp. 621–629 (here pp. 627–628); and Wassen, "'Because of the Angels'".

[59] Thus Wassen, though sympathetic to this understanding of "angels" in 1 Cor. 11:10, seems aware of a one-sided interpretation and thus qualifies it by stressing that, in addition to respect, women are enjoined to make themselves look less female ("'Because of the Angels'", p. 753).

[60] Here the recent studies, which are sensitive to cultural anthropology, are especially important. The observations on the significance of veiling in Greco-Roman antiquity depend to some degree on the following publications: Helen King, "Producing Woman: Hippocratic Gynaecology", in eds. Léonie J. Archer, Susan Fischler, and Maria Wyke, *Women in Ancient Societies* (Houdsmills/Basingstoke/London: MacMillan, 1994), pp. 102–114; Gail Paterson Corrington, "The 'Headless Woman': Paul and the Language of the Body in 1 Cor 11:2–16", *Perspectives in Religious Studies* 18 (1991), pp. 223–231; Anne Carson, "Putting Her in Her Place: Woman, Dirt, and Desire", in eds. David M. Halperin, John J. Winkler, and Froma I. Zeitlin, *Before Sexuality: The Construction of Erotic Experience in the Ancient Greek World* (Princeton: Princeton University Press, 1990), pp. 135–169, esp. pp. 153–164; and Martin, *The Corinthian Body*, pp. 229–249 and 294–300, to whom some of the present discussion is indebted.

women did cover their heads or veiled themselves – whether in public,[62] in relation to marriage rituals,[63] while mourning,[64] or participating in a religious cult[65] – assumptions about the nature of female physiology and, thus, sexuality were being brought to expression. Such would have been especially true in contexts which scholars in the social sciences have termed "strong group".[66] These assumptions reflected, in turn, the male *Angst* in the face of female sexuality. The association of a woman's nature with wetness and porousness was thought to make her especially vulnerable to disease, sexual appetite, irrationality, and pollution. These values in antiquity are even assumed among those who devoted themselves to the science of studying the female anatomy, for example, as in the detailed works of the Hippo-

---

[61] So, e. g., the differences between Romans and Greeks with respect to head coverings in Plutarch, *Moralia, Roman Questions* 14.

[62] See Dio Chrysostom, *Discourse* 33.48–49, who refers to a persisting custom in Tarsus concerning the "the attire of women", meaning that they dress in such a way "that nobody can see any part of them, neither of the face nor of the remainder of the body, and that they might not see anything from the road". Dio's explanation of this practice focuses on control of the woman rather than the man, for he goes on to describe the function of the face covering as a way of keeping out "wantonness" (of the woman!), whereas an uncovered face is as vulnerable as "an uncovered soul." On the propriety of head coverings for women in public in the early Jewish and rabbinic Jewish, see Peter J. Tomson, *Paul and the Jewish Law: Halakha in the Letters of the Apostle to the Gentiles* (CRINT III/1; Minneapolis: Fortress Press, 1990), p. 133. See Philo, *Spec. Leg.* 3.56, in an interpretation of Num. 5 according to which the removal of the suspected woman's head covering symbolizes her loss of innocence.

[63] See Carson, "Putting Her in Her Place", pp. 160–164. Carson refers to a number of sources, from which the following, in terms of exercising social control over (or "civilizing") the bride, seem to be the most significant: the myth which explains cosmology as Zeus' gaining control over the goddess of the underworld by a veiling through which she is transformed into a beautiful and fertile wife Ge. See Hermann Diels and Walther Kranz, eds., *Die Fragmente der Vorsokratiker*, 6th ed. (Berlin: Weidmannsche Verlagsbuchhandlung, 1951), p. 48; Plutarch's reference to the customary Boeotian wedding ceremony, in which "after veiling the bride they put on her head a crown of asparagus, for this plant yields the sweetest fruit from the roughest thorns" so that her "initial unpleasantness" will give way to "a docile and sweet life together" (*Moralia, Conjugal Precepts* 138D). With respect to the protection of the bride's virginity see Lucian, *The Carousal or the Lapiths* 8: the bride on the couch, surrounded by women on both sides "is strictly veiled"; in Homer's *Odyssey* 1.334, Penelope, accompanied by two maidservants on each side, is covered by "a veil across her cheeks" as a symbol of her unavailability to would-be suitors. In addition, there are numerous references among classical sources to the moment of unveiling in a wedding ceremony, at which the protective boundaries around the bride are removed to expose her to the penetrative gaze of her husband; on this see Carson, "Putting Her in Her Place", p. 163 and n. 55, and esp. Cynthia B. Patterson, "Marriage and the Married Woman in Athenian Law", in ed. Sarah B. Pomeroy, *Women's History and Ancient History*, (Chapel Hill: University of North Carolina, 1991), pp. 48–72.

[64] See Plutarch, *Moralia* 267, *Roman Quaestiones* 14.

[65] So Apuleius, *Metamorphoses* 11.10; Varro, *De Lingua Latina* 5.29.130; Juvenal, *Saturnalia* 6.390–392. See also the *Excursus* above.

[66] On this expression as a cultural anthropological category, see Mary Douglas, *Natural Symbols* (New York: Pantheon, 1982), pp. 54–64, and its adaptation for New Testament study by Bruce Malina, *Christian Origins and Cultural Anthropology* (Atlanta: John Knox, 1986), pp. 14–15. The Corinthian situation, we may suppose, fits best the "strong group, low grid" model, according to which the strong concern for purity in a community is combined with the experience of that community being under the threat of pollution from within.

cratic School (beginning in the 4th–5th cents. B. C. E., esp. *Diseases of Women*) and Aristotle (4th cent. B.C.E.; esp. *History of Animals, Parts of Animals,* and *Genera-tion of Animals*).[67] The significance of these sources is not so much their tradition-historical relevance for ideas consciously taken up by Paul or his Corinthian read-ers during the 1st century C. E., but rather it consists in the fact that observations being made among the "sciences" were conditioned by male assumptions about female inferiority. *Socially,* the wearing of something on the head, especially when enjoined on women, would have reflected the wish to exert control over the woman whose very physiology represents a danger to the (male) ordering of society.[68] Within a group for which special importance is attached to defining strict boundaries of "purity" between its members and outside influences (as Paul tries to do for the Corinthians; see 1 Cor. 5:1–2, 9–13; 6:1, 15–20; 8:7, 11; 10:20–21), it should not be surprising that the woman can be regarded as one focal point for the attempt to assert control over the danger of "pollution".[69]

The notion in Greco-Roman antiquity of female vulnerability and inferiority, assumed in many Jewish sources,[70] and the attendant practice of prophylactic head covering fit well with the early Jewish mythological interpretations of Genesis 6:1–4. With regard to this, New Testament scholars have customarily focused on the essentially evil character of the angels who "fell" because they were attracted by the beauty of the "human daughters". This would be much in line with the *Book of Watchers* of *1 Enoch* (see chs. 7–8) and the *Book of Giants*: in these works the more neutral "sons of God" in Genesis 6:1–2, 4 are interpreted as the angels who have introduced evil into the world by siring through woman on earth a race of oppres-sive giants and by instructing them in reprehensible matters. The gigantic offspring are seen as a *mala mixta*, the result of an illegitimate violation of boundaries in the cosmic order *(1 En.* 15:8–16:3). Against such a background, some scholars, even recently, have interpreted "the angels" in 1 Corinthians 11:10 as categorically "bad" angels.[71] The women wear head coverings as protection against precisely *these*

---

[67] See the excellent study of these sources by Lesley Dean-Jones, "The Cultural Construct of the Female Body in Classical Greek Science", in *Women's History and Ancient History*, pp. 111–137 (bibl. in n. 61).

[68] Thus the sexual dimension of head coverings may presuppose a construal of female physiol-ogy which correlates the head and genitalia (i. e., it goes well beyond regarding such a connection as metaphorical); on this, see Dean-Jones, "The Cultural Construct of the Female Body", pp. 124–125 and 136, who is followed by Martin, *The Corinthian Body*, pp. 237–239. See also Gillian Beattie, *Women and Marriage in Paul and His Early Interpreters* (JSNTSup 296; London: T & T Clark International, 2005), pp. 41–46.

[69] It would simply be wrong, therefore, to conclude with Fitzmyer, "A Feature of Qumran Angelology and 1 Cor 11:10", p. 193, with respect to protection, that there is a "lack of evidence showing that a woman's veil was ever thought of as having such a function in antiquity"; in this I concur with Martin, *The Corinthian Body*, p. 299, n. 66.

[70] Josephus, *c. Ap.* 2.201 ("a woman is in all things inferior to a man", γυνὴ χειρῶν ... ἀνδρός εἰς πάντα); Philo, *Spec.Leg.* 3.169–180 (a woman is inferior and oriented towards the senses); and *passim.*

angels because, being invariably cast as male beings, wayward angels pose a sexual threat to the women. However, given our emphasis on the sexual significance of head coverings in antiquity, I would like to suggest that the problem lies less in the sort of angels being referred to than in the assumption of sexual vulnerability of women to pollution. For Paul it is not a matter of offering an explicit argument in chapter 11 about female weakness in the face of angelic threat; rather, his reasons for commending head coverings are unable to break away from the deeply embedded assumption that women constitute the place where boundaries between different parts of the cosmos are most likely to be violated. This view breaks through to the surface of the argument, in spite of all the mutuality between male and female emphasized by Paul (11:11–12).

If the point of departure for female head coverings is located in notions of sexuality and hierarchy in antiquity, then it is unnecessary to consider whether "the angels" are good or bad. In relation to the Jewish apocalyptic traditions, it is important to realize that the "fallen angels" were usually considered "good" to start with. It is only after they have departed from their proper place in creation when the trouble begins. Whereas in the *Book of Watchers* the angelic decision to sire offspring through women on earth takes place in heaven, in *Jubilees* 5:1–11, the "fall" of the angels is delayed; it does not occur in heaven, but happens on earth, while the angels were on a mission to instruct humans "and perform judgment and uprightness upon the earth" (*Jub.* 5:6; cf. also 4:15). The status of angels is, in other words, not static. Whatever their position or nature, angels have the capacity to violate the cosmic order. Despite distinctiveness between human and angelic spheres of existence, Paul and his Corinthian readers shared the worldview that both nevertheless *share social space* (see 1 Cor. 4:9, 15; 6:3; 13:1). Because the understanding of angels was commonly expressed in terms of male sexuality and because women were assumed to be especially "open" to invasion (from whatever source), Paul's reference to the angels betrays a subtle warning that more than just social relationships between men and women are at stake; ultimately, wearing veils is a matter of maintaining the God-given cosmic order on a broader scale. The head coverings are prophylactic in the sense that they protect this order by helping to draw more clearly the boundaries between distinct, yet sometimes socially overlapping, spheres of existence.

These boundaries, which have structured the universe since creation, are to be respected. For Paul, head coverings in worship on the part of women function to keep men and women distinct from one another; in this regard, the notion of dis-

---

[71] See John Hurd, *The Origin of 1 Corinthians* (London: SPCK, 1965), pp. 182–185 (esp. 184 n. 4 with bibl.); Walker, "The Vocabulary of 1 Corinthians 11.3–16", 82; Brian S. Rosner, *Paul, Scripture and Ethics* (AGSU 22; Leiden: Brill, 1994) 139; and L. J. Lietart Peerbolte, "Man, Woman, and the Angels in 1 Cor 11:2–16", in ed. Gerard P. Luttikhuizen, *The Creation of Man and Woman: Interpretations of the Biblical Narratives in Jewish and Christian Traditions* (TBN 3; Leiden / Boston: Brill, 2000), pp. 76–92.

tinctiveness plays into a hierarchical arrangement that reflects a cultural *status quo*. The head coverings also function to keep women distinct from the angels who, for the sake of this argument, belong to an essentially different part of the created order.[72] After all, in analogy to human men, the angels were prone to be cast as beings with a potentially active male sexuality. The veil is thus protective on two fronts[73]: on the one hand, it protects the woman against inadmissible invasions from the outside and, on the other hand, reminds those on the outside (so, from the male point of view!) of the vulnerability to invasion from evil that the woman represents.[74]

Conclusion

In the foregoing analysis, I have tried not to proceed on the assumption that something "normative" is at stake in inquiring into *what* Paul instructs that women in Corinth should do and *why* they should do it. Instead, the discussion has delved into worldviews and tradition-historical backgrounds in order to bring to light a matrix within which Paul's enigmatic statement concerning "the angels" in 1 Corinthians 11:10 might make sense.

The context of 1 Corinthians suggests that Paul and the congregation in Corinth were both familiar with and even understood their worship as participation in the worship of angels. This belief would have reinforced what is at stake in maintaining order (circumscribed by "holiness") in the community, though Paul himself

---

[72] Hence the importance of regarding the offspring sired by these angelic beings as misfits without a proper place within creation; see Chapter One section C.1 above.

[73] This double function is reflected in the account of Dio Chrysostom cited in n. 61 above. In addition, see Tertullian, in *On the Apparel of Women* and *On the Veiling of Virgins:* the veil protects from the outside (e. g., *Veiling of Virgins* 3: "Every public exposure of an honorable virgin is… a suffering of rape") at the same time as protecting the angels (e. g., *Veiling of Virgins* 7: "So perilous a face, then, ought to be shaded, which has cast stumbling-stones even so far as heaven: that, when standing in the presence of God, at whose bar it stands accused of the driving of the angels from their [native] confines, it may blush before the other angels as well; and may repress that former evil liberty of its head,–[a liberty] now to be exhibited not even before human eyes."). Tertullian draws on the watchers myth from the Enochic tradition as the background for 1 Cor. 11:10. However, unlike the Enochic tradition and other Jewish apocalyptic documents, he limits the interest of the evil angels to virgins. There is no indication in 1 Corinthians 11 that Paul is particularly concerned with unmarried women.

[74] It is worth noting that the Jewish interpretations not only considered the "watchers" as having posed a sexual threat to women during the ante-diluvian period *(1 En.* 7–8; 19:1; *Jub.* 4:21– 22; *1 En.* 69:1–15; 86:1–5) but also blamed adorned women themselves for this fall (so *Test. Reub.* 5:1–6). Covering the head would have, of course, covered a prominent area of the woman's body which, when adorned, was frequently associated in Mediterranean antiquity, especially Roman culture, with sexual vices reflecting, according to the traditionally-minded Roman male, foreign influences (e. g., from the East – India, China, Arabia – from which many such goods were imported); see Maria Wyke, "Woman in the Mirror: The Rhetoric of Adornment in the Roman World", in *Women in Ancient Societies*, pp. 134–151.

could relativize the ideal (13:1) if he thought some members of the community were placing it in service of a spirituality that overlooked the dignity and place of others in the community. While the import of angels for the community could be explicitly articulated within the framework of 1 Corinthians, it is unlikely that the mention of angels in 11:10 can be fully explained on this account. Any act of communication – and surely that of Paul is no exception – represents a blend of ideas being consciously articulated and perhaps even unexamined assumptions that underpin these ideas; what is deliberately written and what is left unsaid may correspond to one another or, at times, may conflict. I have presented matters in such a way that, in the case of 1 Corinthians 11, Paul's statements (for instance, those in 11:8–9 and 11–12, respectively) should not be harmonized too quickly, as the apostle fell heir to a worldview, widespread in antiquity, in which veiling or, more simply, covering could not be disassociated from sexual connotations. The mention of "angels", therefore, can be regarded as a reflex of such connotations. Whatever ideologies of worship may be coordinated with the exemplary worship of angels, the potential remains that these angels are sexually vulnerable as well.

In any case, one should recognize that since very early times in the Christian movement 1 Corinthians 11:2–16 has exercised an enormous influence on behavior. As Christian churches almost unanimously agree that Paul's letters belong to a canon of authoritative writings, it is not improper from within the Christian tradition to ask in what way the results of our considerations might be construed as meaningful. The answer, I think lies more in the nature of what Paul is doing than in what he was thinking: here we find him negotiating between a principle of "neither male nor female", which for him counts as ultimate, eschatological reality "in the Lord" (Gal. 3:28; 1 Cor. 11:11–12), and socially-conditioned views and assumptions that have mitigated his vision of what such a principle of equality implies for social relationships between women, men, and even angels. It is hard to escape the notion that Paul's complex instruction in 1 Corinthians 11:2–16 implies that a woman, even when she prays or prophesies, is the social inferior of the man and that this status, for the apostle, is woven into a web of hierarchical relationships within the cosmos (11:3). We are thus left with an irresolvable tension in Paul. Of theological interest is, therefore, less *what* he concludes on the matter, but *that* he was struggling at all to come to terms with his and his readers' religious identity within a complex matrix of ideas received from both sacred Jewish traditions and sexually conditioned mores and social practices of the Mediterranean world. It is such complexity that re-emerges in this text.

Chapter Fourteen

The Apocalypse of John, *1 Enoch*, and the Question of Influence

A. Introduction

A century ago, in his important commentary on *The Book of Enoch or 1 Enoch*, Robert Henry Charles made the following claim:

> The influence of 1 Enoch on the New Testament has been greater than that of all the other apocryphal and pseudepigraphal books taken together.[1]

Since then, a considerable amount of new evidence for Jewish tradition in both the Medieval and Second Temple periods has come to light through not only new discoveries (e.g., Cairo Genizah, Dead Sea Scrolls) but also editions and commentaries that have begun to demonstrate the impact of this material for the interpretation of texts and traditions preserved in Hebrew Bible and the New Testament. The rhetorical claim by Charles regarding the importance of *1 Enoch* was no doubt calculated in order to draw attention to a tradition that had only been reintroduced to the western world during the previous century. Certainly the relative value of this or that tradition in comparison with others for the interpretation of New Testament texts is difficult, if not impossible, to argue with any degree of precision. So, rather than focusing on the grander claim of *1 Enoch*'s "greater influence," one is better positioned to reevaluate the question of influence in itself.

In what follows we would like to discuss the extent to which "*1 Enoch*" may be thought to have shaped particular traditions or ideas found in the Book of Revelation. Theoretically, such a focus is appropriate: if there is anything to Charles' claim about the general importance of the book as an "apocalyptic" text and if Revelation, alongside the book of Daniel in the Hebrew Bible, stands within the emerging stream of early Jewish and Christian apocalyptic traditions, then surely one might plausibly expect there to have been some interface between the two, whether this means dependence in any given instance, indirect influence, or at least a number of shared motifs.[2] Drawing *1 Enoch* into conversation with Revelation is

---

[1] R. H. Charles, *The Book of Enoch or 1 Enoch* (Oxford: Clarendon Press, 1912), p. xcv (cf. further pp. ix–xii).

[2] So R. H. Charles, *Revelation* (2 vols.; ICC; Edinburgh: T & T Clark, 1920). Those, like Charles, who have attempted to read Revelation by including Jewish apocalyptic literature as significant alongside the Hebrew prophets include Johannes Weiss, *Die Offenbarung Johannes: ein Beitrag zur Literatur- und Religionsgeschichte* (FRLANT 3; Göttingen: Vandenhoeck & Ruprecht, 1904); Wilhelm Bousset, *Die Offenbarung Johannis* (KEK 16; Göttingen: Vandenhoeck &

also appropriate because of the breadth of tradition that it represents. In fact, the designation "*1 Enoch*" is in itself misleading; in it we have to do with perhaps as many as twenty distinguishable traditions which can be dated variously within a period of some four hundred years, that is, all the way from the 4th century B. C. E. until the late 1st century C. E.[3] Thus, more than any "document" – this word should be used advisedly – stemming from the Second Temple period, *1 Enoch* includes a wide variety of works, mostly organized around and collected under the ante-diluvian patriarch Enoch's name, that reflects some important motifs articulated, preserved and developed during the time of Alexander the Great to early generations of the fledgling movement represented by the New Testament writings. While it falls outside the scope of the present discussion to elaborate on the developments that can be traced within the early Enochic texts, the theologically significant areas touched on within *1 Enoch* include, for example: the "origin" of evil, theological anthropology, the heavenly cosmos, eschatology, poverty and wealth, socio-religious and political oppression, intermediary figures (angelic beings, messianic figures), demonic and malevolent forces, retelling of Israel's sacred history, predictions of future events based on models of divine activity in the past, early Jewish mystical tradition, prophetic denunciations of wickedness, throne visions, heavenly journeys, offers of reassurance to the righteous, reflection on reality inspired by wisdom tradition, debate surrounding calendar, and the function of gender. This very broad scope of traditions and motifs, when compared not only with the Apocalypse of John but also with numerous other apocalyptic works, makes it possible to locate where, in tradition-historical terms, a given tradition lies within the sometimes complex trajectories that were taking shape within the apocalyptic idiom around the turn of the Common Era.

On the other hand, however, many scholars have been prepared to emphasize how much more the Johannine Apocalypse was indebted to "Old Testament" prophets than to "pseudepigraphal" literature outside the biblical "canon."[4] This view

---

Ruprecht, 1906, 5th ed.); Ulrich B. Müller, *Die Offenbarung des Johannes* (ÖTK 19; Gütersloh: Echter Verlag, 1995, 2nd ed.); David E. Aune, *Revelation* (3 vols.; WBC; Dallas: Word Books, 1997), esp. 1:lxx–xc; Pierre Prigent, *L'Apocalypse de Saint Jean* (CNT 14; Geneva: Labor et Fides, 2000).

[3] These may be summarized, with conventional titles for the major sections, as follows: in the *Book of Watchers*, (1) chs. 1–5; (2) 6–11 – itself a blend of 2–3 sources; (3) 12–16; (4) 17–19; (5) 21–36; the *Book of Parables*, (6) 37–71, into which (7) a number of Noah traditions are interspersed; the *Astronomical Book*, (8) 72–80 (preserving some of the earliest material going back to the 4th cent. B. C. E.); (9) 81:1–82:4a; (10) 82:4b–20; the *Book of Dreams* (11) 83–84, including the *Animal Apocalypse* (12) 85–90; the *Exhortation* (13) 91:1–10, 18–19; the *Apocalypse of Weeks* (14) 93:1–10 + 91:11–17; the *Epistle of Enoch* (15) 92:1–4 + 93:11–94:6 and 104:9–105:2; (16) 94:7–104:8; the *Birth of Noah* (17) 106:1–12 + 106:18–107:3; (18) 106:13–17; and *Eschatological Admonition* (19) 108 (containing some of the latest material that stems from the late 1st century C. E.). An early form of this collection may also have included the *Book of Giants* (if 4Q203 and 4Q204 belonged originally to the same manuscript).

[4] Rendering the contrast in these terms, the merits of comparisons aside, puts the discussion on a misguided footing from the start. Emphasis on continuity between Revelation and the "Old Tes-

is mistakenly coupled with the otherwise valid insight that the writer of the Apocalypse understood himself as a prophet.[5] There is another, pragmatic factor at work as well. Some of the analytical focus linking Revelation to the Hebrew Bible is a matter of convenience and more than simply the outworking of a canonical approach. Due to their complicated text-critical and reception histories, some apocalyptic works relating to the Second Temple period which are predominantly preserved in languages more remote to western scholarship (e. g., Geʿez, Armenian,

---

tament" prophets all too casually becomes a statement about inner-biblical canonicity, while an *a priori* negative valuation of "pseudepigraphal" texts diminishes in principle what one might expect to learn from them. See Isbon T. Beckwith, *The Apocalypse of John* (New York: MacMillan, 1922), pp. 166–197, who distinguished between the borrowing of form from other writings and theological value (canonicity); e. g., on p. 174, while stressing Revelation's indebtedness to the prophets, he states, "It should be distinctly observed that when the characteristics of apocalyptic literature mentioned above are attributed to the Book of Daniel or the Revelation of John, these books of our Bible are not robbed of their religious value or their canonical rank." This perspective, with permutation and with consequences for interpretation, has been sustained by major studies and commentaries who entertain a myopic focus on the influence of the Hebrew Bible or neglect and play down the significance of "non-canonical" Second Temple literature; the more significant voices expressing this view over the years have included, e. g., Henry Barclay Swete, *Commentary on Revelation* (Grand Rapids: Kregel, 1977, repr. 1911); pp. cxl-clviii; Adolf Schlatter, *Das Alte Testament in der johanneischen Apokalypse* (BFCT 16/6; Gütersloh: C. Bertelsmann, 1912); Martin Kiddle, *The Revelation of St. John* (MNTC; New York: Harper, 1940); Austen M. Farrer, *The Rebirth of Images: The Making of St. John's Apocalypse* (Westminster, England: Dacre, 1949); H. H. Rowley, *The Relevance of Apocalyptic* (London: Lutterworth, 1963, rev.'d ed.), pp. 138–149; Akira Satake, *Die Gemeindeordnung in der Johannesapokalypse* (WMANT 21; Neukirchen-Vluyn: Neukirchener Verlag, 1966), pp. 81–86; David Hill, "Prophecy and Prophets in the Revelation of St. John", *NTS* 18 (1971–1972), pp. 401–418 and "On the Evidence of the Creative Role of Christian Prophets", *NTS* 20 (1973–1974), pp. 262–274; Heinrich Kraft, *Die Offenbarung des Johannes* (HNT 16a; Tübingen: Mohr Siebeck, 1974; Jürgen Roloff, *Die Offenbarung des Johannes* (ZB 18; Zürich: Theologischer Verlag, 1974); Frederick David Mazzaferri, *The Genre of the Book of Revelation from a Source-Critical Perspective* (BZNW 54; Berlin: Walter de Gruyter, 1989); Bruce M. Metzger, *Breaking the Code: Understanding the Book of Revelation* (Nashville: Abingdon Press, 1993); Jan Fekkes III, *Isaiah and Prophetic Traditions in the Book of Revelation: Visionary Antecedents and their Developments* (JSNTSup 93; Sheffield: Sheffield Academic Press, 1994); Gregory K. Beale, for example, in *John's Use of the Old Testament in Revelation* (JSNTSup 166; Sheffield: Sheffield Academic Press, 1998). Of course, the sustained attention Charles gave to the Jewish apocalyptic underpinnings of many parts of Revelation while clearly privileging the Christian canonical writings over the Jewish non-canonical texts from the Second Temple period shows how interest in the latter did not necessarily result in a theologically sympathetic treatment.

[5] By drawing a line of continuity between the Hebrew Bible and Revelation as prophecy, this view assumes that "prophecy" does not describe how the authors of pseudepigraphal texts would have styled themselves. The *Epistle of Enoch, Jubilees* and *4 Ezra* (cf. ch. 14) provide several cases to the contrary. On the *Epistle* see Loren T. Stuckenbruck, "The *Epistle of Enoch*: Genre and Authorial Presentation", *DSD* 17 (2010), pp. 387–417 and *1 Enoch 91–108* (CEJL; Berlin: Walter de Gruyter, 2007), pp. 185–216; on *Jubilees* and *4 Ezra* cf. respectively Hindy Najman, "How Should We Contextualize Pseudepigrapha? Imitation and Emulation in 4 Ezra", in eds. Anthony Hilhorst, Émile Puech, and Eibert J. C. Tigchelaar, *Flores Florentino: Dead Sea Scrolls and Other Early Jewish Studies in Honour of Florentino García Martínez* (JSJSup 122; Leiden / Boston: Brill, 2007), pp. 529–536 and "Reconsidering Jubilees: Prophecy and Exemplarity", in eds. Gabriele Boccaccini and Giovanni Ibba, *Enoch and the Mosaic Torah* (Grand Rapids: Eerdmans, 2009), pp. 229–243.

Old Slavonic) have been less easily accessed and therefore more difficult to negotiate for many critical scholars, who find themselves having to rely on modern translations. Here, both familiarity and a principled circumscription of "canonicity" join hands in a way that neglects a constructive attempt to locate Revelation within the wider Jewish literary output of the ancient world.

B. Comparison and Analysis

What can be said about the relationship between the Book of Revelation and the early Enochic literature? In terms of principle, two things should be noted. First, given access to *1 Enoch* in different languages, its complete preservation in only Ge'ez (including two recensions), and its composition over several hundred years, any comparison of the two should involve the recognition of a certain complexity. While Revelation as a whole may also be the product of development, its growth – from traditions that may have initially circulated until the time its visions were organized as messages to the churches of Asia Minor – spanned at most a shorter period of decades towards the end of the 1st century C. E. In other words, while the production of *1 Enoch* as preserved in the Ethiopic text traditions reflects the work of many authors who assumed the name "Enoch" and who entertained different theological outlooks,[6] the book of Revelation by and large is ascribed to the same prophetic figure, John, who was immediately known to the seven churches addressed in the work. It is therefore important to take the different theological perspectives and historical contexts within *1 Enoch* into account as we offer a comparison with selected passages or texts in Revelation. Second, the present discussion, while interested in the question of possible *influence* of Enoch traditions on Revelation, is also concerned with what can be learned about Revelation when both assemblages of tradition are placed in conversation with one another. Thus not only overlapping perspectives but also differences may provide clues on what kinds of traditions John had at hand and what kinds of traditions John may have attempted to avoid.

It is impossible within the present treatment to provide an exhaustive discussion of every possible link that can be subjected to assessment. What we provide below, however, is a list of alleged parallels (columns 1 and 2), and a short summary of what they comprise (column 3), followed by a brief discussion that weighs the relative merits of the parallels. The list is largely drawn from several selected studies and commentaries related to *1 Enoch*,[7] on the one hand, and to Revelation, on

---

[6] On the concurrency of authorial activity under the name of Enoch, see Loren T. Stuckenbruck, "Reflections on Source-Criticism of the Epistle of Enoch and the Significance of *1 Enoch* 104:9–13", in eds. Eric F. Mason *et al.*, *A Teacher for All Generations: Essays in Honor of James C. VanderKam* (2 vols.; JSJSup 135/I and II; Leiden / Boston: Brill, 2012), vol. 2, pp. 705–714.

[7] So esp. Charles, *The Book of Enoch or 1 Enoch*, pp. xcvi–xcix; Matthew Black, *The Book of Enoch or I Enoch*, (SVTP 7; Leiden: Brill, 1985); Nickelsburg, *1 Enoch 1* (Hermeneia; Minneapo-

the other.[8] In order to draw attention to the distribution of parallels in Revelation, the passages supplied follow the sequence of the Book of Revelation, while the discussion and conclusions drawn thereafter will attempt to respect the socio-religious and literary contexts of the Enochic texts in question. References to passages in Revelation which show particular affinity with the Enochic parallel[9] and merit discussion are marked in **bold**. Those passages which show a more general affinity with further parallels in Second Temple Jewish writings (listed in the third column) are left unmarked. Next to each of the Revelation texts, secondary literature from which the parallel was initially derived is indicated by the author's initials (RC = R. H. Charles; DA = David Aune; AYS = Annette Yoshiko Reed; MM = Mark D. Mathews; LS = Loren T. Stuckenbruck), and readers should note the further bibliographical references and discussions in the notes.

Revelation	*1 Enoch*	*Alleged Parallel*
1:1 (LS[10]) – to show the things that must soon take place (4:1; 22:6; cf. 1:19)	**91:1** – "in order that I (Enoch) may show you everything that will happen for ever"[11]	introduction by an intermediary of a document as concerned with the future

An announcement at the beginning of the work that what follows is revealed knowledge about divinely foreordained events is uniquely shared between Revelation and the *Exhortation* of Enoch.

---

lis: Fortress Press, 2001); Patrick A. Tiller, *A Commentary on the Animal Apocalypse of* 1 Enoch (SBLEJL 4; Atlanta, George: Society of Biblical Literature, 1993); and Loren T. Stuckenbruck, *1 Enoch 91–108* (CEJL; Berlin: Walter de Gruyter, 2007).

[8] For the present discussion, in addition to taking note of the bibliography in the previous footnote, we have followed the parallels alleged mentioned in Charles, *Revelation* (bibl. in n. 2), pp. lxxxii–lxxxiii (a much shorter list than in *idem, The Book of Enoch or 1 Enoch*); Aune, *Revelation* (bibl. in n. 2); James H. Charlesworth, "The *Parables of Enoch* and the Apocalypse of John", in eds. Gerbern S. Oegema and James H. Charlesworth, *The Pseudepigrapha and Christian Origins* (Jewish and Christian Texts 4; London: T & T Clark, 2008), pp. 193–242; David E. Aune, "The Apocalypse of John and Palestinian Jewish Apocalyptic", in Oegema and Charlesworth, *The Pseudepigrapha and Christian Origins*, pp. 169–192; Richard Bauckham, "The Use of Apocalyptic Traditions", in *idem, The Climax of Prophecy: Studies on the Book of Revelation* (Edinburgh: T & T Clark, 1993), pp. 38–91; Mark D. Mathews, *Riches, Poverty, and the Faithful: Perspectives on Wealth in the Second Temple Period and the Apocalypse of John* (SNTSMS 154; Cambridge: Cambridge University Press, 2013). A number of commentaries or treatments of Revelation contain a general overview of the early Enochic tradition without, however, assessing its significance in more than very general terms; cf., e. g., Beckwith, *The Apocalypse of John*, pp. 181–183; Leonard L. Thompson, *The Book of Revelation* (New York: Oxford University Press, 1990), pp. 19–21.

[9] Whenever *1 Enoch* is cited, unless otherwise indicated, the translation is that of George W. E. Nickelsburg and James C. VanderKam, *1 Enoch: A New Translation* (Minneapolis: Fortress Press, 2004).

[10] Stuckenbruck, *1 Enoch 91–108*, p. 160.

[11] Translation in Stuckenbruck, *1 Enoch 91–108*, p. 157.

1:4 (RC[12]) – seven spirits before God's throne (cf. 1:20; 3:1–2; 4:5; 5:6; 8:2,6; **15:1,6–8**; 16:1; 17:1)	90:20–21 – summoning of seven "white men" to bring disobedient stars before throne (cf. 20:1–8; 81:5; 87:2)	seven angelic beings before God linked to judgment (Tob. 12:15; *T.Levi* 8:2; cf. Ezek. 8:1–21:9)

If the seven spirits before God's throne in Revelation 1:4 are angelic beings,[13] it is possible that they are linked to those angels who later in the book carry out God's judgment, especially in chapters 8 (by blowing the trumpets) and 15 (by pouring out bowls of wrath). In relation to the broad motif of seven angelic figures, the texts from Revelation come closer to Tobit 12:15 (cf. their intercessory role in Rev. 8:2–5) and to Ezekiel 9:1–11 (cf. their role as executioners of God's wrath in Rev. 15).[14] Unlike *1 Enoch* 90, the activity of the *seven* angels in Revelation is not immediately correlated to the execution of punishment against the fallen stars. Significantly, however, the combination of seven angels as agents of judgment and the motif of a star falling from heaven is only shared with the *Animal Apocalypse* (*1 En.* 86:1; 88:1; Rev. 8:10; 9:1; cf. 12:7–9).

1:7 – every eye will see him; cf. under 6:15–16 below	62:3, 5 – they (all the kings, the mighty, the exalted, those who possess the earth) will see and recognize that he (the Chosen One, v.1) sits on the throne of his glory ... they will see the Son of Man sitting on the throne of glory	eschatological recognition of "son of man" figure by wrongdoers (Mt. 24:30; *Did.* 16:8; Justin *Dial.* 14.8)

The phrase itself, along with the following one ("and those who pierced him"), is an allusion to Zechariah 12:10b. Here, as in Matthew 24:30, *Didache* 16:8 and Justin's *Dialogue with Trypho* 14.8, the Zechariah passage is interpreted together with Daniel 7:13, which refers to a son of man-like figure coming with (Theod.; cf. "with" in Rev. 1:7) or on (MT, Old Grk.; cf. Rev. 14:14) the clouds of heaven. The inclusion of a reference in this combination to "those who pierced him" is shared by Revelation 1:7 and the passage from Justin who, however, attributed the allusion to Hosea and Daniel. The Enochic passage in the *Parables*, in which "the Chosen One" acts as a vice regent also designated as enthroned "the Son of Man" (63:5) may reflect the combination of Zechariah and Daniel, though more remotely. Whereas the *Parables* (the catalogue of wrongdoers) and Justin (non-Christian Jews) emphasize the recognition of God's vice regent by the wicked, Revela-

---

[12] Charles, *The Book of Enoch or 1 Enoch*, p. xcvi. Cf. further Nickelsburg, *1 Enoch 1*, p. 207 ("Excursus: The Four – or Seven – Archangels in Jewish and Early Christian Literature").

[13] On the equivalence between "spirit" and angelic beings, see the discussion in Aune, *Revelation*, vol. 1, pp. 34–35.

[14] Cf. Loren T. Stuckenbruck, *Angel Veneration and Christology* (WUNT 2.70; Tübingen: Mohr Siebeck, 1995), pp. 226–228 (and n. 58).

tion ("every eye"), Matthew ("all the tribes of the earth") and *Didache* ("the world") underscore the universal scope of the vision.

1:14,16; 10:1 (LS[15]) – eyes like a flame of fire (cf. 2:18); face like the sun shining in full strength; face like the sun	106:2 – when he (Noah) opened his eyes, they illuminated the entire house as the sun	the comparison of the brightness of the eyes or face of a divine agent with sunlight (Dan. 10:5; *Gen. Apoc.* 1Q20 v 7; 1Q19 1.5; *Jos. Asen.* 15:9; 22:7; *2 En.* 1:5 A; *Apoc. Zeph.* 6:11)

Just as for Noah at his birth in *1 Enoch* 106:2, the descriptions of Jesus (1:14, 16; 2:18) and of a strong angel (10:1) in Revelation pick up on traditions associated with prominent angelic figures (e. g., Dan. 10:5; *Jos. Asen.* 15:9; *Apoc. Zeph.* 6:11; *2 En.* 1:5 A). No direct connection here between the *Birth of Noah* and Revelation, can, however, be argued.

*2:7 (RC[16]) – to the one who conquers I will grant to eat from the tree of life, which is in the paradise of God (cf. 22:14, 19)	24:4–25:6 – a fragrant tree that no one may touch until the great judgment, when it will be given to the righteous (v. 4) and its fruit as food for the elect (v. 5)	eschatological eating from the tree of life by the righteous (*2 En.* 8–9; 4 Ezra 8:52; *T. Levi* 18:11; *Apoc. Mos.* 28:4; *3 En.* 23:18; *Apoc. Elij.* 5:6)

Access to the tree of life is forbidden after Adam and Eve's disobedience in the garden of Eden (Gen. 3:24). In the *Book of Watchers* Enoch is given to see two prominent trees: (1) a fragrant and beautiful tree, whose fruit will be given to the righteous at the time of judgment (*1 En.* 25:4–5) and (2) a beautiful "tree of wisdom" in "the paradise of righteousness" (*1 En.* 32:3). Unlike the parallel traditions and Revelation, the *Book of Watchers* distinguishes between the "tree of life" (Gen. 2:7; 3:22, 24; cf. *1 En.* 24:4–25:6) and the "tree of the knowledge of good and evil" (Gen. 2:9, 17) in "the garden of righteousness", that is, the one from which Adam and Eve ate (cf. *1 En.* 32:3–6). Like Revelation, *2 Enoch* 8–9 and 4 Ezra 8:52[17] also refer to a tree of life in paradise, but do not expressly state that from it the righteous will eat. The close similarity between Revelation 2:7 and the text of *Testament of Levi* 18:11 is best explained in terms of influence of the former on the latter. If the eschatological tree from which the righteous will eat in *1 Enoch* 24:4–25:6 is to be understood as the "tree of life," then the *Book of Watchers* provides the closest prior existing parallel[18] to the promise to those who conquer in Revelation 2:7.

---

[15] Stuckenbruck, *1 Enoch 91–108*, pp. 628–629.

[16] Charles, *The Book of Enoch or 1 Enoch*, p. xcvii, followed by Loren L. Johns, *The Lamb Christology of the Apocalypse of John* (WUNT 2.167: Tübingen: Mohr Siebeck, 2003), p. 94

[17] 4 Ezra 7:123 refers to paradise and the unsoiled, plenteous and healing fruit without, however, mentioning the tree of life.

[18] The similar tradition is preserved in several compositions that post-date Revelation: *Apoc. Mos.* 28:4, *3 En.* 23:18, and *Apoc. Elij.* 5:6.

*3:5, 7:13 (RC[19]) – the one who conquers will be clothed in white (cf. 3:18; 4:4; 7:9,14)	90:28–32 – in the new house (Jerusalem) three angelic beings are clothed in white and the sheep (the faithful of Israel) are white	association of the faithful with white (clothing) (Hermas, Sim. 8.2.3; 2 Esd. 2:40; b. Shabb. 114a)

In Revelation the color "white" consistently denotes purity,[20] while in the *Animal Apocalypse* the color white is generally applied to those who participate in human lineage (*1 En.* 85:3–Adam; 85:8–Seth; 89:9–Noah and Shem; 89:10–Abraham; 89:11–Isaac; 89:12–Jacob), to angelic beings (87:2; 90:21, 31), to those among Israel deemed to have been loyal (90:6), and to the eschatological faithful sheep of Israel (90:32). Although angelic beings in the *Animal Apocalypse* are the only ones specifically described as "clothed in white," the description of the faithful as white leading up to the time of the great judgment (90:31–32) has its equivalent in Revelation (esp. 3:5; 7:13–14), where being clothed in white signifies faithfulness and religious purity. Among Jewish writings composed prior to the end of the 1st century C. E., the *Animal Apocalypse* offers the closest parallel to Revelation.

3:10 (RC[21]) – "those who dwell upon the earth" cf. under 13:14 below	37:5 – "those who dwell upon the earth"	the phrase in Greek and Geʿez corresponds exactly (4 Ezra 3:12, 34–35; 4:21, 39; 5:1 etc.; 2 Bar. 25:1; 48:32, 40 etc.; T. Abr. 3:12 A; Ps.-Philo 3:3, 9, 12; 4:16; CD x 9)

In addition to sharing the precisely same formulation (οἱ κατοικοῦντες ἐπὶ τῆς γῆς // ʾella yaḥadderu diba yabs), both Revelation (6:10; 8:13; 11:10; 13:8, 12, 14; 17:2, 8) and, for the most part, the Enochic *Parables* (e. g. *1 En.* 40:6–7; 48:5; 54:6, 9; 55:1; 67:7) use it in a negative sense. However, "those who inhabit the land" (יושבי הארץ) is frequently applied to Philistines in the Hebrew Bible (Lam. 4:12; Isa. 24:6, 17; 26:9, 18, 21; Jer. 1:14; 25:29–30; 38:11; Ezek. 7:7; Dan. 4:35; Zeph. 1:18)[22] and occurs in a similar form in a sufficient number of other early Jewish writings that any direct relationship between Revelation and the *Parables* cannot be established.

*3:12 (RC[23]) – the one who conquers "I will make him into a pillar in the temple of God" ... "I will write on him the name of	90:29 – reference to Jerusalem as the "new house" with new pillars, beams, and ornaments; the faithful sheep of Israel will dwell	association of the faithful with a new Jerusalem (including pillars) in which a temple cult is not ultimately envisioned

---

[19] Charles, *The Book of Enoch or 1 Enoch*, p. xcvii.
[20] Cf. Aune, *Revelation*, vol. 1, pp. 222–223.
[21] See also Charlesworth, "The *Parables of Enoch* and the Apocalypse of John", p. 237.
[22] See the discussion in Aune, *Revelation*, vol. 1, p. 240.
[23] Charles, *The Book of Enoch or 1 Enoch*, p. xcvii; not mentioned in Charles, *Revelation*.

my God and the name of the city of my God, the new Jerusalem"; cf. **21:22** – the new Jerusalem is without a temple since "its temple is the Lord God the Almighty and the Lamb."

there; no explicit mention of the Temple (cf. 90:32–35)

While it is now argued that "the new house" referred to in the *Animal Apocalypse* (cf. *1 En.* 90:28–29) describes eschatological Jerusalem and not the Temple as such,[24] it remains that the description of the new Jerusalem contains imagery that also applies to the Temple. While the notion of the heavenly or new Jerusalem was widespread in Jewish literature, the mention of pillars in relation to it is rare, that is, it is only also found in Ezekiel 40:49 and 42:6, and preserved in the *New Jerusalem* fragments from the Dead Sea Scrolls.[25] In Revelation, however, the pillars are associated with "the temple of God" which, in a twist, is expressly stated not to exist as a structure in the new Jerusalem when it is described in chapter 21 (cf. vv. 10–27). Despite the different emphases and the incongruity between the anticipated temple (3:21) and its absence in the conclusion of John's vision (ch. 21), the convergence of the motifs of the new Jerusalem, the presence of pillars and the non-inclusion of the temple as an edifice in the eschatological order of things is only shared by Revelation and the *Animal Apocalypse*.

3:17 (RC[26]) – For you say, "I am rich, I have prospered, and I need nothing." You do not realize that you are wretched, pitiable, poor, blind, and naked. See also under 18:4, 7 below.

97:8–10 – Woe to you, who gain gold and silver which is not through righteousness; and you will say, "We have become wealthy with riches, and we have possessions and own everything that we want. / And now let us do what we have planned, for we have treasured up silver; we have filled our treasures chests, and as much water are the field laborers of our houses." / And like water

speech imputed on wrongdoers who have acquired wealth (Hos. 12:9 Grk.; Epictetus in Arrian, *Epict. Diss.* 3.7.20)

---

[24] So Tiller, *A Commentary on the Animal Apocalypse*, esp. 45–51; Nickelsburg, *1 Enoch 1*, pp. 404–405.

[25] So 1Q32 1.1–2; 5.1; 4Q554 2 iii 22; 5Q15 1 ii 4; 2.4–5; 11Q18 9.2; 11.6 – here the pillars are features of the city, not the Temple *per se*, in contrast, for example, to *Songs of the Sabbath Sacrifice* at 4Q403 i 14 which refers to "pillars" in the heavenly temple and where, interestingly, as in Rev. 3:12, the pillars of the heavenly temple are depicted as animate; see Dale C. Allison, "4Q403 fragm. 1, col. 1,38–46 and the Revelation to John", *RevQ* 12 (1986), pp. 409–414.

[26] Charles, *The Book of Enoch or 1 Enoch*, p. xcvii, though the parallel alleged with *1 En.* 97:8 is not followed up in his *Commentary* on Revelation (vol. 1, pp. 96–97).

> your error will flow away,
> for your wealthy will not
> remain, but will quickly go
> up from you; for you have
> come into ownership of
> everything by means of ini-
> quity, and over to a great
> curse you will be delivered.

The influence behind the imputed speech within the message to the church of Lao-dicea in Revelation 3:17 has been traced to "the discourse of the moral philoso-phers,"[27] sapiential speech underscores the superiority of wisdom over wealth,[28] or, more usually, to the speech of Ephraim in Hosea 12:9 (Grk.[29]): "And Ephraim said, 'Indeed I am rich; I have found relief for myself!' But none of his labors will offset the wrongs he has wicked deeds through which he has sinned."[30] Attributed speech, as such, is common in the Hebrew Bible and Second Temple Jewish texts.[31]

In relation to wealth, such attributed speech also occurs in Ben Sira 11:18–19 (cf. 5:1), while self-glorification speech attributed to Rome is also found in *2 Baruch* 12:3 (cf. Ezek. 28:2). In Ben Sira, however, this device serves an instructional,[32] rather than polemical purpose. In addition, the perspective enjoined in Sirach is not categorically critical of the acquisition of affluence in the present life. Siding on the whole with Deuteronomistic tradition, Sirach, though aware of the pitfalls of wealth, holds that one can enjoy material blessing from God in this life, as long as one guards against greed and does not neglect the poor (4:1, 4; 7:32; 13:24; 14:3; 29:9).

---

[27] As argued by Robert M. Royalty, *The Streets of Heaven: The Ideology of Wealth in the Apocalypse of John* (Macon: Mercer University Press, 1997), pp. 167–172 (cf. n. 51), who appeals to the very similar words of Epicurean perspective made by a Roman official in response to Epictetus' claim that Epicureans are unlikely to subordinate pleasure to social duties: "But I am rich and have need of nothing." Unlike Revelation 3:17, Hos. 12:9 (Grk.) and *1 En.* 97:8–10, however, these words are not formally followed up by a declaration that unmasks the speech's claim.

[28] Cf. J. Massyngberde Ford, *Revelation* (AB 38; Garden City: Doubleday, 1975), p. 421 who refers to Wsd. Sol. 7:9 and Sir. 6:30–31 where, however, the form of imputed speech is lacking.

[29] In contrast to the Heb. (MT), which presents the entirety of the verse as spoken by Ephraim.

[30] So Charles, *Revelation*, vol. 1, p. 96 and, e. g., Swete, *Commentary on Revelation*, p. 61; Ernst Lohmeyer, *Die Offenbarung des Johannes* (HNT 16; Tübingen: Mohr Siebeck, 1970, 3rd ed.), p. 38; Wilfred J. Harrington, *Revelation* (SP 16; Collegeville: The Liturgical Press, 1993), p. 74; Müller, *Die Offenbarung des Johannes*, p. 136; Beale, *The Book of Revelation*, pp. 304–305; Edmundo F. Lupieri, *A Commentary on the Apocalypse of John* (Grand Rapids: Eerdmans, 1999), p. 129.

[31] So, e. g., Deut. 8:17–18; Ps. 10:13; 35:25; Prov. 24:12; Isa. 29:15; 47:8; Jer. 2:23; 13:22; 21:13; 42:13–14; Ezek. 18:19; Hos. 12:9 (Grk., cited above); Amos 7:16; Zech. 11:5; Sir. 5:1; Wisd. Sol. 2:6–10; 5:8, 15–16; *1 En.* 63:10; Lk. 12:19; Jas. 4:13.

[32] Sir. 11:18–19: "One becomes rich through diligence and self-denial, and the reward allotted to him is this: when he says, 'I have found rest, and now I shall feast on my goods!' he does not know how long it will be until he leaves them to others and dies." (NRSV)

[33] See the discussion of these passages in Stuckenbruck, *1 Enoch 91–108*, pp. 537–577.

In its use of the imputed speech form and in overall perspective, Revelation comes closer to the *Epistle of Enoch* than any other document. The *Epistle* expresses five main views regarding wealth: (1) It rejects wealth as a sign of God's blessing in the present age (e.g., *1 En.* 96:4). (2) The Deuteronomistic promise of material reward (Deut. 7:13, 15–16, 20–21; 8:12–13; 9:26; 10:18; 11:6; generally, ch.'s 28–30), is postponed to the eschaton (cf. *1 En.* 103:9–15 with 104:1–6).[33] (3) The acquisition of wealth for the faithful in the present age is categorically rejected. (4) There are warnings that the righteous should not associate with the rich and powerful (*1 En.* 96:4; 104:6; cf. 97:4; 99:10); and finally (5) Although the *Epistle* refers to the unjust wealth (*1 En.* 97:8–10), those who have acquired wealth are irretrievably branded as "sinners"; no effort is made in the *Epistle* to call them to repentance or to instruct them to behave differently. Despite slight differences,[34] John of Revelation also views the present age as a time when the righteous, who are not among the affluent, suffer and, predictably, are going to be materially destitute. In addition, whereas the language that reflects the true state of the rich (wretched, pitiable, poor, blind, naked) has sometimes been explained as related to the banking and wool industry of Laodicea and to medical schools that produced eye salve,[35] the conditions of poverty, blindness and nakedness also occur among the Deuteronomistic curses upon those who are unfaithful to the covenant (Deut. 28:28–29, 48).[36] Coming very close to the *Epistle*, John points out that wealth is not a sign of divine favor, but rather it reflects a state of being unfaithful; moreover, like the *Epistle*, John holds that people are so much more wicked because of their wealth as they have become rich through blatant disobedience to God. Hence the audience of Revelation is exhorted to "come out" of Babylon lest they too become guilty by association (cf. *1 En.* 97:4).

3:20 (RC[37]) – Jesus will eat with those who open the door	62:14 – the Lord of the Spirits will abide over the righteous "and with the Son of Man they will eat"	eating with God's vice-regent is promised to the faithful

Within the context of Revelation, the reference to Jesus' dining with the faithful here is picked up in "the marriage supper of the Lamb" (Rev. 19:9), though the

---

[34] In two respects: (1) Revelation makes no mention of unjust wealth, and (2) the message to Laodicea, together with the appeal to "come out" of Babylon in 18:4, does not regard the materially well-to-do as beyond change (see the summons to repent in 3:19); cf. David A. deSilva, *Seeing Things John's Way: The Rhetoric of the Book of Revelation* (Louisville: Westminster John Knox, 2009), pp. 250–254.

[35] So, e.g., William Ramsay, *The Letters to the Seven Churches of Asia and Their Place in the Plan of the Apocalypse* (New York: Hodder and Stoughton, 1904); Colin J. Hemer, *The Letters to the Seven Churches of Asia in Their Local Setting* (JSNTSup. 11; Sheffield: JSOT Press, 1986).

[36] Mathews, *Riches, Poverty, and the Faithful*, p. 164.

[37] Charles, *The Book of Enoch or 1 Enoch*, p. xcvii; cf. also Charlesworth, "The Parables of Enoch and the Apocalypse of John", pp. 237–238.

latter has a specific event in view and in it the Lamb is assumed to be the host while in the former Jesus is the guest of the one who opens the door to his knocking.[38] The parallel in the *Book of Parables* does not specify anything about the righteous being hosts or guests; however, the shared act of eating, like in Revelation, is considered a reward to be enjoyed and shared between the faithful, on the one hand, and God's primary agent of salvation, on the other. Though the imagery of opening the door for a meal to the one who knocks is already found in Jesus tradition (Lk. 12:35–37)[39] and the tradition of the Last Supper or practice of communion in the church may lie in the background,[40] among the non-Christian Jewish writings from the Second Temple period, only the *Book of Parables* anticipates an eschatological eating with God's heavenly designate who, as Jesus in the New Testament (and in Revelation), is associated with the "son of man"-like figure known from Daniel 7 (*1 En.* 46:3–4; 62:7, 9, 14; 63:11; 69:27, 29) and is called "the Anointed One/Messiah" (48:10; 52:4).

3:21 (RC[41]) – "To the one who conquers I will give a place with me on my throne, just as I myself conquered and sat down with my Father on his throne." Cf. 20:4.	108:12 – "I will let each one (of the righteous) sit on his throne of honor."	enthronement promised to the faithful (1 Sam. 2:8; Job 36:7; 4Q521 2 ii 5–8; Lk. 12:35–37; 22:28–30; cf. *T. Levi* 13:9; *Apoc. Elijah* 1:8)

Taken together with the possible allusion to Luke 12:35–37 in 3:20, some interpreters have stressed the parallel between 3:21 and Jesus' promise to those who persist with him to eat "at my table in my kingdom" which he has received from "the Father" and "to sit on thrones judging the twelve tribes of Israel" (Lk. 22:28–30). These parallels, taken together, might suggest a more immediate frame of reference than either the Enochic *Eschatological Admonition* (*1 En.* 108:12) or the text from 4Q521 2 ii 7 ("for he will honor the pious upon the throne of eternal rule"). In one detail, however, the last mentioned texts agree with Revelation against the parallel from Luke: the faithful will be allowed to sit on the divine throne, not their own individual thrones.[42]

If sitting on the throne is not simply a matter of honor for the faithful but takes the notion of an enthroned messianic figure sitting in judgment of the wicked as its point of departure, then Revelation 3:21 builds on the tradition found also in

---

[38] Martin Karrer, *Die Johannesoffenbarung als Brief* (FRLANT 140; Göttingen: Vandenhoeck & Ruprecht, 1983), p. 215.

[39] Cf. Louis A. Vos, *The Synoptic Traditions in the Apocalypse* (Kampen: J. H. Kok, 1965), p. 100 for the argument of direct dependence on Luke's Gospel.

[40] E. g., Prigent, *L'Apocalypse de Saint Jean*, pp. 167–168.

[41] Charles, *The Book of Enoch or 1 Enoch*, p. xcvii. The Enochic text is not mentioned by Charles in *Revelation*, vol. 1, p. 102.

[42] For a discussion of this motif, see Stuckenbruck, *1 Enoch 91–108*, pp. 735–738.

Revelation 6:16 and 22:1, 3. This, in turn, would have a parallel in the *Book of Parables* where the Chosen One/Son of Man, seated on the divine throne, judges human perpetrators of evil (cf. *1 En.* 45:3; 51:1; 55:4; 61:8; 62:2, 5; 69:26–29).[43] It is not clear, though, whether here the faithful are anticipated to sit with Christ in judgment (Rev. 20:4) or will do so primarily to illustrate the honor that will come to them (as in *1 En.* 108:12; 4Q521 2 ii 7).

4:1 (RC[44]) – "After this I looked, And there in heaven a door stood open! And the first voice … said, 'Come up here …'."	14:8, 15 – "clouds in the vision were summoning me, and mists were crying out to me; … / And look, another open door before me …"	an open door for entry into heavenly space; a sound beckoning the visionary to come (*Aram. Levi Doc.* 4Q213a 2.16–18; *T. Levi* 2:6)

In two details, the *Book of Watchers* parallels the beginning of John's vision of the divine throne room in Revelation chapter 4: (1) the image of an open door as a passageway to heaven (*1 En.* 14:15; *T. Levi* 2:5 – "the heavens were opened") and (2) the sound from above encouraging the visionary to come (14:8; cf. *T. Levi* 2:6).[45] In *1 Enoch* 14:15, the reference to "another door" assumes that the visionary's initial entrance to heaven was a (un-narrated) door. The combination of both details is uniquely shared by Revelation and, among the Hebrew Bible and Second Temple Jewish writings, the *Book of Watchers*.

4:6, 8 (RC[46]) – "around the throne, on each side of the throne, are four living creatures … day and night without ceasing they sing, 'Holy, holy, holy is the Lord God Almighty …'"	40:2 – "on the four sides of the Lord of Spirits, I was four figures different from those who sleep not"; 39:12 – "those who do not sleep bless you … saying, 'Holy, holy, holy is the Lord of Spirits …'" (my translation); cf. 14:23	the location on each side of the divine throne of four creatures in the context of continuous worship (Isa. 6:2–3; Ezek. 1:5–25)

Both the description of the four creatures and their worship of God in the divine throne room in Revelation and the *Book of Parables* are likely influenced by scenes described in Isaiah 6 (the *qedushah* by the four seraphim; see Rev. and *1 En.* 39:12) and Ezekiel 1 (the four living creatures). In addition, the difficult phrase "around the throne" in Revelation 4:6 (lit. "in the midst of the throne", ἐν μέσῳ

---

[43] Aune, *Revelation*, vol. 1, pp. 261–263.

[44] Charles, *Revelation*, vol. 1, pp. 106–107.

[45] Both of these points may be implied by *Aramaic Levi Document* (4Q213a 2.16–18) and *T. Levi* 2:6. For text and commentary of the former, very fragmentary text, see Henryk Drawnel, *An Aramaic Wisdom Text from Qumran* (JSJSup 86; Leiden/Boston: Brill, 2004), pp. 176–179 and 224–228.

[46] Charles, *The Book of Enoch or 1 Enoch*, p. xcvii and *Revelation*, vol. 1, pp. 118–119; Aune, *Revelation*, vol. 1, p. 302; and esp. Charlesworth, "The *Parables of Enoch* and the Apocalypse of John", p. 238.

τοῦ θρόνου) may derive from Ezekiel 1:5 ("in the midst of it [ἐν τῷ μέσῳ – i. e., a great cloud] was the likeness of each of the four sides of the throne"). In addition, unlike Revelation 4:8 neither Ezekiel nor Isaiah state anything about the worship around the divine throne being continuous; in Revelation the uninterrupted continuity of worship is underscored by the phrases "do not have rest" (14:11) and "day and night" (esp. 7:15; cf. 12:10; 20:10) both of which reflect language used elsewhere by John. Both these details are shared with the *Book of Parables* which, using its own phraseology, attributes worship of God and the reciting of the *qedushah* to a class of beings "different" from the four creatures as "those who do not sleep" (*'ella yenawwemu*; *1 En.* 39:12, 13; 40:2). Thus *Book of Parables* and Revelation, which are also the only texts outside of Isaiah before the end of the 1ˢᵗ century C. E. to refer to the *qedushah*, have at least taken their use of the language of Ezekiel and Isaiah in a similar direction; it would be difficult to conclude from this, however, that either of these texts has been influenced by the other.[47]

Significantly, the phrase "day and night" used by John to denote the ceaseless worship of God comes close to what the *Book of Watchers* states about "the holy ones of the watchers (Grk. angels) who approached him (God)" in *1 Enoch* 14:23: "they did not depart by night" and, if we may follow Nickelsburg's emendation of the text, "did not leave <by day>."[48] Only these two texts from the Second Temple period share this language in relation to the *heavenly* worship (also Rev. 7:15), while several documents apply the phrase to the cultic activity of priestly groups (1 Chr. 23:3; Josephus, *Ant.* 7.14.7; 1QS vi 6–12).

5:11 (RC[49]) – "the presence of myriads of myriads and thousands of thousands" around the divine throne	14:22 – "myriads of myriads stood before him"; 40:1 – "thousands of thousands and myriads of myriads"; 71:8 – "thousands of thousands and myriads of myriads" (my translations)	"myriads" and "thousands" (cf. Dan. 7:10 Th.; Ps. 68:17; *Book of Giants* 4Q530 2 ii + 6–7 i + 8–12, lines 16–20; *Apoc. Zeph.* 4:1; 8:1)

Though in reverse order, the presence of "myriads of myriads" and "thousands of thousands" is shared by two passages in the *Book of Parables* (40:1; 71:8; for the same order see *Apoc. Zeph.* 4:1; 8:1; *1 Clem.* 34:6) with Revelation 5:11,[50] whereas

---

[47] Charlesworth, "The *Parables of Enoch* and the Apocalypse of John", p. 238, is more optimistic about the possibility of Enochic influence here. He regards it "probable that one of the sources [i. e., of Revelation 4:8] may ultimately originate with the *Parables of Enoch*" and goes on to postulate that "perhaps the author of the Apocalypse of John is working from memory and had read the *Parables of Enoch*."

[48] Nickelsburg, *1 Enoch 1*, p. 259 n. b (concluding that Rev. 4:8 "seems to have known" *1 En.* 14:23) and pp. 265–266 ("dependent"); cf. Nickelsburg and VanderKam, *1 Enoch: A New Translation*, p. 36; Johns, *The Lamb Christology of the Apocalypse of John*, p. 95.

[49] Charles, *The Book of Enoch or 1 Enoch*, p. xcvii; cf. *idem*, *Revelation*, vol. 1, pp. 148–149. Cf. also Johns, *The Lamb Christology of the Apocalypse of John*, p. 94.

[50] On the sequence, see Aune, *Revelation*, vol. 1, pp. 363–364.

Psalm 68:17 refers to "a myriad thousands," and the *Book of Giants*, in a tradition that relates to Daniel 7, describes the worship of God by "thousands" and "hundreds."[51] The sequence in Revelation, however, corresponds to that of the *Book of Watchers* (*1 En.* 14:22) and to Daniel 7:10, either text of which is likely to have shaped the wording here.

6:9–11 (RC[52]) – the souls of the slain cry out, "Sovereign Lord … how long will it be before you judge and avenge our blood on the inhabitants of the earth?" They were each given a white robe and told to rest a little longer, until the number would be complete … who were soon to be killed as they themselves had been killed.	47:1–4 – prayer of the righteous before the Lord of Spirits and intercession by the holy ones seeking judgment to avenge the blood of the righteous (cf. 8:4–9:2; 9:9–10; 22:12; 97:3–4); "the number of the righteous"[53]	petition for divine judgment to avenge the blood of the faithful (cf. *Sib. Or.* 3.307–313; 2 Macc. 8:2–4; Rheneia inscription; 4 Ezra 4:33–37) with the time specified as completion of "the number"

Petitions and laments seeking and querying divine justice frequently open with the interrogative "how long" (esp. Ps. 4:2; 6:3; 13:1–2; 35:17; 62:3; 74:10; 79:5; 80:4; 82:2; 89:46; 90:13; 94:3; 119:84; Hab. 1:2; Zech. 1:12; 4 Ezra 4:33, 35 – referring to deceased souls; 6:59), while the motif of avenging "the blood" of the righteous though, without the interrogative, is found both in the Hebrew Bible (Gen. 4:10) and in the New Testament (Mt. 23:34–35 par. Lk. 11:51; Heb. 12:24) in relation to Abel's unjust death. One should further note the reference to the spirit of Abel's complaint in the *Book of Watchers* in *1 Enoch* 22:5–7, which is followed by a reference to the spirits of the deceased who were murdered "in the days of the sinners" (22:12; as in *1 En.* 8:4–9:2, 9:9–10, in which the "blood" of the human victims is mentioned).[54] The closest parallel to Revelation 6:9–10 is 4 Ezra 4:35, as "how long" is also uttered there by the souls of the deceased (in their chambers; cf. *1 En.* 22:12) along with a reference to the completion of their "number" (cf. *2 Bar.*

---

[51] Cf. Loren T. Stuckenbruck, "Daniel and Early Enoch Traditions in the Dead Sea Scrolls", in eds. John J. Collins and Peter W. Flint, *The Book of Daniel: Composition and Reception* (VTSupp., 58.2; Leiden/Boston/Köln: Brill, 2001), pp. 368–86 (cf. also Chapter Five above) and Ryan E. Stokes, "The Throne Visions of Daniel 7, 1 Enoch 14, and the Qumran Book of Giants (4Q530): An Analysis of Their Literary Relationship", *DSD* 15 (2008), pp. 340–358.

[52] Charles, *The Book of Enoch or 1 Enoch*, p. xcvii. Cf. further Charlesworth, "The *Parables of Enoch* and the Apocalypse of John", p. 233, the much fuller discussion in Aune, *Revelation*, vol. 2, pp. 403–413; and Johns, *The Lamb Christology of the Apocalypse of John*, p. 95.

[53] Note the plausible emendation to "righteous (ones)" from "righteous one" (Eth. mss. BM 491, Tana 9, IES 392) or "righteousness" (most mss.) by Nickelsburg and VanderKam, *1 Enoch: A New Translation*, p. 61 n. f.

[54] For a fuller discussion of these texts, see John Byron, "The Blood of Righteous Abel", in *idem, Cain and Abel in Text and Tradition: Jewish and Christian Interpretations of the First Sibling Rivalry* (TBN 14; Leiden / Boston: Brill, 2011), pp. 167–205 (here pp. 177–190).

24:3); in 4 Ezra, however, this is not combined with the express mention of "blood." What we have in Revelation, then, is a complex constitution of motifs found in the Hebrew Bible, beginning with the Abel traditions (in addition to the texts cited above, see *Targ. C. Gen.* and *Neophyti* to Gen. 4:10 and Deut. 32:43; Ps. 79:10) and carried over, by the 3rd and 2nd centuries B.C.E., into petitions for justice by the deceased righteous who have suffered at the hands of sinners (*1 En.* 8:4–9:3; 9:9–10; 22:12; 47:1–4; 97:3–4; 99:3, 16; 104:3–4; Rheineia inscription from the 2nd cent. B.C.E.; cf. *T. Moses* 9:6–7).[55] The tradition-historical developments, so strongly represented in Enochic traditions, are nevertheless so broad that any influence on Revelation 6:9–10 from this source cannot be distinguished.[56] However, the Enochic tradition, within the *Book of Watchers,* the *Epistle* and especially the *Book of Parables,* illustrates the trajectory of tradition-historical development which Revelation – this is alongside documents such as *Sibylline Oracles* Book 3 (307–313), 4 Ezra (4:33–37) and *2 Bar.* 23:4–5 – preserves.

6:15–16 (RC[57]) – "the kings of the earth and the great men and the generals and the rich and the powerful, everyone, slave and free, hid in the caves and among the rocks of the mountains .../ calling, 'Fall on us and hide us from the face of the one seated on the throne and from the wrath of the Lamb'." (NRSV) cf. under 1:7 above	62:3, 5 – "all the kings and the mighty and the exalted and those who possess the earth ... and they will be terrified and cast down their faces, and pain will seize them when they see that son of man sitting on the throne of glory"	terror of "kings" and other powerful figures before the divine throne, which is also associated with God's primary agent

The combination of four elements in Revelation and the *Book of Parables* is without parallel in other literature: (a) the holders of power (especially "kings" and

---

[55] Cf. Nickelsburg, *1 Enoch 1,* pp. 185–186, 201, 208, and 305–306 and Stuckenbruck, *1 Enoch 91–108,* pp. 309–313, with a discussion of the Rheineia inscription in Stuckenbruck, *Angel Veneration and Christology,* pp. 183–185 and Pieter W. van der Horst and Judith H. Newman, *Early Jewish Prayers in Greek* (CEJL; Berlin: Walter de Gruyter, 2008), pp. 137–143.

[56] Bauckham, "The Use of Apocalyptic Traditions", p. 54, raises and then dismisses the possibility that the tradition in the *Book of Parables* has shaped that or Revelation which, in turn, underlies that of 4 Ezra and 2 Bar, arguing instead that "the relationships between ... the texts [i.e., *1 En.* 47; Rev. 6; 4 Ezra 4; 2 Bar. 23] ... do not result from direct literary dependence between them, but on a common tradition which had already taken different forms in the sources used by each." Cf. also Aune, "The Apocalypse of John and Palestinian Jewish Apocalyptic", pp. 178–180.

[57] Charles, *The Book of Enoch or 1 Enoch,* p. xcvii and *Revelation,* vol. 1, p. 182; Michael A. Knibb, "The Date of the Parables of Enoch: A Critical Review", *NTS* 25 (1979), pp. 345–359 (here, p. 356); Charlesworth, "The *Parables of Enoch* and the Apocalypse of John", p. 239. The parallel as described here is not picked up in Aune, *Revelation,* vol. 1, pp. 419–421, though is discussed by him in "The Apocalypse of John and Palestinian Jewish Apocalyptic", pp. 173–174.

classes of the wealthy; cf. Rev. 19:18) who (b) cower in fear (c) before the throne of God which (d) is also occupied by or associated with the Lamb (Rev.) / Son of Man (*Book of Parables*).[58] While the text of Revelation alludes to Isaiah 2:19–21 and Hosea 10:6, and *1 Enoch* 62:3–5 draws on the image of the woman in labor in Isaiah 13:8, the possibility of a connection between the two sources cannot be discounted, though it is difficult to argue that the connection is immediate.[59]

7:1 (RC[60]) – "four angels standing at the four corners of the earth, holding back the four winds of the earth"	69:22 – "the spirits of the water, of the winds, and all the breezes and their paths, from all the quarters of the winds" cf. 76:1–14	the responsibility of angelic beings for the winds

This parallel is weak, even if in the *Book of Parables* the "spirits" refers to angelic beings. Ancient sources that relate four winds to four directions of the earth are numerous, preserved in both the Hebrew Bible (Ezek. 37:9; Jer. 49:36; Dan. 7:2; 8:8; 11:4; Zech. 2:6; 6:5) and Second Temple writings (4 Ezra 13:5; Mk. 13:27 par. Mt. 24:31; Josephus, *Bell.* 6.300; cf. *Vit. Ad. et Ev.* 38:3), as well as a wide range of other documents.[61] In the *Book of Watchers*, the visionary sees all classes of winds (*1 En.* 18:1–5), while the *Astronomical Book* (*1 En.* 76:1–14) features twelve winds, in groups of three from each of the four directions. In neither of these Enochic texts are the winds associated with angelic oversight.

7:15 (RC[62]) – "For this reason they are before the throne of God, and worship him day and night in his temple, and the one who is seated on the throne will shelter them." (NRSV)	45:3–4 – "On that day, my Chosen One will sit on the throne of glory, ... I shall make him (my Chosen One) dwell among the chosen ones." (my translation)	the protective force of the divine enthroned presence on behalf of the righteous (Lev. 26:11; Ezek. 37:27)

The phrase in Revelation 7:15, translated in the NRSV as "will shelter them," is σκηνώσει ἐπ᾽ αὐτούς and carries the connotation of presence.[63] The text of *1 Enoch* 45:4 has a similar phrase, though in the causative: ʾanbero māʾkᵉlomu la-xeruyān ("I

---

[58] Aune, "The Apocalypse of John and Palestinian Jewish Apocalyptic", p. 174 argues, in addition, that in both texts there is a similar move from the "kings" and powerful ones to everyone (represented in Rev. by the "slave and free" and in *1 En.* 62:3 by "those who dwell on the earth"). However, Aune's English translation has only limited textual support (Tana 9), while most of the manuscripts from both recensions refer to "those who possess the land", i. e. landowners.

[59] See Aune, "The Apocalypse of John and Palestinian Jewish Apocalyptic", p. 174, who concludes that the texts are "dependent on a common *written* source, which each author partially reformulated in a distinctive way."

[60] Charles, *The Book of Enoch or 1 Enoch*, p. xcvii; idem, *Revelation*, vol. 1, pp. 203–204.

[61] Discussed in Aune, *Revelation*, vol. 2, pp. 450–451.

[62] Charles, *The Book of Enoch or 1 Enoch*, p. xcviii; not mentioned in idem, *Revelation*, vol. 1, p. 215.

[63] Cf. Aune, *Revelation*, vol. 1, p. 476.

will make him dwell among the chosen ones"). Both Revelation and the passage in the *Book of Parables* allude to and draw on Ezekiel 37:27: "my dwelling place shall be with them; and I will be their God, and they will be my people" (NRSV). No relationship between Revelation and the *Book of Parables* can be drawn here, however; whereas the latter applies the tradition to the enthroned Chosen One, who dwells with God's people as the agent of salvation and judgment, the language of Revelation 7 derives the divine presence from language concerned with "the throne of God" alone,[64] something one would not expect were Revelation being influenced at this point by the *Book of Parables.*

7:17 (RC[65]) – "For the Lamb at the center of the throne will be their shepherd, and he will guide them to the springs of the water of life..." (NRSV); cf. 21:6; 22:1, 17	48:1 – the seer beholds "the spring of righteousness, and it was inexhaustible, and many springs of wisdom surrounded it. And all the thirsty drank from them and were filled with wisdom..."	the living water for the righteous to drink (cf. Jn. 4:14; 7:38)

The phrase "he will guide them to the springs of the water of life" has its closest equivalents in Isaiah 49:10 (Grk., "through streams of water he will lead them") and Jeremiah 2:13 (the disobedient "have forsaken me, the fountain of living waters"). The Enochic text from the *Book of Parables* does not expressly refer to the righteous being led to the waters; if the text draws on Isaiah 49:10, the "streams of water" are described as unending and offering wisdom to the righteous elect. Another parallel to Revelation 7:17 occurs in the Johannine tradition at John 4:14 and 7:38 (perhaps also influenced by Isa. 49:10) with the difference, however, that the "spring of water" and "rivers of living water," respectively, are sources located within the transformed human being. In this latter respect, the filling up with wisdom of the chosen ones in *1 Enoch* 48:1 comes closer to the Gospel of John than to the text in Revelation.

8:3–4 (RC[66]) – "Another angel ... was given a great quantity of incense to offer with the prayers of all the saints, on the golden altar	8:4–9:11; 15:2; 40:7, 9; 47:2; 89:76; 97:2, 5; 99:3, 16; 100:10; 104:1 – angelic beings in *1 Enoch* frequently function as media-	angelic mediation of the prayers of the righteous (cf. Zech. 1:12–13; Tob. 12:12; Dan. 10:21; 12:1; *Aram. Levi Doc.* 4Q213a 2.16–18;

---

[64] Without deliberately distancing the Lamb from the throne (cf. 7:9–10, esp. v. 17), the text, then, draws more immediately on the well-developed tradition of *Sukkot*; cf. Håkan Ulfgard, *Feast and Future: Revelation 7:9–17 and the Feast of Tabernacles* (CB.NT 22; Stockholm: Almqvist & Wiksell International, 1989), pp. 86–89 and 120–127.

[65] Charles, *The Book of Enoch or 1 Enoch,* p. xcviii and *Revelation,* vol. 1, p. 217, where he calls this "a remarkable parallel", though finding "the most immediate parallels" in Jn. 4:14; 7:38.

[66] Charles, *The Book of Enoch or 1 Enoch,* p. xcviii; not followed up in *idem, Revelation,* vol. 1, pp. 227–231.

| before the throne, and the smoke of the incense, with the prayers of the saints, rose before God from the hand of the Angel." (NRSV); cf. 5:8 | tors of the prayers of the righteous before God | *T. Levi* 3:5; *T. Dan* 6:2; 3 *Bar.* 11:3–9; *Vit. Ad. et Ev.* 9:3) |

Although the notion of angelic beings acting as intermediaries for prayers and petitions is a characteristic feature of several works within the Enoch tradition (esp. *Book of Watchers, Book of Parables,* and the *Epistle*), it is also shared more widely with a number of writings that preserve Second Temple Jewish tradition.[67] Formally, the closest and more elaborate parallel, which also involves a primary angelic being (Michael), is preserved in *3 Baruch* chapters 11–16.[68] Therefore, any specific relationship between Revelation and the Enoch tradition cannot be postulated. Revelation's use of the motif, therefore, reflects a broad stream of tradition that conveys divine concern to dispense justice in this way on behalf of the righteous who have suffered unjustly.

| 8:8 (RC[69]) – "something like a great mountain, burning with fire" (NRSV); cf. 8:10 | 22:3 – "seven of the stars of heaven, bound and thrown in it together, like great mountains, and burning in fire"; 108:4 – "a flame of fire which was burning brightly, and (something) like brightly shining mountains were turning over and shaking from one side to the other"[70]; cf. 18:13 ("seven stars like great burning mountains"); 52:6 (before the Chosen One, mountains will be "like wax before the fire") | a vision of judgment compared to (a) fiery mountain (s) (Deut. 5:23; Mic. 1:4; Ep. Jer. 63; cf. Psa. 83:14) |

The biblical tradition already associates the burning of mountains with divine judgment (Deut. 5:23; Mic. 1:4; Ps. 83:14; cf. Ep. Jer. 63). The Enochic traditions have also adapted this image in relation to judgment; in the *Book of Watchers* (*1 En.*

---

[67] Cf. Stuckenbruck, *1 Enoch 91–108*, pp. 386–388 and, further, *Angel Veneration and Christology*, pp. 173–179.

[68] For the most complete discussion of this text within its tradition-historical context, see Alexander Kulik, *3 Baruch: Greek-Slavonic Apocalypse of Baruch* (CEJL; Berlin: Walter de Gruyter, 2010), pp. 304–385 (on angelic intercession, pp. 344–346).

[69] Charles, *Revelation*, vol. 1, p. 234; not mentioned in idem, *The Book of Enoch or 1 Enoch*, p. xcviii.

[70] Translation in Stuckenbruck, *1 Enoch 91–108*, p. 707.

21:3) and *Eschatological Admonition* (*1 En.* 108:4), this is presented as a verisimilitude ("like") that is only elsewhere found in Revelation 8:8.[71]

9:1 (RC[72]) – "… I saw a star that had fallen from heaven to earth"; cf. 20:2	86:1, 3 – "I saw the heaven above, and look, a star fell from heaven… I saw many stars descend and cast	descent of a star (angelic being) from heaven to the earth (Lk. 10:18) the identification of the snake in the
12:9 (AYR[73]) – "The great dragon was thrown down, that ancient serpent, who is called the Devil and Satan, the deceiver of the whole world–he was thrown down to the earth, and his angels were thrown down with him." (NRSV)	themselves down from heaven to that first star." cf. 90:21; further, 6:6 69:6 – the fallen angel, Gadreel, led Eve astray	Garden of Eden as a fallen angel or a satan (cf. Lk. 10:18–19; 2 Cor. 11:14; *Apoc. Moses* 17:1; *Vit. Ad. et Ev* 16:3; *3 Bar.* 9:7[74])

The tradition of a falling star, with "star" understood as an angelic being, links Revelation 9:1 with the *Animal Apocalypse* at *1 Enoch* 86:1. Conceptually, however, these texts are very different in terms of what they refer to. At the sounding of the fifth trumpet blast, the "star" in Revelation falls, as a divine emissary, to whom a key is given for unlocking "the bottomless pit" in order to unleash the destructive locusts (9:3; cf. "the angel" with a similar function in 20:1–2). In the *Animal Apocalypse*, however, the falling star represents a lead rebellious angel (*1 En.* 86:1), followed by "many stars" who throw themselves down (86:3), and thus shows the influence of the disobedient angels tradition in the *Book of Watchers* (*1 En.* 6–16; cf. the identification of the transgressing angels with stars in 18:13–16). The language of falling or descent in the Enochic texts has more affinity with the myth about "the Devil … and his angels" in Revelation 12:9. Here both the head figure and his angelic minions are brought down to earth through a defeat at the hands of Michael and his angels, so that there is no place for them in heaven (12:7–8).

Since in the Enoch tradition it is emphasized that the angels' descent occurred by their own volition (*1 En.* 6:6; 12:4; 15:3; 19:1 this seems the case, too, in 86:1, 3),[75] its texts offer an unlikely background against which to interpret Revelation

---

[71] Taking the burning mountain "thrown into the sea" as the point of departure, Aune (*Revelation*, vol. 2, pp. 517–518) discusses the possibility that the image reflects volcanic activity as, e. g., was reported in relation to the eruption of Vesuvius on 24 August 79 C. E. However, if the text contains an allusion to this event, then the hurling of *the mountain itself* into the sea would have to be hyperbolic (i. e., not simply debris from the mountain) and does not match any of the ancient descriptions of what happened (Pliny, *Ep.* 6.16.11, 20; Dio *Hist.* 66.23.1; *Sib. Or.* 4.130–134).

[72] Charles, *The Book of Enoch or 1 Enoch,* p. xcviii and *Revelation,* vol. 1, pp. 238–239.

[73] Annette Yoshiko Reed, *Fallen Angels and the History of Judaism and Christianity: The Reception of Enochic Literature* (Cambridge: Cambridge University Press, 2005), p. 116.

[74] For the rabbinic texts that designate Satan as an "ancient serpent", see the discussion in Aune, *Revelation,* vol. 1, p. 696.

[75] Cf. CD ii 17–19; *Jub.* 4:15; and *2 En.* 18:3–4 A.

12:7–9 as well.[76] Instead, it reflects a storyline, found in other texts, according to which Satan or a primary malevolent figure and accomplices had to be forced out, either because of disobedience (*Vit. Ad. et Ev.* 11–16; cf. *1 En.* 18:15; 21:3–5; Jude 13) or, as perhaps presupposed in Revelation 12, because of a primordial or eschatological attempt at a usurpation of power in heaven (cf., e. g., 11Q13 ii 7–14; 1QM xv–xix; *T. Levi* 3:3; *Sib. Or.* 5.512–513). The mythic *hubris* is more conditioned by the tradition in Isaiah 14:12–21 than by the Enochic fallen angels tradition.

The most important link in Revelation 12 with Enochic tradition resides in the identification in the *Book of Parables* (*1 En.* 69:6) of Eve's deceiver as having been one of the fallen angels, named Gadreel. Such an identification may be implied in Luke 10:18–19, in which the announcement of Satan's fall by Jesus is followed by the power his disciples are given to tread "on snakes and scorpions," or in Paul's statement in 2 Corinthians 11:14 that Satan "disguises" himself as "an angel of light." However, if the Enochic text about Gadreel presupposes a knowledge and reception of Genesis 3, then it is significant that, analogous to Revelation 12:9, the serpent is presented as one of the fallen angels.[77]

9:15–16 (RC[78]) – "So the four angels (i. e. those bound at the river Euphrates, v. 14) were released, who had been prepared for the hour, the day, the month, and the year, to kill a third of humanity." (my translation)	66:1 – "And after this, he showed me the angels of punishment, who are ready to go forth and let loose all the power of the water that is beneath the earth, that it might be for the judgment and destruction of all who reside and dwell on the earth."	angels of punishment who are prepared / ready to inflict destruction on humanity

The connection between Revelation and this text in the *Book of Parables* here is strong. Although the notion of punishing angels is found in a number of further passages in the *Parables* and other sources (e. g., in *Book of Parables* at *1 En.* 40:1–10; 53:3; 56:1; 62:11; 63:1; 1QM ix 15–16; *2 En.* 10:3; *T. Levi* 3:3),[79] only Reve-

---

[76] So correctly Aune, *Revelation*, vol. 1, p. 698; *contra* Yoshiko Reed, *Fallen Angels and the History of Judaism and Christianity*, p. 116 n. 81, who argues that traditions related to the Watchers were "transferred to the beginning of time, to the fall of Satan and his hosts", citing Rev. 9:1; 12:9; and Lk. 10:18 as examples.

[77] Reading *1 En.* 69:6 in relation to 54:6, Charles regarded Gadreel, the fallen angel, as one of Satan's servants who on the Day of Judgment will be thrown down by the angels, Michael, Raphael, Gabriel and Phanuel "into a burning furnace." Cf. Charles, *Revelation*, vol. 1, p. 326. This observation is missed in the commentaries.

[78] Charles, *The Book of Enoch or 1 Enoch*, p. xcviii; esp. idem, *Revelation*, vol. 1, p. 250.

[79] The angels of punishment in these texts are not to be confused with "the angels of destruction" (מלאכי חבל) referred to in a number of the texts among the Dead Sea Scrolls (CD ii 6; 1QS iv 12; 1QM xiii 12; 4Q510 1.5; cf. 4Q495 2.4); see Philip S. Alexander, "The Demonology of the Dead Sea Scrolls", in eds. Peter W. Flint and James C. VanderKam, *The Dead Sea Scrolls after Fifty Years* (2 vols.; Leiden / Boston / Köln: Brill, 1999), pp. 331–353 (here, pp. 332–334).

lation 9:15 and *1 Enoch* 66:1 refer to the angels as "those who are ready" (οἱ ἡτοι-μασμένοι, Eth. *'ella delewān*) to carry out their assigned destructive activities.

| **9:20** (RC[80]) – "The rest of humankind, who were not killed by these plagues, did not repent of the works of their hands or give up worshiping demons and idols of gold and silver and bronze and stone and wood, which cannot see or hear or walk." (NRSV) | 99:7 – "And they (sinners, v. 6) will worship stones, and others will carve images of gold and silver and wood and clay. And others will worship evil spirits and demons and every (kind of) error – and without knowledge – but no help will be found from them."[81] | combination of worshipping idols (listing five materials) and its association with the worship of demons (cf. Dan. 2:32–33; 5:4, 23; 4Q242 1–3.7–8) |

In the Hebrew Bible and Second Temple literature, numerous texts refer to the lifeless materials from which idols were fashioned. Infrequently, however, are more than four of such materials listed. The noticeable exceptions occur in Daniel 2:32–33; 5:4, 20; the *Prayer of Nabonidus* in 4Q242 1.7–8; *Epistle of Enoch* at *1 Enoch* 99:7; and Revelation 9:20. The sequence of materials in the lists compare as follows:

Daniel 2:32–33 – gold, silver, bronze, iron (legs and feet), clay
Daniel 5:4, 23 – gold, silver, bronze, iron, wood, stone
4Q242 1–3.7–8 – silver, gold, [bronze], [iron], wood, stone
1 Enoch 99:7 – stones, gold, silver, wood, clay
Revelation 9:20 – gold, silver, bronze, stone, wood

The closest correspondence occurs between the text in 4Q242 and Daniel 5:23, with the former having the sequence of "silver, gold." The remaining texts differ in number and content with one another, except for the *Epistle* and Revelation which each list five materials used in the making of idols. Significant, however, is not so much the correspondence of materials, but the combination of these lists with the link drawn between idolatry thus described and the worship of demonic beings; Revelation uniquely shares this among ancient sources with the *Epistle of Enoch*.[82]

| 10:7 (RC[83]) – "... the mystery of God will be completed" (my translation) | 16:1 – "the great judgment, when the great age will be consummated" | correspondence in language about the end of the present age |

---

[80] Charles, *The Book of Enoch or 1 Enoch*, p. xcviii; idem, *Revelation*, vol. 1, pp. 252–253.

[81] Translation of the Eth. in Stuckenbruck, *1 Enoch 91–108*, p. 392. The Grk. text is partly preserved: "... and those who carve image[s of silv]er and gold, wood and [stone] and clay, and (who) worship [phan]toms and demons [and abomina]tions and evi[l] spirits and all (kinds of) errors – not according to kno[wledge] – and they will not find any help [from] them."

[82] For a text-, literary-, and tradition-historical analysis of *1 Enoch* 99:7, see Stuckenbruck, *1 Enoch 91–108*, pp. 392–404.

[83] Charles, *The Book of Enoch or 1 Enoch*, p. xcviii; not mentioned in *idem, Revelation*, vol. 1, pp. 264–266.

The text in Revelation is concerned with the blowing of the seventh trumpet (cf. Rev. 11:15–19), when the kingdom of God and God's Anointed One will be established and judgment will be held in relation to the wicked and the righteous and the wicked (cf. Rev. 11:15–19); the "mystery of God," then, when fulfilled, refers to the judgment and visible establishment of God's kingship. Similarly, though in a very different context, the *Book of Watchers* describes the persistence of evil on the earth through the spirits from the giants until the time when, at the great judgment, they will be destroyed; it is at the final judgment that the present age will be rendered complete. In both texts, if one follows the Greek texts for *Book of Watchers*, the verbs are similar (Rev. 10:7 – ἐτελέσθε τὸ μυστήριον τοῦ θεοῦ; *1 En.* 16:1 Cod. Pan. and Sync. – ὁ αἰὼν ὁ μέγας τελεσθήσεται) and bear the connotation of fulfillment in relation to the present world order. However, it would be going too far to draw a genetic link between the passages, especially given their different frames of reference and since the connection with the final judgment in Revelation has to be derived from the larger literary context (Rev. 11:15–19).

11:18 (LS[84]) – "... the nations raged, but your wrath has come" (NRSV)	99:4 – "in those days the nations will be thrown into turmoil, and the tribes of the nations will be raised on the day of the destruction of sin"[85] cf. also 57:1–2	eschatological tumult among the nations (Dan. 12:1; *Jub.* 23:23; 4 Ezra 5:5–6; 9:3; 13:30–31; *2 Bar.* 25:3; 70:2–4, 6–7; *Sib. Or.* 1.156; 3.635–637; *2 Esd.* 15:16–18; 4Q246 ii 2–3; Mk. 13:7–8//Mt. 24:6 and Lk. 21:9, 18, 28)

Drawing on language of Isaiah 19:2 (cf. 2 Chr. 15:5–6), the disarray among the nations during the period leading up to the end of the present age is a very widespread *topos*, for which the *Epistle of Enoch* (along with Daniel and *Jubilees*) provides an early example. No further specific connection between Revelation and either of the Enochic texts can be discerned.

12:8 (MM[86]) – "but they (Satan and his angels, v. 9) were defeated, and there was no longer any place for them in heaven" (NRSV); cf. under 9:1 above	14:5 – "... from now on you will not ascend into heaven for all the ages; and it has been decreed to bind you in bonds in the earth for all the days of eternity"; cf. 15:6–8	forfeiture by rebellious angels of their place in heaven

---

[84] Stuckenbruck, *1 Enoch 91–108*, pp. 388–389 and n. 704.

[85] Translation in Stuckenbruck, *1 Enoch 91–108*, pp. 381–382, 388; the Grk. is: "and then they will be thrown into turmoil, and will rise on the day of the destruction of wickedness."

[86] Mathews, *Riches, Poverty, and the Faithful*, pp. 190–192.

We have already considered (under 9:1 above) the unlikelihood that the down-throw of "the Devil and Satan" (Rev. 12:9) was influenced by the Enochic fallen angels tradition. In addition to the serpent-fallen angel analogy in the *Book of Parables* noted above, an additional detail links with the Enochic tradition at the *Book of Watchers* (cf. 14:5; 15:6–8): the express mention in Revelation that Satan and his angelic forces no longer had a legitimate place in heaven corresponds to the Enochic tradition, worked out in more detail, that the rebellious angels no longer have any claim to their prior existence in heaven. As suggested above (again under 9:1), the reasons given for this forfeiture are different; the text in Revelation assumes that Satan made an attempt to seize power and there-fore was forced out of heaven, while in the *Book of Watchers*, the angels made a deliberate choice to leave heaven, only to learn that there is no chance of return.[87]

12:11 (LS[88]) – "But they have conquered him by the blood of the Lamb and by the word of their testimony, for they did not love their life even to the point of death." (my translation)	108:10 – "And he has ordained for them [i. e. the righteous] their reward, for they were found as (those who) love heaven more than their life which is in the world."	"love of life" contrasted with a willingness to die (Euri-pides, *Hecuba* 348; *Hercules* 518, 531–534; Philo, *Leg. Gaium* 369; Josephus, *Ant.* 6.344, 12.301, 13.198; De-mosthenes, *Or.* 60.28; Jn. 12:25; cf. Mk. 8:35; Mt. 10:39, 16:25; Lk. 9:24, 17:33)

For Revelation 12:11 (οὐκ ἠγάπησαν τὴν ψυχὴν αὐτῶν), Charles regarded John 12:25 as the most immediate background[89]: "Those who love their life (ὁ φιλῶν τὴν ψυχὴν αὐτῶν) their life will lose it, and those who hate their life in this world will keep it for eternal life" (NRSV). On the other hand, commenting on Revela-tion 12:11, Aune argues that "The *topos* of 'the love of life' standing in the way of a willingness to die for an important cause is typically Hellenistic."[90] While Aune's comment applies to the text of the *Eschatological Exhortation* at *1 Enoch* 108:10, it does not illuminate Revelation 12:11 as much as one might initially think. In the latter, "they did not love their life," formulated in the negative, "life" refers to earthly, rather than heavenly existence; the link, therefore, to John 12:25 is much stronger.

---

[87] Cf. Nickelsburg, *1 Enoch 1*, pp. 253 and 271–273.

[88] Stuckenbruck, *1 Enoch 91–108*, pp. 727–728; cf. esp. Aune, *Revelation*, vol. 2, p. 703.

[89] Charles, *Revelation*, vol. 1, p. 329; not mentioned in *idem*, *The Book of Enoch or 1 Enoch*, p. xcviii.

[90] Aune, *Revelation*, vol. 1, p. 703. Aune goes on to cite the texts from Euripides etc. listed above in support.

13:5–6 (LS[91]) – "The beast was given a mouth uttering great and blasphemous words ... It opened its mouth to utter blasphemies against God, blaspheming his name and his dwelling, that is, those who dwell in heaven." (my translation)

5:4 – "... but you have not stood firm nor acted according to his commandments; but you have turned aside, you have spoken great and hard words with your unclean mouth against his greatness." (my translation) also 101:3; cf. 27:2

uttering "great" words against God (cf. Dan. 3:29 [Grk. 3:96]) 7:8, 11, 20, 25; *T. Moses* 7)

The *Book of Watchers* (*1 En.* 5:4) describes the activity of those who do not act in obedience to God (Cod.Pan. and 4Q201 1 ii 13: they utter "great and hard [words]"). In the same way, the *Epistle of Enoch*, influenced by this text, is concerned with sinners who utter "great and hard things" (*1 En.* 101:3). The utterance of such words renders those who speak them in an irretrievable state of wickedness. In the Daniel tradition the fourth beast utters "great things" (7:8, 20-רברבן, μεγάλα; cf. v. 11) and "words against the Most High" (7:25), while in Daniel 3:29 (Grk. 3:96), following the rescue of the pious men from the fiery furnace, Nebuchadnezzar threatens with death anyone who "utters blasphemy" (Grk. Theod.) against their God. The only feature which aligns the Enoch texts (*1 En.* 5:4; 101:3) with Revelation is the double description of sacrilegious speech. Otherwise, especially in making such speech a defining feature of God's (and of God's people) arch-opponent, Revelation picks up more immediately on the Danielic antecedent.[92]

13:14 (RC[93]) – the second beast "leads astray the inhabitants of the earth"

54:6 – the rebellious angels are punished for "leading astray the inhabitants of the earth"; cf. 67:7

primary agents of sin as those who "lead astray the inhabitants of the earth"

Under the note to 3:10 above, the propensity for both Revelation and the *Book of Parables* to use the phrase "inhabitants of the earth" was observed. This designation in itself does not signal a relationship between the two works; however, these are the only two writings which combine the motif of deception by (a) notorious agent(s) of wrongdoing with "inhabitants of the earth" as the object.

---

[91] Stuckenbruck, *1 Enoch 91–108*, pp. 475–476.

[92] So correctly Beale, *The Book of Revelation*, pp. 695–696, who also notes the parallel phraseology (Rev.-"a mouth speaking great things was given to it"; Dan. 7:6, 8 Grk.-"a tongue was given to it ... a mouth speaking great things"). Beale, however, makes no mention of any of the Enochic texts.

[93] Charles, *The Book of Enoch or 1 Enoch*, p. xcviii; not mentioned in idem, *Revelation*, vol. 1, pp. 359–360.

14:4[94] – the 144,000 are those who "have not defiled themselves with women, for they are virgins"[95]

7:1; 9:8; 10:11; 12:4; 15:3, 4 – "they (the rebellious angels) have defiled themselves with women" (esp. 9:8; 12:4; 15:3);[96] cf. *Book of Giants* at 4Q531 1.1

purity defined through lack of sexual contact

The term for "virgins" is masculine, so that the background to the text is initially to be found in purity regulations related to male behavior.[97] While several texts in the Hebrew Bible, especially in Ezekiel, frequently apply such language to idolatry (e. g., Jer. 7:30; 32:34; Ezek. 14:11; 20:7, 18, 30, 31, 43; 22:4; 23:20; 33:26; 37:23), the closest language to that of Revelation 14:4 is found in the *Book of Watchers*, in which the activity referred to is that of the rebellious angels. Significantly, as in the Enochic text, the emphasis is not *women* who are defiled, but rather on the ritual impurity of those who initiate (and therefore are responsible for) the activity.

While the linguistic parallel to the fallen angels tradition is strong, it is more difficult to determine whether any aspect of the myth carries over into Revelation 14. In particular, the problem relates to how one interprets "virgins", not least since this term occurs nowhere else in Revelation and does not appear in the Enochic tradition. William Loader, for example, proposes that the term be understood literally as a reference to believers who espouse a life of celibacy and who, in this state, did not act like the Watchers.[98] Along different lines, Daniel Olson, following Adela Yarbro Collins, has suggested that the Enochic background strengthens the view that the 144,000 redeemed believers live in an angelic state, so that their lack of defilement is to be understood in contrast to that of the wayward angels.[99]

---

[94] Adela Yarbro Collins, "Women's History in the Book of Revelation", *SBLSP 1987* (Atlanta: Scholars Press, 1987), pp. 80–91; Daniel C. Olson, "Those Who Have not Defiled Themselves with Women", *CBQ* 59 (1997), pp. 492–510; and Ruben Zimmermann, "Die Virginitätsmetapher von Apk 14,4–5 im Horizont von Befleckung, Loskauf, und Erstlingsfrucht", *NovT* 45 (2003), pp. 45–70 and *idem*, "Nuptial Imagery in the Revelation of John", *Bib* 84 (2003), pp. 153–183.

[95] The text reads: οὗτοί εἰσιν οἳ μετὰ γυναικῶν οὐκ ἐμολύνθησαν παρθένοι γάρ εἰσιν.

[96] The Grk. texts read as follows: μιαίνεσθαι ἐν αὐταῖς (7:1 Cod.Pan. and Sync.ᵃ); ἐμιάνθησαν (9:8 Cod.Pan. and Syncᵃ); (τοῦ) μιανθῆναι ἐν αὐταῖς (10:11 Cod.Pan. and Syncᵃ); μετὰ τῶν γυναικῶν ἐμιάνθησαν (12:4 Cod.Pan.); μετὰ τῶν θυγατέρων τῶν ἀνθρώπων ἐμιάνθητε (15:3 Cod.Pan.); and ἐν αἵματι τῶν γυναικῶν ἐμιάνθητε (15:4 Cod.Pan.).

[97] Therefore the background is not to be sought in texts that regard a woman as having polluted herself or having been defiled by men (Gen. 34:5, 17, 27; Lev. 21:7, 14; Num. 5:13–14, 20, 28–30; Ezek. 18:6, 11, 15; 22:11).

[98] William G. Loader, *The New Testament on Sexuality* (Grand Rapids: Eerdmans, 2012), pp. 478–481.

[99] Olson, "Those Who Have not Defiled Themselves with Women", pp. 496–500 and 505 and Zimmermann, "Die Virginitätsmetapher von Apk 14,4–5", p. 56. Zimmermann adds to Olson's argument that "virgins" is a metaphor for the believing community as it is being prepared for marriage (the bride of Christ) and associates the motif with the notion of being purchased from the earth (*ibid.*, pp. 61–66); cf. Yarbro Collins, "Women's History and the Book of Revelation" (bibl. in n. 94).

Within this perspective, "virgins" would be understood metaphorically, that is, it applies to all believers, women or men, and the defilement does not refer literally to sexual behavior, but rather function as an image for faithfulness (in the sense that sexual imagery is applied in the message to Thyatira in Rev. 2:20, 22).

14:9–10 (RC[100]) – "those who worship the beast ... will be tormented with fire and sulfur in the presence of the holy angels and in the presence of the Lamb." (NRSV)	48:9 – the kings of the earth and the landowners (v. 8) "As straw in the fire... they will burn before the face of the holy ones, and they will sink before the face of the righteous ones..."	punishment by fire in the presence of "holy ones"

Both texts emphasize how the punishment of the wicked will be seen in the presence of "the holy ones." The notion of the righteous being able to see the sinners' torment in the context of a vision is also found elsewhere (e. g., *Book of Watchers* at *1 En.* 27:2–3; *Animal Apocalypse* at 90:26–27; 4 Ezra 7:36); however, what Revelation 14:9–10 and the *Book of Parables* (*1 En.* 48:9) share in addition, and uniquely so, is the announcement that those deemed wicked will perish in fire in the presence of "holy ones." Although the Enochic text probably applies "holy ones" to the human righteous and Revelation probably has angelic beings in view, the precise meaning of the designation vacillated easily between one meaning and the other.[101]

14:11 (LS[102]) – "...there is no rest day or night for those who worship the beast..." (NRSV) cf. under 4:6, 8 above; **14:13**	99:14 – those "who reject the foundation (stone) and eternal inheritance of the fathers and who pursue the spirit of error ... will have no rest"	lack of "rest" for the wicked (cf. Isa. 23:12; Deut. 28:65), together with a promise of "rest" for the faithful

In the Enoch tradition and elsewhere, the usual pronouncement against notorious wrongdoers is "you will have no peace" (cf. the parallel in *1 En.* 99:13);[103] only in the *Epistle* at *1 Enoch* 99:14 is the phrase "you will have no rest" used (Grk. οὐκ ἔστιν ὑμῖν ἀναπαύσαι; Eth. *'esma 'i-yekawwen lakemu 'eraft*), while there is a contrasting promise of "rest" for the righteous in the *Epistle* at *1 Enoch* 96:3. Variations of this pronouncement occur in descriptions of divine punishment in Deuteronomy 28:65 and, especially Isaiah 23:12; however, these texts do not promise rest for those obedient to the covenant. Similar to the *Epistle*, on the other hand,

---

[100] Charles, *The Book of Enoch or 1 Enoch*, p. xcviii; *idem, Revelation*, vol. 2, p. 17. See also Charlesworth, "The *Parables of Enoch* and the Apocalypse of John", pp. 233–234.

[101] On this broad usage within the Enoch tradition and elsewhere, see Stuckenbruck, *1 Enoch 91–108*, pp. 314–315.

[102] Stuckenbruck, *1 Enoch 91–108*, p. 423.

[103] See Stuckenbruck, *1 Enoch 91–108*, pp. 261–262 for a discussion of the literature.

Revelation couples the pronouncement (lit. "they have no rest," οὐκ ἔχουσιν ἀνά-
παυσιν) with the promise, in 14:13, that "those who from now on die in the Lord
... will rest (ἀναπαύσωνται) from their labors." This combination of rest and no rest
to the righteous and wicked, respectively, is only shared by these texts.

14:13 (RC[104]) – pro-nouncement of a blessing on "the dead who from now on die in the Lord"	**81:4** – "... Blessed is the one who dies righteous and good; regarding him no book of wickedness has been written and no day of judgment will be found."	makarism on the faithful who die

Apart from the testamentary conclusion to the *Astronomical Book* at *1 Enoch* 81:4,
no other text composed before Revelation preserves the pronouncement of a blessing on those who die in a state of faithfulness to God.[105]

14:14–15 (JC[106]) – "Then I looked, and there was a white cloud, and seated on the cloud was one like the Son of Man... And another angel..."	**46:1–2** – "There I saw one who had a head of days ... And with him was another, whose face was like the appearance of a man; and his face was full of gracious-ness, like one of the holy angels. And I asked the angel of peace, who went with me and showed me all the hidden things, about that son of man-who he was and whence he was (and) why he went with the Head of Days."	vision of the "son of man" as an angelic being

The similarities between the texts can be reduced to the vision of the "the Son of
Man" figure whose own being is expressly identified as or compared with angels
(respectively, Rev. 14:15 and *1 En.* 46:1). Taking the whole of the *Book of Parables*
into consideration, Charlesworth argues, that "The author of the Apocalypse of
John develops and brings into focus his creative Christology by stressing the judgment given to the Son of Man, a theme created and developed in *1 Enoch* 37–
71."[107] This possibility, given the extensive influence of Daniel (in this case, Dan.

---

[104] Charles, *The Book of Enoch or 1 Enoch*, p. xcviii; not mentioned in idem, *Revelation*, vol. 1, p. 370.

[105] Without mentioning the parallel in *1 En.* 81:4, Aune cites the nearly contemporary *1 Clem.* 44:5 as a parallel (*Revelation*, vol. 2, p. 839): "Blessed are those presbyters who have travelled on before, who had a perfect and fruitful departure, for they are no longer concerned that anyone remove them from the place established for them."

[106] Charlesworth, "The *Parables of Enoch* and the Apocalypse of John", pp. 234–235.

[107] Charlesworth, "The *Parables of Enoch* and the Apocalypse of John", p. 235.

7:9–14) on Revelation, is too general to confirm that, in this case, the presentation of "the son of man" of Revelation draws or is reliant on the direction of the interpretation taken up in the *Book of Parables*.

14:19–20 (RC[108]) – "So the angel swung his sickle over the earth and gathered the vintage of the earth, and he threw it into the great wine press of the wrath of God. / And the wine press was trodden outside the city, and blood flowed from the wine- press, as high as a horse's bridle..." (NRSV)	100:3 – "And a horse will go up to its chest in the blood of sinners, and the chariot will sink up to (its) height. And in those days the angels will descend to the hidden places and gather into one place all those who have given aid to sin."[109]	great slaughter of sinners illustrated through the height of their blood in relation to a horse, combined with angelic harvest of sinners

While the phrase "the wine press was trodden" at the beginning of Revelation 14:20 echoes language from Isaiah 63:3 (cf. Lam. 1:15), the following phrase links the wine press to a motif about the blood of sinners flowing up to a certain height on a horse. The *Epistle* (*1 En.* 100:3) offers an early image of a horse wading in blood that is picked up in later Christian (Rev. 14:20; *2 Esd.* 15:35–36 – adds "a man's thigh and a camel's hock" to the comparison) and Jewish texts (*Lam. Rabba* 2.2.4; *b. Ta'anith* 69a; *b. Gittin* 57a).[110] If a source for the text in Revelation is to be traced, *1 Enoch* 100:3 provides the best candidate. What makes the *Epistle* even more likely as a source here, however, is the location it assigns to the motif of angels acting as harvesters of sinners alongside the vivid imagery regarding the height of the sinners' blood. This is precisely what the text of Revelation 14:19–20 does, albeit in reverse order.

16:5 (RC[111]) – "the angel of the waters"	66:1–2 – the angels of punishment ready to go forth (v. 1); "And the Lord	angelic being(s) with responsibility over waters (cf. over elements: *Jub.* 2:2; 1QH[a] ix

---

[108] For Rev. 14:20, see Charles, *The Book of Enoch or 1 Enoch*, p. xcviii; *idem, Revelation*, vol. 2, p. 24; cf. Mazzaferri, *The Genre of the Book of Revelation*, p. 49. On Rev. 14:19–20 in relation to *1 En.* 100:3–4, see Stuckenbruck, *1 Enoch 91–108*, pp. 433–435 and Matthias Hoffmann, *The Destroyer and the Lamb* (WUNT 2.203; Tübingen: Mohr Siebeck, 2005), p. 55

[109] Translation by Stuckenbruck, *1 Enoch 91–108*, pp. 426, 433–434; the Grk. reads: "And a horse will go up to its chest through the blood of sinners, and the chariot will sink down to its axles."

[110] See Richard Bauckham, "The Use of Apocalyptic Traditions", pp. 38–91 (esp. pp. 40–48). Aune, *Revelation*, vol. 2, pp. 847–848, in noting the parallel with *1 En.* 100:3, resists, perhaps too categorically, that the *Epistle* could have exerted any influence on Revelation here, as "there is no evidence of any literary borrowing among these [*1 Enoch*, 6 Ezra=*2 Esd.* 15–16] sources."

[111] Charles, *The Book of Enoch or 1 Enoch*, p. xcviii; *idem, Revelation*, vol. 2, p. 44; cf. Aune, *Revelation*, vol. 2, p. 884; Hoffmann, *The Destroyer and the Lamb*, pp. 56–62.

of Spirits commanded the angels who were going forth, that they not raise their hands, but that they keep watch; for these angels were in charge of the power of the waters." 60:22 – "For the waters are for those who dwell on the land ... and the angels are given charge of it." cf. 69:22; 75:3	8–13; *2 En.* 2–4, 19:1– 4[112])

The text in Revelation assumes that material elements of the world are placed under the charge of angelic beings (see *1 En.* 60:11–22). The link between the angel in Revelation 16:5 is stronger with the *Book of Parables* at *1 Enoch* 66:1–2, since the context of both is that of punishment. However, though the angel in Revelation 16:5 speaks when the third bowl of wrath has been poured out (v. 4), this angel simply declares God's ways to be just, without actually functioning as an agent of the unfolding acts of divine wrath. The *Book of Parables* is the only other early Jewish text outside Revelation that specifically connects angelic oversight with water.

16:12–16 (Aune[113]) – "kings of the east," also called "kings of the whole earth," being assembled by demonic spirits for the great battle at Harmagedon cf. 19:19–21	56:5 – angels "hurl themselves toward the East against the Parthians and Medes". They will stir up the kings... to "trample the land of his chosen ones" and to come up against Jerusalem	spiritual forces arouse kings in the East to engage in military activity in Palestine

Several texts anticipate a single king from the East (*T. Moses* 3:1; *Sib. Or.* 4.120, 139 – the return of Nero myth). Only these passages in Revelation and the *Book of Parables* refer to the activity of "kings" while attributing this to the work, respectively, of demonic or angelic forces.[114]

17:14 (RC[115]) – the warring Lamb is called "Lord of lords and King of kings"; cf. 19:16	9:4 – (Cod.Pan.) "you are Lord of lords and God of gods and king of the ages" (Sync. a,b) "you are God of	similarity of divine title (cf. Dan. OG 4:37)

---

[112] Cf. Aune, *Revelation*, vol. 2, pp. 884–885 for later rabbinic and magical sources that regard angels as being in charge of rain or water.

[113] Aune, *Revelation*, vol. 2, p. 891 and esp. pp. 866–867.

[114] This attribution could explain why the notoriously evil Nero could be readily identified with Belial in *Sib. Or.* 3.63–74 and *Asc. Isa.* 4:1–12 (Beliar).

[115] Charles, *The Book of Enoch or 1 Enoch*, p. xcviii; *idem*, *Revelation*, vol. 2, p. 75.

gods and Lord of lords and
King of those who reign
and God of the ages" (Eth.)
"Lord of lords and God of
gods and King of kings"
(4Q202 1 iii 14) "you are]
our great Lord, [(you) ar]e
the Lord of the world, [...]"

The angels' address to God in the *Book of Watchers*, in its Greek and Ethiopic versions, attests to the combination of the two titles applied to the Lamb in Revelation 17:14 and 19:16. Matthew Black accounted for the difference between the Aramaic text of 4Q202 and the later Greek and Ethiopic versions by positing the addition in the latter of the titles "Lord of lords" and "God of gods" on the basis of designations for God in the Greek translation tradition of the Hebrew Bible (esp. Deut. 10:17; Ezek. 26:7; Dan. 2:23; Ezra 7:12).[116] If Black was correct, the question is whether or not these formulations existed prior to the composition of Revelation. Beale, on the other hand, has argued that underlying the title in Revelation is the Old Greek version of Daniel 4:37, where it is without an equivalent in the Aramaic text: "he is God of gods and Lord of lords and King of kings."[117] Both the Daniel (OG) and the *Book of Watchers* (cf. Jude 14–15) existed by the end of the 1st century. The verbal parallel to Revelation 17:14 and 19:16 is closest in the Danielic text. If one leaves open whether or not the Enochic text tradition might have influenced the Old Greek translation of Daniel at this point (or vice versa), the affinity between the latter and the Lamb's title in Revelation is striking.[118] Since this Greek text to Daniel (as Grk. and Eth. *1 En.* 9:4) preserves the threefold title, it is improbable that it has been influenced by the text of Revelation. If a background therefore to be sought, it is best found in the Danielic, not the Enochic tradition.

17:14 (RC[119]) – the Lamb who conquers when warred against by the kings allied with the beast	90:9, 12–13 – "I saw until horns came out on those lambs ... and I saw until a great horn sprouted on one of the sheep. ... And those	the notion of a warring lamb figure (cf. Dan. 7:21, 25; *T. Joseph* 19:8–9)

---

[116] Matthew Black, *The Book of Enoch or 1 Enoch* (SVTP 7; Leiden: Brill, 1985), p. 130.

[117] Beale argues this in several publications; see esp. *idem, The Book of Revelation: A Commentary on the Greek Text* (Grand Rapids: Eerdmans, 1999), pp. 881–882, where he draws attention, in addition, to the titles for Nebuchadnezzar in the Old Greek version to Daniel 2:37 and 3:2 (respectively, "king of kings" and "king of kings and lord of the world").

[118] Despite some of the problems noted in Beale's argumentation by Aune, *Revelation*, vol. 3, pp. 953–954.

[119] Charles, *Revelation*, vol. 1, p. 141 (on Rev. 5:6); see also, e.g., Robert H. Mounce, *The Book of Revelation* (NICNT; Grand Paids: Eerdmans, 1998, 2nd ed.), p. 145; George R. Beasley-Murray, *The Book of Revelation* (NCBC; Grand Rapids: Eerdmans, 1981, repr. 1974), pp. 124–125; Beale, *The Use of Daniel in Jewish Apocalyptic Literature and in the Revelation of St. John* (Lanham: The

> ravens were struggling and
> fighting with it (one of the
> lambs, v. 8)..., but did not
> prevail against it. And I saw
> until the shepherds and the
> eagles and those vultures
> and the kites came, and
> they cried to the ravens to
> smash the horn of that ram,
> and they made war with it,
> and it was struggling with
> them ..."

In addition to emphasizing the image of Jesus as a "slaughtered" Lamb (5:6), the Lamb functions as a warrior who defeats the enemies of God and of God's people as well.[120] While the former image comes to terms with Jesus' death within the framework of Passover and related traditions,[121] scholars have debated whether or not the latter had any precedent in Second Temple Jewish tradition. The primary focus of this discussion has centered on the *Animal Apocalypse* in which the Maccabeans, with Judas at their head, wage war, depicted as horned "lambs" (*1 En.* 90:9a),[122] in response to Antiochus Epiphanes' persecution. A related question, and more easy to assess, is the degree to which any link can be discerned in the *Animal Apocalypse* between such lamb imagery and the primary figure of power in *1 Enoch* 90:37–39. Beginning with the latter question, we may note that the divine agent in the eschatological vision is symbolized by a "bull," not a lamb. If that divine agent were to be understood as a "messianic" figure, then the lamb symbolism does not play a role.[123] Thus, although one can argue, despite textual and source-critical complexities in *1 Enoch* 90:6–16,[124] that Revelation has some precedent in the *Animal Apocalypse* in its present form for a combative lamb figure, the background is weak; Judas Maccabeus, as a horned lamb (v. 9b) is given provisional, though not ultimate support in the work,[125] and it would be difficult to explain how the Enochic work would have provided John in Revelation with any warrant to transfer the lamb symbol to God's primary agent.

University Press of America, 1984), pp. 71–75 and *idem, The Book of Revelation,* p. 881 (focusing esp. on *1 En.* 90:12–13).

[120] So Hoffmann, *The Destroyer and the Lamb,* pp. 169–211.

[121] Johns, *The Lamb Christology of the Apocalypse of John,* pp. 108–149.

[122] By contrast, the lamb seized by the ravens (the Gentile oppressors) in *1 En.* 90:8 is likely to refer to the high priest Onias III (cf. also 90:12).

[123] Cf. the discussion of the textual evidence in scholarly analysis by Johns, *The Lamb Christology of the Apocalypse of John,* pp. 90–92. Johns is correct in noting the disjunction between "lamb" or "ram" in the *Animal Apocalypse* and the bull figure in *1 En.* 90:37–39, though strains to draw a distinction between the more fluid "lamb" and "ram" imagery in the text.

[124] See Tiller, *Commentary on the Animal Apocalypse,* pp. 352–353 and Nickelsburg, *1 Enoch 1,* pp. 396–401.

[125] Tiller, *Commentary on the Animal Apocalypse,* pp. 109–115.

18:4, 7 (MM[126]) – the exhortation to "come out of" Babylon "lest you participate in her sins," for "she has glorified herself and lived in luxury" (cf. above 2:9; 3:17)	104:6 and 108:8–15 – do not fear and do not become companions with strong and prosperous sinners	the critique of wealth and of associating wrongdoers with the prosperous

Critiques of wealth to varying degrees are well attested in the Hebrew Bible and Second Temple writings (including the New Testament).[127] Several texts also warn against collusion with sinners: Proverbs 13:20; Ben Sira 12:14; 37:11–12; *Jubilees* 22:16; and the *Epistle of Enoch* (*1 En.* 94:2–4; 97:4). The critique of wealth in Revelation (2:9; 3:17) is amplified in the warning, announced by a heavenly voice, to disassociate from Babylon (18:4), who then is linked to living in luxury (18:7). Apart from the *Epistle of Enoch* (*1 En.* 104:6; cf. more generally 108:8–15) there is no other Jewish text that combines a critique of wealth with an injunction not to associate with wealthy sinners.

18:6–7 (MM) – Render to her as she herself has rendered, and repay her double for her deeds; mix a double draught for her in the cup she mixed. / As she glorified herself and lived luxuriously, so give her a like measure of torment and grief.... (NRSV)	91:12 – After this there will arise an eighth week of righteousness, in which a sword will be given to all the righteous, to execute righteous judgment on all the wicked, and they will be delivered into their hands. cf. 38:5; 90:19; 95:3; 96:1; 98:12	the righteous to carry out judgment against the wicked (cf. 2 Macc. 15:15–16; *Jub.* 23:30; *Apoc. Abraham* 29.17–20)

The motif of "double" repayment for wrongdoing is well attested in the Hebrew Bible. The summons to "render to her as she herself has rendered, and repay her double for her deeds" is very close to the Greek text for Jeremiah (27:29, Heb. 50:29), to which it may be an allusion.[128] Significantly, those who are exhorted to be agents of punishment against Rome are "my people" of Revelation 18:4.[129] Parallels for this idea exist in several early Jewish writings, though it is best attested in the *Animal Apocalypse* (*1 En.* 90:19), *Epistle of Enoch* (95:3; 96:1; 98:12), and *Book of Parables* (38:5). A reliance of Revelation on the Enochic texts, however, is hard to establish since none of specific terms used in Revelation 18:6–7 reflect any ver-

---

[126] Mathews, *Riches, Poverty, and the Faithful*, pp. 198–202.

[127] See Catherine M. Murphy, *Wealth in the Dead Sea Scrolls and in the Qumran Community* (STDJ 40; Leiden: Brill, 2002) and Mathews, *Riches, Poverty, and the Faithful*.

[128] On double retribution see Exod. 21:24–25; Lev. 24:19–20; Deut. 19:21; Isa. 40:2; and Jer. 16:18, all passages in which it is considered unjust; cf. Aune, *Revelation*, vol. 3, pp. 992–993 (also for parallels in classical Grk. literature).

[129] Cf. Aune, *Revelation*, vol. 3, p. 994.

bal link with these traditions. At most, Revelation shares the motif with a number of writings, for which several sections of *1 Enoch* provide examples.

18:10 (MM[130]) – the kings of the earth (v. 9) say, "Woe, woe, O great city, Babylon, the mighty city! For in one hour your judgment has come!" (cf. 8:13; 9:12; 11:14; 12:12; 18:10, 16, 19)	*Epistle of Enoch* alone has 32 woe-oracles,[131] most of which are followed by a 2nd person address (94:6–8; 95:4–7; 96:4–8; 97:7–10; 98:9, 98:11–99:2; 99:11–16; 100:7–9; 103:5–8)	woe oracles with 2nd person (*passim* in the Heb. Bible)

The "woe-oracle" form, which functions to denounce perpetrators of wrongdoing, occurs frequently among the prophets of the Hebrew Bible (e. g., Isa. 3:11; 10:1, 5; Jer. 22:13; 48:1; Ezek. 13:3, 18; 34:2; Amos 5:18; 6:1). Up to fifty-four such oracles can be identified within the entirety of the Hebrew Bible,[132] while it is in Isaiah that twenty of these instances can be accounted for.[133] Against this background, there is an unusually high proportion of woe-oracles in the *Epistle of Enoch*, where alone they number to thirty-two, of which thirty occur in collections of two to six oracles.[134] Both the Hebrew Bible texts and the *Epistle of Enoch* follow a pattern which, following the "woe" itself, includes (a) an accusation and (b) a threat. There may be reason to doubt that Revelation has been influenced here by the Enochic tradition, though the latter provides the fullest use of the woe-oracle among Jewish apocalyptic writings, especially in that the *Epistle*, as Revelation, characteristically makes this form function as a formal announcement that guarantees the punishment of the wicked at the time of eschatological judgment.[135]

18:20 (MM[136]) – "Rejoice over her, O heaven, you saints and apostles and prophets! For God has given judgment for you against her." (NRSV) cf. 19:1–4	94:10 – denunciation of the rich: "… with regard to your fall there will be no compassion, and your Creator will rejoice over your destruction." (89:58)	rejoicing over the destruction of the wicked (cf. Jer. 51:48; 4Q225 = 4QPsJub[a] 2 ii 6–7)

---

[130] Mathews, *Riches, Poverty, and the Faithful*, pp. 211–215.

[131] For a list of the texts and discussion, see Nickelsburg, *1 Enoch 1*, pp. 416–418 and Stuckenbruck, *1 Enoch 91–108*, pp. 193–197.

[132] So Claus Westermann, *Basic Forms of Prophetic Speech*, trans. Hugh Clayton White (Louisville: John Knox Press, 1991), p. 191.

[133] J. William Whedbee, *Isaiah and Wisdom* (Nashville: Abingdon Press, 1971), p. 80.

[134] In addition to the discussions by Nickelsburg and Stuckenbruck mentioned in n. 115 above, see Robert A. Coughenour, "The Woe-Oracles in Ethiopic Enoch", *JSJ* 9 (1978), pp. 192–197 (here p. 192).

[135] Mathews, "Riches, Poverty, and the Faithful", pp. 215

[136] Mathews, "Riches, Poverty, and the Faithful", p. 212.

A divine response of rejoicing at the destruction of the wicked for their wrong-doing is denied in Ezekiel (18:23, 32; 33:11). The motif in Revelation 18:20 is very different: the righteous thought to have suffered because of Babylon's deeds are exhorted to rejoice at God's judgment against her. The closest parallel to this is the rejoicing of "heaven and earth and all that is in them" over the destruction of Babylon in Jeremiah 51:48. In the Enochic *Animal Apocalypse* (*1 En.* 89:58) and *Epistle* (94:10), a similar motif can be found. However, there are three differences. The first is that, unlike Revelation, the righteous are not expressly told to rejoice in this way. Secondly, in the Enochic texts, the rejoicing is ascribed to God, not to the righteous. Thirdly, the 2nd person in the *Epistle* is directed at the wicked, not the righteous (*1 En.* 94:10), while in the *Animal Apocalypse* tells of God's rejoicing, in the 3rd person, at the devouring of Judah by the Babylonians when the Temple was destroyed (89:58). Although the motif of rejoicing when the wicked are punished or destroyed is rare in the Hebrew Bible and Jewish apocalyptic traditions, the differences just noted render it unlikely that the Enochic tradition explains its use in Revelation.

19:12[137] – Christ "has a name inscribed that no one knows but himself" (NRSV)	69:13–29 – Michael has a "secret name" that forms part of an oath through which the heavens, earth, and sea were created	possession of an unknowable (probably the ineffable) name

In two further traditions, Judges 13:17–18[138] and *Joseph and Aseneth* 15:11–12,[139] an angelic figure withholds revealing his name when asked by the human in the encounter what it is. In Revelation 19, however, the name that Christ possesses is not referred to in the context of a visionary encounter. In the *Book of Parables* in *1 Enoch* 69:13–14 the name that Michael possesses is not one that is only known to him; another angel, Kasbe'el, the "chief of the oath", also knows it, having been taught the name by Michael (69:14). If the name Christ bears is the divine name, then other parallels come into view: Exodus 23:21 (the angel who guides Israel in the wilderness), *Apocalypse of Abraham* 11 (Yahoel), and the later *3 Enoch* 12 (Metatron). The limited value of these parallels, not least the one in *1 Enoch* 69, is reinforced by the fact that the notion of a secret name in Revelation is not exclusive to Christ. At the conclusion to the message to the church at Pergamum, the faithful are promised a white stone on which is inscribed a "new name that no one knows except the one who receives it" (2:17). While the superiority of Jesus suggests that his secret name is greater than that of believers, the text of Revelation

---

[137] Darrell D. Hannah, *Michael and Christ: Michael Traditions and Angel Christology in Early Christianity* (WUNT 2.109; Tübingen: Mohr Siebeck, 1999), pp. 144–145: "Christ has not only taken over Michael's role as leader of the heavenly hosts – he also possesses the divine Name as Michael does in *1 En.* 69.13–25" (p. 145).

[138] Hoffmann, *The Destroyer and the Lamb*, p. 195.

[139] Stuckenbruck, *Angel Veneration and Christology*, pp. 168–170.

uses this motif to strengthen the analogy between Christology and those who are faithful to God.

20:4 – the beheaded "came to life and reigned with Christ a thousand years" (NRSV)	91:12–13 – in "the eighth week of righteousness ... a sword will be given to all the righteous, to execute righteous judgment on all the wicked, and they will be delivered into their hands. / And at its conclusion, they will acquire possessions in righteousness, and the temple of the kingdom of the Great One will be built for all the generations of eternity."	temporary kingdom for the righteous

The comparable point between Revelation and the *Apocalypse of Weeks* is the limited duration of control or rule given to those who are faithful, in the former a thousand years and in the latter the period covered by the eighth week. In addition, both texts anticipate the reign of the righteous in the near future, that is, after an initial punishment is carried out against the wicked. Beyond the notion of reigning, however, there are no verbal links between the texts.

20:7–9 (RC[140]) – "When the thousand years are over, Satan will be rereleased from his prison, / and will come out to deceive the nations at the four corners of the earth, Gog and Magog, in order to gather them for battle; they are as numerous as the sands of the sea. / They marched up over the breadth of the earth and surrounded the camp of the saints and the beloved city. And fire came down from heaven and consumed them." (NRSV)	56:5–8 – "In those days, the angels will assemble themselves, and hurl themselves toward the East against the Parthians and Medes. They will stir up the kings, and a spirit of agitation will come upon them, and it will rouse them from their thrones... They will begin (to make) war among themselves... / They will go up and trample the land of his chosen ones ... / but the city of my righteous ones will be a hindrance to their horses. / In those days, Sheol will open its mouth, and they will sink into it. And their destruction will be at an end; Sheol will devour the sinners from the presence of the chosen."	nations roused by powers make war on Jerusalem, but are defeated by divine activity

---

[140] Charles, *Revelation*, vol. 2, p. 188.

The text in the *Book of Parables* does not mention Satan, nor does it name the nations gathered to attack Jerusalem Gog and Magog (cf. Ezek. 38:14–18 where, however, God stirs up the nations). In broad terms, these texts correlate, and Jerusalem is linked with the faithful. However, correspondences in detail and vocabulary are lacking, so that any direct connection between the texts is difficult to maintain.[141]

20:12 (RC[142]) – "And I saw the dead, great and small, standing before the throne, and books were opened. Also another book was opened, the book of life. And the dead were judged according to their works, as recorded in the books." (NRSV) cf. Rev. 3:5	90:20 – "I saw until a throne was constructed in the pleasant land and the Lord of the sheep sat upon it, and he took all the sealed books and opened those books before the Lord of the sheep." 47:3 – "In those days I saw the Head of Days as he took his seat on the throne of his glory, and the books of the living were opened in his presence..." 108:3 – "... their (those who do evil) names will be erased from the book of life and from the books of the holy ones, and their seed will be destroyed forever..."[143]	the opening of books for judgment in the divine court (cf. Dan. 7:9–10; *Book of Giants* at 4Q530 2 ii 6–12 (?), lines 16–20); book of life / living

Among the texts given above only Revelation 20:12 distinguishes the opened "book of life" from the books opened for judgment. In Revelation the expression "book of life" (τὸ βιβλίον τῆς ζωῆς) occurs a number of times (Rev. 3:5; 13:8; 17:8; 20:15; 21:27), while elsewhere in the New Testament it appears only in Philippians 4:3. An approximate form of the expression, "book of the living (ones)", is attested in the *Book of Parables* at *1 Enoch* 47:3 and in Psalm 69:28 ("let them [the enemies] be blotted out from the book of the living and let them not be enrolled among the righteous", NRSV to Heb.). A more exact equivalent is preserved in the *Eschatological Admonition* of *1 Enoch* 108:3 (*maṣḥafa ḥewiyān*), where it is twinned with "the books of the holy ones". The latter text announces that the names of the wicked "will be erased from the book of life", a phrase that has its negative equivalent in Revelation 3:5: "To those who conquer ... I will not blot your name out of

---

[141] Cf. Charlesworth, "The *Parables of Enoch* and the Apocalypse of John", pp. 235–236.

[142] Charles, *The Book of Enoch or 1 Enoch*, p. xcviii (for v. 12: the opening of books for judgment).

[143] The translation is taken from Stuckenbruck, *1 Enoch 91–108*, pp. 697–698.

the book of life". Both Revelation 3:5 and *1 Enoch* 108:3 are allusions to Psalm 69:28 and, perhaps secondarily, to Exodus 32:32 ("[b]ut now, if you will only forgive their sin – and if not, blot me out of the book you have written"); they go beyond the texts from the Hebrew Bible, however, in regarding the book of life as a list of names of those who will survive the eschatological judgment, an idea which among literature composed before the Common Era is also found in Daniel 12:1 and *Jubilees* 36:10 (cf. also *1 En.* 103:2; 104:1).[144] Since the motif is broadly shared, it is difficult to isolate influence on or an immediate link with Revelation from either the *Book of Parables* or *Eschatological Admonition*.

A similar conclusion can be reached in relation to the books of judgment referred to as "opened" in Revelation 20:12. The important parallels in *Animal Apocalypse* (*1 En.* 90:20), the *Book of Giants* (4Q530 2 ii + 6–12 (?), lines 16–20) and Daniel 7:9–10 demonstrate how much currency traditions formed during the 2nd century B.C.E.[145] still had when Revelation was composed. More specifically, Revelation envisions the opened books relating to the expanse of deceased humanity ("great and small"), while the texts in Daniel 7 and the *Book of Giants* are concerned with the judgment to be executed against the fourth beast (Dan. 7:8) and the ante-diluvian giants, respectively. The Enochic *Animal Apocalypse*, on the other hand, conceives of the judgment in the broadest possible terms; it is meted out to several groups, all who "were found to be sinners": the fallen stars (*1 En.* 90:21), the seventy angelic shepherds (90:22), and the "blinded sheep", that is, the disobedient of Israel (90:26–27). In a different vein, however, Revelation relates the books to the human dead (Rev. 20:12–13), not to the judgment of demonic powers (20:9). Conceptually, the scope of judgment in the *Animal Apocalypse* provides the nearest antecedent to Revelation; however, it is difficult to establish that the inclusion of the deeds of dead humans in the opened books can be explained on the basis of literary influence.

20:13 (RC[146]) – "And the sea gave up the dead that	51:1 – "In those days the earth will restore what has	the return of the dead from the netherworld for judg-

---

[144] Moreover, erasure "from the book of life" may be inferred from the fragmentary *4QNon-Canonical Psalms^b* = 4Q381 B 31.8 in which the writer refers to the death of his enemies. The more contemporary and later texts containing this motif include *Jos. and Asen.* 15:4; *T. Levi* 18:59–60 (Grk. ms. Athos Koutloumous 39); the parallel petitions in the *Shemoneh Esreh* 12th benediction (Pal. recension); and *Pistis Sophia* 1.33. See also the more wide-ranging discussion of the notion of citizen enrolment in classical Greece by Aune, *Revelation*, vol. 1, pp. 224–225. A number of rabbinic discussions pick up on the motif, albeit while more immediately concerned with Ps. 69:28 and Exod. 32:32; see Hermann Strack and Paul Billerbeck, *Kommentar zum Neuen Testament* (6 vols.; München: Beck, 1922–1961), 2:170.

[145] These three texts, with the *Book of Giants* preserving the tradition in its earlier form, are roughly contemporary and can be interpreted in relation to one another; cf. Loren T. Stuckenbruck, "Daniel and Early Enoch Traditions in the Dead Sea Scrolls", in eds. John J. Collins and Peter W. Flint, *The Book of Daniel: Composition and Reception* (2 vols.; VTSup 58; Leiden/Boston/Köln: Brill 2001), 2:368–86 (and Chapter Five above).

[146] Charles, *The Book of Enoch or 1 Enoch*, p. xcix and *idem*, *Revelation*, vol. 2, p. 195.

were in it, Death and Hades gave up the dead that were in them, and all were judged according to what they had done." (NRSV)

been entrusted to it, and Sheol will restore what it has received, and destruction will restore what it owes."

ment (cf. literature mentioned below)

The notion of a resurrection of the dead, whether spiritual or physical, for judgment is of course well attested in ancient Jewish and early Christian tradition.[147] Revelation 20:13, more particularly, shares a tradition with a number of other writings that presents resurrection as taking place when (a) the abode of the dead returns the dead and (b) this abode returns what was entrusted to it (*1 En.* 51:1; *4 Ezra* 4:41–43; 7:32; *Ps.-Philo* 3:10; 33:3; *Apoc. Peter* 4:10–12; *Midr. Psa.* 1:20; *Pirq. R. Eliezer* 34; *Pes. Rabbati* 21:4).[148] In no respect does the text of Revelation 20:13, which goes its own way among these texts by including the sea as a repository for the dead, share with the *Book of Parables* at *1 Enoch* 51:1 any detail not also found elsewhere. It is therefore difficult to posit any form of connection beyond the observation that Revelation draws on a widely shared tradition.

20:15 (RC[149]) – "and anyone whose name was not found written in the book of life was thrown into the lake of fire." (NRSV)

90:26 – "And I saw at that time that an abyss like it was opened in the middle of the earth, which was full of fire. And they brought those blinded sheep, and they were all judged and found to be sinners. And they were thrown into that fiery abyss, and they burned."

image of the wicked being thrown into a fiery place

The expression "lake of fire" (ἡ λίμνη τοῦ πυρός) occurs six times in the context of final judgment in Revelation (19:20; 20:10, 14 *bis*, 15; 21:8). Into it are thrown "the beast" and "false prophet" (19:10), "the devil" (20:10), "Death and Hades" (20:14), and those not in "the book of life" (20:15), including a catalogue of wrongdoers (21:8). Although fire is frequently associated with eschatological pun-

---

[147] Texts featuring in reviews of this literature include Dan. 12:2–3; *1 En.* 51:1–2; *4 Ezra* 6:18–29; 7:31–38; *2 Bar.* 21:23, 24; *Ps.-Philo* 3:10; *Sib. Or.* 2.221–237; 4.179–191. See the different treatments on the texts in question and their relationship with the Dead Sea Scrolls by Émile Puech, *La croyance des esséniens en la vie future: immortalité, résurrection, vie éternelle?: histoire d'une croyance dans le judaïsme ancien* (2 vols.; Paris: J. Gabalda, 1993); John J. Collins, "Resurrection and Eternal Life", in *idem, Apocalypticism in the Dead Sea Scrolls* (London and New York: Routledge, 1997), pp. 110–129; and George Nickelsburg, *Resurrection, Immortality, and Eternal Life in Intertestamental Judaism and Early Christianity* (HTS 56; Cambridge, Massachusetts: Harvard University Press, 2006, 2nd ed.).

[148] These texts and their constituent elements are discussed by Bauckham, "The Use of Apocalyptic Traditions", pp. 56–70.

[149] Charles, *The Book of Enoch or 1 Enoch*, p. xcix.

ishment in Jewish literature (1QS ii 7–8; CD ii 5; *1 En.* 10:6; *Sib. Or.* 2.195–205; cf. Ezek. 38:22; Mk. 9:43; Rev. 14:10–11), the image of being "thrown" into a fiery place is limited to Revelation (ἐβλήθη) and, among the early apocalyptic texts, to the *Animal Apocalypse* at *1 Enoch* 90:26. In the Enochic text, as in Revelation 20:15, it is human wrongdoers who are judged in this way, and the equivalents to Revelation would be the Ethiopic *wa-tawaddeyu westa zeku 'emuqa 'essāt* (lit. "and they were thrown into that deep place of fire"). If we focus on the combination of the verb and the place of punishment, *Animal Apocalypse* offers the closest linguistic parallel to Revelation.

21:1 (RC[150]) – "Then I saw a new heaven and a new earth; for the first heaven and the first earth had passed away, and the sea was no more."	91:16 – "And the first heaven shall disappear and pass away, and a new heaven shall appear, and every power of the heavens shall shine sevenfold forever."[151]	the disappearance of "the first heaven" at the appearance of "a new heaven"

The anticipation of "a new heaven and new earth" in Revelation 21:1 is traditional; see especially Isaiah 65:17; 66:22; and 2 Peter 3:3. Indeed, it is from Isaiah that Revelation has derived this language. On the other hand, outside Revelation only the *Apocalypse of Weeks* at *1 Enoch* 91:16 refers to the passing away of "the first heaven".[152] While this correspondence might appear minor, it is possible to discern, based on the comparisons made above, a further correspondence in the sequence of eschatological events between the *Apocalypse of Weeks* and the later chapters of Revelation:[153] (1) the motif of the righteous executing judgment against the wicked (*1 En.* 91:12, eighth week; Rev. 18:6–7); (2) a period of temporary dominance by the righteous on the earth (*1 En.* 91:13–14, eighth and ninth weeks; Rev. 20:4); (3) eschatological judgment (*1 En.* 91:15, tenth week; Rev. 20:11–12); and (4) the establishment of a new cosmic order (*1 En.* 91:16; Rev. 21:1).[154] This broad correlation, coupled with the verbal linkage, suggests that if the text of Revelation does not know the *Apocalypse of Weeks* directly, it was shaped by an otherwise unknown tradition that stemmed from it.

---

[150] Charles, *The Book of Enoch or 1 Enoch*, p. xcix.

[151] Translation in Stuckenbruck, *1 Enoch 91–108*, p. 145.

[152] As noted by Daniel C. Olson, *Enoch: A New Translation* (North Richland Hills, Texas: BIBAL Press, 2005), p. 222 and Mathews, *Riches, Poverty, and the Faithful*, p. 211 n. 74. No mention is made of a recreation of the "earth" for the tenth week in the *Apoc. of Weeks* because the seventh, eighth and ninth weeks are concerned with events on earth; cf. Stuckenbruck, *1 Enoch 91–108*, p. 149 and n. 303.

[153] So Charles, *The Book of Enoch or 1 Enoch*, pp. 260–265; Mathews, *Riches, Poverty, and the Faithful*, p. 211.

[154] A similar sequence, though with less immediate correspondence to Revelation, is discernable in *1 En.* 50:1–51:5.

22:2 (RC[155]) – "the throne of God and of the Lamb"	51:3; 61:8; 62:2–3, 5; – the Chosen One sits on the throne of God's glory, cf. 45:3; 51:1; 55:4; 69:27, 29	a primary divine agent seated on the throne of God (Mt. 25:31)

Though it is not clear that the Enochic tradition in the *Book of Parables* has influenced the assimilation of the Lamb to God's throne, it does attest the possibility that non-Christian tradition could envision the heavenly enthronement of a principal mediator figure. This notion of placing of God's designate on a throne to vanquish God's enemies is probably influenced by Psalm 110:1, interpreted in relation to a divine agent. However, these texts go beyond Psalm 110 to specify the place of seating is none other than the divine throne itself. This idea already occurs in Matthew 25:31, which anticipates that at the final judgment "the Son of Man will sit on the throne of his (God's) glory", language that comes much closer to the formulations in the *Book of Parables*, as the divine throne in Revelation is never described as such in relation to "glory".

22:3 (RC[156]) – "Nothing accursed will be found there anymore. But the throne of God and of the Lamb will be in it, and his servants will worship him." (NRSV)	25:6 – "Then they (the righteous) will rejoice greatly and be glad, and they will enter into the sanctuary. Its fragrances <will be> in their bones, and they will live a long life on the earth, such as your fathers lived also in their days, and torments and plagues and suffering will not touch them."	the combination of nothing harmful in the new cosmic order with the worship of God by the faithful

The presentation of the future Jerusalem as a place unaffected by manifestations of evil in Revelation 22:3 alludes to Zechariah 14:11; though it is possible, too, that the *Book of Watchers* at *1 Enoch* 25:6 alludes to Zechariah as well, it implies that the joyful righteous who enter the Temple will worship God. In Revelation, the cultic worship (λατρεύσουσιν) by the faithful is explicit, with God and the Lamb constituting the heavenly Temple (Rev. 21:22).

C. Conclusions

Having reviewed fifty-one alleged parallels between the Apocalypse of John and *1 Enoch*, we are in a better position to summarize what can be said about the significance of the latter for the former. We do so by means of the following five points.

---

[155] Charles, *Revelation*, vol. 2, pp. 175–176.
[156] Charles, *The Book of Enoch or 1 Enoch*, p. xcix.

First, in most of the cases identified and discussed, Revelation has been shown to participate alongside other writings in developments of apocalyptic tradition that can be observed in other early Jewish writings. In these instances, Revelation preserves nothing, whether conceptually or in a given detail, that corresponds with the Enochic tradition in a way not found in other traditions. We have found this to be the case in the following twenty-three passages of Revelation: 1:7; 1:14, 16 (cf. 10:1); 3:21; 5:11; 6:9–11; 7:1; 7:15; 7:17; 8:3–4; 9:1; 10:7; 11:18; 12:11; 13:5–6; 17:14; 18:6–7; 18:10; 18:20; 19:12; 20:4; 20:7–9; 20:12; and 20:13. These general and widely shared traditions demonstrate at least how much Revelation stands generally within the Jewish apocalyptic tradition.

Second, a further group of thirteen parallels reflects more strongly a specific affinity between Revelation and the Enochic tradition. In these cases, the correspondences are based on a uniquely shared *combination* of ideas or motifs in Revelation and in one of the sections of *1 Enoch*. Though sometimes there is a correspondence in detail, the combination occurs mostly on a conceptual level of commonly held motifs. The texts and Enochic parallels in question are as follows, with the stronger cases for Enochic influence on Revelation marked with an asterisk:

Rev. 1:1   *Exhortation* 91:1–2
– Introduction of a document as concerned with the future by an intermediary

Rev. 1:4; 9:1; and 15:5–6   *Animal Apocalypse* 86:1; 88:1
– Seven angels associated with the divine throne who act as agents of judgment with the motif of a falling star

*Rev. 3:12 and 21:22   *Animal Apocalypse* 90:29; 90:32–25
– Location of the faithful in the New Jerusalem (including association with pillars) in which a Temple structure is not ultimately envisioned

*Rev. 4:1   *Book of Watchers* 14:8, 15
– An open door in heaven with a sound that beckons the visionary to come

*Rev. 4:6, 8   *Book of Parables* 40:2; 39:12
– Four creatures on each side of the throne singing the Trisagion in the context of continuous worship

*Rev. 6:15–16   *Book of Parables* 62:3, 5
– The terror of kings and the mighty before the divine throne which, in turn, is associated with a primary agent

*Rev. 9:20   *Epistle of Enoch* 99:7
– The combination of a list of materials used to make idols, idolatry, and the worship of demonic beings

Rev. 12:9   *Book of Parables* 69:6
– The identification of the serpent in the Garden of Eden with a demonic being

*Rev. 14:11, 13   *Epistle of Enoch* 99:14
– No rest for the wicked with promise of rest for the righteous

Rev. 14:19–20   *Epistle of Enoch* 100:3
– A great slaughter of sinners, resulting in flow of blood to a height comparable to parts of a horse combined with the angelic harvest of sinners

*Rev. 16:12–16   *Book of Parables* 56:5
– Spiritual forces arouse kings from the East to military activity in Palestine

Rev. 18:4, 7   *Epistle of Enoch* 104:6; *Eschatological Admonition* 108:8–15
– The critique of wealth with condemnation of those who associate with rich wrongdoers

Rev. 22:3   *Book of Watchers* 25:6
– Nothing harmful in the new world order together with the worship of God by the faithful

Third, in fifteen instances the correspondences between Revelation and *1 Enoch* can be observed in exclusively or almost exclusively shared significant terms or closely comparable phrases, especially if the remaining parallels, if they exist, are preserved in later literature. Again, the stronger parallels that open the possibility of Enochic influence on Revelation are marked with an asterisk:

Rev. 2:7   *Book of Watchers* 24:4–25:6
– The eschatological eating from the tree of life by the righteous

Rev. 3:5, 7:13   *Animal Apocalypse* 90:28–32
– The association of the faithful with white clothing

*Rev. 3:20   *Book of Parables* 62:14
– Promise that the faithful will eat with God's vice regent

Rev. 8:8   *Book of Watchers* 22:3
– Vision of (a) fiery mountain(s) in the context of divine judgment

*Rev. 12:8   *Book of Watchers* 14:5; cf. 15:6–8
– Rebellious angels forfeit their assigned position in heaven

*Rev. 13:14   *Book of Parables* 54:6
- The primary agents of sin lead astray those who inhabit the earth

Rev. 14:4   *Book of Watchers* 7:1; 9:8: 10:11; 12:4; 15:3, 4
- Defiling themselves with women

Rev. 14:9–10   *Book of Parables* 48:9
- Punishment by fire in the presence of the holy ones

*Rev. 14:13   *Astronomical Book (addition)* 81:4
- Blessing pronounced on the faithful who die

*Rev. 14:14–15   *Book of Parables* 46:1–2
- Vision of the "son of man" as an angelic being

Rev. 16:5   *Book of Parables* 66:1–2; cf. 60:22
- Angels with assigned responsibilities over water

Rev. 17:14   *Animal Apocalypse* 90:9, 12–13
- A warring lamb figure

*Rev. 20:15   *Animal Apocalypse* 90:26
- The wicked thrown into a fiery place

*Rev. 21:1   *Apocalypse of Weeks* 91:16
- The passing away of the first heaven when the new heaven appears

Rev. 22:2   *Book of Parables* 51:3; 61:8; 62:2–3, 5
- God's vice regent seated on the divine throne

Fourth, certain parts of *1 Enoch* can be determined which have featured the stronger parallels (from the last two lists) more than others. The largest number of significant parallels (marked with an asterisk) suggesting the possibility of Enochic influence on Revelation has to do with the *Book of Parables* (six). This signifies an affinity that can be explained by the relative contemporaneity of the *Book of Parables* with Revelation or by the use of one by the other, with the direction of influence most likely being from the *Book of Parables* to Revelation. The other writings with potentially significant parallels are *Book of Watchers* (three), *Animal Apocalypse* (two), *Epistle of Enoch* (two), *Exhortation* (one), *Astronomical Book (testamentary addition)* (one), and *Apocalypse of Weeks* (one). On the whole, this makes it likely that the writer of Revelation was either directly acquainted (through literary or oral transmission) with several of the major sections of *1 Enoch* or at least had access to traditions that were influenced by these writings. While most recent scholarly attention has understandably focused on the correspondences between

Revelation and the *Book of Parables*, our analysis has demonstrated that the importance, perhaps even impact, of the Enochic tradition on the interpretation of Revelation does not stop there.

Fifth and finally, at no point can it be demonstrated that the Apocalypse of John quotes from any passage in *1 Enoch*. The same is true, of course, for most of the remaining books of the Hebrew Bible, though the books of Exodus, Daniel, Isaiah and Ezekiel stand out as having wielded considerable influence on the shape and concepts of the Revelation. Leaving these four books aside, we would not be far wrong to claim that the works brought together into *1 Enoch* are, collectively, at least as important as most of the other biblical books. How this compares, for example, with the traditions Revelation shares with the more contemporary works of 4 Ezra and *2 Baruch* is a matter for further investigation.

Cumulative Bibliography

Abegg, Martin. "Messianic Hope and 4Q285: A Reassessment", *JBL* 113 (1994), pp. 81–91.

Adams, Edward. *Constructing the World: A Study in Paul's Cosmological Language*. Edinburgh: T & T Clark, 2000.

Adler, William R. and James C. Vander Kam. *The Jewish Apocalyptic Heritage in Early Christianity*. CRINT III.4. Assen: Van Gorcum, and Minneapolis: Fortress Press, 1996.

Adler, William R. and Paul Tuffin. *The Chronography of Geeorge Synkellos: A Byzantine Chronicle of Universal History from the Creation, Translated with Introduction and Notes*. Oxford: Oxford University Press, 2002.

Albinus, Lars. "The Greek δαίμων between Mythos and Logos". In eds. Armin Lange, Hermann Lichtenberger, and K. F. Diethard Römheld, *Die Dämonen – Demons. Die Dämonologie der israelitisch-jüdischen und frühchristlichen Literatur im Kontext ihrer Umwelt*. Tübingen: Mohr Siebeck, 2003. Pp. 425–446.

Alexander, Philip S. "Wrestling Against Wickedness in High Places: Magic in the Worldview of the Qumran Community". In eds. Stanley E. Porter and Craig A. Evans, *The Scrolls and the Scriptures: Qumran Fifty Years After*. JSPSup 26. Sheffield: Sheffield Academic Press, 1997. Pp. 319–330.

Alexander, Philip S. "The Demonology of the Dead Sea Scrolls". In eds. Peter W. Flint and James C. VanderKam, *The Dead Sea Scrolls after Fifty Years. A Comprehensive Assessment*. 2 vols. Leiden / Boston / Köln: Brill, 1999. Vol. 2, pp. 331–353.

Alexander, Philip S. and Geza Vermes. "4QSefer ha-Milhamah". In eds. Stephen Pfann *et al.*, *Qumran Cave 4. XXVI: Cryptic Texts and Miscellanea, Part 1*. DJD 36. Oxford: Clarendon Press, 2000. Pp. 228–246.

Allison, Dale C. "*4Q403* fragm. 1, col. 1,38–46 and the Revelation to John", *RevQ* 12 (1986), pp. 409–414.

Allison, Dale C. "A Plea for Thoroughgoing Eschatology", *JBL* 113 (1994), pp. 651–668.

Allison, Dale C. *Jesus of Nazareth: Millennarian Prophet*. Minneapolis: Fortress Press, 1998.

Alter, Robert. "How Convention Helps Us Read: The Case of the Biblical Annunciation's Type-Scene", *Prooftexts* 3 (1983), pp. 115–130.

Amihay, Aryeh and Daniel A. Machiela. "Traditions of the Birth of Noah". In eds. Michael E. Stone, Aryeh Amihay, and Vered Hillel, *Noah and His Book(s)*. SBLEJL 28. Atlanta: Society of Biblical Literature, 2010. Pp. 53–70.

Andersen, Francis I. "2 (Slavonic Apocalypse of) Enoch". In ed. James H. Charlesworth, *The Old Testament Pseudepigrapha*. 2 vols. Garden City, New York: Doubleday, 1983–1985. Vol. 1, pp. 91–221.

Annus, Amar. "On the Origin of Watchers: A Comparative Study of the Antediluvian Wisdom in Mesopotamian and Jewish Traditions", *JSP* 19 (2010), pp. 277–320.

Arrington, French L. *The Acts of the Apostles. An Introduction and Commentary*. Peabody, Massachusetts: Hendrickson, 1988.

Attridge, Harold W. "Historiography". In ed. Michael E. Stone, *Jewish Writings of the Second Temple Period*. CRINT II.2. Assen: Van Gorcum, and Minneapolis: Fortress Press, 1984.

Auffarth, Christoph and Loren T. Stuckenbruck, eds. *The Fall of the Angels*. TBN 6. Leiden: Brill, 2004.

Aune, David E. "Magic in Early Christianity". In ed. Wolfgang Haase, *Aufstieg und Niedergang der römischen Welt*. II.23.2. Berlin / New York: Walter de Gruyter, 1980. Pp. 1507–1557.

Aune, David E. *Revelation*. 3 vols. WBC. Dallas: Word Books, 1997.

Aune, David E. "The Apocalypse of John and Palestinian Jewish Apocalyptic". In eds. Gerbern S. Oegema and James H. Charlesworth, *The Pseudepigrapha and Christian Origins*. Jewish and Christian Texts 4. London: T & T Clark, 2008. Pp. 169–192.

Baillet, Maurice. "2Q19–20". In eds. Maurice Baillet, Józef T. Milik, and Roland de Vaux, *Les 'Petites Grottes' de Qumran: Exploration de la falaise, Les grottes 2Q, 3Q, 5Q, 6Q, 7Q, à 10Q, Le rouleau de cuivre*. DJD 3. Oxford: Clarendon Press, 1962. Pp. 77–79.

Baillet, Maurice. "3Q5". In eds. Maurice Baillet, Józef T. Milik, and Roland de Vaux, *Les 'Petites Grottes' de Qumran: Exploration de la falaise, Les grottes 2Q, 3Q, 5Q, 6Q, 7Q, à 10Q, Le rouleau de cuivre*. DJD 3. Oxford: Clarendon Press, 1962. Pp. 96–98.

Baillet, Maurice. "6Q7pap". In eds. Maurice Baillet, Józef T. Milik, and Roland de Vaux, *Les 'Petites Grottes' de Qumran: Exploration de la falaise, Les grottes 2Q, 3Q, 5Q, 6Q, 7Q, à 10Q, Le rouleau de cuivre*. DJD 3. Oxford: Clarendon Press, 1962. Pp. 114–116.

Barde, Édouard. *Commentaire sur les Acts des Apôtres*. Lausanne: Bridel, 1905.

Barrett, Charles Kingsley. *A Commentary on the First Epistle to the Corinthians*. New York: Harper & Row, 1968.

Barrett, Charles Kingsley. *Das Evangelium nach Johannes*. Translated by Hans Bold. KEK. Göttingen: Vandenhoeck & Ruprecht, 1990.

Barrett, Charles Kingsley. *The Acts of the Apostles*. 2 vols. ICC. Edinburgh: T & T Clark, 1994–1998.

Barrett, Charles Kingsley. *Acts. A Shorter Commentary*. Edinburgh: T & T Clark, 2002.

Barthélemy, Dominic. "1Q71–72". In eds. Dominic Barthélemy and Józef T. Milik, *Qumrân Cave 1*. DJD 1. Oxford: Clarendon Press, 1955. Pp. 150–151.

Barton, Stephen C. "Paul's Sense of Place: An Anthropological Approach to Community Formation in Corinth", *NTS* 32 (1986), pp. 225–246.

Bashem, Donald. *Deliver Us from Evil*. Washington Depot, CT: Chosen Books, 1972, repr. 2005.

Bauckham, Richard. "The Use of Apocalyptic Traditions". In *idem, The Climax of Prophecy: Studies on the Book of Revelation*. Edinburgh: T & T Clark, 1993. Pp. 38–91.

Baumgarten, Joseph M. "The 4Q Zadokite Fragments on Skin Disease", *JJS* 41 (1990), pp. 153–165.

Baumgarten, Joseph M. *Qumran Cave 4 XIII: The Damascus Document (4Q266–273)*. DJD 18. Oxford: Clarendon Press, 1996.

Beale, Gregory K. *The Use of Daniel in Jewish Apocalyptic Literature and in the Revelation of St. John*. Lanham: The University Press of America, 1984.

Beale, Gregory K. *John's Use of the Old Testament in Revelation*. JSNTSup 166. Sheffield: Sheffield Academic Press, 1998.

Beale, Gregory K. *The Book of Revelation: A Commentary on the Greek Text*. Grand Rapids: Eerdmans, 1999.

Beard, Mary. "The Sexual Status of Vestal Virgins", *Journal of Roman Studies* 70 (1980), pp. 12–27.

Beasley-Murray, George R. *The Book of Revelation*. NCBC. Grand Rapids: Eerdmans, 1981, repr. 1974.

Beattie, Gillian. *Women and Marriage in Paul and His Early Interpreters*. JSNTSup 296. London: T & T Clark International, 2005.

Becker, Jürgen. *Das Evangelium nach Johannes*. 2 vols. ÖTK 412. Gütersloh: Gerd Mohn / Echter Verlag, 1984.

Becker, Jürgen. *Jesus of Nazareth*. Translated by James E. Crouch. Berlin: Walter de Gruyter, 1998.

Beckwith, Isbon T. *The Apocalypse of John*. New York: MacMillan, 1922.

Bedale, Stephen. "The Meaning of *Kephale* in the Pauline Epistles", *JTS* 5 (1954), pp. 211–215.

Beker, Johan Christiaan. *Paul the Apostle: The Triumph of God in Life and Thought*. Edinburgh: T & T Clark, 1989 repr. 1984.

Beker, Johan Christiaan. *The Triumph of God: The Essence of Paul's Thought*. Translated by Loren T. Stuckenbruck. Minneapolis: Fortress Press, 1990.

Bell, Richard H. *Deliver Us from Evil: Interpreting the Redemption from the Power of Satan in New Testament Theology*. WUNT 21. Tübingen: Mohr Siebeck, 2007.

Belset, Johann Evangelist. *Die Apostelgeschichte*. Münster: Aschendorff, 1910, 3rd ed.

Bergmaier, Roland. *Gerechtigkeit, Gesetz und Glaube bei Paulus: Der judenchristliche Heidenapostel im Streit um das Gesetz und Seine Werke*. BTS 115. Neukirchen- Vluyn: Neukirchener Verlag, 2010.

Bernstein, Moshe J. "Divine Titles and Epithets and the Sources of the Genesis Apocryphon", *JBL* 128 (2009), pp. 291–310.

Beyer, Klaus. *Die aramäischen Texte vom Toten Meer*. Göttingen: Vandenhoeck & Ruprecht, 1984.

Beyer, Klaus. *Die aramäischen Texte vom Toten Meer. Ergänzungsband*. Göttingen: Vandenhoeck & Ruprecht, 1994.

Beyer, Klaus. *Die aramäischen Texte vom Toten Meer. Band 2*. Göttingen: Vandenhoeck & Ruprecht, 2004.

Beyerle, Stefan. *Die Gottesvorstellungen in der antik-jüdischen Apokalyptik*. JSJSup 103. Leiden / Boston: Brill, 2005.

Bhayro, Siam. *The Shemihazah and Asael Narrative of 1 Enoch 6–11: Introduction, Text, Translation and Commentary with Reference to Ancient Near Eastern and Biblical Antecedents*. AOAT 322. Münster: UGARIT-Verlag, 2005.

Black, Matthew. "The Twenty Angel Dekadarchs and 1 Enoch 6, 7 and 69", *JJS* 33 (1982), pp. 227–235.

Black, Matthew. *The Book of Enoch or 1 Enoch: A New English Edition*. SVTP 7. Leiden: Brill, 1985.

Blanch, Stuart Y. *Encounters with Jesus*. The Jesus Library. London: Hodder and Stoughton, 1998.

Boccaccini, Gabriele. *Beyond the Essene Hypothesis: The Parting of the Ways between Enochic and Qumran Judaism*. Grand Rapids: Eerdmans, 1997.

Boccaccini, Gabriele and Giovanni Ibba, eds. *Enoch and the Mosaic Torah: The Evidence of Jubilees*. Grand Rapids: Eerdmans, 2009.

Bockmuehl, Markus. *Jewish Law in Gentile Churches: Halakhah and the Beginning of Christian Public Ethics*. Edinburgh: T & T Clark, 2000.

Borg, Marcus. *A New Vision*. San Francisco: Harper & Row, 1988.

Borgen, Peder. *Philo of Alexandria. An Exegete for His Time*. NovTSup 86. Leiden: Brill, 1997.

Borger, Rijkle. "Die Beschwörungsserie *bit meseri* und die Himmelfahrt Henochs", *JNES* 33 (1974), pp. 183–196.

Böttrich, Christfried. "Die vergessene Geburtsgeschichte. Mt 1–2/Lk 1–2 und die wunderbare Geburt des Melchizedek in slHen 71–72". In eds. Hermann Lichtenberger and Gerbern S. Oegema, *Jüdische Schriften in ihrem antik- jüdischen und urchristlichen Kontext*. JSHRZ 1. Gütersloh: Gütersloher Verlagshaus, 2002. Pp. 222–248.

Böttrich, Christfried. "The 'Book of the Secrets of Enoch' (2En) Between Jewish Origin and Christian Transmission. An Overview". In eds. Andrei A. Orlov and Gabriele Boccaccini, *New Perspectives on 2 Enoch: No Longer Slavonic Only*. SJS 4. Leiden / Boston: Brill, 2011. Pp. 37–68.

Bousset, Wilhelm. *Die Offenbarung Johannis*. KEK 16. Göttingen: Vandenhoeck & Ruprecht, 1906, 5th ed.

Brandon, Samuel G. F. *Jesus and the Zealots: A Study of the Political Factor in Primitive Christianity*. Manchester: Manchester University Press, 1967.

Braun, Herbert. *Qumran und das Neue Testament*. 2 vols. Tübingen: Mohr Siebeck, 1966.

Bremmer, Jan N. "Remember the Titans". In eds. Christoph Auffarth and Loren T. Stuckenbruck, *The Fall of the Angels*. TBN 7. Leiden / Boston: Brill, 2004. Pp. 35–61.

Brenk, Frederick E. "In the Light of the Moon: Demonology in the Early Imperial Period". In ed. Wolfgang Haase, *Aufstieg und Niedergang der römischen Welt*. II.16.3. Berlin: Walter de Gruyter, 1986. Pp. 2068–2145.

Brooke, George J. "Between Qumran and Corinth: Embroidered Allusions to Women's Authority". In ed. James Davila, *The Dead Sea Scrolls as Background to Parabiblical Judaism and Early Christian*. STDJ 46. Leiden / Boston: Brill, 2003. Pp. 157–176.

Brown, Raymond E. *The Gospel According to John*. AB 29–30. Garden City, New York: Doubleday, 1979.

Brown, Raymond E. *The Community of the Beloved Disciple*. New York: Paulist Press, 1979.

Brown, Raymond E. *The Birth of the Messiah: A Commentary on the Infancy Narratives in the Gospels of Matthew and Luke*. ABRL. Garden City, New York: Doubleday, 1993.

Bruce, Frederick F. *1 and 2 Corinthians*. London: Butler and Tanner, 1971.

Bruce, Frederick F. *The Acts of the Apostles*. Grand Rapids: Eerdmans, 1990, 3rd ed.

Bullard, Roger Aubrey. *The Hypostasis of the Archons*. NHC II.4. Patristische Texte und Studien 10. Berlin: Walter de Gruyter, 1970.

Bultmann, Rudolf. *History of the Synoptic Tradition*. Translated by John Marsh. London / New York / Hagerstown / San Francisco: Harper & Row, 1963, revd. ed..

Bultmann, Rudolf. *Das Evangelium des Johannes*. 2 vols. KEKNT. Göttingen: Vandenhoeck & Ruprecht, 1950.

Bultmann, Rudolf. *The Gospel of John: A Commentary*. Translated by George R. Beasley-Murray, Rupert W. N. Hoare, and John K. Riches. Philadelphia: Westminster, 1976.

Burridge, Richard A. *What are the Gospels? A Comparison with Graeco-Roman Biography*. Grand Rapids: Eerdmans, 2004, 2nd ed.

Byron, John. "The Blood of Righteous Abel". In *idem*, *Cain and Abel in Text and Tradition: Jewish and Christian Interpretations of the First Sibling Rivalry*. TBN 14. Leiden / Boston: Brill, 2011. Pp. 167–205.

Cadbury, Henry J. "A Qumran Parallel to Paul", *HTR* 51 (1958), pp. 1–2.

Caird, George B. *Principalities and Powers*. Oxford: Clarendon Press, 1956.

Cantwell, Laurence. "The Parentage of Jesus: Mt. 1:18–21", *NovT* 24 (1982), pp. 304–315.

Capes. David B. *Old Testament Yahweh Texts in Paul's Christology*. WUNT 2.47. Tübingen: Mohr Siebeck, 1992.

Capps, Donald. *Jesus the Village Psychiatrist*. Louisville / London: Westminster John Knox Press, 2008.

Carson, Anne. "Putting Her in Her Place: Woman, Dirt, and Desire". In eds. David M. Halperin, John J. Winkler, and Froma I. Zeitlin, *Before Sexuality: The Construction of Erotic Experience in the Ancient Greek World*. Princeton: Princeton University Press, 1990. Pp. 135–169.

Carson, Donald A. *The Gospel According to John*. Pillar New Testament Commentary. Grand Rapids: Eerdmans, 1991.

Carson, Donald A., Peter T. O'Brien, and Mark A. Seifried, eds. *Justification and Variegated Nomism*. 2 vols. WUNT 2.140, 181. Tübingen: Mohr Siebeck, 2001 and 2004.

Carter, Warren. *Matthew: Storyteller, Interpreter, Evangelist*. Peabody, Massachusetts: Hendrickson, 2004.

Caudill, Earl M. "The Two-Age Doctrine in Paul: A Study of Pauline Apocalyptic". Ph.D. Dissertation, Vanderbilt University, 1972.

Chance, J. Bradley. *Acts*. Macon: Smyth & Helwys, 2007.

Charles, Robert Henry. *The Book of Enoch or 1 Enoch*. Oxford: Clarendon Press, 1912.

Charles, Robert Henry. *Revelation*. 2 vols. ICC. Edinburgh: T & T Clark, 1920.

Charles, Robert Henry. *Eschatology. The Doctrine of a Future Life in Israel, Judaism, and Christianity: A Critical History*. New York: Schocken Brooks, 1963 repr.

Charlesworth, James H., ed. *The Old Testament Pseudepigrapha*. 2 vols. Garden City, New York: Doubleday, 1983–1985.

Charlesworth, James H. "John the Baptizer and the Dead Sea Scrolls". In ed. James H. Charlesworth, *The Bble and the Dead Sea Scrolls*. 3 vols. Waco, Texas: Baylor University Press, 2006. Vol. 3, pp. 1–35.

Charlesworth, James H. "The *Parables of Enoch* and the Apocalypse of John". In eds. Gerbern S. Oegema and James H. Charlesworth, *The Pseudepigrapha and Christian Origins*. Jewish and Christian Texts 4. London: T & T Clark, 2008. Pp. 193–242.

Chrysovergi, Maria. *Attitudes towards the Use of Medicine in Jewish Literature from the Third and Second Centuries BCE*. JSJSup. Leiden: Brill, 2014.

Coblentz Bautch, Kelley. "Heavenly Beings Brought Low: A Study of Angels and the Netherworld". In eds. Friedrich Reiterer, Tobias Nicklas, and Karin Schöpflin, *The Concept of Celestial Beings. Origins, Development and Reception. Deuterocanonical and Cognate Literature Yearbook*. Berlin / New York: Walter de Gruyter, 2007. Pp. 59–75.

Coblentz Bautch, Kelley. "Decoration, Destruction and Debauchery: Reflections on 1 Enoch 8 in Light of 4QEn^{b}", *DSD* 15 (2008), pp. 79–95.

Coblentz Bautch, Kelley. "Putting Angels in Their Place: Developments in Second Temple Angelology". In eds. Károly Dániel Dobos, Gábor Buzási, and Miklós Kószeghy, *"With Wisdom as a Robe": Qumran and Other Jewish Studies in Honour of Ida Fröhlich*. Sheffield: Phoenix Press, 2009. Pp. 174–188.

Collins, John J. "Apocalyptic Eschatology as the Transcendence of Death", *CBQ* 36 (1974), pp. 21–43.

Collins, John J. "Methodological Issues in the Study of 1 Enoch. Reflections on the Articles of P. D. Hanson and G. W. Nickelsburg". In *SBLSP 1978*. 2 vols. Missoula: Scholars Press, 1978. Vol 1, pp. 315–322.

Collins, John J. "Introduction: Towards the Morphology of a Genre". In ed. John J. Collins, *Apocalypse: The Morphology of a Genre*. Semeia 14. Missoula: Scholars Press, 1979. Pp. 1–20.

Collins, John J. and Peter W. Flint. "4Q243–244 (4QpsDana-b)". In eds. George J. Brooke *et al.*, *Qumran Cave 4. XVII: Parabiblical Texts, Part 3*. DJD 22. Oxford: Clarendon Press, 1996. Pp. 95–151.

Collins, John J. and Peter W. Flint. "4Q245 (4QpsDanc)". In eds. George J. Brooke *et al.*, *Qumran Cave 4. XVII: Parabiblical Texts, Part 3*. DJD 22. Oxford: Clarendon Press, 1996. Pp. 153–164.

Collins, John J. "*Pseudo-Daniel* Revisited", *RevQ* 17 (1996), pp. 111–150.

Collins, John J. *Apocalypticism in the Dead Sea Scrolls*. New York / London: Routledge, 1997.

Collins, John J. *Seers, Sybils and Sages in Hellenistic-Roman Judaism*. Leiden / New York / Köln: Brill, 1997.

Collins, John J. *The Apocalyptic Imagination*. Grand Rapids: Eerdmans, 1998, 2nd ed.

Collins, John J. *Beyond the Qumran Community: The Sectarian Movement of the Dead Sea Scrolls*. Grand Rapids: Eerdmans, 2010.

Colson, F. H., G. H. Whitaker, and R. Marcus. *Philo in Ten Volumes (and Two Supplementary Volumes)*. LCL. London: Heinemann, 1929–1962.

Conrad, Edgar. "The Annunciation of Birth and the Birth of the Messiah", *CBQ* 47 (1985), pp. 656–668.

Conzelmann, Hans. *Die Mitte der Zeit: Studien zur Theologie Lukas*. BHT 19. Tübingen: Mohr Siebeck, 1964, 5th ed.

Conzelmann, Hans. *Acts of the Apostles*. Translated by James Limburg, A. Thomas Kraabel, and Donald H. Juel. Hermeneia. Philadelphia: Fortress Press, 1987.

Cope, Lamar. "1 Cor 11,2–16: One Step Further", *JBL* 97 (1978), pp. 435–436.

Corrington, Gail Paterson. "The 'Headless Woman': Paul and the Language of the Body in 1 Cor 11:2–16", *Perspectives in Religious Studies* 18 (1991), pp. 223–231.

Cranfield, Charles E. B. *The Epistle to the Romans*. 2 vols. ICC. Edinburgh: T & T Clark, 1975.

Cross, Frank Moore. "The Development of Jewish Scripts". In ed. G. Ernest Wright, *The Bible and the Ancient Near East: Essays in Honor of William Foxwell Albright*. New York: Doubleday, 1961. Pp. 133–202.

Cross, Frank Moore. *The Ancient Library of Qumran*. The Biblical Seminar 30. Sheffield: Sheffield Academic Press, 1995, 2nd ed.

Crossan, John Dominic. *The Historical Jesus: The Life of a Mediterranean Jewish Peasant*. San Francisco: HarperSanFrancisco, 1991.

Crossan, John Dominic. *Jesus: A Revolutionary Biography*. San Francisco: HarperSanFrancisco, 1994.

Coughenor, Robert A. "The Woe-Oracles in Ethiopic Enoch", *JSJ* 9 (1978), pp. 192–197.

Coulot, Claude. "L'instruction sur les deux espirits (1QS III.13-IV.26)", *RSR* 82 (2008), pp. 147–160.

Cullmann, Oscar. *Christ and Time*. Translated by Floyd V. Filson. Philadelphia: Westminster Press, 1964, revd. 1946 (German).

Dalley, Stephanie. "Gilgamesh in the Arabian Nights", *JRAS* 1 (1991), pp. 1–16.

Davidson, Maxwell J. *Angels at Qumran: A Comparative Study of 1 Enoch 1–36, 72–108 and Sectarian Writings from Qumran*. JSPSup 11. Sheffield: JSOT Press, 1992.

Davies, Philip. "*Hasidim* in the Maccabean Period", *JJS* 28 (1977), pp. 127–140.

Davies, W. D. *Paul and Rabbinic Judaism*. Philadelphia: Fortress Press, 1980, 4th ed.

Davis, Charles Thomas. "Tradition and Redaction in Matthew 1:18–2:23", *JBL* 90 (1971), pp. 404–421.

Daley, Brian E. "The Word and His Flesh: Human Weakness and the Identity of Jesus in Patristic Christology". In eds. Beverly Roberts Gaventa and Richard B. Hays, *Seeking the Identity of Jesus: A Pilgrimage*. Grand Rapids: Eerdmans, 2008. Pp. 251–269.

Das, A. Andrew. *Paul, the Law, and the Covenant*. Peabody, Massachusetts: Hendrickson, 2001.

Dautzenberg, Gerhard. *Urchristliche Prophetie: Ihre Erforschung, ihre Voraussetzung im Judentum und ihre Struktur im ersten Korintherbrief*. Stuttgart: Kohlhammer, 1975.

Dautzenberg, Gerhard. "Zur Stellung der Frauen in den paulinischen Gemeinden". In eds. Gerhard Dautzenberg, Helmut Merklein, and Karheinz Müller, *Die Frau im Urchristentum*. Quaestiones Disputatae 25. Freiburg im Breisgau: Herder, 1983. Pp. 182–224.

Davis, Stephan K. *The Antithesis of the Ages: Paul's Reconfiguration of Torah*. CBQMS 33. Washington D.C.: The Catholic Biblical Association of America, 2002.

Dean-Jones, Lesley. "The Cultural Construct of the Female Body in Classical Greek Science". In ed. Sarah B. Pomeroy, *Women's History and Ancient History*. Chapel Hill: University of North Carolina, 1991. Pp. 111–137.

de Boer, Martinus C. *The Defeat of Death: Apocalyptic Eschatology in 1 Corinthians and Romans 5*. JSNTSup 22. Sheffield: JSOT Press, 1988.

de Boer, Martinus C. "Paul and Apocalyptic Eschatology". In ed. John J. Collins, *The Encyclopedia of Apocalypticism. Volume 1: The Origins of Apocalypticism in Judaism and Christianity*. New York / London: Continuum, 2000. Pp. 345–383.

Delcor, Martin. "Le myth de la chute des anges et de l'origine des géants comme explication du mal dans le monde dans l'apocalyptique juive histoire des traditions", *RHR* 190 (1976), pp. 3–53.

Denis, Albert-Marie. *Fragmenta Pseudepigraphorum Quae Supersunt Graeca. Una Cum Historicum et Auctorum Judaeorum Hellestarum Fragmentis*. PVTG 3. Leiden: Brill, 1970.

Deselaers, Paul. *Das Buch Tobit. Studien zu seiner Entstehung, Komposition und Theologie*. OBO 43. Freiburg, Schweiz: Universitätsverlag, and Göttingen: Vandenhoeck & Ruprecht, 1982.

DeSilva, David A. *Seeing Things John's Way: The Rhetoric of the Book of Revelation*. Louisville: Westminster John Knox, 2009.

Diagnostic and Statistic Manual of Mental Disorders. Washington D.C.: American Psychiatric Association, 2000, 4th ed.

Diamond, Stephen A. *Anger, Madness, and the Daimonic*. Albany: State University of New York Press, 1996.

Diamond, Stephen A. "The Devil Inside: Psychotherapy, Exorcism, and Demonic Possession". www.psychologytoday.com/blog/evil-deeds/201201/the-devil-inside-psychotherapy exorcism and demonic possession. Dated 2012. Accessed 15 October 2013.

Dietzfelbingen, Christian. *Sohn: Skizzen zur Christologie und Anthropologie des Paulus*. BTS 188. Neukirchen-Vluyn: Neukirchener Verlage, 2011.

Dimant, Devorah. "'The Fallen Angels' in the Dead Sea Scrolls and in the Apocryphal and Pseudepigraphic Books Related to Them". Ph.D. thesis, Hebrew University, 1974. (mod. Heb.)

Dimant, Devorah. "1 Enoch 6–11: A Methodological Perspective". In *SBLSP 1978*. 2 vols. Missoula: Scholars Press, 1978. Vol. 1, pp. 323–339.

Dimant, Devorah. "The 'Pesher on the Periods' (4Q180 and 4Q181)", *IOS* 9 (1979), pp. 77–102.

Dimant, Devorah. "The Biography and the Books of Enoch", *VT* 33 (1983), pp. 14–29.

Dimant, Devorah. "Qumran Sectarian Literature". In ed. Michael E. Stone, *Jewish Writings of the Second Temple Period*. CRINT II.2. Assen: Van Gorcum, and Philadelphia: Fortress Press, 1984. Pp. 483–550.

Dimant, Devorah. "The Qumran Manuscripts: Contents and Significance". In eds. Devorah Dimant and Lawrence H. Schiffman, *Time to Prepare the Way in the Wilderness*. STDJ 26. Leiden: Brill, 1995. Pp. 23–28.

Dimant, Devorah. "Between Qumran Sectarian and Non-Sectarian Texts: The Case of Belial and Mastema". In eds. Adolfo Roitman, Lawrence H. Schiffman, and Shani Tsoref, *The Dead Sea Scrolls and Contemporary Culture*. STDJ 93. Leiden / Boston: Brill, 2010. Pp. 235–256.

Dimant, Devorah. "The Flood as Preamble to the Lives of the Patriarchs: The Perspective of Qumran Hebrew Texts". In eds. Reinhard Kratz and Devorah Dimant, *Rewriting and Interpreting the Hebrew Bible*. BZAW 439. Berlin: Walter de Gruyter, 2013. Pp. 101–134.

Doak, Brian R. *The Last of the Rephaim: Conquest and Cataclysm in the Heroic Ages of Ancient Israel*. Ilex Foundation Series. Cambridge, Massachusetts / London: Harvard University Press, 2012.

Dodd, Charles H. *Apostolic Preaching and its Development*. London: Hodder and Stoughton, 1936.

Dodd, Charles H. *The Parables of the Kingdom*. London: Nisbet, 1936, 3rd ed.

Dodd, Charles H. *History and the Gospel*. London: Hodder and Stoughton, 1964, revd. 1938.

Dodd, Charles H. *The Interpretation of the Fourth Gospel*. Cambridge: Cambridge University Press, 1965.

Dodd, Charles H. *The Founder of Christianity*. New York: Macmillan, 1970.

Doran, Robert. "Pseudo-Eupolemus: A New Translation and Introduction". In ed. James H. Charlesworth, *The Old Testament Pseudepigrapha*. 2 vols. Garden City, New York: Doubleday, 1983–1985. Pp. 873–879.

Douglas, Mary. *Natural Symbols*. New York: Pantheon, 1982.

Drawnel, Henryk. *An Aramaic Wisdom Text from Qumran*. JSJSup 86. Leiden / Boston, 2004.

Drawnel, Henryk. "Knowledge transmission in the Context of the Watchers' Sexual Si with the Women in *1 Enoch* 6–11", *BibAn*2 (2012), pp. 123–151.

Duhaime, Jean. "Dualistic Reworking in the Scrolls from Qumran", *CBQ* 49 (1987), pp. 32–56.

Duke, Robert. *The Social Location of the* Visions of Amram *(4Q543–547)*. Studies in Biblical Literature 135. New York: Peter Lang, 2010.

Dunn, James D. G. *Jesus and the Spirit: A Study of the Religious and Charismatic Experience of Jesus and the First Christians as Reflected in the New Testament*. London: SCM Press, 1975.

Dunn, James D. G. *Romans 1–8*. WBC 38A. Dallas: Word Books, 1988.

Dunn, James D. G. *The Theology of St. Paul the Apostle*. Grand Rapids: Eerdmans, 1998.

Dunn, James D. G., ed. *Paul and the Mosaic Law*. Grand Rapids: Eerdmans, 2001, repr. 1996.

Dunn, James D. G. *Christianity in the Making, Volume 1: Jesus Remembered*. Grand Rapids: Eerdmans, 2003.

Dunn, James D. G. *The New Perspective on Paul*. Grand Rapids: Eerdmans, 2008.

Dunn, James D. G. *Christianity in the Making, Volume 2: Beginning from Jerusalem*. Grand Rapids: Eerdmans, 2009.

Ehrman, Bart D. *Jesus: Apocalyptic Prophet of the New Millennium*. Oxford: Oxford University Press, 1999.

Eisenman, Robert H. and James M. Robinson, *A Facsimile Edition of the Dead Sea Scrolls*. 2 vols. Washington D.C.: Biblical Archeological Society, 1991.

Eisenman, Robert H. and Michael O. Wise. *The Dead Sea Scrolls Uncovered*. Shaftsbury, UK and Rockport, Maine: Element, 1992.

Eitrem, Samson. *Some Notes on the Demonology in the New Testament*. Symblae orloenses Fasc. Supplet 20. Oslo: Universitetsforlaget, 1966, 2nd ed.

Elgvin, Torleif. "The *Yahad* is more than Qumran". In ed. Gabriele Boccaccini, *Enoch and Qumran Origins: New Light on a Forgotten Connection*. Grand Rapids: Eerdmans, 2005. Pp. 273–279.

Ellens, J. Harold. "Biblical Miracles and Psychological Process: Jesus as Psychotherapist". In ed. J. Harold Ellens, *Miracles: God, Science, and Psychology in the Paranormal*. Westport, CT: Praeger, 2008. Pp. 1–14.

Ellis, Earle E. "Traditions in 1 Corinthians: For Martin Hengel on His Sixtieth Birthday", *NTS* 32 (1986), pp. 481–502.

Ellis, Earle E. "The Silenced Wives of Corinth (1 Cor 14,34–5)". In eds. Eldon J. Epp and Gordon D. Fee, *New Testament Textual Criticism: Its Significance for Exegesis*. Oxford: Clarendon Press, 1981. Pp. 213–220.

Engberg-Pedersen, Troels. *Cosmology and the Self in the Apostle Paul. The Material Spirit*. Oxford: Oxford University Press, 2010.

Eshel, Esther. "Demonology in Palestine During the Second Temple Period". Ph.D. Dissertation, Hebrew University, 1999.

Eshel, Esther. "Genres of Magical Texts in the Dead Sea Scrolls". In eds. Armin Lange, Hermann Lichtenberger, and K. F. Diethard Römheld, *Die Dämonen – Demons. Die Dämonologie der israelitisch-jüdischen und frühchristlichen Literatur im Kontext ihrer Umwelt*. Tübingen: Mohr Siebeck, 2003. Pp. 395–415.

Eshel, Esther. "The *Imago Mundi* of the *Genesis Apocryphon*". In eds. Lynn R. LiDonnici and Andrea Lieber, *Heavenly Tablets: Interpretation, Identity and Tradition in Ancient Judaism*. JSJSup 119. Leiden / Boston: Brill, 2007. Pp. 111–131.

Eshel, Esther. "The Aramaic Levi Document, the Genesis Apocryphon, and Jubilees: A Study of Shared Traditions". In eds. Gabriele Boccaccini and Giovanni Ibba, *Enoch and the Mosaic Torah: The Evidence of Jubilees*. Grand Rapids: Eerdmans, 2009. Pp. 82–98.

Eve, Eric. *The Jewish Context of Jesus' Miracles*. JSNTSup 231. Sheffield: Academic Press, 2002.

Falk, Daniel K. *The Parabiblical Texts: Strategies for Extending the Scriptures in the Dead Sea Scrolls*. LSTS 63. London: T & T Clark, 2007.

Farrer, Austen M. *The Rebirth of Images: The Making of St. John's Apocalypse*. Westminster, England: Dacre, 1949.

Fee, Gordon D. *The First Epistle to the Corinthians*. Grand Rapids: Eerdmans, 1987.

Fekkes, Jan. *Isaiah and Prophetic Traditions in the Book of Revelation: Visionary Antecedents and their Developments*. JSNTSup 93. Sheffield: Sheffield Academic Press, 1994.

Fitzmyer, Joseph A. "The Aramaic 'Elect of God' Text from Qumran Cave 4". In *idem*, *Essays on the Semitic Background of the New Testament*. SBLSBS 5. Missoula: Scholars Press, 1979, repr. from 1965. Pp. 127–160.

Fitzmyer, Joseph A. "A Feature of Qumran Angelology and 1 Cor. 11:10". In *idem*, *Essays on the Semitic Background of the New Testament*. SBLSBS 5. Missoula: SBL and Scholars Press, 1974. Pp. 187–204.

Fitzmyer, Joseph A. *The Gospel According to Luke*. 2 vols. AB 28–28A. Garden City, New York: Doubleday, 1981–1985.

Fitzmyer, Joseph A. *Romans*. AB 33. Garden City, New York: Doubleday, 1992.

Fitzmyer, Joseph A. "4Q196 (4QToba ar)", "4Q197 (4QTobb ar)", "4Q198 (4QTobc ar)", "4Q199 (4QTobd ar)", and "4Q200 (4QTobe hebr)". In eds. Magen Broshi *et al.*, *Qumran Cave 4 XIV. Parabiblical Texts, Part 2*. DJD 19. Oxford: Clarendon Press, 1995. Pp. 1–76.

Fitzmyer, Joseph A. "The Aramaic and Hebrew Fragments of Tobit from Cave 4", *CBQ* 57 (1995), pp. 655–675.

Fitzmyer, Joseph A. *Tobit*. CEJL. Berlin: Walter de Gruyter, 2003.

Fitzmyer, Joseph A. *The Genesis Apocryphon of Qumran Cave 1: A Commentary*. BibOr 18. Rome: Pontifical Biblical Institute, 1966, 1st ed.; 1977, 2nd ed.; 2004, 3rd ed.

Flint, Peter W. "4Qpseudo-Daniel arc (4Q245" and the Restoration of the Priesthood", *RevQ* 17 (1996), pp. 137–150.

Flint, Peter W. *The Dead Sea Psalms Scrolls and the Book of Psalms*. STDJ 17. Leiden: Brill, 1997.

Flint, Peter W. "The Daniel Tradition at Qumran". In eds. John J. Collins and Peter W. Flint, *The Book of Daniel: Composition and Reception*. 2 vols. VTSup 83.1–2. Leiden / Boston / Köln: Brill, 2001. Vol. 2, pp. 329–367.

Flusser, David. "Qumrân and Jewish 'Apotropaic' Prayers", *IEJ* 16 (1966), pp. 194–205.

Foerster, Werner. "ἐξουσία". In ed. Rudolf Kittel, *TDNT*, vol. 2. Translated by Geoffrey Bromiley. Grand Rapids: Eerdmans, 1964. Pp. 562–574.

Foh, Susan T. *Women and the Word of God: A Response to Biblical Feminism*. Grand Rapids: Baker Academic, 1979.

Ford, J. Massyngberde. *Revelation*. AB 38. Garden City, New York: Doubleday, 1975.

Fornberg, Tord. "The Annunciation: A Study in Reception History, the New Testament". In eds. Morgens Müller and Henrik Tronier, *The New Testament as Reception*. JSNTSup 30. Sheffield: Academic Press, 2002. Pp. 157–180.

Freed, Edwin D. *The Stories of Jesus' Birth: A Critical Introduction*. The Biblical Seminar 72. Sheffield: Academic Press, 2001.

Freud, Sigmund. *Totem and Taboo: Resemblances Between the Psychic Lives of Savages and Neurotics*. Translated by James Stracey. London: Routledge, 1950, repr. 1913.

Freudenthal, Jacob. *Alexander Polyhistor und die von ihm erhaltenen Reste judäischer und samaritanischer Geschichtswerke, Hellenistische Studien*. Breslau: Grass, 1987.

Frey, Jörg. *Die johanneische Eschatologie*. 3 vols. WUNT 2.96, 110, 116. Tübingen: Mohr Siebeck, 1997.

Frey, Jörg. "Different Patterns of Dualistic Thought in the Qumran Library". In eds. Moshe Bernstein, Florentino García Martínez, and John Kampen, *Legal Texts and Legal Issues. Proceedings of the Second Meeting of the International Organization for Qumran Studies, Published in Honour of Joseph M. Baumgarten*. STDJ 23. Leiden: Brill, 1997. Pp. 275–335.

Frey, Jörg. "Die paulinische Antithese von 'Fleisch' und 'Geist' und die palästinisch- jüdische Weisheitstradtion", *ZNW* 90 (1999), pp. 45–77.

Frey, Jörg. "The Notion of 'Flesh' in 4QInstruction and the Background of Pauline Usage". In eds. Daniel K. Falk *et al. Sapiential, Liturgical and Poetical Texts from Qumran: Proceedings of the Third Meeting of the International Organization for Qumran Studies, Oslo 1998*. STDJ 35. Leiden: Brill, 2000. Pp. 197–226.

Frey, Jörg. "Flesh and Spirit in the Palestinian Jewish Sapiential Tradition and in the Qumran Texts: An Inquiry into the Background of Pauline Usage". In eds. Charlotte Hempel,

Armin Lange, and Hermann Lichtenberger, *The Wisdom Texts from Qumran and the Development of Sapiential Thought*. BETL 159. Leuven: Leuven University Press and Peeters, 2002. Pp. 367–404.

Frey, Jörg. "Die Apokalyptik als Herausforderung der neutestamentlichen Wissenschaft. Zum Problem: Jesus und die Apokalyptik". In eds. Michael Becker and Markus Öhler, *Apokalyptik als Herausforderung neutestamentlicher Theologie*. WUNT 2.214. Tübingen: Mohr Siebeck, 2006. Pp. 23–94.

Frickenschmidt, Dirk. *Evangelium als Biographie: Die vier Evangelien im Rahmen antiker Erzählkunst*. TANZ 22. Tübingen: Mohr Siebeck, 1997.

Friedrich, Johannes. "Die hethitischen Bruchstücke des Gilgameš-Epos", *ZA* 39 (1930), pp. 1–82.

Fröhlich, Ida. "Les enseignments des veilleurs dans la tradition de Qumran", *RevQ* 13 (1988), pp. 177–187.

Fröhlich, Ida. "Theology and Demonology in Qumran Texts", *Henoch* 32 (2010), pp. 101–129.

Fröhlich, Ida. "Evil in Second Temple Texts". In eds. Ida Fröhlich and Erkki Koskenniemi, *Evil and the Devil*. LNTS 481. London: Bloomsbury T & T Clark, 2013. Pp. 23–50.

Froitzheim, Franzjosef. *Christologie und Eschatologie bei Paulus*. FB 35. Würzburg: Echter Verlag, 1979.

Funk, Robert W. and Roy W. Hoover. *The Five Gospels: The Search for the Authentic Words of Jesus*. New York / Toronto: Macmillan, 1970.

Gantz, Timothy. *Early Greek Myth. A Guide to Literary and Artistic Sources*. Baltimore / London: The Johns Hopkins University Press, 1993.

García Martínez, Florentino. "The Book of Giants". In *idem*, *Qumran and Apocalyptic. Studies on the Aramaic Texts from Qumran*. STDJ 9. Leiden / New York: Brill, 1992. Pp. 97–115.

García Martínez, Florentino. "4QPseudo Daniel Aramaic and the Pseudo-Danielic Literature". In *idem*, *Qumran and Apocalyptic. Studies on the Aramaic Texts from Qumran*. STDJ 9. Leiden / New York: Brill, 1992. Pp. 137–149.

García Martínez, Florentino. "The Origins of the Essene Movement and of the Qumran Sect". In eds. Florentino García Martínez and Julio Trebolle Barrera, *The People of the Dead Sea Scrolls: Their Writings, Beliefs and Practices*. Leiden: Brill, 1993. Pp. 77–96.

García Martínez, Florentino. "11Q11". In eds. Florentino García Martínez, Eibert J. C. Tigchelaar, and A. S. van der Woude, *Qumran Cave 11.II: 11Q2–18, 11Q20–30*. DJD 33. Oxford: Clarendon Press, 1998. Pp. 198–201.

García Martínez, Florentino and Eibert J. C. Tgchelaar. "11Q12". In eds. Florentino García Martínez, Eibert J. C. Tigchelaar, and A. S. van der Woude, *Qumran Cave 11.II: 11Q2–18, 11Q20–30*. DJD 33. Oxford: Clarendon Press, 1998. Pp. 207–220.

García Martínez, Florentino and Eibert J. C. Tigchelaar. *The Dead Sea Scrolls Study Edition*. 2 vols. Leiden / Boston / Köln: Brill, 1998.

Garlington, Don B. *Faith, Obedience, and Perseverance: Aspects of Paul's Letter tot he Romans*. WUNT 2.79. Tübingen: Mohr Siebeck, 1994.

Garrett, Susan R. *The Demise of the Devil*. Minneapolis: Fortress Press, 1989.

Gärtner, Bergil. *The Temple and the Community*. SNTSMS 1. Cambridge: Cambridge University Press, 1965.

Gaston, Lloyd. *Paul and the Torah*. Vancouver: University of British Columbia Press, 1987.

Gaventa, Beverly Roberts. *Mary: Glimpses of the Mother of Jesus*. Columbia, South Carolina: University of South Carolina Press, 1995.

Geffcken, Johannes. *Die Oracula Sibyllina*. Leipzig: J. C. Hinrichs, 1902.

George, Andrew. *The Epic of Gilgamesh: The Babylonian Epic Poem and Other Texts in Akkadian and Sumerian*. New York: Barnes & Noble, 1999.

Gitin, Seymour, Trude Dothan, and Joseph Naveh. "A Royal Dedicatory Inscription from Ekron", *IEJ* 47 (1997), pp. 1–16.

Glasson, Thomas Francis. *Greek Influence in Jewish Eschatology with Special Reference to the Apocalypses and Pseudepigrapha*. London: SPCK, 1961.

Goff, Matthew J. "Gilgamesh the Giant: The Qumran *Book of Giants'* Appropriation of *Gilgamesh* Motifs", *DSD* 16 (2009), pp. 221–253.

Goff, Matthew J. "Subterranean Giants and Septuagint Proverbs: The 'Earth-born' of LXX Proverbs". In eds. Károly Dániel Dobos, Gábor Buzási, and Miklós Kószeghy, *"With Wisdom as a Robe": Qumran and Other Jewish Studies in Honour of Ida Fröhlich*. Sheffield: Phoenix Press, 2009. Pp. 146–156.

Goff, Matthew J. "Monstrous Appetites: Giants, Cannibalism, and Insatiable Eating in Enochic Literature", *JAJ* 1 (2010), pp. 12–42.

Goff, Matthew J. "Ben Sira and the Giants of the Land: A Note on Ben Sira 16:7", *JBL* 129 (2010), pp. 645–655.

Grabbe, Lester L. *Etymology in Early Jewish Interpretation. The Hebrew Names in Philo*. Brown Judaic Studies 118. Atlanta: Scholars Press, 1988.

Green, Joel B. "The Problem of a Beginning: Israel's Scriptures in Luke 1–2", *BBR* 4 (1994), pp. 61–86.

Green, Joel B. *The Gospel of Luke*. NICNT. Grand Rapids: Eerdmans, 1997.

Greenfield, Jonas, Michael E. Stone, and Esther Eshel. *The Aramaic Levi Document*. SVTP 19. Leiden / Boston: Brill, 2004.

Gross, Heinrich. *Tobit und Judit*. NEBAT 19. Würzburg: Echter Verlag, 1987.

Gundry, Robert H. *Matthew: A Commentary on his Literary and Theological Art*. Grand Rapids: Eerdmans, 1982.

Gundry-Volf, Judith. "Paul on Women and Gender: A Comparison with Early Jewish Views". In ed. Richard N. Longenecker, *The Road from Damascus: The Impact of Paul's Conversion on His Life, Thought, and Ministry*. Grand Rapids: Eerdmans, 1997. Pp. 184–212.

Hagner, Donald A. *Matthew 1–3*. WBC 33A. Dallas: Word Books, 1993.

Hahn, Ferdinand. *The Titles of Jesus in Christology: Their History in Early Christianity*. Translated by Harold Knight and George Ogg. London: Lutterworth, 1969.

Hahne, Harry Alan. *The Corruption and Redemption of Creation*. LNTS 336. London: T & T Clark, 2006.

Halpern-Amaru, Betsy. "The First Woman, Wives, and Mothers in Jubilees", *JBL* 113 (1994), pp. 609–626.

Halpern-Amaru, Betsy. *The Empowerment of Women in the Book of Jubilees*. JSJSup 60. Leiden: Brill, 1999.

Hamilton, James M. "'The Virgin Will Conceive': Typological Fulfilment in Matthew 1:18–23". In eds. Daniel M. Gurtner and John Nolland, *Built upon the Rock: Studies in the Gospel of Matthew*. Grand Rapids: Eerdmans, 2008. Pp. 187–206.

Hannah, Darrell D. *Michael and Christ: Michael Traditions and Angel Christology in Early Christianity*. WUNT 2.109. Tübingen: Mohr Siebeck, 1999.

Hanson, Paul D. *The Dawn of Apocalyptic: The Historical and Sociological Roots of Jewish Apocalyptic Eschatology*. Philadelphia: Fortress Press, 1979, revd. ed.

Hanson, Paul D. "Rebellion in Heaven, Azazel and Euhemeristic Heroes in 1 Enoch 6–11", *JBL* 96 (1977), pp. 195–223.

Harmon, Austin Morris. *Lucian.* 8 vols. LCL. Cambridge, Massachusetts: Harvard University Press, 1969.

Harrington, Wilfred J. *Revelation.* SP 16. Collegeville: The Liturgical Press, 1993.

Harris, Russell. "Embracing Your Demons: An Overview of Acceptance and Commitment Therapy", *Psychotherapy in Australia* 12 (2006), pp. 2–8.

Harris, Sam. *The End of Faith.* New York: W. W. Norton, 2004.

Hayward, Robert. "The Priestly Blessing in Targum Pseudo-Jonathan", *JSP* 19 (1999), pp. 81–101.

Heil, Christopher. *Die Ablehnung deer Speisegebote durch Paulus: Zur Frage nach der Stellung des Apostels zum Gesetz.* BBB 96. Weilheim: Beltz Athenäum, 1996.

Hellholm, David. *Apocalypticism in the Mediterranean World and the Near East: Proceedings of the International Colloquium on Apocalypticism, Uppsala, August 12–17, 1979.* Tübingen: Mohr Siebeck, 1989, 2nd ed.

Hemer, Colin J. *The Letters to the Seven Churches of Asia in Their Local Setting.* JSNTSup 11. Sheffield: JSOT Press, 1986.

Hempel, Charlotte. "Kriterien zur Bestimmung 'essenischer Verfasserschaft' von Qumrantexten". In ed. Jörg Frey, *Qumran kontrovers.* Einblicke 6. Paderborn: Bonifatius, 2003. Pp. 71–85.

Hempel, Charlotte. "The *Treatise on the Two Spirits* and the Literary History of the *Rule of the Community*". In ed. Geza Xeravits, *Dualism in Qumran.* LSTS 76. London: T & T Clark International, 2010. Pp. 102–120.

Hendriksen, William. *Exposition of the Gospel According to John.* Grand Rapids: Baker Academic, 2002, repr. 1952.

Hengel, Martin. *Judaism and Hellenism.* Translated by John Bowden. Translated by John Bowden. 2 vols. London: SCM Press, 1974.

Hengel, Martin. *The "Hellenization" of Judaea in the First Century after Christ.* London: SCM Press, 1989.

Henning, Walter B. "The Book of Giants", *BSOAS* 11 (1943–1946), pp. 52–74.

Henze, Matthias. *Jewish Apocalypticism in Late First Century Israel.* TSAJ 142. Tübingen: Mohr Siebeck, 2011.

Héring, Jean. *The First Epistle of Saint Paul tot he Corinthians.* Translated by Arthur W. Hethcote and Philip J. Allcock. London: Epworth, 1962.

Hicks-Keeton, Jill. "Already/Not Yet: Eschatological Tension in the Book of Tobit", *JBL* 132 (2013), pp. 97–117.

Hill, David. "Prophecy and Prophets in the Revelation of St. John", *NTS* 18 (1971–1972), pp. 401–418.

Hill, David. "On the Evidence of the Creative Role of Christian Prophets", *NTS* 20 (1973–1974), pp. 262–274.

Hitchens, Christopher. *God is not Great: How Religion Poisons Everything.* New York: Warner, 2007.

Hoffmann, Matthias. *The Destroyer and the Lamb.* WUNT 2.203. Tübingen: Mohr Siebeck, 2005.

Holladay, Carl H. *Fragments from Hellenistic Jewish Authors. I. Historians.* Texts and Translations 20. Chico: Scholars Press, 1983.

Hooker, Morna D. "Authority on Her Head: An Examination of 1 Cor XI.10", *NTS* 10 (1963–1964), pp. 410–416.

Horsley, Richard A. *Jesus and the Spiral of Violence: Popular Jewish Resistance in Roman Palestine.* San Francisco: Harper & Row, 1987.

Horsley, Richard A. *The Liberation of Christmas: The Infancy Narratives in Social Context.* New York: Crossroad, 1989.

Huggins, Ronald V. "Noah and the Giants: A Response to John C. Reeves", *JBL* 114 (1995), pp. 103–110.

Hull, Jonathan M. *Hellenistic Magic and the Synoptic Tradition.* SBT 2.28. London: SCM Press, 1974.

Hurd, John. *The Origin of 1 Corinthians.* London: SPCK, 1965.

Hutter, Manfred. "Lilith". In eds. Karl van der Toorn, Bob Becking, and Pieter W. van der Horst, *Dictionary of Deities and Demons in the Bible.* Leiden: Brill, 2nd ed. Pp. 520–521.

Jackson, David R. *Enochic Judaism: Three Defining Paradigm Exemplars.* LSTS 49. London: T & T Clark International, 2004.

Jacoby, Felix. *Fragmente der griechischen Historiker. Erster Teil: Genealogie und Mythographie.* Leiden: Brill, repr. 1957 from 1923.

Jacoby, Felix. *Fragmente der griechischen Historiker. Band 3: Geschichte von Staedten und Voelkern.* Leiden: Brill, 1985.

Jastrow, Marcus. *Dictionary of the Targumim, the Talmud Babli and Yerushalmi, and the Midrashic Literature.* New York: Judaica Press, 1971 repr. 1903.

Jaubert, Annie. "La voile des femmes (1 Cor. xi.2–16)", *NTS* 18 (1972), pp. 419–430.

Jervell, Jacob. *Die Apostelgeschichte.* KEK 3. Göttingen: Vandenhoeck & Ruprecht, 1998.

Jervis, Lee Ann. "'But I Want You to Know ...' Paul's `midrashic Intertextual Response to the Corinthian Worshipers (1 Cor 11:2–16)", *JBL* 112 (1993), pp. 231–246.

Jewett, Robert. *Romans.* Hermeneia: Minneapolis: Fortress Press, 2007.

Johns, Loren L. *The Lamb Christology of the Apocalypse of John.* WUNT 2.167. Tübingen: Mohr Siebeck, 2003.

Johnson, Timothy Luke. *The Acts of the Apostles.* SP 5. Collegeville, Minnesota: The Liturgical Press, 1992.

Karrer, Martin. *Die Johannesoffenbarung als Brief.* FRLANT 140. Göttingen: Vandenhoeck & Ruprecht, 1983.

Käsemann, Ernst. "The Beginnings of Christian Theology". In *idem. New Testament Questions of Today.* Philadelphia: Fortress Press, 1969. Pp. 82–107 (repr. 1960).

Käsemann, Ernst. "The Righteousness of God in Paul". In *idem. New Testament Questions of Today.* Philadelphia: Fortress Press, 1969. Pp. 168–182 (repr. 1961).

Käsemann, Ernst. *Commentary on Romans.* Translated by Geoffrey W. Bromiley. Grand Rapids: Eerdmans, 1980, 4th ed.

Kee, Howard Clark. "Medicine and Healing". In ed. David Noel Freedman, *Anchor Bible Dictionary.* 6 vols. Garden City, New York: Doubleday, 1992). Vol. 4, pp. 660–662.

Keith, Chris. *Jesus Against the Scribal Elite.* Grand Rapids: Baker Academic, 2014.

Kerényi, Karl. *The Gods of the Greeks.* Translated by Norman Cameron. New York / London: Thames and Hudson, 1951.

Kiddle, Martin. *The Revelation of St. John.* MNTC. New York: Harper, 1940.

King, Helen. "Producing Woman: Hippocratic Gynaecology". In eds. Léonie J. Archer, Susan Fischler, and Maria Wyke, *Women in Ancient Societies.* Houdsmills / Basingstoke / London: MacMillan, 1994. Pp. 102–114.

Kingsbury, Jack Dean. *Matthew as Story.* Philadelphia: Fortress Press, 1988, 2nd ed.

Kister, Menahem. "Demons, Theology and Abraham's Covenant (CD 16:4–6 and Related Texts)". In eds. Robert A. Kugler and Eileen M. Schuller, *The Dead Sea Scrolls at Fifty: Proceedings of the 1997 Society of Biblical Literature Qumran Section Meetings*. SBLEJL 15. Atlanta: Society of Biblical Literature, 1999. Pp. 167–184.

Klinghardt, Matthias. *Gesetz und Volk Gottes. Das lukanische Verständnis des Gesetzes.* WUNT 2.32. Tübingen: Mohr Siebeck, 1988.

Klutz, Todd E. "The Grammar of Exorcism in the Ancient Mediterranean World". In eds. Carey C. Newman, James R. Davila and Glady S. Lewis, *The Jewish Roots of Christological Monotheism*. JSJSup 63. Leiden / Boston / Köln: Brill, 1999. Pp. 156–165.

Knibb, Michael A. *The Ethiopic Book of Enoch: A New Edition in Light of the Aramaic Dead Sea Fragments*. 2 vols. Oxford: Clarendon Press, 1978.

Knibb, Michael A. "The Date of the Parables of Enoch: A Critical Review", *NTS* 25 (1979), pp. 345–359.

Knibb, Michael A. *The Qumran Community*. Commentaries on Writings of the Jewish and Christian World 2. Cambridge: Cambridge University Press, 1987.

Knibb, Michael A. "The Book of Enoch or Books or Enoch?". In eds. Gabriele Boccaccini and John J. Collins, *The Early Enoch Literature*. JSJSup 121. Leiden / Boston: Brill, 2007. Pp. 21–40.

Kobelski, Paul J. *Melchizedeq and Mechireša'*. CBQMS 10. Washington D.C.: Catholic University of America Press, 1981.

Kollmann, Bernd. "Göttliche Offenbarung magisch-pharmakologischer Heilkunst im Buch Tobit", *ZAW* 106 (1994), pp. 289–299.

Kollmann, Bernd. *Jesus und die Christen als Wundertäter. Studien zu Magie, Medizin und Schamanismus in Antike und Christentum*. FRLANT 170. Göttingen: Vandenhoeck & Ruprecht, 1996.

Konradt, Matthias. *Israel, Kirche und die Völker im Matthäusevangelium*. WUNT 215. Tübingen: Mohr Siebeck, 2007.

Köstenberger, Andreas J. *John*. BECNT. Grand Rapids: Baker Academic, 2004.

Kraft, Heinrich. *Die Offenbarung des Johannes*. HNT 16a. Tübingen: Mohr Siebeck, 1974.

Kreitzer, L. Joseph. *Jesus and God in Paul's Eschatology*. JSNTSup 19. Sheffield: JSOT Press, 1987.

Krodel, Gerhard. *Acts*. Minneapolis: Augsburg Publishing, 1986.

Kroeger, Richard and Catherine Clark. "An Inquiry into Evidence of Maenadism in the Corinthian Congregation", *SBLSP 1978*. 2 vols. Missoula: Scholars Press, 1978. Vol. 2, pp. 331–346.

Krüger, Thomas. "Das menschliche Herz und die Weisung Gottes". In eds. Thomas Krüger and Reinhard G. Kratz, *Rezeption und Auslegung im Alten Testament und in seinem Umfeld*. OBO 153. Freiburg: Universitätsverlag Fribourg, and Göttingen: Vandenhoeck & Ruprecht, 1997. Pp. 65–92.

Kugel, James. "Which is Older, *Jubilees* or *Genesis Apocryphon*? An Exegetical Approach". In eds. Adolfo Roitman, Lawrence H. Schiffman, and Shani Tsoref, *The Dead Sea Scrolls and Contemporary Culture. Papers in Celebration of the 60th Anniversary of the Discovery of the Dead Sea Scrolls*. STDJ 93. Leiden: Brill, 2011. Pp. 257–294.

Kugler, Robert. *From Patriarch to Priest. The Levi-Priestly Tradition from Aramaic Levi to Testament of Levi*. SBLEJL 9. Atlanta: Scholars Press, 1996.

Kuhn, Heinz-Wolfgang. *Enderwartung und Gegenwärtiges Heil*. SUNT 4. Göttingen: Vandenhoeck & Ruprecht, 1966.

Kuhn, Heinz-Wolfgang. "The Impact of Selected Qumran Texts on the Understanding of Pauline Theology". In ed. James H. Charlesworth, *The Bible and the Dead Sea Scrolls: The Second Princeton Symposium on Judaism and Christian Origins. Volume 3: The Scrolls and Christian Origins*. Waco, Texas: Baylor University Press, 2006. Pp. 153–185.

Kulik, Alexander. *3 Baruch*. CEJL. Berlin: Walter de Gruyter, 2010.

Kümmel, Werner Georg. "Paulus". In *idem, Heilsgeschehen und Geschichte: Gesammelte Aufsätze 1933–1964*. Marburg: Elwert, 1965. Pp. 439–456.

Kuula, Karl. *The Law, the Covenant, and God's Plan*. Publications of the Finnish Exegetical Society 72. Göttingen: Vandenhoeck & Ruprecht, 1999.

Kvanvig, Helge S. *The Roots of Apocalyptic: The Mesopotamian Background of the Enoch Figure and of the Son of Man*. SMANT 61. Neukirchen-Vluyn: Neukirchener Verlag, 1988.

Kvanvig, Helge S. *Primeval History: Babylonian, Biblical, and Enochic. An Intertextual Reading*. JSJSup 148. Leiden: Brill, 2011.

Laato, Timo. *Paulus und Judentum: Anthopologische Erwägungen*. Åbo: Åbo Akademis Förlag, 1991.

Lagrange, Marie-Joseph. *Évangile selon Saint Jean*. Études Bibliques. Paris. J. Gabalda, 1936. 5th ed.

Landry, David T. "Narrative Logic in the Annunciation to Mary. Luke 1:26–38", *JBL* 114 (1995), pp. 65–79.

Lange, Armin. *Weisheit und Prädestination: Weisheitliche Urordnung und Prädestination in den Textfunden von Qumran*. STDJ 15. Leiden / New York, 1995.

Lange, Armin. "1QGenAp XIX19–XX12 as Paradigm of the Wisdom Didactive Narrative". In eds. Heinz-Josef Fabry, Armin Lange, and Hermann Lichtenberger, *Qumranstudien. Vorträge und Beiträge der Teilnehmer des Qumranseminars auf dem internationalen Treffen der Society of Biblical Literature, Münster, 25.-26. Juli 1993*. Schriften des Institutum Judaicum Delitzschianum 4. Göttingen: Vandenhoeck & Ruprecht, 1996. Pp. 191–204.

Lange, Armin. "The Essene Position on Magic and Divination". In eds. Moshe Bernstein, Florentino García Martínez, and John Kampen, *Legal Texts and Legal Issues. Proceedings of the Second Meeting of the International Organization for Qumran Studies, Published in Honour of Joseph M. Baumgarten*. STDJ 23. Leiden: Brill, 1997. Pp. 377–435.

Lange, Armin and Hermann Lichtenberger. "Qumran. Die Textfunde von Qumran". In eds. Gerhard Müller *et al.*, *Theologische Realenzyklopädie*. 36 vols. Berlin: Walter de Gruyter, 1997. Vol. 28, pp. 45–65, 75–79.

Lange, Armin. "Die Endgestalt des protomasoretischen Psalters und die Toraweisheit: Zur Bedeutung der nichtessenischen Weisheitstexte aus Qumran für die Auslegung des protomasoretischen Psalters". In ed. Erich Zenger, *Der Psalter in Judentum und Christentum*. HBS 18. Freiburg: Herder, 1998. Pp. 101–136.

Lange, Armin. "Kriterien essenischer Texte". In ed. Jörg Frey, *Qumran kontrovers*. Einblicke 6. Paderborn: Bonifatius, 2003. Pp. 59–69.

Lange, Armin. "Considerations Concerning the 'Spirit of Impurity' in Zech 13:2". In eds. Armin Lange, Hermann Lichtenberger, and K. F. Diethard Römheld, *Die Dämonen – Demons. Die Dämonologie der israelitisch-jüdischen und frühchristlichen Literatur im Kontext ihrer Umwelt*. Tübingen: Mohr Siebeck, 2003. Pp. 254–268.

Langlois, Michael. *Le premier manuscrit du Livre d'Hénoch. Étude épigraphique et philologique des fragments araméens des 4Q201 à Qumrân*. Paris: Éditions du Cerf, 2008.

Langton, Edward. *Essentials of Demonology: A Study of Jewish and Christian Doctrine: Its Origin and Development*. London: Epworth Press, 1949.

Leaney, Alfred R. C. *The Rule of Qumran and Ist Meaning. Introduction, Translation, and Commentary.* Philadelphia: Fortress Press, 1966.

Le Cornu, Hilary and Joseph Shulam. *A Commentary on the Jewish Roots of Acts.* Jerusalem: Academon, 2003.

Leipholdt, Johannes. *Die Frau in der antiken Welt und im Urchristentum.* Gütersloh: Gerd Mohn, 1962.

Leonhardt-Balzer, Jutta. "Gestalten des Bösen im frühen Christentum". In eds. Jörg Frey and Michael Becker, *Apokalyptik und Qumran.* Einblicke 10. Paderborn: Bonifatius, 2007. Pp. 203–235.

l'Eplattenier, Charles. *Livre des Actes: Commentaire pastorale.* Paris / Outremont: Centurion and Novalis, 1994.

Levison, John R. "The Two Spirits in Qumran Theology". In ed. James H. Charlesworth, *The Bible and the Dead Sea Scrolls.* 3 vols. Waco, Texas: Baylor University Press, 2006). Vol. 2, pp. 169–194.

Lewis, Scott M. *What Are They Saying about New Testament Apoacalyptic?* New York: Paulist Press, 2004.

Lichtenberger, Hermann. *Studien zu Menschenbild in den Texten der Qumrangemeinde.* SUNT 15. Göttingen: Vandenhoeck & Ruprecht, 1980.

Lichtenberger, Hermann. *Das Ich Adams und das Ich der Menschheit: Studien zum Menschenbild in Römer 7.* WUNT 164. Tübingen: Mohr Siebeck, 2004.

Lightfoot, John. *Horae Hebraicae et Talmudicae.* 6 vols. Cambridge: John Field, 1958–1678.

Lincoln, Andrew T. *Paradise Now and Not Yet: Studies in the Rule of the Heavenly Dimension in Paul's Thought with Special Reference to His Eschatology.* SNTSMS 43. Cambridge / New York: Cambridge University Press, 1981.

Lincoln, Andrew T. *The Gospel According to Saint John.* Black NT Commentaries. Peabody, Massachusetts: Hendrikson, 2005.

Lincoln, Andrew T. *Born of a Virgin? Reconceiving Jesus in the Bible, Tradition, and Theology.* London: SPCK, 2013.

Lincoln, Andrew T. "Luke and Jesus' Conception: A Case of Double Paternity", *JBL* 132 (2013), pp. 639–658.

Loader, William G. *Enoch, Levi, and Jubilees on Sexuality.* Grand Rapids: Eerdmans, 2007.

Loader, William G. *The New Testament on Sexuality.* Grand Rapids: Eerdmans, 2012.

Lohfink, Norbert. "'Ich bin Jahwe, dein Arzt' (Ex 15,26). Gott, Gesellschaft und menschliche Gesundheit in einer nachexilischen Pentateuchbearbeitung (Ex 15,25b.26)". In Norbert Lohfink *et al.*, *"Ich will euer Gott werden". Beispiele biblischen Redens von Gott.* SB 100. Stuttgart: Verlag Katholisches Bibelwerk, 1981. Pp. 11–73.

Lohmeyer, Ernst. *Die Offenbarung des Johannes.* HNT 16. Tübingen: Mohr Siebeck, 1970, 3rd ed.

Loisy, Alfred. *Remarques sur la literature épistolaire du Nouveau Testament.* Paris: Nourry, 1935.

Longenecker, Bruce W. *Eschatology and the Covenant: A Comparison of 4 Ezra and Romans 1–11.* JSNTSup 57. Sheffield: JSOT Press, 1991.

Longenecker, Richard N. *New Testament Social Ethics for Today.* Grand Rapids: Eerdmans, 1984.

Lüdemann, Gerd. *Early Christianity According to the Traditions in Acts. A Commentary.* Translated by John Bowden. Minneapolis: Fortress Press, 1989.

Lupieri, Edmundo F. *A Commentary on the Apocalypse of John.* Grand Rapids: Eerdmans, 1999.

Luz, Ulrich. *Matthew 1–7: A Commentary.* Translated by Wilhelm C. Linss. Edinburgh: T&T Clark, 1989.

Lyons, W. John and Andrew M. Reimer. "The Demonic Virus and Qumran Studies: Some Preventative Measures", *DSD* 5 (1998), pp. 16–32.

Macaskill, Grant. *Revealed Wisdom and Inaugurated Eschatology in Ancient Judaism and Early Christianity.* JSJSup 115. Leiden / Boston: Brill, 2007.

Macaskill, Grant. "Manuscripts, Recensions, and Original Language". In eds. Andrei A. Orlov and Gabriele Boccaccini, *New Perspectives on 2 Enoch: No Longer Slavonic Only.* SJS 4. Leiden / Boston: Brill, 2011.

Macaskill, Grant. *The Slavonic Texts of 2 Enoch.* SJS 6. Leiden / Boston: Brill, 2013.

MacDonald, Dennis R. "Corinthian Veils and Gnostic Androgynes". In ed. Karen L. King, *Images of the Feminine Gnosticism.* Philadelphia: Fortress Press, 1988. Pp. 276–292.

MacGregor, George H. C. *The Gospel of John.* MNTC. London: Hodder and Stoughton, 1942.

Machen, John Gresham. *The Virgin Birth of Christ.* New York: Harper & Row, 1932.

Machiela, Daniel A. *The Dead Sea Genesis Apocrphon: A New Text and Translation with Introduction and Special Treatment of Columns 13–17.* STDJ 79. Leiden / Boston: Brill, 2009.

Machiela, Daniel A. and Andrew B. Perrin. "That you may know everything with certainty: A New Reading in 4QEnGiantsb ar (4Q530) and a literary connection between the Book of Giants and Genesis Apocryphon", *RevQ* 25 (2011), pp. 113–125.

MacNutt, Francis. *Healing.* New York: Bantam Books and Ave Maria Press, 1974.

MacNutt, Francis. *Deliverance from Evil Spirits: A Practical Manual.* Grand Rapids: Chosen Books, 1995, repr. 2009.

Macquarrie, John. *Mary for All Christians.* Edinburgh. T&T Clark, 2001, 2nd ed.

Malina, Bruce. *Christian Origins and Cultural Anthropology.* Atlanta: John Knox, 1986.

Maloney, Francis J. *The Gospel of John.* SP 4. Collegeville, Minnesota: The Liturgical Press, 1998.

Manson, T. W. *On Paul and John.* SBT 38. London: SCM, 1963.

Marsh, John. *Saint John.* Westminster Pelican Commentaries. Philadelphia: Penguin Books, 1978.

Martin, Dale B. *The Corinthian Body.* New Haven: Yale University Press, 1995.

Martyn, J. Louis. "Epistemology at the Turn of the Ages: 2 Corinthians 5.16". In *idem, Theological Issues in the Letters of Paul.* Edinburgh: T&T Clark, 1987, repr. 1967. Pp. 87–110.

Martyn, J. Louis. "Apocalyptic Antinomies in the Letter to the Galatians". in *idem, Theological Issues in the Letters of Paul.* Edinburgh: T&T Clark, 1987, repr. 1967. Pp. 111–123.

Martyn, J. Louis. *The Gospel of John in Christian History.* New York: Paulist Press, 1978.

Martyn, J. Louis. *History and Theology in the Fourth Gospel.* Louisville: Westminster John Knox, 2003, 3rd ed.

Martyn, J. Louis. *Galatians: A New Translation and Commentary.* AB 33A. New Haven: Yale University Press, 2010, repr. 1997.

Mateos, Juan and Juan Barreto. *El Evangelio de Juan.* Vol. 4. Madrid: Ediciones Cristiandad, 1982, 2nd ed.

Mathews, Mark D. *Riches, Poverty, and the Faithful: Perspectives on Wealth in the Second Temple Period and the Apocalypse of John.* SNTSMS 154. Cambridge: Cambridge University Press, 2013.

Matlock, Barry R. *Unveiling the Apocalyptic Paul: Paul's Interpreters and the Rhetoric of Criticism*. JSNTSup 127. Sheffield: Sheffield Academic Press, 1996.

Mäyrä, Frans Ilkka. *Demonic Texts and Textual Demons*. Tampere: Tampere Univesity Press, 1999.

Mazzaferri, Frederick David. *The Genre of the Book of Revelation from a Source-Critical Perspective*. BZNW 54. Berlin: Walter de Gruyter, 1989.

McNicol, Allan J. *Jesus' Directions for the Future: A Source and Redaction-History Study of the Use of the Eschatological Traditions in Paul and in the Synoptic Accounts of Jesus' Last Eschatological Discourse*. Macon: Mercer Press, 1996.

Meeks, Wayne. "The Man from Heaven and Johannine Sectarianism", *JBL* 91 (1972), pp. 44–72.

Meeks, Wayne. "The Image of the Androgyne: Some Uses of a Symbol in Earliest Christianity", *History of Religions* 13 (1974), pp. 165–208.

Meier, John P. *A Marginal Jew: Rethinking the Historical Jesus*. 4 vols. Garden City, New York: Doubleday, 1991.

Meggitt, Justin. "The historical Jesus and healing: Jesus' miracles in psychosocial context". In ed. Fraser Watts, *Spiritual Healing. Scientific and Religious Perspectives*. Cambridge: Cambridge University Press, 2011. Pp. 17–43.

Mertens, Alfred. *Das Buch Daniel im Lichte der Texte vom Toten Meer*. SBM 12. Stuttgart: Echter, 1971.

Metso, Sarianna. *The Textual Development of the Qumran Community Rule*. STDJ 27. Leiden: Brill, 1997.

Metzger, Bruce M. *Breaking the Code: Understanding the Book of Revelation*. Nashville: Abingdon Press, 1993.

Michel, Otto. *Der Brief an die Römer*. KDKNT4. Göttingen: Vandenhoeck & Ruprecht, 1978, 5th ed.

Milik, Józef T. "Livre de Jubilés". In eds. Dominique Barthélemy and Józef T. Milik, *Qumran Cave I*. DJD 1. Oxford: Clarendon Press, 1955. Pp. 82–84.

Milik, Józef T. "'Livre de Noé' (PL XVI)". In eds. Dominique Barthélemy and Józef T. Milik, *Qumran Cave I*. DJD 1. Oxford: Clarendon Press, 1955. Pp. 84–86.

Milik, Józef T. "'Apocalypse de Lamech' (PL XVII)". In eds. Dominique Barthélemy and Józef T. Milik, *Qumran Cave I*. DJD 1. Oxford: Clarendon Press, 1955. Pp. 86–87.

Milik, Józef T. "Le Testament de Lévi en araméen: fragment de la grotte 4 de Qumran", *RB* 62 (1955), p. 404.

Milik, Józef T. "'Prière de Nabonide' et autres écrits d'un cycle de Daniel: Fragments araméens de Qumrân 4", *RB* 63 (1956), pp. 411–415.

Milik, Józef T. "La patrie de Tobie", *RB* 73 (1966), pp. 322–330.

Milik, Józef T. "Turfan et Qumran: Livre des géants juif et manichéen". In eds. Gerd Jeremias, Heinz-Wolfgang Kuhn, and Hartmut Stegemann, *Das frühe Christentum in seiner Umwelt. Festgabe für Karl Georg Kuhn zum 65. Geburtstag*. Göttingen: Vandenhoeck & Ruprecht, 1971. Pp. 117–127.

Milik, Józef T. *The Books of Enoch: Aramaic Fragments from Qumrân Cave 4*. Oxford: Clarendon Press, 1976.

Miller, Robert J. *Born Divine: The Birth of Jesus and Other Sons of God*. Santa Rosa, CA: Polebridge Press, 2003.

Minear, Paul S. "Luke's Use of the Birth Stories". In eds. Leander E. Keck and J. Louis Martyn, *Studies in Luke-Acts*. Philadelphia: Fortress Press, 1980, repr. 1966. Pp. 111–130.

Mitchell, Margaret M. *Paul and the Rhetoric of Reconciliation: An Exegetical Investigation of the Language and Composition of 1 Corinthians.* HUT 28. Tübingen: Mohr Siebeck, 1991.

Mittmann (-Richert), Ulrike. *Der Sühnetod des Gottesknechts.* WUNT 220. Tübingen: Mohr Siebeck, 2008.

Moffatt, James. *The First Epistle of Paul to the Corinthians.* London: Hodder and Stoughton, 1947.

Moore, Carey A. "Scholarly Issues in the Book of Tobit Before Qumran and After: An Assessment", *JSP* 5 (1989), pp. 65–81.

Moore, Carey A. *Tobit. A New Translation with Introduction and Commentary.* AB 40A. Garden City, New York: Doubleday, 1996.

Morris, Leon. *The Gospel According to John.* NICNT. Grand Rapids: Eerdmans, 1971.

Mosshammer, Alden A. *Georgii Syncelli Ecloga chronographica.* Leipzig: Teubner, 1984.

Mounce, Robert H. *The Book of Revelation.* NICNT. Grand Rapids: Eerdmans, 1998, 2nd ed.

Müller, Ulrich B. *Die Offenbarung des Johannes.* ÖTK 19. Gütersloh: Echter Verlag, 1995, 2nd ed.

Müller-Kessler, Christa. "Lilit(s) in der aramäisch-magischen Literatur der Spätantike", *AF* 28 (2001), pp. 338–352.

Munter, Sussman. "Medicine". In eds. Cecil Roth and Geoffrey Wigodor, *Encyclopaedia Judaica.* 16 vols. New York: Keter, 1971. Vol. 11, pp. 1178–1185.

Murphy, Catherine M. *Wealth in the Dead Sea Scrolls and in the Qumran Community.* STDJ 40. Leiden: Brill, 2002.

Murphy-O'Connor, Jerome. "La genèse littéraire de la Règle de la Communauté", *RB* 76 (1969), pp. 528–549.

Murphy-O'Connor, Jerome. "The Non-Pauline Character of 1 Cor 11,2–16?", *JBL* 95 (1976), pp. 615–621.

Murphy-O'Connor, Jerome. "Sex and Logic in 1 Corinthians 11:2–16", *CBQ* 42 (1980), pp. 482–500.

Murphy-O'Connor, Jerome. "1 Corinthians 11:2–16 Once Again", *CBQ* 50 (1988), pp. 268–269.

Myers, Ched. *Binding the Strong Man: A Political Reading of Mark's Story of Jesus.* Maryknoll, New York: Orbis, 1988.

Na'aman, Nadav and Ran Zadok. "Sargon II's Deportations to Israel and Philistia (716–708 B.C.)", *JCS* 40 (1988), pp. 36–46.

Na'aman, Nadav. "Population Changes in Palestine Following Assyrian Deportations", *TA* 20 (1993), pp. 104–124.

Najman, Hindy. *Seconding Sinai: The Development of Mosaic Discourse in Second Temple Judaism.* JSJSup 77. Leiden / Boston: Brill, 2003.

Najman, Hindy. "How Should We Contextualize Pseudepigrapha? Imitation and Emulation in 4 Ezra". In eds. Anthony Hilhorst, Émile Puech, and Eibert J. C. Tigchelaar, *Flores Florentino: Dead Sea Scrolls and Other Early Jewish Studies in Honour of Florentino García Martínez.* JSJSup 122. Leiden / Boston: Brill, 2007. Pp. 529–536.

Najman, Hindy. "Reconsidering Jubilees: Prophecy and Exemplarity". In eds. Gabriele Boccaccini and Giovanni Ibba, *Enoch and the Mosaic Torah.* Grand Rapids: Eerdmans, 2009. Pp. 229–243.

Najman, Hindy, Eva Mroczek and Itamar Manoff, "How to Make Sense of Pseudonymous Attribution: The Cases of 4 Ezra and 2 Baruch". In ed. Matthias Henze, *Companion to Biblical Interpretation in Early Judaism*. Grand Rapids: Eerdmans, 2012. Pp. 308–336.

Nanos, Mark D. "Paul's Relationship to Torah in Light of His Strategy 'to Become Everything to Everyone' (1 Corinthians 9:19–22". In eds. Reimund Bieringer and Didier Pollefeyt, *Paul and Judaism: Crosscurrents in Pauline Exegesis and the Study of Jewish-Christian Relations*. London / New York: T & T Clark International and Continuum, 2012. Pp. 106–140.

Naveh, Joseph. "Writing and Scripts in Seventh-Century BCE Philistia: The New Evidence from Tell Jemmeh", *IEJ* 35 (1985), pp. 8–21.

Naveh, Joseph. "Fragments of an Aramaic Magic Book from Qumran", *IEJ* 48 (1998), pp. 252–261.

Newsom, Carol A. "The Development of 1 Enoch 6–19. Cosmology and Judgment", *CBQ* 42 (1980), pp. 310–329.

Newsom, Carol A. "4Q370: An Admonition Based on the Flood", *RevQ* 13 (1988), pp. 23–43.

Newsom, Carol A. "'Sectually Explicit' Literature from Qumran". In eds. William H. Propp, Baruch Halpern, and David Noel Freedman, *The Hebrew Bible and Its Interpreters*. Winona Lake: Eisenbrauns, 1990. Pp. 167–187.

Newsom, Carol A. "370. Admonition Based on the Flood". In eds. Emanuel Tov *et al.*, *Qumran Cave 4 XIV: Parabiblical Texts, Part 2*. DJD 19. Oxford: Clarendon Press, 1995. Pp. 85–97.

Nickelsburg, George W. E. "Apocalyptic and Myth in 1 Enoch 6–11", *JBL* 96 (1977), pp. 383–405.

Nickelsburg, George W. E. "Social Aspects of Palestinian Jewish Apocalypticism". In ed. David Hellholm, *Apocalypticism in the Mediterranean World and the Near East*. Tübingen: Mohr Siebeck, 1989, 2nd ed. Pp. 641–654.

Nickelsburg, George W. E. "Eschatology, Early Jewish". In David Noel Freedman, *Anchor Bible Dictionary*. 6 vols. Garden City, New York: Doubleday, 1992. Vol. 2, pp. 579–594.

Nickelsburg, George W. E. "Patriarchs Who Worry about their Wives: A Haggadic Tendency in the Genesis Apocryphon". In eds. Michael E. Stone and Esther G. Hazon, *Biblical Perspectives: Early Use and Interpretation of the Bible in Light of the Dead Sea Scrolls. Proceedings of the First International Symposium of the Orion Center for the Study of the Dead Sea Scrolls and Associated Literature, 12–14 May 1996*. STDJ 28. Leiden: Brill, 1998. Pp. 137–158.

Nickelsburg, George W. E. *1 Enoch 1: A Commentary on the Book of 1 Enoch, Chapters 1–36; 81–108*. Hermeneia. Minneapolis: Fortress Press, 2001.

Nickelsburg, George W. E. "Patriarchs Who Worry about Their Wives". In eds. Jacob Neusner and Alan J. Avery-Peck, *George Nickelsburg in Perspective: An Ongoing Dialogue of Learning*. 2 vols. JSJSup 80. Leiden: Brill, 2003. Pp. 200–212.

Nickelsburg, George W. E. *Jewish Literature between the Bible and the Mishnah*. Minneapolis: Fortress Press, 2005 2nd ed.

Nickelsburg, George W. E. *Resurrection, Immortality, and Eternal Life in Intertestamental Judaism and Early Christianity*. HTS 56. Cambridge, Massachusetts: Harvard University Press, 2006, 2nd ed.

Nickelsburg, George W. E. and James C. VanderKam. *1 Enoch 2: A Commentary on the Book of 1 Enoch Chapters 37–82*. Hermeneia. Minneapolis: Fortress Press, 2012.

Niehr, Herbert. "JHWH als Arzt. Herkunft und Geschichte einer alttestamentlichen Gottesprädikation", *BZ* 35 (1991), pp. 3–17.

Nitzan, Bilhah. *Qumran Prayer and Religious Poetry*. STDJ 23. Leiden: Brill, 1994.

Noack, Bent. *SATANÁS und SOTERÍA: Untersuchungen zur neutestamentlichen Dämonologie*. Copenhagen: G. E. C. Gads Forlag, 1948.

Noack, Christian. *Gottesbewußtsein. Exegetische Studien zur Soteriologie und Mystik bei Philo von Alexandria*. WUNT 2.116. Tübingen: Mohr Siebeck, 2000.

Novenson, Matthew V. *Christ among the Messias: Christ Language in Paul and Messiah Language in Ancient Judaism*. Oxford: Oxford University Press, 2012.

Økland, Jorunn. *Women in Their Place: Paul and the Corinthian Discourse of Gender and Sanctuary Space*. JSNTSup 269. London: T & T Clark International, 2004.

Olson, Daniel C. "Those Who Have not Defiled Themselves with Women", *CBQ* 59 (1997), pp. 492–510.

Olson, Daniel C. *Enoch: A New Translation*. North Richland Hills, Texas: BIBAL Press, 2005.

Orlov, Andrei A. "Overshadowed by Enoch's Greatness: 'Two Tablets' Traditions from the Book of Giants to Palaea Historica", *JSJ* 32 (2001), pp. 137–158.

Orlov, Andrei A. "The Flooded Arboretums: The Garden Traditions in the Slavonic Version of 3 Baruch and the Book of Giants", *CBQ* 65 (2003), pp. 184–201.

Oster, Richard F. "When Men Wore Veils to Worship: The Historical Context of 1 Corinthians 11.4", *NTS* 34 (1988), pp. 481–505.

Oster, Richard F. "Use, Misuse, and Neglect of Archaeological Evidence", *ZNW* 72 (1990), pp. 52–73.

Padget, Alan. "Paul on Women in Church: The Contradiction of Coiffure in 1 Cor 11,2–16", *JSNT* 20 (1984), pp. 69–86.

Pate, C. Marvin. *The End of the Age Has Come: The Theology of Paul*. Grand Rapids: Zondervan, 1995.

Patterson, Cynthia B. "Marriage and the Married Woman in Athenian Law". In ed. Sarah B. Pomeroy, *Women's History and Ancient History*. Chapel Hill: University of North Carolina, 1991. Pp. 48–72.

Patterson, Stephen J. *The God of Jesus: The Historical Jesus and the Search for Meaning*. Harrisburg: Trinity Press International, 1998.

Pearson, Brook W. R. "Resurrection and the Judgment of the Titans: ἡ γῆ τῶν ἀσεβῶν in LXX Isaiah 26.19". In eds. Stanley E. Porter, Michael A. Hayes and David Tombs, *Resurrection*. JSNTSup 186. Sheffield: Sheffield Academic Press, 1999. Pp. 33–51.

Peerbolte, L. J. Lietart. "Man, Woman, and the Angels in 1 Cor 11:2–16". In ed. Gerard P. Luttikhuizen, *The Creation of Man and Woman: Interpretations of the Biblical Narratives in Jewish and Christian Traditions*. TBN 3. Leiden / Boston: Brill, 2000. Pp. 76–92.

Penner, Ken M. "Did the Midrash of Shemḥazai and Azael Use the Book of Giants?". In eds. James H. Charlesworth, Lee Martin McDonald, and Blake Jurgens, *Sacra Scriptura: How "Non-Canonical" Texts Functioned in Early Judaism and Early Christianity*. JCTCRS 20. London: Bloomsbury T & T Clark, 2014. Pp. 15–45.

Penney, Douglas L. and Michael O. Wise. "By the Power of Beelzebub: An Aramaic Incantation Formula from Qumran (4Q560)", *JBL* 113 (1994), pp. 627–650.

Pero, Cheryl S. *Liberation from Empire: Demonic Possession and Exorcism in the Gospel of Mark*. SBL 150. New York: Peter Lang, 2013.

Perrin, Norman. *Jesus and the Language of the Kingdom: Symbol and Metaphor in New Testament Interpretation*. Philadelphia: Fortress Press, 1976.

Peters, Dorothy M. *Noah Traditions and the Dead Sea Scrolls: Conversations and Controversies of Antiquity.* SBLEJL 26. Atlanta: Society of Biblical Literature, 2008.

Pfann, Claire Ruth. "A Note on 1Q19: The 'Book of Noah'". In eds. Michael E. Stone, Aryeh Amihay, and Vered Hillel, *Noah and His Book(s).* SBLEJL 28. Atlanta: Society of Biblical Literature, 2010. Pp. 71–76.

Pfann, Stephen J. "4QDanield 4Q115: A Preliminary Edition with Critical Notes", *RevQ* 17 (1996), pp. 37–71.

Piper, Ronald A. "The Absence of Exorcisms in the Fourth Gospel". In eds. David G. Horrell and Christopher M. Tuckett, *Christology, Controversy, and Community: New Testament Essays in Honour of David R. Catchpole.* NovTSup 99. Leiden / Boston / Köln: Brill, 2000. Pp. 252–278.

Plevnik, Joseph. *What are They Saying about Paul and the End Time?* New York: Paulist Press, 2009, revd. ed. from 1986.

Polhill, John. *Acts.* Nashville: Abingdon Press, 1992.

Popović, Mladen. *Reading the Human Body: Physiognomics and Astrology in the Dead Sea Scrolls and Hellenistic-Early Roman Period Judaism.* STDJ 67. Leiden / Boston: Brill, 2007.

Porter, Stanley E. and Christopher D. Stanley. eds. *As It Is Written: Studying Paul's Use of Scripture.* SBLSymS 50. Atlanta: Society of Biblical Literature, 2008.

Pouilly, Jean. *Le Règle de la Communauté. Son evolution littéeraire.* Cahiers de la Revue Biblique 17. Paris: J. Gabalda, 1976.

Preisendanz, Karl *et al.,* eds. *Papyri Graecae Magicae.* 2 vols. Stuttgart: Teubner, 1973–1974, 2nd ed.

Prigent, Pierre. *L'Apocalypse de Saint Jean.* CNT 14. Geneva: Labor et Fides, 2000.

Puech, Émile. "Le Testament de Qahat en araméen de la grotte (4QTQah)", *RevQ* 15 (1991), pp. 23–54.

Puech, Émile. "Le deux derniers psaumes davidiques du ritual d'exorcisme 11QPsApa IV,4-V,14". In eds. Devorah Dimant and Uri Rappaport, *The Dead Sea Scrolls: Forty Years of Research.* STDJ 10. Leiden: Brill, 1992. Pp. 64–89.

Puech, Émile. *La croyance des Esséniens en la vie future: immortalité, resurrection, vie éternelle.* Paris: Gabalda, 1993.

Puech, Émile. "Messianism, Resurrection, and Eschatology at Qumran and the New Testament". In eds. Eugene Ulrich and James C. VanderKam, *The Community of the Renewed Covenant: The Notre Dame Symposium on the Dead Sea Scrolls.* CJA 10. Notre Dame, Indiana: University of Notre Dame Press, 1994. Pp. 235–256.

Puech, Émile. "Les fragments 1 à 3 du Livre des Géants de la grotte 6 (pap 6Q8)", *RevQ* 19 (1999), pp. 227–238.

Puech, Émile. "Les songes des fils de Semihazah dans le *Livre des Géants* de Qumrân", *Comptes Rendus de l'Académie des Inscriptions et Belles Lettres* janvier-mars (2000), pp. 7–26.

Puech, Émile. "4Q530; 4Q531; 4Q532; 4Q533 [and 4Q206a 1–2]. 4QLivre des Géantsb-e ar". In ed. *idem, Qumrân Grotte 4 XXI: Textes Araméens Première Partie 4Q529–549.* DJD 31. Oxford: Clarendon Press, 2001. Pp. 9–115.

Puech, Émile. "4QNaissanc de Noéa-c". In ed. *idem, Qumrân Grotte 4 XXI: Textes Araméens Première Partie 4Q529–549.* DJD 31. Oxford: Clarendon Press, 2001. Pp. 118–170.

Puech, Émile. "Quand on retrouve le Livre des Géants", *Le Monde de la Bible* 151 (2003), pp. 24–27.

Puech, Émile. "560: 4QLivre magique ar". In *idem, Qumrân Grotte 4 XXVII: Textes Araméens Deuxième Partie. 4Q550–4Q575a, 4Q580–4Q587 et Appendices*. DJD 37. Oxford: Clarendon Press, 2009. Pp. 291–302.

Ramsay, William. *The Letters to the Seven Churches of Asia and Their Place in the Plan of the Apocalypse*. New York: Hodder and Stoughton, 1904.

Rausch, Thomas. *Who Is Jesus? An Introduction to Christology*. Collegeville, Minnesota: Liturgical Press, 2003.

Reed, Annette Y. "The Trickery of the Fallen Angels and the Demonic Mimesis of the Divine: Aetiology, Demonology, and Polemics in the Writings of Justin Martyr", *JECS* 2 (2004), pp. 141–171.

Reed, Annette Y. *Fallen Angels and the History of Early Christianity and Judaism*. Cambridge: Cambridge University Press, 2005.

Reed, Annette Y. "Pseudepigraphy, Authorship, and the Reception of 'the Bible' in Late Antiquity". In eds. Lorenzo DiTommaso and Lucian Turcescu, *The Reception and the Interpretation of the Bible in Late Antiquity*. BAC 6. Leiden: Brill, 2008. Pp. 467–490.

Reeves, John C. *Jewish Lore in Manichaean Cosmogony: Studies in the Book of Giants Traditions*. HUCM 20. Cincinnati: Hebrew Union College Press, 1992.

Reeves, John C. "Utnapishtim in the Book of Giants?", *JBL* 112 (1993), pp. 110–113.

Reimer, Andy M. "Rescuing the Fallen Angels: The Case of the Disappearing Angels at Qumran", *DSD* 7 (2000), pp. 334–353.

Reynolds, Bennie H. "What Are Demons of Error? The Meaning of שידי טעותא and Israelite Child Sacrifice", *RevQ* 88 (2007), pp. 593–613.

Ribi, Alfred. *Demons of the Inner World: Understanding Our Hidden Complexes*. Translated by M. Kohn. Boston: Shambhala, 1990.

Robertson, Archibald and Alfred Plummer. *A Critical and Exegetical Commentary on the First Epistle of St Paul to the Corinthians*. ICC. Edinburgh: T & T Clark, 1914, 2nd ed.

Roloff, Jürgen. *Die Offenbarung des Johannes*. ZB 18. Zürich: Theologischer Verlag, 1974.

Roloff, Jürgen. *Apostelgeschichte*. NTD 5. Göttingen: Vandenhoeck & Ruprecht, 1981.

Rösler, Wolfgang. "Die Entdeckung der Fiktionalität in der Antike", *Poetica* 12 (1980), pp. 283–319.

Rosner, Brian S. *Paul, Scripture and Ethics*. AGSU 22. Leiden: Brill, 1994.

Rowland, Christopher. *The Open Heaven: A Study of Apocalyptic in Judaism and Early Christianity*. New York: Crossroad, 1982.

Rowley, H. H. *The Relevance of Apocalyptic: A Study of Jewish and Christian Apocalypses from Daniel to Revelation*. New York / London: Lutterworth, 1963.

Royalty, Robert M. *The Streets of Heaven: The Ideology of Wealth in the Apocalypse of John*. Macon: Mercer University Press, 1997.

Runia, David. *Philo of Alexandria and the* Timaeus *of Plato*. Philosophia Antiqua 44. Leiden: Brill, 1986.

Russell, D. S. *The Method and Message of Jewish Apocalyptic*. London / Philadelphia: Westminster Press, 1964.

Sacchi, Paolo. *Jewish Apocalyptic and its History*. Translated by William J. Short. JSPSup 20. Sheffield: JSOT Press, 1990).

Sanders, Ed Parish. *Paul, the Law, and the Jewish People*. Philadelphia: Fortress Press, 1983.

Sanders, Ed Parish. *Jesus and Judaism*. Philadelphia: Fortress Press, 1985.

Sanders, James A. "Psalm 154 Revisited". In eds. Georg Braulik, Walter Gross, and Sea McEvenue, *Biblische Theologie und gesellschaftlicher Wandel. Festschrift für Norbert Lohfink S. J.* Freiburg: Herder, 1993. Pp. 296–306.

Sanders, James A. *The Psalms Scroll of Qumrân Cave 11 (11QPsa)*. DJD 4. Oxford: Clarendon Press, 1996.

Sanders, James A., James H. Charlesworth, and Henry W. L. Rietz. "Non-Masoretic Psalms". In ed. James H. Charlesworth, *Pseudepigraphic and Non-Masoretic Psalms and Prayers*. PTSDSS Project 4a. Tübingen: Mohr Siebeck, and Louisville: Westminster John Knox, 1997. Pp. 155–215.

Sanders, Joseph N. *The Gospel According to Saint John*. London: Adam and Charles Black, 1968.

Sandmel, Samuel. *Philo's Place in Judaism. A Study of Conceptions of Abraham in Jewish Literature*. Cincinnati: Hebrew Union College Press, 1956.

Satake, Akira. *Die Gemeindeordnung in der Johannesapokalypse*. WMANT 21. Neukirchen-Vluyn: Neukirchener Verlag, 1966.

Schaberg, Jane. "Feminist Interpretations of the Infancy Narrative of Matthew", *Journal of Feminist Studies in Religion* 13 (1997), pp. 35–62.

Schaberg, Jane. *The Illegitimacy of Jesus: A Feminist Theological Interpretation of the Infancy Narratives*. San Francisco. Harper & Row, 1987, expanded ed. in 2006.

Schäfer, Peter. *Jesus in the Talmud*. Princeton: Princeton University Press, 2007.

Schlatter, Adolf. *Das Alte Testament in der johanneischen Apokalypse*. BFCT 16/6. Gütersloh: C. Bertelsmann, 1912.

Schmidt, Johann Michael. *Die jüdische Apokalyptik: Die Geschichte ihrer Erforschung von den Anfängen bis zu den Textfunden von Qumran*. Neukirchen-Vluyn: Neukirchener Verlag, 1969.

Schmithals, Walter. *Die Apostelgeschichte des Lukas*. ZBK 3/2. Zürich: Theologischer Verlag, 1982.

Schnackenburg, Rudolf. *Das Johannesevangelium*. 3 vols. HTKNT 4. Freiburg / Basel / Vienna: Herder, 1975.

Schnelle, Udo. "Die Abschiedsreden im Johannesevangelium", *ZNW* 80 (1989), pp. 64–79.

Schnelle, Udo. *Das Evangelium nach Johannes*. THNT 4. Leipzig: Evangelische Verlagsanstalt, 2004, 3rd ed.

Schofield, Alison. *From Qumran to the Yaḥad: A New Paradigm of Textual Development for The Community Rule*. STDJ 77. Leiden / Boston: Brill, 2009.

Schreiner, Thomas R. *New Testament Theology: Magnifying God in Christ*. Grand Rapids: Baker Academic, 2008.

Schüssler-Fiorenza, Elisabeth. *In Memory of Her: A Feminist Theological Reconstruction of Christian Origins*. London: SCM Press, 1983.

Schweitzer, Albert. *The Quest for the Historical Jesus: From Reimarus to Wrede*. Translated by W. Montgomery. London: Black, 1954, 3rd ed.

Schweitzer, Albert. *The Mysticism of the Apostle Paul*. Translated by William Montgomery. Baltimore: The Johns Hopkins Press, 1998, repr. 1931.

Scroggs, Robin. *The Text and the Times. New Testament Essays for Today*. Minneapolis: Fortress Press, 1993.

Segal, Michael. "The Literary Relationship between the Genesis Apocryphon and Jubilees: The Chronology of Abram and Sarai's Descent to Egypt", *Aramaic Studies* 8 (2010), pp. 71–88.

Sherwood, Aaron. *Paul and the Restoration of Humanity in Light of Ancient Jewish Traditions*. AJEC 82. Leiden: Brill, 2013.

Simpson, David Capell. "The Chief Recensions of the Book of Tobit", *JTS* 14 (1913), pp. 516–530.

Smith, Morton. *Jesus the Magician*. London: Gollancz, 1978.

Smith, Robert S. *Justification and Eschatology: A Dialogue with "the New Perspective on Paul"*. RTRSup 1. Doncaster, Australia: Reformed Theological Review, 2001.

Söding, Thomas. "Wenn ich mit dem Finger Gottes die Dämonen austreibe ...' (Lk 11,20): Die Exorzismen im Rahmen der Basileia-Verkündigung Jesu". In eds. Armin Lange, Hermann Lichtenberger, and K. F. Diethard Römheld, *Die Dämonen – Demons. Die Dämonologie der israelitisch-jüdischen und frühchristlichen Literatur im Kontext ihrer Umwelt*. Tübingen: Mohr Siebeck, 2003. Pp. 519–549.

Sorensen, Eric. *Possession and Exorcism in the New Testament and Early Christianity*. WUNT 2.157. Tübingen: Mohr Siebeck, 2002.

Spong, John Shelby. *Born of a Woman: A Bishop Rethinks the Birth of Jesus*. San Francisco: HarperSanFrancisco, 1992.

Stanley, Christopher D., ed. *Paul and Scripture: Extending the Conversation*. SBLECL 9. Atlanta: Scholars Press, 2012.

Starcky, Jean. "Un texte messianique araméen de la grotte 4 de Qumrân". In *École des langues orientales anciennes de l'Institut Catholique de Paris. Mémorial du cinquantenaire 1914/ 1964*. Travaux de l'Institut Catholique de Paris 10. Paris: Bloud et Gay, 1964. Pp. 51–66.

Stegemann, Hartmut. *The Library of Qumran: On the Essenes, Qumran, John the Baptist, and Jesus*. Grand Rapids: Eerdmans, and Leiden: Brill, 1998.

Stokes, Ryan E. "The Throne Visions of Daniel 7, 1 Enoch 14, and the Qumran Book of Giants: An Analysis of Their Literary Relationship", *DSD* 15 (2008), pp. 340–358.

Stone, Michael E. and Jonas C. Greenfield. "The Prayer of Levi", *JBL* 112 (1993), pp. 247–266.

Stone, Michael E. and Jonas C. Greenfield. "Aramaic Levi Document". In eds. George J. Brooke *et al.*, *Qumran Cave 4. XVII: Parabiblical Texts, Part 3*. DJD 22. Oxford: Clarendon Press, 1996. Pp. 25–36.

Strack, Hermann and Paul Billerbeck. *Kommentar zum Neuen Testament*. 6 vols. München: Beck, 1922–1961.

Strugnell, John and Daniel J. Harrington, eds. *Qumran Cave 4. XXIV: Sapiential Texts, Part 2: 4QInstruction (Musar le Mevin): 4Q415ff. with a Re-edition of 1Q26*. DJD 34. Oxford: Clarendon Press, 1999.

Stuckenbruck, Loren T. *Angel Veneration and Christology*. WUNT 2.70. Tübingen: Mohr Siebeck, 1995.

Stuckenbruck, Loren T. *The Book of Giants from Qumran: Texts, Translation, and Commentary*. TSAJ 63. Tübingen: Mohr Siebeck, 1997.

Stuckenbruck, Loren T. "The Sequencing of Fragments in the Qumran Book of Giants: An Inquiry into the Structure and Significance of an Early Jewish Composition", *JSP* 16 (1997), pp. 3–24.

Stuckenbruck, Loren T. "The Throne-Theophany of the Book of Giants: Some New Light on the Background of Daniel 7". In eds. eds. Stanley E. Porter and Craig A. Evans, *The Scrolls and the Scriptures: Qumran Fifty Years After*. JSPSup 26. Sheffield: Sheffield Academic Press, 1997. Pp. 211–220.

Stuckenbruck, Loren T. "4Q201 2; 1Q23–24; 2Q26; 4Q203; 6Q8". In eds. Stephen J. Pfann *et al.*, *Qumran Cave 4, XXVI: Cryptic Texts and Miscellanea, Part 1*. DJD 36. Oxford: Clarendon Press, 2000. Pp. 3–94.

Stuckenbruck, Loren T. "4QInstruction and the Possible Influence of Early Enochic Traditions: An Evaluation". In eds. Charlotte Hempel, Armin Lange, and Hermann Lichtenberger, *The Wisdom Texts from Qumran and the Development of Sapiential Thought.* BETL 159. Leuven: Leuven University Press and Peeters, 2002. Pp. 245–261.

Stuckenbruck, Loren T. "Giant Mythology and Demonology: From the Ancient Near East to the Dead Sea Scrolls". In eds. Armin Lange, Hermann Lichtenberger, and K. F. Diethard Römheld, *Die Dämonen – Demons. Die Dämonologie der israelitisch-jüdischen und frühchristlichen Literatur im Kontext ihrer Umwelt.* Tübingen: Mohr Siebeck, 2003. Pp. 318–338.

Stuckenbruck, Loren T. "Deliverance Prayers and Hymns in Early Jewish Documents". In eds. Gerbern S. Oegema and Ian Henderson, *The Changing Face of Judaism and Christianity.* Gütersloh: Gerd Mohn, 2005. Pp. 146–165.

Stuckenbruck, Loren T. "Pleas for Deliverance from the Demonic in Early Jewish Texts". In eds. Robert Hayward and Brad Embry, *Studies in Jewish Prayer.* JSSSup 17. Oxford: Oxford University Press, 2005. Pp. 55–78.

Stuckenbruck, Loren T. "The Early Traditions Related to 1 Enoch from the Dead Sea Scrolls: An Overview and Assessment". In eds. Gabriele Boccaccini and John J. Collins, *The Early Enoch Literature.* JSJSup 121. Leiden / Boston: Brill, 2007. Pp. 41–63.

Stuckenbruck, Loren T. *1 Enoch 91–108.* CEJL. Berlin: Walter de Gruyter, 2007.

Stuckenbruck, Loren T. "The Book of Jubilees and the Origin of Evil". In eds. Gabriele Boccaccini and Giovanni Ibba, *Enoch and the Mosaic Torah.* Grand Rapids: Eerdmans, 2009. Pp. 294–308.

Stuckenbruck, Loren T. "The Eschatological Worship by the Nations: An Inquiry into the Early Enoch Tradition". In eds. Károly Dániel Dobos, Gábor Buzási, and Miklós Kószeghy, *"With Wisdom as a Robe": Qumran and Other Jewish Studies in Honour of Ida Fröhlich.* Sheffield: Phoenix Press, 2009. Pp. 191–208.

Stuckenbruck, Loren T. "'Apocrypha' and 'Pseudepigrapha'". In eds. John J. Collins and Daniel C. Harlow, *Dictionary of Early Judaism.* Grand Rapids: Eerdmans, 2010. Pp. 179–203.

Stuckenbruck, Loren T. "The *Epistle of Enoch*: Genre and Authorial Presentation", *DSD* 17 (2010), pp. 387–417.

Stuckenbruck, Loren T. "The Interiorization of Dualism in the Human Being in Second Temple Judaism: The Treatise on the Two Spirits (1QS iii 13 – iv 26) in its Tradition-Historical Context". In eds. Eric Myers, Armin Lange, and Randall Styers, *Light Against Darkness: Dualism in Ancient Mediterranean Religion and the Contemporary World.* JAJSup 1. Göttingen: Vandenhoeck & Ruprecht, 2010. Pp. 159–184.

Stuckenbruck, Loren T. "Pseudepigraphy and First Person Discourse in the Dead Sea Documents: From the Aramaic Texts to Writings of the Yaḥad". In eds. Adolfo Roitman, Lawrence H. Schiffman, and Shani Tsoref, *The Dead Sea Scrolls and Contemporary Culture. Papers in Celebration of the 60th Anniversary of the Discovery of the Dead Sea Scrolls.* STDJ 93. Leiden: Brill, 2011. Pp. 295–326.

Stuckenbruck, Loren T. "Demonic Beings and the Dead Sea Scrolls". In ed. J. Harold Ellens, *Explaining Evil. Volume 1: Definitions and Development.* Santa Barbara, CA: Praegers, Publishers, 2011. Pp. 121–144.

Stuckenbruck, Loren T. "The 'Heart' in the Dead Sea Scrolls: Negotiating between the Problem of Hypocrisy and Conflict within the Human Being". In eds. Armin Lange, Emanuel Tov, and Matthias Weigold, *The Dead Sea Scrolls in Context. Integrating the the Dead Sea Scrolls in the Study of Ancient Texts, Languages, and Cultures.* 2 vols. VTSup 140. Leiden / Boston: Brill, 2011. Pp. 237–253.

Stuckenbruck, Loren T. "Reflections on Source-Criticism of the Epistle of Enoch and the Significance of *1 Enoch* 104:9–13". In eds. Eric F. Mason *et al.*, *A Teacher for All Generations: Essays in Honor of James C. VanderKam.* 2 vols. JSJSup 135/I and II. Leiden / Boston: Brill, 2012. Pp. 705–714.

Stuhlmacher, Peter. *Paul's Letter to the Romans.* Translated by Scott J. Hafemann. Louisville: Westminster John Knox, 1994.

Sturm, Richard. "Defining the Word 'Apocalyptic': A Problem in Biblical Criticism". In eds. Joel Marcus and Marion L. Soards. JSNTSup 24. Sheffield: JSOT Press, 1989. Pp. 17–48.

Sundermann, Werner. "M5900 Recto? and Fragment 'L' page 1, Verso, line 5". In *idem, Mittelpersische und partische kosmogonische und Parabeltexte der Manichäer.* Berlin Turfan Texte 4. Berlin: Brepols, 1978.

Sundermann, Werner. "Ein weiteres Fragment aus Manis Gigantenbuch". In *Orientalia J. Duchesne-Guillemin emerito oblate.* Textes et Memoires 12. Leiden: Brill, 1984. Pp. 491–505.

Suter, David W. "Fallen Angel, Fallen Priest. The Problem of Family Purity in 1 Enoch 6–16", *HUCA* 50 (1979), pp. 115–135.

Swete, Henry Barclay. *Commentary on Revelation.* Grand Rapids: Kregel, 1977, repr. 1911.

Talbert, Charles H. *What is a Gospel? The Genre of the Canonical Gospels.* Philadelphia: Fortress Press, 1977.

Talbert, Charles H. *Reading Corinthians: A Literary and Theological Commentary on 1 and 2 Corinthians.* New York: Crossroad, 1987.

Talbert, Charles H. *Reading Acts. A Literary and Theological Commentary.* Macon: Smyth & Helwys, 2005.

Tannehill, Robert C. *The Narrative Unity of Luke-Acts: A Literary Interpretation. Volume One: the Gospel According to Luke.* Philadelphia: Fortress Press, 1986.

Tàrrech, Armand Puig i. *Jesus: A Biography.* Waco, Texas: Baylor University Press, 2011.

Tatum, W. Barnes. "The Origin of Jesus Messiah (Matt 1:1, 18a). Matthew's Use of the Infancy Traditions", *JBL* 96 (1977), pp. 523–535.

Telford, William R. *The Theology of the Gospel of Mark.* New Testament Theology. Cambridge, UK / New York: Cambridge University Press, 1999.

Thackeray, H. St. John and Ralph Marcus. *Josephus. Jewish Antiquities V: Books V–VIII.* LCL. Cambridge, Massachusetts: Harvard University Press, 1938.

The World Health Organization Report 2001: Mental Health: New Understanding, New Hope. Geneva: The World Health Organization, 2001.

Thomas, John C. *The Devil, Disease and Deliverance: Origins of Illness in New Testament Thought.* JPTS 13. Sheffield: Sheffield Academic Press, 1998.

Thompson, Cynthia L. "Hairstyles, Head coverings, and St. Paul: Portraits from Roman Corinth", *BA* 51 (1988), pp. 99–115.

Thompson, Leonard L. *The Book of Revelation.* New York: Oxford University Press, 1990.0.

Thyen, Hartwig. *Das Johannesevangelium.* HNT 6. Tübingen: Mohr Siebeck, 2005.

Tigay, Jeffrey. *The Evolution of the Gilgamesh Epic.* Philadelphia: University of Pennsylvania Press, 1982.

Tiller, Patrick A. *A Commentary on the Animal Apocalypse of 1 Enoch.* SBLEJL 4. Atlanta: Scholars Press, 1993.

Tomson, Peter J. *Paul and the Jewish Law: Halakha in the Letters of the Apostle to the Gentiles.* CRINT III.1. Minneapolis: Fortress Press, 1990.

Trompf, Garry W. "On Attitudes toward Women in Paul and Paulinist Literature: 1 Cor 11:3–16 and Its Context", *CBQ* 42 (1980), pp. 196–215.

Trotter, Jonathan R. "The Tradition of the Throne Vision in the Second Temple Period: Daniel 7:9–10, 1 Enoch 14:18–23, and the Book of Giants (4Q530)", *RevQ* 99 (2012), pp. 451–466.

Twelftree, Graham H. *Jesus the Exorcist: A Contribution to the Study of the Historical Jesus.* Peabody, Massachusetts: Hendrickson, 1993.

Twelftree, Graham H. *In the Name of Jesus: Exorcism Among Early Christians.* Grand Rapids: Baker Academic, 2007.

Uhlig, Siegbert. "Das äthiopische Henochbuch". In ed. Werner Georg Kümmel, *Jüdische Schriften aus hellenistisch-römischer Zeit* V/6. Gütersloh: Gütersloher Verlagshaus, 1984. Pp. 461–780.

Ulrgard, Håkan. *Feast and Future: Revelation 7:9–17 and the Feast of Tabernacles.* CBNT 22. Stockholm: Almqvist & Wiksell International, 1989.

Ulrich, Eugene. "Daniel Manuscrpts from Qumran. Part 1", *BASOR* 268 (1987), pp. 17–37.

Ulrich, Eugene. "Daniel Manuscripts from Qumran. Part 2", *BASOR* 274 (1989), pp. 3–26.

Ulrich, Eugene. "112–116. 4QDana-e". In eds. Eugene Ulrich *et al.*, *Qumran Cave 4. XI: Psalms to Chronicles.* DJD 16. Oxford: Clarendon Press, 2000. Pp. 239–254.

van der Horst, Pieter W. and Judith Newman. *Early Jewish Prayers in Greek.* CEJL. Berlin: Walter de Gruyter, 2008.

VanderKam, James C. *Textual and Historical Studies in the Book of Jubilees.* HSM 41. Missoula: Scholars Press for Harvard Museum, 1977.

VanderKam, James C. *Enoch and the Growth of an Apocalyptic Tradition.* CBQMS 16. Washington D.C.: The Catholic Biblical Association of America, 1984.

VanderKam, James C. *The Book of Jubilees: Translated.* CSCO 511 and Scriptores Aethiopici 88. Leuven: Peeters, 1989.

VanderKam, James C. "The Birth of Noah". In ed. Zdzislaw J. Kapera, *Intertestamental Essays in honour of Józef Tadeusz Milik.* Qumranica Mogilanensia 6. Cracow: The Enigma Press, 1992. Pp. 213–231.

VanderKam, James C. and Józef T. Milik. "4Q216–224". In eds. Harold W. Attridge *et al.*, *Qmran Cave 4. VIII: Parabiblical Texts, Part 1.* DJD 13. Oxford: Clarendon Press, 1994. Pp. 1–140.

VanderKam, James C. *Enoch: A Man for All Generations.* Columbia: University of South Carolina Press, 1995.

VanderKam, James C. "1 Enoch, Enochic Motifs, and Enoch in Early Christian Literature". In eds. William R. Adler and James C. VanderKam, *The Jewish Apocalyptic Heritage in Early Christianity.* CRINT III.4. Assen: Van Gorcum, and Minneapolis: Fortress Press, 1996. Pp. 33–101.

VanderKam, James C. "The Demons in the *Book of Jubilees*". In eds. Armin Lange, Hermann Lichtenberger, and K. F. Diethard Römheld, *Die Dämonen – Demons. Die Dämonologie der israelitisch-jüdischen und frühchristlichen Literatur im Kontext ihrer Umwelt.* Tübingen: Mohr Siebeck, 2003. Pp. 339–364.

van der Ploeg, J. "Fragments d'un manuscrit de Psaumes de Qumran (11QPsb)", *RB* 74 (1967), pp. 408–413.

van der Toorn, Karel. "Hubaba". In eds. Karel van der Toorn, Bob Becking, and Pieter W. van der Horst, *Dictionary of Deities and Demons in the Bible.* Leiden: Brill, 1999, 2nd ed. Pp. 431–432.

van der Toorn, Karel. "Echoes of Gilgamesh in the Book of Qohelet?". In eds. W. H. van Soldt *et al.*, *Veenhof Anniversary Volume: Studies Presented to Klaas R. Veenhof on the

Occasion of His Sixty-Fifth Birthday. Leiden: Netherlands Institute for the Near East, 2001. Pp. 503–514.

van Kooten, George H. *Paul's Anthropology in Context: The Image of God, Assimilation to God, and Tripartite Man in Ancient Judaism, Ancient Philosophy and Early Christianity*. WUNT 232. Tübingen: Mohr Siebeck, 2008.

van Ruiten, Jacques T. A. G. M. "The Flood Story in the Book of Jubilees". In eds. Florentino García Martínez and Gerard P. Luttikhuizen, *Interpretations of the Flood*. TBN 1. Leiden / Boston: Brill, 1998. Pp. 66–85.

Verbrugghe, Gerald and John Moore Vickersham. *Berossos and Manetho, Introduced and Translated: Native Traditions in Mesopotamia and Egypt*. Ann Arbor: University of Michigan Press, 1996.

Verheyden, Joseph. "The Fate of the Righteous and the Cursed at Qumran and in the Gospel of Matthew". In ed. Florentino García Martínez, *Wisdom and Apocalypticism in the Dead Sea Scrolls and in the Biblical Tradition*. BETL 168. Leuven: Peeters, 2003. Pp. 427–449.

Vermes, Geza. *Jesus the Jew: A Historian's Reading of the Gospels*. Philadelphia: Fortress Press, 1973.

Vermes, Geza. "2. The Genesis Apocryphon from Qumran". In Emil Schürer, *The History of the Jewish People in the Age of Jesus Christ*, revd. by Geza Vermes, Fergus Millar, and Martin Goodman. 3 vols. Edinburgh: T & T Clark, 1973–1987. Vol. 3, pp. 318–325.

Vielhauer, Philipp. "Apocalyptic". In eds. E. Hennecke and William Schneemelcher, revd. by Georg Strecker, *New Testament Apocrypha*. 2 vols. Louisville: Westminster John Knox Press, 1990–1992. Vol. 2, pp. 581–600.

Vielhauer, Philipp. "Apocalyptic in Early Christianity". In eds. E. Hennecke and William Schneemelcher, revd. by Georg Strecker, *New Testament Apocrypha*. 2 vols. Louisville: Westminster John Knox Press, 1990–1992. Vol. 2, pp. 608–642.

von der Osten-Sacken, Peter. *Gott und Belial*. SUNT 6. Göttingen: Vandenhoeck & Ruprecht, 1969.

Wacholder, Benjamin Zion. "Pseudo-Eupolemus' Two Greek Fragments on Abraham", *HUCA* 34 (1963), pp. 83–113.

Wacholder, Benjamin Zion. *Eupolemus. A Study of Judaeo-Greek Literature*. HUCM 3. Cincinnati: Hebrew Union College Press, 1974.

Waddell, James A. *The Messiah: A Comparative Study of the Enochic Son of Man and the Pauline Kyrios*. JCTLS 10. London: T & T Clark, 2011.

Waetjen, Hermann. *A Reordering of Power: A Sociopolitical Reading of Mark's Gospel*. Minneapolis: Augsburg Fortress Press, 1989.

Wagner, J. Ross. *Heralds of the Good News: Isaiah and Paul "in Concert" in the Letter to the Romans*. NovTSup 201. Leiden / Boston: Brill, 2002.

Wainwright, Elaine M. *Towards a Feminist Critical Reading of the Gospel according to Matthew*. BZNW 60. Berlin: Walter de Gruyter, 1991.

Walker, William O. "1 Corinthians 11.2–16 and Paul's Views Regarding Women", *JBL* 94 (1975), pp. 94–110.

Walker, William O. "The 'Theology of Woman's Place' and the 'Paulinist' Tradition", *Sem* 28 (1983), pp. 101–112.

Walker, William O. "The Vocabulary of 1 Corinthians 11.3–16: Pauline or Non-Pauline?", *JSNT* 35 (1989), pp. 75–88.

Walter, Nikolaus, "Pseudo-Eupolemos (Samaritanischer Anonymus)". In ed. Werner Georg Kümmel, *Jüdische Schriften aus hellenistisch-römischer Zeit*, I/2. Gütersloh: Gerd Mohn, 1976. Pp. 137–143.

Wassen, Cecilia. "'Because of the Angels': Reading 1 Cor 11:2–16 in Light of Angelology in the Dead Sea Scrolls". In eds. Armin Lange, Emanuel Tov, and Matthias Weigold, *The Dead Sea Scrolls in Context: Integrating the Study of the Dead Sea Scrolls in Ancient Texts, Languages, and Cultures*. 2 vols. SVTP 140. Leiden / Boston: Brill, 2011. Vol. 2, pp. 735–754.

Watson, Francis. *Paul, Judaism, and the Gentiles: Beyond the New Perspective*. Grand Rapids: Eerdmans, 2007.

Weeks, Stuart, Simon Gathercole, and Loren Stuckenbruck, eds. *The Book of Tobit: Texts from the Principal Ancient and Medieval Traditions*. FoSub 3. Berlin: Walter de Gruyter, 2004.

Weeks, Stuart. "Some Neglected Texts of Tobit: the Third Greek Version". In ed. Mark Bredin, *Studies in the Book of Tobit: A Multidisciplinary Approach*. LSTS 55. London / New York: T & T Clark, 2006. Pp. 12–42.

Weiss, Johannes. *Die Offenbarung Johannes: ein Beitrag zur Literatur- und Religionsgeschichte*. FRLANT 3. Göttingen: Vandenhoeck & Ruprecht, 1904.

Weiss, Johannes. *Der erste Korintherbrief*. KEK 5. Göttingen: Vandenhoeck & Ruprecht, 1910, 9th ed.

Wengst, Klaus. *Das Johannesevangelium*. 2 vols. TKNT. Stuttgart: Kohlhammer, 2001.

Werman, Cana. "Qumran and the Book of Noah". In eds. Esther G. Chazon and Michael E. Stone, *Pseudepigraphic Perspectives: The Apocrypha and Pseudepigrapha in Light of the Dead Sea Scrolls*. STDJ 31. Leiden: Brill, 1999. Pp. 171–181.

Werner, Martin. *The Formation of Christian Dogma: An Historical Study of Its Problem*. Translated by Samuel G. F. Brandon. London: Adam and Charles Black, 1957, German 1941.

Westermann, Claus. *Basic Forms of Prophetic Speech*. Translated by Hugh Clayton White. Louisville: John Knox Press, 1991.

Westermann, Claus. *Genesis 1–11. A Continental Commentary*. Translated by J. J. Scullion. Minneapolis: Fortress Press, 1994.

Wevers, John William. *Genesis*. SVTG 1. Göttingen: Vandenhoeck & Ruprecht, 1974.

Whedbee, J. William. *Isaiah and Wisdom*. Nashville: Abingdon Press, 1971.

Wickham, Lionel R. "The Sons of God and the Daughters of Men: Gen 6:2 in Early Christian Exegesis". In eds. James Barr *et al.*, *Language and Meaning: Studies in Hebrew Language and Biblical Exegesis*. OtSt 19. Leiden: Brill, 1974. Pp. 135–147.

Wilk, Florian and J. Ross Wagner. *Between Gospel and Election: Explorations in the Intepretation of Romans 9–11*. WUNT 257. Tübingen: Mohr Siebeck, 2010.

Williamson, Lamar. *Mark*. NTL. Louisville, Kentucky: Westminster John Knox Press, 2009.

Winandy, Jacques, "Un curieux *casus pendens*: 1 Corinthiens 11.10 et son interprétation", *NTS* 38 (1992), pp. 621–629.

Wintermute, Orvil S. "Jubilees". In ed. James H. Charlesworth, *The Old Testament Pseudepigrapha*. 2 vols. Garden City, New York: Doubleday, 1983–1985. Vol. 2, pp. 35–142.

Wire, Antoinette Clark. *The Corinthian Women Prophets: A Reconstruction through Paul's Rhetoric*. Minneapolis: Fortress Press, 1990.

Wise, Michael O., Martin G. Abegg, and Edward M. Cook. *The Dead Sea Scrolls*. London: Harper Collins, 1996.

Witherington, Ben. *Conflict and Community in Corinth: A Socio-Rhetorical Commentary on 1 and 2 Corinthians*. Grand Rapids: Eerdmans, 1995.

Witmer, Amanda. *Jesus the Galilean Exorcist: His Exorcisms in Social and Political Context*. LNTS 459 and LHSS 10. London: T & T Clark, 2012.

Wold, Benjamin G. *Women, Men, and Angels: The Qumran Wisdom Document* Musar LeMevin *and Its Allusions to Genesis Creation Traditions*. WUNT 2.201. Tübingen: Mohr Siebeck, 2005.

Wright, Nicholas T. *The Climax of the Covenant: Paul and the Law in Pauline Theology*. Edinburgh: T & T Clark, 1991.

Wright, Nicholas T. *Jesus and the Victory of God*. London: SPCK, 1996.

Wright, Nicholas T. *The New Testament and the People of God*. London: SPCK, 1992.

Wright, Archie T. *The Origin of Evil Spirits*. WUNT 2.198. Tübingen: Mohr Siebeck, 2005.

Wyke, Maria. "Woman in the Mirror: The Rhetoric of Adornment in the Roman World". In ed. Sarah B. Pomeroy, *Women's History and Ancient History*. Chapel Hill: University of North Carolina, 1991. Pp. 134–151.

Yarbro Collins, Adela. "Women's History in the Book of Revelation", *SBLSP 1978*. Atlanta: Scholars Press, 1987. Pp. 80–91.

Zetterholm, Magnus. "Paul and the missing Messiah". In *idem, The Messiah in Early Judaism and Christianity*. Minneapolis: Fortress Press, 2007. Pp. 33–55.

Zimmermann, Ruben. "Die Virginitätsmetapher von Apk 14,4–5 im Horizont von Befleckung, Loskauf, und Erstlingsfrucht", *NovT* 45 (2003), pp. 45–70.

Zimmermann, Ruben. "Nuptial Imagery in the Revelation of John", *Bib* 84 (2003), pp. 153–183.

Zumstein, Jean. *L'Évangile selon Saint Jean*. 2 vols. CNT 4b. Geneva: Labor et Fides, 2007.

Index of Passages

A. Hebrew Bible

B. New Testament

C. Jewish "Apocrypha"

D. Old Testament "Pseudepigrapha"

E. Philo

F. Josephus

G. Dead Sea Scrolls

H. Ancient Near Eastern Texts

I. Rabbinic, Hekhalot, and Medieval Jewish Literature

J. Targumic Literature

K. Early Christian and Gnostic Writings

L. Manichaean Sources

M. Greek and Roman Literature

Index of Modern Authors

Index of Subjects (with Proper and Place Names)